close relations

AN INTRODUCTION TO THE SOCIOLOGY OF FAMILIES

susan a. mcdaniel
University of Alberta

lorne tepperman
University of Toronto

Prentice Hall Allyn and Bacon Canada
Scarborough, Ontario

Canadian Cataloguing in Publication Data

McDaniel, Susan A., 1946–
  Close relations : an introduction to the sociology of families

Includes index.
ISBN 0-13-749862-4

1. Family—Canada. I. Tepperman, Lorne, 1943– . II. Title.

HQ560.M285 2000   306.85'0971   C00-931059-3

© 2000 Prentice-Hall Canada Inc., Scarborough, Ontario
Pearson Education

Prentice-Hall, Inc., Upper Saddle River, New Jersey
Prentice-Hall International (UK) Limited, London
Prentice-Hall of Australia, Pty. Limited, Sydney
Prentice-Hall Hispanoamericana, S.A., Mexico City
Prentice-Hall of India Private Limited, New Delhi
Prentice-Hall of Japan, Inc., Tokyo
Simon & Schuster Southeast Asia Private Limited, Singapore
Editora Prentice-Hall do Brasil, Ltda., Rio de Janeiro

ISBN 0-13-749862-4

Vice President, Editorial Director: Laura Pearson
Acquisitions Editor: Nicole Lukach
Signing Representative: Andy Wellner
Developmental Editor: Dawn du Quesnay
Production Editor: Avivah Wargon
Copy Editor: Gilda Mekler
Production Coordinator: Peggy Brown
Art Director: Mary Opper
Photo Research: Sarah Wittmann, Susan Wallace-Cox
Permissions: Bernard Munich, Susan Wallace-Cox
Cover Design: Sarah Battersby
Cover Image: Leon Zernitsky
Page Layout: Gerry Dunn (Pixel Graphics)

 2 3 4 5   WEB   04 03 02 01 00

Printed and bound in Canada

Contents

Preface

Family is a hot topic as we begin a new millennium. Talking about our own family experiences and relationships is endlessly interesting, and family is a common theme in politics and on radio and television talk shows. Family is what we say we value most in life (Vanier Institute, 1994). Yet families are rife with contradictions. Although we value our families, increasing numbers of us abandon them. Family is a place of love, in which we seek solace from the world; yet it is also a place where abuse and violence are prevalent. Politicians seem to value families, commonly using terms such as "family responsibilities" and "family values," and yet they blame families for social problems.

Family life is still a fundamental part of life throughout the world, and certain general features characterize most families: extended kinship ties, provision of resources and social support, relative stability and permanence, and a (fading) association with the sacred. However, marital, divorce and childbearing behaviours, attitudes, values and norms have changed rapidly and dramatically, showing just how fragile the traditional system really is.

The Approach of This Book

As recently as twenty years ago, books on the family were often simple "how-to" guides to family life. Sometimes called "matching, hatching, and dispatching" books, they had subtitles such as "dating and courtship" and "family and you." This approach was possible a few decades ago since the ways in which people lived in families tended to be less diverse than in the 1990s, and the diversity that did exist was neither portrayed nor celebrated in family texts. Consistent with Talcott Parsons' structural functionalism, then the overwhelmingly dominant perspective on families, it was thought useful to society for students to have guides on preferable ways to live in families.

It is possible that families do fulfil some of Parsons' "functions," including those related to work. The observation that families have certain structures and forms under certain conditions—for example, that the nuclear family form is prevalent in industrial societies—is an important link between families and the economy and the world of work.

Far more interesting than the regularities in close relations, though, are the variations in form or structure. Modern families are remarkably diverse. It is largely in response to that empirically verifiable fact that we have felt called on to write this book. This book sets itself the task of being different from many other family books in use today. Its focus is on applications and theory: what works for families, for us as individuals, and for society. Several themes characterize our book:

1. We know families to be immensely varied and characterized more by processes than by the forms they take.

2. Family is becoming more, not less, important to us as individuals and to societies. Recent research and theory has shown clearly that family health affects individual health and longevity and the population health of entire countries (Evans & Stoddart, 1994; McDaniel, 1998).

3. Old expectations about family may no longer work. New solutions to family problems, based on what is known from family research, are needed and are offered here.

4. There is a constantly changing interplay among families, schools, and work. Family is both part of the problem and part of the solution, as shown in this book in a variety of ways.

5. Historical changes and cross-national comparisons help to make families today understandable and interpretable.

Throughout this book, we look at families as plural and diverse. We focus on families in terms of what they do rather than the shape they take.

Canadian Content

Speaking of diversity, this is a Canadian book intended primarily for Canadian students and classrooms. While some generalizations based on American data apply to Canadian situations as well, others do not. Our laws are somewhat different, as are also our histories, traditions, values, norms, and customs relating to family and marriage. At the same time, it is difficult to write a text based entirely on the findings of Canadian research. The body of available Canadian research is not only smaller than one might hope, but also uneven in scope. So, a Canadian text has to use whatever Canadian research is available and also borrow from the findings of other research. Thus, what we attempt here is a careful triangulation, using research from Canada, the United States, and elsewhere. Where we are convinced that distinguishing between countries is critical, we indicate whether the findings of the studies we use to make generalizations are Canadian or American. On the other hand, we do not draw attention to the nationality of a finding if we think that doing so adds nothing to a student's understanding of the research on families.

Brief Overview

Chapter 1 begins with an exploration of the variety of interesting shapes and processes of families and family-like relationships. We then explore how families begin with a look at dating, mating, cohabitation, and marriage patterns and dynamics. There follows a chapter on marriage and well-being, in which we discuss satisfactions and points of dissatisfaction, particularly in relation to communication, trust, and sex.

People sometimes consider the real beginning of family to be entry into parenthood, a time increasingly fraught with changes and challenges as choices simultaneously widen and contract. That is the subject of Chapter 4. In Chapter 5, we consider parenting and the multiple challenges it poses today. We propose several approaches to parenting supported by research, and some solutions to parenting problems.

In Chapter 6, we discuss the division of domestic labour, a source of conflict as families and expectations of family members change. Work in relation to family, the subject of the next chapter, is a topic of strong interest in the 1990s, as most adult members of families must balance family life with paid work.

Violence and stress in families, the topic of Chapter 8, is crucial to understand if we are to solve or even ameliorate these problems. In Chapter 9, the trends, myths, causes and consequences of divorce are considered. If couples divorce, some people remarry, and some experience stepparenthood. Other families, over the life course, go through the stages of children growing up and leaving home. Fresh starts for families, in all their diversity, are the topic of Chapter 10. Chapter 11 offers a glimpse into families of the future, emphasizing how, to some extent, families will create their own futures within both the opportunities and the constraints societies offer.

Each chapter of the text begins with a chapter outline. Anecdotes and excerpts from the popular media and from scholarly works are set off from the text throughout each chapter, to highlight related attitudes, debates, and current features of family.

Study tools at the end of each chapter include a chapter summary and questions for review and discussion. Related Web sites are also provided, along with a brief description of the site's contents. A glossary of important terms is included at the end of the book.

Supplements

Instructor's Manual. An instructor's manual is available with this edition. Its features include chapter outlines, key terms and concepts, motivational activities, answers to review questions in the text, critical thinking exercises, debate suggestions, group activities, project suggestions, and film and video suggestions

Test Item File. A comprehensive test item file, including approximately 50 multiple choice and 5 essay questions per chapter, is available in print and computerized forms. Prentice Hall Test Manager II is a test generator and classroom management system designed to provide maximum flexibility in producing and grading tests and quizzes. It is available in Windows and Macintosh formats.

Acknowledgments

The preparation of this book benefited from the efforts of many people. To begin, many talented students helped with the content of the book: University of Alberta graduate students Teresa Abada, Sandra Badin (now at Columbia University), Rob Cartwright, Delaine Jodain, Sheryl McInnes, and Line Pinsent; Ryerson Polytechnic University undergraduate Nicole Greenspan; University of Toronto undergraduates Megan Bockus, Sally Safa, and Cheryl Stewart; and Toronto graduate student Kathy Osterlund. University of Toronto undergraduate Sarah Wittman located a selection of suitable photographs. Bernard Munich, another University of Toronto undergraduate, hunted up usable visual materials, and requested permission to reprint textual material from other sources.

We have attempted to seek permission and to acknowledge all use of copyrighted material. If we have inadvertently failed to attribute any such material to its correct source, we will be pleased to correct such errors in future editions.

Colleagues kind enough to read and criticize the first draft included Bonnie Fox and Nancy Howell of the University of Toronto, Murray Pomerance of Ryerson Polytechnic University, and Ed Thompson of Sheridan College. Charles Tepperman helped with some of the charts and graphics. As always, Susan McDaniel thanks Kerri Calvert of the University of Alberta Sociology Information Centre for her generous assistance with literature searches. We also thank the following reviewers for their candid and helpful suggestions and comments on an earlier draft: Satadal Dasgupta, University of Prince Edward Island; Karen March, Carleton University; Beverly J. Matthews, University of Lethbridge; Don Swenson, Mount Royal College; and James M. White, University of British Columbia. Lorne Tepperman would like to thank Charles Jones (University of Toronto) and Susannah Wilson (Ryerson Polytechnic University) for all he learned from them while collaborating on earlier books about the family.

Both of us are grateful to the professionals at Prentice Hall Canada for making this process of book writing and book publishing as easy as it could be. This has included the kind efforts of acquisitions editors Rebecca Bersagel and Nicole Lukach; developmental editors Lisa Berland and Dawn du Quesnay; and production editor Avivah Wargon. A special thank-you goes to copy editor Gilda Mekler, who clarified our muddy writing in a great many places. (Any mud remaining is our own fault.) Gilda reorganized the first chapter and drew out our thoughts in dozens of places throughout the book.

We must also thank our families for their support and tolerance of time spent away from them. Susan thanks her spouse, Douglas, without whom writing about families would have less meaning. Lorne thanks his wife Sandra and three sons Andrew, Charles, and Alexander. It was life with them (and other kin) that made sociology of the family a personally compelling topic. Lastly, we thank each other for patience and tolerance as the project evolved in the midst of two immensely busy schedules. The authors met in person only once during the course of the project, and communicated over increasingly long distances as McDaniels' sabbatical in 1998 took her to an island off the coast of British Columbia. This book is truly a late-twentieth-century collaboration via cyberspace, courier, and fax.

We hope you learn as much reading this book as we learned writing it, and that you look into studying families further.

Close Relations:

Families and Other Close Relations

"I don't know how anyone gets along without a family," declared an Ontario grandmother in a focus group on families (Vanier Institute of the Family, 1994:12). Her comments reflected the attitudes of most Canadians—and most people. Among our deepest and most abiding human needs is to have someone close to us who understands and loves us and in whom we can confide and trust. In a world that is at times uncertain and insecure, we seek solace from close relations.

Families belong to a large class of relationships we would character-ize as "close," including intense friendships, love affairs, and long-term work relationships. What characterizes all close relationships is a strong at-tachment or bonding between the partners. Of course, not all family mem-bers feel strongly attached or bonded to each other. However, what people commonly imagine when they think of the word *family*—what the word *family* evokes in our culture—is attachment, sentiment, and emotional in-tensity. For most of us, families are our most important relationships, our first connection to the social world, and one that remains important throughout our lives.

This book explores the dimensions of close relations, the changes, the challenges we face, the ways in which close relations are affected by and affect school, work, society, and social policy. Drawing on the best avail-able social research, we discuss new, creative solutions to family problems. We examine the diversity of close relations now and in the past. And we consider how close relations and families may be becoming more, not less im-portant in our lives.

The Importance of Family

"The reports of my death," Mark Twain once remarked dryly, "are greatly exaggerated." It would be easy to conclude from media reports and casual comments at the end of the millennium that the family is, if not dead, at least in serious trouble. Doomsayers point to the upsurge in single-parent households and in children born outside of marriage, and to high divorce rates (actually, while divorce rates are certainly much higher than they were in the 1960s, rates have been falling ever since 1987). Has social change de-stroyed the family? Do people no longer care?

On the contrary, close personal relationships remain fundamentally important to people. Public opinion polls consistently find that family is tremendously important to Canadians (Vanier Institute of the Family, 1994:13). If anything, family and close relations are increasing in impor-tance to Canadians (Angus Reid, 1994). Young people are no less enthusiastic about families than are older people. A study of family attitudes in Canada done in conjunction with the 1994 International Year of the Family (Angus Reid, 1994:71–75), found that youth maintain many traditional views about the value of family and close relations in their lives, and feel a strong sense of belonging in their current families. They also express confidence about their future families, with 91 percent anticipating marriage and 89 percent children.

Why do people value family so highly? Throwing one's lot in with someone else's may seem at times irrational. Are people simply irrational, failing to act in their own best interests? Sociology has always been fascinated by the study of behaviour that makes no rational sense (see Parsons, 1937, for example). When looking closely, sociologists usually have found that behaviour that seems, at first glance, to be irrational turns out to be *non-rational*. That is to say, people are acting rationally in pursuit of objectives that are determined by values and beliefs beyond the realm of logic. Seen from this perspective, family life "makes sense" in the same way as most other social, religious, and cultural customs.

One explanation attributes family to a blind following of custom: people get married and have children simply because that's the way it's always been done. Are we driven by tradition? Are people locked into "traditional" ways by habit, fear, or ignorance? If ignorance is a factor, we would expect education to change behaviour. Yet, in fact, evidence shows that highly educated Western people are just as likely to marry, raise children, and form new relationships after divorce as other people are. It is true that highly educated, "post-traditional" people marry later, raise fewer children, and have more tolerance for a variety of intimacies (for example, homosexuality) than less educated, more traditional people do. Otherwise, no differences are apparent, so the "traditionalism" explanation for family behaviours seems unsupported.

Another explanation is that family meets our human needs, both economic and emotional. Like other close relations, family relations involve some form, often many forms, of dependency. There may be financial dependency, especially among children who depend on adult parents and among work-at-home wives who depend financially on their husbands ... or, increasingly, among out-of-work husbands who rely on their wives financially. There is an old saying that two can live as cheaply as one. While this may not be strictly accurate, there is an overall economic benefit to pooling material resources and labour; conversely, as we will discuss in Chapter 9, there is a cost to separating.

Often, there is also emotional dependence, based on trust and intimacy. Evidence suggests that men are particularly dependent emotionally on their wives, while wives are a little less emotionally dependent on their husbands (Angus Reid, 1994:20). Family members often depend on one another for understanding. This understanding is based on familiarity and trust, and also on reciprocity, an expectation that emotional support given by one will be returned by the other at some time in the future.

Family also meets our need for stability and predictability in life. It is no accident that the word *familiar*, which means close, well-known, or intimate, originates in the word *family*. Consider the human value of the familiar. It provides everyday life with form, content, and meaning. It may be true that we crave the *un*familiar (some of us more than others). That is why we travel, change jobs, seek educational opportunities, and do crazy things from time to time. It may also explain why some people change spouses. Yet, for most of us, the unfamiliar has appeal only against the backdrop of the familiar. A steady diet of the unfamiliar would be chaotic and (probably) harmful to health and sanity, as well as to work and economic stability. This may be why young people find such comfort in their families. The stability of their families enables them to explore their options and to develop confidence in who they are.

What families provide us is a set of familiar faces, activities, and routines. Family routines, like all routines, *can* be boring. Nonetheless, routines serve to structure the world for us. In fact, we come to love them *because* they are comfortable and predictable. We even attribute meaning to our routine relationships and activities. They humanize an otherwise indifferent universe, and structure our days and lives. Family life, despite its changes and diversity (or perhaps because of it) is our first and best source of the "familiar" in our lives. Social research shows that people need the familiar, and families will likely remain one of the best social institutions for providing it.

What Is a Family?

Families are important to us. But what *is* a family? Most people think of families as groups of people related to one another through marriage, descent, or adoption. But is that description specific enough? Is it inclusive enough? Is it possible to delineate the boundaries between families, friendships, and other close relations?

To some people the answer seems obvious. They argue that the term *family* should only be used to describe "traditional families." But what is a traditional family? The exact meaning varies with the speaker. Families have varied in form throughout history and still vary from one society to another; and the families now regarded as traditional are themselves a significant departure from earlier traditions. Where, then, do we draw the line?

The other problem with a rigid "traditionalist" stance is that it doesn't seem to match the realities of life for many families. For example, if a couple marries and has children, with every intention of making it a life-long commitment and the marriage fails, are the ex-spouses and the children of that union no longer a family? The subsequent arrangement may depart from the ideal traditional family or from both partners' original expectations and hopes, but a family remains nonetheless. Similarly, does a family come to an end when the children grow up and leave home? What about a woman who flees an abusive partner with her children?

Defining the Family

The answers to these questions are not merely academic. How family and close relations are defined matters to us personally—to our values, our dreams, our aspirations as individuals. Definitions also matter to our rights in terms of law and policy, and to our entitlements to benefits, pensions, schools, and a myriad of other social resources. Debates rage in the media about whether common-law spouses should have the same rights as married spouses, about spousal rights for gays and lesbians, and about the financial responsibilities and the rights (to custody, access, etc.) of divorced people. Let's look now at some definitions of family.

Murdock: Three Relationships

For many years, sociologists used as a benchmark George Murdock's (1949:1) definition of family as

> a social group characterized by a common residence, economic co-operation and reproduction [including] adults of both sexes, at least two of whom maintain a socially approved sexual relationship, and one or more children, own or adopted, of the sexually cohabiting adults.

Note that by this definition, three basic relationships—co-residence, economic cooperation, and reproduction—must all be present to qualify a social group as a family. Murdock's definition excludes many groups that most of us would consider families: childless married couples, for example, and single parents and their children. Same-sex unions are excluded, as are married couples who are separated. Celibate couples, according to Murdock, cannot be a family even if they have children, live together, and share other kinds of intimacy. (This means that you might have to question a couple about their sex life to determine whether they and their children constitute a family!) What about two sisters who live together? They cannot be a family, according to Murdock. Thus, Murdock's definition does not seem to allow for the variability among families that exists among various cultures, or even within our own.

Core Relationships

Trost (1988) has suggested a definition focusing on two of the family's core relationships: "spouse-to-spouse" and "parent-to-child," or the "spousal unit" and "parent-child unit" respectively. By this standard, a family is a group consisting of at least one parent-child unit and/or at least one spousal unit. This definition is far more inclusive: it allows a couple with no children to be accepted as a family—even if they do not live together. A single parent with a child or children could also be a family.

There are many advantages to this approach. It frees us from having to specify exactly who will be considered members of families, and how they will behave toward one another. On the other hand, this definition is very abstract and gives us little information about what we would expect to find happening among a group of people who consider themselves a family. Thus, Trost's definition may suit the needs of sociologists but it does not meet the standard of common sense and everyday experience.

Statistics Canada

Statistics Canada (1992:133) defines family as "… a now married couple (with or without never-married sons and/or daughters of either or both spouses), a couple living common-law (again with or without never-married sons and/or daughters of either or both partners), or a lone parent of any marital status, with at least one never-married son or daughter living in the same dwelling."

Household versus Family

Market researchers and census takers often try to sidestep difficulties of definition by distinguishing between "household" and "family." That distinction allows us to talk about changes in households without necessarily implying changes in families or family life. But this approach, too, presents problems. As pointed out clearly by Eichler (1997), more and more families live in separate households but maintain ongoing family relationships. The prime example is divorced families in which custody is joint or shared (discussed in detail in subsequent chapters). In these situations, when child care and household responsibilities are shared but the adults live separately, family and household are not congruent.

There have always been married couples who lived apart because of illness, because one partner was in prison, or for job-related reasons such as migrant labour or military service. Commuter marriages are a contemporary example of this phenomenon, which Gerstel and Gross (1982) see as a response to economic and cultural pressures that force couples to live apart.

A "household" may contain only one person or many unrelated members—roommates, boarders, or residents in a group home. Or, it may contain a nuclear family, an extended family, or multiple families (for example, communes or families sharing living space to save money). In short, a household can contain many families, or none at all. Conversely, a family may spread across many households. But usually families and households coincide, giving rise to "family households."

In the United States, **family households** are officially defined as married couples with or without children under 18, or one-parent families with children under 18. Or they may be other households composed of related individuals (for example, two sisters sharing a household, or a parent and a child 18 years old or over). By contrast, **nonfamily households** contain unrelated individuals or people who live alone.

Process versus Structure

The United Nations (1991) prefers to define family by the important socio-economic functions it performs, such as providing emotional, financial, and material support to its members, caring for each other, preserving and transmitting cultural values, and serving as a resource for personal development.

The International Year of the Family in 1994 spotlighted families around the world. Diversity was vividly demonstrated at conferences where different kinds of families were celebrated in photos, videos, art, words, speeches, and music. It became clear that families matter greatly to people everywhere, but that how they see families varies as much as the need for them is constant (McDaniel, 1995a). This observation led to deep consideration in Canada about what *family* is, and what families are. The question was taken up by family researchers, by the Vanier Institute of the Family, and by the Canada Committee for the International Year of the Family on which one of the authors of this book (McDaniel) served. The conclusion was reached that ultimately families are defined not by the shape they take but by what they do (Vanier Institute of the Family, 1994:9). As Moore-Lappe (1985:8) puts it:

> ... families are not marriages or homes or rules. Families are people who develop intimacy because they ... share experiences that come ... to make up their uniqueness—the mundane, even silly, traditions that emerge in a group of people who know each other. ... It is this intimacy that provides the ground for our lives.

To acknowledge the diversity of family and close relations, broad inclusive definitions are needed that encompass the *dynamics* of family and close relations over time. Consistent with much of family research, it is *process* rather than *form* that defines families. This idea has worked well and is used throughout this book.

Over the past two decades or so, a broad definition of family has become generally accepted by most Canadians (see Angus Reid, 1994). Much of family law and policy reflects the move toward inclusion of families that are diverse.

> To arrive at a definition, we need to be sensitive to and in touch with family life as Canadians live it ... we must ... acknowledge that there are a lot of different types of families out there ... [and] look at the social environment in which people live (Vanier Institute of the Family, 1994:5).

Some groups, however, particularly some fundamentalist religious groups of various denominations, explicitly oppose inclusive definitions. The diversity of families is controversial. It challenges vested interests, myths, misunderstandings, and idealized images of what families should be. Some of the idealization is based on religious belief or interpretation, some of it on political belief. At times, politics and religion join in political movements with religious overtones, such as the "family values" campaigns in the United States. Families have become, as one family scholar (Skolnick, 1991) puts it, "embattled paradise." As contested territory, what are called "nontraditional families" may call into question what families are or should be.

Gay and lesbian families have become a touchstone in many contemporary debates about what is and is not family and what rights and entitlements those who are deemed family ought to have. Similarly, immigration and growing ethnic diversity have meant challenges to how we form, maintain, define, and connect in close relations.

Common Elements of Family Life

The social groups we think of as families typically share many features in common. It is therefore possible to say some things in general about families—things that can help us begin to understand the nature of families. But keep in mind that families are extraordinarily diverse, and becoming more so, so it is difficult to make general rules about them. We progressively have to widen and revise our notions of what close relations in general, and family relations in particular, look like. Typically, families, as social units, are made up of people who have lived together over an extended period of

---

Children Raised by Gay Parents Are Not Different, Advocates Say

Children raised by gay or lesbian couples are no different from those raised by heterosexuals and no more likely to be gay or lesbian, say advocates of the government's same-sex rights legislation. A review by University of Virginia professor Charlotte Patterson of more than 30 independent U.S. studies carried out since the mid-1970s ... concluded there is "no evidence to suggest that psychosocial development among children of gay men or lesbians is compromised in any respect relative to that among offspring of heterosexual parents."

[Bill 167, which would have given same-sex couples many of the same rights as common-law heterosexual couples, was put forward in Ontario in 1994 but was not passed.]

Suzanne Scorsone, spokesperson for the Catholic Archdiocese of Toronto which is vigorously opposed to the bill, says there isn't enough information to make a definitive judgment. "This is so new we don't know what is going to happen when they (children raised by gays or lesbians) grow up," Scorsone says.

Dr. Miriam Kaufman, a pediatrician raising two children with her longtime lesbian partner, says the quality of family relationships is the most important factor. "What children need is to be brought up in homes where they are loved, where they are cared for and where their parents nurture their sense of self-esteem. And that bears no relationship to what [sexual orientation] the parents are," she says.

Source: Bruce deMara. 1994. Reprinted with permission of The Toronto Star Syndicate. Abridged from an article originally appearing in *The Toronto Star* (June 5, 1994).

time, or intend to do so. They are connected by legal contract or emotional commitment, or both. They may care for one or more dependent relatives, whether children, aged adults, or disabled or ill members.

Dependency and Intimacy

All close relations have in common attachment and some kind of dependency or interdependency. Most close friendships and work relationships include some degree of emotional dependency, based on familiarity and expectations of reciprocity. However, one marked difference is that adult partners within a family typically have a long-term, exclusive sexual relationship—often a fundamental aspect of closeness between spouses—whereas among co-workers and among friends, sexual relations are either absent or of short duration. Family relations are also special in that they tend to include long-term commitments both to each other and to the family unit.

For most of us the essential quality of family life is strong emotional commitment. Good families are supposed to provide intimacy (close, satisfying relationships), promote children's upbringing and schooling, enhance members' material well-being and health, raise self-esteem, and help in mental adjustment (Pullium, 1986). **Affective nurturance** or love is one of the crucial ties among family members. The family is said to be the place to go to heal the wounds all of us may sustain at times from society, and a place where we will always be loved no matter what.

Of course, these ideal conditions are not always realized in practice. A family relationship is no guarantee of emotional commitment. In fact, unmarried people can, and do, share relationships as close as many married couples'. Family members do not always support one another, financially or psychologically.

Sexuality

In families, as we noted earlier, sexual relations are permitted and expected between certain members but socially prohibited between other members. Taboos against incest ostensibly forbid sexual relations with a family member other than a spouse, but sexual abuses of children and elders occur within families. Norms of sexual propriety are much stronger in families than they are in friendship or work groups.

Women's sexual activity and sexuality has almost always been more closely controlled than men's. This is because in male-dominated societies people have felt that families' property rights related to women's reproductive and sexual capacities. They saw marriage as the capture and possession of "erotic property" (Collins, 1988). Women were defined by law as the sexual property of their husbands, and could not, in legal terms, be sexually assaulted by their husbands, since sexual access was the husband's right. As well, inheritance of property depended on women's sexual fidelity so that a man could be ensured that the children to whom he left his property were indeed his. We'll discuss sexual mores in more depth in the next chapter.

Protection

Effective families keep their members under guard against all kinds of internal and external dangers. There is a clear cultural expectation that families will protect their members. Parents and grandparents are supposed to keep children safe from accidents, household dangers (falls, house cleaning products that may be poisonous, etc.), and away from drugs, alcohol, predators, and other forms of harm. Spouses are supposed to protect one another; parents are supposed to protect their children, and adult children to protect and help their parents. In reality, family members often fail to do this sufficiently, and in spite of their best efforts, harm befalls a family member. Worse, many people neglect, exploit, or abuse family members.

Risk and Power

Risk is built into family living, sometimes considerable personal risk. Remember that households and families are small social groups whose members spend a lot of time together and depend on each other to fill both economic and non-economic needs. There are large differences in power, strength, age, and social resources among members. It is this imbalance that makes **patriarchy**, control of the family by a dominant male (typically, the father), a central fact in the history of family life in most known societies. Simply put, men dominated because they possessed and controlled more of the resources and because society gave them privileges, with the two forces interlinked. In any group, those with the most resources can exercise the most control ... though, of course, they may choose not to exert this control.

Violence has always existed in families. In the last two decades, there have been growing reports of violence within the family. Some estimate that one woman in ten will be assaulted at some time in her life; others put the estimate higher, and some lower. In most cases the assailant is a spouse or boyfriend. Date rape and dating physical abuse occur about as often as wife abuse. Researchers estimate that one girl in four and one boy in ten is sexually abused before the age of 16, often by friends or relatives. Violent relationships generally do not begin in adulthood. As we will see in the course of this book, children who grow up in violent homes are more likely to enter violent partnerships. But it must be emphasized that children who have experienced violence can overcome their past and become non-violent members of families and society.

The figures on intimate violence are alarming indeed. They seem to point to a huge, too-hidden problem in everyday family life, what sociologists used to call "social pathology." Alarming evidence on family violence leads sociologists to ask whether this pathology is growing, or whether family life has always been stressful and violent and we are now just becoming more aware of it. To answer questions like these, sociologists must distinguish actual from idealized patterns of family life.

What Makes Strong Families?

We said earlier that families could be defined by what they do. Let's look more closely at these functions. Six basic functions are typically cited as characteristic of families:

- physical maintenance and care

- adding new members to society—procreation and adoption

- socialization of children

- social control of members of families

- maintenance of family morale and motivation

- production and consumption of goods and services

(Zimmerman, 1988:75–76)

Efforts to broaden and improve the definition of family, to establish norms for family life, and to solve family problems have led to research on what makes for functioning families. The underlying logic is simple: any social grouping that functions like a "good family" is, effectively, a family. The key is fulfilling the purposes of families in society.

A recent review of the research literature on family strengths finds many common themes in the work of varied family researchers. According to Schlesinger (1998:4–5): "Family strengths are relationship patterns, intrapersonal and interpersonal skills and competencies, and social and psychological characteristics that:

1. create a sense of positive family identity;

2. promote satisfying and fulfilling interaction among family members;

3. encourage the development of the potential of the family group and individual family members;

4. contribute to the family's ability to deal effectively with stress and crisis; and

5. contribute to the family's ability to be supportive of other families."

Typically, a strong family is a well-functioning, durable family. Characteristics of such families include clear roles and responsibilities, clear and fair rules, the legitimate exercise of authority, accepted procedures for resolving conflict, the sharing of tasks, and a respect for individual needs and differences. These elements comprise what might be considered the structure and subculture of successful family life. As you can see, they are not very different from the structure and subculture of a successful sports team, business office, or sociology class.

When a family is healthy, strong, and durable, it works in certain characteristic ways. For example, a functional family is more likely to be relaxed, to have fun, and to deal with conflicts quickly and openly. It is likely to have traditions, rituals, a particular way of viewing the world, and a group identity.

How do people create and maintain such healthy family structures and subcultures? Research on strong families finds a surprising number of common means. They include communication, cooperation, support, respect, time investment, and patience. Communication is key: everyone has to be listened to. Members of healthy families spend a good deal of time talking to each other. Cooperation is also critical: members of healthy families promote each other's well-being, in the knowledge that the welfare of each contributes to the welfare of all. Each supports the other, showing respect and tolerance. Cooperation, of course, takes time: there is no shortcut to a healthy family life, and no real way to substitute quality time for quantity time (though obviously lots of high-quality time is better than lots of low-quality time). And, because none of this is fast or easy, patience is needed. No lasting human structure, whether the city of Rome or the Smith family, is built in a day.

Some researchers have tried to boil this prescription down further to a few variables. For example, it is fair to say that every strong, healthy family requires *cohesion*, a sense of bonding between the members, and *flexibility*, an ability to change rules and roles in response to new opportunities and stresses. Certainly, without sufficient cohesion and flexibility, a family is unlikely to be able to maintain its communication, cooperation, etc. in the face of new, ever-changing challenges. At the same time, with too much cohesion comes suffocation; with too much flexibility comes chaos.

With all this in mind, we can say that a family is a group of people with a stable, characteristic pattern of rules and roles, who view themselves and are viewed by others as cooperating to support one another emotionally, materially, and otherwise. They are in frequent communication, know each other well, and recognize that, for better or worse, their fates are tied together. There are a large number of ways to tie family members together, which is why we keep insisting that family processes are the key to understanding family life. Many social groupings make possible family-like communication, cooperation, and so on. But no family-like structure, even the so-called traditional nuclear family with the expected number of opposite-sex parents and biological children, will ever be mistaken by sociologists for a strong (or durable or healthy) family if it is deficient in communication, cooperation, etc.

A Historical, Cross-Cultural Perspective

Before we consider some of the contemporary changes in family life, let's step back and look at what families were like in the past. The vast majority of people who ever lived have farmed the earth, herded animals, hunted, fished, or harvested wild plants. In such economies, activities tend to be gendered: women do one thing and men another. It should be noted, however, that the exact division of labour has varied from one time and place to another. As well, children and the elderly tend to have a clear place. Since an extra pair of hands is always useful in subsistence societies, training in economically productive activities starts at an early age.

In these societies, kinship relations are very important. Families succeed by multiplying and prospering, increasing the number of cows or camels or sheep, or improving the yield of rice, wheat, millet, or sorghum in their fields. Families die out if no children survive and none are adopted. For societies on the edge—which still includes many peoples in the world—survival of the group is the central aim. People tend to seek happiness collectively, if they consciously seek it at all. Personal freedom is not highly valued.

Indeed it may be difficult even to explain our notions of individual freedom to people in many other societies. We find far more ideas about property than ideas about freedom and happiness. Virtually all societies have customs regulating the ownership of animals, the use of certain areas of land, the right to harvest wild plants in a given location, and the practice of certain trades. Tellingly, these rules are often defined for families, clans, or descent groups, not for individuals *per se*. As children reach adulthood, they can inherit property under certain conditions, not others. And when young adults marry into another family group, they take limited property with them. They also take on rights and duties as part of the family they marry into. In these cultures, marriage is seen more as a union of groups or families than of individuals. Romantic love does exist, but is not considered an important goal or a foundation of marriage.

The most familiar example of such a traditional culture is ancient Israel, as described in the Old Testament. Have you ever wondered why the Old Testament contains such long lists of people begetting other people? It is because these genealogies establish the membership of descent groups. This is enormously important, since kinship is what justifies people's claims to land ownership, and land ownership is the means of survival. It also gives people a clear sense of belonging to a group, a family, a tribe, a culture.

Issues of kinship are critically important. Kinship affects the right to choose a marriage partner, the adoption of potential heirs, and the legitimacy of children. The position of the family in the community and the individual within the family determine people's ability to participate in the society's economic activities. We see some of this system in hereditary monarchies such as the royal family in the United Kingdom.

Kinship, Clan, and Community

A **kinship group** is a group of people who recognize a blood relationship and have positions in a hierarchy of rights over the property. What counts as a kinship relationship varies from one society to another. This is important, for kinship determines which of your relatives count as potentially useful to you. Kinship relationships may also determine whom you can marry, where you are to live, and the degree to which women or men specialize in child rearing and "kin-keeping" activities.

Logically speaking, there are only so many possible variations of kinship. Some societies count relationships through the male line, so that who you are is determined by who your father is; we call such kinship systems **patrilineal**. Others count relationships through the female line and use expressions such as "coming from the same womb"; they are **matrilineal** systems. Still others count relationships through both lines; they are **bilateral** kinship systems.

If the kinship system is patrilineal, a person gains a position in the community just by being the child of his or her *father*. In a matrilineal kinship system on the other hand, a person has certain property rights because of being the child of his or her *mother*. However, the kinship system is independent of which sex holds more authority in society. Men can be the dominant sex even in a matrilineal society. In this case, the person whose kinship link is most important to a child is not the biological father. It is the mother's brother, as among the Ashanti in West Africa or a number of North American aboriginal societies.

The Huron, for example, measure descent through the female line. Their system is matrilineal and a person's clan membership is reckoned through his or her mother. These matrilineal clans are **exogamous**, meaning you must marry someone from another clan. Even distant relatives on your mother's side of the family are off-limits as potential marriage partners. Most married couples live close to the wife's mother's kin, and at one time they lived in group residences called longhouses. Each longhouse would contain several nuclear families, these families being linked to each other because sisters or female cousins were the women of those families, while their male partners were from a different clan or clans. As anthropologists

Some aboriginal societies are matrilineal, measuring descent through the female line. However, even a patrilineal kinship system can have *matrifocal* characteristics, meaning women play an important role in maintaining family contacts.

would say, the Huron are *matrilineal* and *matrilocal*—people live with or near their mothers' families. Those two characteristics do not necessarily mean they are **matriarchal**—men might still have held the power in such societies. However, many scholars have argued that the combination of matriliny and matrilocality empowers women or, at least, limits the possibilities for male dominance. In fact, Huron women are often prominent in decision making.

As in other matrilineal societies, family property can only be inherited from the mother's side of the family. In the Ashanti tribe, for example, it is better to have a rich mother than a rich father, because a father's wealth goes to his sisters' children; a mother's wealth goes to her own children.

Because of the clan exogamy rule, a person's kin on each side will belong to different clans. Thus, the Huron have names to distinguish a person's relatives on the mother's side from those on the father's side. The children of a person's mother's brother and father's sister are classified as his or her "cross-cousins." The children of a person's mother's sister and father's brother are classified as sisters and brothers (Anderson, 1982: 116; Buchler & Selby, 1968).

Western Europeans and North Americans have no special words to distinguish kin on the father's side from kin on the mother's side. For emotional purposes, it does not matter whether a first cousin, uncle, or aunt is on the mother's or father's side. However, our system is mildly patrilineal. For example, a woman has historically taken her husband's family name, not the reverse, and this name is the one that passes to the children.

(It should be noted, however, that this is not the case everywhere in the West. In Quebec, for example, women are prevented by law from taking their husband's name on marriage.)

Among Scottish clans, a Macdonald woman who married a Stuart man would become attached to the Stuart clan. Her daughters would be Stuarts, with a weak connection to the Macdonalds. If a blood feud broke out between the two clans, they would side with the Stuarts, however regretfully. Similar clan systems, with well-developed rules about alliances during a blood feud, have been found in Iceland, the mountains of Albania, Papua New Guinea, and other parts of the world.

In the Western pattern, property is also typically inherited along the male line. Likewise, where families settle down is traditionally determined by the husband's job, not the wife's, although this too is changing.

However our society also has certain *matrifocal* characteristics. Because women have been defined as the primary **kin-keepers**—the people who maintain family contacts—children tend to have stronger ties with their mothers' kin than with those of their fathers (Rosenthal, 1985; Thomson & Li, 1992:15). They also maintain closer contacts with their mothers when they grow up and the mothers grow old. When parents of grown children live separately, fathers are less often visited, called, and relied upon than are mothers.

Even at the best of times, kinship rules produce conflicts. That is because, in many such kinship systems, marriage rules are exogamous. People marry outside the kinship group, even into families with whom hostilities may arise. In such cases, the local people may wryly inform anthropologists, "We marry our enemies." Such marital alliances provide the basis by which different kin groups can unify against a common enemy, should one emerge. But people may also find their loyalties to a spouse's kin and their own kin repeatedly tested by conflicts between the two groups.

The basic relationships in a nuclear family—spouse-to-spouse and parent-to-child—still exist within such kinship systems. However, they are less important in the kinds of societies described above than in our own society. By contrast, relations with cousins, uncles, and siblings are *more* important than in our society. That is because more of these kin live close by, even if not in the same household.

In traditional societies, the kinship group's approval or disapproval exercises a strong control over people's behaviour. This can also be the case in farm families in Canada today. A woman marrying a farmer is said to marry him, his land, and his family's land. Anyone marrying into a family business marries more than an individual.

The Extended Family

As agriculture becomes less important, so does the larger kin group. Over time, kin life shades into family life as we know it. An important example of this is what the nineteenth-century sociologist Frederic Le Play called the "stem family." Over the centuries, the stem family maintains a small farm as a family-run enterprise, and only one of the children (often the eldest son) inherits ownership of it. The rest move out upon marriage or remain unmarried. At some times in the family life cycle, several generations of the family may be living under the same roof. At other times, they are off on their own living independently.

Most cultures have a saying equivalent to "Many hands make light work" and peasant families have traditionally borne large numbers of children. Many family sociologists have believed that big, complex families are happy families. Le Play described the "ideal typical" household of such a family as follows:

> The heir and his wife, aged 25 and 20; the father and mother, the heads of the household, married for 27 years and now aged 52 and 47; a grandfather aged 80; two unmarried kinsfolk—brothers or sisters of the head of the family; nine children, of whom the eldest are nearly as old as the brother who is the heir; and the youngest is a baby, often still at the breast; finally, two servants living on terms of complete equality with the other members of the family (cited in Flandrin, 1979: 52).

This ideal, however, was probably attained only rarely. Stem family households were only possible under certain conditions. In rural European communities of the Middle Ages, a wealthy man might have a large number of relatives, servants, and apprentices living in his household. In general, the richer the household, the larger it was. But for the most part, peasants remained poor, died young, and lived out their lives in nuclear families.

Canadian Kinship and Family Patterns

Aboriginal families in Canada have always been diverse. Some, like the Iroquois Confederacy of which the Mohawks are part, were matriarchal, with women making the important political decisions while men were the warriors. This was apparent a few years ago in the Oka crisis in Ontario, where Mohawk people protested the building of a golf course on what was their ancient burial ground. At one point, television crews captured images of the Mohawk women ordering the warriors to back down from confrontation. And they did, much to the surprise of some viewers and commentators. This is consistent with the Iroquois traditions and customs. Other aboriginal groups are more patriarchal in family and social behaviours.

With contact with explorers, fur traders, and settlers aboriginal family practices changed, as did the practices of some of the settlers. Early settlers in Canada developed strong relationships of mutual aid with their aboriginal neighbours. Blood Nation women helped homesteading women in the prairies with childbirth and with house building so as to stay warm in the harsh winters. The settlement of New France (now Quebec) and Upper Canada (now Ontario) brought families of aboriginal groups together with those of the colonists. In the early days, some children born to settler women who were unmarried were adopted out to aboriginal families. The American Revolution brought to Canada the United Empire Loyalists, including significant groups of African Americans. The latter settled largely in Nova Scotia and in southern Ontario.

Later, in the early twentieth century, African-American families settled as homesteaders in central Alberta (Hooks, 1997). Gwen Hooks, the daughter of original homesteaders, describes how they banded together in families and communities to make a new and happy life on the prairies. She also states how homesteaders of all ethnic groups tended to band together to build community facilities such as schools. Later immigrants, of course, have included peoples from all regions of the world who are seeking a better life and who bring with them rich family traditions and strong beliefs. With time, some of their family practices change in the new situation and others enrich the traditions of those with whom they have contact.

Changes in Family, in Canada and Worldwide

Struggles to define and redefine families are ongoing throughout the industrialized world (Baker, 1995). Indeed, industrialization had a huge impact on family living. The separation of public and private domains took place as men left the household/farm to earn a living in the new factories. In the last hundred years, more and more societies have industrialized.

A number of changes in close relations seem to accompany modernization. These consequences of modernization for close relations are especially evident in Eastern Europe, Asia, and Africa, where the nuclear family has not had the same historic prominence as it's had in Western Europe. For example, with opportunities for paid employment, **neolocal residence**—a pattern in which adults live in nuclear families apart from their own parents—becomes more common. They may continue to live near their parents, but may be drawn away to wage employment in urban centres.

Urbanization has had as great or greater an effect on family life than industrialization, although the two typically go hand in hand (see Finlay, Velsor & Hilker, 1982). That is mainly because households—or who lives with whom—are determined by property ownership arrangements, which vary between urban and rural areas. Typically, households are larger (i.e., extended) and family life is more psychologically important to people in rural than in urban areas—or so we have been taught to think. That history has some surprises for those who look closely will be apparent in subsequent chapters. In many parts of the world, people still spend substantial parts of their lives in extended households, though they increasingly spend significant parts of their lives in nuclear families.

Prospective brides and grooms become less willing to accept a mate their parents have selected for them, although arranged marriages still occur with considerable regularity, even in Canada among some ethnic groups. Where **polygamy** existed before, even if only as an ideal, it tends to diminish. **Endogamy** may persist, but it does so in a modified form. For example, people may continue choosing mates from within their group (village, county, region, ethnic group, tribe, etc.), but not from among their kinfolk.

Changes in Relationships within Families

Throughout the world, women increasingly seek more education with industrialization and modernization. Families have changed dramatically as women have become more able to control their childbearing and to support themselves economically. Attitude change has also had a lot to do with changing patterns of intimacy. This trend parallels delayed marriage, and delayed (as well as restricted) childbearing. Men tend then to value and to seek more educated wives and wives closer to them in age. In general, marriages tend to become somewhat more egalitarian, in that family power is shared between spouses more equally than in the past.

This is not to say that all marriages become equal and fair; they do not. But marriages used to be even less equal and fair than they tend to be today. Despite the desire to imagine a "Golden Age" of family life to which we might someday return, families in the past had a great many shortcomings, especially for women and children. In truth, there never was a Golden Age of the family against which we should compare modern families.

Even where traditional family forms persist most strongly, in small rural areas, parent-child relations are changing (Caldwell, Reddy & Caldwell, 1984). Children, on average, are gaining more autonomy and power in interactions with parents. These changes demonstrate the pervasive influence of Western cultural notions, specifically notions about childhood and adolescence, but also, more generally, notions about the life cycle. It also shows the growing importance of education and media even in rural areas, and the socialization of new generations in preparation for an urban, industrial lifestyle.

Everywhere, a modern industrial economy means people earn wages that their families cannot control (see Melikian & al-Easa, 1991, writing about Qatar, in the Persian Gulf). Young people rely on schooling and the media for more of their knowledge and information than generations before them, and they learn to value a high material standard of living. These changes may conflict with traditional family norms, values, and expectations. They certainly have the potential to set up conflicts between the parental generation and their children and, often, between religious and state institutions. These changes may be particularly challenging in countries in which the state and religion are not separate, such as Iran or Israel. Yet outcomes are not preordained; there is no certainty, for example, that the family in a modernizing Muslim region will be identical to the modern Christian, Hindu, or Jewish family.

Another factor that changes family life is political will and ideology. China, for example, has attempted to mobilize families in support of social development. Planned change of the family has gone hand in hand with economic and political change. In research by Kejing (1990), both the hardship and the progress along this road are apparent. Many conditions of life in China remain difficult, yet there is no doubt that family life is improving, especially for women. Despite a lack of prosperity, state efforts to regulate marriage, fertility and the rights of women are starting to pay off with smaller families and increased gender equality, though at the expense of personal liberty.

The Ultimate Motherhood Issue

The modern landscape of motherhood is a confusing, conflicted place made all the more tangled because, obviously, it is a sacred subject infused with myriad prejudices, expectations and tyrannies. Overarching the debate about motherhood and parenthood is the appalling want of many children in North America, even in the midst of plenty. For those born in poverty what's wanted is food, shelter, protection from neglect. For many born in material comfort the want is perhaps more subtle but just as malignant: a need for nurturing—actually, a need for parenting.

Which brings us to the debate about day care versus mother care. The heat surrounding this issue is at least in part explained by the strong emotions it stirs up in mothers. Most of us are convinced at some level that what our children need most is us, and we feel guilty about relegating their care to someone else.

But the issue is murky. Mother care is not the panacea it seems. For some children, good day care is better than being at home. For most, however, it's still not clear how beneficial or harmful other care really is, because most of the studies done to quantify the effects of day care versus mother care on young children (and to assure mothers that day care is okay) compare luxury day-care centres and middle-class, advantaged mothering for their measurements. The harm of giving day care the thumbs up is that scenario is not the reality for the vast majority of children in the United States and Canada.

The guilt and fear and blame that suffuse child-rearing makes the motherhood issue difficult to talk about honestly. There's no denying that across all income strata we've got serious problems with behaviour and values in a lot of children these days. The right's call for a return to "family values" is an attempt to address some of this, and as ridiculous as the yearning for the Leave-It-To-Beaver era is, the underlying proposition—that children need an involved parent or two—is not.

Source: Patricia Best. 1997. (abridged). Reprinted with permission from *The Globe and Mail*.

In the West, where industrialization occurred a century or more ago, economies have continued to change to a pattern sometimes called "late industrial," "post-industrial," or "the information age." Along with these changes have come shifts in family. Families have become both smaller and less stable, and have been affected by the changing role of women, who have entered the labour market in large numbers. This is a function of changing economies as well as changing opportunities for women in society. It also relates to the demise of what was known as the family wage, the payment of a wage sufficiently high to enable an entire family to live on it. With the end of this notion, families had little choice but to send out an additional worker to make ends meet. Interestingly, early in this century it was more often children who entered the market to earn the extra money families needed to survive. Now, it is more common for both spouses to work while the children do not. But there are hints in the 1990s of a strong tendency for families once again to be relying on the earnings of adolescent children—as well as both parents' earnings—in order to manage.

Declining Fertility and the Value of Parenthood

One of the most profound changes in family life has been a change in family size. Since the 1870s, fertility in the West has declined steadily (see Figure 1.1). Today, most European and North American countries are at, or just below, population replacement levels. This means that, unless there is a radical shift in fertility or immigration, Western populations will get smaller and older during the next century. This process is already well underway in Sweden and France, as well as in Japan. Whether this is a problem—for families and for societies—depends on who is deciding and how the situation is defined. It is a topic to which we will return as we proceed.

A significant blip on this downward fertility curve was the post-war "baby boom." The baby boom, however, was only a temporary reversal of the long-term trend and was largely confined to North America. The "boom" was also misnamed. Higher birth rates, in fact, were the result not of increasing family size but of compressing two decades of births into a decade and a half (roughly 1947–1962). In other words, it was the result not so much of increased fertility but of postponed fertility due to World War II. Several different age groups then had their desired number of children within a short time frame, leading to a dramatic increase in birth rate for those years. By and large, however, the long-term downward trend in fertility over the course of the twentieth century has never really stopped.

The First and Second Demographic Transitions

A demographic transition also occurred, from high mortality and fertility to low mortality and fertility, which transformed the social meaning of children, childrearing, and women's place in the family. We shall have much more to

Figure 1.1 **TOTAL FERTILITY RATE FOR CANADIAN WOMEN, 1920–1990**

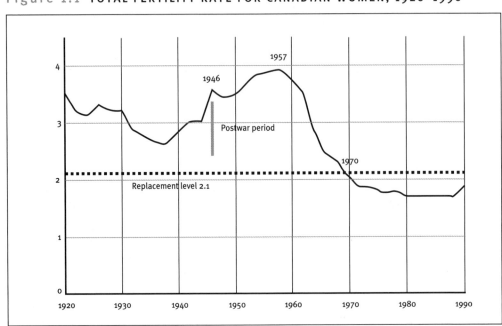

Source: Statistics Canada. *Vital Statistics*, Vol. 1, adapted from *Births and Deaths* (Catalogue # 84-204) and *Health Reports*, Supplement # 14 (Catalogue # 82-003). Reprinted with permission.

say about these never-ending changes in later chapters.

This transition to low fertility in the West, which began around 1870, is called the *first demographic transition*. This brought births into line with a sharply reduced death rate, so the theory argues. Since 1965, we have seen a new force for lower fertility in the West. Demographers have called this new phase the "second demographic transition" (Van de Kaa, 1987). This contemporary transition has brought birth rates into line with new lifestyle goals and family practices. Wherever we find the second demographic transition well advanced, we find a profusion of new ("non-traditional") family styles, women working in the paid labour force in large numbers, and people seeking autonomy and fulfilment in their personal lives.

The second demographic transition is particularly advanced in Northern and Western Europe. Renewed concerns have been expressed in these regions about depopulation and a shortage of young people in the future. In Europe, the fertility rates needed to replace the population—about 2.1 lifetime births per woman—are found only in Ireland, Malta, Poland, Albania, Turkey, and some countries of the former USSR. None of these countries is a highly industrialized, Protestant country. All of them have made a virtue of large family size or limited access to birth control. It must be remem-

The postwar "baby boom" produced a significant blip in the downward fertility curve. However, the long-term downward trend has never really stopped.

bered that Canada did this as well until very recently.

In most Protestant industrial countries, fertility rates hover around 1.5 children per woman. Japan's fertility rate has dropped too, from an annual level of 2.14 in 1973 to 1.57 in 1989, the lowest ever recorded there. A continuing decline in fertility will leave Europe's population with a growth of only 6 percent between 1985 and 2025, while the world's population overall nearly doubles. As a result of low fertility, by 2025 one in every five Europeans will be 65 or older.

The effects of this transition are profound and subtle. A long decline in fertility, together with increased life expectancy, has led to an aging population. People have fewer young kin today than they did in the past. Many of us have (or will have) fewer daughters and sons, nephews and nieces, grandsons and granddaughters than did our parents or grandparents. On the other hand, we are much more likely to have many generations alive at once than at any previous time in history, with some families having as many as five or even six living generations (McDaniel, 1996b). Remarried and reconstituted families also expand our kin networks into stepchildren and step-grandchildren, as well as his-and-hers extended families. And, largely because of urbanization, more people today live alone or outside conventional families than their parents or grandparents would have done. In general, domestic lives are becoming more varied and complex.

Several explanations exist for these recent fertility declines. We are hard-pressed to assign priority to one or another factor. Women have been taking advantage of more access to education and employment. Couples have delayed marrying. When people delay marriage, they are somewhat less likely ever to marry (although this is less so now than in the past) and, if they do marry, likely to have fewer children. At the same time, the costs of raising children, both economic and social/personal, rose dramatically during the twentieth century. Children are particularly expensive if they need daycare by someone other than the mother (whose child care was in the past presumed to be costless) or if caring for them means forgoing a parent's income and career aspirations for several years. And, of course, who among us would not want our children to have "quality" lives? This term may be defined differently by each of us, but may include such costly items as hockey, ballet, and music lessons. As well, children today remain in a state of economic dependency for longer than in the past, sometimes for surprisingly long times, as we shall see in later chapters. Finally, children often contribute less to the family economy than they used to in pre-industrial times and in the early part of the twentieth century.

The number of people who remain childless has also grown in many Western countries; only, however, in comparison to recent decades. Among women now in their eighties, approximately 25 percent are childless (Rosenthal, 1999), a higher proportion than among younger women or than is likely in the immediate future. A small number of childless couples are desperately eager to make use of new reproductive technologies or to adopt a child. Most childless women and men, and couples, however, are content to be childless. For some proportion (it is not known how many), childlessness is a chosen option, one they enjoy. In short, people think about parenting and having children in different ways today than they used to in the 1950s and 1960s.

Contraception and Childbearing Choice

A very important factor in fertility decline may be technological. During the 1960s, safe, reliable contraception became easily available. The first demographic transition was accomplished through a combination of strategies including late marriage, abstinence from sex, awkward methods of birth control, and dangerous, illegal abortion. The second demographic transition has occurred in the midst of a liberalizing sexual revolution and new accessible means of contraception. Thanks to the Pill and other relatively readily available forms of contraception—including IUDs (intrauterine devices), spermicidal gels and foams, and higher-quality condoms—more and more women and couples are able to choose if and when to become pregnant.

Women are extending their education, entering careers, and postponing marriage and/or childbearing to do so. Many are not ready to begin parenthood before their thirties and few are willing, or able, to take much time off work to do so. The result is a late, brief explosion of births among women who, by world and historical standards, are "older" first-time mothers. In the last twenty years, we have seen an overall decrease in the numbers of children born to women aged thirty and over, but an increase in first births among these same women (Statistics Canada, 1992). These statistics represent changing preferences of women, including planned delay.

Abortion

Sterilization and abortion also play important roles in fertility reduction today. Overall, abortions have had less impact on the North American fertility rate than contraceptives (pills, condoms, and the like). However the same is not true everywhere. For example, legal abortions have had strong effects on fertility in Eastern Europe and Latin America. Not enough is known about the effects of abortion on fertility in China and in other less developed regions of the world to be able to make claims with any certainty. Eastern European women, however, have an average of 1 to 2.5 legal abortions in their lifetimes, in contrast to .2 and .6 in other parts of Europe. Whether these high rates will continue or increase with the "fall of the Berlin Wall" remains to be seen.

Contraception has been generally scarce in Eastern Europe. The average woman in the former Soviet Union and Romania in the mid-1960s would have had seven abortions during her lifetime. Van de Kaa (1987) notes the dramatic rise in third and higher-order births after the repeal of legal abortion legislation in Romania, while the Ceaucescu regime maintained an iron-fisted stance against birth control in a deliberate attempt to increase the birth rate. What this shows is that abortion had been playing a large role in controlling fertility, where other means of birth control were unavailable. Once abortion was ruled out, people abandoned their babies to the care of the state. The net result was a huge number of Romanian babies and children crammed into orphanages under appalling conditions.

Though less dramatically, easier access to legal abortion has also influenced fertility in the West (Krannich, 1990). Up to the 1890s, abortion was tolerated in many jurisdictions, including in Canada. Women who wanted to end their pregnancies could do so with the assistance of surgeons, herbalists, or midwives. Abortion was in fact legal in most North American states until the 1890s. Then it became illegal for seventy years as a result of pressure exerted by social purity movements. Legalizing abortion once again made the process safer and more medically controlled. The (legal) abortion rate rose briefly after the mid-1960s, with a more liberal interpretation of the laws, but the rate soon tapered off (Krannich, 1990:368).

The most important factor promoting a decline in the incidence of abortion is the use of contraception, which enables avoidance of unwanted pregnancies. As in so many areas of life, preventing problems is easier, safer, and surer than remedying them after the fact. So as contraceptive knowledge and use have spread, abortion has become a less often relied-upon means of limiting fertility. However, the debate over abortion has not ceased, nor is it likely to. All pregnancies are not planned or wanted or safe for the health and well-being of either the woman or the fetus. The need for abortion as an option is not likely to disappear anytime soon.

This revolution in birth control has had profound effects on relations between women and men. Before effective antibiotics and birth control methods existed, there was a strong prohibition on male-female relationships, even friendships, outside of marriage. People were afraid they would lead to sexual intercourse, loss of a young woman's virginity, and pregnancy or killer venereal diseases such as syphilis. (Ironically, the prevalence of contraceptive pill use may have contributed to the spread of HIV/AIDS as well as some of the newer venereal diseases such as chlamydia.) Where sexual purity was an issue, a double standard has always been applied. Moreover, sexual prohibition or abstinence was enforced more or less strongly in different times and places. We'll discuss sexual mores more fully in the next chapter.

Family and Household Size

As fertility has declined, the number of people in the average household has become smaller. The average Canadian household has shrunk by 50 percent, from around six people in 1681 to just under three people in 1981. What's more, complex family households, containing a variety of people who are not part of a nuclear family, have almost vanished. The proportion of two-family households dropped by 75 percent between 1931 and 1981. The proportion of households with lodgers also fell, from 14.9 percent in 1931—more than one household in seven—to nearly zero fifty years later (Bradbury, 1984). All these trends, however, may be changing slightly with tough economic times, as families double up more to share expenses (Mitchell & Gee, 1996).

At the same time, a major change in family life has been a rise in the proportion of single-person households (Sweet & Bumpass, 1987:340)—the proportion has more than tripled since 1931, when they made up 7 percent of all households. Since 1971 alone, there has been an 88 percent increase in non-family households (Vanier Institute of the Family, 1994:29), while the proportion of people overall living in families declined from 89 percent in 1971 to 84 percent in 1991 (Vanier Institute of the Family, 1994:29). Today, more people prefer to, and can afford to, live alone, something to which we will return in a later chapter.

Curiously, while households have been growing smaller, houses have been growing bigger. Victorian-era houses were intended to serve as single-family homes with space for one or two live-in servants. When immigration was at a peak, as many as 15 people occupied these houses (Iacovetta, 1992). In pre-industrial times, even more people shared living quarters. But today, most single-family houses are occupied by couples with fewer than three children, or none at all. Yet suburban middle-class houses of the 1930s that were big enough for raising four children now seem too small for raising two children (Rybczynski, 1992). As families have shrunk, desires for space and privacy have increased.

In North America, home life and family life imply intimacy but also privacy. Intimacy and privacy demand a suitable physical environment. In practice, this means enough room (and rooms) to separate the household from the community and family members from one another within the household.

Changing Attitudes to Marriage

Traditionally, marriage was viewed largely in terms of rights, duties, and obligations. Throughout the West, a major attitude shift has placed greater emphasis on the personal or emotional side of close relations.

As far back as 1981, only one in five North Americans surveyed expressed "traditional" family attitudes (Yankelovich, 1981). Likely, this number has since shrunk. Another one in five believed life is about self-fulfilment, not duty to others in either family or society. Marriage and family life may be valued so long as they complement—or at least do not interfere with—personal aspirations and self-fulfilment. The remaining three in five North Americans, the majority, fall between these two extremes. For most, the quality of a relationship is more important than its structure (e.g., married versus common-law). The important question for three-fifths of people is

Formal weddings and legal ceremonies of marriage have more to do with marking a transition or gaining social approval than with emotional commitment.

"What makes an intimate relationship satisfying?" not the legal or societal arrangements under which the relationship exists.

Why, then, do people still keep up the old forms? Why do so many still get married, many of them in churches, dressed in immensely expensive white bridal gowns and formal black tuxedos with cummerbunds? We shall discuss these questions in a later chapter. In short, formal weddings and going through the legal ceremony of marriage have more to do with marking a transition and/or gaining social approval than with emotional commitment. Many people still find the idea of legal marriage compelling, despite what they know about the realities of marriage and divorce. Enormous numbers of North Americans are neither rejecting the family or other long-lasting, close relationships nor accepting family in a traditional form. Most are hoping to revitalize and reinterpret family (Scanzoni, 1981a, 1981b, 1987), making families suited to themselves and their needs.

Yet in some parts of Canada and the world, and in the future, marriage may no longer be the close relationship in which people spend most of their adult lives. People are already less inclined to marry than they were in the past. They are more likely to view cohabitation or singlehood positively.

Cohabitation: Trial Marriage or an Alternative?

One significant change in family life in the Western world has been an increase in cohabitation—people living together without being legally married (see Figure 1.2). Living together, also called cohabitation or common-law union, used to be more prevalent among working-class people. It also used to be seen as a lesser form of relationship than marriage. Now, however, it has lost its stigma, and is much more accepted. In Quebec, cohabitation has become the norm for younger couples, with legal marriage decidedly less preferred.

Cohabitation is, however, a less stable form of union than legal marriage. It describes many different kinds of relationships, including some that may be less serious from the outset. This does not mean that there are not long-lasting, happily cohabiting couples, for there are many. Some people may prefer cohabitation precisely because it does not have the same expectation of permanence, but for others cohabitation is seen as permanent. It gives people many of the expected benefits of family life—emotional and sexual satisfaction, and mutual dependency and support, for example—while they retain (or at least perceive) a greater degree of choice and freedom.

Increasingly, couples in cohabiting relationships have children. In 1993–94, 20.4 percent of all Canadian children were born to women living in common-law unions with the child's father (Vanier Institute of the Family, 1994). Legal marriage appears to be less the basis of family formation and childbearing than it used to be. The old stigma of illegitimacy, or birth "out of wedlock," is largely gone, particularly when the parents are in a stable, car-

Figure 1.2 FAMILY STRUCTURE IN CANADA, 1986 AND 1996

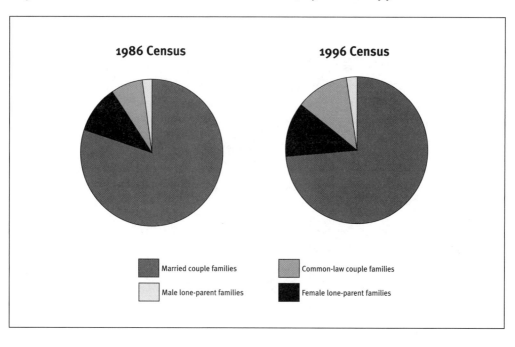

Source: From the Statistics Canada Web page (http://www.statcan.ca). Reprinted with permission.

ing relationship. Especially in Quebec, people now see cohabitation as a lifelong way of family life, a close, committed relationship in which to have and raise children (see Figure 1.3).

If cohabitation is trial marriage (and increasing evidence suggests that it is an alternative form of family union instead), one might think that the longer the cohabitation period, the more stable the subsequent marriage. However, there is not much difference in divorce rates between women who had previously cohabited one year, two years, or three years. One study, though, shows that women who cohabit premaritally for more than three years before marrying have higher divorce rates than women who cohabit for shorter durations (Halli & Zimmer, 1991). It may be that it is not the cohabitation *per se* that relates to the higher risks of splitting up, but the social risk factors that people bring into the relationship. Evidence shows that people who cohabit tend to be "divorce-prone," or already divorced once. If so, the difference in divorce rates may not be a result of cohabitation but a reflection of the characteristics of a self-selected group. We will discuss this further in a later chapter.

It may be coincidental that the growth in cohabitation has coincided with later marriage, higher divorce rates, and lower rates of childbearing.

Figure 1.3 **COMMON-LAW FAMILIES AS A PROPORTION OF ALL FAMILIES, 1996**

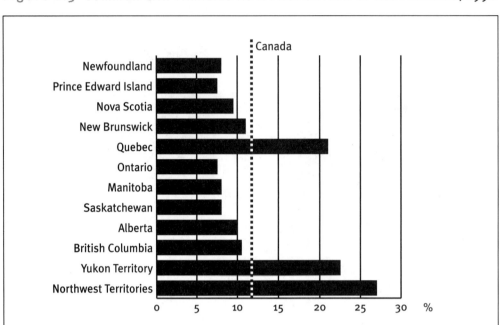

Source: From the Statistics Canada Web page (http:/www.statcan.ca). Reprinted with permission.

More and more often, people think of spousal relations as being about love and sexual attraction, not childbearing and cementing families together. People have come to expect more satisfaction of their emotional and psychological needs in their close relationships. Women, particularly, are less economically dependent on their partners than they used to be. These shifting norms, opportunities, and expectations have all contributed to a decline in the stability of married and cohabiting life.

Variation in Life Course

In the past, people expected a certain sequencing of family-related events. They expected, for example, young people to complete their educations before marrying, marry before having children, get old before becoming a grandparent, and so on. So predictable was the pattern that sociologists spoke confidently about a normal life cycle of family events. Today, the timing and sequencing of events are too varied to be easily categorized. A woman can be a grandmother and a mid-career professional at the same time, or a new mother at midlife while starting a career. Patterns of family life have become more complex: for example, a child whose biological parents have joint custody may call two houses "home" and claim four (or more) sets of grandparents. Some middle-aged adults have to cope with the anxieties of dating again after becoming newly single. A woman can safely have a first child, with or without a long-term partner, after age forty.

Childbearing Alone

Childbearing is no longer seen as inevitably associated with marriage, or even cohabitation. In 1993–94, 8.7 percent of Canadian children were born to women who were not living with the child's father. Of these, over half were born to women who had never lived with the child's father. Data from Canada's Longitudinal Study of Children and Youth reveal that when babies are born to single mothers, it is less common for the father to eventually move in. More than half the children born to single mothers in 1983–84 witnessed the completion of the family unit when the father came to live with the mother after the birth. By 1992, the movement was the other way: in more than half the births to women living apart from the baby's father, the parents had lived together when the baby was conceived, but the father moved out before the birth.

Pregnancy in the absence of marriage may be a deliberate choice among women who strongly desire motherhood but not marriage. And a man who wishes to become a father may do so without being married or in a committed relationship by enlisting the services of a surrogate mother.

Teen Pregnancy

One variation in life course that has been the focus of a great deal of public concern is "children having children." There has been, until very recently, a steady decline in births to adolescents in Canada. In the late 1990s the rate has increased a little, but still remains considerably lower than teen pregnancy rates in the United States (Baker, 1996a). Teen pregnancy rates vary enormously across the industrialized West. Teen pregnancy, for example, is rare in Sweden, where childbearing among women below age 18 has almost disappeared (Hoem, 1988:22). By contrast, the United States has the highest rate of unmarried teen pregnancy in the world; 33 percent of live births in 1990 were to teenaged mothers (Baker, 1996a; Ryder, 1992).

In part, the rise in teen births in the U.S. is a function of an increase in the number of teenagers. However it mostly reflects a growing acceptance of unmarried pregnancy. More of these young mothers, too, are keeping their babies and raising them alone: both "shotgun weddings" and giving babies up for adoption have become less common.

Some people believe that the economic social supports available to single mothers—social assistance payments, food stamps, Medicaid—contribute to teen pregnancies. This seems unlikely, however, since tightening entitlement criteria for such benefits in the 1980s did not stop the rise in teen pregnancy rates. Comparative research (Jones, *et al.*, 1987) suggests, instead, that American teenagers are sent very mixed messages about sex-

---

Most Teenaged Mothers Have History of Abuse

Teenage girls who get pregnant tend not to be just ordinary kids who make a mistake—most have had a life full of them. The majority of teenage mothers come from homes where they were physically or sexually abused and where there were drug and alcohol problems and divorce.

A study that has followed 300 teenage mothers in southwestern Ontario for the past 12 years shows the teens got pregnant with considerably older men. "I confess I imagined teenage pregnancy as some-

thing that happened to a couple of otherwise normal teenage kids who were doing okay, and that's not so," said Ann Marie Sorenson, who co-authored the study with Carl Grindstaff of the University of Western Ontario.

Most have not managed to escape the deprivation they grew up with. In a follow-up seven years later only 15 per cent had completed high school, just one-third were working, and most were living below the poverty line.

Source: Elaine Carvey. 1997. Reprinted with permission of The Toronto Star Syndicate. Abridged from an article originally appearing in *The Toronto Star* (October 31, 1997).

uality. The media bombard them with urgent messages about the thrill of sexual love. Yet religious fundamentalists make it difficult for governments and public schools to provide children with information and contraception that would prevent unwanted pregnancies. Recent analyses have also argued that among African-American teenaged girls, the high rates of pregnancy are related to the lack of other options for self-fulfilment and achievement. We'll talk more about teen childbearing in Chapter 4.

New Ways to Understand Family Diversity

Life course approaches offer sociologists new ways to study family change over our lives. They enable us to follow the variety of social and interpersonal dynamics of close relations and how these change throughout our lifetimes (Elder, 1992; Kohli, 1986). For example, it is possible to see the ways in which the times (women's greater socioeconomic opportunities, for example) affect how families are shaped by individuals over their lives. It is also possible with the life course approach to see the full range of diversity in close relations over lifetimes.

Another new approach is to look at family relations from the perspectives of different family members. Much of family research up until the early 1970s was done from a male perspective. A popular phrase of the time that has stuck is "bedroom communities," which described suburban communities in which families lived and women often worked at home. These were living communities and could be seen as bedrooms only if seen from the point of view of men who worked elsewhere. Many other examples exist. What do family life and changes in close relations among adults look

Canadian Children Doing Well, Study Says

"The majority of Canadian kids are doing well, and the reason they are doing well is because government communities and families have put an enormous investment into the well-being of our children," Katherine Scott, the project director, said yesterday.

"Our concern is that there are a number of danger signs on the horizon, and without continued investment in public education, health programs and other community services, the well-being of kids today could actually deteriorate in the future."

Nearly 80 per cent of children, new-born to age 11, live with two biological parents, and only 1 per cent live with teen-age mothers, says the report, entitled The Progress of Canada's Children, 1996. It was prepared by the Canadian Council on Social Development and drawn from Statistics Canada data.

The report says nearly nine in ten children aged four to nine have a positive attitude toward learning and look forward to going to school.

Canada has high rates of youth literacy compared with other countries, the report concludes. But the study also notes a large number of discouraging signs:

• One in five children—or 1.4 million—live in poverty. Forty per cent of welfare recipients are children.

• Since 1984, parents in two-parent families have increased their work time by an average of 5.7 weeks a year and are having increased difficulties balancing their work and family responsibilities.

• The number of single-parent families is increasing, and they are more likely to be poor—56 per cent compared with 13 per cent for two-parent families. One child in seven lives in a single-parent household.

• Children in poor households are twice as likely as others to have low scores on school-readiness exams.

• Earnings are dropping for young families.

• Funding for kindergarten classes is being cut, depriving children of access to high-quality preschool programs.

• Nearly 6 per cent of babies have low birth weights, which often lead to lifelong problems.

• Violent crimes by youths aged 12 to 17 doubled between 1986 and 1992.

• The teen-age suicide rate, particularly among boys, has soared in the past 30 years.

Source: Edward Greenspon. 1996. (Abridged). Reprinted with permission from *The Globe and Mail*.

like from the viewpoint of children, for example? They look profoundly different, as we are now discovering (Marcil-Gratton, 1993). Children live in numerous and varied kinds of families while still dependent, and changes in family are happening earlier in their lives than for children in times past. Looking at shifting close relations among adults from the viewpoint of children's living situations gives us a new and important vantage point on families.

Yet another new approach is to collect data in new ways so that family diversity can be studied over time. One example is Statistics Canada's Survey of Labour and Income Dynamics (Statistics Canada, 1996), which builds a picture of the changes in people's work and family lives over time. For the first time, it is possible to know fully about the changes that occur in individual families over time. Cheal (1997), for example, relies on the new survey (known as SLID) to examine the longer-term effects of being in a financially dependent family while young or at various life course stages. He finds that the effects of dependence and of poverty of youth increase intergenerational inequities over time.

Some researchers call our attention to the fact that all families change, and the times change families. For example, Whitehead (1990:1) tells us that "Today's stay-at-home mother is tomorrow's working mother." She further points out that families are changeable according to the times: "One day, the Ozzie and Harriet couple is eating a family meal at the dining room table; the next day, they are working out a joint custody agreement in a law office."

Another overview is provided by Statistics Canada's Longitudinal Survey of Children (to which we have already referred), which follows children's lives through until adulthood, collecting data on family changes, schooling, health, and a whole range of variables that affect children's lives. Early findings from this study have enabled us for the first time to learn, for example, that the effect on children of living with a single parent is more than the result of the low incomes often faced by such families. The good news from the early findings is that good parenting can, to a large degree, overcome these detrimental effects. (We'll look at the effects of single parenthood more closely in Chapter 5.) Much is to be learned by following the same people (children or adults) for a long period of time and seeing how their changing family situations affect them.

Social Support: The Role of Family and State

Around the world, both families and states provide social support for dependent social groups: children, old people, the infirm, and others who may need support. However, demographic changes associated with modernization have reduced the size of the kin networks most people have. Increased longevity and decreased fertility have meant lesser portions of our lives spent parenting, smaller families, and fewer siblings. These changes have also lengthened pre-childbearing and "empty nest" periods for intact couples and extended parental survival and the probability of dependency in late life. In turn, this has reduced the potential quality and quantity of the family support that dependent people can obtain (Keyfitz, 1988; Matras, 1989).

As families have changed and evolved with respect to meeting people's needs for support, state support has also developed and changed. Major cycles of change in state support for families have occurred through recent times, with sharp reductions occurring at present. As well, gaps in service exist and there is wide variation from society to society.

Families remain socially and economically important. The allocation of resources, for example, even in modern society, is often based on families and family relations. One benefits from having a family with resources, and one suffers from being in a family without resources. These resources may be money, connections, and other concrete benefits. They may also include the sharing of caring, the capacity to mobilize opportunities, or the presence of a dependable shoulder to lean on. In times of uncertainty, when services and supports are cut and so many people face insecure jobs and futures, families are the providers of resources. As we shall see in later chapters, families may be becoming the central safety net for many people as other options shrink.

Variation Despite Convergence

As we have seen throughout this section, changing economies and societies have played a major role in changing both the form and content of family life, both in countries just becoming industrialized and in the Western world, where economic change continues. Many social scientists perceive these changes as part of an inevitable and universal progress toward a single worldwide culture of modernity. **Convergence theory** presents a rosy picture of family modernization, as though families and individuals are choosing to change and are all changing effectively. In fact, families have been forced to change. William Goode (1984:57–8) has pointed out that families change when societies industrialize precisely because industrialism "fails to give support to the family":

> 1. The industrial system fires, lays off, and demands geographical mobility by reference to the individual, ignoring the family strains these actions may cause.

> 2. The economy increasingly uses women in the labor force, and thus puts a still larger work burden on them; but few corporations have developed programs for helping women with child care, or making it easier for men to share in these tasks.

> 3. The industrial system has little place for the elderly, and the neolocal, independent household with its accompanying values in favor of separate lives for each couple leaves older parents and kin in an ambiguous position ...

> 4. The family is relatively fragile because of separation and divorce, but the larger system offers little help in these crises for adults and their children.

Industrialization produces great opportunities, but also great perils, for families and family life. Some societies, and some families, respond better than others. In some industrial countries, families receive much more support from the state than they do in other countries. By its laws and policies, a state can influence the costs to individuals and to society associated with marriage, divorce, childbearing, childrearing, and elder care. In this way, it can influence the patterns of family life in that society. That is, in part, why industrial societies do not have identical family forms, why families in modern societies are far from uniform.

There is no evidence of a single evolutionary path in family life—from simple to complex, extended to nuclear family. Even nuclear families, thought to be the most distinctive feature of modern family life, are not a linear product of industrialization. Because the effects of industrialization have been so all-encompassing, social scientists have been tempted to search for the origins of the Western family with industrialization. But, as Goldthorpe (1987:10) points out, many features of the Western family—neolocal residence, bilateral kinship recognition, and possibly monogamy—go back to pre-Christian history. Nuclear families were common in England long before industrialization. English adults apparently never had an overwhelming desire to live with their parents, with their grown children, or with uncles, aunts, or cousins. Like us, the pre-industrial English preferred to set up their own households, containing only spouses and children, and did so whenever they could. A similar pattern is found in pre-Confederation Newfoundland (McDaniel & Lewis, 1997).

Industrialism does not by itself create nuclear families, nor does it necessarily destroy them. Mitterauer and Sieder (1986) have shown that throughout European history, multiple family forms have co-existed. Families of the past, like our own families today, were full of variety, change, movement, and uncertainty. Just as they do today, families in the past changed with the economic, political, legal, and social conditions surrounding them, yet made some choices about what they would change and what they would let be.

Major forces of social change like industrialization, urbanization, and education certainly affect family life; yet the relationships are not simple, nor are the outcomes predictable. Indeed, in two of the most industrialized countries, Japan and Sweden, we find very different family forms. In Japan, we find traditional family and gender norms persisting; in Sweden, by contrast, there is a very high rate of cohabitation, divorce, and women working in the paid work force (although mostly in traditional female sectors). Throughout this book we argue that many family forms are not only possible but desirable, and, indeed, work well—in Canada and throughout the world.

There are no obvious conclusions to be drawn about what a family is, what causes families to change, or whether family life is getting better or worse. Those who want simple answers may find this ambiguity disappointing. Those who want to understand the modern family will find that the many open questions make for an exciting and intellectually challenging area of sociology.

Concluding Remarks

It seems that everywhere, family relationships are in flux. In Africa and Asia, industrialization and urbanization are destroying extended kinship networks and bringing a drastic change in the nature of family obligations. In North America, people value family life. However they are spending a smaller and smaller fraction of their lives in anything resembling a traditional family. And North American families today show more signs of stress and conflict than ever before.

Current family trends are the result of long-term worldwide changes in social life. New laws and new contraceptive technology have given rise to new sexual permissiveness. Fertility has continued to fall for more than a century. Divorce rates have reached historically high levels everywhere, especially in the United States. These long-term trends have been given a boost by rapid increases in the labour force participation of mothers of young children. In turn, their behaviour is the culmination of a struggle for equality with men that began in earnest two centuries ago with such early feminists as Mary Wollstonecraft.

The process of industrialization has set in motion irresistible, irreversible social forces that transform the content of everyday life. They include the development of a consumer culture, market economy, welfare states, and a mobile, urban social structure. As well, new technology prolongs life, prevents unwanted births, and creates life outside the womb. In future, many scientists expect that it will even create new sentient creatures through genetic engineering and artificial intelligence.

The sociological study of family life offers a good illustration of the relationship between social structures and social processes, between choices and constraints, between similarity and diversity. Some aspects of family life—for example, the norm of marital fidelity—are slow to change. *The family* as a cultural ideal exists outside and beyond individual people, in the ways that people of a particular society think about love, marriage, parenthood, the domestic division of labour, and so on. What is amazing about family life today is the contrast between people's idealization of family life "in the old days" and people's never-ending creativity in the face of a rapidly changing everyday reality.

Family life is constantly being constructed, and every family bears the unique stamp of its members. No two families enact love, marriage, parenthood, or domestic work in precisely the same way. If anything, the study of families makes clear that social life is a process of continued uncertainty, variety, and negotiation. We get the families we struggle for, although some family members have more power than others in the struggle.

Yet families *have* changed dramatically in the last thirty or so years. Accepted ways of thinking, speaking, and behaving have changed because dozens, then thousands, then millions of family members have changed their way of doing things. We should not conclude that we are in the midst of a breakdown of the family, in which a mate is no more than erotic property, and a child no more than a consumer durable. The way most people continue to struggle and sacrifice for their family suggests that the family means a great deal more.

In the chapters that follow, we study a variety of families as they form, develop, grow, and, occasionally, shatter. We begin with a discussion of dating and mating.

CHAPTER SUMMARY

In this chapter, we have discussed what defines families, as well as some of the issues that make this a difficult task. Recent definitions have focused more on the processes than on the precise features of families. However, families do tend to share certain features, including for example strong emotional ties, norms, and taboos pertaining to sex and sexuality, and dependence and trust between members.

Historically, families have been important bases for identity and for resource allocation. In many cultures, broader family structures such as kinship groups and clans have played a large role in determining relationships and social position.

On the whole, over time there has been increasing acceptance of more diverse forms of families beyond the traditional nuclear family. In certain instances it is helpful to delineate the concepts of household and family, as is done by U.S. census-takers. In Canada families are defined in a somewhat different way, but one that reflects this increasing acceptance of family diversity, and recognizes that considerable change has taken place in the family since the nineteenth century. Family-related events, such as marriage and childbearing, no longer invariably follow a certain sequence. In many instances, family life has become more complex. Yet many, if not most, Canadians continue to consider family to be of key importance in their lives.

A key change in the twentieth-century family pertains to fertility, which has, with the exception of the brief post-War blip, shown a steady decline with industrialization. Several accounts of this decline were discussed, particularly the role of technology. Family life has also changed in conjunction with changes in the status and roles of women. Cohabitation as a precursor or alternative to marriage is increasingly accepted, even preferred among certain social groups. These and other changes suggest a greater equity within intimate relations, along with widening options to achieve satisfying relationships.

Industrialization and modernization have had an enormous impact on family lives. In contradiction to Convergence Theory, which presents familial change as both inevitable and beneficial, some argue that these processes have forced families to change or face peril. But the diversity of family life in the present suggests that there is no simple path leading to the idealized nuclear family from historical forms.

KEY TERMS

Affective nurturance: Caring for another with emotional attachment.

Bilateral: Referring to a kinship system in which descent or lineage is traced through the families of both the mother and the father.

Convergence theory: A sociological theory that holds that social forces such as urbanization, industrialization, and education lead inevitably to changes in social and family structure, so that ultimately family structures will be much the same the world over; and that these changes are beneficial.

Endogamy: Marriage to a partner from the same social group or geographical locale (village, area, etc.).

Exogamy: Marriage to a partner from outside one's social group or geographical locale.

Family household: A household whose members are related to each other by blood, marriage, or adoption.

Kin-keeper: The family member who keeps the family in contact through holidays, special occasions, letter-writing or phone calls, arranging family reunions, or by other means.

Kinship group: A group of people who recognize a blood relationship and have positions in a hierarchy of rights over the property.

Matriarchy: A society of family type/system in which women have more power or authority than men.

Matrilineal: Referring to a kinship system in which descent or lineage is traced through the family of the mother.

Neolocal residence: Wife and husband (bride and groom) live in a residence separate from their parents.

Nonfamily household: A household containing unrelated individuals or people who live alone.

Patriarchy: A society or family type/system in which men have more power and authority than women.

Patrilineal: Referring to a kinship system in which descent or lineage is traced through the family of the father.

Polygamy: A system of marriage in which adults are allowed to marry more than one person at time, even if they do not actually do so.

SUGGESTED READINGS

Coontz, Stephanie. *The Way We Never Were: American Families and the Nostalgia Trap*. New York: Basic Books, 1992. This book explores the myths and realities of twentieth-century family history from a social problems perspective. Also consider:

Coontz, Stephanie. *The Way We Really Are: Coming to Terms With America's Changing Families*. New York: Basic Books, 1997. An extension of the earlier book, this book addresses contemporary historical and sociological perspectives on change and chal-

lenges within American families.

Conway, John F. *The Canadian Family in Crisis*, 3rd Edition. Toronto: James Lorimer and Co., 1997. This book addresses changes in the Canadian family and the social, economic, and psychological consequences of this "crisis." Recommendations are made in the form of social and feminist policy reforms.

Hochschild, Arlie. *The Second Shift: Working Parents and the Revolution at Home*. Toronto:

Viking Penguin Inc., 1989. A discussion by case studies of the problems faced by men and women as they attempt to negotiate the difficulties presented by the (usually) female problem of the "second shift" of unpaid labour in the home.

Gittins, Diana. *The Family in Question:* *Changing Households and Familiar Ideologies,* 2nd Edition. London: Macmillan Press, 1993. A feminist discussion of changes to the family in Britain with an emphasis on understanding the ideologies, such as patriarchy and conservatism, that influence our perceptions.

REVIEW QUESTIONS

1. Provide two different definitions of family and discuss why each is useful and why it is also problematic.

2. Identify and give examples of the main functions or processes of the family within society.

3. Is a cohabiting couple with no children a family? Why or why not?

4. Highlight the important ways in which family life has changed since the 1870s in Canada. What factors have helped to create these changes?

5. Distinguish between the first and second demographic transitions, keeping in mind the importance of social and historical context.

6. What has been the overall consequence of women's changing roles in society for families and close relations?

7. How has the value we place on parenting and becoming parents changed over the past three decades?

8. Compare and contrast the organization of close relations in industrialized and subsistence societies, being careful to clearly define all terminology (e.g., kinship group, exogamy).

9. What are the main characteristics of strong or healthy families?

10. What are the main changes in Canadian families in the last fifty years, and what caused those changes?

DISCUSSION QUESTIONS

1. What are the essential differences between family relations and other kinds of close relations? Why do these matter to us and to society?

2. If emotional intimacy is so central to what families are, then why do our friends sometimes matter more to us than our families?

3. Is the sequencing of "love, marriage, and baby carriage" changing? Does this matter to our concepts of family and close relations?

4. Choose two very different ways of living in families and discuss how both work to promote close relations.

5. In what ways do ideas about family and close relations affect our choices in our own lives?

6. Why do you suppose that family and close relations are so much discussed and debated in the 1990s?

7. Single-parent families as well as gay and lesbian families have been quite controversial in recent years. Discuss in terms of the definitions of family, as well as broader political and social issues.

8. In media and politics we can often see a pronounced nostalgia for the ideal nuclear family of the past. Based on your reading, how likely is this ideal to have actually existed?

9. Weigh the pros and cons of cohabitation with a partner before or as an alternative to marriage. Now consider it from your parents' viewpoint, then your grandparents'.

10. New reproductive technologies offer an intriguing set of issues for family sociologists. Are such technologies likely to change our experience and concepts of family and close relations? In what ways?

WEBLINKS

http://socialunion.gc.ca/ncb_e.html

The Social Union

An initiative of the federal government, this site is a key resource for students studying recent developments in Canadian family and social policy, including the National Children's Agenda and the National Child Benefit Program.

http://www.comnet.ca/~gilseg/chnbkmrk.htm

Canadian Social Research Links: Children, Families and Youth

Includes many useful links to local, provincial, and federal organizations and initiatives relevant to family research, as well as links to non-governmental organizations (NGOs) and international sites. Topics include daycare, child poverty, legislation, children's rights, education, etc.

http://familyforum.com/

Family Forum

A free service for the public and professionals in family services, including resources for families and researchers, mainly in the form of links grouped by subject matter.

http://www.bccf.bc.ca/

Family Connections

Hosted by the British Columbia Council for Families, this site is intended to provide resources for families (self-help information), researchers (online and traditional media), and those in the helping professions; the site also discusses the Council's advocacy and lobbying efforts.

http://www.hrdc-drhc.gc.ca/hrdc/corp/stratpol/arbsite/publish/may96_e.html

National Longitudinal Survey of Children and Youth

This site provides information as it becomes available from the ongoing National Survey, and will provide instructions for acquiring data and reports as they are generated.

http://familyforum.com/vanier/index.htm

Vanier Institute of the Family

Hosted by a national charitable organization dedicated to the study of the economic, demographic, social, and other influences on Canadian families; includes many links to online articles produced by the Institute.

http://www.trinity.edu/~mkearl/family.html

Kearl's Guide to the Sociology of the Family

An informative and up-to-date site about the sociology of the family and its major areas of concern, particularly why families are such a hot topic in the U.S. in the 1990s.

http://www.personal.psu.edu/faculty/n/x/nxd10/family3.htm

Family Relations

An initiative from the Department of Sociology and students at Penn State University, this site offers resources for the study of the family with an emphasis on relations within the family.

http://www.ncfr.com/body.html

The National Council on Family Relations (NCFR)

NCFR provides a forum for family researchers, educators, and practitioners to share in the development and dissemination of knowledge about families and family relationships, establishes professional standards, and works to promote family well-being.

CHAPTER TWO

How Families Begin:

Dating, Cohabitation, Marriage

Dating and mating is what most often comes to mind first when we think about close relations. Falling in love, being loved, cherished, indulged, forgiven our faults, and sharing everlasting sexual intimacy is the popular image of dating and mating in North American societies. It is where families begin in North America, for better or for worse. It is also the basis of much trouble in families, as you perhaps know from some of your own experiences or those of others close to you.

In this chapter, we will discover that romantic love is not the only, nor even necessarily the best, way to begin families; that it is a relatively modern human invention (although some see it as having a biological basis); that power matters in how families begin and how they develop; and that the ways in which we form family-like intimate relationships are changing dramatically in the 1990s. We look at sexual intimacy, the negative sides of dating relationships, and how having someone close who cares about you can be good for your health and overall well-being, a theme to which we return in the next chapter.

Love and Family Beginnings

Love and Sociology

Curiously, love and sociology are linked almost as closely as love and marriage are thought to be. Émile Durkheim, one of the founding fathers of sociology, discovered in the earliest sociological research that close social ties make a difference to survival (married people are less likely to commit suicide, for example), and that ceremonies and symbols (such as weddings, and wedding rings) tend to bring communities together for common purposes (Durkheim, 1915/1957). We will talk more about the importance of symbols and rituals in the next chapter when we focus on the effects of close relations for well-being, both individual and social.

Durkheim saw marriage partners and their dependent children as a freeing family form that evolved as the **extended family** retreated in importance (Sydie, 1987:17). Along with the reduction in family members, according to Durkheim, was an intensification of ties between marital partners, as well as between parents and their children. It is in the attachment of husbands and wives that the basis of societal solidarity is found, argues Durkheim. This view was echoed in the slogan chosen for the International Year of the Family: "The family is the heart of society." **Attachment** is characterized by common sentiments and shared memories, as well as shared purpose in work and life.

Max Weber, another founding father of sociology, reveals the centrality of marriage in his exploration of feudalism (Sydie, 1986:73–77). The chivalry of knighthood required personal bonds and unity among knights. Women of feudal nobility were often the managers of estates and huge feudal households in partnerships with their husbands. Marriages were the means to cement clans or family groups, so that in some instances, men marrying women who owned fiefdoms took the woman's name on marriage.

Frederick Engels, who along with Karl Marx is also a father of sociology, outlined a theory of marriage (Sydie, 1986:96). With the availability of additional resources, Engels argues, women and men became **monogamous** (married to only one partner for life). The link between economic production and marriage is that men would be able to pass their wealth to their offspring with some certainty about their role in fatherhood. Women's faithfulness in marriage then becomes part and parcel of an economic system. Here, argues Engels, is found the origin of modern marriage. Here is also found one basis of inequality between men and women in marriage, and one way in which marriage gives men power over their wives.

Love and sociology go together in another sense too. It was often in courses in sociology of marriage and the family, the "how to make a family" courses we refer to in the introduction, that men and women sought their future spouses, or at least did some scouting around for possibilities. Even if they did not succeed in this quest, students learned how to propose, how to date, and what weddings were all about; so the sociology of family was, in those days, truly an applied science. It may still be.

Love in the Past

The origins of sociology clearly begin with theories about marriage and family. There is nothing natural about the connection of love and marriage. Many people think that they have always gone together, like the horse and carriage. Yet, the togetherness of love and marriage is a relatively new concept, and one not endorsed by all, even today in North America.

Most people in the world think that the purpose of marriage is to benefit the family group, not necessarily the individuals who are marrying. Therefore, they prefer to arrange marriages that are mutually advantageous to families. Negotiating these connections in the best interests of the community or social group matters more to many in the world than whether the couple love each other *per se*. We shall see when we discuss arranged marriages, however, that love can be found in marriages arranged by one's parents or other relatives. This is not always the case, of course; but relationships that begin with romantic love don't always work well either.

The idea of **romantic love** is a social construction, something invented by people to serve a social purpose, although some argue that it has a biological basis (Fisher, 1992). Morton (1992) tells of how the idea of love as a basis for marriage grew out of questioning the traditional social and eco-

A Girl Like Diana

Not selected by the Royal Family, as is widely believed, Diana was coldly thrust forward by her own family, when efforts to interest Charles in her older sisters failed ... Earl Spencer ... was not averse to the chance for the Spencers to condescend to the House of Windsor....

Everyone involved knew that Diana was no match for the moody, sensitive Charles. But the Spencers pressed on with their dynastic designs, just as the Howards placed not one, but three, Howard girls in the King's bed (Henry VIII).

Source: Rosalind Miles. 1997. "A Girl Like Diana," *Saturday Night* November 18 (abridged).

nomic grounds for marriage. It is not that love itself is at all a new concept. Ancient myths and age-old stories have love at their core. For example, Krishna, one of the popular gods of Hinduism, is often shown as a flute-playing suitor of a maiden (Coltrane, 1998:36). In Krishna, erotic and romantic love are combined with the quest for salvation. Ancient legends of Japan also have themes of love. Greek philosophers wrote about love. Although love is the focus in all these instances, mythic love or love as salvation is not quite the kind of love that we today think of as linked with marriage, or the basis on which families are formed today. We tend to be more earthbound and, on average, aspire to be more egalitarian.

Romantic love, indeed, was seen by many people as a kind of taking over of the person by spirits or by something else decidedly unreasonable. There are still those who see romantic love as such an aberration that it has been equated with a form of mental illness. In some ways, this makes sense. Think of someone in love being preoccupied, distracted, not eating, walking about as if in a trance—not so very different from the symptoms of some mental illnesses! No wonder so many people question this as the basis on which to launch families!

As capitalism developed, households shrank. As the number of family-only households increased rapidly, the traditional bases of marriage came into question. Ultimately, marriage as it was then known was transformed. Love came to be the basis on which families began. Divisions of labour emerged between the marriage partners, including different standards for sexual behaviours and for sharing and passing along family resources. Power differentials sharpened between men and women on the domestic front as they were no longer equal partners in work.

Think of the concept of romantic love suddenly emerging—for women in particular. They had to transform themselves from farm and castle workers into love objects; in this role, adornment and looks mattered more than their actual contributions to the table or the family's coffers or the unit's overall well-being. Women went from being partners in work, where family meant work, to being weaker, more passive decorations (Abu-Laban & McDaniel, 1998). The differences between men and women became more exaggerated, as social and economic power in society and in marriage shifted more to men.

Throughout history, people paired off or married in some way, not out of love (romantic or otherwise), but because they needed to do so to survive in the world. Some see in this a biological imperative. As we have seen, the well-to-do married to join families or consolidate land holdings. Marriage was international or inter-castle diplomacy. With the emergence of middle classes for the first time in early towns and villages, marriage was a purposeful sharing of labour. Wives were needed to work in the new shops and crafts industries along with their husbands and children. The poor married, or paired off, to help them survive in a difficult world. Pooling resources was useful. In all of these types of marriage, however, sex was part of the deal, and usually so was reproduction. Pairing off ensured that children would be brought into the world, decidedly important to the continuation of humanity, as well as of family lines. Again, this has been argued as evidence for the biological basis of love and marriage, although the evidence for this is not clear.

Courtly love, the likely origin of romantic love as we know it today, emerged in Europe in the Middle Ages. This was a period of lords and ladies, troubadours and knights. Many images of romantic love in the late twentieth century still retain aspects of this period. Think of finding one's "Knight in Shining Armour" or one's beautiful princess, serenading one's love, or offering gifts of love, hope, and good intentions. Knights sometimes wore some token from their ladies, such as a scarf or handkerchief, as they entered into battle. No wonder that, on Valentine's Day each year, out come the images of romantic love, many of them medieval in origin.

Courtly love affairs were not simple, as the story of Romeo and Juliet makes abundantly clear to us. The difference with the emergence of courtly love was the placing of the woman, as the object of male affections, on a kind of pedestal. She was worshipped and seen as the embodiment of spiritual love as well as earthly love. She was to be won, though remaining, in a fundamental sense, unattainable. These ideas, too, exist in our modern thinking about love and sex. Along with them goes the well-entrenched idea of a sexual double standard, which places a high value on women's sexual purity—virginity—on marriage and their fidelity afterward. Men's sexual experience prior to marriage and fidelity afterwards was seen as somewhat less important. Do current events—for example, the intense public and political attention paid to the revelation of widespread sexual infidelity among U.S. leaders—suggest that mores have changed?

The traditional **sexual double standard**, as described above, was the premise for dating rituals (or "scripts") that existed in North America from about the 1920s through the 1950s and most of the 1960s (despite popular images of that decade as the era of "free love"). **Sexual scripts** saw boys as initiators, calling girls for dates and often paying for everything. Girls were expected, by the same scripts, to be chaste and virginal until marriage. In fact, couples negotiated dating plans and intimacy. The game, however, was a difficult one for women. Schwartz and Rutter (1998:79) note that girls were cast as "good" if they were chaste, and "bad" ("loose," "easy," and worse) if they followed masculine rules of sexuality. This led to an impossible situation for girls and women, with men cast in the dual role of sexual predators whom they must fight off to protect their reputations, and protectors from other men who might be worse. No wonder that honest communication sometimes failed to develop between women and men!

Laumann, Gagnon, Michael and Michaels (1994), relying on data from the United States' National Health and Social Life Survey, find that the sexual double standard is shifting dramatically. They zero in on people on their eighteenth birthday: in particular, what proportion have not had sexual intercourse as yet, and what proportion have had five or more partners? They compare results over four decades, considering men and women who turned 18 in the 1950s through the 1990s. Not surprisingly, there are fewer 18-year-old virgins than there were in the 1950s. And the differences between men and women are smaller than they used to be. However, the big change occurs in the proportion who have had five or more sexual partners by age 18. Almost four times as many women in the 1990s fall into this category than did in the 1950s. In contrast, the proportion of young men who have had more than five sexual partners by age 18 has not changed much.

The concept today of love in marriage involves companionship and mutual emotional bonds. This is the era of **companionate marriage**. We expect marriage partners to be everything to each other: friends, lovers, companions. We are so fond of romantic love as the basis of marriage that we have come to see it as natural, the only real way to launch a marriage. If it is natural, however, it wasn't so for much of human history, and still is not the norm in many societies. Mutual caring is also expected to be part of marriage. Sex is seen as a part of sharing and caring for each other. We strongly resist any suggestion that sex may be controlled, bartered, or economically valued in families. Yet the sexual double standard remains a part of companionate marriage, with fewer adverse consequences for men who engage in recreational sex than for women who do the same. The sentimental ideal of modern love in companionate marriage sees women as loyal and true, while men, who tend to be valued more for their public roles, are permitted more sexual freedom, and are more likely to be excused. In the way in which we treat sex and sexuality, much about our deep-seated beliefs and assumptions about dating and mating become clear.

In the Victorian era, the banishing of sex from public view reached its now famous apex. Legs on tables were covered for fear that, in their naked state, they would make people think of sex. Pregnancy was disguised, hidden, or denied. Feminine ankles were thought too alluring for men to observe. Nonetheless, during this period a world of men's pubs, clubs, and male occasions such as hunting flourished, as did a thriving prostitution trade and some lurid novels. Sex certainly did not cease to exist.

By the late nineteenth century, sex began to be seen as a central part of marriage and sexual attraction a crucial part of courtship. Ward (1990: 9–11) relies on the diaries of George Stephen Jones, a young Quebec City clerk who between 1845 and 1846 kept note of his growing feelings for Miss Honorine Tanswell, whom he describes as "that most amiable young Lady Miss Tanswell." George describes himself as feeling the first stirrings of romance but being uncertain of his new-found emotions. He learns, after making his feelings known to Honorine, that her parents intend for her to marry a Monsieur Gingras. Poor George, not certain what basis for marriage he is dealing with now, tells his diary, "If she dose [*sic*] I will be the most mesirable [*sic*] man on earth and I will never marry. No never" (Ward, 1990:11).

At the end of the twentieth century, images remain of pure, virtuous women who search for knights in shining armour. Romance writers grow rich describing these images, as do others in the romance trade. Marriage is seldom considered clearly by dewy-eyed youth engaged often not in planning lives together, but in planning romantic, and increasingly expensive, weddings. Interestingly, in weddings today, all but the most ultra-modern brides still look like fairy princesses and grooms remain one step short of riding in on white chargers. Brides are still "given away" by their fathers (or both parents) to their husbands. And important rituals are shared by families brought together for the wedding.

What Is This Thing Called Love?

Love has always had some mystery about it; perhaps that is part of what we love about it. Modern-day social science approaches to love tend to focus on how we fall in love, and with whom. Love, it turns out, is not a random selection process. It has been found that we most commonly locate that special someone by doing activities related to our class, education, work, ethnicity, religion, or neighbourhood. And we are most likely to fall for someone similar to us and with a similar background.

This should not be entirely surprising, since we interact most with those with whom we have things in common. **Propinquity** (or proximity) **theory** says that people are more likely to find a mate among those with whom they associate. The theory of **homogamy** takes this further, suggesting that people tend to fall in love within their own social group, as defined by class, educational level, religion, and race or ethnicity. Indeed, most intimate relationships involve people of remarkably similar backgrounds. One study (Laumann *et al.*, 1994:255) of a national population sample in the United States found that 93 percent of marriages and 89 percent of long-term relationships involve people of similar race or ethnicity, while 82 percent of marriages and 83 percent of long-term relationships involve people with similar education. In Canada, the 1996 Census suggests a growing tendency to intermarry among ethnic groups, leading to more persons with multiple ethnic origins than in the past (Statistics Canada, 1998c:3). Yet, the overwhelming tendency remains to marry or settle down with someone like ourselves.

Yet, this does not tell us much about love itself. What is this thing called love?

> Friendship is love minus sex and plus reason. Love is friendship plus sex and minus reason. (Mason Cooley, "Thought du Jour," *The Globe and Mail*, 20 January 1998:A20).

Despite the interests of the early sociologists, remarkably little research exists on love in marriage and families. One Australian study tries to define the love that supports marriage and families (Noller, 1996). Love is found to be socially constructed and shaped by cultural beliefs. Love has a behavioural, an emotional, and a cognitive component; it can exist in a mature or an immature form.

Mature emotional love involves passion and companionship which can begin with young people and extend throughout life. *Immature* emotional love is exemplified by love addiction and infatuation—not, according to Noller (1996), the best bases on which to build strong marriages and families. Mature love, she finds, is best conceptualized as creating an environment in which both the lovers and those who depend on them can grow and develop. This is consistent with falling in love with someone who is part of your community and of whom both families approve, so that love will be nurtured by others who love you as well as the lover.

Whom do we find lovable? Contrary to popular belief, both men and women consider a potential partner's attractiveness and earning capabilities (Landolt, Lalumière & Quinsey, 1995).

In personal ads, it has been found that men tend to emphasize looks and physical attributes (weight, height, ethnicity, even eye and hair colour) more than women do. For example, terms such as *attractive, slender, petite,* or *sexy* are used much more often by men in their ads to describe the person for whom they are looking (Coltrane, 1998:47; Smith, Waldorf & Tremblath, 1990). For women, common keywords include *secure, professional, successful,* or *affluent* along with terms to describe physical features and age in the man of their dreams.

Love, Marriage, and Baby Carriage

Everyone knows that old song "First comes love, then comes marriage. ..." But the link is no longer inevitable; nor is the link between marriage and babies. And even when all three coexist, they do not always happen in that sequence.

That younger people are less committed to the idea of marriage *per se* than older people is telling of rapidly changing attitudes, which may reflect underlying social and moral values. The age difference is found in analyses of the 1995 General Social Survey in Canada (Canadian Council, 1997:14). No difference exists, however, in the importance young and old attach to forming lasting relationships. On a list of what Canadians say they need for a happy life, topping the list by far is a lasting relationship. It is marriage that younger people do not feel is essential to a happy life. As to babies, young people feel that having children is important, although not as important as forming a lasting relationship. More on this in Chapter 4.

Meeting and Mating

Meeting a potential mate is not what it used to be, as anyone who goes to college or university in the 1990s knows. Yet some older traditions remain and some new traditions emerge as the older ones are updated. When Ann Landers ran, in 1997, a series of letters on "How We Met," some readers expressed frustration and boredom with the old-fashioned stories of how couples met. The implication is that none of that sort of thing happens any more, which may or may not be true.

The range of ways to meet one's life partner has certainly widened in

The Way We Met

On a late January evening in 1941, I arrived home to find a strange guy sitting, fully dressed, in my bathtub. His company had sent him the wrong day to tile our bathroom and my roommate had let him in. I had a bridge party scheduled for that night and he knew I would be angry at the clutter in the bathroom, but he stuck around anyway. He had made quite a mess, and I was furious.

Ten days later, he called me. He apologized profusely for his behaviour and asked me for a date. I reluctantly accepted his apology and agreed to have dinner with him the following evening. After six months of a romantic courtship, he paid a preacher $15 to marry us in the funeral parlour chapel.

Our romantic date lasted 50 years, including four years of separation during the war. We had one son and four grandchildren. He is gone now, but our life was never dull. He kept me entertained for a lifetime.

Source: "Ann Landers Advice," *The Edmonton Journal*, 18 October 1997:G7 (abridged).
Permission granted by Ann Landers and Creators Syndicate.

Arranged Marriage Goes Modern

When the time comes to marry, it will happen something like this: Boy meets girl. Boy likes girl. Boy tells his mother; Mother calls the girl's mother: The two families arrange to meet. The courtship begins. Both parties can back out if the courtship goes badly.

"This is the modern way, actually," says ... Hamed Madani, a professor of political science at Tarrant Junior College Southeast Campus. "The traditional way, the boys and girls know nothing about it."

Mitra Madani [Hamed's daughter] said she is entrusting her marriage to fate and to her parents with whom she has a close relationship.

"Even for me, it is confusing. The ideal situation would be: I'll get my degree [in Computing Science at the University of Texas], I'll have a lot of people asking for me and I'll get to pick."

Source: Brady, Matthew. 1998. "Finding a Mate in Texas Often a Matter of Faith," *The Edmonton Journal*, 8 February 1998:A2.

recent years. Many meet in the usual places of shared activities—schools and universities, workplaces, religious places, neighbourhoods, sporting groups, or events. Others meet through common friends or relatives. Still others are put together by relatives or traditional marriage brokers in **arranged marriages** or semi-arranged marriages. How common this is in North America is not fully known. In Canada in the 1990s, with higher rates of immigration than the United States, it is known that arranged marriages occur regularly among several ethnic groups.

Exposure to potential mates is a first step in the meeting and mating process. As we have shown, this process, far from being random, is structured or arranged by our social characteristics. There is a range of possibilities extending from the more constrained choices of arranged marriage systems to the more open, but still constrained, process of falling in love with someone you meet at school, in your neighbourhood, or at your church, temple, or mosque.

Thinking of a mating or marriage market may seem too economistic or rational a description of a process we tend to view as largely emotional. And yet, there is much that is market-like about finding a mate. One, for example, can think in terms of exchanges. Each potential partner brings to the potential relationship something that is of value to the other: personality, skills, physical attractiveness, earnings potential, etc. Personal ads (to which we shall turn in a moment) make clear that an exchange of characteristics in demand is proposed.

Whether participants admit it or not, rating and ranking is part of the mate market. Meeting, mating, and marrying involve a giant sorting process whereby our "market values" are matched with the market values of others. It can be a cold calculation, as when for example, a man seeks a wife who will "look good on his arm." We even have a name for such wives, although

Though the script has been updated over the years, flirting is still an important part of the meeting-and-mating scenario.

interestingly not for the men, typically men climbing the rungs of success in business or politics, who seek them. They are called "trophy wives." They are visible at country clubs and in some elite social circles, beautiful as well as being beautifully groomed, coiffed, and dressed. Sometimes their husbands match them well in terms of appearance and style, but sometimes they do not. The husband's allure is his earning power. He does not need good looks so much. We can all likely bring to mind numerous examples of these kinds of couples.

More often, the rating and ranking process is less calculated. Watch people at a singles bar or a campus event. They—both men and women—eye those they wish they might have. But in the end they woo those more like themselves. People are seen as "catches" in the mate market, as if it were a fishing derby. Each of us constantly compares our self-perceived market value, sometimes based on testing the "mate market" in high school, university or college, or in the work world, with what we think we can achieve in the marketplace of love. Confidence in one's ability to "strike a deal" often determines how far one can reach. Popular movies notwithstanding, in reality, princes and billionaires seldom wed paupers or street prostitutes.

Sociology has examined the romance market carefully. In addition to the market basket of values each of us brings to the mate market, we must play our social cards carefully and well to win at love. Most everyone who has survived high school knows this intuitively, even if they might not voice it quite so starkly. Consistent with the image of the woman in courtly love stories of the past, a woman must construct herself as desirable but not completely attainable, so as to maximize her market value (Cancian, 1987; Hendrick & Hendrick, 1996).

The cruel way this works in the high school market is that, even today, girls who are too generous with their sexual favours get quickly labelled with "reputations." Yet, being too unattainable is seen as disinterest, causing other labels to emerge, such as "grind," "nerd," or "lesbian." Essentially, the difficult balance to be achieved for women is to have men interested in them, so that they can show that they have market value, but to maintain their unattainability so as to maintain and elevate their marketability. It is a careful dance, indeed, and one in which women receive little training and no practice.

A central part of the mate market is the politics of attractiveness. Good looks make a difference, for both men and women, in getting attention in the mate market. Looks matters just as much in the gay market as in the heterosexual market. For women, attractiveness is a life's project (Abu-Laban & McDaniel, 1998). Immense amounts of time, effort, and products go into the construction of female attractiveness. Women pluck, wax, and shave unwanted hair, carefully groom the wanted hair, shape and flatten unwanted bulges, and enhance wanted ones. On it goes. All this is packaged in the latest fashions after being "worked out" into the shape of the day, sometimes even called "body sculpting." Impression management also matters in the attractiveness project; it must appear as if "the look" is achieved effortlessly.

Even aspects of the dating script contribute to the decorative potential of women. Often, gifts from the adoring man are decorative to the woman. Certainly, engagement rings have this decorative purpose. The well-entrenched concept is that the ring should cost X percent of the man's earnings, the latest being about two months' salary. The woman then wears the ring as a symbol with dual meanings: that she is desirable on the mate market, and that her intended makes sufficient money (or comes from sufficient family money) so that she can be decorated well. This suggests that she will be "kept well" during their married life and announces to all who see her ring that she has made a "good catch." Among younger people, token gifts are often adornments as well. They include anything from scarves to hats, to shirts, to friendship or "pre-engagement" rings, lockets, bracelets, or temporary tattoos.

In the mate market, flirting matters. However the flirting script, like the dating market, has been considerably updated. Women being sexually aggressive are still seen as offputting to most men (Coltrane, 1998:33). Yet, flirting by women, as well as by men, is still an important part of the meeting and mating scenario. Women are expected to flirt with a blend of innocence and interest; the mix must be exact so as not to convey unintended messages. Flirting prior to the 1990s was heavy on the innocence, light on the sexual innuendo. Now, the content ratio is reversed, with women expected to be sexual in flirting, though not too aggressive (Coltrane, 1998:34).

With no lack of emphasis on romance in the 1990s, both women and men are taught to expect never-ending courtship-like romance. Little is written into romance novels or Hollywood movies about what the "and then they lived happily ever after" really entails. The meeting, dating, and mating rulebook does not do so well at preparing people for housework, childbirth, and child rearing, as well as tough decisions about money, about jobs, about who will do what when a job opportunity in another place arises for one but not both spouses. At times, the surprises of reality are shocking and diminish romantic ideals. The growing old together part, although in reality potentially romantic, can have its creaky problems along the way.

With greater equality between men and women in the present, it may be thought that meeting romantic partners takes on more equality than it did in the past. The image of the past is the woman waiting for the man to ask her out, ask her to dance or to phone her. Yet women were not entirely passive in this process, even in the dim past of the 1960s. Numbers of ways to convey interest in particular men were mastered by women. Among the most popular was to "put out the word" with your friends and his that you are interested. This is similar to parents of girls eligible for marriage in some parts of Mediterranean Europe putting a symbolic pot of herbs on the windowsill announcing the daughter's availability for suitors.

Some women, of course, still sit and wait for men to take dating initiatives. The patterns of dating are different, however, in the 1990s. Groups of young people of both sexes often go out together. The cues of who likes whom are hard to read for any but the initiated. It is the special look, the holding of the door only for you, the talking to you more than the others that must be read like tea leaves for signs of interest beyond friendship.

At times, the reading of the signs is so complex that both women and men ask others, sometimes even strangers, to help them interpret what meanings lurk in behaviours. One teenaged girl who worked in the local grocery store asked the advice of one of the authors in interpreting the behaviour of a young man she "really, really liked." Did his holding the door especially for her but not for the other girls in the group mean that he actually "liked" her?

The question of whether wooing is more equal remains. In some ways, it is, since both sexes take initiatives in singling out the person they particularly like. However, a gender imbalance remains. Several studies of first date initiation find that men tend to evaluate woman-initiated first dates in more sexual ways than do women (Mongeau & Carey, 1996). Those who initiate

---

Friends and Companions: A Sampler

RUGGED old sea dog offers reliable/slender young protegee opportunities to travel ...

RUSSIAN charming ladies, free brochure, tours ...

MR. RIGHT ANSWER! If you are a professional man over 40 who has dignity, values & is seeking a quiet family life to complete your busy, lonely life ...

ARE YOU LOOKING FOR YOUR PERFECT PARTNER? ... HEARTS Introduction Service is Canada's only traditional matchmaker.

Source: "Friends and Companions," *The Globe and Mail*, 17 January 1998:A11 (abridged).

---

dates are seen by a group of impartial observers as being more sociable, more liberal, but less physically attractive than the person being asked (Mongeau & Carey, 1996). Despite a welcome tendency toward more equality in dating initiatives, it could still be that the women who initiate dates are viewed differently from the men, who are expected to initiate dates.

Personal ads have grown both in popularity and acceptability in the latter part of the twentieth century. What used to be called "lonely hearts" ads —for the truly desperate who were unable to get dates any other way—are now mainstream, appearing in respectable newspapers, and used by respectable people. One recent U.S. study (Merskin & Huberlie, 1996) discovered that mate finding is becoming more and more a matter of mediated information rather than traditional selection. More people than ever are turning to the want ads or to Internet dating services to meet that someone special.

Of course, this does not mean that mate selection is any more random than it ever was, only that the pools of potentials within the socially preferred categories have been enlarged. Maybe this is yet another dimension of globalization.

A study of personal ads in a Canadian newspaper between 1975 and 1988 found a sixfold increase in the number of ads placed (Sev'er, 1990). The ratio of males to females placing ads was about 4 to 1. In some newspapers, the ratios may differ and favour women's ads instead. A stunning finding is that although the means used in the mate market has changed, the gender expectations of meeting and mating have not. Women are still presenting themselves in their ads in terms of physical attractiveness, and men are still seeking good-looking women with specified physical attributes. It may be that in this still not completely conventional means of mate seeking, gender stereotypes matter more than in more conventional mate markets. Or, it could be that people placing personal ads are particularly "consumer"-oriented: they want a good "product." Sev'er (1990:76) concludes that "... even in this unconventional market, the rules of the mating game have remained extremely traditional. Women (especially older women) are at a disadvantage, both as choosers and as potential chosen. The personal ads market seems to be a traditional market in disguise, "a new bottle for the same old wine."

Sexual Intimacy

A dramatic shift has occurred in the age at which sexual activity begins. Brumberg (1998) notes that the average age for starting intercourse for girls in the United States is now 16 years old. Today's girls, notes Brumberg, are sexually active before the age at which their great-great-grandmothers had even begun to menstruate.

This is not surprising when we think that in grandmother's time, the standard—although not always the reality—was abstinence until marriage. Now, the standard has become "the love standard" (Hobart, 1996): sexual relations are fine as long as the couple love each other. With evidence presented earlier on the increase in sexual activity for women by age 18, there must be a lot of love out there! For francophone young men in Canada, Hobart found that (1996:149) the "fun standard" (sex is okay if it is enjoyable) takes priority over the love standard.

Many discrepancies exist between what people do privately and what they say they do. Nowhere is this more the case than with sexuality, whether premarital, extramarital, or marital. People underestimate, overestimate, and misrepresent. It is challenging indeed for family sociologists to sort out what is really occurring from what people may wish were occurring. Even presidents are reluctant to talk openly about their sexual encounters. From multiple studies (Hobart, 1996:150 summarizes the Canadian studies), it is known, however, that the majority of youth today report having had sexual experiences. They also have few qualms about premarital sex; the vast majority do not think it is wrong.

A minority movement has developed in the late 1990s in favour of abstinence until marriage. This is a serious, committed group of people, often of fundamentalist religious groups; adherents claim their numbers are increasing. Its presence and the interest of some parents in having their children marry as virgins has led to the concept of "born again" virgins. One such marriage is known to one of the authors: at the wedding, the parents of the groom touted their son's virginity and had special toasts to his virtue. The reality was that his bride was five months pregnant. When the baby was born, simple announcements were sent, with no comment on the surprisingly early birth date.

Another counter to sexual intimacy in uncommitted relationships has been the threat of AIDS and venereal diseases in the latter part of this century. The threat has been controversial and misinformation has abounded; many young people mistakenly believe that heterosexuals are not vulnerable to AIDS. Nonetheless, the lethal threat of AIDS has affected the enthusiasm of some young people for sexual intimacy, at least unprotected sexual intimacy.

Sexuality is still seen differently for women than for men. Some of these differences are apparent in approaches to contraception and are discussed more in Chapter 4. The concept of exchange seems to mean that women are expected to provide sexual favours in exchange for dinner, movies, etc. In the 1990s, the old sexual double-standard takes a new form: some men perceive that women who dress in styles they consider provocative—tight, short dresses, skin-tight jeans, halter tops, even dangling earrings—are "asking for it." The young women themselves, in contrast, typically do not see their fashion statements as anything but trendy. Communication between men and women remains as imprecise and inadequate as ever. In inadequate communication about sexual expectations can lie the seeds of sexual violence.

Not All Wine and Roses: Dating Violence

Abuse of women in dating relationships is found from research to be relatively widespread but underreported and understudied (DeKeseredy & Schwartz, 1994). There may be a pattern of perpetuation of violence by men and acceptance of violence by women that starts as early as elementary school.

A national Canadian study of 1835 girls/women and 1307 boys/men (DeKeseredy & Schwartz, 1994) found that girls who experience violence while in elementary school are more likely to be victims of dating violence in high school and college/university. And boys who are violent while young are more likely to perpetuate violence in dating relationships. These men are also more accepting of rape myths (such as the myth that women enjoy sexual assault, or that sexual assault can only be perpetrated by strangers, etc.) than are non-violent men.

The 1993 Violence Against Women Survey in Canada, about which more will be said in Chapter 8, found that 16 percent of women in Canada had experienced some kind of violence in a dating relationship (Statistics Canada, 1993:2). Violence was found to be widespread, with over one-half of Canadian women experiencing at least one incident of physical violence since age 16. The survey addressed only behaviours such as hitting, threatening, etc. defined as crimes in the Criminal Code of Canada. Women aged 18–24 and women with some post-secondary education were the most likely to have experienced violence in the 12 months prior to the survey, suggesting that dating violence is relatively widespread. Interestingly, about 20 percent of the women interviewed for this survey said that they had never before told anyone about the violence they had experienced. The Canadian survey, the first of its kind anywhere, is being replicated in other countries in the late 1990s.

Marriage Trends and Patterns

Two trends characterize contemporary marriage: decline in marriage rates and the continuing popularity of marriage. These two trends seem contradictory but are really not. More people marry at some point in their lives now than did in the 1910s (Gee, 1986:266). So marriage remains popular. At the same time, there has been a decline in rates of marriage since the 1960s. (See Figure 2.1.) This trend continues in the most recent data available (Statistics Canada, 1998b) which shows that the marriage rate dropped 2.2 percent between 1995 and 1996 in Canada. If common-law or cohabiting unions, which are growing rapidly in popularity, are added to rates at which couples form relationships, then family starts are in excellent shape. More on non-marital unions in a moment.

"Over the past three decades, the institution of marriage has been questioned by a growing number of Canadians," note Nault and Belanger (1996:1). Alternative ways to begin lasting relationships have sprung up. Living together (cohabitation) is the major alternative. But there are others.

For example, a growing number of stable relationships are developing without the spouses living together at all. This has been termed by some

Figure 2.1   **PERCENTAGE OF MEN AND WOMEN WHO ARE NOT MARRIED AND HAVE NEVER BEEN MARRIED**

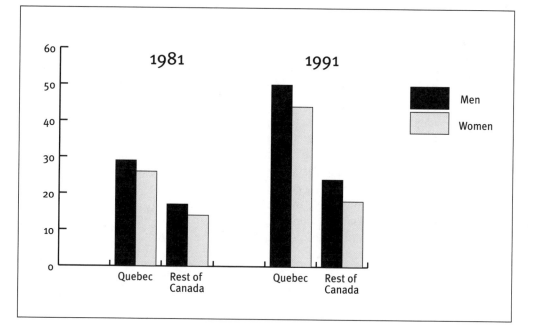

European sociologists as "living together apart." Committed relationships, or what Nault and Belanger (1996:1) term "true couple relationships" are established with each spouse maintaining their own residence, sometimes distant from each other. One of the authors (McDaniel) knows of several long-term committed commuting marriages. The two most extreme are one where the husband lives in Canada and the wife in Europe, and one where the wife lives in California and the husband in New York. Both of these marriages have lasted twenty years or more and are viable and ongoing. Nault and Belanger (1996) also note committed long-term relationships in which both spouses live with their parents. This is an aspect of the growing "cluttered nest" phenomenon when adult offspring return to the family home, or never leave it. This will be explored in more detail in Chapter 10 when we consider fresh starts in family.

In the decade 1981–1991, first-marriage rates declined by 25 percent in Canada and 42 percent in Quebec (Nault & Belanger, 1996:2). Put another way, the proportion of Canadian men who ever get married dropped from 80 percent in 1981 to 70 percent in 1991 (Nault & Belanger, 1996:32,36). For Québécois men, the comparable proportions of men ever marrying fell from 71 percent in 1981 to 50 percent in 1991. For women in Canada, 83 percent in 1981 would marry, compared to 75 percent in 1991; for Québécoise women, the proportions are 74 percent in 1981 and 56 percent in 1991 (Nault & Belanger, 1996:38,42). While these are large declines, the fact remains that, even in Quebec, the majority of both men and women do marry at some point. Before we conclude that marriage is going the way of the dinosaur, we need to consider what else is happening with the formation of couple unions.

First, people tend to marry later now than they did in the 1960s and 1970s. Even though The Sixties was supposedly a time of "free love," the age at marriage during that period was lower than it had been for a long time and lower than it has been since (about 22 for women, 25 for men) (Ram, 1990:80). The long-term trend toward postponement of marriage continues (see Table 2.1); by 1996, women were 27.1 on average at first marriage, and men 29.3 (Statistics Canada, 1998f). The tendency is slightly greater for women than for men to postpone first marriage.

The reasons for later marriage are complex and related to social and economic opportunities and expectations. One factor is today's uncertain job prospects for young people. A large factor seems to be people's interest in pursuing non-family interests such as education, travel, or work. Young people still seem to value marriage and family, as we have seen, although marriage is valued considerably less by younger than older people. Younger people seem to prefer not to jump into marriages early.

Table 2.1   **AVERAGE AGE AT FIRST MARRIAGE IN CANADA**

	MEN	WOMEN
1921	28.0	24.5
1930	27.7	24.2
1940	28.2	24.9
1950	26.6	23.6
1960	25.4	22.6
1970	25.1	22.7
1980	25.7	23.5
1990	27.9	26.0

Source: Statistics Canada data.

Living Together Goes Mainstream

There have always been people who have lived together without the blessings of churches/temples/mosques or civil authorities. In recent decades two trends have emerged: massive growth in the number of couples who live together rather than legally marry, and a greater diversity. This is consistent with an overall trend in North America toward non-traditional attitudes and behaviours with respect to family, sex, and close relations.

Cohabitation is no longer limited to "trial marriage," as used to be thought. The majority of Canadians now live common-law in their first conjugal relationship (Statistics Canada, 1997). It is more often now the basis of long-term, sometimes lifelong committed unions, in which increasing numbers of couples have children and even grandchildren.

In Canada, the growth in common-law unions has been dramatic, up nearly 40 percent in the 1981-1991 decade (Nault & Belanger, 1996:19). The proportion of adult Canadians living in common-law unions increased from 3.8 percent in 1981 to 6.9 percent in 1991, and in Quebec from 4.9 percent in 1981 to 11.2 percent in 1991. For those aged 20–34, the proportion in common-law unions was 9 percent in 1991, and then drops little by little with age. Among aboriginal Canadians, from the 1996 Census, the proportion of children (0–14) who live with common-law parents was 24.7 percent in 1996, up from 10.5 percent in 1986 (Statistics Canada, 1998a:5). The longest duration common-law unions occur in Quebec, but time spent in common-law unions is increasing in all parts of Canada.

Common-law unions are now increasing among all age groups in Canada, although the rate of increase is less among older than among younger people. One of the authors (McDaniel) knows of a couple in their late eighties who are living together. They were married to each other and divorced more than 65 years ago; each married someone else and raised a family in the interim. Now, with both second spouses deceased, these two somehow found each other again and are happily cohabiting.

Why is there a move away from traditional marriage (though it is still the majority choice) and toward common-law unions? Some see the trend as a result of greater opportunities for women, enabling them to rely less on marriage as a kind of occupational choice. Similar reasons are used to explain higher divorce rates, as we shall see in Chapter 9. It is not at all clear, however, that this is actually a factor (Oppenheimer, 1997); this will be discussed in a moment. Another potential explanation focuses on men's deteriorating employment and income prospects so that they are seen by women as less stable providers (see, for example, Easterlin & Crimmins, 1991). Changing values about traditional marriage also may play a role. Distrust of traditional institutions could be part of the explanation too.

Quebec is interesting in that common-law unions are more popular there than anywhere else in North America. Quebec is only different by North American standards, however. In comparison to patterns of cohabitation in Europe, Quebec is way behind (Baker, 1995:50–52). In Sweden, for example, it is estimated that over 60 percent of young couples live in common-law unions rather than in marriages. The distinction is blurred in Europe, in policy and sometimes in law (Baker, 1995). Some have suggested that indifference to traditional institutions may be the result of Quebec's shedding traditional strict adherence to Catholic Church doctrine with the Quiet Revolution in the 1960s (Nault & Belanger, 1996:25). Surprisingly, if living together is seen as a trial marriage, the probability of divorce is greater, on average, for couples who marry after having lived together than for couples who marry without living together (Baker, 1995:51). The reasons for this are complex and maybe even contradictory. Individuals who live together prior to marriage may have different characteristics than those who do not, in terms of religion, family supports, perhaps class or ethnic backgrounds, so they may not be directly comparable to those who marry.

It may be, as well, that there is considerable diversity among those who live common-law, with many living in committed long-term relationships and others living in shorter-term, less committed relationships. When the two are lumped together and compared with those who marry, the result can seem to be that living common-law prior to marrying puts couples at greater risk of divorce than actually may be the case.

Most provinces in Canada treat common-law unions that last for some specific period, typically more than two years, the same as they treat married unions. The obligations to partners and children are the same. The split of property if the union ends is the same as it would be for married couples.

However, since some jurisdictions, such as Alberta, do not recognize common-law unions, it is wise for couples living common-law to have legal contracts and wills that protect them, their children, and their property. Just putting into writing each person's understanding of the relationship can be helpful in sorting things out should the relationship end or one partner die.

For example, if an older couple of similar means decide to share a domicile but wish for their estates to go to their adult children rather than to each other should one die, it is wise to have this in writing. Wills should also deal with occupancy arrangements. Otherwise a surviving partner could be evicted by the government or the partner's children from a house viewed as her or his own. New types of unions require new and sometimes careful steps.

What are young people's attitudes toward living together? A cross-national study of white high-school seniors (Lye & Waldron, 1997) is revealing, but not the final word since non-white students are not included in the sample. As expected, students who are concerned with social issues, particularly males, were more favourably inclined toward cohabitation. The findings suggest that concerns about social fairness and the well-being of others translates into support for gender equality and acceptance of cohabitation. By contrast, more conservative political beliefs were found to be associated with traditional attitudes toward both gender issues and cohabitation.

Marriage Timing

"Oh dear, oh dear, I shall be too late," the White Rabbit exclaimed as he examined his watch fob (Lewis Carroll, *Alice in Wonderland*).

People tend to live their lives according to some sense of the appropriate timing of life events. Where this sense comes from is not entirely clear. It may be simply a sense of what is appropriate, or it may be pressure from parents, peers, the media, or some other source.

There are hints that the pressure some women feel to have children at, or by, certain ages, comes from fears that infertility may set in or that risks to the pregnancy and/or the baby increase with age. There *is* some slight increase in risks (of, for example, Down syndrome) but the risks are not nearly high enough to account for the fears women have about not having children "on time." That these fears are often not particularly well grounded has little effect on the deep sense of the appropriate timing of life events people seem to have.

Gee (1990) shows in a Canadian study that women measure the success of their lives, in part, on the basis of how closely they approximate the internalized ideals of family life events. This standard contradicts the increas-

People tend to live their lives according to some sense of the appropriate timing of life events. Most North Americans today postpone marriage until they have completed their education.

ing diversity of people's life courses. Women, for example, may get married or establish their first conjugal relationship in their teens or in their forties or older. The social rules are more flexible than ever, but people's internal sense of timing remains.

Computation of probabilities of marrying at certain ages then can have surprising consequences on attitudes and behaviours. A famous example occurred a few years ago when the media reported, falsely as it turned out, that women's probabilities of marrying after a certain age were abysmal. The story was carried in a wide range of media for months, although the researchers whose work was reportedly being quoted denied that this was their conclusion. The result was massive fear by women that if they did not marry by that age, they would probably never marry.

The possibilities that this media-propagated fear might induce are difficult to imagine—settling for the next available man perhaps. The story would be only an amusement were it not still cropping up in classes when age at marriage is discussed. Even though the media reports were not based on true research findings, the consequences of the reports were real nonetheless.

Most North Americans today tend to postpone marriage or establishment of a long-term committed relationship until they have completed their education. For many it is something beyond high school, such as technical training, college, or university. This means that most marry in their mid-twenties or older, a pattern that is similar to what it was a century ago. In both Canada and the United States, many young people come to marriage with considerable experience with dating and sexual experimentation; many have lived with someone, either the new spouse or someone else. This generally adds a maturity to the beginning of a marriage that can be important for its strength and survival. Age and education are also good predictors of marriage success and survival.

Unequal Matches

If the sexual double standard is being, at least partially, replaced with greater equality, and if young men and women are both coming into marriage with experience with sex and with various conjugal living arrangements, why is it that we still talk about marriage mismatches?

One of the most consistent and persistent facts of life with respect to marriage comes from sociology. It is the age gap in marriage. Men marry women a little younger than they are; women marry men a little older. Surprisingly, despite the reality that everyone knows a couple where the woman is a little older than the man, or where the couple is the same age, this pattern is a clear and persistent one over many, many years—although the age gap today is a little smaller than it used to be.

In the days when marriage meant financial security, women may have looked for a financially secure man who could provide for them. That often meant an older, established man. Now, marriage is more than security for women, yet the age difference persists. It could be argued that with the gender gap in earnings potential, marriage is still a matter of security for many women who cannot earn as much by their own labours in the market as they can by marrying someone who has higher earning power.

Age difference can reflect different power and experience, although of course, this is not always true. It can mean that men exercise greater financial leverage in marriage. The younger partner may be in a weaker bargaining position. It is also possible, even probable, that if the man is a little older, it is his career that is more established and sets the course for the marriage in terms of who is likely to follow whom for a job or a promotion, or a transfer. These differentials tend to widen further with the birth of a child.

The **marriage gradient**, a well-known sociological concept, takes unequal marriages one step further. First discovered by Jessie Bernard in the 1970s, the marriage gradient reveals that we sort ourselves into couples not only by age, but also by differential status (or as sociologists are fond of saying, socioeconomic status). Men, on average, tend to marry women with a little less education or a slightly lower occupational status than their own.

The interesting consequence of this is twofold. First, when taken together, the unequal matches form an off-centre parallelogram, of higher-status men linked with slightly lower-status women. Since the world comprises men of all statuses and women of all statuses, there are bound to be some men and some women prevented from making marriage matches. But, they are not the same kinds of people. Men who are left out of the marriage gradient are those at the bottom for whom there is no one of lower status to marry. Women who are left out of marriage are those at the top for whom there is no one of higher status to marry.

Thus, one must be wary when comparing the married with the unmarried: unmarried men and unmarried women may be profoundly different.

The second consequence is just as interesting. When men and women pair off unequally by status, age, and even height, the impression is created that differences between men and women are larger than they actually are. It works like this: we see couples walking around in which she is shorter, younger, and lower in status than he is. The conclusion: this is a natural sex difference. In fact, social choices in marriage partners tend to exaggerate existing sex differences.

Living Solo

Marriage is not for everyone. Over the last two decades, one-person households have increased substantially in Canada; 21 percent of all households in Canada consist of a person living alone. The reasons for singlehood are many: never marrying, separation or divorce, widowhood. Some may be married and in a commuting relationship.

The growing popularity of living alone may be, in part, a function of people having sufficient money to indulge their preferences. At the same time as living solo is increasing, so are the cluttered or refilled nests of family homes in which families double or triple up. In part, the growth in living alone is due to an aging population containing more widowed people. It also reflects the divorce rate, in that more people at any given time may be between relationships and thus living alone.

However, it is also clear that some singles have made clear choices to live alone, to buy homes alone and to develop a single lifestyle that they fully enjoy, a point of view expressed by a character in Jane Urquhart's 1997 novel, *The Underpainter*:

> I had never even considered marriage, could not imagine domesticity, the contractual companion, household chores. I was dependent on being single, wanted to avoid the daily structures that a constant woman guaranteed.

To live without a life partner is not new, nor is it even more common now than it was in the early part of this century, though more concerns are expressed about it now. Alone, however, need not mean lonely. Many who live solo are not isolated at all from their communities or circles of friends. People who are devoted to their work may prefer not to have a life partner. Many great artists and writers have remained unmarried and some unattached in any permanent way. And the need for marriage for security and acceptability for women has declined, even though it is not gone.

Romantic Love Over the Life Course: Wane or Change?

Dance Me to the End of Time. (Leonard Cohen)

A popular perception is that love and romance are for the young. With age, so the belief goes, romance—or at least the day-to-day experience of it—wanes. That this is not necessarily so has been shown in recent research (see Abu-Laban & McDaniel, 1997, for example). Happy marriages remain happy into old age. And happy couples remain sexually involved with each other, too.

Marriages or relationships that survive long-term are more often (but not always, as we shall see in a moment) based on shared interests, humour, respect, and friendship. Adams and Jones (1997) find, in a study of marital commitment, that three primary dimensions exist: attraction based on devotion, satisfaction, and love; a moral imperative component based on personal responsibility for maintaining the marriage; and the belief that marriage is an important social and religious institution accompanied by fear of the costs (social, emotional, and financial) of ending the relationship. These three dimensions are found to correspond well with couples' personal accounts of what it feels like to be in a committed relationship.

Many couples who reach their fiftieth wedding anniversaries are clearly

A Rose Every Friday

When I first met my lady, 50 years ago, she was playing Gershwin on a baby grand piano...

How to woo this lady? I bought her a red rose and won her heart...

Every subsequent Friday ... I gave her a rose.

Every Friday I take a rose to Avril in [hospital] and, although I am gradually losing her, I know she recalls ... when we fell in love with the help of Gershwin and flowers.

Source: "A Rose Every Friday...," *Gulf Islands Driftwood*, 24 December 1997. Reprinted with permission, Alex Mitchell, *Gulf Islands Driftwood*.

and visibly in love with each other. People who have known close couples in their own families recognize the glow they have when they look at each other. Television and radio, on special occasion programs, sometimes allow us a glimpse of long-term married couples where it is apparent that they love and respect each other deeply. A lifetime of sharing can bring comfort with each other and shared memories that pull them even closer. These relationships exemplify the supportive transactions that sustain solid relationships, to which we shall return in Chapter 8 when we discuss how to avoid violence and stress in families.

At the same time, marital duration is not always indicative of happiness. We all know couples, or know of couples, who stay together not because they are in love or happy with each other but for practical reasons: the children, too much shared to separate, too much invested to leave the relationship, or fears of the consequences of leaving.

Romantic love can be discovered later in life too. Some whose first marriages have ended in divorce or widowhood find love the second time around. Their attitudes may be more mature but are no less romantic. Few studies have focused on love in mid life or later life, but what exists offers hints that love can indeed be sweet and long-lasting when people find each other after having some life experience. Among the most romantic of scenarios is the couple that lose each other when young, marry others and then, when widowed, find each other again and renew their love. These stories are almost epic in the feelings they evoke of love discovered. The struggles and the separation from each other sweeten the sense of romance once they find each other at long last.

Still others in midlife find love in coming to grips with their sexual orientation. A man who is father to three children, who had lived his life not admitting to himself or to others that he is gay, comes out and, for the first time, feels contentment and self-security in his identity. A woman realizes she is lesbian after marrying, mothering five children, and divorcing; she finally finds love and commitment with another woman. These are real-life examples of people known to one of the authors. Dunne (1997), in a study of lesbian lifestyles, invites us to look more closely at the nature and implications of heterosexual relations. Dunne argues that heterosexuality is an institution that regulates everyday social life and is more likely to make women dependent, to limit their participation in the labour force, and to legitimize unequal relationships. This linking of sexuality and sexual relations to economic systems and constraints parallels Engels' theory discussed earlier.

Marital/Relational Conflicts

Close relationships, whether marriage or cohabitation, are never conflict-free. Yet conflicts do not mean that the people do not love each other. On the contrary, acquiescing to a partner without respecting one's own views can be a sign of trouble and differential power in the relationship. Some couples handle conflicts much better than others. In this section, we will look at what existing family research can teach us about marital/relationship conflicts and about how to resolve them. In a subsequent chapter (Chapter 8 on stress and violence in family), we will see how economic pressures increase stress in marriages and family relationships.

Early in relationships, conflicts most often centre on jealousy, on power, and on sex. As the relationship develops, money and the division of labour become larger issues. Commitment to each other helps to get over the rough spots, and love and forgiveness help, but they are not enough. Both individuals in the couple must work to develop skills and mechanisms to resolve conflicts as they arise. Communication and flexibility have been found to be key components. Choices exist and change is possible, even in marriages or relationships that seem difficult.

One large change to marriage and long-term intimate relationships is that, if they last a lifetime—and many do—a lifetime is much, much longer than it was for our grandparents. When couples today make vows of lifetime commitment to each other, either in a formal marriage ceremony or privately, they are committing themselves for an average of well over 50 years, compared to less than 35 years for the generation born at the turn of the century (Gee, 1986:273).

Remarkably few couples take any pre-marriage counselling or courses in marriage. We take courses in driving; we even take lessons to develop skills in hobbies such as golf or tennis. Yet when it comes to a crucial life step such as marriage or committing oneself to a long-term relationship, we somehow think that simply living into our mid-twenties gives us all the knowledge we need!

One pastor, when counselling pre-marital couples, focuses on "fighting," probably to the surprise of some engaged couples. Chris Levan (1998:F4) says that "Apart from the pre-apple Adam and Eve, there hasn't been a couple who didn't fight…. Strong partnerships are not built because we avoid couple combat, but because we fight honestly and openly." He counsels four rules of couple fighting for strength in their relationship:

> Rule #1 about fighting: we all do it … accept that no matter how good your navigation, your ship of marital bliss will go through the tempests of stormy waters …

> Rule #2 in fighting fairly is to keep the arguing above the table. As soon as we repress our anger or direct it against something else—the dog, the traffic, the office crowd—we're in trouble.

> Rule #3: don't use old ammunition. How often do we fly off the handle in the midst of a fight and dredge up past offenses and insults to fire back at our partner? This is a non-starter.

Rule #4: keep a close grip on your own feelings. Try to insert what's happening in your gut into the conversation ... use statements which express your inner 'I' and avoid the wagging-the-finger 'you' statements (Levan, 1998:F4).*

"Fighting for Your Marriage" workshops exist in many communities, as well as many other marriage counselling courses. This is a program to counsel couples that developed out of research done at the University of Denver. A component of this program is videotapes of couples learning, and others who have successfully learned, how to problem-solve, how to be a team and get back to being best friends again as they were before all the demands of family life began to impose on their relationship. Seeing what is possible helps couples see that they can change and together make a better relationship.

Some argue that marital counselling is political (Jacobson, 1989) in that couples are not free-floating entities but are shaped by societal expectations. It is, argues Jacobson, difficult to counsel couples struggling with conflicts over closeness and independence when the real conflict is not between the two people but relates to how to make societal expectations their own.

Jacobson came to this conclusion because he found that the communication skills he and his partner taught often worked only temporarily for couples under controlled conditions. Later the conflicts escalated into intense, angry outbursts. He says that "It gradually became apparent that high-conflict couples exhibited characteristic 'dances' that seemed to encompass most or all of their arguments" (Jacobson, 1989:30). Eventually, in working to "re-choreograph" the dance of conflict, Jacobson and his partner came to understand that social-learning-based marital therapy, although important, cannot solve all couples' conflicts because conflicts are scripted by gender and unequal power.

Jacobson concludes (1989:32) that "Marital therapists come face to face on a daily basis with the products of an antiquated, patriarchal marital structure which manifests itself in a power differential almost always favouring men." He suggests then that the solutions to marital conflict should be based both on enhancing communication and understanding between the couple, and, importantly, on improving the inequalities that both women and men suffer in light of societal expectations about marriage.

Putting the individual together with the social/political, what practical conclusions can we reach about how best to resolve conflicts in marriages or relationships? Several lessons emerge. First, not all conflicts are solvable. Some are best left alone. A couple can agree to differ; or, when the conflict is serious, may take it as a sign that the relationship is truly unworkable. The wisdom to know which is which is key not only to the success of the marriage but to individual happiness as well.

Reprinted with the permission of Chris Levan, Principal, St. Stephen's College.

Second, being the individual you are nurtures rather than detracts from healthy relationships. Much 1990s popular advice on marriage starts and ends with the idea that we each should mould or submerge ourselves to please the other partner (Coltrane, 1998). This is particularly typical of the advice women are receiving. Family sociology research generally does not support this as an effective long-term strategy. On the contrary, it is known that strong and secure individuals generally make for stronger and happier close relations. Along with this strength, of course, must go some degree of accommodation and tolerance. Submerging of self to the other, no matter what society encourages, is likely to lead ultimately to a self resentful of the other partner.

Third, softening the edges is known to be helpful. Partners who listen to each other, tolerate each other's habits and views, and savour the differences between them are more likely to have longer, happier unions than those who expect or hope for unanimity on everything. Humour also is known to be a key determinant of long-term successful marriages or unions. Taking time out from responsibilities to play, relax, or simply be together is also key. Much more will be said about the challenges and workable solutions to marital conflicts in the next chapter.

The Power of Love

Having someone with whom you are close can save your life, or at least add years to your life expectancy. The fundamental relationship between social support and health and well-being is such a well-known and consistent sociological research finding that it's sometimes called the "big effect." The benefits of social support, particularly loving support, for individuals and for families, is a recurrent theme throughout this book.

The role of supportive transactions in preventing and dealing with family violence is discussed, for example, in Chapter 8 as part of considering stress and violence in families. McDaniel (1997), in a paper prepared

Santa's Health and Mrs. Claus

Even with his red nose, "bowl full of jelly" tummy, love of fat-laden cookies, and late-night work hours, Santa's health may not be as bad as you might think.

New medical evidence published since last Christmas suggests that his jolly disposition and close ties to Mrs. Claus and the elves may help stave off the effects of heart disease.

"The fact that he has been around for so long can be attributed to a number of things, including his cheerfulness, broad social network and high job satisfaction," said Dr. Joseph Lieberman....

Source: *The Globe and Mail*, December 23, 1997: A10 (abridged).

Having someone with whom you are close can add years to your life expectancy.

for the National Forum on Health, brings together existing research on how the "power of love" in families contributes to well-being and survival. This vast and growing research literature suggests that love is like chicken soup: it is good for your health, though we can't explain exactly why and how.

Another theme that emerges from the research on the health benefits of having a close life partner is that *too much* closeness can undermine these benefits. This finding supports the idea that we need a degree of personal independence and autonomy in healthy relationships.

A different take on the healthful effects of marriage in particular comes from Waite (1995). In her presidential address to the Population Association of America, she argues that marriage partners derive special benefits that other close relationships do not provide. Why? She concludes that "Spouses act as a sort of small insurance pool against life's uncertainties, reducing their need to protect themselves by themselves from unexpected events" (Waite, 1995:498).

Married people, in fact, have a slightly higher average socioeconomic status than the unmarried or than common-law couples. It has further been suggested (McDaniel, 1997) that marriage "protection" may be different for men than for women. Women may derive a financial co-insurance benefit, while men derive emotional co-insurance. Both are good for well-being.

In times of trouble or health crises, having someone to care about can

Svend and Max

MP Svend Robinson says thoughts of his partner Max Riveron propelled him to drag himself to safety after falling while hiking.

Glancing to the opposite side, he was startled to realize that he was at the top of a cliff right beside an 18-metre drop.

He noted the time, 1:45 p.m., reached out—and that was the last thing he remembers before waking up at the bottom of the cliff.

Without panicking, he took stock of his condition. He was in terrible pain. His right leg was covered in blood, bones were sticking out of his foot; he had huge gashes in his head and his right knee. Breathing was difficult.

"The worst of it was my jaw." He felt as if he no longer had a chin. Bones were sticking out inside his mouth and his teeth were loose.

"I lay there and began to think about what it means to die." He thought about the friends and family he would not see again.

And then he thought about [Max] Riveron. As he recalled that moment, tears welled in his eyes. "We've been together for 3 1/2 years and I ... just, it's so powerful. I love him so much."

Mr. Robinson said that emotion and the prospect of leaving the Cuban expatriate [Max] alone in his adopted country renewed his determination to survive.

Source: "MP Battered but Not Beaten," *The Globe and Mail*, January 19, 1998:A4. Reprinted with the permission of *The Globe and Mail*.

pull one that extra little bit away from the abyss. The death and dying literature has many stories of how constant thoughts of a loved one led to rescue from an accident, survival against the odds, or surviving longer than anticipated from a life-threatening illness. In Chapter 3 we will explore other ways in which love and close relations matter to our lives.

Policy Challenges and Debates

Marriage and families are hot topics in policy circles in Canada and even more so in the United States. The crux of the debates on family and family policy is marriage: its changes, its solidity, its future. The centrality of this concern was apparent in the outcry that followed Statistics Canada's proposal in 1996–97 to no longer publish marriage data in the traditional format, a decision subsequently reversed. It is also apparent in recent public debates on both sides of the border about what governments should or should not do to promote or encourage marriage or traditional families.

Generally, the involvement of the state (with all of its agents and agencies) in marriage has been limited to laws about who cannot marry whom, and what procedures must be followed to enter legal wedlock. There has been some resistance on the part of governments to involve themselves closely in what is largely seen as a private family matter.

Of course, the reality is that the state and state policies have actively shaped the ways in which we form and live in families, as well as our sense of family. Ideas about individual responsibility, about the vulnerable dependent, about sex and morality, about life chances and choices, are all reaffirmed through our laws and policies. Therefore, it is not surprising that changes to these basic ideas cause concern and debate about family policies.

Two factors propelling the re-evaluation of policies on marriage and mating are recent concerns about family poverty, particularly the poverty of children in mother-headed lone parent families, and the rapid growth in women's labour force participation.

The issue of persistent poverty among female-headed single parent families has raised questions about what policy steps might be taken to address the problem. Among the answers are improved subsistence for single mothers, more job opportunities, gender equity in pay and work opportunity, more child support from absent fathers, and better access to affordable daycare so that single mothers can more readily seek work.

All of these are viable and reasonable policy options on which volumes have been written by sociologists as well as policy analysts. However, other solutions have been proposed. One is that governments, through policy, should promote marriage continuity (*The Globe and Mail*, 1993). The logic is simple: since it is divorce and separation that is behind most mother-only single parent families, the way to prevent the poverty so many of them subsequently face is to make marriages more stable.

Proposed methods to achieve this goal include making divorce more difficult to get, requiring conciliation counselling or divorce school for those who are seeking divorce or legal separation, and working to change attitudes, convincing women to expect less romance in marriage and men to value more highly their family roles (Richards, 1998; *The Globe and Mail*, 1993:A17).

The rapid growth in women's labour force participation has been repeatedly cited as a central reason for marriage not being as stable and secure as it was presumed to be in the past. The labour market is seen as competing with marriage for women's basis of security. "Once marriage provided a woman with the best guarantee of financial security. Now she can more easily escape from an unhappy marriage—even though the escape often leads to poverty" (*The Globe and Mail*, 1993:A17). The exact means by which women's labour market participation is linked with marriage instability has not been well spelled out.

Oppenheimer (1997:449) contributes by sociologically examining the presumption, carefully relying on existing research. Her conclusions bear sharing:

> Although the popularity of the women's economic independence explanation of marriage behavior remains strong in the 1990s, this review of the literature found little empirical support for the hypoth-

esis.... [We find that] women's educational attainment, employment, and earnings either have little or no effect on marriage formation or, where they do have an effect, find it to be positive, the opposite effect of that hypothesized.

She adds two additional important conclusions. "The apparent congruence in time-series data of women's rising employment with declining marriage rates and increasing marital instability is partly a result of using the historically atypical postwar behavior of the baby boom era as the benchmark...." (Oppenheimer, 1997:431). Then she makes a crucial point about presumed marital mismatches: "The frequent tendency to equate income equality between spouses with women's economic independence and a lowered gain to marriage fails to distinguish between situations where high gains to marriage may be the result of income equality from situations where the result is a very low gain to marriage" (Oppenheimer, 1997:431).

Focusing on the relative levels of couples' incomes ignores the contexts in which incomes are earned and the fact that those contexts are changing.

It has also been suggested that marriage laws may be a disincentive to marriage. Laws may discourage couples from marrying if aspects of legal marriage are seen as bringing major, and possibly unwanted, changes in a couple's relationship.

On the other hand, if legal marriage is seen as changing nothing much they may not find it attractive as an alternative to living common-law. As common-law unions and legal marriages become more similar under the law, as they are in many jurisdictions, then marriage *per se* may seem less attractive.

In Quebec, for example, the province with the highest rates of common-law living in Canada, there has been a seemingly progressive law on the books for 15 years that a woman may not take her husband's name. She can, if she insists, use his name in social contexts, but all legal documents will be issued in her maiden name. This was followed in 1989 by a law that specified that in case of divorce, all assets, even those acquired prior to the marriage, must be divided equally. There is no opting out. So, couples may feel, on the one hand, that there is little difference between marriage and living together since both parties keep their own name anyway. On the other hand, they may feel that legal marriage compromises their preferences about property ownership and prefer to make their own personalized conjugal agreements. If societies value marriage, it is argued, then laws and policies ought to more consistently favour it.

At the same time, a strong argument is emerging from the family economy literature that many tax policies are based on an outdated view of what families are. Given that, increasingly, Canadian family policy is delivered through the income tax system, it does make a difference what model of family is used. Men are defined much more often as the economically dominant partner in a marriage or common-law union, and women as the subordinate partner. All kinds of tax options encourage the husband to purchase retirement plans in his wife's name, and to assign income to the lesser paid spouse.

> Our tax system cannot achieve the modern social welfare and equity
> goals claimed for it so long as we continue to base policy decisions on
> an image of family that belongs to old reruns (Phillips, 1995:31).

Another policy debate is the question of who should be entitled to the workplace benefits that marriage permits. Groups have lobbied for a broad definition of spouse in spousal entitlements. Access to such benefits, including health care, is especially important in the U.S. In Canada, public health care insurance makes the issue less pressing, but an incentive for being declared a spouse remains.

In both countries, common-law spouses may wish to marry to take advantage of benefits packages, including access to pensions, to survivors' benefits, and to bereavement and care leaves. This has also been a motivator for common-law unions to be declared "as married" or "equivalent to married." It has also been the essential reason for gays and lesbians to lobby for access to legal marriage or to "equivalent to married" status. This position, however, is not without controversy among gays and lesbians, many of whom see their relationships as innovative and pioneering, and marriage as a heterosexual institution.

There may be a difference emerging between recent immigrants and the Canadian-born in terms of marriage policy. Immigration policy in Canada has long emphasized, along with market forces, family reunification. The definition of what a family is, of course, is paramount in implementing family reunification.

Who exactly counts as family and is thus eligible for immigrant status in Canada has narrowed over recent years. The shrinking definition of family has excluded adult children of a couple, for example. A paradox emerges. Although in Canada, as we have seen, more couples are living common-law, for purposes of immigration, a person does not qualify as a spouse unless there has been a formal, binding, traditional marriage. Thus policy maintains a widening gap between new and other Canadians.

Concluding Remarks

It is apparent that the quest for a close, committed, intimate relationship has changed dramatically in recent times in North America. What has not changed is the importance it has in our lives and to our sense of well-being. Dating and mating has been of sociological interest since the beginning of sociology. The interest and the surprises its study brings never stops. Neither will our personal interest in sharing as closely as we can our lives with someone special.

Chapter Summary

We have seen in this chapter that romantic love is only one way to begin a close relationship, and, as a basis for forming lasting close relations, is relatively new in human history. We have also explored the close connection between the findings of the early sociologists and the fundamental role of close relations to our lives.

Our particular cultural approach to mating grew out of the development of a market economy and courtly love during the Middle Ages. Many vestiges of that knightly period remain in our approaches to courtship and love. Power, particularly of systems like the economic system, the class system, and gender structures, also closely determines how families begin and what roles we end up playing. Even though some of these structures have changed and are changing, they still influence our lives and choices about close relations.

The struggles men and women have in sorting out the sexual scripts involved in pairing off are outlined as well as the changes that have occurred. That violence occurs in dating relationships is important to know and understand.

Increasingly, families begin with cohabitation rather than marriage today, and they may begin over again several times as couples dissolve their close relationships to form new ones or to restart the existing relationship in a new way.

Key Terms

Arranged marriage: A marriage in which the bride and groom are chosen for each other by their relatives.

Attachment: The close relationship that develops between individuals with strong emotional ties.

Companionate marriage: Marriage in which the partners are in love and find pleasure in each other's company.

Extended family: A multigenerational family in which grandparents, parents, children, and perhaps other relatives (aunts, uncles, cousins, etc.) share a household; or a description of such rela-

tives even if they do not live together.

Homogamy: A tendency for people to marry people from similar socioeconomic and cultural backgrounds, partly because they have more opportunities to meet such people.

Marriage gradient: The tendency of men, on average, to marry someone who is a little younger, a little less well educated, a little lower in socioeconomic status and slightly shorter than they are; or conversely, of women to marry men who are a little older, a little more educated, a little higher in socioeconomic status, and slightly taller than they are. This results in a gradient of marriage partners that leaves out tall women and short men differentially, as well as very well-educated, well-off women and poor men with little education.

Monogamy: The system of marriage in which one is married to one person to whom one is expected to be loyal and faithful.

Propinquity theory: The theory that peo-ple tend to associate with and eventually marry those who live near them or work or go to school or university with them.

Romantic love: Idealized or sentimental love.

Sexual double standard: Social rules governing appropriate sexual conduct that differ markedly for men and women, and typically also by class, race, and ethnicity.

Sexual script: The social rules of sexual behaviours for men and for women.

SUGGESTED READINGS

Abu-Laban, Sharon & Susan A. McDaniel. 1998. "Beauty, Status and Aging," pp. 78-102 in Nancy Mandell (Ed.), *Feminist Issues: Race, Class and Sexuality*. Scarborough, Ontario: Prentice Hall Allyn Bacon. This article shows how beauty and the quest for it by women is shaped by society and by the expectations of a sexualized dating game. It continues by discussing how beauty standards change with age.

Fisher, H. 1992. *Anatomy of Love: A Natural History of Mating, Marriage and Why We Stray*. New York: Fawcett. This book develops the argument that love, monogamy, and adultery have biological bases.

Morton, Suzanne. 1992. "The June Bride as the Working Class Bride: Getting Married in a Halifax Working Class Neighbourhood in the 1920s," pp. 360-379 in Bettina Bradbury (Ed.), *Canadian Family History: Selected Readings*. Toronto: Copp Clark Pitman. This article shows how weddings used to be simple, taking place on weekdays in registry offices, with the most popular colour of the bride's dress being brown. It also reveals how marriage was seen as a life goal for women, necessitating that they leave work.

Risman, Barbara. 1998. *Gender Vertigo: American Families in Transition*. New Haven: Yale University Press. Based on original research by the author on single fathers, married baby boom mothers, and heterosexual egalitarian couples, this book reveals how gender as a structure in society becomes a crucial part of the families we build. She then shows how we as individuals can work to change those families and ourselves.

Schwartz, Pepper & Virginia Rutter. 1998. *The Gender of Sexuality*. Thousand Oaks, California: Pine Forge Press. This book offers a sociological framework and analysis of sexuality. It integrates the most useful of biological and sociological perspectives and includes an in-depth analysis of recent changes, largely focusing on the United States.

REVIEW QUESTIONS

1. What is the origin of romantic love and how is it linked to early sociology?

2. How is it that arranged marriages often work out and at times lead to the development of love?

3. Under what circumstances in the past would a man take the woman's name on marriage?

4. What is the link between monogamous marriage and the economic system? How does it work theoretically?

5. Whose benefit is most important to consider in planning a marriage in the eyes of much of the world outside of North America, and even in some subgroups on this continent?

6. What is the sexual double standard and how is it changing in the 1990s?

7. What is companionate marriage and why is it important to us?

8. What are the trends in cohabitation overall, and what are they by age group?

9. Identify two issues relating to the establishment and maintenance of close relations that are the subject of a good deal of attention and proposed policy change.

10. What are some future challenges to understanding/explaining the beginnings of family relationships?

DISCUSSION QUESTIONS

1. Why is romantic love as a basis for establishing lasting close relations troublesome at times for us? For society?

2. If monogamy was initially developed in conjunction with a change in the economic system, as Engels theorized, then could current economic changes bring about a new kind of marriage system? What might it look like?

3. What would happen to meeting and mating rituals if couples were to become more realistic in their expectations and plans? Is this approach possible in our society? Would it truly bring the benefits we desire or would it create additional problems?

4. As globalization of economies, jobs, and education occurs, do you think the same will happen with the mate market? How? What would be the implications?

5. What reasons exist for the growing preference for cohabitation rather than marriage in Canada, and in particular in Quebec?

6. Why do you suppose that the age gap persists between men and women at marriage?

7. Discuss the relationship of happiness to divorce. Does divorce always result from unhappiness or do other factors matter too?

8. Would promotion of policies that make divorce more difficult make for happier and more stable families?

9. Why are single-parent families headed by women such a touchstone for concern and a focus for debate on policy changes?

10. What would you say is the future of meeting and mating in Canada?

WEBLINKS

http://www.acs.ohio-state.edu/units/ research/archive/oldfight.htm

An article showing that marital arguments lead to weakened immune system in older couples.

http://www.apa.org/releases/relation.html

An article on why relationships last and who best predicts how long they will last.

http://www1.od.nih.gov/obssr/marstres.htm

Stressful marital relationships: Immunological and endocrinological correlates.

http://www.ryerson.ca/family-soc/ cas-coh1.htm

Case studies on cohabitation.

http://www.jinjapan.org./stat/stats/ 02VIT34.html

An international comparison of cohabitation rates.

Marriage and Well-Being:

The Role of Love and Communication

"All happy families are alike but an unhappy family is unhappy after its own fashion," begins Tolstoy's classic Russian novel, *Anna Karenina*. Is there only one way for a family to be happy but many ways for families to be unhappy? If so, why should that be? Suppose that every family is unhappy in a unique way. How can today's readers of *Anna Karenina*, the story of a very unhappy family, hope to understand the problems confronting the main characters in the story if every unhappy family is unique?

Most social scientists would disagree with Tolstoy. Research suggests that there are many ways to be happy, both individually and within close relationships, and many ways to be unhappy. Still, there are a few recipes for increasing the likelihood of happiness that we will explore in this chapter. As we will see, the variety of routes to happiness in close relations is large but not endless.

In this chapter we consider the reasons why some people have closer, more fulfilling relationships than others. In Chapter 1, we discussed what we mean by *relationship* and *closeness*, and how we might measure closeness. Here, we consider why married people or people in committed long-term relationships are, on average, happier and healthier than unmarried people. We try to understand why married people enjoy more material, physical, and mental well-being, however those are measured. These questions interest not only family researchers but also those who study health and illness.

We also consider the reasons why some marriages are more fulfilling than others. We focus mostly on marriages because most of the research on satisfaction with intimate relationships has focused on marital relationships. The central question, however, is what makes any close relationship work. We suspect, but cannot prove, that the answer is much the same for marriage and cohabitation, for same-sex and opposite sex relationships. Further research on intimate, non-marital relationships will determine whether they work in similar ways.

Some readers may wonder if our tone is prescriptive. Are we telling you to marry rather than stay single, to marry someone as much like yourself as possible, to have or to avoid having children? Are we encouraging you to report being happy even when you are not? Not at all. We do feel that regularities in the research findings of scores of studies point to generalizations. However, let us rush to assure you that we have no grand scheme here. There is no right path for all people, all children, or all parents. Research evidence must always be taken with a grain of salt: the more general the evidence, the more superficial it becomes; the more specific the evidence, the more situations it fails to take into account. Moreover, one may doubt that anyone—still less any young person—ever makes important life decisions based on the evidence of social scientists or the advice of others, especially perhaps of middle-aged sociologists.

So, instead, read this chapter to see what answers the research evidence suggests to questions that you may be asking yourself. If you find yourself thinking about your own situation and your options in a different, perhaps a clearer way, we will have achieved our goal.

Marriage and Well-Being

Marriage and Satisfaction

The first key finding is that married people are generally more satisfied people. Sociologists have measured the link between marriage and well-being in at least three ways: (1) by examining suicide rates, (2) by asking people to report their feelings of happiness or satisfaction with life, and (3) by looking for signs of deficient personal well-being (e.g., poor mental or physical health or changes from previous healthfulness).

One of the earliest sociological studies, Émile Durkheim's classic *Suicide*, discovered something that today we think of as almost common sense. In looking at the patterns of French suicide rates in the late nineteenth century, he found that socially integrated people are less likely to take their lives than people who are more isolated. As well, people whose lives are unregulated by social ties are more likely to kill themselves. They often suffer from a state of normative confusion he called **anomie**, which increases the risk of suicide. Emotional ties connect married people to the people with whom they live. Obligations to protect and support these people regulate their lives. They have agreed to curb their sexual desires, for example. On the other hand, single people, especially unmarried people with no children or other close family (e.g., dependent parents, brothers or sisters), are more free to go where they want, when they want, and with whom they want. With more integration and regulation, married people are less likely to commit suicide than unmarried people. Of course, this is not to say that married people never take their own lives; we are talking here about probabilities. Today's statistics support Durkheim's theory: suicide rates remain higher among unmarried than among married people, just as they were a century ago.

In Durkheim's frame of analysis, there can be no fulfilment or satisfaction without human association and involvement with others in close relationships.

Until the second half of this century, few Canadians divorced because of structural barriers that made it difficult to do so. Divorce in Canada was only possible with a special act of Parliament. Christianity has historically opposed divorce, so Western society has often stigmatized divorced people. Cut off from membership in the religion and from religious members of the society, divorced people have historically experienced anomie and isolation, even more so than widowed or never-married people. As Durkheim's theory predicts, suicide rates are consistently found to be higher among the divorced than among widowed and never-married people.

However, researchers rarely use suicide statistics to measure the well-being of married couples. Although suicide may be a sign of unhappiness, most people who are unhappy do not commit suicide. Moreover, marriage breakups are not the only cause of suicide. Therefore, sociologists have developed a variety of ways besides suicide rates to measure the happiness, satisfaction, or well-being of married people. They focus their attention on the measurement of marital quality, since bad marriages often lead to divorce, diminished well-being, or both.

Satisfaction as a Measure of Marital Quality

Space does not permit an exhaustive summary of the progression of sociological thinking about marital quality. Research on the topic began with Locke in the 1930s. Later work by Spanier (1979) established that marital happiness and marital satisfaction, one visceral, the other cognitive, are so highly correlated as to be virtually the same thing. Further research has examined the question of whether marital quality is multidimensional or unidimensional, generally opting for the latter (see, for example, Karney & Bradbury, 1997).

Much of the current literature focuses on marital commitment, rather than marital satisfaction or quality. This is because, for reasons that become clear in Chapter 9 (on divorce), factors other than marital quality influence the decision to break up a marriage. Nonetheless, satisfaction and quality remain the place to start our discussion. They have *some* influence on people's divorce decisions and, more important, people believe that they *ought* to feel satisfied with their marriage.

Surveys show that people's feelings about their marriage range from the peak of satisfaction to the trough of despair. Most people, most of the time, report being satisfied with their marriage. Moreover, married people, both men and women, are twice as likely to be satisfied with their lives than separated or divorced people. On average, never-married people are less satisfied than married people (not surprising in view of the importance people place on marriage), but more satisfied than divorced or separated people (Campbell, 1980; Tepperman, 1994).

According to some Canadian research, the strength of the relationship depends on age and, in general, may be vanishing, thus challenging the view that marriage is a source of well-being in Canada (McDaniel, 1998a; White, 1992). In contrast, relying on evidence from Europe, Veenhoven (1983) argues that marriage is actually gaining in its importance to our well-being. Marital satisfaction spills over into many domains of life. Married people continue to be happier (especially in the most modernized European countries), less disturbed, healthier, and live longer than unmarried people. Since 1950, these benefits of marriage have increased. As a result, overall life satisfaction today is more strongly correlated with marital satisfaction than it was several decades ago.

Health is another area in which Canadian and European data disagree. Though Veenhoven's summary of European data shows that married people are healthier than unmarried people, Canadian data suggest that overall, single people are healthier than married people (McDaniel, 1998a; White, 1992). The differences in findings may be attributable to differences in research methodology, such as how health is defined and whether the study examines married people as a whole or looks at results for subgroups. Marital status may affect health in a number of ways, as shown in Figure 3.1.

Despite these differences, a growing body of research shows that marital status still contributes to people's health, wealth, and happiness.

Now let's consider other measures of well-being. Marital happiness and stability are the strongest predictors of a mother's personal happiness, self-esteem, and absence of depression (Demo and Acock, 1996). A good remarriage, for all the problems remarriage sometimes can entail, is almost as beneficial in terms of well-being as is a good first marriage. Though moth-

Figure 3.1 PATHWAYS THROUGH WHICH MARITAL STATUS IS ASSUMED TO AFFECT HEALTH

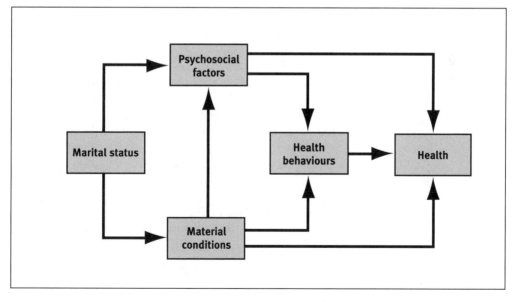

Source: I.M.A. Joung, K. Stronks, H. Van de Mheen, F.W.A. Van Poppel, J.B.W. Wan der Meer, J.P. Mackenbach. 1997. "The contribution of intermediary factors to marital status differences in self-reported health." *Journal of Marriage and the Family*, 59:2, p. 478. Online courtesy: UMI Proquest Direct. Copyrighted 1997 by the National Council on Family Relations. Reprinted by permission.

The Trick: Love, Honour, and Negotiate

Alas, marriage licences don't come with a users' manual, so sooner or later, the honeymoon ends. But it doesn't have to. Not if we know how to love, honor—and negotiate. We can learn those skills to keep rekindling the flame of romantic love, say increasing numbers of therapists, counselors and authors who are helping couples acquire the tools to make a modern-day marriage work.

At any stage of a relationship, couples can learn to negotiate to get their needs met, they say. Even couples headed for divorce can learn to happily-ever-after. "There is no magic formula," says newlywed Zac Shiel, who admits he needed help to learn how to negotiate. "To negotiate you've got to listen; really listen."

Family therapists point to our lack of relationship skills for the spiraling divorce rates. One Canadian couple divorces for every 2.4 marriages and more than 30,000 kids each year suffer a split in their families.

Source: Sharon Adams, 1996. "How to Live Happily Ever After," *Calgary Herald*, October 13, D1, D3 (abridged). Reprinted with permission.

---

ers in their first marriage enjoy the greatest well-being, remarried mothers fare nearly as well. Divorced and single mothers score lowest on well-being.

However, the health benefits of marriage occur only if it is a "good marriage." "Bad marriages" destroy well-being, however it is measured. Good marriages range from stable, conventional, and boring to exciting and fun. From the outside, the people in a particular marriage may seem conservative, smug, or lacking in ambition. What matters, however, is how the marriage seems to the participants. People's needs and wishes vary, but in general people can tolerate a lot more boredom in their family lives than they can tolerate danger and uncertainty.

A good marriage is particularly important to people who are sick, weak, or otherwise vulnerable. Marriage helps if the spouse is loving and supportive. For example, pregnant women particularly benefit from being in a good marriage with a supportive and understanding spouse since they may often feel vulnerable or even unwell. The quality of the attachment between a pregnant woman and her husband affects the woman's sense of well-being (Zachariah, 1996). Moreover, this effect continues after the child is born. Hock, Schirtzinger and Lutz (1995) collected data during pregnancy and after the infant's birth. Reports from both spouses reveal that marital satisfaction influences whether a mother shows symptoms of depression nine months after the birth of her child. The late Princess Diana, for example, is reported to have suffered a loss of self-esteem during her pregnancies and after the births of her sons, which may have been accentuated by being in a bad marriage.

In short, if husbands do not take into account a spouse's pregnancy or illness in making demands, their wives are worse off when pregnant or sick than they would be alone, or with their mothers. However, if the marriage is good, its effects are particularly beneficial when the partners are most needy.

His and Hers Marriage

Is marriage better for men or for women? In a sexist society, marriage, like most everything, would be better for one sex than for the other. In our society, research, not surprisingly, has suggested that marriage is better for men than for women. Indeed, men and women often even have different experiences of marriage. This insight led sociologist Jessie Bernard (1973) to speak of "his marriage" and "her marriage" as two very distinct versions of what many would suppose to be the same reality. Some critics (e.g., Glenn, 1975; 1878) have accused Bernard of perhaps overstating the differences. Evidence shows that marriage benefits both men and women, though not equally. Schumm and colleagues (1985), using data from three samples of married couples, find that, while men and women are equally happy on average, when there is an extremely wide difference in marital satisfaction, it is almost always the woman who is less satisfied. "Her marriage" is quite different from "his." As well, Glenn (1975) found that, although husbands and wives report similar levels of marital happiness, marital happiness has a stronger effect on overall happiness for the wives than for the husbands. As with any social reality, there is no single unified experience of family. Members of the same family can have different, and even opposing, views.

Marital quality means somewhat different things to men and women. The stability and constancy of "being married" may be the most important aspect of marriage for men, especially perhaps for older men. Yet men have a different set of needs than women, reflected in the traditional household division of labour. Marital closeness seems to dampen husbands' sense of well-being (Tower and Kasl, 1996). Among couples aged 65 and over, husbands are happiest when they have emotionally independent wives who don't need much attention. By contrast, wives are happiest and least depressed when they feel important to their husbands and can depend on them emotionally. The same is not clearly true of younger couples.

Different ideas about marriage contribute to the gap between men's and women's experience of and happiness with marriage. Both married men and women report more life satisfaction than unmarried people. However, husbands and wives get different amounts of well-being from marriage. Comparative measures of longevity confirm that women get less benefit from marriage than men do. Canadian married men have a life expectancy five years longer than single men, while married women live only one-and-a-half years longer than unmarried women (Keyfitz, 1988). (Keep in mind, however, that women as a whole live longer than men as a whole.) The precise causal connection between marriage and longevity is yet to be determined.

Men also gain more satisfaction out of marriage because men and women hold different structural positions in society. Therefore, they have access to different kinds of rewards and opportunities. Women as a group have less power. They get paid less, and society and employers discriminate against them in other ways. Because they do not as often occupy positions of social or political power equal to men, women are more vulnerable to exploitation, be it economic or sexual. Thus, even before marriage, women are less able to achieve the same level of life satisfaction as men and then less likely to derive as many benefits after marriage.

Women may benefit less from marriage than men because in a society characterized by gender inequality, marriage tends to be an unequal relationship. In that sense, it is a sealing, bonding, and prediction of future inequalities. People entering unequal relations, or entering relations unequally, are likely to experience inequality afterward. Women suffer disadvantages in marriage for at least two reasons. One is the prior social gender inequality that exists in our society. The other is gender inequality within marriage, such as the domestic division of labour, discussed in more depth in Chapter 6.

After marriage, gender-based disadvantages continue, both in the workplace and at home. Marriage functions to perpetuate exploitation of women. Personal conflict at work is more likely to disadvantage women who are also experiencing conflict in their marriages. Conflicts at work less often seriously harm men's well-being; nor do they cause as much harm to women in good marriages. Additionally, the pressures to get married, from society, families, and personal expectations, are stronger for women than for men. Thus, women may be more likely to marry for the wrong reasons and perhaps to have unrealistically high expectations. This, too, increases the likelihood they may gain less satisfaction from marriage than men.

Even if marriage yielded women as much mental, emotional, and financial benefit, they would profit less than men because they had invested more. This is especially true where the spouses have children to care for. As we will see in a later chapter, women still do the lion's share of the housework, whether or not they also work outside the home. When the household division of labour is unequal (favouring husbands), wives, especially employed wives, are more likely to become unhappy and depressed (Pina & Bengston, 1995). On top of that, women often take time out from work to bear and raise children. Along with housework, women spend more time than men raising children. Constantly attending to children raises their stress level. Depression and stress reduce women's satisfaction with marriage.

To repeat an earlier point, marriage tends to be more satisfying for both men and women than never marrying or being single again after separation or divorce. However, a bad marriage is far worse, especially for women, than singlehood or divorce, which explains why many people divorce or avoid marrying in the first place. For many women and children, the family is the primary locus of violence in their lives. It is where they experience danger and pain. For them, well-being may only come after they have escaped abuse at the hands of their intimates.

We will discuss divorce and family violence more in later chapters. For now, note that marriage provides life well-being for most people, but it is dangerous and even life-threatening for many others. A bad marriage affects every aspect of well-being, including life satisfaction and physical and emotional well-being.

Often, marital dissatisfaction and unhappiness take physical forms. Our immune system declines, we catch colds or infectious diseases, and recover slowly from whatever illnesses we might get. Symptoms of stress from marital dissatisfaction occur in an apparently ever-widening range of illnesses. For example, people with cancer vary in their adjustment to the illness. Cancer patients in bad marriages report more depression and anxiety, less commitment to good health, and more illness-related family problems than patients in good marriages (Rodrigues & Park, 1996).

Moreover, people in unhappy marriages often show signs of psychological difficulty. The symptoms include a weaker will to live, less life satisfaction, and reported poorer health, compared to people in happy marriages (Shek, 1995a). A bad marriage may even lead to work loss, especially for men in the first decade of an unhappy marriage (Forthofer, Markman & Cox, 1996). That is because our bodies show physically how we feel emotionally. Emotional suffering can make it hard to be productive in one's job.

What Makes a Marriage Satisfying?

What is it about a good marriage that increases life satisfaction, health, and longevity to such a degree? Or, if you are prone to skepticism, what factors predispose people to attribute satisfaction to their marriages? Does marriage serve some primitive and basic need for closeness which, if unsatisfied, dooms us to a briefer and more miserable life? Or are the problems associated with singlehood social, in the sense that we have structured society to enforce the idea that there is something wrong with people who never marry? The answers to these questions are complex.

For happily married couples, marriage means achieving a good fit between the spouses' individual needs, wishes, and expectations, a fit which they regard as unique and irreplaceable (Wallerstein, 1996). Such couples believe that maintaining a good marriage throughout life means establishing and maintaining a good sex life and providing a safe place for expressing deep feelings. People, especially married people, think they know what makes for a happy marriage. Yet do they really? Social scientists are not quite so certain. In studying the factors associated with marital satisfaction, distinguishing the causes from the effects is often difficult. For example, couples who report talking to each other a lot also report trusting each other, having satisfying sex, and, generally feeling satisfied with their marriage. However, this finding is open to interpretation. Is it frequent conversation that increases trust, sexuality, and satisfaction? Perhaps cause-and-effect run in the opposite direction. Perhaps marital satisfaction causes spouses to talk to each other more. Or all the factors reinforce each other again and again over time.

This problem of causality is challenging in all studies of marital quality. It arises because most research on the topic is cross-sectional. That is, most research examines the correlation between two or more variables, such as levels of conversation and marital satisfaction, at one point in time. Solving the problem of cause-and-effect means identifying which variable changes first. To do this, we ideally require an experiment or a longitudinal study. However, no one wants their marriage experimented on, and longitudinal research, though possible and done on occasion, is rare because of the expense and the long delay in finding out anything.

The Life Cycle of a Typical Marriage (With Children)

Some problems that we face in marriages are avoidable and others are apparently not. Marital satisfaction usually decreases over time, a finding reported in both longitudinal and cross-sectional studies (see, for example, Adelmann, Chadwick & Baerger, 1996). This decline is particularly marked for couples with children. Willen and Montgomery (1996) refer to the "Catch 22" of marriage: Wishing and planning for a child increases marital happiness, but achieving this wish reduces the happiness.

The birth of a child, and the resulting intense mother-child relationship, tends to strain marital relations, just as a troubled marital relationship strains parenting (Erel & Burman, 1995). New parents experience reduced marital happiness and more frequent, sometimes, violent, conflicts with their spouse after the baby arrives (Crohan, 1996). Some evidence suggests that conflict may even begin before the baby arrives, during pregnancy. More will be said about this when we discuss family violence in a later chapter.

Marital satisfaction decreases with the arrival of children because children drastically reduce the time wives have for their husbands. Childbirth reduces by up to 80 percent the proportion of activities wives do alone, or parents do as a couple or with non-family members. (See Figure 3.2.) This radical shift from spousal (adult) activities to parenting activities creates an emotional distance that the partners find hard to bridge. Romance and privacy disappear. Sleepless nights increase. Mothers, the main providers of child care, change their time use much more than fathers. Particularly after the birth of a first child, marital quality and the quantity of time spouses

Figure 3.2   **MARITAL COMPANIONSHIP: LEISURE TIME TOGETHER WITH AND WITHOUT CHILD (MINUTES PER DAY)**

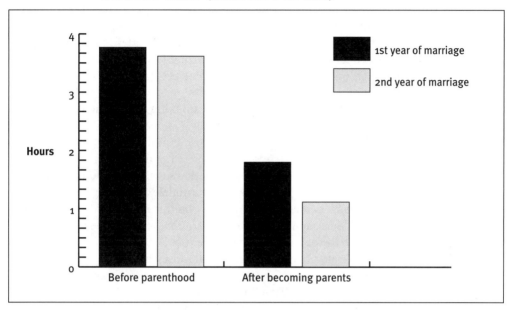

Source: Ted L. Huston and Anita L. Vangelisti. 1995. "How Parenthood Affects Marriage." In: Mary Anne Fitzpatrick and Anita L. Vangelisti (eds.), *Explaining Family Interactions*. Thousand Oaks, CA: Sage, 161. Copyright ©1995 by Sage Publications. Reprinted with permission of Sage Publications, Inc.

spend together declines immediately. Mothers report feeling more anger and depression than before (Monk, Essex, Snider, Klein *et al*, 1996; for Canadian evidence on this topic, see Cowan & Cowan, 1992).

Researchers report findings similar to these in both cross-sectional and longitudinal studies, in which people report on their current experiences; and in retrospective studies, where they recall what happened to them at different stages in their parenting experience. For evidence drawn from longitudinal research, see Belsky and Rovine, (1990), and Volling and Belsky (1991). The convergence of these different types of evidence makes it unlikely that popular myths about parenthood overly colour these conclusions.

Whatever the types of evidence, research finds that marital satisfaction decreases much more for first-time mothers than for any other parents (Wilkinson, 1995). However, the problem doesn't end with the first child. Bearing and caring for children continues to impair the psychological health of even experienced parents. For both mothers and fathers, stress increases with the number of children in the household. This stress reduces the parents' psychological well-being, which, in turn, reduces marital satisfaction (Lavee, Sharlin & Katz, 1996).

Even the closest, happiest couples experience distress after having a baby. Regrettably, few professional services are available to smooth this transition (Cowan & Cowan, 1995; but see also Kermeen, 1995 on an innovative program to improve the sexual aspects of marriage postpartum). After the emotional roller-coaster of new parenthood, reality sets in. The spouses are often too busy to spend even limited "quality time" with each other. This change to their relationship is long-lasting. For example, sexual activity falls off dramatically and never returns to its original level. Researchers report that with preschoolers present in a household, sexual inactivity is likely and prolonged. It is amazing that some couples with preschoolers actually have another child!

Space does not permit a detailed discussion of marital sexuality. Be assured, however, that researchers widely accept the quality and frequency of sexual intercourse as an indicator of marital satisfaction and marital "quality." At the same time, recognize that marital sexuality typically declines with circumstances that may or may not be traceable to declines in satisfaction: with illness, aging, frequent separation, and childbearing. In these cases, a decline in sexual activity may reduce marital satisfaction, or may be spuriously related to declines in marital satisfaction (meaning, the decline in both sexuality and satisfaction is due to a common cause).

Typically, marital satisfaction, which decreases with the arrival of children, reaches an all-time low when the children are teenagers. Once the children leave home, creating what some sociologists call an "empty nest," many marriages, however, improve to near-newlywed levels of satisfaction. Parental (and other work) responsibilities decline, largely explaining the return of marital satisfaction in later life (Orbuch, House & Mero, 1996). Many couples rediscover each other at this time. They have more leisure time to become reacquainted. Thus, compared to younger married couples, older couples show much less distress, less desire for change in their marriage, and a more accurate understanding of the needs of their partners (Rabin & Rahav, 1995).

Parenthood is, in some ways, like a classic experiment conducted on naive subjects. One set of well-functioning couples introduce the experimental condition, a child. Other matched "control" couples do not. In the experimental group, marital satisfaction plummets; in the control group, it continues to decline slowly (if at all) as the marriage wears on. At a later stage in the experiment, the condition removes itself. The child grows up and, with luck, leaves home. Marital happiness returns to earlier levels. The conclusion is obvious.

Our first point, then, is that marital satisfaction varies normally and predictably over the life cycle. It typically declines over time, and declines most rapidly and extremely with the presence of children. Then, satisfaction typically recovers when the children leave home. So, unless you avoid having children, this is likely to happen in your own marriage. Knowing this pattern, however, means that extra efforts can be taken to keep the spark in your marriage. Having children has satisfactions too. Bear in mind as well that children are not the only causes of marital problems, nor does the avoidance of parenting ensure happiness. In fact, many couples who are involuntarily childless are unhappy as a result. Less is known about couples who are voluntarily childless, but there are strong hints that they tend to be happy. Recognize too that our culture continues to stigmatize people, especially women, who choose not to bear children, regarding them as selfish or unloving (Veevers, 1980). Happily, the stigma has faded in recent years as women's lives have become more diverse.

There are other marital problems that can also be predicted and avoided. We will discuss separately several factors that affect marital satisfaction.

Homogamy

First, marital satisfaction depends on how similar the spouses are. Generally, husbands and wives who are more alike get along together better and report being more satisfied with their marriage.

Your common sense might tell you otherwise. In fact, sociologist Robert Winch theorized that "opposites attract." Couples who are dissimilar, he argued, should be more satisfied with their marriages because their differences (in personality or skills) are complementary. Marriage is a series of exchanges, Winch reasoned. Therefore, couples will be more satisfied if each spouse offers something that the other cannot provide for himself or her-

Having children typically lessens marital satisfaction for a significant period, but parenthood has its satisfactions too.

self. A marriage with little similarity between the partners' respective skills and aptitudes would be more efficient.

Winch's (1962) initial qualitative study of couples supported his theory. However, this finding is the exception, not the rule. Typically, more researchers find that "like attracts like" than that "opposites attract." The marriage of like to like, or *homogamy*, does not necessarily mean that spouses are similar in every respect. However, as discussed in Chapter 2, some kinds of social similarity, such as age, education, race, religion, and geographic location, are particularly common and, therefore, perhaps particularly important. As well, some shared physical traits (e.g., physical attractiveness) and psychological traits (e.g., intelligence) increase the likelihood that two people will be attracted to each other. They also increase the likelihood that mates will be happy with each other (Buss, 1985).

It is not clear precisely how these similarities affect the mating process. For example, large people tend to marry large people (Allison *et al*, 1996). It is not clear why. Nor do similarities always ensure the survival of a marriage. To continue the same example, mate similarities in weight before marriage do not reduce the likelihood of divorce. Other similarities do. Behaviours, interests, personality traits, and attitudes about men's and women's roles do tend to matter. They help to decide who will mate with whom, and who will stay with whom. People usually pair with partners who hold similar attitudes, and couples who are similar in their attitudes toward gender roles turn out to have better marriages (Aube & Koestner, 1995). The ultimate homogamy is homosexuality, leading one to predict that homosexual unions would be particularly happy and long-lived. There is no evidence so far addressing this prediction, but it would be difficult to test, since discrimination and social censure make gay and lesbian relationships challenging in our society.

Overall, homogamy is strongly correlated with marital satisfaction: the more similar two spouses are, the more likely they will be satisfied with their marriage. Homogamous couples also adjust to marriage better, in the sense that their marriages work better (Weisfeld *et al.*, 1992; Creamer & Campbell, 1988). Long-term spouses tell researchers that agreement on a variety of issues contributes to the longevity of their marriage, to marital satisfaction, and to overall happiness (Lauer *et al.*, 1990).

Homogamy increases marital satisfaction because mate selection based on value and role similarity reduces the number of issues the couple may disagree on and so the number of areas of potential conflict. In marriage two people build a shared life, together facing the little injuries and major tragedies life has in store. Doing this is easier when spouses view the world in similar terms, and when each knows, understands, and respects the other's point of view. Similarity in education, age, and cultural background guarantees nothing but tends to make this easier on average.

Spouses also become more like each other over time, and this strengthens the relationship. Again, this reminds us that mating and marriage is a shared construction project—specifically, the shared construction of a narrative about life, oneself, and others. How well spouses work together to construct this narrative predicts the quality of their marriage. Spouses who can't talk about their lives together in similar ways are unlikely to work together agreeably.

In a test of this hypothesis, researchers asked parents to describe the birth of their child and then, separately, to complete a test of marital satisfaction. They found that the emotional expressiveness and coherence of the couples' narratives—how thoroughly, clearly, and similarly they described their child's birth—predicted how satisfied they were with their marriage at the time they constructed the narrative, and also one and two years later (Oppenheim, Wamboldt, Gavin, *et al.*, 1996).

Sometimes, an assumed similarity between spouses is as important as real similarity. Other things being equal, spouses who think they are a lot alike express more satisfaction with their marriage. They also speak to each other in more positive ways than spouses who think they are very different (Thomas, Fletcher & Lange, 1997). That may be because people consider people like themselves to be more attractive and likeable than people who are different. They are also more likely to forgive indiscretions in spouses they consider to be like themselves.

Because of the tendency for like to marry like, and for homogamous marriages to be more satisfying, **heterogamous** marriages are less common and less satisfying. The effects of racial and religious heterogamy (or "intermarriage") are less harmful today than they once were, or people had once thought they were. Nevertheless, they are occasionally harmful. For example, (heterogamous) couples in which the man is Nigerian and the woman African-American consistently express more distress and dissatisfaction over finances, child rearing, and time spent together than (homogamous) African-American couples (Durodoye, 1997). Likewise, intermarriages of Filipinas to American white men can have many problems, perhaps because of the economic goals and reasons for migrating that underlie many of these marriages (Paredes-Maceda, 1995). Other things being equal, spouses in minority male-white female marriages are less happy than spouses in same-race marriages (Chan & Smith, 1996).

Perhaps the troubles intermarrying couples face are due to discrimination; when racially or ethnically mixed couples are more common, there may be fewer problems. The point is, similarity makes a difference to marital well-being. Ultimately, however, relationship dynamics are more important than background similarities in predicting marital satisfaction (Fowers & Olson, 1989).

Love

Relationship dynamics include interaction patterns, communication styles, and intimate practices between the spouses. All are very important. However, as we saw in the last chapter, many people consider that love is more important than anything else.

What, then, of marriages that are not initially based on romantic love? In many societies, as discussed in Chapter 1, arranged marriages are the norm. The mates may "learn to love one another" or may never learn to love each other as they may have hoped. These marriages may indeed prove satisfying to the spouses. Given that arranged marriages are built on perceptions of shared attributes between the partners, parents very often choose wisely for their children. Arranged marriages tend to be very stable and sometimes immensely happy. Folk mythology argues that arranged marriages become, over time, more satisfying than love marriages (as shown in Figure 3.3a). There is no evidence, however, that this is so. On the contrary, even in societies like China, where arranged marriage has a long history, love marriages are more satisfying at every stage or duration. As shown in Figure 3.3b, arranged marriages tend to become more satisfying over time, but do not, on average, reach the level of satisfaction found with love marriages (Xiaohe & Whyte, 1990).

Given that finding, how can we compare the stability of arranged marriages with the higher satisfaction of love marriages? Marital stability can be a good thing for couples and for society. Ideally, marital stability is a product of marital satisfaction. Where the two diverge, a person must often choose. It would be helpful to know whether stability or satisfaction contributes more to individual health and longevity, to children's well-being, and to society as a whole. However, we cannot give a clear general answer to this question.

In any case, in Canadian society most people marry for love. They see love as the basis of their union, without which the marriage would not satisfy either partner. We are all of us, to a greater or lesser extent, enthralled by the myth of Romantic Love. Yet, as we said in Chapter 2, romantic love has a very particular social and cultural history. The demand for love in marriage is neither universal nor timeless. Typically, it is associated with economic security. People who must live hand-to-mouth cannot afford to think as much about love. (This is not to say that wealth brings love. Beyond a certain level of comfort, an increase in income does not increase the chance of love flourishing.) That is why people pay more attention to romantic love in industrialized, or "Westernized," societies. Those in the upper classes, who set the ideals for the rest of us, pay the most attention of all.

Thus, college students from Western or Westernized nations rate love as more important than anything else for the establishment and maintenance of a good marriage. Typically, people in nations with a high stan-

Figure 3.3   **TRENDS FOR MARRIAGE SATISFACTION IN LOVE MATCHES AND ARRANGED MARRIAGES, ACCORDING TO POPULAR CONCEPTION (PART A) AND AS OBSERVED BY XIAOHE & WHYTE (PART B)**

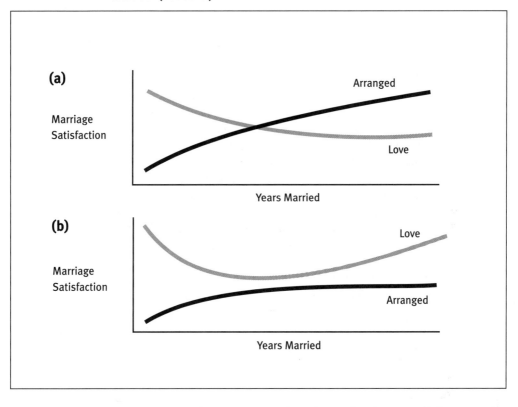

Source: Adapted from Xiaohe, Xu and M.K. Whyte. 1990. "Love Matches and Arranged Marriages." *Journal of Marriage and the Family*, 52 (August):709–721. Copyrighted 1990 by the National Council on Family Relations. Reprinted by permission.

dard of living, high marriage and divorce rates, and low fertility rates assign the most importance to love as a basis for marriage and as a source of happiness (Levine, Sato, Hashimoto & Verma, 1995).

In marriage, feelings of passion and companionship usually continue throughout life, yet some types of love are more common than others at particular stages of a marriage (Noller, 1996). What some consider immature love—exemplified by limerence, love addiction, and infatuation—is characteristic of the first year or two of an intimate relationship.

Limerence is that package of experiences which includes preoccupation with the loved one, wild fluctuations in mood, ecstatic feelings of well-being, and depths of despair. That is the stage when lovers convince themselves they are walking on clouds, when they are smiling to themselves, ever ready to think and talk about their beloved. They can't get enough of their mate. Their moods can swing chaotically from euphoric highs to black depressions as they review what they said and how they looked when they last saw their lover. They can spend much time thinking over how likely they are to win, please, and keep their beloved. Limerence has sometimes been seen as a kind of mental illness. Indeed, there are similarities.

Mature love, on the other hand—the kind that allows the lovers and those who depend on them to grow and develop—provides constraint, stability, and certainty. This kind of love, less euphoric and less chaotic, supports marriage and family life, and it can continue throughout life. Mature love is more common later in a romantic relationship. It typically sets in after the lovers have promised to stay with each other. The thrill of discovery and threat of loss has abated; familiarity sets in. The partners settle down to building a life together.

Commitment of this kind has at least three components (Adams & Jones, 1997). The *attraction* component includes sexual attraction, satisfaction, and devotion. The *moral* or *normative* component is based on a sense of personal responsibility for maintaining the marriage, and on the belief that marriage is an important social and religious institution. Finally, the *constraining* component is based on fear of the social, financial, and emotional costs of ending the relationship. Part of the attraction component is a fantasy—the illusion that the love object is much different from, and usually better than, oneself. Often it includes the willing suspension of disbelief in another person, or in the institution of marriage itself. However, fantasy serves as a powerful glue in most social relations, whether we are consid-

Religious Observance, Marriage, and Family

Canadians who attend religious services every week report having happier, less stressful lives and happier relationships with their partners than those who do not attend services at all. The odds of having a very happy marital relationship were 1.5 times greater for people who attended religious services weekly than for those who did not attend at all (after accounting for differences in age, education, income, religion, province, employment status and the decade when the marriage began).

Accounting for similar socio-demographic factors, the odds of a marriage dissolving for those attend-ing religious services every week were less than half of those who never attended.

About 57% of people who attended religious services weekly reported that they would stay married for the sake of the children compared with 36% of those who did not attend religious services.

Weekly attenders were less likely to view lack of love and respect, and a partner's drinking too much as sufficient grounds for divorce. However, religious people were just as unwilling to forgive a spouse's unfaithful behaviour as those who did not attend religious services.

Source: Statistics Canada. Adapted from *The Daily*. September 15, 1998. Catalogue No. 11-001. Reprinted with permission.

ering religion, politics, leisure, or family life. Positive illusions about one's marriage are good: they are found in most of the happiest marriages (Fowers, Lyons & Montel, 1996). When people speak about their mate or their marriage in glowing, idyllic terms they are merely exaggerating (or noting to themselves and those who matter to them) an already high degree of satisfaction with the relationship.

Some idealization or illusion may be a necessary part of any satisfying love relationship. Intimates see their partners in an even better light than partners see themselves. Typically, the impression they have of their partner reflects their own self-image and ideals, rather than their partner's self-reported attributes. Yet, the more that people idealize their mate in this way, the more they report being satisfied with their relationship (Murray, Holmes, Griffin & Dale, 1996). Perhaps that is because expressing these illusions endears us to our mate, who expresses endearing illusions in return. So, in each other's eyes, and then in our own eyes, we become perfectly matched spouses.

Under certain social conditions the ability to idealize someone successfully (i.e., unchallenged) is crucial to success. Marriage can create favourable conditions for such idealizing. In marrying, we find someone we can idealize who won't stop us from doing so.

People in highly satisfied unions are more willing to attribute good qualities to their spouse. For example, a loving, satisfied spouse is more likely to give credit to his or her partner when something works well. Interestingly, when it doesn't work well, women are more likely to take responsibility for the failure. Sometimes, we can see this most easily when couples break up and the partner who is left blames himself or herself for the failure of the relationship. The tendency to feel "part of a couple"—merely one-half of a pair—means that often people will still carry around the idea that they are a "couple" in their heads long after experiencing psychic (and even physical) separation.

Mutual attribution can increase the satisfaction of both spouses, who each come to view the other partner as a major contributor to their good marriage. Conversely, people who take to routinely blaming their spouse for failure later report less marital satisfaction, even when we control for depression, self-esteem, and initial marital satisfaction. Blaming one's spouse— whether justifiably or otherwise—sets in motion dynamics that reduce the love and satisfaction between the two spouses.

In a loving relationship, people often speak of the qualities they admire in their partner. They use the terms "we" and "us" a lot, and glorify struggles rather than brood about them. However, in a failing relationship, spouses play out a different script. For example, the husband becomes disillusioned, one spouse criticizes the other, and both are reluctant to talk about the relationship. In interviews, the spouses are eager to tell about unexpected problems and hardships (Leonard, 1995).

As we mentioned, the love that partners feel in the early stages of a relationship rarely remains at that initial, feverish intensity for long. As the passion gradually dies down, something else typically replaces it, a deeper, more compassionate, less intensely sexual kind of love that is based on sharing a life together. The moral normative component or commitment to marriage becomes increasingly important. The felt obligation to one's spouse, and in return, the perceived or imagined commitment of one's spouse, is the most powerful influence on the relationship (Nock, 1995). People who are religious tend to be more satisfied with their marriage, and more stably married, a finding confirmed in a late 1990s study by Statistics Canada. This may be because religious people are more accustomed to making and maintaining moral, normative commitments.

When one spouse helps the other pursue a personal or relationship goal satisfaction with the relationship is enhanced (Brunstein, Dangelmayer & Schultheiss, 1996). For example, women who care for their aged parents are usually under much stress, and stress typically reduces marital satisfaction. However, caregiving women who receive much support from their husbands are typically much more satisfied with their marriage (Franks & Stephens, 1996).

Couples show their lasting strengths and weaknesses early; likewise, the willingness to provide support is established early in a relationship. So, for example, Pasch and Bradbury (1998) invited 57 couples, all married less than six months, to discuss a problem that each partner was having. Two years later, nine of these couples had separated and five other marriages were "in trouble." Trouble had arisen in only those marriages where the spouses, as newlyweds, had provided little support and encouragement.

Intimacy, like love, helps mates to establish and maintain a close bond based on attraction, trust, and respect. It is expressible in words, but is also expressed physically, as affection and sexuality.

Intimacy

The origins of the word "intimacy" are informative. "Intimacy" comes from the Latin word meaning "inward" or "inmost." It connotes, on the one hand, "familiarity" and on the other hand, "secrecy." Now, consider the connections among these three words— "inward," "secret," and "familiar." We are, each of us, uniquely familiar with our secret, inward thoughts, hopes, and fears. To become intimate with someone else means admitting them to our (partly) private, unique world, which in turn means trusting them with our most valued possessions. Building and maintaining this intimacy with a partner is the key to a mature, surviving relationship.

From these beginnings, the word "intimacy" in our culture has come today to mean little more than sexual intercourse. When we say that X and Y have been intimate, we normally mean that they have had sexual relations.

This implies that our culture equates sexuality with trust, privacy, familiarity, and closeness. The reality is far different: many who are sexually active are not truly intimate with each other, and many who are truly intimate have no sexual relations. Consider the peculiar status of friendship—especially, same-sex friendship—in our culture: often, our friendships are far more intimate (in the original sense of the word) than our sexual relationships.

What actions are considered a violation of intimacy—what we usually call "cheating"? The criteria vary from one relationship to another, and are different for men and women. Typically, men consider cheating by their spouse to mean sexual intimacy with another man. Women may also consider emotional intimacy with another woman to be cheating, whether sexual relations occurred or not. The fact that, traditionally, people have viewed marriage as the acquisition of sexual property by men may account for this difference. For women, it has been the acquisition, if anything, of financial security.

In good marriages, we find intimacy of both kinds, sexual and psychological. Satisfied spouses are more sexually intimate with each other, as measured by how often they display affection physically, touch each other, kiss each other, cuddle and have sex. These affectionate behaviours, like the expressions of liking we discussed earlier, are reciprocal. Shows of affection by one spouse usually prompt affectionate behaviour by the other spouse. What is more, they promote other positive actions. Often, they also prompt respectful behaviour (Gaines, Jr., 1996).

Intimacy grows naturally in a supportive social relationship. However, intimacy doesn't come easily to everyone. Knowing how to be intimate with another person is something that we learn, more by example than by instruction, from the moment of earliest infancy. A loving, committed couple can have problems with intimacy if one or both partners never learned how to be intimate. They may have trouble trusting or confiding in others generally, or particularly in others of the opposite sex. They may have trouble expressing affection because they grew up in a family in which people never did so. Or, they may have trouble with sexual behaviour because of an earlier sexual trauma, or because they never saw their parents relate to each other as sexual beings.

People in different social and ethnic groups vary in the ways they express intimacy and the meanings they attach to it. For example, Spanish-speaking Mexican Americans are less idealistic about sex than Anglo Americans (Contreras, Hendrick & Hendrick, 1996). That is, they don't make such a big deal about it. In Anglo American culture (and English-Canadian culture is similar in this regard), sexual satisfaction is correlated with greater self-esteem, positive regard, communication, and cohesion between the spouses (Song, Bergen & Schumm, 1995). In other words, sexual satisfaction is central to marital satisfaction in an Anglo relationship.

Anglo-American (and Canadian) culture places a high premium on sex, both as a source of pleasure and an indicator of intimacy and marital happiness. We look at non-monogamous relationships and think "There must be something wrong; they can't last." Indeed, sexual satisfaction contributes significantly to marital satisfaction (Kumar & Dhyani, 1996). Couples in which sexual activity is rare and one or both partners show little sexual desire may have problems getting along together. They can show signs of anxiety and depression. Usually, the spouse with less sexual desire tends to be the wife (Trudel, Landry & Larose, 1997), but this is not always the case. Little is known about couples who are not sexually intimate much in marriage but still have strong and affectionate relationships. (For an overview of who is having sex how often, see Figure 3.4.)

Why is sexual intimacy, like marriage generally, experienced differently by the two sexes? When it comes to sexual and emotional intimacy in our society, women and men seem to want, need, and expect different things. So much is this the case that they might be on different planets (or, as one very popular book title suggests, *Men Are From Mars, Women Are From Venus*). This difference in experience sometimes leads to breakdowns in communication. Women want more disclosure than men. Men don't understand what the fuss is all about. Women need to talk about their feelings and they want their men to do the same. Some men act as if the whole exercise is a big waste of time. Some have argued that this proves men and women are genetically different in emotionally relevant ways. An alternative, and more convincing explanation is that we raise boys to avoid emotional discussions while we raise girls to engage their emotions. Showing emotion is seen by some men as a sign of weakness or even manipulation, and thus, different attitudes to emotional expression relate to the inequality of power between men and women.

More than talk is at issue here. Husbands report more sexual satisfaction than wives. Sex occurs within an unequal society. Marital sex occurs in a context shaped by the structural and cultural realities of people's lives. Many women have to find sexual pleasure within a marital relationship that also provokes feelings of powerlessness, anxieties about contraception, and exhaustion from child care and outside employment.

For many reasons, sexual frequency declines over a marriage. Age, duration of marriage, and the presence of children all affect the frequency of marital sex. Allowing for age, duration of marriage, and the presence of children, happily married people have sex more often than less happily married people. Again, the cause-and-effect relationship is unclear. Is it that people who are happy together are more inclined to make love, that making love often helps a couple stay happy together, or that other factors affect both happiness and sexual frequency? Perhaps it may be some of each.

Controlling for age and other relevant factors, people who cohabited before marrying, and people in their second or later marriages, have sex more often (Call, Sprecher, & Schwartz, 1995). The reasons likely are due

Figure 3.4 **SEXUAL ACTIVITY BY MARITAL STATUS**

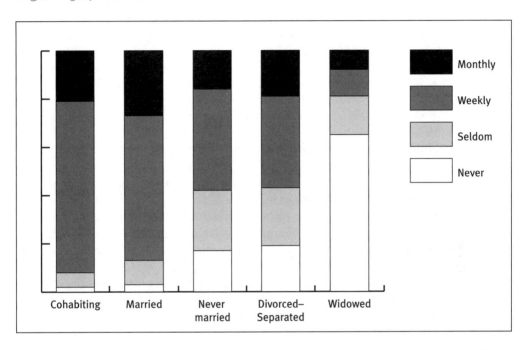

Source: Reginald W. Bibby. 1995. *The Bibby Report: Social Trends Canadian Style.* Toronto: Stoddart, 66.

to selectivity. Typically, people who cohabit have, at least until recently, been different kinds of people from those who marry directly and stay married. It seems likely that these kinds of people put more store by intimacy, especially sexual intimacy, as a basis for marriage. Therefore, they have sex more often, or stop being married.

Coping and Conflict Management

We have already discussed conflicts between intimates in an earlier chapter, and will talk at greater length about stress and coping in a later chapter, but we must say something about it here. For how well a couple copes with stressors and manages the conflicts that arise in any long-term relationship influences their marital satisfaction.

Financial strain, for one, increases the likelihood of depression in both spouses. Depression leads the partners to withdraw social support and undermine the other. These behaviours, in turn, reduce marital satisfaction and intensify the depression, in a vicious cycle (Vinokur, Price & Caplan, 1996).

Health-induced strains also influence marital satisfaction. Taking care of a chronically ill spouse puts an enormous strain on a marriage. It leads to dissatisfaction for the caregiving spouse, especially one who feels the ill person brought on his or her own health problems, or who has other reasons for feeling cheated in the relationship (Thompson, Medvene & Freedman, 1995).

As we said earlier, the birth of a child reduces marital satisfaction by increasing conflict and parenting stress (Lavee, Sharlin & Katz, 1996). The problem is greatest if a couple has been unable to resolve important relationship issues before the birth (Heinicke & Guthrie, 1996). The death of a child also reduces marital satisfaction, by reducing emotional and sexual intimacy for years afterward. Death itself may have less effect than the way each spouse reacts to it and to the other spouse's reaction (Gottlieb, Lang & Amsel, 1996). Often, marriages fall apart after a child's death. Each spouse has a hard time thinking and talking about their suddenly changed lives, with their child missing. The grieving parents may need help to reorganize the ways they think and talk about themselves and their family (Riches & Dawson, 1996).

As we will see in Chapter 8, a problem like this can reflect the couple's inability to cope with stressors. It does not necessarily show that marital satisfaction was lacking, or artificial, before the trauma—only that the couple found themselves without sufficient resources once a crisis arose. Often, couples don't know how well they can function until they are forced to deal with stressors like this.

The stresses of work can also reduce marital satisfaction. Often, conflicts resulting from a spouse's employment cause distress. By producing hostility and reducing warmth and supportiveness between the spouses, these conflicts reduce the quality and satisfaction of a marriage (Matthews, Conger & Wickrama, 1996). Unemployment due to job loss also causes marital conflict. It may be due to a loss of customary ways of family living or unwanted role reversal (particularly for males). Material deprivation and marital conflict over financial issues also play a part (Lobo & Watkins, 1995). When husbands lose their jobs, wives experience half as much family income and have the husband at home twice as much.

Retirement from work can either increase marital satisfaction or decrease it. Retiring from a high-stress job normally increases satisfaction. On the other hand, poor health and other changes that often cause or accompany retirement, which may reverse gender roles or reduce social support, reduce satisfaction (Myers & Booth, 1996). Retirement changes the relationship dynamics—the balance in incomes and status that existed before retirement. Couples made up of a retired husband and employed wife are often less satisfied, especially if they hold traditional ideas about gender roles. That is because retirement, like unemployment, shifts authority away from the husband who is traditionally the breadwinner and boss. On the other hand, employed husbands with retired wives report even more marital satisfaction than husbands in dual-earner couples, possibly because the new arrangement is more like a traditional marriage (Szinovacz, 1996).

Married people cannot avoid conflicts, and trying to avoid disagreements altogether is usually unwise. Marital adjustment is more a function of interrelationship skills and beliefs than of the presence or absence of extra-relationship hardships. To a large degree, the couple's belief in their ability to resolve disagreements is the best predictor of marital adjustment (Meeks, Arnkoff, Glass & Notarius, 1986). Couples who use passive-aggressive behaviours, such as whining or playing on guilt feelings, may have trouble "making space" for themselves in relationships, that is, dealing with seemingly incompatible characteristics, personalities, or behaviours. This failure to confront differences may itself produce difficulties in adapting. So we are not arguing against confrontation. As with much else in life, it's not what you do that counts, it's how you do it.

Though confronting disagreements is better than trying to avoid them, there are better and worse ways of doing this. In older couples, conflict resolution is usually less hostile and more affectionate than in young and middle-aged couples. With the passage of time, many couples figure out how to defuse and laugh at their disagreements. Styles of conflict resolution also vary by sex. Generally, wives tend to be more emotional than husbands. Husbands are more defensive and less expressive (Carstensen, Gottman & Levenson, 1995).

In his book, *Why Marriages Succeed or Fail*, John Gottman (1994) notes that successful marriages resolve conflicts through validation or conflict-avoidance. Marriages are destroyed through criticism, contempt, defensiveness, and stone-walling. A great deal of what couples do to support or antagonize each other is nonverbal. For this reason, it is often possible for marriage counsellors to help the couple diagnose the type and seriousness of a marital problem, using videotapes of distressed couples (Gottman, Markman & Notarius, 1977). Expressions of feeling, nonverbal behaviour during message delivery, feeling probes, and positive and negative reciprocity all help to identify the quality of the relationship.

In good marriages, spouses can read each other's nonverbal cues better than anyone else (Gottman & Porterfield, 1981). In particular, the husbands of satisfied wives are more able to read their wives' nonverbal cues than are strangers, while the husbands of dissatisfied wives are less able to read them. There is strong evidence of gender differences in the emotional expressiveness and physiological reactivity of spouses. Though men show a stronger physiological reactivity (measured by skin conductance) to their spouses' emotions than women, they respond more neutrally or positively than women (Notarius & Johnson, 1982).

According to Gottman (1982), what distinguishes happy from unhappy marriages is not so much the reciprocation of positive affect as the de-escalation of negative affect. In other words, whether your compliments or words of love are returned does not matter so much as simply not being hurtful in interactions with the spouse, or reducing any hurtful interactions. The underlying mechanism that maintains closeness in marriage is balanced emotional responsiveness, particularly in low-intensity interactions such as sharing events of the day.

Not surprisingly, people in unhappy marriages express more negative emotion than people in happy marriages. However, though it is good to express emotion, expressing too much negative emotion may not be. Becoming quiet and withdrawn does more to keep the peace and maintain marital happiness, providing this is not simply a means of avoiding problems. Many new parents adapt (effectively) to the increased stress accompanying childbirth by adopting this strategy of quiescence (Crohan, 1996). It can have the extra benefit of letting the newborn sleep!

Once tempers die down, dealing with the disagreement in a moderate and thoughtful way becomes easier. By contrast, verbally attacking the spouse or leaving the scene of the conflict leads, not surprisingly, to marital unhappiness. Spontaneity, though attractive and valuable in many areas of life and marriage, may not play a useful role in resolving marital conflicts.

If the relationship has become a constant power struggle, certain combative types of communication that may have developed make it worse. As

If a relationship has become a constant power struggle, the couple may have developed combative types of communication that will only make matters worse.

each partner tries to one-up the other, the argument may spiral out of control. Sometimes no one wants to be the first to stop arguing. The argument, even the game of it, becomes more important than the relationship. If, from the beginning of the disagreement, the couple recognizes that they are "in it together," they have more chance of solving the disagreement without either member losing face. Losing face or the fear of it can affect the balance of power in a relationship, which in turn reduces marital satisfaction.

Violence is never a satisfactory way to deal with marital conflict. It neither makes the disagreement disappear nor improves the marriage. Spouses in violent relationships often respond to each other's comments with one-up moves. Violence can escalate quickly. This interaction pattern, in which both spouses assert but neither accepts the other's effort at control, may reflect poor skills in arguing constructively (Sabourin, 1995). In some couples, one or both spouses excuse violence on the grounds of drinking or another extenuating circumstance. As a result, the violence has less impact on marital satisfaction and thoughts of divorce (Katz, Arias, Beach *et al.*, 1995). However, the violence problem does not go away.

More than 60 percent of couples who seek marriage counselling have experienced physical violence in their relationship. However, fewer than 10 percent of these couples spontaneously report or identify the violence as presenting a problem. Many spouses fail to report it because the violence is infrequent and it is secondary to, or caused by other problems (like excessive drinking). Also, they may be ashamed to have experienced or perpetuated violence. Both men and women, perpetrators and victims, use these excuses (Ehrensaft & Vivian, 1996). We will have much more to say about violence in Chapter 8.

Gender Role Attitudes and Equity

People are more satisfied with a marriage that meets their expectations of what a marriage should be, and how a spouse should treat them. This means that increasingly in our society, people are much more satisfied when their spouse treats them as an equal in the marital relationship. This is particularly the case for women.

Over the past twenty years, we have seen an increase in the sense of injustice associated with an unfair domestic division of labour. In fact, this is often a greater source of marital tension than sex. The most dissatisfied wives today are younger mothers who are doing most of the household work, as well as much more often working outside the home (Stohs, 1995). On the other hand, when husbands adopt a less traditional attitude, they tend to feel more satisfied with their marriages. Likely, such spouses are sharing the domestic workload and their spouses appreciate it (Amato & Booth, 1995), so everyone benefits.

Couples fight more about household work than about paid work or anything else. (We will return to the division of household labour in more detail in Chapters 6 and 7.) Conflicts about paid work usually revolve around the husbands' working hours, with most wives preferring their husbands to spend less time at work (Kluwer, Heesink & Van de Vliert, 1996). Child care is an area of particular contention. Mothers with paid jobs who provide most or all the child care are often stressed, resentful, and dissatisfied with their marriages. The problem is further complicated among parents of children with disabilities. In these families, more participation by the father in child care increases marital satisfaction for both parents substantially (Willoughby & Glidden, 1995). The feelings of facing a common, shared responsibility is no doubt a key factor.

In contemporary society, men are more ready to subscribe to the ethos of gender equality than they are to take on an equal share of the domestic work. They "talk the talk" of equality, but don't "walk the walk." In some families this doesn't pose a problem. Some couples develop a myth of equality that helps them maintain stability in the relationship by avoiding any serious examination of the issues they face (Knudson-Martin & Mahoney, 1996). Some women who hold traditional gender attitudes are less likely to see inequalities in the division of household labour as unjust. So, among these families, inequalities do not reduce marital satisfaction. However, among women who hold nontraditional attitudes, inequalities in the division of household labour deeply affect their assessment of the quality of their marriage (Greenstein, 1995).

No one has yet resolved the anomaly of seeming inequality and perceived fairness, but there are clues. Data collected by Statistics Canada (1997b) show that when you measure the market value of husbands' and wives' labour around the house, men do more work than women. However, when you measure only hours, and not value, women do more work than men. This difference, of course, reflects societal discrepancies in pay between women and men. Wives may vary in whether they assess their husband's contribution in units of hours or dollars. Other things being equal, those who assess hours will perceive less fairness, and be less satisfied, than those who do the latter. Most women focus on hours contributed to family life.

Good Communication

The primary area of marital discord revolves around communication. But there is no absolute "good" form of marital communication that works for all couples. Each couple has their own needs, standards, and traditions in this area. So, we get nowhere by merely urging people to improve their communications.

Having said that, trite and commonplace observations about good communication point in the right direction. Both quantity and quality of communication are important in relationship dynamics. *Quantity* includes how often spouses talk with each other. *Quality* includes (1) how open spouses are with one another; (2) how well they listen to one another; (3) how attentive and responsive they are to one another; (4) whether and to what extent they confide in one another. These are all important to the establishment of a good, satisfying relationship.

Successful couples make lots of conversation, even if they have tight schedules and little time to spend together. How much time spouses spend in discussion influences their satisfaction with the relationship. More satisfied couples engage in much more communication than dissatisfied couples. Dissatisfied couples engage in little communication on most of the topics commonly discussed by marital couples (Richmond, 1995). Putting this another way, satisfied couples chitchat: they make small talk, banter, and joke around. Dissatisfied couples talk less, or mainly talk about weighty matters.

One question researchers have asked time and again is whether good communication is a cause or an effect of a good, satisfying relationship. Probably, as with good sex, the answer is "a bit of both." Spouses who are satisfied with their marriage are more likely to talk often and talk openly with each other. On the other hand, good communication also increases satisfaction by bringing partners closer together. It also keeps them regularly in touch with each other's lives.

Communication and Gender

Communication is a gendered relationship challenge, in the sense that women perceive more communication problems than men, and are more likely to perceive men as the source of these problems. Men, on the other hand, view the communication problem, if it is a problem at all, as mutual (Eells & O'Flaherty, 1996). Some supposed gender differences in language are stereotypical and have not been empirically confirmed. However, researchers have found gender differences in such dimensions as how much women and men talk, length of utterance, use of qualifying phrases, swearing, breaking of silences, and compliment styles (O'Donohue & Crouch, 1996; Tannen, 1993). There are also differences in the emotional content of the talk, with women being more expressive of emotions than men on average, as we discussed above.

So, men and women speak differently and this difference can become a problem. Successful marriages handle the problem better than other marriages.

Consider an important form of marital communication called **debriefing**—conversation about what happened during the day. Men view their debriefing talk as having an informative-report function, that is, to bring their spouse up to speed on current events around the office or in other parts of their life. Women, for their part, see debriefing talk as having an equally important emotional or rapport function (Vangelisti & Banski, 1993). In women's view, the talk may be about current events at home or at work but the real purpose is downloading grievances, receiving and providing support, and renewing contact with the mate.

Homogamy between partners, which we discussed earlier, is one factor that leads to easier and better communication. People with a similar history, who grew up believing similar things and behaving in similar ways, have an easier time talking with each other. Members of homogamous marriages also have more similar expectations about the role that each is to fill in the marriage. So homogamy increases the likelihood each mate will satisfy the other by behaving in the expected ways. This advantage is especially valuable in the early stages of marriage, when both partners try to define their respective roles.

Encoding and Idioms

Communication is the transmission of information from one person or group to another. To transmit information successfully, the sender must present the message encoded as clearly as possible. That way, the receiver can understand the message with the least loss of meaning and then respond.

Sometimes, problems in communication arise from one person assuming that the other person is using the same codes (or shorthand). A word, phrase, or even type of body language can have profoundly different meanings for different people. It is partly to avoid these problems that many couples develop elements of their own private language to use with each other. Such a language involves the use of "idioms." Couples often create idioms to separate their relationship from others. By using a different language, they are defining themselves as a couple, both as a notice to outsiders and as a reminder to themselves of their special relationship. These idioms take a variety of forms: for example, special pet names for each other, "inside" jokes about other people, words or phrases that denote intimate activities (e.g., for sexual behaviour or parts of the body), special or ritual activities, occasions or places, and so on.

The use of idioms also improves communication, because the couple has defined their meanings together. This vastly decreases misunderstanding. As a result, satisfied couples use more idioms than couples who report lower levels of marital satisfaction.

Couples in the earliest stages of marriage report using the most idioms, and those in later stages use the fewest, for a variety of reasons. One is the appearance of children. When teaching children to speak, you want to teach them words that will help them in the outside world. Family idioms will not do that. Another reason is that, when a couple is close and secure, they do not need the public declaration of togetherness that idioms provide. So, long-established couples have less need for idioms.

Nonverbal Communication

Another important part of successful communication is the encoding and decoding of nonverbal information. Nonverbal communication includes

Blue-Collar Marriage and the Sexual Revolution

"Experimental? Oh, he's much more experimental than I am. Once in awhile, I'll say, 'Okay, you get a treat; we'll do it with the lights on.' And I put the pillow over my head." [Thirty-year-old woman, married twelve years]

"Experimental? Not Ann. I keep trying to get her to loosen up; you know, to be more—What should I call it?—adventurous. I mean, there's lots of different things we could be doing. She just can't see it. Sometimes I mind; but then I think, 'After all, she was brought up in a good family, and she always was a nice, sweet girl.' And that's the kind of girl I wanted, so I guess I ain't got no real right to complain. [Twenty-seven-year-old man, married seven years]

Not one couple is without stories about adjustment problems in this difficult and delicate area of marital life-problems not just in the past, but in the present as well. Some of the problem areas—such as differences in frequency of sexual desire between men and women—are old ones. Some—such as the men's complaints about their wives' reluctance to engage in variant and esoteric sexual behaviors—are newer. All suggest that there is, in fact, a revolution in sexual behavior in the American society that runs wide and deep—a revolution in which sexual behaviors that formerly were the province of the college-educated upper classes now are practiced widely at all class and education levels.

Source: Lillian Breslow Rubin, 1976. Abridged from Chapter 8 of *Worlds of Pain: Life in the Working Class.* New York: Basic Books. Reprinted with permission.

posture, the direction of the gaze, and hand position. Researchers find that dissatisfied couples are particularly prone to misunderstanding each other's nonverbal cues. This lack of understanding can cause problems when nonverbal cues contradict the speaker's verbal cues. For example, if one partner is apologizing sincerely, and the other spouse misreads nonverbal signals as suggesting insincerity, a simple miscue can turn into a full-blown argument. Nonverbal accuracy increases over time in marriages, but it increases more for those who are satisfied with their marriages.

Research highlights the importance of good communication for good marital relations in a study comparing couples with and without a history of abuse. Researchers asked each couple to discuss their daily routines, and then analyzed the conversations. The researchers identified seven communication-based differences between the abusive and non-abusive couples. In their conversations, the non-abusive couples were optimistic, complimentary, collaborative, and mutually helping. They spoke precisely about particular topics, and considered effective ways of changing their routines. By contrast, in their conversations the abusive couples were pessimistic, complaining, opposed, and interfering. They spoke vaguely about relationships, events or problems, and were ineffective in considering ways of changing their routines or solving problems (Sabourin & Stamp, 1995).

As we mentioned earlier, the cause-and-effect relationship is hard to detect. We can interpret these results in either (or both) of two ways. First, they may mean that unhappy, non-communicative couples are more likely to become abusive. Because they are unhappy, they speak about their lives and their relationships in negative, pessimistic ways. Or, alternatively, the results may mean that couples who don't know how to talk well with each other grow unhappy about their relationships. Then they resort to violence in case of disagreement. We cannot decide between these two plausible interpretations without better data or a longitudinal study.

Rules for Successful Communication

Talking openly when we are already satisfied with our marital relationship may be easier. However, good communication is hardly ever the automatic result of a good relationship. Couples who love each other intensely and are committed to one another may still have to learn to talk effectively, and it may take a long time. Like all our other social skills, communication is something we learn, and continue to learn about throughout our lives. It is not something we are born knowing how to do. In extreme cases of poor communication, marital therapy may help. We will discuss this later in this chapter.

What counts as good, effective communication varies over time and across cultures. In our own society, however, most people agree that certain forms of communication harm the relationship because they undermine the listener's self-esteem. For example, personal insults, ridicule, undermining a person's authority or competence, or dismissing or belittling the person's achievements are hurtful, even emotionally abusive, forms of communication. Yet, not communicating is sometimes just as harmful as communicating negatively. Giving your partner the cold shoulder can hurt even more than a personal insult.

From a certain standpoint, we can see marital communication as part of a social system that mediates relations through theatrical imagery. Communication, after all, is a way of dramatizing a relation. It may be important to learn this as a central feature of relationships. Thus, a marriage works best when the "players" know the script that permits them to express their needs, wishes, and beliefs. This script is different for every marriage. However, no marriage can work without some kind of script, nor can it work if one or both players refuse to follow the script. It also sometimes helps to watch ourselves as we communicate as if we were actors in a play or a TV drama. What would we think of ourselves if we heard our own words and saw our own body language, but had no access to motives or any past history of the relationship? This kind of approach is sometimes used, to good effect, as part of marriage counselling.

Some rules of successful communication emerge from sociological research on families. One purpose of communication is to convey information, either of a factual or an emotional nature. The first rule then is that *communication must be clear* if it is to be effective. Both partners should say what they mean and mean what they say. This rule may seem self-evident.

However, it is surprising how many spouses regularly fail to observe it. Part of the reason is that many learned at an early age that communication is not only a tool for making our thoughts and feelings known; it is also a powerful tool for hurting and controlling people. Children who see conversation used regularly to inflict pain and establish control often end up forgetting how to talk any other way. They are often unaware of how damaging their words can be, and may end up destroying their marriages because they cannot stop hurting the people they love.

Another reason is that many people, at least at certain points in their lives, don't *know* what they mean or what they want. Or, if they do, they may not be able to express it. This can be especially true during conflicts or crises, when objectivity and calmness are hard to maintain. How can you communicate clearly what you mean when you don't know what you mean?

The second golden rule of communication is: *Be willing to hear and to respond to your partner's comments, complaints, and criticisms.* A key to establishing and sustaining good communication is the recognition of our own deficiencies and a sincere willingness to work on remedying them. Communication is important at all stages of a close relationship, but it can be especially important in the beginning. This is because during the so-called honeymoon period, there is an increased sensitivity to the communication of the other as well as a strong desire to please and to understand the other person. It is during this period that couples establish the basic interactional patterns of the marriage. Indicators of marital quality, such as the methods that a couple uses in solving problems, are often first observed at this time.

Later, often during transition periods, other behaviours, such as the establishment of meaningful family rituals, can help a couple to establish and project stability. Among couples with small children, marital satisfaction is highest for people who have created family rituals and believe that these rituals are important. Such rituals may include regular daily events, such as having dinner together, weekly events such as a Sunday afternoon outing, or seasonal events such as going to the cottage or going skiing. Typically, family rituals, particularly the seasonal ones, include special clothes, foods, and behaviour. Often, they also include the retelling of family stories: how Mom and Dad met and fell in love; why Grandpa is so forgetful; how Uncle Sid crashed his car into the SkyDome; how hard it was snowing the day Joey was born; what Sarah said when we brought Sam home from the hospital, and so on.

Ways to Increase Marital Well-Being

Marriages survive as emotionally satisfying only if they are "good," which is to say that the spouses feel the marriage is giving them something they value. And it is important that both spouses feel this way. Marriages must be mutually satisfying. They must increase and maintain the participants' sense of well-being, if they are to survive. Marriages that fail to satisfy, whether because of dissimilarity of the spouses (having little in common), absence of love, too little intimacy, too much conflict (or abuse or violence), or poor communication, will fail to survive.

Ultimately, marital quality (or satisfaction) depends on a couple's ability to adapt effectively in the face of stressful events, given their own enduring vulnerabilities (Karney & Bradbury, 1995). Every person, and every couple, has vulnerabilities. Every person, and therefore every couple, faces stressful events and must find ways of adapting or coping if the relationship is to survive. No marriage, however good, is sure of surviving; none will survive without changing and adapting in the face of difficulties. From this perspective on satisfaction, there are only three ways to increase marital well-being: (1) by better adapting to stressful events, (2) by better avoiding stressful events, and (3) by reducing the couple's vulnerabilities.

Many couples try to increase their marital well-being on their own, and do this successfully. Others seek help with their family-related problems from a variety of others. These include family and friends and a variety of discreet and sympathetic but unspecialized advisors such as priests/ministers/rabbis/mullahs, family doctors or lawyers, or teachers. Little is known about the effectiveness of the advice these sources provide. Sometimes (perhaps more often than we would suppose) people talk with wise amateurs:

Talk to Our Kids about Sex?

We are surrounded by messages about sexuality. Messages vary from the obvious to the subtle, from the written and visual images of mass media to "dirty" and sexist jokes. Even buying our children toys is full of sexuality messages regarding gender roles. The blue and pink aisles correspond to the trucks, guns and rough and tumble figures marketed to boys with the dolls and often sickly sweet items for "feminine" girls. We're surrounded by sexuality, but do we reflect on these messages or comment on their meaning to our children? Do we encourage questions about sexuality and are we comfortable with our answers?

Sexuality is a part of our lives that can bring fulfillment, excitement and satisfaction. We are sexual beings from birth until death. In fact, infancy may be the most sensual time of our lives. Constantly held and cuddled, kissed, caressed, cleaned and powdered and talked to in warm, loving tones, an infant learns how to be loved and to trust others. Many parents jump to the conclusion that talking about sexuality with their children means talking about sexual intercourse. Sexuality refers to much more than sexual intercourse. It involves how we feel about ourselves as boys and girls, men and women and how we present ourselves to members of the same and opposite sex. It is an integral part of our self-esteem and body image. It is also our sexual behaviour, including, but far from limited to, sexual intercourse. Sexuality is a significant part of our physiological, psychological, social and spiritual selves.

bartenders, cabbies, dental assistants, hairdressers. And they talk to TV and radio talk show hosts increasingly, it seems, or write to newspaper advice columnists.

Others, or sometimes the same people, consult specialized advisors, including psychologists, psychiatrists, and marriage and family therapists. Although information is incomplete, we know something about contacts with marriage and family therapists. In Minnesota, for example, marriage and family therapists (MFT) practise short-term therapy, with the average case involving 11 sessions over a four-month period. Therapy for families (an average of eight sessions) and couples (10 sessions) is typically briefer than for individuals (14 sessions). Inevitably, MFTs treat a wide range of serious problems associated with marital problems (Simmons & Doherty, 1995).

Does Marital Therapy Work?

A survey of the outcomes of marital and family therapy finds moderate but significant effects (Shadish *et al.*, 1995). In short, yes, therapy does help couples, on average. Of course, couples who seek MFT want to be helped so this increases the odds that they will be helped by the process.

No consideration of theories about the family, and specifically about marital satisfaction, can be complete without some discussion of family therapies. In a perfect world, theories would drive all therapies, just as they do in the best-developed areas of medicine. Conversely, no family theory would be considered proven until it had yielded testable and verified results in clinical, therapeutic trials. Regrettably, however, we do not live in a perfect world. Today, many family therapies continue without a theoretical basis. Equally, many family theorists ignore the therapeutic literature as though they stand to learn nothing from clinical trials which, whatever their conceptual grounds, improve family functioning in dramatic ways. Indeed only a few researchers on family issues, most notably Gottman (1979) and Notarius and Johnson (1982), have tried to link therapeutic approaches to social science research on marital interaction.

The difficulties we have in making sense of research on treatment effectiveness have to do, first, with the problems of cause-and-effect discussed throughout this chapter. As well, there are problems of generalizing from research to everyday clinical practice. For example, randomized experiments may yield different answers from non-randomized experimental studies, which in turn may yield different answers from non-experimental (observational) studies of clinical outcomes. Beyond that, therapists practise a variety of treatments. So, we are far from being able to say conclusively how well marital therapy works, or what kind of treatment works best for what kinds of problems.

The findings on treatment effectiveness vary widely. Leading marital therapists no longer consider the 50 percent success rate of most marital therapies—whether they define success as improvement or recovery—an acceptable standard (Johnson, 1997). There is general agreement that marital therapy can be effective in reducing marital conflict and promoting marital satisfaction, at least in the short term (Bray & Jouriles, 1995). Research examining the long-term efficacy of couples therapy for the prevention of marital separation and divorce is sparse but promising.

The overwhelming majority of couples begin with true love and great hopes, yet divorce still claims more than one-third of all first marriages. The treatment literature, like the research literature, shows that many couples do not know how to handle the bad feelings that are an inherent by-product of the differences between people. Many researchers have concluded that, instead of therapy, unhappy couples need to learn crucial psychological skills, called "psychoeducation," to help them avoid escalating conflict (Marano, 1997).

Recognize that the goal of the therapist, or of one or both parties, may be to eliminate conflict without solving, or even recognizing, the problem that is causing the conflict. So, for example, the underlying problem may be spousal inequality, family poverty, or alcohol addiction. Merely helping a couple to avoid escalating its conflicts may mask the problem temporarily. Pretending that conflict is unnatural, or that we can prevent conflict through skilful communication, is no more likely to work in a family or a couple than it is in a factory or a legislature. The problem here is not merely theoretical: it concerns inducing cooperation in a system of human relations that has a history and is loaded with emotional freight.

Who Is Helped by Marital Therapy?

Whether a program of treatment is effective is determined in part by the treatment goal. Is the goal, for example, to improve the well-being of the relationship as a whole, or of one spouse? Increasingly, marital therapists are seeing just one partner, and they need to consider methods of treating relationship distress within this mode (Bennun, 1997). It is not clear that helping one spouse helps the relationship, nor that helping the relationship helps either or both spouses. Some spouse-aided therapy with depressed patients leads to reduced depression and less dysfunctional thinking. However, there is no evidence this treatment affects marital satisfaction or communication and expressed emotion between the spouses (Emanuels-Zuurveen & Emmelkamp, 1997).

Some couples therapy produces improvement in both individual psychological functioning and relationship satisfaction. This shows that couples therapy can accomplish both goals simultaneously, while individual therapy cannot (Hannah, Luquet & McCormick, 1997). One study (Vansteenwegen, 1996a) finds that, seven or more years after completing couples therapy, the individual changes were longer-lasting than changes in

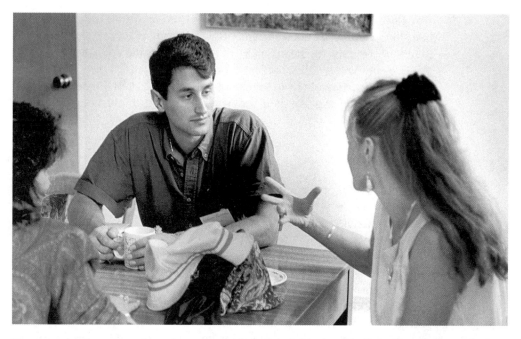

Some couples therapy produces improvement in both individual psychological functioning and relationship satisfaction.

the marital relationship itself. Thus, often, therapists must decide whether to apply psychological theories to help individual clients in a troubled marriage, or to apply sociological theories to help improve the relationship itself.

Some kinds of couples also make "better use" of therapy than others. Assessment and response by therapists produce small positive changes in already well-functioning relationships. These changes may account for a large fraction of the changes observed in relationship-enrichment programs. Thus, change may come easiest, or most assuredly, to those who are already best able to make changes and are therefore more readily suited to the therapeutic intervention (Worthington, McCullough & Shortz, 1995). This may also explain why couples who participate in premarital programs do not show more improvement than couples who do not participate. One group didn't need the help (Sullivan & Bradbury, 1997) and the other wasn't ready to take it.

Among distressed couples, some respond to marital therapy better than others. Gray-Little, Baucom and Hamby (1996) find that what they call wife-dominant couples improve more than any others from therapy. Egalitarian couples continue to function well before and after therapy, while anarchic couples—those who operate without stable rules or expectations—and, to a lesser degree, husband-dominant couples, change little and continue to function poorly.

Research suggests that clients themselves are good judges of what helps them and what does not. Clients generally find a treatment helpful if they start by granting the expertise of the therapist and consider the therapist to be empathetic (Bischoff & McBride, 1996). Couples most likely to be satisfied by emotionally focused marital therapy (EFT) start out believing that EFT will help them solve their problems and, accordingly, cooperate with the therapist (Johnson & Talitman, 1997).

Concluding Remarks

Much of what happens in our lives is due to chance, which is beyond our control. There are no guarantees in life, and no fixed rules we can follow to ensure a satisfying marriage. Yet, one reason we place so much importance on marriage and family life is that these are areas over which we can have a good deal of control. In our culture, we choose our spouses and—at least to a degree—decide whether to have children, when to have them, and how many to have. We may divorce if we no longer want to be married to our spouse, remarry, perhaps encourage adult children to leave the house, and so on.

It is because we think of our family lives as domains over which we have some control that we also expect that they will bring us great satisfaction. We assume that they will bring us satisfaction if only we make the right choices and the right decisions. But is this assumption valid? Are there right and wrong choices, right and wrong decisions? What can sociology tell us in this regard?

As we have seen throughout this chapter, there are a few things we can do to increase our chances of finding satisfaction in marriage. The first is to get rid of the myth that happiness is all wrapped up in finding the

Staying in Love

Adult love relationships have a complex implicit purpose: Partners are chosen in the tacit hope that they will accompany, assist, emotionally stabilize, and enrich us as we evolve, mature, and cope with life's other demands. Adult love is expected to combine three elements for each partner as the couple moves through the life cycle: sexual pleasure, cherishing of the partner, and behavioral caring for the partner.

To realize these lofty purposes, each of us must rely at times on mechanisms of defense, including idealization, denial, and rationalization. Idealization enables us to hover closer to our ideal of loving and being loved. We idealize our partners in return for their devotion to us; it is an unconscious bargain we make with them: I will continue to bestow love onto you and you will continue to bestow love onto me.

Source: Stephen B. Levine. 1998. Abridged from Chapter 1 of *Sexuality in Mid-Life*. New York: Plenum Press. Reprinted with permission.

perfect mate. No one is perfect—or not for long. Conflict is bound to arise, and a successful marriage is one in which conflict is managed well. As we've said before, the key to this is good communication.

Long before marriage, couples should start to discuss what they expect from marriage, what they want from life, what they are willing to give up and what they are not. Most people who are about to get married discuss few of the important things that could lead to conflict in the future. They may discuss whether they are going to have children, when, and how many. They may devote less time to thinking through together the implications for each of them of having children and how that will be handled. However, they are unlikely to discuss the possibility that one of them may be sterile or infertile, and how they would deal with that: whether they would opt for artificial insemination, surrogacy, adoption, or give up trying to have children altogether. Nor do they often discuss the possibility of giving birth to a child with a disability, and what kind of adaptations or arrangements they would be comfortable making for the child's care.

Couples who are planning to get married may discuss where they want to live. However, they rarely discuss what they will do if one of them gets a promotion that forces them to move to another city, and how they will decide. Nor do they discuss the possibility that their parents will reach an age when they will no longer be able to take care of themselves, but must be taken care of by others. Will they let their parents come to live with them, or put them in a nursing home? In either case, who will have the final word in these decisions?

Miraculously, in many marriages people never have these discussions, yet their marriages appear to succeed anyway. This tells us that, on the one hand, people have much tolerance for relationships that work passably well or even poorly; they aren't going to look for ways to improve their marriage. Inertia, stability, and complacency are the dominant factors. On the other hand, it tells us that relationships that look satisfactory from the outside, and appear to be succeeding, may not really be succeeding at all when viewed from the inside.

No one can anticipate all problems, much less solve them, in advance. A marriage is, in the end, a plan to solve problems together. People who can't solve problems together won't be married for long, or if married, they will be miserably unhappy. When it comes to marriage, or to any kind of close relationship, we can only regulate our expectations by communicating with one another. Only in that way are you likely to have some idea of what is in store when you say "I do." On the other hand, be aware that society has socialized you to pair off and marry even without having the faintest idea what is in store!

CHAPTER SUMMARY

In this chapter, we have shown that married people are happier and healthier, on average, than divorced people and even single people or widowed people. We have considered some reasons for this and have concluded that Durkheim was right: well-being has something to do with social integration and regulation.

Among people who are married, or in another steady relationship, some are happier and healthier than others. We noted that men and women have different experiences in marriage, so that evaluating any given marriage is difficult. It looks different to the husband and wife. Nonetheless, in some marriages both the husband and wife are more satisfied than spouses in other marriages. We asked why.

Marriages have a life cycle with periods of more and less satisfaction. Typically, spouses lose satisfaction as the marriage goes on, but they do so most rapidly and dramatically in marriages with children. Marriages reach a low point in satisfaction when the children are in their teens, then recover after the children leave. Factors increasing marital satisfaction are homogamy, feelings of love, expressions of intimacy, good skills for coping with stress and conflict, equity and fairness, and good communication between the spouses.

Since problems in a marriage often arise through failures of communication, improving communication can often solve them. We considered the evidence that we can improve communication and discussed a few of the ways therapists go about doing this.

KEY TERMS

Anomie: A state of normative confusion; a lack of rules and regulations.

Debriefing: Conversation between spouses about what happened during the day, which may serve both to convey information and to share support.

Heterogamy: Marriage between people who are significantly different in race, religion, or sociocultural background.

Idioms: Expressions that form a private language for a couple, including pet names, inside jokes, and special words or phrases for intimate or special activities.

Relationship dynamics: The patterns of interaction, communication styles, expressions of emotion, and intimate practices between spouses.

SUGGESTED READINGS

Beeghley, Leonard. *What Does Your Wife Do? Gender and the Transformation of Family Life*. Boulder, CO: Westview Press, 1996. This book provides empirical data on changes in social life that have affected family life and how men and women interact with each other, focusing on premarital sex, abortion, divorce, and employment/income. Cross-cultural and historical comparisons are explored.

Blossfeld, Hans Peter. *The New Role of Women: Family Formation in Modern Societies.* Boulder, CO: Westview Press, 1995. This book explores the relationship between women's increased education attainment and the decline in rates of marriage and fertility in the industrialized world. Empirical data are provided from the United States and eight European nations.

Dench, Geoff. *Transforming Men: Changing Patterns of Dependency and Dominance in Gender Relations.* New Brunswick, NJ: Transaction Publishers, 1996. This book challenges the view that men are really as important or powerful as feminist theory proposes (with the concept of patriarchy). It argues that for men to become caring members of society, they need to have a greater stake than women in the public realm and be allowed to be the main family providers.

Fineman, Martha Alberto. *The Neutered Mother, the Sexual Family, and Other Twentieth Century Tragedies.* New York: Routledge, 1995. This book examines the historical, legal, and cultural processes by which the sexual-intimate connection between spouses came to be the dominant element in the modern definition of family life. This book argues that, instead, the mother-child bond should be protected and subsidized as the basis of society's protection of family life.

Popenoe, David; Elshtain, Jean Bethke; and David Blankenhorn (eds.) *Promises to Keep: Decline and Renewal of Marriage in America.* Lanham, MD: Rowman and Littlefield Publishers, 1996. A collection of 13 essays that examine the nature and underlying causes of the decline of marriage in the United States. Strategies—political, economic, and cultural—are proposed to encourage the reinstitutionalization of marriage.

Pyke, Karen D. *Family Diversity and Well-Being.* Thousand Oaks, CA: Sage Publications, 1994. Data from a national survey of families and households are used to explore whether family members are better served by the traditional family or by today's diverse arrangements. The data include reports of nearly 2500 mothers belonging to four different family "types"—traditional, two-parent, first marriages; two-parent step families; single-parent families headed by a divorced mother; and single-parent families headed by a never-married mother. The results strongly suggest that structure itself is not an important determinant of well-being.

REVIEW QUESTIONS

1. What are the three components of married life described in this chapter? Explain each.

2. Explain the term homogamy. Give some reasons why homogamous couples are likely to be more satisfied than other couples.

3. What measures of marital quality are discussed in this chapter? How are they related?

4. A couple's satisfaction typically follows a U-shaped pattern over the course of a marriage. Describe the factors that change spouses' level of satisfaction over time.

5. What is the difference between "romantic love" and "mature love," as discussed in this chapter?

6. Briefly explain the difference between satisfaction and happiness, as described in this chapter. Why do we

rely more on satisfaction to assess marital quality?

7. Explain a few of the gender-related differences in marital satisfaction. What are some reasons for the gender differences? Do men or women benefit more from marriage, and why?

8. Discuss three stressors that could lead to marital conflict. How do these stressors cause conflict?

9. Briefly discuss the differences in the ways women and men communicate.

10. What is the current success rate of marital therapies? Is it considered acceptable? Why or why not?

DISCUSSION QUESTIONS

1. This chapter stated that "felt obligation" to one's spouse is the most powerful influence on the relationship. Do you agree?

2. Throughout the chapter we have seen that married people enjoy greater well-being than single or divorced people. What kinds of data were used to prove this point? Do you agree with Durkheim's argument? Why or why not?

3. How is it possible that (some) arranged marriages can be satisfying even if the bride and groom do not know each other before marrying?

4. You are paid to advise unhappily married couples. One young couple comes to your office. They have stopped talking to each other in order to avoid conflict. When they do speak, they express anger toward each other. From what you have learned in this chapter, what do you suggest?

5. Outline some of the problems that intermarriages are likely to face.

6. Cite some examples from the mass media (TV, movies, magazines) that might cause young people to rate love as more important than anything else in the establishment and maintenance of a good marriage. Does this message from the mass media create a problem for marrying couples, and, if so, are the media at the root of the problem?

7. Which kind of intimacy—sexual or psychological—is more important in maintaining a good marital relationship? Explain your answer.

8. What are some of the health problems caused by unsatisfactory marriages? Explain the link between marital dissatisfaction and poor health.

9. What are some of the best ways for married couples to resolve their problems or conflicts, according to what you have learned in this chapter?

10. "Marriage usually ensures that someone is there to look after us when we are sick, a person we can lean on when something bad happens, who makes us feel needed, talks and listens to us, laughs with us, and lets us show our vulnerable side." What are some of the consequences when these elements are not present in the marriage?

WEBLINKS

http://www.utexas.edu/courses/pair/ CaseStudy/ED2e.html

These two sites provide statistics about satisfaction and variables that are correlated with satisfaction. There is also text discussing marital satisfaction in general.

http://www.gwdg.de/~rbeer/marital/links. html

This Web site provides links to other sites that deal with marital satisfaction.

http://www.whosoever.org/Issue1.html

This is the address of an online same-sex marriage magazine. It contains information about same-sex marriage and leads into information about satisfaction and conflict.

http://www.public.iastate.edu/~wpanak/ p230/lect6.html

This Web site gives a breakdown and general overview of satisfaction and marriage, including predictors of a good marriage, conflict resolution, and the family cycle as it relates to marital satisfaction.

http://www.ncpa.org/~ncpa/pd/social/ sociale.html

This site provides good information on marital satisfaction, love and ambivalence, satisfaction with domains of marriage, perception of a spouse's traits, and other relevant issues.

http://www.utexas.edu/courses/pair/ CaseStudy/ED.html

This Web page contains good information on sex and marital satisfaction.

http://www.hope.edu/academic/ psychology/335/webrep/marital.html

A brief discussion of the relationship between sex and marital satisfaction that reviews recent research findings.

CHAPTER FOUR

Entering Parenthood:

Family Planning, Childbearing, and the
Parenthood Transition

Chapter Outline

Parenthood, to many, *is* family. To societies, parenthood is the way in which society reproduces itself. More than anything else, families are vital to society because they provide new members (new workers, new consumers, and new citizens). For individuals, entering parenthood marks the most fundamental family transition in their lives. In some societies, entering parenthood is the sign that one has become an adult. Becoming parents can be a sign that the families of the wife and of the husband are one.

In this chapter, we shall explore the many ways that becoming a parent has changed and is changing for both women and men, the different ways people enter parenthood, new reproductive and contraceptive technologies, the emergence of choices and options about entering parenthood, and implications of the entry (and non-entry) to parenthood for individuals, families, and countries.

Is Parenthood Family?

Do you have a family? Are you planning on having a family? Is she "in the family way"? People asking questions like these are not talking about extended families. They are not talking about a couple as family. They are likely not talking about whether you have a mother or father, or sisters and brothers. They are asking about childbearing, about entering parenthood.

Entering parenthood, in our society as in many others, is almost synonymous with family. This tells us a great deal about the social importance of having children in our society. Becoming a mother is often the definition of womanhood in our society. Manhood, too, can be defined by becoming a father, although in our society occupational status matters more. Fathering children matters more in other societies and cultures, such as Latin America. It is what small children say first when asked what the difference is between women and men: women are mommies and men are daddies. This is said as if it is natural and universal for adult women to be mothers and adult men to be fathers.

Women's identities and lives are more caught up in whether or not they are mothers than are men's in whether or not they are fathers. In fact, several royal women in history were put to death because they could not have children. Marriage partners are sometimes selected for childbearing capacity or potential, which may be part of the reason men often marry younger, attractive women. Men also sometimes choose women who they think would be good mothers for their children. This quality of being a good mother may be what distinguishes a woman for dating from a woman for marrying; a man would presumably want a "good girl" rather than a "bad girl" to raise his children. Women are taught that becoming mothers is the way to be familial, to be accepted as women, to be fulfilled.

In many (perhaps most) cultures in Canada, marriage is, first and foremost, about having children. Marriage without children is not seen by many as marriage at all, not what a family is supposed to be. (This may, however, be changing with recent generations, particularly in urban centres.) Parents will often endlessly question a couple on when they intend to "start a family." Historically, the tradition was, and still is in some cultures, that a marriage was not "real" until it was consummated by sexual intercourse of the newlyweds. Before widespread use of contraception, this may have been a way to ensure that the marriage was "fruitful." In some African cultures, childbearing is so fundamental to family that only women who have had a child (or children) are considered good candidates for marriage. In Canada, by contrast, women who have had children are less likely to marry or remarry than those who have not.

Some Scenarios

To give a sense of the diverse ways in which individuals and couples enter parenthood, we will introduce a few fictional scenarios, to which we will return throughout the chapter.

Dear Diary, I'm Pregnant

At 18, Lisa was a mother, and trying to run a household on her own. She was 16 when she got pregnant, 17 when she had her daughter, Erica, and 18 when she had an abortion. It was a rough couple of years. She had met James when she was 13. By the time she got pregnant, the two had been together about three years and were having sex and using birth control. Both were living at home and going to school. Lisa was her mother's only child. Her parents had divorced when she was about six. She lived with her mother right up until she was about nine months pregnant, then she moved out and now she, James, and Erica live on their own.

At Least We're Married

When Salimah and Ahmed met, she was in grade 10 and he in grade 12. She initially didn't like him much. He was handsome but seemed more traditional than she was, although she was dutiful in obedience to her parents' wishes and her Muslim faith. She changed her mind about Ahmed after they had talked a few times at school. When he called her at home, her parents didn't like it. Salimah and Ahmed sneaked a few phone calls but were never alone together, although they wanted to date. When she had just turned 17, Ahmed proposed, not to Salimah, but to her father, asking him to let Salimah marry. After much thought, Salimah's father agreed. While still 17, Salimah gave birth to a baby boy, and then when she was 18 and Ahmed was 20, with both still in school, they became parents of a baby girl. Salimah's father says that he was surprised that she had a baby so soon after marrying, but at least Salimah and Ahmed were married.

The Roller Coaster

Sung-Min and Ji-Hee had been married for six years. They wanted nothing more than to become parents, but so far no pregnancy. Their friends and relatives told them to relax and not to worry, that soon Ji-Hee would be pregnant. Sung-Min and Ji-Hee had postponed getting married until she had completed her Ph.D. and he his law degree. They were getting worried now that time was passing and their chances for having a child of their own might be getting smaller. Sung-Min and Ji-Hee made an appointment at an in vitro fertility clinic where they were both examined and medical histories taken. They were informed that the chances of success were not large, but this information was buried in their minds along with all the technical information about tests, procedures, temperature-taking, and how carefully they must follow the prescribed regime. Ji-Hee was given fertility drugs, which she dutifully took. She underwent several surgical procedures to test and clear her fallopian tubes and to "harvest" eggs. After each procedure, their hopes were raised that this might just be the procedure that worked.

After years of trying and dashed hopes, in addition to considerable expense and time away from work, each other, and other family, they are still childless and on a long waiting list to adopt a child. They remain hopeful.

What a Surprise!

Jane and Christopher had everything they wanted in life, including two fine children: Sean, in first year university, and Kelly, in grade 11. They have a nice house, two cars, and a summer holiday cabin on a lake. Both Jane and Christopher were doing well in jobs they loved. Jane and Christopher had been high-school sweethearts and married right after graduation. They had taken turns going to university and college while the kids were growing up. They were still very much in love and looking forward to the time they would have together once the kids were on their own. Jane's periods had been irregular lately but Jane and Christopher chalked it up to menopause until Jane started feeling queasy in the mornings. Checking it out with their family doctor, she discovered that she was pregnant. Christopher's response to the news: "What a surprise!"

Two Mothers Are Better Than One

Karen and Ellen shared everything, the expenses, the housework, and the wish to become mothers. They were in love and had been ever since they first met five years earlier on a hiking trip to the mountains. Both had decent jobs; they had bought an older house that they were renovating. It was a friendly house near a creek with a beautiful backyard bordered by berry bushes. Karen and Ellen decided they wanted to have a baby. The first decision was which of them would become pregnant. The second decision was how they would arrange for the insemination. It turned out that the first decision was the easier one. Karen had a less secure job with lower income. In addition, she was eager for the experience of pregnancy. The decision on how to proceed with the insemination proved more challenging. Karen and Ellen tried the infertility clinic at the local hospital but were turned away. The clinic told them that they had no infertility problem, and furthermore, that the clinic's policy was to help only heterosexual couples in stable relationships who had no children of their own. Ellen, early in her adult life, had been married briefly and had a grown child, but Karen had no children of her own.

They finally settled on a gay friend of theirs, Kevin, who volunteered a sperm sample on the provision that he could have some role in raising any child that resulted. Today, Karen and Ellen (and Kevin) are the happy parents of a baby boy, Stephen.

Entering Parenthood in the Past

Sometimes in the 1990s, people think that our grandparents and great-grandparents had no control over the timing and numbers of children they had. Only in the 1960s, they imagine, did control over fertility develop with the birth control pill. This is not true, as we shall see, although on average, large families were more common in the past.

Ellen Gee (1986:269) shows from historical records how strong the Canadian decline was, from the mid-nineteenth to the mid-twentieth century, in average numbers of children born. Women born in Canada in 1817–1831, for example, had about 6.6 children, compared to 1.7 for women born in 1947–1961. In Quebec, an even sharper decline occurred over a much shorter time. For example, "Between 1959 and 1969 Quebec cut its **crude birth rate** (live births per 100,000 population) in half, accomplishing in ten years what it had taken the rest of the country over a century" (McLaren & McLaren, 1986:125). By the beginning of the 1970s, Quebec had the lowest birth rate in Canada, a distinction it maintains today (LeBourdais & Marcil-Gratton, 1994:103–104).

The decline in numbers of children born in families was largely due to the changing social and economic circumstances in which families lived. As industrialization developed, fewer children were needed to work on the farms. Children in towns and cities were also more costly to raise than children on farms. Housing in towns and cities was more cramped, too. Children, thus, changed from a labour source to a cost. Birth control had a role in fertility decline, but not as large a role as is often thought. More on this in a moment.

Family size and birth rates in Canada have always been political issues. The term used to describe Quebec's historically high birth rates (before they fell sharply from the late 1950s on) was "**the revenge of the cradle**," an image reflecting the belief that Quebec's long-standing sense of political injustice might be countered by having more Quebec (French-speaking) citizens (see Henripin & Peron, 1971). Quebec's birth rate remains a political issue in the 1990s (Baker, 1994). Family researchers who study birth rates—known as **demographers**—are household names to Quebeckers; not so in the rest of Canada. Early birth control promoters, such as A.R. Kaufman of Kitchener, Ontario, were concerned about the French in Canada "outbreeding" the English (see McLaren & McLaren, 1986:124).

Children in New France were the basis of settlement of the St. Lawrence valley (Landry, 1992) in the late 1600s and early 1700s. Wives and children were necessary to run farms and businesses. All were expected to work. Men who did not marry often left the colony. The basis of the legendary high birth rates in Quebec is traced to this period when girls as young as twelve were chosen as wives by the men of New France, and became mothers of many children. Moogk (1982:26–27) has shown that all was not entirely well, however, with high fertility in New France.

> Illegitimate births were an increasing problem in eighteenth century New France ... indicative of the breakdown of communal social restraints....

> In the villages of the Christian Amerindians, [were] observed numerous illegitimate children of the French colonists ... adopted by the native peoples and they fully accepted the aborigines' way of life.

Eighteenth-century New France may not have been so different from the world of Lisa in our 1990s scenarios, except that Lisa would likely have been older when she got pregnant than the unmarried mothers of New France.

Prizes were given by the Quebec Government in the 1930s and 1940s to women who bore many children. Their photos would appear in newspapers, the television of the past. Both the church and the government encouraged families to have more children. This policy was formalized with baby bonuses, which increase with each additional child born. The present Prime Minister of Canada, Jean Chrétien, is the 18th of 22 children. The shift from large to small families in Quebec has occurred rapidly indeed, leaving many Quebec families with older and younger generations of vastly different sizes.

Native peoples in Canada also had high birth rates in the past. In the 1970s and into the 1980s, births to native peoples were just starting to decline. Recently, however, native birth rates have increased and the First Nations are now the fastest growing group in Canada (Statistics Canada, 1998). As a result, 12.4 percent of the aboriginal population are in the youngest age group (0–4 years old) compared to only 6.7 percent of the Canadian population at large (Statistics Canada, 1998). The prime working-age aboriginal population will grow by 41 percent by 2006, according to 1996 census findings, with the numbers of aboriginal children and teens swelling considerably in the immediate future. Enormous diversity in family size exists among

Sarah Abel of Old Crow

Born in 1886, Sarah Abel ... is a much esteemed Vuntut Gwitch'in elder. She was widowed when her husband of 32 years died of tuberculosis, leaving her to raise their 17 children on her own. The youngest child was 11 at the time she was widowed.

She supported her large family by hunting and trapping by dog sled, tanning skins and making boots. Her granddaughter has this to say: "She was a strong woman ... very strict ... she's had 17 kids and she's still standing."

Source: Brend, Yvette. 1997. "Why History Lives in Old Crow," *The Globe and Mail*, 11 November 1997:A2. Reprinted with the permission of *The Whitehorse Daily Star*.

various native peoples, however, as well as between those who live on reserves and those who live in cities.

Native entry into parenthood occurs in a radically different family form than it does for many other Canadians. The 1996 Census shows that 32.1 percent of aboriginal children under 15 live with a single parent, compared to 16.4 percent for all Canadians. The proportions are close to one-half in Winnipeg, Regina, and Saskatoon. Nearly a quarter of aboriginal children live with parents who are common-law, compared with 10.5 percent of all Canadians. And about 11 percent of aboriginal children under 15 live with neither parent, compared with 2.1 percent of all Canadian children. This group includes children living in a variety of situations; foster care is the most common, but some live with relatives, often grandparents.

It is not only that Canadian families are now having fewer children than previously. It is also that expectations about marrying and having children have changed dramatically. When asked by family researchers today, most young people say that they expect to get married and have children (Vanier Institute, 1994). Interestingly, few expect ever to be divorced! In the late nineteenth century and early part of this century, many more people than now never married at all. For example, Gee (1986:266) finds from historical records that in 1911 12 percent of Canadians never married. This compares with only 5.8 percent in 1981. It has dropped to about 2 percent today. Not marrying in the past generally meant not entering parenthood. So, in fact, parenthood in the past was not part of as many people's lives as it is now. In the past, a lower percentage of the population got married, but those who did had many more children, on average, than couples do today.

Parenthood Timing in the Past

Our grandmothers and great-grandmothers not only had more children, on average, than we do today, but they spent a much larger portion of their lives bearing and raising children. This is both because we live longer today and because our patterns of entering parenthood have changed. For instance, Ellen Gee (1986:273) has found that Canadian women born between 1831 and 1840 spent an average of 14 years between their first and last births. This compares with an average of 1.8 years for women born between 1951 and 1960. With a life expectancy of about 60 years, women born in the middle of the nineteenth century had little time, either before or after parenthood, to do anything else. A woman today can anticipate that her last child will, on average, be grown up before she reaches age 50. With life expectancy for women in Canada at 82 years today, there is ample time to have careers after children, or while the children are growing up. This may be why family in the past was seen as such a dominant aspect of people's lives, particularly women's lives. It literally took most of their time!

In the 1990s, we tend to have fewer children and have them closer together. There is a huge range of possibilities in entering parenthood in the 1990s, as our scenarios show. Yet, most Canadians enter parenthood in their mid- to late twenties. It is as if our entry to parenthood has become more efficient so as to take up less of our lives. More of us have the parenthood experience than in the past, but we have it less frequently, we start later, and we compress parenting into a shorter period of our lives. This opens the door, along with other social and economic changes, for women to balance paid work with families. It also means that many women experience long careers in paid work, both during and after their children are born. Other factors also enter into these changes, factors that are discussed in other chapters.

Choosing Parenthood in the Past

In the past, women found a major source of identity in having children and being a mother. This was the case in such different situations as urban Quebec in the seventeenth century, and the early frontier societies in the West of Canada. Silverman (1984:59) tells us that giving birth and raising children was the answer often given to the question, "What are women for?"—an answer given by women as well as by men. Until recently, both women and men agreed that childbearing and child rearing gave women's lives meaning. Entering parenthood was also vital to populate Canada, particularly in settling the West, and, as we have seen, in the earliest settlements in Quebec.

The popular belief that couples in the past would accept however many babies God gave them is not quite true. There have always been attempts, some of them successful, to regulate pregnancy and births. Although officially illegal in Canada until 1969, some couples used birth control to choose how many children they would have and when they would have them. As now, not all birth control worked. You remember Lisa's story of her two pregnancies *while using birth control* in the 1990s.

Among the most common birth control methods in the past were abstinence and prolonged breastfeeding. One woman who homesteaded on the Prairies tells in her diary, "A woman I knew when I was quite young nursed her baby until she was four years old so that she wouldn't have another one" (Silverman, 1984:60). The woman reporting this adds, "That wouldn't have worked for me at all." Other popular birth control methods used in Canada's past include barrier methods, timing or rhythm approaches, withdrawal, abortion, and as one wise advisor to young married women suggested in her 1908 marriage manual, "twin beds" (McLaren & McLaren, 1986:19–20).

Abortion was common in the past in Canada, with methods of "bringing down the menses" routinely advertised in daily newspapers and early magazines (McLaren & McLaren, 1986:33–35). There were ads for Radway's

Pills for "female irregularities," the New French Remedy, Sir James Clarke's Female Pills, Dr. Davis' Pennyroyal, and on the list goes. Cook's Cottonroot Compound was argued to be "used successfully by over 10,000 ladies" (McLaren & McLaren, 1986:33). It is only in recent decades that abortion has come to be seen as an important public, moral issue. Interestingly, several of the well-known nineteenth-century abortifacients (herbs or potions that brought on a miscarriage) are still in use today for inducing labour.

Family planning and abortion may have been the means by which women could have identities apart from being mothers, and lives outside motherhood. It may be that information about birth control and abortion was commonly shared among women, along with important information about parenting and caring for their own and their children's health. The beginnings of schools and health care provision, often with emphases on maternal and child health, were ways that women created communities in frontier societies.

Family Planning Today

Most people who are sexually active in the 1990s know something about contraception. Some use various methods regularly and reliably, others only occasionally. Why this varies remains to be fully understood, but family research provides some answers. Let's look first at young people's approach to intimate relations and contraception.

Sexuality is a marketable commodity, as we emphasized in Chapter 2. Look at Hollywood movies and television. Sexuality is romanticized, with women often caught in the allure of the Madonna/whore images. "Love babies" are popular among cultural icons in music and film in today's world. It is easy to understand how adolescents can be attracted by these glamorous images. D'Emilio and Freedman (1988:358) suggest that "... not only did modern capitalism sell sexual fantasies and pleasures as commodities, but the dynamics of a consumer-oriented economy has also packaged many products in sexual wrappings."

The rational, clinical aspects of birth control contrast vividly with romantic, glamorous images of love and sex. Besides, relying on birth control may suggest an admission to anticipating sex and acknowledging that one is not being entirely "swept off one's feet." Birth control may make sex seem less spontaneous and romantic. Links between sexuality and birth control are not always made. Sex education in schools is sometimes perceived as education about frogs or other animals more than about human sexuality, or more about the mechanics of "sexual plumbing" than about feelings, values, or how to make important decisions about sexuality. Lessons taught and lives lived may not seem to be at all the same thing.

In Canada, knowledge about contraception is widespread (Balakrishnan,

Lapierre-Adamcyk & Krotki, 1993:197); however, it cannot be assumed that knowledge is always used, or reliably used, by everyone. It is a myth that every entry into parenthood in the late 1990s is planned and wanted. Nonetheless, the practice of contraception by Canadians is common. In 1984, in the only nationwide survey of fertility and contraception ever done in Canada, about 68 percent of women of childbearing ages were using one or another form of contraception, with only 5 percent of currently married women not using contraception (Balakrishnan, Lapierre-Adamcyk & Krotki, 1993:198).

Of those not using contraception, most were not sexually active. Sterilization (where one or both partners are sterilized for either contraceptive or other medical reasons) was the single most popular birth control approach in use in Canada in the mid-1980s, accounting for almost one-half of contraceptive usage and testifying to the seriousness with which we in Canada take the choice to enter or not enter parenthood (Balakrishnan, Lapierre-Adamcyk & Krotki, 1993:200–201). Even more surprising was the discovery that sterilization was common (49 percent) among women as young as 25–29 when they had a birth prior to turning 18 (Balakrishnan, Lapierre-Adamcyk & Krotki, 1993:45–46). Rates of sterilization are higher among those who have had a birth earlier in their lives, or among those who have had all the children they wish to have. (See Table 4.1.) More recent data in Canada (Statistics Canada, 1998b) have found that 4.5 million couples where the woman is under age 50, or 46 percent of all couples in reproduc-

Table 4.1   WOMEN INFERTILE BY STERILIZATION* OF SELF OR HUSBAND/ PARTNER BY AGE AT WHICH THEY HAD A FIRST BIRTH (1984)

AGE	25–29	30–34	35–39
AGE AT 1ST BIRTH	PERCENTAGE STERILIZED		
<17	49	79	79
18–19	43	70	65
20–21	43	61	70
22–24	15	57	65
NO BIRTH			
<25	3	22	48
Total	20	43	59

*Includes contraceptive sterilization of either partner, medical sterilization, and known infertility of either partner.

Source: Adapted from Balakrishnan, T.R., Evelyne Lapierre-Adamcyk and Karol J. Krotki. 1993. *Family and Childbearing in Canada: A Demographic Analysis*. Toronto: University of Toronto Press, p. 46.

tive ages, were sterile for natural, medical, or contraceptive reasons.

Family planning methods include the Pill, particularly popular with married women, but also among single women; **IUDs** (intrauterine devices) among married women; condoms, used by unmarried couples; and the usual array of diaphragms, foams and jellies, rhythm, withdrawal (*coitus interruptus*), and douches. Widespread use of contraception has been a fundamental factor in the decline in the Canadian birth rate and in family size— but it is not the cause of this decline but rather the *means*. Still, it is worthy of note that widespread use of contraception that is effective allows a separation of sexual intercourse from risks of pregnancy, which changes both sex and the perception and process of entering parenthood.

The consequence is that many people now see the entry into parenthood as a distinct choice, for good or bad. This perception, and the newness of it, has had serious social implications, particularly for single women who become mothers. The perception that childbearing is a choice may lead to holding pregnant single women responsible for their presumed choice, with all its consequences and risks. However, we emphasize, pregnancy can still occur by accident or by violent assault. It is not always a choice women or men make.

In other parts of the world, contraceptive use varies. Europe, particularly Czechoslovakia and western/northern Europe, has the highest usage of contraception in the world (*Statistical Record of Women*, 1991:522–523). Japan also has high rates, as do China, Korea, and Singapore. Low rates occur in Pakistan (8 percent), Haiti (7 percent), Senegal (11 percent), and Kenya (17 percent) (*Statistical Record of Women*, 1991:521). In the less developed regions of the world, the most common family planning methods are female sterilization and IUDs (intrauterine devices), while in more developed regions, the birth control pill, condoms, and withdrawal are the common methods (*Statistical Record*, 1991:523). The percentage of governments that limit access to contraception has steadily decreased in recent decades.

The promotion of contraceptive use worldwide is controversial. Some feminists argue that family planning promotes choices for women (see Correa, 1994 for examples) and is related to women's levels of education. More likely, the causal effect works the other way round: women's enhanced educational opportunities lead to a sense of reproductive rights, which then leads to contraceptive use (McDaniel, 1996c; Watkins, 1993). Women's opportunities for education and work may, however, be enhanced by reliance on contraception. Family researchers have argued that without effective control over one's fertility and choices over when to enter parenthood, women's options are sharply limited.

In countries where male dominance is most pronounced, fertility rates tend to be highest (Keyfitz, 1986). When societies become less unequal, women's education and contraceptive use increase, reducing fertility. Dixon-Mueller (1993) points out that in patriarchal societies women have little con-

In countries where male dominance is most pronounced, fertility rates tend to be highest.

trol over the circumstances under which they live, the returns on their labour, their sexuality, or the number and timing of their children. The current attitude on promoting family planning worldwide is that it makes little sense to promote policies encouraging contraception without, at the same time, addressing larger issues of social and economic constraints on women's opportunities.

Compulsory Motherhood?

The concept that all women ought to be mothers, or that women's role is to mother, is prevalent enough in society that it has been called "compulsory motherhood" (Pogrebin, 1983). Women's sense of self, and even femininity itself, is thought to be tied to women's caring for others. The caring ideal carries into work, where women are expected, for example, to care for patients or pupils not only as a job, but because "they care." Occasionally, when nurses or teachers strike or demand higher pay or better working conditions, it is argued that they should be more concerned with patients or students than with themselves.

Women who are mothers tend to be seen as better people, as fulfilled and complete women. This is despite evidence that mothers of small children report having more stress and being overall less well and happy than child-less women or mothers of grown children (Glenn, 1994). Women who choose to be childless are often seen, and may even come to see themselves, as selfish.

The curiosity of compulsory motherhood is that motherhood for women is seen as natural, and yet something women are taught to deliberately seek and want. This pressure can lead to a number of dilemmas for both moth-ers and non-mothers. It can also lead to the quest for parenthood through reproductive technologies, sometimes risky and typically costly in both money and energy. (More on that in a moment.) Mothering, or *motherwork* as some researchers term it (McMahon, 1995; Hays, 1997), can foster a num-ber of contradictions for a woman, such as having the most loved person in her life, her child, be the source (or one of the sources) of her lack of options in life (Sogner, 1993).

Entering Parenthood Young

Early parenthood is a topic of much public interest in North America. In the United States, it has become a "hot button" political issue, one raised centrally in the last U.S. presidential election and routinely in state politics. The "family values" advocates see unmarried teen mothers as worrisome at best, even demonizing them as "bad girls" or welfare queens. There is a popular perception that some teens may get pregnant deliberately in order to obtain welfare benefits or to get their own places. Research suggests that there is more myth than reality in these images.

A curiosity in the growing concerns about teen pregnancy is that, despite headlines expressing worry about the rates of teen pregnancy and childbearing, the rates in Canada have not actually been increasing. This is not revealed in the every-so-often headline. Pregnancies to adolescent girls rose in the 1970s and then levelled off in the 1980s and early 1990s. Recent data shows an upturn once more, but still they are rates that do not war-rant headlines.

Kristin Luker (1996) convincingly argues that teenage pregnancy in the United States is a scapegoat for seemingly insoluble social problems. She suggests that poverty, race, gender, and sexuality come together in a rich stew of mythology about teen moms. Several flaws are revealed in the views, for example, of those who think that limiting welfare benefits will reduce teen pregnancy. Most notable is that the United States at present has the highest rates of teen pregnancy in the developed world, and the low-est benefits for single mothers. The liberal view that teen women will make informed choices, if only the choices are made available to them, is accord-ing to Luker also flawed.

The problem, says Luker, is *not* raging, uncontrolled hormones among teens who know nothing, or nothing much, of how to prevent pregnancy, but poverty. She argues, with chilling power, that teens who live in poverty and lack any sense of opportunity may not feel that there is much to lose by bearing children young. This supports the liberal argument that teens who are not suffocated by poverty and lack of hope can make choices (to use contraceptives, to seek abortions, not to engage in sexual activities, etc.). The key, however, is that they must have not only the capacity to make such decisions, but the contexts in which those decisions matter and can be realized.

Luker's analysis is supported by another recent study, of African-American teen motherhood in the United States. Kaplan (1997) tells of the skyrocketing growth in single-parent black families headed by women in the U.S. (from 25 percent of black families in 1957 to 61 percent of black families in 1997), with many of these being teen mothers. She quickly counters the political face of the black teen mother on welfare by pointing to the fact that most of those on welfare are not blacks but whites. It is true, however, that single mothers make up a large portion of welfare cases, and that there are many black communities with high rates of teen pregnancy.

Kaplan's analysis argues that all the major theories of why black teens become mothers so early are wrong. There are essentially three such theories. The first is that of Daniel Patrick Moynihan, now a U.S. Senator but a former sociologist: he argues that the black teen mother is the product of pathological family breakdown. A second prevalent theory is that of noted Harvard sociologist William Julius Wilson, himself African American. He argues that the economic despair of the black community in the U.S. has left black men without future prospects, making them unattractive as husbands, and thus making single motherhood acceptable. The third theory, of Carol Stack, argues that black families have always been outside the mainstream norm of family life in the U.S., so that single parents may be another form of difference.

Kaplan (1997), for her part, argues that what she calls "the poverty of relationships" creates early mothers among black teens. If society abandons black girls on all fronts (home, school, communities, work prospects, access to health care, etc.) then teen girls may be trapped in a world where the only way to have love from someone is to have a baby.

Kaplan puts her argument about the stigma associated with teen pregnancy in black communities in vivid terms: that there is a taboo on out-of-wedlock teen births, such that even black teens who are pregnant tend to denounce other black teens in a similar situation. It is a socially constructed self-hatred that leads to a search for love in a way that adds to, rather than solves the problem. Kaplan (1997) contributes to our understanding of teen pregnancy by showing how the structures of poverty and of race relate to individual behaviours.

Clear research evidence, over a long period, has shown that many women who enter parenthood while teenagers *never* make up the lost opportunities for education and work. Having a baby while a teen disadvantages a woman, *regardless of her class background* (Furstenberg, Brooks-Gunn & Morgan, 1997). Similar findings have come out of Canadian research (Grindstaff, 1990). In other words, entering parenthood too early can negate for women many of the benefits of being born into the middle class or above. Lisa, in the scenario at the beginning of this chapter, is unlikely to achieve high status in her life through education or employment, or even through marriage, though her probabilities may be enhanced if she comes from a better-off family.

Early entry to parenthood can have profound, life-long effects on women's opportunities. On the other hand, these effects are not always written in stone, as Salimah's scenario reveals. Although the ultimate outcome of her life story is yet to be told, she differs in two ways from many adolescent mothers: she is married and enjoys the benefits, economic and otherwise, that shared parenthood can bring; and she seems to have the support, both emotional and financial, of her own and Ahmed's families, enabling them both to continue their educations. The title of their scenario may be a central determinant of their and their children's life chances: "At Least We're Married."

A study that followed poor, black teens who had a child (Harris, 1997) finds surprises. It is women who had a birth while in their teens and cycle on and off welfare who are most disadvantaged by early entry into parenthood. Women who had a birth while they were young who exit welfare tend to do so after achieving some education or developing a work skill. Women who are persistent welfare users often manage to stabilize their lives eventually and get off welfare. Reentry to welfare among the women who cycle on and off welfare is found to be precipitated more often by a life event, such as a subsequent birth or losing a job, than by any prior family characteristic. Interestingly, more than half of the women who were on welfare at some point in the study had been working when they had their teen birth. Harris's policy suggestions, arising from this research, are several: supplements to minimum wages, child care subsidies, and low-income tax credits.

If a pregnancy while an adolescent can be damaging, on average, to a woman's future prospects, consider the consequences of more than one adolescent pregnancy. Unfortunately, there is not much research on this, though it occurs more than we would think. The research evidence that does exist, however, is clear: the negative effects for women's life opportunities are further restricted (Gillmore *et al.*, 1997). And the likelihood of an immensely disrupted life increases, with histories of problems in school, drug use, fighting, breakups with boyfriends, etc. Harris (1997), in the study mentioned earlier of long-term effects, finds that women who have more than one birth while teens are most likely to have disrupted relationships and to cycle on and off welfare.

Attitudes toward one's first pregnancy can also have important consequences for parenting. For example, recent research (Groat *et al.*, 1997) shows that those who find parenting rewarding tend to be drawn disproportionately from among those who felt good about their first pregnancies. Positive feelings increase with age at first birth and with marriage and, interestingly, decrease with value placed on material possessions. Another factor in attitudes toward parenting is number of children. Parents of three or more children find parenting less rewarding than parents of fewer children.

Far less is known about the fathers of babies born to teen mothers. One enlightening new Canadian study found, for the first time, that many of these fathers were indeed not teens! Using birth records, Millar and Wadhera (1997) discovered that more than 77 percent of births to teen mothers involved men who were older, by an average of 4.1 years. An incredible 24 percent were six or more years older. These findings raise a number of questions about responsibility for pregnancy and for contraception, and call into serious question the popular belief that teen pregnancy results from an unanticipated grope in the back seat of a car by two teens. Older men would likely have had more sexual experience and know more about contraception. A pressing question then is why that greater knowledge and experience is not being translated into pregnancy prevention with their younger girlfriends.

That so little is known about the fathers in pregnancies among teen women is telling. Adolescent pregnancy has been defined, occasionally with the tacit agreement of family researchers, as a women's problem. As one study puts it, "The study of teen pregnancy has become almost synonymous with the study of teen mothers..." (Thornberry, Smith & Howard 1997:505). Street language reflects this when people say, "She got herself pregnant!" This has to be a biological impossibility, even with new reproductive technologies, yet it shows the ways in which pregnancy and reproduction have been defined as women's issues and concerns.

Of those pregnancies to teen mothers that involve teen fathers (which may not be a large proportion, as we have seen), the little evidence that exists suggests that there are negative consequences for both babies and teen fathers (see Thornberry, Smith & Howard, 1997). When the pregnant young women receive help and support, including prenatal care, the outcomes for their children are better. Teen fatherhood is found to be associated with a number of risks such as low school achievement, lower social class, early sexual activity, and drug use.

Most importantly, research finds that teen fatherhood is strongly related to risk accumulation, so that the life chances of teen men are affected as well by teen pregnancy (Thornberry, Smith & Howard, 1997). It must be emphasized that the consequences of early childbearing, although not good for teen fathers, are far less dire for them than for teen mothers. More research is needed on teen fatherhood as well as on the fathers of teen mothers' babies, who we know now may not be teens themselves. More research is also needed on the consequences for babies born to teen mothers.

A significant shift has occurred in recent decades in the attitudes of adolescent women toward their pregnancies. It used to be that pregnant teens were urged by their families, and often by authorities, to give their babies up for adoption. For many, this was a wise decision, although undeniably difficult to make and then to implement. Recently the story of singer Joni Mitchell's experience has come to light, highlighting the torment often faced by pregnant unmarried women (and still faced by many). As described by Gale Garnett (1997),

> [Joni] Mitchell's recent reunion with the daughter whom she, as a too-young mother, gave up for adoption, gives added depth and poignancy to *Little Green*, which now reads as a protective talisman, tied to a child left on a safer doorstep; this is sisterly familiar territory to any of us who are or were simultaneously intoxicated by eroticism and emancipation. 'We love our livin', but not how we love our freedom.'"

Most birth mothers at the time Joni Mitchell gave up her daughter for adoption had little choice. Their predicament was a product of the sexual revolution's mixed messages for women: being sexual was acceptable, but was to be kept silent; in other words, "Okay, as long as you don't get pregnant." Many stories of that period are only now beginning to come to light.

Madeleine's Story: Any One of Us?

When you look at Madeleine's life, what's frightening is not the fact that she is always one step away from living on the streets, but that her story could easily belong to any one of us.

A couple of decades ago, she left ... home to attend university ..., became head of the youth wing of the Liberal Party, read the news on the student radio station and was a straight A student. The world, as they say, was her oyster.

Then, in her second year, she got pregnant. Two months into the pregnancy, the father left her and instead of having an abortion, Madeleine opted to drop out of school and raise the child herself. Young, poor and inexperienced with the challenges of motherhood, Madeleine eventually decided to let her mother raise the child.

"Sometimes I think more with my heart and emotions rather than with my head and I suffer because of that," she said. "I had a beautiful apartment, a child and I lost it all."

She held down odd jobs in restaurants, selling flowers and working in a travel agency, but none lasted long. Madeleine suffered severe depression and, after being hospitalized several times and three suicide attempts, she was eventually diagnosed as manic depressive.

... Madeleine ... has been finding support at a downtown drop-in centre for women in crisis. She goes there every day to have a hot meal, visit with other women and has started taking classes in word processing in hopes of finding work.

Source: Montgomery, Sue. 1997. "Madeleine Fights to Turn Her Life Around," *The Gazette* (Montreal), 19 November, A3. Quoted with the permission of *The Gazette* (Montreal) and Sue Montgomery.

The consequences of teen or young mothers raising their children themselves, a trend apparent in the 1980s and 1990s, can be devastating.

The trend apparent in the 1980s and 1990s is for teen mothers to keep their babies, raising them themselves, or having relatives, most often mothers, raise them. This can strain family relations, to say the least. It can also create a new kind of family, comprising multiple mothers and consisting of strengths created by adversity (Kaplan, 1997). The role, if any, played by the fathers of the babies is not much known. An indirect consequence of teen mothers keeping their babies is that there are fewer babies for infertile couples (such as Sung-Min and Ji-Hee, in the scenarios above) to adopt.

Consequences for the teen or young mother of the decision to raise the child herself can be devastating, as the real-life experience of Madeleine reveals.

The reinforcing consequences of leaving school, facing work in a market that is often not friendly to single mothers, and the vulnerability that can come from the transition to a precarious motherhood, can make life much more difficult for young, single mothers than they might anticipate.

The profound stigma of teen pregnancy even in the 1990s can lead to horrific consequences, as teen mothers attempt to deny or cover up their pregnancies. At best, they and their fetuses may not receive the kind of preventive health care that could ensure a healthy baby and mother. At worst, the baby could be murdered at birth (called **neonaticide**).

> Samantha Pearson, an 18-year-old Burleson High School dropout, was indicted last month on charges of killing her newborn son ...

> The highly publicized recent cases are those of "Prom Mom" Melissa Drexler of New Jersey, and high school sweethearts Amy Grossberg and Brian Peterson, Jr., who could face the death penalty ... if they are found guilty of killing their newborn son.

> There are more cases in the headlines, but are neonaticides actually increasing?

> Experts, and federal statistics are divided on the issue (Wissenstein, 1997).

What can or should be done about too-early entry to parenthood and its often devastating consequences for young women, but also for young men and the babies born to teens? The evidence from family research is clear; however, implementation of the actions known to work has been highly controversial. It is, paradoxically, because of the conceptualization of teen pregnancy as a moral and political issue that the problem cannot be solved. At the macro- or societal level, it is well understood that teen pregnancy is related strongly to lack of opportunities for young people, both female and male. It is also related to lack of education and lack of access to birth control and abortion services. At the micro-level, teen pregnancy can be a cry of despair in a difficult family situation, or a quest for someone to value the young woman as a person. The problem of teen pregnancy may begin to be solved, or at least reduced, if we can enhance communication within families and communities, provide real opportunities to young women, and value them for their contributions rather than their sexuality.

Yet, it may be that societies in general in North America are valuing their young people, both female and male, less; persistently high youth unemployment is only one indicator.

Deciding about Entering Parenthood

Motherhood or fatherhood is not a status that is entered without consideration, and often agonizing deliberation. Even in the case of unexpected, unwanted pregnancies such as Jane's in the scenarios, there is often a process of deciding whether the pregnancy will proceed or not. This process of decision making about the entry into parenthood is of strong interest to family researchers. It is also difficult to study, since researchers can seldom be present while such decisions are being made.

Several theories exist about the ways in which decisions about entering parenthood are made. One presumes that the couple has some sort of a plan, about which they may or may not talk with each other, and then they approximate their expectations by starting and/or stopping contraception. Built into this approach is the possibility of surprises such as Jane and Christopher (in the scenarios) experienced. This approach would see the role of family and religious background as being fundamental to the couple's decisions about parenthood.

At the other end of a decision-making continuum is a theory which sees the couple making informed decisions and doing a complicated cost/benefit analysis of childbearing. Into the equation would go such factors as the costs of having children, lost income opportunities for whoever takes on the largest part of child care, the other goods (new house, car, travel, etc.) the couple may forgo to have a child, and any other relevant factors.

This approach is known as the "new home economics." One can imagine a calculator under each double bed to work out all the costs and benefits! Likely, the process involved in deciding to enter parenthood is a combination of longing, life hopes for parenthood, background factors and influences, and estimated costs and benefits (McDaniel, 1996c).

A new approach to childbearing decisions focuses on mothers and their self-identities (McMahon, 1995). With an emphasis on identity transformation, McMahon shows how the effects of motherhood can be transforming of self and result in an enormous social power. Contrary to popular images of self-sacrificing mothers, the mothers McMahon interviewed did not see themselves as denying their own identities, although the choice of motherhood was not really a choice for women. Instead, motherhood was seen as an opportunity for personal growth and development. The women found in motherhood the possibility of developing themselves as people. Nelson (1996) finds parallels, with differences, in lesbian families. It would be interesting to study fathers with a similar focus on identity.

People deciding about entering parenthood usually do so without much training for making such a decision. Some schools have programs that give high school students a little experience with parenting by asking them as "couples" (which may be assigned) to "care for" an egg for a period of time. They must treat it like a baby, never leaving it, never dropping it or letting harm come to it. Students describe this as an important learning experience, but it does not prepare them for making the decision about entering parenthood.

There is a strong recent trend toward postponement of childbearing decisions. Postponement is, in fact, a decision: a decision not to have children at that moment. This choice increases the probabilities, for both biological and social reasons, that the woman (or the couple) will not have a child. Biologically, with aging, the probabilities of infertility increase. This is the well-discussed "ticking biological clock" that pressures many women to make a decision about childbearing sooner than they might wish. Socially, some people gradually become comfortable with the way they live, and some become reluctant to change that with an addition to the family. Other couples, however, such as Sung-Min and Ji-Hee, as well as Karen and Ellen, in the scenarios at the beginning of the chapter, feel the opposite: their interest in becoming parents increases as they grow older and more settled.

Childlessness: Voluntary and Not

Despite the societal push toward parenthood, particularly for women, there has been growth in the number of people who are childless. As mentioned in Chapter 1, however, this growth is only evident in comparison to recent decades. Overall, the proportion who are childless is not very different from what it was in 1898 in Canada. In Canada, it is estimated that the proportion who are married and childless has increased from about 14 percent in 1961 to about 23 percent now (Balakrishnan, Lapierre-Adamcyk & Krotki, 1993:28-3). In the United States, there has been a comparable increase (United States Bureau of the Census, 1995). There is a challenge, however, for researchers in deciding the point at which a person or couple is declared childless. It might be that they are postponing entry to parenthood, and ultimately will become parents one way or another.

Some of the childless may be infertile rather than choosing to be childless. There is evidence that infertility is growing among both men and women in North America. (Note that, up to now, we have been discussing *fertility* in the demographic sense of birth rate. We are now talking about a physical *inability* to conceive and bear children.) There is also an indication that prolonged use of certain forms of contraception might lead to greater rates of infertility for some people. Moreover, since fertility naturally declines with age, people who wait to have babies are more likely to have trouble conceiving. In addition, there is at times an unrealistic expectation that the moment contraception is stopped, pregnancy should occur. If a pregnancy does not happen when they think it should, the couple might feel as if they were infertile (Balakrishnan, Lapierre-Adamcyk & Krotki, 1993).

A relationship is known to exist between marital situation and the choice of childlessness. Lapierre-Adamcyk (1987), for example, finds that of women who live common-law, approximately 30 percent expect to have no children. The proportion of women overall who expect never to have children is 9.6 percent (Balakrishnan, Lapierre-Adamcyk & Krotki, 1993:28). Among currently married women, only 5.5 percent expect to remain childless. It is striking, however, that among all young women in Canada, a significant proportion anticipate having no children at all (15 percent of those aged 15 to 19 and 9 percent of those aged 20 to 24) (Balakrishnan, Lapierre-Adamcyk & Krotki, 1993:30). Some of these women may change their minds as they go through life.

Adoption

Entry into parenthood not by biologically reproducing, but by adopting a child, has a long history. Some have called adopted children "chosen children" to emphasize that they are wanted and special to parents.

Custom adoptions (adoption of a child that does not go through legal processes but is based on traditional understandings and customs) among First Nations peoples in Canada are part of ancient cultures that see children as belonging to communities or groups of families rather than to a couple alone. The Inuit in Canada's north adopt out children to the childless or to relatives who may wish for another child. Birth parents, in custom adoptions, are known to the child and often participate in child rearing, but the child lives largely with the adoptive parents. This is a cultural separation of social and biological parenting, where children may have more than one mother and father. High-tech reproduction also separates social and biological parenting, but in a different way. This is the case for the son of Karen and Ellen (and Kevin) in the scenarios.

Adoption is probably as old as the family itself, going back to biblical times and earlier (Kirk & McDaniel, 1984). Among the ancient Greeks and Romans, adoption allowed continuation of a lineage and subsequently ancestral worship in families where no sons were born, thereby serving both a family and a religious purpose. In feudal Japan, adoption was a means of increasing property holdings and making alliances. Most non-modern adoptions tended to be limited to males, both as adopters and as children being adopted. In what anthropologists call "primitive" societies, it has been found that adoption is central to understanding social structure, how families are perpetuated, and how they value others and their communities and cultures.

The concept of entering parenthood by parenting children not born to the parental couple raises a number of fundamental questions about what family is and what taken-for-granted assumptions we make about family. The profoundly important research of Canadian David Kirk on adoption (see Kirk, 1984; 1988) reveals how adoption can be the lens through which we see family afresh. For example, he asks (Kirk, 1988:9):

- How much do we see 'parental adequacy' in terms of instinctual forces, such as maternal instinct?

- Is personality development seen in terms of hereditary endowment in families?

- How much do we emphasize 'blood lines' as important in families?

- How much of the perception of adoptive families as 'not quite' families or lesser than biological families stems from ambivalent thinking about sexuality and reproduction?

In considering entry to parenthood and family in terms of something other than biological reproduction, we may be posing vital questions about what families are. These questions lie behind adoption policies and practices and recent challenges and changes to these practices. Not long ago, adoption was handled quietly and the records of the adoption largely closed to the child as well as to the adoptive and birth parent(s). The intention was, as shown by Kirk and McDaniel (1984), to make the adoptive family as equivalent as possible to the non-adoptive family, thereby removing any notion of difference. This went so far as to alter birth certificates so that the adoptee would have the adoptive parents' name retroactively from birth.

The birth parents were, in essence, erased from existence in the child's life.

In the everyday lives of families, the practice encouraged was for parents not to tell the adopted child that he or she was adopted. The fear was that the sense of difference would affect the adopted child adversely. The fiction or hoax of the adoptive family as identical with non-adoptive families was not to be disturbed, even in relations between parent and child. The reality of perpetrating such a fiction with a child often led to problems once the child discovered the truth.

What is called the "equivalence doctrine" (i.e., working to make adoptive and non-adoptive families as identical as possible) was institutionalized in policy in North America (Kirk & McDaniel, 1984). Everything possible was done to reinforce the equivalence by law, policy, and practice. This occurred even in circumstances where obvious physical differences between adopted children and parents existed, such as aboriginal children or black children being adopted by whites. Policies on adoption, in fact, deliberately reinforced the strength of our hopes for traditional families formed by biological reproduction. Paradoxically, damage may have been done to adoptive families, particularly to adopted children. Opportunities for creating families in new ways may also have been missed.

Adoption has been subject to considerable debate in recent decades as old practices and policies have been questioned, revised, or dispensed with. Opening adoption records in various ways with various constraints has opened new possibilities for families. Reunions between children and birth mothers are not always happy. Yet, the adult adoptee can know parents who are biological and parents who are social, and in the best of reunions, incorporate both into a family world. The open acknowledgement of difference enables the adoptive parents and child to explore together and derive strength. The adoptive family as a voluntaristic family is a kind of futuristic family by choice. This potential can only be seen, however, if the equivalence doctrine is superseded.

Adopted children today have several choices, depending on jurisdiction. It is possible to register with a "finders" group or a government agency, so that if your birth mother also consents to be found, contact may be established. If, however, one or both parties does not wish to be found, the adopted child may never know his or her biological parents. It is agreed by most family researchers today that it is preferable for adopted children to be told, with sensitivity, that they are adopted as soon as they are old enough to understand what that means. Adoptive families have come a long way.

A new variant on adoption is for North American couples or single women or men to adopt children internationally. Some Canadians and Americans have adopted Romanian orphans, for example, or babies from China (especially girls) who may be unwanted with the one-child policy that favours boys, or children from various parts of Africa, Asia, or Latin

America where strife has occurred. This practice is not without controversy, however; some of the adopted children are found not to be orphans at all but to have been kidnapped or sold by desperately poor parents. Other children are held by so-called adoption agencies until more and more fees are paid by the parents. Then there are issues of international relations and cultural differences in the ways children are seen. It may be that some countries would not favour what they might see as the exporting of their children. It is also likely that the children could have difficulty growing up in a culture in which they are seen as different. This has certainly been the case for aboriginal children adopted by white families.

Gays and Lesbians Becoming Parents

Until recently, family studies, for the most part, excluded same-sex couple families. Instead, gay and lesbian lives were studied largely by sociologists of deviance. This was unfortunate (as well as being bad sociology) since some of the rich diversity of family lives was being overlooked, resulting in an incomplete picture of what families are and do. Even in family books in the late 1990s, references to gay and lesbian families are scant.

Data on how many gays and lesbians are parenting children are scarce because official definitions of family still often exclude gay/lesbian families, and because some gays and lesbians are not "out" but keep their sexual preferences secret. Also, many official means of artificial insemination or adoption have not been, or are still not, available to same-sex couples. As in the scenario with Karen and Ellen, arrangements are made privately, away from public scrutiny and knowledge. Best estimates are that a significant minority of gay and lesbian couples are parenting and raising children, either in couples or as single parents (see Laumann *et al.*, 1994; Epstein, 1996). To address the absence of gay/lesbian family experiences in courses and curriculum, specific approaches have been developed. Eichstedt (1996), for example, suggests that gay and lesbian experiences be included routinely in sociology courses in inequality, in race and ethnicity, in contemporary society, and in family, as part of the multiple dimensions of power, oppression, and diversity. In this way, she argues, the topic of homosexuality will be seen not as an "add-on" to other ways of living or as an "exotic" lifestyle, but as a fundamental component of living in society. Others, such as Steven Bruhm at a university in Nova Scotia (MacDonald, 1998), are developing curriculum material for teaching school children about gay and lesbian families.

Books such as *Heather Has Two Mommies* have created controversy in regions where heterosexual parents have pushed to have them withdrawn from the curriculum. Nevertheless, inclusive learning materials teach children and university students to be tolerant and accepting of gay/lesbian parents, and, more importantly, make children who are growing up in gay/lesbian families visible.

Gay/lesbian families face immense challenges in being accepted by law and society. These challenges are multi-layered, and in many ways go to the heart of the view that having children is what makes a couple a family, which is where this chapter started. In most, if not all, debates about gay and lesbian families, the point is raised—usually by opponents of gay families—that gays and lesbians cannot have babies. The conclusion is that therefore they are not raising children and are not families. The erroneous nature of this position becomes clear when people realize that many gays and lesbians are parents.

One well-publicized case, that of Ms. T in Alberta in 1997, brought to the fore implicit but strongly held attitudes toward raising children in same-sex-couple families (Abu-Laban & McDaniel, 1998:82). The Province of Alberta deemed Ms. T, a woman who had successfully raised 17 foster children over many years, an unfit foster mother when it was discovered that she had moved from a heterosexual to a lesbian relationship. Such questions about her capacity to parent were not raised when she was seen as a heterosexual. In the wake of this ruling, existing research on lesbian and gay parenting was brought together and publicized.

The Globe and Mail (16 July 1997:A7) concludes in an article entitled "Homosexuality No Barrier to Good Parenting" that a stable home environment is found, from research, to be more important than the mother's sexual orientation. Rosemary Barnes, former chief psychologist at the Women's College Hospital in Toronto, notes that there are no differences between children raised by heterosexual mothers and those raised by lesbian mothers. The Ms. T. case remains before the courts.

In sharp contrast to the ruling in Alberta on Ms. T, *The Globe and Mail*, Canada's self-professed national newspaper, argues in a 1997 editorial that gays and lesbians are, indeed, family:

> Most Canadians accept the fundamental goodness of love between adults, whatever its sexual expression—as you would expect most Canadians to do. Our governments shouldn't rely on the courts to stop being stupid and callous in the application of laws to gay and lesbian households. The more functional families in our communities the better (Editorial, *The Globe and Mail*, 28 June 1977:D6).

"Normalizing" the same-sex family is not without problems, however—problems that partly arise from the immense diversity among gay and lesbian couples. In short, there is no one gay/lesbian family type, just as there is no one heterosexual family type. Not all gays and lesbians want to legally marry or to have children; nor do all heterosexuals. The normalizing approach is seen by some gays and lesbians as "assimilationist." It could be seen as resembling the "equivalence doctrine" as applied to adoptive families. It works no better for gays and lesbians, who are also creating new ways to live in families and new ways to have children.

The dilemma gays face in having families equivalent to heterosexual families are many. Some of these have been brought to the fore as part of a proposal to open a gay "bathhouse" in a major Canadian city in early 1998. Neighbours expressed worry about degeneracy and health problems. Commentators argued that the gay lifestyle could not be seen as both familial and part of a bathhouse culture where sexual encounters could occur. This is a curious argument, since prostitution, pornographic movie houses, and peep shows thrive among heterosexuals, in parallel with family lives. One thoughtful letter to the editor put it this way:

> I must wonder if the use of bathhouses, public washrooms or parks would be utilized if we lived in a world which saw homosexuality as perfectly normal. Imagine a society where a person would not blink an eye if they saw a same sex couple holding hands, read in the paper their engagement (put there by their parents) or the adoption of their lovely baby girl. If we lived in a society where the majority of homosexuals were not afraid to love, maybe anonymous sex would not be required (*The Edmonton Journal*, 18 January 1998:A9).

Adding further complexity, the experience of lesbian motherhood is profoundly different from that of gay fatherhood, as the research of Nelson (1996) shows. For example, lesbian mothers pursue and achieve pregnancy (to paraphrase Nelson, 1996:133), giving more thought to the decision than heterosexual women generally do. Children in lesbian families often have two mothers, like Karen and Ellen in our scenarios, one of whom is most often the child's biological mother. It is also true that with gay fatherhood, often one member of the couple is the child(ren)'s biological father. Not as much is known about gay parenting, but it seems that being raised by two fathers may be a different experience in our society than being raised by two mothers. The parenting quality may be the same, but the ways in which the child fits into our gendered society may differ. We do know, however, as we stated above, that few differences are found between children raised by same-sex parents, whether gay or lesbian, and children raised by heterosexual parents.

One way in which one partner in gay and lesbian couples may enter parenthood is through the custody awarded to the partner of their child(ren) from a previous, usually heterosexual relationship. Custody is such a huge challenge for gays and lesbians in North America that fear of losing custody is one determinant of how lesbian couples go about achieving pregnancy (Nelson, 1996:47). They are reluctant to have contracts in which the biological father is identified, for example. However, although lesbians are denied custody in the majority of Canadian cases, there have been cases where custody was granted to an "out" lesbian (Nelson, 1996:47). Eichler

(1997:56) concludes that the odds are heavily stacked against gay and lesbian couples having child custody.

Brave New Worlds of Reproduction

Entering parenthood was never a simple process. In the later part of this century, however, undreamed-of possibilities have become reality. Grandmothers have given birth to their own grandchildren; women in their sixties have given birth; babies have been born with three mothers (a genetic mother—the egg donor, a gestation mother who gives birth; and a mother who raises the child). Even though these kinds of events may not be everyday occurrences, the fact that they can and do occur at all changes our ideas and thinking about entering parenthood.

> The cloning of Dolly, the sheep, in late 1997, added another possibility ... Dolly, the lamb, the first animal cloned from a cell taken from an adult. It was a feat that science had declared impossible.
>
> In the hubbub that ensued, scientist after scientist and ethicist and ethicist declared that Dolly should not conjure up fears of a Brave New World. There would be no interest in using the technology to clone people, they said.
>
> They are already being proved wrong (Kolata, 1997).

All too soon, a U.S. physicist was proposing to clone humans in private enterprise.

Many questions arise from this prospective way to enter parenthood. Would a person who had himself or herself cloned be a parent to the clone? What would it be like to be an identical twin with a child? Who among us would so like the way we are that we would seek to have ourselves cloned (with no alterations, of course)? And—a big question—would anyone see cloning as a way at long last to get around being born at the wrong time, saying, for example "If only I had been born with all the advantages kids have today, why look what I might have become!"? And they could do it and see! Then there are the fears that possibilities will be opened for only the rich to reproduce, or that an army of clones will be created. The possibilities are mind-boggling.

The new reproductive technologies as a whole pose a number of possibilities for couples and individuals wishing to enter parenthood, but also raise challenges, dilemmas, and perhaps unrealistic expectations about having children. What are called the new reproductive technologies are a range of different approaches including surrogate motherhood (where a woman agrees by contract to have a baby for a man or a couple), artificial insemination with sperm donors, *in vitro* (or test-tube) fertilization, embryo transfers, and a long list of other procedures. In fact, there is nothing at all new about some "new" reproductive technologies. Surrogate motherhood occurred in the Bible (McDaniel, 1988), for example, and artificial insemination has been occurring since the early part of this century. Nonetheless, the image of babies being conceived in test-tubes is like science fiction to many.

New reproductive technologies have enabled some people who might otherwise have remained childless to have children. Many are immensely happy that they have that option. However, the "roller coaster" experience of Sung-Min and Ji-Hee is more typical. Hopes and expectations are raised by the existence of new reproductive technologies for childless couples who wish for parenthood, but the realistic probabilities of success with many procedures is not high at all. In vitro fertilization, for example, results in a healthy baby in only a small percentage of cases treated (McDaniel, 1988). Artificial insemination has a little higher rate of success, but success is not guaranteed. Many couples like Sung-Min and Ji-Hee experience disappointment, frustration, and emotional turmoil as they go through the process of seeking fertility treatment.

Others experience big surprises. Such was the experience of Bobbi McCaughey and her husband; she gave birth to septuplets after being on fertility drugs.

> The Alberta relatives of Bobbi McCaughey, the Carlisle, Iowa, super-mom who gave birth to four sons and three daughters ... say that icing an entire hockey team of children—with subs—is something of a family tradition.

> McCaughey is the eldest of six children. Her Dad ... is one of eight. And her uncle ... has a family of nine. Oh, and by the way, her grandfather is from a family of 17 (Gordon & Sesku, 1997).

Septuplets have since been born to two women in Saudi Arabia, one of whom was known to be taking fertility drugs. And 1998 marked the first time a set of octuplets all survived birth; they were born to Nkem Chukwu of Texas, who had also been taking fertility drugs. (One of the eight babies has since died.) In the case of Ms. McCaughey, there was an attempt to normalize the birth of seven babies at once by suggesting that large families ran in her family line. That may be true, but there had not been any previously known cases, even in her family of large families, of seven babies being born at one time!

The new reproductive technologies raise a host of legal and social questions about entry to parenthood, most of which society has yet to deal with. In Canada, a Royal Commission on Reproductive Technologies worked for years to come up with recommendations on how society and governments ought to handle the situations that occur when babies are conceived and born in high-tech ways. Most of its many recommendations have yet to be heeded. Central social questions are raised: Who are the child's parents? To whom should one turn if something goes wrong with the process? There are also issues for the children born with high-tech intervention. Imagine sitting in a college classroom and looking around at someone who looks so like you that he could be your brother. With new reproductive technologies, he might just be!

There are further issues related to the costs of the new reproductive technologies and who will pay for them. Will it be Canada's public health care insurance schemes? Or will they be open only to those who can afford to pay directly for the full costs? Custody issues may also arise as the biological parents (whoever they are and however they might be defined or define themselves) struggle with social parents over parental rights and responsibilities for children needing special care.

Children's and Women's Options

There are increasing numbers of ways to enter parenthood, as we have seen. There are also diverse consequences of entering parenthood, particularly for women. We have seen above that those consequences can be particularly disadvantaging to women who become mothers while young. But for many women, the entry into parenthood is the point at which differences between men's and women's opportunities become most pronounced. Until Canadian women are married with children, their incomes for comparable work tend to be not much different than men's. However, the presence of children works against women's pursuit of other opportunities.

In North American societies, a woman who works at home is considered "not in the labour force." The implication has been that mothering work and caring for one's family and home is not really work, and hence, given the value placed on paid work in our society, not valued to the same degree.

Every Mother Is a Working Mother

There are many reasons why women fall into the ranks of the uncounted and the undervalued, but the main reason is children. And this, according to feminist critic Elisabeth Fox-Genovese, is why children have become this generation's version of what Betty Friedan called the "problem that has no name."

In her 1996 book, *Feminism Is Not the Story of My Life*, Ms. Genovese writes, "Children, not men, restrict women's independence. Children, not men, tend to make and keep women poor. Few but the most radical feminists have been willing to state openly that women's freedom requires their freedom from children. Yet the covert determination to free women from children shapes much feminist thought and most feminist politics."

Source: Brooks, Paula. 1997. "Every Mother Is a Working Mother," *The Globe and Mail*. 26 October: D1. Quoted with the permission of Paula Brooks.

This issue, as we will discuss in greater detail in Chapter 6, is beginning to be addressed with, for example, the inclusion of questions about unpaid work on the 1996 Census of Canada. Feminist economists, in conjunction with statisticians at national offices such as Statistics Canada, are devising ways to measure the value of unpaid work at home, done largely by women. This could have the consequence of increasing the value people place on motherwork.

Because children place limitations on women, and because most mothers of young children in Canada today also work outside the home, the issue of child care is central to women's interests. It is also in the interests of families, who benefit from the earned incomes of women as well as their family contributions (McDaniel, 1993c). Child care is known to be a factor in decisions about entry to parenthood. It matters, as well, to children's learning opportunities in early life.

It is not only that children restrict women's opportunities; women's opportunities also restrict childbearing. In societies where women have more opportunities, families are smaller and more likely planned. Women have more education, are better off economically, and can be better mothers. The societal benefits overall tend to be large (McDaniel, 1995), including improvements in life expectancies.

How Parenthood Affects Marriage/ Relationships

The entry to parenthood has major effects on marriages/relationships. It can affect the career patterns of both parents, patterns of household work, distribution of power, marital satisfaction, and economic well-being. The pre-

Population Stability Is a Women's Opportunity Issue

Population growth in the world's poorest countries is still booming even as it levels off in richer nations that encourage the education and employment of women, the Population Institute reported yesterday.

"What made that slowdown happen [in the industrialized world] is they had universal access to education for girls, so wherever a woman has achieved an eighth-grade education she has half the number of pregnancies of an uneducated sister," Werner Fornos, Population Institute President, said. "Once you get an eighth grade education, you don't turn a woman into a baby factory again."

Mr. Fornos also urged men to take a larger role in population control: "If there's one obstacle that all of us ought to address, it's that if we can achieve a much faster or greater male responsibility in the reproductive act, these numbers will start to come down even more significantly."

Source: "Gender Equality Key to Population Cuts," *The Globe and Mail*, 31 December 1997:A11. Reprinted with the permission of *Reuters* News Service, Copyright *Reuters* Limited 1999.

sumption that marriage and children go together, or that childbearing is women's natural destiny, may mask a number of important changes that occur in marital relationships with parenthood.

The most consistent finding about the consequences of parenthood on marriage is that marital tensions tend to increase (Glenn, 1990; Lupri & Frideres, 1981). The commonly expressed view that having a child cements relationships is generally not borne out by research. Two threads of family research are important here. First, research on childless couples finds them generally happier than those with children. Second, couples with children report being happier prior to the arrival of their first child and just after the last child leaves home (Lupri & Frideres, 1981). The pattern of marital satisfaction tends to be U-shaped.

The costs to a marriage or intimate relationship of entering parenthood are several. Tension may develop over questions of who takes what responsibility, for example. The child may have the perceived unattractive personality traits or appearance of one partner, thereby increasing strains. Children, particularly babies, are demanding and self-centred, and may not return their parents' love and consideration, making them feel tired and even used. Opportunity costs for parents to do other things such as work, travel, or even go out for an evening may dramatically increase, adding to tensions and conflicts from which there may be little relief.

As we mentioned in Chapter 3, new parents experience a significant drop in the time they spend together as a couple. There can be increased worries about the child's safety or well-being, worries that may not be shared equally or perceived in the same way by

Having children increases marital tensions, sometimes over the question of who takes on which responsibilities in the household.

both parents. And last but far from least, there are the financial burdens of entering parenthood, which can be enormous. It is estimated that the direct costs of raising one child are close to $150 000 (Scott, 1996:18). This can add immense stress for the couple. The effects of becoming a parent tend to be more detrimental for women than for men.

Not all the consequences of entering parenthood are bad for marriages/relationships. A marriage can benefit from the shared miracle of the newborn, a new link in the kin network. A child can symbolize immortality for both mother and father, linking them to the future and to their families' past. Entering parenthood has been found to give the new parents a sense of meaning and direction that they might not have had before. Becoming parents can also enhance their status, particularly in the eyes of their families but also in society, and signify entry into adult responsibilities.

In large part, the effects of entering parenthood are filtered through the way parenting is seen and defined by the couple, their families, and society. This is the core of the parenting role and experience, discussed in detail in the next chapter.

The responsibilities of parenting become more onerous and the potential costs to marriages greater if children are seen as vulnerable, easily damaged by stress, trauma, or poor parenting (as Freud argues), or as malleable by their environments (as behaviourism suggests). The evidence on these views is decidedly mixed, with some research suggesting that nurturing is critical to a solid social identity, while other research finds that children from troubled families can nonetheless develop solid senses of self and have happy homes of their own (Cook & Fine, 1995). There are fads in beliefs about the importance of nurturing and socializing children by parents, which means that one generation's beliefs may not be those of the subsequent generation.

An alternative model of parenting, which can reduce the negative effects of parenthood on marriage, takes the view that parents are important to a child, but not the only factor. The child is not an empty vessel into which parents pour identity but an active social being who shapes his or her parents as much as they shape him or her. Other social actors also play vital roles in children's lives, such as other family members, siblings, the media, schools, doctors and other professionals, and so on. Social structural forces also matter greatly, such as class, ethnicity, race, recency of immigration, language, location, and importantly, the degree of support the parents have in entering parenthood.

Parental satisfaction is key to how parenthood affects marriage/relationships but has been difficult to assess (see Waldron-Hennessey & Sabatelli, 1997). Satisfaction is found to be related to the expectations each parent has about entering parenthood. The higher the expectations, the greater the likely disappointments and possible dissatisfactions. Stage of parenthood also matters. Greater satisfactions are felt by parents of young children, a research finding supported by new approaches to assessment of parental satisfactions (Waldron-Hennessey & Sabatelli, 1997:830), although, as we noted in the previous chapter, marital satisfaction can suffer. Not surprisingly, the quality of the marital relationship matters to satisfaction with parenthood (Belsky, 1990). And both emotional support from a spouse and help with tasks smooth the entry to parenthood.

The research is clear on how best to have a satisfying entry to parenthood. Have a planned child after the age of twenty (at least), a child whom both parents want and for whom both are willing to sacrifice. Talk openly with your partner about who will do what when the baby arrives, and how you will handle the new stresses and conflicts. Most importantly, realize that babies are needy in terms of both time and family resources. Start saving early for the baby's arrival and make a clear plan for how to work around any forgone income.

Concluding Remarks

We have seen that entering parenthood is vastly different today than it was in the past, and yet parallels and continuity with the past are apparent. It emerges that having children remains an important, if not universal, aspect of close relations in families. Entry to parenthood is not always welcome or happy but always transforms relationships in families and self-identities. The most positive experiences in entry to parenthood are achieved when a decision is made by mature adults with sufficient education and resources to become good parents.

CHAPTER SUMMARY

In this chapter, we have considered the many and complex ways that becoming a parent has changed and is changing for both men and women. In particular, we focused on the diversity of the entry to parenthood and the implications these different approaches and contexts have for families.

We discussed how becoming a parent is often seen as the first step toward becoming a family and how perceptions about parenting and family have changed—and have not changed—in the 1990s. We discovered that the past is not what many of us think it is. Although some families had many children, there were large numbers of people who remained unmarried and childless. Couples and individuals are more committed to choice about childbearing than they ever have been, although even today not every pregnancy is wanted. Contraceptive use and knowledge is widespread. The popularity of sterilization suggests that Canadians do not want accidental pregnancies.

Becoming a parent, despite its happy image, can have unhappy consequences for adolescents or for women who have little choice about motherhood. We discussed some of the political issues related to single parents, particularly teen mothers, as well as the role of teen fathers and fathers of babies born to teen mothers (who may not be teens themselves).

There is an increasing tendency to postpone entry to parenthood. Although personal satisfaction tends to increase with entry to parenthood, marital satisfaction does not.

Gay and lesbian families must struggle against bias and discrimination, but the children raised in gay/lesbian families are no different in the problems they face than children raised in heterosexual families.

The new reproductive technologies both enable more choices in becoming parents and emphasize social biases in who should become parents. Adoption brings similar tensions between individual choices about entry to parenthood and legal and cultural practices and possibilities.

Key terms

Coitus interruptus: A natural contraceptive method whereby the man withdraws from sexual intercourse prior to ejaculation.

Crude birth rate: Number of live births per 100 000 population.

Custom adoption: Adoption of a child, especially among First Nations peoples, which does not proceed through legal processes but instead is based on traditional understandings and customs.

Demographers: Researchers who study the processes of population, most notably fertility, mortality, and migration.

IUD (Intrauterine Device): A contraceptive device medically inserted into a woman's uterus that prevents conception.

Neonaticide: The murder of a newborn.

The revenge of the cradle: A historical term used to describe Quebec's long-standing high birth rates as "revenge" against perceived social injustices felt by the Quebec people surrounded as they were (and are) by an anglophone country and continent.

Suggested Readings

Furstenberg, Frank F., Jr., J. Brooks-Gunn & P. Morgan. 1987. *Adolescent Mothers in Later Life*. New York: Cambridge. This original research focuses on the long-term consequences of early childbearing among a group of teens in the United States. It finds that although some of the losses in opportunities can be made up later in life, for the majority of teen mothers, there is no catching up with the lost opportunities they

experience by having children while young.

Kirk, H. David. 1984. *Shared Fate: A Theory and Method of Adoptive Relationships*. New York: Free Press. This is the classic book on adoption as an emergent family form. It looks at the doctrine of sameness (to non-adoptive families) and the damage this can do to adoptive parent-child relations. It develops a method and approach for the study of adoptive families.

Luker, Kristin. 1996. *Dubious Conceptions: The Politics of Teenage Pregnancy.* Cambridge, MA: Harvard University Press. This book looks at the social contexts of teen pregnancies from the teens' viewpoints, and from the point of view of U.S. politics of the 1990s.

McLaren, Angus & Arlene McLaren. 1986. *The Bedroom and the State: The Changing Practices and Politics of Contraception and Abortion in Canada, 1880-1980.* Toronto: McClelland & Stewart. This book is a historical study of the legality and illegality of contraception and abortion in Canada over the course of a century. It examines forced use of contraception by one Canadian employer, the changing relation of the state to contraception, the eugenics movement in Canada, and the process of growing liberalization of laws on contraception and abortion.

Nelson, Fiona. 1996. *Lesbian Motherhood: An Exploration of Canadian Lesbian Families.* Toronto: University of Toronto Press. This book reports original Canadian research on lesbians pursuing parenthood separate from men. It looks at reproductive decision-making, how motherhood is achieved in lesbian families, and the challenges and benefits of becoming a lesbian family with children.

Review Questions

1. In which part of the world are women who have had a child seen as better candidates for marriage?

2. What has happened to Quebec birth rates during this century?

3. Which province in Canada has the lowest birth rate today?

4. In eighteenth-century Quebec, which group most commonly adopted children born outside of marriage?

5. Which group in Canada has the highest birth rates today?

6. Are marriage and parenthood less popular now than they used to be?

7. Is it true that the Pill brought about control over childbearing for the first time in history?

8. What were the main birth control approaches used in the past?

9. What generally are the effects of entering parenthood on individual and marital satisfaction?

10. What are two processes couples use to make decisions about becoming parents?

Discussion Questions

1. Why is family seen by many as involving parenting?

2. Motherhood and femininity seem socially intertwined. Do you see this changing as women's roles change?

3. Why are birth rates and family size such political issues?

4. As the world in the 1990s and beyond becomes more globalized, would you expect more international adoptions? What challenges might this trend pose to families? To social and family policies and practices?

5. Why are rates of childbearing higher

in more male-dominant societies?

6. What can be learned about the gender dimensions of entering parenthood from studying gay and lesbian families and parenthood?

7. Why were family and children seen as so dominant a part of our lives in the past?

8. Without access to contraception, would it be possible for women to aim for higher education, careers, and social equality?

9. How is not using birth control by teens seen by them as more romantic?

10. Why is sterilization so popular as a contraceptive method?

WEBLINKS

http://www.jstor.org/journals/ 00393665.html

Studies in Family Planning (a journal)

http://www.undp.org/popin/journals/ifpp/ ifpptoc.htm

International Family Planning

A number of online articles on topics related to family planning.

http://www.msh.org/pop/POPHOME.HTM

Population and Family Planning

http://snycorva.cortland.edu/~king/ Outline14.htm

Family and the Transition to Parenthood

This Web site has demographics and definitions.

http://www.geocities.com/Heartland/ Prairie/2324/transitions.html

An online paper arguing that while our parents knew what to expect from marriage and gender roles, we have redefined what these things mean.

http://www.mentalhealth-net.com/ research/projects/0080/

Promoting Parenthood

The psychosocial transition to first-time parenthood is a period of intense adjustment for new parents.

http://ws1.kidsource.com/kidsource/ content/news/teen_pregnancy.html

Groundbreaking study on teenage childbearing quantifies devastating consequences to parents, children, and society.

Parenting:

Socialization and Discipline

In interactions with people, we tend to make assumptions about what they are thinking, how they will react to anything we do or say, and what their fears or aspirations may be. We make these assumptions even when (or especially when) we don't know the other people well. Assumptions help us to decide how to interact, and what we will say or do to create the impression that we are trying to project. Usually, other people respond as we expect—if not totally, at least within the expectations of civilized society. That shows us that both participants in the interaction have been socialized well to act in similar ways in given situations, and to be attentive to how others react to us. Think of what life would be like without these assumptions and expectations. It would be like a jungle, or a circus. Nothing would ever get done because we would spend all our time trying to figure out how to interact in simple ways with our fellow humans.

Our parents are largely to be credited with this achievement. As our first socializers, mother and father have an enormous influence on our lives even after we have left home. It is our parents who mainly shape our original templates for seeing, thinking about, and dealing with the world. Parents are aided in this by public education systems and other social institutions such as law, mass media, and religion.

On the other hand, some people may seem to us on any given day to act completely unexpectedly, at least according to our own values and principles. This is probably because they were taught a different set of norms and values than we were, or are less fully socialized to the abiding norms of society. Differences in norms and expectations cause uncertainty and disorientation for everyone concerned. Again, that is because we have all learned that most people act according to rules similar to our own. Though experience usually bears this out in everyday life, it masks the differences between, and even within, cultures and subcultures. These difficulties are often the result of differences in the content and degree of children's socialization.

Socialization

Sociologists define **socialization** as the social learning process a person goes through to become a capable, functioning member of society. The process is social because it is through interaction with others and in response to social pressures that people acquire the **culture**—the language, perspective, and skills, the likes and dislikes, the cluster of norms, values, and beliefs—that characterizes the group to which they belong. Socialization is one of the most important processes by which social structure constrains and transforms us, and at the same time, enables us to take full advantage of the opportunities society has to offer each of us.

Primary socialization is learning that takes place in the early years of a person's life. It is extremely important in forming an individual's personality and charting the course of future development. Most often, primary socialization takes place within the context of a family. Here, a young child learns the many social skills needed to participate effectively in a variety of social institutions.

The primary socialization of children is usually the responsibility of the child's family. It has a profound impact on the individual's life, by helping to set the child's future values, aspirations, and, to a certain extent, personality. Although the family is not the only early socializer, it is arguably the most important, especially during the child's infancy. It is in the family that a child first learns how to gain rewards by performing set tasks, and how to negotiate to achieve a consensus on rules. It is also the family that first exposes the child to social inequality, as parents have almost total control over the child's life, and it is only by pleasing the parent that the child can gain relative autonomy. Most importantly, most children learn that they are valued human beings to their parents, showing them that other human beings ought to be valued too.

Most children seem to follow something of a set pattern of growth, physically, mentally, emotionally, and morally, within a range. Barring any disabilities or other impediments to development (which we will discuss later) these patterns seem universal, within the limits of human diversity. A child learns to sit up before learning to stand, and stands before walking. Children walk before they run, dance, or jump. This developmental sequence seems obvious to us. Each development is necessary before the next can be achieved, and each new step develops the skills necessary for the next task or achievement. A child who cannot hold up his or her head will find it difficult to achieve the balance or muscles needed to sit up.

Cognitive abilities progress in a similar pattern. A baby learns to coo, then babble, then usually moves on to saying one-word sentences, and gradually progresses until he or she can carry on an intelligent conversation. The family environment affects these seemingly unstoppable patterns by encouraging each step and by modelling for the baby how to communicate. Children who are never talked to learn language later, if at all. A baby who is swaddled for the first few months of life—tightly wrapped in cloth that impedes movement—will accomplish the various motor skills later than children whose parents constantly stimulate and teach physical skills before they are ready. If these hindrances last a short time, babies can compensate and their ultimate performance will be largely unaffected. If parents restrict a child's movement for longer periods of time, they will stunt the baby's motor abilities. The baby's body may have grown into a shape that makes it impossible to walk. Even if the gross motor skills are learned, fine motor skills, like manipulating a fork or spoon, may be unachievable.

Most children tend to grow up securely attached to their family or other caregivers and able to take their place in society. It is in this secure family context that they begin to learn social roles, of which one of the earliest and most consequential is their *gender*. People learn their gender-based habits of behaviour through **gender socialization**. The socialization process links gender to personal identity—in the form of *gender identity*—and to distinctive activities—in the form of *gender roles*. The major agents of socialization—family, peer groups, schools, and the mass media—all serve to reinforce cultural and conventional definitions of masculinity and femininity.

Consider the obvious difference between men's and women's interest in hockey or football. Men are more likely to play hockey or football and watch games than women, but the difference doesn't end there. Men also use hockey or football playing and watching as an occasion for male bonding. Televised hockey or football games model a certain style of male talk and behaviour.

Gender-based communicative differences extend into all areas of life. For example, male and female doctors exhibit different attitudes toward their patients, and this shows up in the way they ask questions and give advice. Female doctors tend to be more interested in their relationship with the patient. Male doctors tend mainly to be interested in getting and giving information.

Learned gender differences in communication also show up in our intimate relations. For example, women are generally taught to behave in a demure, innocent and uninterested fashion when sex is the topic of discussion with men. (They are more forthcoming in discussions with other women.) In short, learned patterns of communication create and maintain gender distinctions and reinforce social arrangements between the sexes. Often, they complicate our understanding of what is going on between the sexes, as we began to explore in Chapter 2.

Such differences in communication between the sexes are largely socially created. Often they are maintained by the different positions men and women hold in the occupational structure. Since bosses are more often men than women, women often have to adopt "men's ways" of doing things if they are to succeed. For example, people resolve conflicts differently at home and at work, using more competitive styles at work and more accommodating styles at home. But at work, at most managerial levels, men and women tend to do it the male way, because that is the way in which women have been able to achieve promotion in male-dominated workplaces. In female-dominated workplaces, women use a somewhat more consensual, less hierarchical style of management. In her many studies of gender and talk, Deborah Tannen argues that conversation itself is hierarchical with men and consensual with women (1993).

As we have said, several agents of socialization ensure that the sexes learn proper gender behaviours and characteristics. The most important of these agents are the family, schools, and mass media; each reinforces exist-

ing patterns. Gender socialization begins as soon as an infant's sex is identified and continues through pre-school and primary school. Young children learn gender identities when they experiment with hair and clothing
styles, role-playing games, and body decoration, and also by observing others at nursery school or daycare. Their imitative efforts all reflect enormous
pressures to conform to assigned gender identities.

Parents routinely assign more household tasks to daughters than to
sons. The tasks people assign to their sons are more usually "handyman"
tasks, and less often cleaning, child care, or meal preparation—probably
reflecting their own patterns of household activities (see Figure 5.1). Not
surprisingly, children often form traditional, gender-based attitudes toward
housework before the end of high school. In this way, they perpetuate age-
old stereotypes without being aware of doing so. Men, older people, and
poor people are particularly likely to hold and teach traditional, gendered,
attitudes. As a result, fathers demand more help from teenaged daughters
than from teenaged sons.

Even parents who believe they treat their children equally often treat

Figure 5.1   **PERCENTAGE OF WOMEN AND MEN PERFORMING SELECTED
HOUSEHOLD CHORES**

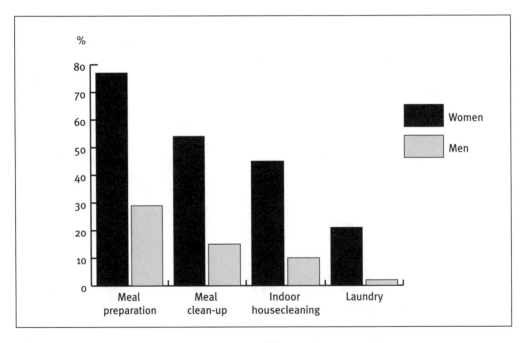

Source: Statistics Canada, General Social Survey, 1986, from *Canadian Social Trends*, Catalogue No. 11-008, Spring 1990, No. 16.
Reprinted with permission.

Raising a Tomboy ... Without Lowering Her Confidence

Raising a girl who acts like "one of the boys" is easier nowadays, when individual differences are more respected than in the past. Most child-development experts reject the notion of "gender-appropriate behaviour" for children. "Rather than forcing their daughter into a mold she's uncomfortable with, parents should ask themselves, 'What is my daughter good at? What does she like to do?' Activities should stem from her interests," says Jeffrey A. Kelly, Ph.D., professor of psychology at the University of Mississippi Medical Centre.

Parents can, however, help their daughters find friends of both sexes by being alert to interests that might include other girls. For instance, one mother of a ten-year-old encouraged her daughter to join a photography group in addition to the karate class in which she was the only girl.

Most important is that children feel loved by their parents as they are, not as the parents would prefer them to be.

Is tomboyish behavior ever a cause for concern? Only, according to Anke Erhardt, Ph.D., of Columbia University, when a girl is extremely unhappy about being a girl. "It's not the behavior itself, but the child's degree of unhappiness that parents should use as a barometer in whether to seek psychological assistance for their child," she notes.

Source: Wendy Schuman. 1986. *Parents* (abridged). Reprinted with the permission of *Parents* magazine.

boys and girls differently. And even the children of parents who reject traditional gender roles are affected by the stereotypes around them. For example, where gender identity, role, and sexual orientation are concerned, the adult daughters of lesbian mothers do not differ from those of heterosexual mothers. Children in these "nontraditional" families learn essentially the same gender attitudes as their peers.

To summarize, families are important because they prepare new members of society to participate in society's key institutions. We might even say that they are responsible for reproducing society, since they both produce the next generation and prepare people for full participation in social life.

In this chapter, we show that family researchers have found there are better and worse ways of preparing children to participate in society. In saying this, we recognize that societies—and within societies, subgroups—differ in their parenting behaviours. Some parents put a high value on obedience, other parents value independence. Some parents want their children to be cooperative and adaptable; others, to be competitive and ambitious.

It is not the job of sociologists to decide which goals are the "right" goals, or the best ones. However, most (if not all) sociologists, and most (if not all) parents, would agree on a few minimum standards for parenting. For example, they would think it better if children do well in school, obey the law, respect others, and enjoy good mental health. As parents, they wouldn't like their children to fail or drop out of school, commit delinquent acts, or become deeply depressed, addicted, or suicidal.

If a child is failing, delinquent, or disturbed, this is not necessarily the result of poor parenting. Genetic factors increase the risks of childhood failure, delinquency, and depression. Outside social influences—for example, peer groups, mass media, the school or neighbourhood, the lack of resources or opportunities—also increase the risks. The best parenting in the world cannot prevent these factors from having a harmful influence. Moreover, they put some children at higher risk than others of being labelled failures, delinquents, or slackers in school. We have no way of telling, at this stage in the development of sociology, the relative sizes of the genetic, extra-familial, and parental influences.

The best we can do is look for trends in the research findings, while taking into account, or *controlling for*, other factors. Doing this leads the open-minded observer to conclude that there really are better and worse parenting strategies, and this chapter will describe what they are. We begin by examining some keys to good parenting practice, and note the results of bad parenting practice. Then we consider factors that influence the ways in which parents raise their children.

Parenting Processes

"Parenting" involves much more than taking care of a child's basic needs for food and shelter. It means helping turn that child into a functioning member of society. This, in turn, requires that parents create the right conditions for the emotional and cognitive development of their children. These "right" parenting conditions include providing love and attachment, emotional stability, protection and control, and fair and moderate discipline. We will look at each of these important conditions in turn.

Love and Attachment

The vast majority of parents probably love their children, just as one would hope. Problems can occur, however, when parents do not know how to express love to their children (Perez, 1978), and when children who feel unloved by their parents suffer emotional damage. One study compared delinquent with non-delinquent boys, finding that delinquents are much more likely to have been deprived of parental affection (Bruce, 1970). Another comparative study finds that the delinquents receive much less support and communication from their fathers. Their fathers talk to them less, praise them less, and show them less understanding (Cortex & Gatti, 1972).

A comparison of delinquent and non-delinquent girls yields similar findings (Riege, 1972). Delinquent girls are more likely to say that their mothers and fathers should spend more time with them. They are also more likely to have experienced separation from their parents, especially in their early adolescent years. Often, they feel that neither parent gives them the right amount of love; and they report spending less time in leisure with their parents than the average girl. In short, they often feel deprived of parental attention and affection.

Why are children who feel unloved more likely to break society's rules? Explanations vary. Perhaps, only delinquent peers are available to the unloved children, and they learn delinquent ways from the peers from whom they are seeking friendship and acceptance. Or, perhaps they are angry at their parents for (apparently) not loving them, so they deliberately choose friends of whom their parents will disapprove. By engaging in delinquent activity, they may also be seeking attention which they feel they do not get from their parents otherwise. Children who receive too little attention at home may look for it elsewhere, even if that means attaching themselves to delinquent groups. Delinquent activity strengthens feelings of attachment within the peer group, compensating for a lack of attachment to family members. Linden and Hackler (1973) find that a lack of ties to parents is associated with delinquency even among youth with no close ties to delinquent peers.

Criminologist Travis Hirschi talks about the importance of social bonds that keep people from resorting to delinquency. His and other research suggests that a feeling of **attachment** to one's parents is critically important. In turn, the three strongest influences on feelings of attachment are control and supervision, identity support, and instrumental communication

From Crib to Criminal: The Social Stew That Turns Kids Bad

Every killer was once an innocent baby. So what is it that happens between the time the diapers get changed and the moment a person kills? A Statistics Canada report ... documents a trend of increasingly serious violence by youths aged 12 to 17.

The *Child at Risk* report, based on testimony from 27 witnesses, concludes there is no single factor in childhood that leads to later criminal behavior. It's more like a stew—genetic and/or environmental influences that can create a monster....

The report cites a study of the personal history of murderers which found that all had lacked loving care as a young child.

Another strong influence leading to criminality is exposure to violence, be it emotional or physical, direct or indirect, or all of these. This can refer to child abuse or even watching violent TV programs. Poverty is also a factor that can predispose a troubled child to criminality.

The report is conclusive on the following controversial point: "Much of the violent crime committed by adults can be traced to a breakdown of parenting in the early childhood period."

Source: Barbara Yaffee. 1995. *The Vancouver Sun*, August 5 (abridged). Reprinted with permission.

(Cernkovich & Giordano, 1987). **Control and supervision** refers to the extent to which parents monitor their children's behaviour. **Identity support** refers to the parents' respect, acceptance, and emotional support for the adolescent. **Instrumental communication**, finally, refers to the frequency with which an adolescent talks to his or her parents about problems at school, job plans, and problems with friends.

In short, a child who feels attached to his or her parents is one they watch (and watch over), respect, and listen to. This feeling of attachment, in turn, reduces the likelihood of delinquent behaviour. Children are less likely to become delinquents if their parents keep an eye on what they are doing, offer them support, and give them a chance to discuss whatever it is that is bothering them. This is true of children in two-parent families, mother-only families, and mother-stepfather families. It is the quality of family relationships and family dynamics that counts in forming and socializing children.

Researchers on child development continue to debate the process by which attachment occurs between a child and his/her parents. The conventional wisdom is that attachment between infant and mother occurs almost immediately after birth and is permanent. A baby who is securely attached cries upon being separated from its mother but is gladdened and consoled by her return. A baby who is insecurely attached ignores the mother, and is indifferent or refuses to be consoled by her return. According to this theory, the quality of this attachment forms the basis for all subsequent social relations.

More recent research, however, has challenged the view that secure attachment in infancy is either necessary or sufficient for solid and rewarding attachments and relationships in adulthood. Longitudinal research finds that insecure infants can grow up to be secure adults. And, many intervening events—for example, abuse or divorce—can interrupt a secure attachment formed in infancy. Finally, though insecure attachment in infancy can create problems, other childhood experiences do too. Other factors beside attachment to parents also influence the risk of delinquent behaviour. For example, marital unhappiness increases the risk (Gove & Crutchfield, 1982), as does abuse in the family.

At least two plausible explanations account for this relationship between the parents' unhappy marriage and the children's delinquency. First, an unhappy marriage can cause children to feel unloved. Unhappily married people often spend too little time with their children. The parents are depressed, stressed-out, and self-absorbed. Second, marital conflict disrupts the normal practices of discipline, especially by mothers, who are typically the family disciplinarians in Canadian society. This, in turn, reduces the attachment between parent and child. (Rule enforcement is another form of attachment between parents and their children—a way that parents show concern for their children.)

Besides feeling unloved, the children of unhappily married parents may feel angry or guilty that their parents cannot get along, often obliging them to take sides in an argument. These angry children may want to escape from family life overall. Running away is one such escape for some children. We will discuss runaways shortly. Some escape socially into groups of friends who have also rejected family life to seek thrills by challenging authority (parental) figures of all kinds. Most delinquent behaviour (e.g., activities like vandalism or assault) is symbolic or expressive. In delinquency, children "act out" against parents on a larger, public stage. In effect, delinquent behaviour can in many instances be seen as a public argument with one's parents.

Remember that children—indeed, people of all ages—form judgments about themselves by responding to how others treat them. That is the essence of what sociologists call the **looking-glass self**. People learn how to conform to rules, and how to obey authority, by generalizing from particular situations. Society is a "generalized other," in the words of sociologist George Herbert Mead. We form our impressions of society, as we do of ourselves, from concrete, limited experiences. Many of these formative experiences occur within our family homes.

Children with more supportive, encouraging parents usually get higher grades at school, have more social competence, and get into less trouble with teachers. Other things being equal, these children see themselves as having more scholastic and athletic ability, take more pride in their physical appearance, and rate their overall worth more highly than other children. Finally, children with supportive parents feel that their teachers and friends also support them. In short, they generalize from a loving, supportive home to imagine that they live in a loving, supportive world. Feeling valued inside the home, they feel valued outside the home. Feeling loved and valued, they conform more enthusiastically to the rules of social institutions like the school.

This observation proves the validity of a principle attributed to the early American sociologist, W.I. Thomas, and commonly called the **Thomas Dictum**: "A situation that is believed to be real is real in its consequences." What people believe to be true about their lives is usually more important in shaping their close relations than what is objectively true— that is, what therapists, sociologists, friends, or strangers might think is true.

So, true or not, a world that is believed to be supportive and loving "produces" a different kind of child than a world believed to be hostile and cruel. In short, parents who want their children to feel good about themselves, get along well with others, and do well at school, should teach their children that the world is supportive and loving. This they do by themselves being supportive and loving to the child.

Parental involvement is another important form that love often takes, and research shows that involvement matters. Parents who are more involved with their children spend more time with them, talk with them more, and think and talk *about* them more. Research shows that more involved parenting reduces delinquency among inner-city boys. It also increases the effect of preschool programs on later school success up to seven years after children have completed the programs. Children with more involved parents feel more loved, and children who feel loved get more engaged in what they are doing, and draw more benefit from it. They don't break the rules because they don't view the rules as alien and repressive. They use what they learned in preschool because they like school and want to do well.

Attachment and involvement aren't all that goes to make up parental love. A warm, nurturing parenting style increases the child's own sense of effectiveness, competence, and worth. Parents who take the trouble to nurture their child in a warm, careful way are showing the child consideration and respect. This increases the child's sense of his or her own value. No wonder: in our society we equate the spending of time with preferences and values. We all take more time with people we care about. People we don't care about—whom we don't value highly—are people we rush, avoid, delay, or brush off. We don't return their phone calls, for example, or return them less promptly.

Warm, supportive parenting leads to good social, psychological, and school adjustment. Even in adolescence, often a time of big changes and uncertainties, children whose parents are supportive do better. Teenagers with inattentive parents get poorer grades and have more problems with each passing year, unless they acquire other attachments—for example, to school. As well, children with a more positive self-concept have better relations with peers.

By contrast, adolescents with unsupportive parents are also more likely than other adolescents to start smoking cigarettes. The health hazards of tobacco aside, cigarette smoking in adolescence also predicts a variety of substance abuse. Whether this indicates nonconformity, risk-taking, or self-destructiveness, adolescents with unsupportive parents are different. It also could be the stronger influence of peer pressure on adolescents who lack parental support, or feel that they do. The strong role of peer pressures on adolescents who smoke has been well substantiated in research (Van Roosmalen & McDaniel, 1989; 1992).

Emotional Stability and Family Cohesion

Emotional stability ranks close behind love as a contributor to the healthy development of children. Anything that reduces the parents' ability to provide stable, consistent support runs the risk of producing school problems, delinquency, or depression in the child. This can include spousal conflict, addiction, depression, or physical illness. Children whose parents are emotionally unstable are more anxious, less secure, and more likely to act out than children whose parents are emotionally stable. Similarly, children whose parents argue and fight a lot have lower self-esteem than those whose parents get along.

Of course, all couples fight on occasion. Couples vary in how often they fight, and how violent their fights become. Generally, how they fight makes a big difference, as we noted in Chapter 3, to marital satisfaction and overall family well-being. Frequent, violent fights pose a serious problem for the entire family, not only for the fighting spouses but also for the healthy development of children. However, emotional instability can take other dangerous forms, too—for example, depression. Some couples are severely depressed and silently hostile. They may not fight loudly but the signs of animosity are there, and children pick up on them. In this respect, children are like powerless people everywhere. They are vigilant and always watching out for the slightest sign that the social situation is going to improve or worsen, and worry about how it might affect them.

In some families, the parents rarely spend time with each other. They rarely speak to each other. There are no regular family meals because the family members, especially the parents, have difficulty being in each other's presence. These family patterns can be very harmful for the children. Researchers report that children who live in families that have sit-down meals together at least three times a week are much less likely to become delinquents in their adolescence, or to turn to crime in adulthood. Family dinners are a sign of **family cohesion** and stability, which contribute to the healthy emotional development of children. Likewise, families that have recreational activities together are much less likely to produce delinquent children than families in which members each do their own thing.

Such family rituals and routines are important not for the activities themselves but as symbols of sharing. Physiologically, eating a hamburger in the company of your parents and siblings is no different from eating it alone in front of the television set. The body chemistry is the same. However, the cultural and psychological meaning is completely different. By the rituals and routines it enacts, a group declares its importance to itself, its members, and even to outsiders. The absence of family ritual hurts a child because it implies that the family and its members are not important. It also tends to reinforce the belief that the child is not valued by others, or worse yet, is being shunned.

Conflict disrupts family ritual, and increases stress, resulting typically in poor parenting. Spousal conflict can have a variety of sources—for example, addiction or substance abuse by one or both parents. Children of alcoholics report feeling more rejection than love from the alcoholic parent. They experience more stress across their entire life course, more family disruption, and more drug use. Active alcoholism often breaks up families, especially where children are involved. Many addicted parents are too preoccupied with their relationship to the addictive substance to provide care and support for anyone else. They, their children, their spouses, and most aspects of their lives tend to be neglected.

Alcoholic women jailed for drunk driving, for example, have difficulty caring for their children after release from jail (Goldberg, Lex & Mello, 1996). Sometimes they abandon their children to live with alcoholic men who do not want children around. Sometimes, representatives of the state take their children into foster care, in the (perhaps correct) belief they are receiving inadequate care. It has been shown, unfortunately, that some foster homes may be as bad as the original home situation, but of course, some are excellent family homes.

Other factors, such as chronic depression, may have the same effect as addiction on family stability and cohesion. Depression hinders a parent's ability to care for children. Frequent, serious depressive episodes cause parents to have poorer communication and problem-solving skills. And, these problems may make the depression worse. Depression can also distort their perceptions of the children's behaviours, leading to more intense and frequent conflict, both between the spouses and between the parent and child.

Physical illness may also affect family life, a topic we will discuss at length in Chapter 8 when we consider stress and its effects on close relations. For example, breast cancer hinders family functioning by increasing maternal depression and by creating feelings of fear, anger, and confusion among the family members. Often, these feelings change to guilt and self-loathing as family members take themselves to task for resenting the intrusion of the illness. They may even resent the family member who has the illness for bringing the intrusion into their lives. Because of the emotional turmoil, family expectations constantly change. Children are left in a state of uncertainty about the kinds of behaviour that are, and are not, permitted.

Protectiveness and Control

No less important than love and stability is parental control: how firmly, consistently, and fairly a parent makes and enforces rules for the child. Good rules guide and protect the child. They signify the parent's concern and attachment. Good rules also reduce normative uncertainty.

On the other hand, too many rules enforced coldly or unfairly can be as bad as no rules at all. A survey of adolescents in Scotland identified four parenting styles, distinguished by their degree of acceptance and control of adolescent behaviour. (By "acceptance" the researchers mean that parents like and respect their children.) Researchers (Shucksmith *et al.*, 1995) found these types:

1. permissive (high acceptance, low control; 37.8 percent of families);

2. unengaged (low acceptance, low control; 16.8 percent of families);

3. authoritarian (low acceptance, high control; 15.3 percent of families);

4. authoritative (high acceptance, high control; 23.7 percent of families).

Of course, parents may lie at different points along the spectrum for both acceptance and control, and the same parents will vary from time to time in their style.

The **authoritative parenting** style (high acceptance, high control) turns out children who achieve the highest levels of academic performance and mental well-being. They are also more likely than other adolescents to have a strong community orientation, are less self-centred, and are less likely to engage in deviant behaviour. At home, parental authoritativeness is positively correlated with cohesion, organization, achievement, and intellectual orientation (Radziszewska *et al.*, 1996; for African Americans, Taylor *et al.*, 1995). Thus, well-functioning families typically have an authoritative parenting style and produce children who are happy and successful outside the home.

Other forms of parenting produce less desirable outcomes. For example, **authoritarian parenting** (low acceptance/high control) hinders the development of expressiveness and independence. This parenting style also tends to increase the risk of adolescent drug use. Children whose parents are highly controlling but not as caring are more likely to become delinquents (Mak, 1996), to become depressed, and to fail in school (Radziszewska *et al.*, 1996). Where emotional warmth and nurturance are lacking, parental control simply feels like bullying to the child.

This doesn't argue in favour of lax parental control, however. **Unengaged parenting** (low acceptance/low control) can also be harmful. For example, children under the age of 11 are more likely to use alcohol, tobacco, and drugs if their parents fail to monitor the children's behaviour closely. Likewise, among middle school students, **latchkey youth** (who are home alone two or more days per week) are four times more likely to get drunk than youth who have parental supervision (five or more days a week). They are also more likely to smoke cigarettes, sniff glue, and use marijuana (Mulhall *et al.*, 1996).

Permissive parenting produces poor results too. Along similar lines, a study of high school students in the San Francisco Bay area found that permissive (high acceptance/low control) parenting produces poor grades (Vergun, Dornbusch & Steinberg, 1996). Poor students are more likely to come from families with permissive parenting styles (Bronstein, Duncan & D'Ari, 1996; Radziszewska *et al.*, 1996). What's more, differences in adjustment accumulate over time, and the harmful effects of neglectful parenting continue to take their toll as behaviour problems, internal distress, and poor

The authoritative style of parenting offers the best mixture of love and control.

school performance (Steinberg *et al.*, 1994).

Thus, children whose parents are authoritarian, unengaged, or permissive are the children who are most likely to show problems of adjustment, poor academic achievement, or substance abuse. The authoritative parenting style offers the best mixture of love and control—not too much or too little of either. Adolescents with authoritative parents turn out "best"—whether we consider depressive symptoms, smoking, or school grades.

Fair and Moderate Discipline

The issue of discipline is related to control. A desire for control leads to the creation of rules, and **discipline** is the enforcement of these rules. The two go together, but they are different—like law courts and police forces. Overzealous discipline may wipe out the benefits of control, and so may inattentive discipline. So we must consider disciplinary practice as a parenting concern in its own right.

Research shows that too much discipline is a bad thing and so is too little discipline. For example, Wells and Rankin (1988) report that delinquency is less likely when parental strictness is moderate, rather than high or low.

Hoffman (1979) differentiates between three basic types of disciplining technique: power assertion, love withdrawal, and induction. In **power**

assertion, a parent or other caregiver threatens a child with punishment for noncompliance. Typically, punishment is to be delivered in a physical form. The child changes his or her behaviour to avoid punishment; however, this compliance is not based on moral learning. Rather, the child's seemingly moral behaviour is externally, not internally, driven. Similarly, in **love withdrawal**, a parent threatens a child. Instead of the punishment taking a physical form, it takes an emotional form—producing in the child anxiety over the loss of love. As with power assertion, the child complies with parental demands to avoid punishment. There is no moral learning—no internalization of ideas of good and bad.

Induction, on the other hand, emphasizes the possible benefits of the child's behaviour for others. Inductive discipline—teaching good behaviour by setting a good example, then rewarding imitation—is better for the child than power assertion. When children break the rules, they become aware of contributing to another's distress and feel guilty; they also learn how to prevent that from happening. Feelings of guilt, unlike feelings of fear, exercise an **internal moral control** over our behaviour. Therefore, they represent moral learning and are the most effective means of maintaining prosocial behaviour. Adolescents taught using inductive techniques make decisions more independently, for they have learned how to make moral judgements.

Moral internalization is fostered by parental affection and inductive discipline, and it is harmed by power assertion (Hoffman, 1979). Identification with the parents contributes to certain visible moral attributes. As children grow older, parental influence wanes and peer interaction tends to undermine rather than uphold parental teaching. This is particularly true for boys; girls are more morally internalized than boys, probably as a result of gender socialization.

It is through early compliance to maternal socialization that self-regulation develops, leading to a growth of conscience—i.e., a general moral orientation and feelings of guilt. Longitudinal research (Kochanska, Padavich & Koenig, 1996) finds that children who experience more power-assertive maternal discipline are less likely than other children to imagine solving moral dilemmas in a socially responsible way. As well, their behaviour—both observed on videotape and reported by their mothers—is more antisocial. Conversely, maternal rearing behaviours that de-emphasize the use of power are associated with children's internalized conscience six years later (Kochanska, 1991).

Inductive techniques offer many benefits: typically, they force parents to explain and demonstrate good behaviour, for example. Yet, four American parents in five use some degree of physical punishment—a form of power assertion—as a disciplinary tool. Unlike inductive discipline, power assertion is quick and simple. Physical punishment, and power assertion more generally, appeals to parents who don't have the time, patience, or inclination to teach rules inductively. Often it is a result of marital conflict: hostile family interactions are more likely to produce maternal power assertion—especially against boys—which, in turn, leads to children misbehaving (Erel, Margolin & John, 1998) as well as becoming hostile, depressed, or anxious (Margolin & John, 1997).

To see discipline in a natural setting, researchers spent hundreds of hours watching parents threaten their children in indoor malls and other public spaces (Davis, 1996). They noted that, when parents use physical punishment as a form of discipline, usually they want compliance with some very simple demands. For example, the parent wants the child to sit still, be quiet, come with the parent, stay close, or stop touching things. Children typically respond as if nothing is happening: they are doing nothing wrong and the parents aren't threatening them. Only a handful challenge the legitimacy of the threat. About half the adults making these threats also hit the children.

What we learn from this scenario is that parents use physical punishment—perhaps power assertion more generally—routinely and perhaps thoughtlessly, and it is ineffective! Seventy-seven percent of surveyed mothers of three-year-olds spank their children at least once in a two-week interval; they do so an average of 2.5 times per week. Though parents may try to get the child to internalize blame—thus justifying the punishment—children do not feel guilty. They know they have done nothing wrong by squirming, fidgeting, wandering, or otherwise trying to deal with boredom. In this situation, physical punishment by the parent is as automatic and unproductive as fidgeting by the child. It produces no lasting benefit. In the long run, punitive discipline often produces delinquency and low self-esteem (Peiser & Heaven, 1996).

The use of physical punishment as a disciplining tool varies from one social group to another. For example, parents with conservative scriptural beliefs practise physical punishment more often than parents with less conservative theological views (Ellison, Bartkowski & Segal, 1996; Ellison, 1996). Disciplinary techniques also vary from one ethnic group to another (see, for example, Papps, Walker, Trimboli & Trimboli, 1995) and vary by the education of the caregiver (Scott-Little & Holloway, 1994).

Research also shows that the probability of physically punishing children varies according to the age of the mother. Teenage mothers are more likely to punish their children physically, and the youngest adolescent mothers advocate the use of physical punishment more strongly. They also report more personal unhappiness than other adolescent mothers. Perhaps these two factors relate. Teenage mothers may experience more feelings of inadequacy and of being overwhelmed by a task (raising children) with which they have no experience. Studies of teenage mothers also find evidence of distress, rigid parenting attitudes, and inappropriate expectations of children.

Research findings show overwhelmingly that the power assertion method of discipline—especially in its more extreme forms—is harmful to children. Not only are verbal and physical punishment ineffective ways of gaining obedience, but they also leave scars within the child. Among women, the experience of verbal abuse in childhood predicts marital conflict in adulthood (Belt & Abidin, 1996). Physical punishment experienced in childhood predicts marital conflict for men (*ibid.*) and increases the risk of bulimia in women (Rorty, Yager & Rossotto, 1995).

A broad range of studies has found that harsh childhood discipline produces harmful consequences for both sexes in adulthood. Among them are depression, alcoholism, low self-esteem, aggressive behaviour, moral uncertainty, suicide, and a tendency to physically abuse wives and children. Anger and abusiveness directed toward wives is highly correlated with a man's recollection of his parents shaming him. Men who recall receiving childhood punishments that were excessive, public, and random—in short, humiliating—are more likely to beat their wives. Thus, by lowering self-esteem, physical punishment in childhood produces a cycle of abusive behaviour.

Physical punishment reduces people's confidence in themselves. For example, physical punishment in childhood leads to concerns about parenthood. College students who have suffered physical punishment by their father, or who have witnessed father-to-mother violence, are likely to express concerns about their own ability to be good parents. Mistreatment in childhood also increases the likelihood of criminal behaviour, though it is a better predictor of juvenile delinquency than of adult criminality. Harsh discipline can even undo the good work of love and attachment. A study of nearly two thousand adolescents found that, even after controlling for the effects of attachment to parents, discipline that is extremely harsh increases the risk of delinquency.

As the harshness and frequency of punishment increases, so does delinquency. Perhaps that's because physical punishment leads children to think of violence as an effective means of solving problems. It implicitly condones the thoughtless and violent use of power by people who (like parents) are in positions of authority. Therefore, abused children may engage in criminal behaviour because they find it acceptable to use harsh, irrational means to deal with their problems.

Parents use physical punishment for a variety of reasons. Drinking problems contribute to the use of violence against children, as do high levels of stress and anger. A lack of preparation for parenting—including a lack of knowledge about child development and negative attitudes toward children—also predicts the use of physical punishment.

Nonetheless, the single most important factor predicting physical punishment by an adult is violence that adults have experienced during their own childhood. People whom parents yelled at and spanked frequently as children are more likely to yell at and spank their own children. The childhood experience of physical punishment apparently leads to approval of physical

"Spare the Rod" Gaining in Popularity

There is a growing pressure on the federal government to change a Criminal Code section that provides a limited defense against assault charges for parents who use "force by way of correction ... if the force does not exceed what is reasonable under the circumstances." ...

Psychologists Joan Durrant and Linda Rose-Krasner say in a report, "Although corporal punishment has been used by a majority of Canadian parents, its justifiability is increasingly being called into question as research consistently reveals that it not only lacks effectiveness but that it carries significant risks for children's developmental outcomes." ...

In Sweden and other countries where corporal punishment has been banned, there is a strong emphasis on public education to equip parents with non-violent problem-solving strategies. Such an approach should be adopted in Canada, said Ross Dawson, managing director of the Toronto-based Institute for the Prevention of Child Abuse.

Source: Virginia Gault, *The Globe and Mail*, April 25, 1995, A7 (abridged). Reprinted with permission from *The Globe and Mail*.

punishment (Barnett, Quackenbush & Sinisi, 1996).

Such attitudes are widespread. In one study, parents in waiting rooms at pediatric clinics completed an anonymous questionnaire about their childhood punishment experiences and their current approval of various types of punishment (Buntain-Ricklefs *et al.*, 1994). The findings reveal that 45 percent had experienced certain common punishments (e.g., being shaken by a parent) in their childhood, and 17 percent currently approved of parents doing this. Ninety-four percent had been spanked and 88 percent approved of it. Having experienced a type of punishment in childhood strongly predicts approving of that type of punishment today. Therefore, efforts to identify and educate parents who approve of harsh or dangerous punishments should focus on people who themselves experienced such punishments while growing up.

Skills and Coping Resources

It is sometimes difficult for parents to give their children the love, supervision, and discipline they need. Thus, an important part of the parenting equation is the possession of parenting skills (including good parenting knowledge, attitudes, and practices), coping resources, and social supports. Giving children enough love, supervision, and stability places enormous demands on the parents. Parents—being only human—sometimes run out of the time, money, energy, patience, optimism, creativity, or self-confidence needed to give their children all this good parenting.

Parenting is incredibly hard work. It is full of surprises and (often) dangers. It calls for poise and calm. However, most parents have to do this difficult task while struggling to also be a good employee, a good spouse, a good child, and a good friend, and maybe even to find a moment or two for themselves. It is not surprising that parents, especially those who are stressed, find themselves getting angry more often than people without children (see Figure 5.2). Some people need to find ways of dealing with multiple, sometimes conflicting, demands which include parenting. Good parenting skills are valuable, too. As we have seen, they include knowing how to express your affection openly, supervise your child in a fair and consistent way, and create an atmosphere of emotional safety. Good parents apply appropriate norms and standards; they avoid the use of verbally or physically abusive discipline.

Finally, social supports are important. People who receive emotional and practical support from extended family, friends, or trained professionals parent more effectively than people who receive no support. Outside supports help by lightening the parent's burden. Research shows that women with larger support networks interact more responsively with their infants. They also give their children more stimulating environments than mothers with smaller social networks. Thus, supportive social networks improve

Figure 5.2 **LEVEL OF ANGER FOR WOMEN WITH AND WITHOUT CHILDREN**

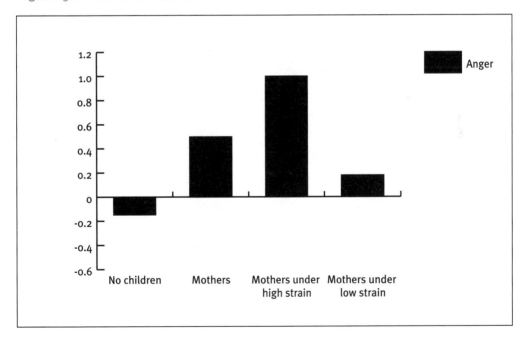

Note: The 0 line represents the mean response to a telephone survey in which people were asked how often they had felt angry or yelled at someone within the last week. "High strain" and "low strain" were defined in terms of economic hardship, difficulty arranging and paying for child care, and responsibility for child care.

Source: Catherine E. Ross and Marieke Van Willigen. 1996. "Gender Parenthood and Anger," *Journal of Marriage and the Family* 58:3. Copyrighted 1996 by the National Council on Family Relations. Reprinted with permission.

maternal caregiving. Informal social support (e.g., friends, aunts) can be as nurturing as formal social support (e.g., psychologists, social workers).

In particular, grandparents are becoming important again as surrogate parents who provide care to their grandchildren and support to their children. Grandparenting in the 1990s has increasingly become second-time-around parenting because of factors that include alcohol and drug abuse, teenage pregnancy, divorce, incarceration, and AIDS (Minkler & Roe, 1996; Minkler & Robinson-Beckley, 1994). Grandparent caregiving, though found in all socioeconomic and ethnic groups, is particularly prevalent in low-income, inner-city areas.

Grandparents are effective because they give their daughters an opportunity to learn from skilled caregivers. As a result, young African-American mothers who live in three-generation households with their own mothers give their children better quality care than other young mothers. Such support also increases the self-reliance and grades of African-American adolescent children and reduces the risk of problem behaviour.

Runaways

Sociologists always have to watch out for personal bias. We have to be certain that the types of parents we have labelled "bad" are not simply bad in our own eyes. One approach is to find out how their children view them and how their children turn out. We have already done this in the foregoing sections. Another approach is to seek information on the reasons why some children reject their families and become runaways. If our foregoing analysis is correct, research will show that runaways include a disproportionate number of children from families that lack love, stability, cohesion, control, fair discipline, and good parenting skills.

A Profusion of Types

However, in sociology nothing is ever as simple as it seems. Research shows that runaways overlap, in experience and background, with a variety of other social types. To their parents, they are merely "missing children." Yet, as Finklehor, Asdigian and Hotaling (1996) point out, the federal government defines four categories of missing children: children missing due to injury in an accident; due to delinquent or rebellious behaviour; due to getting lost; and due to miscommunication among adult care givers. We can debate the merit of this categorization. What is important is the finding that some kinds of families are more likely to lose their children than others. Vulnerability in all these circumstances is associated with certain family characteristics, suggesting that they are not simply accidental occurrences.

For his part, Payne (1995) identifies five different kinds of young people who go missing: runaways, pushaways, throwaways, fallaways, and take-aways. Adams, Gullotta and Clancy (1985) identify three categories of homeless adolescents: runaways, throwaways, and societal rejects. As the names suggest, young people have a variety of reasons for leaving home. Some are distinguished by their lack of bonds with friends and other non-family acquaintances. Others show a lack of assertiveness and poor bonding with their mothers. Others still have positive community bonds, though many lack community bonds entirely (Cherry, 1993).

One recurrent distinction in the literature is between "runaways," who have left home on their own volition and "throwaways," who have been forced to leave (Hier, Korboot & Schweitzer, 1990). True "runners" leave their homes with no intention of returning, and thus they extend their runs. "In and outers" use the run as a temporary coping mechanism. Their runs tend to be impulsive and of short duration. Generally, the greater the distance from home and length of time on the run, the greater the risk of being drawn into illegal activities (Kufeldt & Nimmo, 1987).

A review of runaway behaviour patterns reveals different reasons for running, and changes in reasons with time or living situation. Causes and patterns of running vary historically. Thus, industrialization increased the incidence of running in the nineteenth century. In the early twentieth century, the Great Depression also increased it. In the 1960s, so did the countercultural youth movement (Wells & Sandhu, 1986). Recently, the population of runaway and homeless youth has changed, with youth running away from abuse, neglect, and disintegrated families rather than seeking economic opportunities or excitement.

Despite the variety and diversity of "runaways," note the uniformity of views among people who work with runaway children and other homeless people. They repeatedly assert that runaways are reacting to a family problem. Interpersonal and family relationships influence adolescents' decisions to run away. So do difficulties at school, problems with siblings, and friends whose influence is not in the best interest of the adolescent (Spillane-Grieco, 1984). Most street youth are from families suffering serious emotional, mental, or substance abuse problems. These youth are not necessarily on the street due to socioeconomic pressures (Price, 1989), though family financial difficulties increase the likelihood of physical abuse. (Sexual abuse is different: it is more common in reconstituted families that are financially stable, or in broken families that are financially unstable, according to McCormack, Burgess & Gaccione, 1986.)

The Family Problems of Runaways

Whitbeck, Hoyt, and Ackley (1997) conclude that families of runaways tend, on average, to give their children less support, supervision, and acceptance than other families. Higher levels of youth conduct problems are also present, whether as cause or effect of family rejection. Even parents at times concede they may have been guilty of minor abusive acts, though they are less willing than their children to report more severe forms of abuse. Runaways, however, can occur in families where children have been provided many advantages and suffered no abuse.

Typically, runaways go through a similar sequence of stages. Relations with their parents become problematic. A fight with the parents ignites. Then, the young person runs. Running away could be avoided at any of the three stages. As we have seen, some children return once or even repeatedly (Ek, Steelman & Carr, 1988). Whatever the pattern, running usually poses a problem as well as a solution (Miller, Eggertson-Tacon & Quigg, 1990). Researchers estimate that only one-third of the runaways can return home after receiving social services (Shane, 1989).

In short, most runaways are children escaping dysfunctional families. Abuse aside, the children tend to come from "chaotic/aggressive families" and to reveal a mixed pattern of youth aggression and parental skill deficiency (Teare, Authier & Peterson, 1994). Running away is most often, but not always, a response to neglect, abandonment, and physical or sexual violence (Cote, 1992). Abused runaways are even more likely than those who were not abused to describe their parents in ways that suggest serious antisocial personality and drug problems (Stiffman, 1989a). Evidence also suggests that the parents of runaways themselves had a history of running away from home when they were children (Plass & Hotaling, 1995).

Parents are often portrayed as the villains in these stories. Powers, Eckenrode and Jaklitsch (1990) report that, of New York runaways and homeless youth, 60 percent had suffered physical abuse, 42 percent emotional abuse, 48 percent neglect, and 21 percent sexual abuse. Biological mothers were the most often cited perpetrators of maltreatment (63 percent), followed by biological fathers (45 percent). More than one-third of the homeless youth had been pushed out of their homes by their parents.

A Canadian study concurs. Janus and colleagues (1995) estimate that 74 percent of runaway males and 90 percent of the females had been physically abused at least once. Most of these adolescents have been victims of chronic, extreme abuse, experienced at a young age, often perpetrated by the biological parents (most often the mother) and initiated before the first runaway episode. Once youths left home, the physical abuse experiences decreased in frequency but grew in severity.

People who work with runaways and homeless people generally agree that there is a far higher incidence of physical and sexual abuse among runaways than in the general population of children. Runaway males are much more likely to have been sexually abused than prior research has reported (Rotherham-Borus et al., 1996). Among adolescent runaways interviewed in a Toronto shelter, one in three males and three in four females report having been sexually abused. These abused runaways report more anxiety and suicidal feelings than their non-abused counterparts. Many male victims of sexual abuse report a fear of adult men; female victims report confusion about sex. Another Toronto study of street youth also reports high rates of substance use and abuse, attempted suicide, loneliness and depression among the street youth population (Adlaf, Zdanowicz & Smart, 1996).

Common to runaways studied in Toronto (Janus, Burgess & McCormack, 1987) are problem families, high rates of delinquency, depression, tension, low self-image, and a history of physical abuse. Sexually abused male runaways show extreme withdrawal from all types of interpersonal relationships.

A history of childhood abuse is strongly associated with deviant peer group affiliation for survivors of both sexes, and associated with deviant subsistence strategies (such as prostitution) for males. Deviant peer group affiliation is strongly associated with deviant subsistence strategies for females (e.g., prostitution) but the association is not as clear for males. Frequency of running away is positively associated with deviant behaviour on the streets for both sexes (Whitbeck & Simons, 1990).

As we have already indicated, runaways run a heightened risk of suicide attempts. Thirty percent of runaways report having attempted suicide in the past. Suicide attempters in runaway shelters have many more behavioural and mental health problems, and report having more family members and friends with problems than do other runaways (Stiffman, 1989b). Suicide attempts by runaway youths are most commonly caused by trouble at home, arguments, disappointments, humiliations, trouble at school, assault, and sexual abuse (Rotherham-Borus, 1993).

The once-popular conception of a runaway as an out-of-control escapee from restrictive parents is not realistic. Two main reasons why teenagers run away from home are breakdown of the relationship between parent and child and disruption of the family. Interviews reveal that many runaways leave home because of parental neglect, in search of real or substitute family support (Bernier, Morisette & Roy, 1992).

Accordingly, the main reason that runaways remain on the street, refusing to return home or to try foster care, is their stated belief that family conflict is inevitable. Runaways develop their own surrogate families on the street, largely among other street people, rather than risk further rejection and/or potential further abuse (Holdaway & Ray, 1992). Some runaways who become residents of child welfare institutions opt not to run away. What determines whether they stay or run is the perceived level of emotional warmth or coldness in the institution (Angenent et al., 1991).

Many chronic runaways grow up to be homeless adults. Homeless adults who display higher than average rates of criminal behaviour, substance abuse, and other forms of deviant behaviour tend to come from more abusive and deprived childhoods (Simons & Whitbeck, 1991). A history of foster care, group home placement, and running away is particularly common among homeless adults (Susser *et al.*, 1991).

In short, the evidence from research on runaways supports our contention that good parenting must include love, stability, protection, discipline, and social support for parents and children. Families that fail to provide these—that give abuse in place of protection, or rejection in place of love—produce runaways. Runaways are not glamorous adventurers: they are depressed, troubled young people who would rather brave the streets than stay with their families. They are the product of bad parenting, and they know it.

Variations on a Theme

Well-intentioned, thoughtful parents can do a lot to create good conditions for their children. However, many things that can harm children are beyond the reach of parents to control. Desperate poverty, peer pressure toward delinquent or criminal behaviour, and single parenthood are conditions within which many parents raise their children. A complete discussion of parenting would have to consider the effects of economic, political, and structural variables on the lives of parents, and thus on their ability to care for their children. Workplace stress, unemployment, and racial discrimination, for example, all affect children directly or indirectly. This all makes the task of producing happy, successful children decidedly more difficult.

Parenting also varies from one ethnic group to another, and from one social class to another. Within a given culture and class, parenting varies from one family to another and, within any given family, it even varies from one year to another. Parenting styles vary as time passes. Young newlyweds' ideas of parenting may be different from those of "empty-nest" couples'. Parenting style also varies according to the child that parents are bringing up. A son's experience is likely to be different from a daughter's, and a firstborn (or only) child's experience different from that of a middle or youngest child.

Thus, diversity is normal and natural. Different kinds of parents can do an equally good job of raising their children as long as they provide the basics of "good parenting" that we have already considered. On this theme, consider a few variations: same-sex (gay or lesbian) parents, single parents, adolescent parents, communal parents. Consider, also, the different approaches of parents who belong to various cultural or socioeconomic groupings.

Gay and Lesbian Families

Research finds stereotypical views about homosexuality even among young, highly educated people. They include the beliefs that homosexual parents create a dangerous environment for the child, provide a less secure home, and offer less emotional stability. Such views are more common among older, less educated, rural respondents, among people who are highly religious (particularly fundamentalists of whatever faith), and among people who are generally worried and tense about the state of the world, and specifically, fearful about sex.

Yet, as we discussed in Chapter 1 and Chapter 4, research on same-sex couples does not provide any grounds for these concerns. Contrary to popular belief, gay and lesbian parents often raise fine, healthy families. Research in the United Kingdom, for example, finds that young adults raised by lesbian mothers are happy and well (Golombok & Tasker, 1994; Tasker & Golombok, 1995). Further, there is no more chance of children growing up gay or lesbian in a same-sex family than in a heterosexual family.

Same-sex (especially lesbian) parents may, in fact, be especially proficient in raising children. Research finds that a pattern of more equal sharing of household, child care, and paid work is the norm among lesbian parents (Epstein, 1996; Nelson, 1996). Therefore, the stress level may be lower in a lesbian household than in a heterosexual household. As well, children are more likely to see something like spousal equality. Of course, the very real fact of discrimination against lesbians and gays may affect the children of same-sex families despite the parents' best efforts.

A survey of the quantitative literature (Allen & Burrell, 1996) finds no differences between heterosexual and homosexual parents on any measures of the parenting style or emotional adjustment of the children. Though the children of lesbian families are more likely to accept and explore same-sex relationships, they are no more likely to become lesbians and usually identify themselves as heterosexual. Thus, the data fail to support the fears of some about same-sex parents (Epstein, 1996; Weston, 1991).

Single Parents

Single-parent families have drawn the most criticism, along with same-sex families, often from the same family "traditionalists." For generations, the folk wisdom has linked delinquency to "broken homes" and researchers continue to find an association between the two. Single-parent homes produce a disproportionate share of delinquency and of more serious forms of delinquency, but this is by no means a definitive relationship. There are many highly successful people who have come from single-parent families. Chilton and Markle (1972), however, find more marital disruption in delinquent families than in the general population. This may show that marital disruption contributes to delinquency. However, it could also indicate that families that experience marital disruption also experience other kinds of disruption that may be harmful for the children's well-being, such as poverty, violence, or neglect. Children in single-parent families tend to score lower on tests of intelligence, drop out of school earlier, and have higher rates of delinquency and depression. Likewise, a disproportionate percentage of homeless and runaway youth come from female-headed, single-parent families (Shane, 1991). But it must be kept in mind that, although single parenthood may occur among people of any background, it is most common among the poorest in society, not only in income but also in social resources.

Some argue that it is poverty, not family disruption, that produces more delinquency in single-parent homes. Since single-parent families often live below the poverty line, they experience many of the same problems as other families with low incomes. The presence of only one parent may heighten these problems. But, of course, it could decrease the problems, too, if it means an abusive parent is no longer involved with the child. Economic problems may also force the family to move frequently, causing instability, stress, and insecurity by disrupting the children's routines and their schooling and friends. Frequent moving also cuts off connections with outsiders who could provide help and social support.

The conclusion that economic problems are a large part of the issue is supported by evidence from the Canadian National Longitudinal Study of Children and Youth. These data show that children in low-income single-parent families are much more likely than children in low-income two-parent families to show a variety of emotional, behavioural, and academic problems. However, children in medium- and high-income single-parent families are much less likely to do so, and are only slightly more likely to show these problems than children in same-income two-parent families.

This suggests that the source of the single-parent family consequences for children is both social and economic. The role of the social effects of single parenthood does not completely disappear with economic resources, but the problems are reduced. Laub and Sampson (1988), for example, report that single-parent homes are no more likely to produce delinquents than two-parent homes, once we control for attachment, supervision, and discipline. Likewise, Van Voorhis and colleagues (1988) report that children in single-parent homes are no more prone to delinquency, once we control for the quality of family life. This is also supported by the Canadian Longitudinal Study of Children and Youth, which finds that quality of parenting and types of parental discipline and encouragement are what matter to children's outcomes.

Researchers find that children raised in single-parent homes can become fully successful, competent adults if two compensating factors are present: money and social support. Strong social support, along with unwavering attachment between child and parent, can even overcome the adverse consequences of lack of money. In fact, in some instances, lack of money can be a creative challenge for some children, encouraging resourcefulness. Autobiographies and biographies of many famous people bear this out. However, with only one parent, and perhaps only one income, economic problems today can cause severe difficulties for children. A second adult

A Failure to Teach Girls about Poverty

A week before Christmas, my seven-year-old daughter and three of her little friends convened around our kitchen table to pass an afternoon making cheesy crafts, such as glitter-sprinkled pinecones and candy-cane reindeer. As the girls tested their fine-motor skills gluing googly eyes onto candy canes, my daughter Kathryn asked, from out of nowhere, "So, have you guys given any thought to what you might like to be when you grow up?" (Her words, I swear.)

"Well, a mom of course," answered Lauren, not looking up from her project. The other girls nodded their agreement.

"Well, of course, a mom," sniffed Kathryn. "But I mean, what are you going to do *for your money?*" (Emphasis hers.)

"Well, I won't need money because I'll be married," said Lauren, the daughter of a working mother.

At the pre-Christmas party that followed my daughter's craft party, I lamented to a friend that I remembered having almost an identical conversation with my own girlfriends when I was six. We all believed princess to be a serious career aspiration. Had the women's movement accomplished nothing in the intervening 30 years? Take heart, my friend advised, do the math. In one generation, one little girl's attitudes had been changed. By the time my daughter's daughter sits down to decorate candy canes with her friends, there should be at least two little girls at the table who have given a thought to what they might want to do when they grow up.

Source: Julie Ovenell-Carter. 1996. *The Globe and Mail*, February 26, A18 (abridged).
Reprinted with the permission of Julie Ovenell-Carter.

can provide more income; and perhaps more support.

In short, family interaction and parenting skills are what seem to explain the association between single parenthood and adverse outcomes for children, along with economic circumstances. When we control for the quality of family interaction, the relationship between single-parenting and delinquency disappears. Said another way, children from unhappy homes are just as likely to commit delinquent acts when they live with two parents as when they live with one. The critical factor is the quality of family life.

Other things being equal, however, single-parent families have a harder time than two-parent families maintaining a high quality of life for themselves and their children. For example, the most important factor in recent years in poverty prevention among families, with all its risks for children, is the number of wage earners a family has. A study of adolescents in Rochester, New York (Stern & Smith, 1995) finds that difficulties caused by single-parenting are the result of an interaction between lack of partner support, life distress, social isolation, and shortage of money.

According to one study, single parents may be less strict with their children. Called upon to play two parental roles, they parent less completely or competently, or, at least, so their children believe. For these and other reasons, the children may be less persistent in pursuing their educational ambitions (Bosman, 1994). Children from single-parent, typically mother-headed, families are less inclined to follow rules, on average, at

Even without economic hardship, the children of single-parent families still have more problems than the children of two-parent families.

home and at school. American research (Zinsmeister, 1996) shows that children with a single parent present also receive much less help with school planning and homework than do children in two-parent families. This may be a simple function of lack of time.

Even in families without economic hardship, the children of single-parent families still have more problems than the children of two-parent families. Likely, this is due to a shortage of time and social support. It can also be, in part, the result of societal labelling of the inadequacies of single parents and the stigma to which their children may be subjected. Research suggests that better coping resources are associated with more optimism about the future, fewer financial problems, more confidence in parenting ability, and a more satisfactory relationship with the former spouse (O'Leary *et al.*, 1996). While any given single-parent family may be stable and happy, and some single parents are excellent parents, stresses beyond the parent's control mean that a two-parent family has a greater chance of being stable and happy. That's because there are two people to share the burden. It is also because this type of family receives the support of society more often and more substantially.

Adolescent Mothers

In much of the industrial West, particularly in the United States, there is a heightened concern about adolescent mothers. Generally, women who are young when they deliver a child are more likely to reject the child emotionally, in part because of the heavy burden and the stigma they all too often experience. Others who do not reject the child emotionally have little confidence in their parenting skills, have inappropriate parenting values, and, understandably, have very high levels of stress.

Generally, people who enter parenting unprepared and unexpectedly are likely to find the parenting role stressful and their children difficult. Beyond this, adolescent women often have little understanding of the developmental milestones in their infants' behaviour. They may therefore fail to encourage their own infants' development and may see their children as less competent than other infants, or more troublesome.

Adolescent mothers who are better prepared for parenting, mentally and emotionally, have children who develop better intellectually and show fewer behaviour difficulties. Outside support often helps an adolescent mother to handle the demands her child poses. Researchers (Luster, Perlstadt, & McKinney, 1996) report that adolescent mothers receiving an intensive family support program provide higher-quality care for their infants than mothers who receive less intensive support. A highly successful program in New Brunswick (McIlroy, 1998) does double duty. It provides children born to adolescent mothers a jump start on life with adequate nutrition and exposure to learning opportunities they might not have at home. In addition, while the children are away at nursery school, parents get lessons and examples in how to parent, all offered in a kind and caring way, not punitively as in some jurisdictions.

Multi-Parent Families

If two parents are better than one (generally), are more than two even better? Many children of divorce and separation have three or four, actively involved parents, although they do not all live together. Children can benefit from the additional support and from seeing different parenting styles. Many cultures develop multiple parenting systems where all of the mother's or the father's sisters act as mothers, or all of the mother's or the father's brothers act as fathers.

Alternative family structures and approaches go back to the beginnings of families in history. Experiments with multi-parent families were common in the nineteenth and early twentieth centuries, and again in the 1970s, when some young people lived in communes and shared the work, the resources, and the parenting, sometimes as part of a religious or cult movement. Today, few of these experiments remain.

As another, longer-lived example of multiple parenting, consider the early Israeli **kibbutz**. In these small agricultural communities, families had their own sleeping quarters but ate in a common dining room. Most communities expected, but did not oblige, children to sleep in a common sleeping area. In the early Israeli kibbutzim, communal living was a necessity due to space availability. To adapt to these circumstances, antifamilistic values were encouraged, using mechanisms like the common stove, the disparagement of weddings, the rejection of symbols of family ties, and the acquisition of parental rights by the kibbutz.

The purpose of the kibbutz arrangement was to ensure that all children received similar, high quality care and socialization from specialized kibbutz care givers. It was also to socialize children, from an early age, into a cooperative peer environment, whether for learning, working, or playing. Additionally, the system allowed both mothers and fathers to work full days and serve in the military. In the establishment of the new state of Israel out of the challenges of World War II, these social innovations were seen as necessary.

Much research has been done, over the years, on the results of kibbutz child rearing. Such research, for the most part, has not strongly supported the kibbutz approach. For example, Sagi and colleagues (1994) report that, other things being equal, home-based infants on a kibbutz are nearly twice as likely as the infants in communal sleeping arrangements to be securely attached to their mothers. There is little evidence that communal parenting provides children with better parenting, at least by some standards.

On the other hand, children raised in semi-communal situations are more securely attached to their peers. Because of cooperative learning, kibbutzim children are much more likely than urban Israeli children to cooperate and rely on peers to help them master their environment (Butler & Ruzany, 1993). Perhaps this is a beneficial quality for kibbutzim members to have. It also might be highly marketable in an economy reliant on teamwork.

Kibbutz-reared males are also more likely than urban males to have androgynous attitudes and values (rather than being rigidly masculine), to tolerate cross-sex behaviour, and to display gender egalitarianism (Parker & Parker, 1992). Researchers believe this flexible gender identity development can contribute to identity conflict which, in turn, produces excessively masculine behaviour and military valour. It is argued that this may account for the disproportionately large number of male kibbutz soldiers volunteering for service in high-risk units and being killed or wounded (Snarey & Son, 1986). (Other factors, of course, could play a role as well since in major wars, rural young men are often killed and wounded in disproportionate numbers.)

Where the kibbutzim are concerned, Israelis have "voted with their feet," and the kibbutzim have changed accordingly. In the 1970s, 42 percent of the females and 29 percent of the males left the kibbutzim where they had been born and raised (Nathan et al., 1981). By the 1990s, the kibbutzim are mainly family-centred, with children, though still educated communally, living and sleeping with their parents. Women on the kibbutzim now concentrate in education and social work occupations, in a gender-typed division of labour. They also have shorter working hours, a morning break for visiting children, and special educational duties that deter them from holding more male-dominated jobs. These changes in the organization of kibbutz life, a process of "familism," are not a result of biological imperatives nor do they show a lack of real change in the gendered division of labour. Mainly, they reflect the diminished adherence to egalitarian values in the kibbutz and changes in the structure of the larger Israeli society (Palgi, 1993).

As well, the choice of (traditionally favoured) communal sleeping arrangement over (currently favoured) familial sleeping arrangement reflects a difference in family attitudes and organization. For example, women whose children sleep at home are more active in leisure behaviours, and report having more interesting work. Perhaps because of a fuller schedule, they are less punctual at work (Isralowitz & Palgi, 1993). Or, interpreted another way, men and women with family sleeping arrangements report more tardiness and absence from work and less ability to meet work responsibilities than do parents with communal sleeping arrangements. Yet, despite these adverse effects on work, family sleeping arrangements are becoming more common on Israeli kibbutzim because people believe them to strengthen family ties (Isralowitz & Palgi, 1992).

In Loco Parentis

As children spend more of their time away from family, in schools and other public arenas, public institutions assume more responsibility for parent-

---

Abandoning Ownership: A Philosophical Approach to Adoption

Despite recent changes in family forms, it appears that the concept of ownership of children based on blood ties is still very prevalent. In most alternative family forms in today's society—single-parent, common-law or blended families, for example—children are still biologically connected to at least one parent. A large proportion of adoptive families, on the other hand, are formed without a biological basis. In that sense, adoptive families have been on the leading edge of alternate kinship forms in Western societies. And in so doing, they are in many ways defying the "laws of natural order" as they relate to the Western concept of family. Therefore ... adoptive families can be said to be unconventional. In families that adopt older children, this unconventional status is more pronounced in that they lack a shared history with the child. Being unconventional poses a number of conflicts and stressors for adoptive families. They are confronted with a lack of societal supports and resources for themselves and their children.

Source: Terri Spronk. September, 1992. *Transition*, a publication of the Vanier Institute of the Family. Reprinted with permission.

like protection of children. This is what we mean by the term *in loco parentis*, literally, "in the place of parents." As this has happened, the rights and duties of parents, and parent substitutes (such as guardians and grandparents) have been both clarified and narrowed.

The *in loco parentis* role is an elaboration and specification of the parental relationship. The parent-child relationship is typically asymmetric, due to different power as well as abilities. The caregiver's ultimate goal should be to transform the relationship into one of symmetry, a relationship between equals. Or, as has been the cultural ideal in North America, the parental goal has been to propel the children as adults into a higher status than the parents achieved. And many employer-employee or student-mentor relationships are meant to work the same way. They are based on the belief that if a superordinate enacts a kind of parent-like role with a subordinate, the latter's chances for success are increased. Not everyone, however, is lucky enough to receive this kind of treatment. Since people are more likely to bond with people similar to themselves, and white males fill most superordinate roles, minorities are more likely to fail than non-minorities. This helps explain, in part, the perpetuation of gender and racial or ethnic inequalities (Molseed, 1995).

In particular, schools and colleges have been forced to clarify their *in loco parentis* role in the lives of their students. Historically, the doctrine of *in loco parentis* gave teachers the right to act as parents would when responding to disciplinary problems. The progressive movement of the 1900s opposed the corporal punishment approach of nineteenth-century classrooms, although strapping of children in schools continued well into the middle of the twentieth century in many places in Canada. Because of the progressive movement, teachers knew what not to do (corporal punishment), but not necessarily what should replace it. The management of student behaviour in classrooms continues to be a challenge (Conte, 1994).

An extreme version of *in loco parentis* was the residential schools for aboriginal children, which operated in Canada from the late nineteenth century until the last one was closed in the 1980s. The teachers, often members of religious groups or orders, served as "parents" to the children, who often did not see their own parents for up to 10 months a year. Children were forbidden to speak their own languages, wear their own clothes, or maintain cultural traditions or religions. Harsh punishment was meted out to children reluctant to obey their masters in the schools. Arranged marriages were sometimes worked out by the priests/teachers/school authorities for the children when they grew old enough (Fiske & Johnny, 1996). Essentially, these children were being re-parented and resocialized for assimilation into mainstream society. This "experiment" in cultural domination has long since been declared a disaster—not only for aboriginal families, who lost cultural traditions and often could not learn the skills needed to parent their own children, but for the entirety of Canadian society.

Increasingly, teachers today are rejecting the *in loco parentis* role. Devine (1995) argues that the rejection of this role has contributed to the growing prevalence of urban school violence. But are school teachers really to be held responsible for school violence? Likewise, are university or college administrators responsible for regulating students' behaviour, such as hate speech on campus? Do university administrators owe it to their students to protect them against the emotional distress that hate speech might cause? (Collier *et al.*, 1995). The doctrine of *in loco parentis* originally permitted colleges to act as students' "parents." Colleges did this by enforcing both academic and nonacademic codes of conduct, to protect the safety, morals, and welfare of all students. However, dramatic changes following World War II, and particularly since the late 1960s, resulted in schools losing the authority to discipline students without due process. Recently there has been a trend to reestablish institutional authority, for a variety of reasons. These include student conservatism, an increased incidence of injuries and deaths associated with fraternity hazings, increased bias-related incidents, and concern over alcohol- and drug-related problems. Today, administrators devise new policies, for example, in relation to alcohol possession and consumption, to govern the students' quality of life (Thomas, 1991).

Schools aside, people raise *in loco parentis* issues concerning children living in step-families. What should be the rights and obligations of members of a step-family? For example, should step-parents have a legal authority to act on behalf of their stepchildren? Should they have rights or obligations to their stepchildren following the divorce, death or incapacity/abandonment of the spouse? (Duran-Aydintug & Ihinger-Tallman, 1995). And can we rely on them to provide satisfactory parenting, as though they were parents with all the rights and obligations of biological or adoptive parents? Research in Hamilton, Ontario (Daly & Wilson, 1985) finds that abuse and police apprehension are least likely for children living with both natural parents. Preschoolers living with one natural and one step-parent are 40 times as likely to become child abuse cases than are those living with both natural parents.

Cultural Variation

In many respects, members of the same culture often behave in somewhat similar ways and differ from people of other cultures. Likewise, people of the same social class share certain behaviours which they do not share with people of different classes. So, explaining variations in the family experiences of different individuals is taken a long way by examining variations by culture and class.

A great deal could be said about these cultural and class variations in parenting practice. We will, however, limit ourselves to a few of the themes that are commonly discussed, for several reasons.

First, as important as cultural and class variations in parenting are, they are always changing, indeed, changing more rapidly than ever. Reasons for rapid change include globalization of the economy and global mass media influences, which increase the similarity among different social and cultural groups. Second, it is important to remember that, in a society as mobile and urbanized as Canada's, we are forever coming into contact with people of other cultures and social classes. A central result is the growing variation of parenting attitudes and practices *within* each culture and social class. That is, people *within* cultural or class groups are becoming more different, while the groups as a whole become more similar.

Finally, we have emphasized throughout this chapter—indeed, this book—that processes, not structures, are key to understanding how close relations work. From this standpoint, it is of relatively little importance whether a parent belongs to a culture or class that subscribes to belief X rather than belief Y. What matters is whether that parent, in teaching a child belief X or belief Y, does so lovingly, consistently, fairly, and supportively. In this sense, to use a phrase made famous by Canadian scholar Marshall McLuhan, the medium (or manner of parenting) is the message (or outcome).

In North American culture, one common element is the work ethic, sometimes associated (as by sociologist Max Weber) with the rise of certain Protestant sects in the early days of capitalism. According to Weber, the Protestant work ethic is highly compatible with the capitalist drive for material success. Postponed gratification, ambition, and diligence in wage work are the keys not only to material success in this life, but also to reward in an afterlife. In this scheme, the willfully unemployed have some explaining to do. On the other hand, retired people and full-time homemakers are seen as having contributed—or as contributing in a different but equal way—to society, their own well-being, and their futures in the afterlife. Worst of all are those who have never done any paid work, who may be considered not to have had a full life.

The fact of cultural variation is evident whenever we look at a group which does not come out of the Anglo/Christian tradition—for example, the Chinese. In China, two compelling but sometimes contradictory ideologies face parents. Traditional Confucianism stresses large families and loyalty to family elders. Communism stresses small families and loyalty to the state. Chinese parents now worry whether they have what it takes to raise children or whether they lack needed insight into contemporary childhood experience. Modern Chinese parents are more open to Western ideas about democratic parenting than their parents would have been. Nonetheless, their children report that Chinese parents are still using authoritarian child-rearing techniques.

The difficulties Chinese parents face in making a transition to Western

Child-Rearing Lessons Emerge in the Third World

On a high plateau in Ecuador, a mother and her 4-month-old baby prepare for the day together. She wraps her newborn with more than five kilograms of wool cloth to protect him from the very cold and dry winds that will blow all day. The infant catches his mother's eye and chirps with a lovely smile. Mother bends closer, smiling too, and kisses his cheek. She finishes by wrapping his arms by his sides. He seems unable to move. Yet he looks lovingly up at her. She picks him up, and they bounce together, as they watch the herd of goats. ....

Recent studies show that Ecuadorean infants, cared for in this traditional way, develop into happy, functional children.

In a central African community, a baby, eight weeks old, and her mother have some intimate moments together—just the two of them. Like the Ecuadorean baby, this girl is an expert at catching her mother's eye. Mother and infant gaze at each other tenderly....This girl is being cared for in a way that is traditional for her village. During the first two months of her life, an average of nine people hold, feed and care for her each day.... Often her mother cares for and breast feeds other babies of similar age.

Babies raised in these traditional tribal ways, like the Ecuadorean infants, develop into normal children....

A middle-class mother in Houston holds her daughter of eight weeks who, like other babies, tries to catch her mother's eye. For a moment she does. She stops and grimaces.... Mother continues to look at this baby and hold her carefully. But her expression remains unchanged: neutral, still gazing, but with almost no emotion. This mother loves her wanted baby. But she has felt depressed, "cut off from people" and very fatigued since her baby's birth.

... There is significant likelihood that this baby will develop abnormally....

How can it be that such large differences and apparent inconsistencies and deprivations (by Canadian and U.S. standards) cause no problems while relatively small differences in our cultures result in significant medical and emotional handicaps?

We can only surmise that the answer has to do with intentions. The baby on the cold, windy plateau, and the baby with multiple care givers in the jungle somehow understand that they will be safe....

The baby in Houston may be unable to understand her mother's intentions. Her mother is unable to communicate with gazes and smiles because of her depression. This baby will, after many frustrated attempts to get her mother to interact, give up. She will begin to make abnormal gestures with her hands, and relate with her own body, or an object rather than her mother.

Source: Dr. Charles Schwarzbeck, 1994. *Winnipeg Free Press*, March 15 1994 (abridged), Scripps Howard News Service. Reprinted with permission.

styles of parenting are even more marked outside the People's Republic of China. For example, lower-class Chinese adolescents in Hong Kong report their parents are warm, but overly controlling. In terms of Shucksmith's parenting styles, they would be seen as somewhere between authoritative and authoritarian. As control increases and warmth declines, conflict between parents and children becomes more frequent and intense. Among Chinese immigrants in North America, the **cultural gap** becomes even wider. Chinese mothers place a tremendous emphasis on formal education and ensuring that their child conforms to the family and to the larger society. They are willing to make a big investment of time and energy to get their children educated (e.g., to oversee homework completion and disciplinary matters). In short, Chinese mothers score very highly on what Chao (1994) calls "training ideologies"—a form of parental control that some mistake for authoritarianism.

By contrast, European-American mothers tend to take a child-centred approach. They put more emphasis on developing social (or relational) skills rather than academic skills and on building their children's self-esteem. Unlike Chinese mothers, who directly intervene in their children's schooling, European-American mothers are less directive. They focus on easing educational opportunities where their children have already expressed an interest. For example, they would make it easier for children to study swimming, ballet, hockey, or computers, if that is what their children seem to want to do.

In Japanese families, there is less need than in Chinese families to enforce discipline continuously. This is because the Japanese cultural practice of maintaining bodily closeness with infants creates *amae*, a desire for bodily closeness with family and friends. This desire leads to a need for attachment, social acceptance, and involvement that many have likened to a dependency or addiction. As the child gets older, cuddliness is replaced by coldness and unconditional love is replaced by love that is conditional. Commonly, the condition is success at school and professional achievement. Given Japanese children's fear of rejection and isolation, particularly from their parents, enforcing a high level of discipline and productivity at school is easy. The high degree of interdependency, familism, and communitarianism in Japanese culture makes shaming a more common and effective parenting practice than it is among other groups, for example, African-Americans (see Zhang, 1995).

Consistent with media images, American fathers spend more time, on average, with their children than Japanese fathers. This interaction influences American children's perceptions of their fathers: that is, fathers who spend more time are considered "better fathers." However, this is not so in Japan, where children's views of their fathers are not strongly associated with amount of interaction. In Japanese culture everyone, children included, expects that fathers will spend long hours away from home working or commuting to and from work, or socializing with workmates rather than with family members. Although expected and even sanctioned, this separation of child from father may feel like coldness or rejection, given the intense closeness that characterizes the child's earliest years.

Most cultural variation in parenting is due to differences in cultural preconceptions about infants, children, and adolescents. North Americans view their children as helpless and needing to form a distinct self, so they emphasize the growth of independence and physical mobility. By contrast,

Vietnamese mothers see their children as unique individuals who require strong moral teachings to bind them to the family and to society. The parents of these infants thus take very different approaches to their children, and socialize them in different ways. Differences in early socialization lead to profound differences in a person's later personality. For the most part, for example, North Americans are more independent and feel less connected to their historical, cultural, and familial roots than do Vietnamese.

In a study (Pomerleau *et al.*, 1991) of two cultural groups residing in Montreal, researchers showed that differences in parental beliefs have a profound impact on their subsequent rearing of their children. The study focused on two groups: Québécois and immigrant Vietnamese. Differences in parental beliefs are striking. We often assume that certain things about child rearing are self-evident, and that everyone else interprets behaviours in the same way as we do. One example of this phenomenon is how parents interpret their baby's putting objects in his or her mouth. Québécoise mothers are likely to think that babies put objects in their mouths to explore their world. Vietnamese mothers, instead, consider the child's motive to be hunger or an instinct to suck. This difference in interpretation will lead to major differences in how they respond to a child who exhibits this behaviour. For example, the Québécois may expect children to routinely explore and learn from their surroundings while the Vietnamese parents would see children as searching the environment for what they need.

In the same study, researchers asked the mothers to teach their child several tasks that were impossible for the children to do at their present stage of development. They gave the parents no chance to prepare their children. Parents only had one minute to teach their six-month-old child tasks like banging a toy on the table or playing peek-a-boo. The tasks were intentionally difficult (indeed, impossible) because the researcher's goal was not for the children to accomplish them, but to observe how the mothers tried to teach them.

The cultural beliefs of the mothers strongly influenced the way they attempted to teach their children. Since the Québécoise mothers believe that mouthing objects is important for children, they allowed their children to mouth the object instead of completing the task. They viewed their child's overall development as more important than finishing a set task within an allotted time. The Vietnamese mothers, in contrast, removed the object from the child's mouth and tried to focus the child's attention on finishing the task within the allotted time.

The Québécois emphasis on personal development and the goal orientation of the Vietnamese immigrants will produce widely differing results in the socialization of their children (Pomerleau *et al.*, 1991). When these children reach adulthood, the cultural beliefs which parents employed in raising them will likely colour their approaches to problem solving.

Québécois children will likely feel more free to explore the world and be less concerned about following conventional societal rules than Vietnamese children.

Anglo culture has characterized the permissiveness of traditional Inuit parenting as indulgence and non-control. However, this view of Inuit parenting style is ethnocentric. In fact, Inuit children are controlled by parents, but mostly through the use of inductive rather than power-assertive techniques. They are prepared for their dangerous physical environment and for appropriate behaviour in their culture through example, praise, and withdrawal of approval more than direct order or instruction.

How closely parents feel the need to control children varies. For example, Figure 5.3 shows differences among black, white, and Hispanic parents in the United States in their attitude toward leaving an adolescent home alone.

In many cultures, parents exert a high degree of close control for extended periods. Jewish mothers are legendary, and often stereotyped, for this quality. Often, a high degree of control is associated with the use of shaming, guilt, or love withdrawal as tactics in exercising control. Research verifies that some groups—for example, Greek and Lebanese mothers—use this approach more often than other groups—for example, Vietnamese mothers.

Close parental control of children, especially by mothers, is probably the norm in most societies. There may be many reasons. Sociobiologists might look for an explanation in our genetic makeup or evolutionary heritage. Further research could tell if this line of thinking bears fruit; we believe it is premature to decide on the merits of this approach. In the North American context, for many women who are homemakers throughout their married lives, mothering is their job, their calling, and an opportunity to create something special. Many grew up at a time when careers were not open to married women with children. Many companies in Canada, for example, required women to resign from their jobs on marriage. It is not surprising if full-time mothers take this role extremely seriously. For them, their children are their "products," their life's work. They therefore have a great deal invested in the children and expect them to turn out well and to reflect their mother's work and self-sacrifice.

Members of different cultures enforce parental control differently. Take the adoption of medical discourse by Jewish-American immigrant mothers in the first half of this century. Jewish mothers adopted medicalized mothering practices, an emphasis on healthy eating, sleeping, etc., to control their children and enhance their own images as women of knowledge and modern ideas. This behaviour raised their status; it also produced healthy children and perhaps accounts for an overrepresentation of Jewish doctors today.

Figure 5.3 WILLINGNESS TO LEAVE ADOLESCENT HOME ALONE

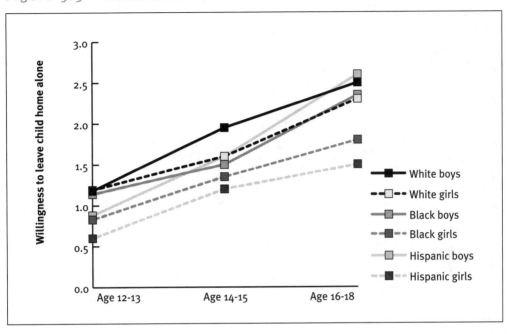

Source: Richard A. Bulcroft, Dianne Cyr Carmody, and Kris Ann Bulcroft. 1996. "Patterns of Independence Giving for Adolescents: Variations by Race, Age, and Gender of Child." *Journal of Marriage and the Family* 58:4.

Using superior or the latest knowledge is an interesting way of exerting parental control. However, many cultures continue to rely on physical punishment. The conditions under which a mother or father may use physical punishment, however, vary with the family's social characteristics. There is evidence that Hispanic parents use controlling, authoritarian, and punitive child-rearing techniques more often than Anglo parents. Defiance, running away, and failing to study are some common reasons these parents (usually the mother) cite for using physical punishment.

People in some cultures readily turn to specific coping resources. For example, African-Americans find kinship networks and church organizations very important in enforcing children's discipline and helping families to survive overall. Recall that research shows that kinship support provided to mothers or female guardians increases maternal well-being and leads to more adequate mothering practices.

Class Variation

Cultural ideologies affect family process, and so does the family's social class. Even within the same cultural group, differences in social class can

Differences in culture and class account for many of the differences in people's family experiences, including how parents perceive their children and how much they attempt to control them.

have a profound impact on the socialization of children. Since children often stay in the same social bracket as their parents, their parents often train them for their prospective areas of work. (For general discussions of this theme, see Lillian Rubin's *Worlds of Pain* (New York: Basic Books, 1969) and Mirra Komarovsky's *Blue-Collar Marriage* (New Haven: Yale University Press, 1987).)

In North America, parents holding blue-collar jobs tend to stress obedience and respect for authority and are more inclined to use physical punishment. Though class differences may be narrowing, blue-collar parents are more likely to discipline according to the character of their child's misbehaviour. Parents holding white-collar jobs, by contrast, stress self-motivation and independence. They are also more likely to use reason or verbal threats to force the child to comply with household rules.

Many poor parents do not have enough time for their children, and are too stressed to spend quality time with them when they are home. Time shortage, of course, is a problem not limited to the poor. However, it may be more common among the poor, who are struggling to make ends meet, perhaps working longer hours or at multiple jobs. High-powered professionals are often guilty of spending too little time with their children. However, they can decide to cut back their hours, or take time off to spend with their families. When parents are holding down three jobs just to feed their children and to make monthly bill payments, they often cannot even take a day off to care for a sick child without having their pay reduced or possibly their jobs imperilled. Poverty has a great effect, not only on parenting styles, but on the family as a whole.

Economic pressures can have many harmful effects on families, including parental depression, hostility, marital conflict, and conflict between parents and adolescents over money and what to spend it on. Hostile and coercive exchanges between parents and adolescents, in turn, can lead to adolescent emotional and behavioural problems.

Furthermore, children growing up in poverty are more likely to spend time by themselves or with their friends—in either case, unsupervised—while their parents are out working or socializing. They may feel neglected as a result, and are therefore more likely to become delinquent. Children who grow up in poverty are also more likely to associate with others who are engaged in delinquent behaviour, and they may fall into it via peer pressure. This, however, does not imply that poor children are all delinquent or that only poor children fall into delinquency.

Social and economic change have produced a rash of difficult life conditions, cultural beliefs, and social conditions, such as poverty and discrimination against minority groups. These all hinder family life and parenting.

Historically, the more unequal a nation and the poorer the social class or individual family, the more it displays violent behaviour. The United States and South Africa, although having high standards of living, also have the highest crime rates in the developed world. Both have more inequalities in their societies than other industrialized countries. Thus, it is speculated that the rise in youthful violence may be an effect of an increase in economic inequality since 1979. Nevertheless, in truth, we really don't know all the dynamics of these complex relations.

Concluding Remarks

Families are complex and important. How well families raise their children affects what kind of world we will live in, and what kind of adults those children will become. How well parents have managed to strike a balance between discipline and freedom will affect how the children act and feel when they become teenagers. In North America, teenagers who see their parents as accepting and warm, and as less controlling, have higher self-esteem than other children. In turn, parents with higher self-esteem are more likely to give their children freedom and acceptance, and to have better communication with the children as a result.

As we have seen and will explore in greater detail in Chapter 8, people

Trust Not Hurt by Child Care, Study Finds

[A] new study was designed to try to answer one of the most emotionally charged issues in society today: Does a mother put her child at risk by working outside the home? ...

It reported that the sense of trust 15-month-old children feel in their mothers was not affected by whether or not the children were in day care, by how many hours they spent there, by the age they entered day care, by the quality or type of care or by how many times care arrangements were changed.

Instead, what affected that trust was a mother's sensitivity and responsiveness to her child.

"Part of what elicited this study was real worries that child care in and of itself was unhealthy," said Dr. Deborah Lowe Vandell, one of the 25 researchers on the project, which was sponsored by the National Institute of Child Health and Human Development, part of the National Institutes of Health.

"I think that is the wrong analysis. One message from the study is that if the quality of the interaction with the mother is sensitive, then the child is likely to develop a secure relationship with her. I'm sure that will be reassuring to many mothers and families."

But the U.S. researchers cautioned that the study found some aspects of child care appeared to pose risks for certain vulnerable children. When a mother does not handle her child sensitively, the likelihood of a troubled mother-child bond can be increased by child care that is of poor quality, changes several times or extends more than 10 hours a week....

exposed to family violence as children are more likely than others to end up abusing their own spouses and children. Childhood experiences resonate through adult life. Similarly, children whom parents have punished physically are more likely to grow up to be aggressive toward other family members. A particularly explosive recipe is infrequent reasoning and frequent spanking. Treating children this way dramatically increases their potential for violence as teenagers.

Nevertheless, not all family difficulties (or lucky breaks, for that matter) are the result of parental influences and choices. Many important forces are not under parental control. Sometimes factors beyond the parents' control, such as the sickness of a family member or a sudden change in socioeconomic circumstances, interrupt the socialization process. We are only starting to understand the full effects of disrupted development and the problems that are likely to emerge later. Also, bear in mind that not only do parents socialize their children, but the children socialize their parents too. Children's influence over their parents is more powerful under some conditions than others. For example, a parent who feels guilty about neglecting the child or about divorcing a spouse, or who feels unloved or otherwise emotionally insecure and therefore depends on the child for important gifts of affection and attention, may change parenting styles to get the desired effect.

As we have seen in this chapter, parenting makes a tremendous difference to the ways that children grow up. Good parenting translates into good child and adult outcomes. Bad parenting produces the opposite. But parenting is not the full story either.

A recent book by Judith Rich Harris, *The Nurture Assumption: Why Children Turn Out the Way They Do* (1998), has caused a stir by suggesting that, contrary to the conventional wisdom of psychologists and sociologists, parents don't really count for much in the socialization of children. Harris defends this claim with a variety of evidence showing the importance of genes and of peers. Genes, we are learning, have a great impact on people's basic personality traits, from the moment of birth onward. Peers, and to a lesser degree schools and the mass media, also play a large role in shaping people's attitudes and behaviours. By implication, little is left for the parents to influence.

The social science establishment has answered that, although genes, peers, schools, the media, and other influences do play a central part in shaping a child, parents play a critical role. Harris is failing to assess this role correctly because, they say, the parental influence works far below the surface level of behaviours, attitudes, values, and personality traits. It works on such basic dimensions as whether a person is able to trust or identify with other people. Moreover, the role of peers and other nonparental socializers is culturally specific; its importance varies over time and from one culture to another. The role of parents is significant, indeed critical, in every culture.

Parenting varies from one culture to another, because cultures vary in the ways they conceive of "good" and "bad" parenting. Yet, whatever the culture, good parenting demands resources. In our own society, people have unequal chances to be good parents, because they have unequal chances for a good income, good daycare, and good social supports. Most of these inequalities are socially structured, in the sense that they are a result of the way we distribute scarce resources in our society. Therefore, we can remedy most of these inequalities through social change, especially legislation to improve the social safety net for poor people, single mothers, and wives and children in abusive families.

In the next chapter, we further explore a topic mentioned in this chapter and one with much significance for both parent-child relations and the functioning of the family as a whole: namely, the domestic division of labour.

CHAPTER SUMMARY

This chapter explores factors affecting the development of children, focusing on parental influences. We begin by discussing what characterizes successful parenting practices. To sum up our findings, parents who are attached, loving, and emotionally stable produce children who can thrive in society. A lack of these qualities contributes to delinquency, depression, and school failure.

We discuss how parents navigate the difficulties associated with control and discipline of their children. Parenting styles discussed include authoritative, authoritarian, permissive, and unengaged; authoritative parenting (combining control with acceptance) tends to produce the best outcomes. Discipline styles include power assertion, love withdrawal, and reasoning. Physical punishment, despite its prevalence in society, is surprisingly ineffective and can do lasting harm.

To illustrate, we discuss runaways, who are generally escaping a bad home situation; a large proportion of these troubled youngsters were physically abused.

Our discussion then focuses on family diversity. Whether parents are gay or lesbian, single, or multiple, the most important factor is the quality of family interactions. We end with a discussion of how cultural, class, and financial variations—all external or societal factors—affect parenting processes. Though social institutions cannot make successful parenting a certainty, or even easy, they can make successful parenting more difficult. A society with an interest in healthy children needs to invest more resources, both financial and social, in its parenting and its parents.

KEY TERMS

Amae: In Japanese culture, a desire for bodily closeness with family and friends developed by frequent and intense bodily contact between parents and infants.

Attachment: A state of intense emotional dependence on someone (especially a parent); a social bond involving affection and a feeling of belonging.

Authoritarian parenting: A style of parenting characterized by low acceptance (i.e., little liking and respect is shown for children) and high control.

Authoritative parenting: A style of parenting characterized by high acceptance (i.e., liking and respect for children) and high control.

Control and supervision: The extent to which parents monitor and influence their children's behaviour.

Cultural gap: Conflict between parents and children based on differing expectations that occur either in a rapidly changing culture or among immigrants.

Culture: The language, perspective, and skills, the likes and dislikes, and the cluster of norms, values, and beliefs that characterize a group of people.

Discipline: The enforcement of rules to control children's behaviour (not necessarily through punishment).

Family cohesion: Sticking together as a family, with its own group identity, social life, and activities that involve the members.

Gender socialization: The part of the socialization process through which people learn gender-based habits of behaviour, as they learn to associate gender with their personal identity and with distinctive activities.

Identity support: Parents' respect, acceptance, and emotional support for a child.

In loco parentis : Literally, "in the place of parents"; refers to the assumption of parent-like responsibility by public institutions, such as schools, or by individuals such as step-parents, grandparents, or other caregivers.

Induction: A type of discipline based on teaching good behaviour by example and rewarding imitation.

Instrumental communication: The frequency with which an adolescent talks to his/her parents about problems, plans, etc.

Internal moral control: Control of one's own behaviour because of a feeling of right and wrong, rather than to avoid punishment.

Kibbutz: A quasi-communal, usually agricultural community in Israel; in early kibbutzim children were largely raised communally in a vast social experiment at replacing the family with the community as the chief socializing influence.

Latchkey youth: Children who are home alone two or more days per week.

Looking-glass self: A self-concept constructed from the way we appear to others, which is then reflected back to us.

Love withdrawal: A type of discipline based on threatened emotional punishment (withholding parental affection) for

a child who does not comply with rules.

Parental involvement: Emotional and practical commitment of parents to children, shown by spending time with them, talking with them, and thinking and talking about them.

Permissive parenting: A style of parenting characterized by high acceptance (i.e., liking and respect for children) and low control.

Power assertion: A type of discipline based on threatening to punish a child for noncompliance with rules.

Primary socialization: Learning that takes place in the early years of a person's life.

Socialization: The social learning process a person goes through to become a capable, functioning member of society.

Thomas Dictum: The observation that a situation that is believed to be real is real in its consequences.

Unengaged parenting: A style of parenting characterized by low acceptance (i.e., little liking and respect is shown for children) and little control.

SUGGESTED READINGS

Blankenhorn, David. 1995. *Fatherless America: Confronting Our Most Urgent Social Problem*. New York: Basic Books. Using secondary sources, this book examines the causes and consequences of fatherless households. In many cases, social problems, such as poverty and violence, are ultimately due to fatherlessness. Without drastic action now, the future world will divide into two groups: the socially/economically advantaged and the disadvantaged.

Dickerson, Bette. J. (Ed.) 1995. *African-American Single Mothers: Understanding Their Lives and Families*. Thousand Oaks, CA: Sage Publications. A collection of 10 essays by sociologists, psychologists, and others who

study family relations. As the title suggests, the essays focus on how black families differ from white families, and single-parent families from two-parent families.

Lykken, David T. 1995. *The AntiSocial Personalities*. Lawrence Erlbaum Associates. The author argues that a common set of characteristics distinguishes the most criminal element from the rest of society. Along with biochemical and psychological factors, a dysfunctional family environment in childhood is key. Most violent crime, he says, stems from sociopathic behaviour— a result of inadequate or inappropriate socialization, in turn the result of poor parenting and family instability.

Marsiglio, William (Ed.) 1995. *Fatherhood: Contemporary Theory, Research and Social Policy.* Thousand Oaks, CA: Sage Publications. This volume of 13 chapters, written by sociologists and professionals in family social work, includes empirical and theoretical research on fathers. It focuses on legal, economic, and policy questions, in addition to father-child interactions, family life in the inner city, and single-parent custody.

Ribbens, Jane. 1994. *Mothers and Their Children: A Feminist Sociology of Childrearing.* London: Sage Publication. Based on interviews with 24 young mothers, this book focuses on mothers' own understandings of their parenting practices and reveals how differences are rooted in fundamental ideas about social life and the place of the family within it. Despite social gains outside the home, women still give priority to child rearing. The position of fathers in relation to children's care has become increasingly anomalous, with trends to shared parenting (on the one hand) and absent fathers (on the other).

Spiro, Melford E. *Gender and Culture: Kibbutz Women Revisited,* 2nd ed. 1996. New Brunswick, NJ: Transaction Publishers. A revised and augmented study of an Israeli kibbutz first studied in 1951, then studied again in 1975, with a report on radical changes over the last twenty years in gender relations, the character of marriage, the structure of the family, patterns of child rearing, and the sexual division of labour.

REVIEW QUESTIONS

1. What do family dinners signify?

2. List some factors that lead to emotional instability in a child.

3. Name and describe the three types of disciplining techniques.

4. How does divorce disrupt parenting ability?

5. What determines the effect of work on parenting in a dual-earner family?

6. What factors do the Chinese, Euro-American, and Vietnamese cultures emphasize in their parenting practices?

7. Compare the control techniques most commonly used by Jewish parents and Hispanic parents.

8. How does the typical parenting style of working-class people differ from that of upper-middle-class people?

9. Name three factors that explain why children run away from home.

10. What is the most common source of informal social support for parents?

DISCUSSION QUESTIONS

1. "The government should test people to find out their ability to be good parents; only those scoring above 75 percent should be allowed to reproduce." Do you agree or disagree? Why?

2. Is the use of a mild form of physical punishment (like spanking) necessary in parenting? Why or why not?

3. Can same-sex couples provide the same quality of parenting as heterosexual couples? Explain your answer.

4. What was the purpose of comparing the Québécois and immigrant Vietnamese parenting styles?

5. Which explanation for the cause of

delinquency in a two-parent household is most convincing? Why?

6. "Power assertion and love withdrawal are two disciplining techniques that fail to create internalized moral standards." Do you agree with this statement? Why or why not?

7. How and why does a mother's engagement in paid work outside the home affect healthy child development? What are some of the issues surrounding "substitute" care?

8. Why are some parents particularly likely to use physical punishment?

9. "It is good that working-class parents stress obedience and respect for authority as opposed to self-motivation and independence since that is what their children will need to be prepared for a blue-collar job." Comment.

10. To what degree can problems such as poverty and discrimination be held responsible for an upsurge in youth violence?

WEBLINKS

http://www.cfc-efc.ca/vif/index.htm

Vanier Institute of the Family

This section contains great information on parenting; it also contains a search engine.

http://panopticon.csustan.edu/syllabi/lerno.htm

Explores the question of whether or not homosexual couples should be allowed to parent.

http://www.todaysparent.com

Today's Parent

Contains all sorts of information on parenting and the problems faced today by parents.

http://www.calib.com/naic/factsheets/gay.htm

Interesting information on working with gay and lesbian adoptive parents.

http://www.positiveparenting.com/696news.html

Advice on positive parenting.

http://m2.medialinx.ca:1245/healthyway/DIRECTORY/B9-C15.html

A good source of general information on parenting.

http://www.tnpc.com/

Includes a search engine for articles on parenting-related topics.

CHAPTER SIX

The Domestic Division of Labour:

Gender and Housework

Families do not just happen, as we have seen in previous chapters; nor do they maintain themselves well without tending. Families require considerable efforts to stay well, to thrive in the world, to get along, to learn and to enjoy life. Housework is the not entirely appropriate term that is used to describe all the various kinds of work needed to keep families going. **Family work** may be a better term. It includes far more than the menial chores that might come to mind when we think of housework. A major component of housework or domestic labour in the 1990s is coordinating family activities and family with paid work. Another major component is child care and child rearing.

Before you turn to (or away from) this chapter with the yawns that often greet the mention of housework, think of this: It may be issues related to family work that most often determine whether close relations will thrive or perish. Dividing the work in the home may be the next big frontier of equality between men and women. And it may be that without serious attention to division of domestic work, intimacy and interpersonal closeness in relationships suffer. In this chapter, we will look at how we tend to see domestic work and why it is both so invisible and so vital to our close relations. We consider myths and realities of who did what on the home fronts of the past, and just what the introduction of labour-saving devices into homes did to domestic work.

Lately, governments have become interested in measuring the worth of unpaid work; we look at why and how and what they come up with. The double days of paid and unpaid work have changed the lives of many women; we consider recent evidence. Child care is the big component of domestic work and the big challenge for families where both mother and father work outside the home. Mr. Mom, although a popular image, is alive and well mainly in Hollywood. Conflicts over housework are determinants of marital relations and sometimes whether marriages last, or last happily. The effects of family work on paid work and the effects of paid work on domestic work are considered, as are challenges to domestic arrangements over the life cycle. Homemakers who are displaced by divorce or death lose not only their close relations but their occupation; what does this fact mean to the lives of women and men and should society do anything about it?

Two new challenges on the family work front are the importation of housewives (nannies, domestic workers) to meet the demand for work on the home front while North American women go out to work, and the growing needs of elderly relatives for care. We shall look at these and what they mean for us and for policy.

How We See Domestic Work

John Lennon is reported to have remarked during his caring-for-Sean-while-Yoko-worked phase that it was tough being a stay-at-home Dad. He said that every day he baked bread and everyone ate it all up and asked for more, and he never even got any royalties!

Domestic work has a way of being or becoming invisible. Baked bread gets eaten; clean floors, dishes, and clothes get dirty again; taking a child to hockey practice or ballet once is not often enough; and family members' hurts and problems occur over and over again and need to be tended and mended. To make it all more complicated, this work occurs in a private sphere, inside homes, without any accounts or public scrutiny. How, then, are we to see domestic labour? How is it to be made visible to us?

Just how invisible housework is was made clear to one of the authors (McDaniel) when, as a graduate student, she shared a bathroom in a rooming house with a young man down the hall. When approached about how the work of cleaning the shared bathroom would be shared, the young man (of about 22) looked distressed. He replied sharply that he did not understand why the question would be posed. He had never seen a bathroom, he emphatically stated, that had ever needed cleaning! The young man had moved from his parents' home, where his mother had (unbeknownst to him, apparently) regularly cleaned the bathroom. The labour of cleaning the shared bathroom was not divided, but the times between cleaning were extended a little to let the young man see that bathrooms indeed do need cleaning! In another true story, a woman asked her new husband to clean the bathroom. He vacuumed it and looked puzzled when she suggested that it wasn't cleaned yet!

There may be no sphere of close relations in which change is so pronounced as it has been in expectations about the domestic division of labour. Essentially, the traditional bargain struck between men and women—financial support by the man in exchange for domestic services by the woman—is no longer the bargain. This means that both men and women enter marriage with high expectations of personal communication, intimacy, romance, sexual gratification, and financial security that they will both provide. The modern or postmodern bargain struck by men and women includes images of having children, but seldom does it ever include any (or much) discussion about division of household work. Most young couples seem to enter marriage in the hope that housework will do itself. With more women in the paid workforce, they have less time and inclination to do all the household work as well. With the demise of the presumptions of the past (at least on the part of some women) about domestic division of labour, housework and who will do what becomes a big problem, bigger than almost anything else the couple might face, except for money troubles or questions of marital fidelity.

Domesticity and caring are commonly viewed as women's attributes. They are seen as so closely allied with womanhood that they may even be part of the definition of femininity. A good woman is a caring, family-oriented woman who puts the needs of others ahead of her own. A woman who is not domestic, not interested in families or motherhood or caring for a home, is seen by many as selfish, as unfeminine. Marge Reitsma-Street (1991), in a study of delinquent teenage girls, shows the extent to which these ideas are embedded in society and in us as individuals. She describes how the law and the courts work to make delinquent girls into non-delinquent (good) girls. Girls are "policed to care." For women, learning to be a proper, acceptable woman means learning to be domestic and caring. Girls and women, according to Reitsma-Street, are routinely asked to bear the costs of caring for others ahead of themselves, willingly, and with feminine grace and forbearance.

Just Who Did What in the Past?

Housework and child rearing, contrary to popular beliefs, have not always been women's responsibility. Men took a more active role than women in caring for and raising children in pre-industrial and early industrial times. Children were not seen the way they are today, as being in need of long and careful tending and nurturing. The older concept of child rearing was that children should be toughened up for the real world of earning a living to help the family, a task to which they were often put when they were barely old enough to walk and talk. Children at age six were often working on farms and ranches, in the early factories and mines, and selling newspapers, picking rags or shining shoes on the streets of towns and cities.

Our images of life on the home front before industrialization are romanticized. Typically, we picture young women by their spinning wheels before a bubbling pot of stew on the open hearth, or mothers tending lovingly to their children while they toiled in sumptuous kitchen gardens or fields. Men are thought to have been occupied as craftspeople, hunters, or farmers. Division of labour is imagined to be clear, sharp, agreed upon and happy, but incontestable. However, the realities of domestic divisions of labour in pre-industrial times were much more complex. In fact, after industrialization women lost market ties and the independence that permits.

Men's and women's work were largely separate in pre-industrial times, and the female sphere was more often confined to the domestic arena, more broadly defined than it is now to include farm animals, some manufacturing, social services to others in the community, and so on (Cross & Szostak, 1995). Men also had domestic responsibilities such as farm work, child discipline, and some provisioning of the larder. It was in many ways a partnership of women and men. The division of who did what was crossed by both women and men. This was a function of necessity. Because resources were limited, both men and women had to work to be able to clothe and feed themselves and their children.

In North America the pre-industrial division of labour was coloured by contact with the new land and its long-time aboriginal inhabitants. Among many First Nations people, women were more often in positions of power than they tended to be in Victorian society. These differences made settlers question the traditional sharp division of labour they had brought with them from Europe.

Early settlers may have preferred a more strict division of labour at home than they, in fact, experienced. Land was sometimes owned and worked by unmarried women, for example, a practice unheard of in the "old country" of England and most of Europe. The motivation was less an interest in gender equality than in increasing the output of agriculture lands. The ongoing demands of provisioning required children, elders, and women to participate in work. Because men often had to leave homesteads, farms, and early crafts shops to work at other jobs or to obtain supplies, women ran many domestically based businesses. The high mortality rate, particularly of men, meant that married women could anticipate being left as widows, usually with dependent children still at home. This gave some women considerable power and autonomy in both their families' enterprises and in the wider society.

"The notion of 'home, sweet home' as a place of family togetherness, comfort and refuge from the world of business and work was largely an invention of the industrial era" (Cross & Szostak, 1995:41). Pre-industrial homes involved a lot of work—hard work. Although much of what women did in pre-industrial times was domestic, it involved direct production. Such activities as spinning yarn, making butter, keeping chickens and collecting eggs, making jams, baking, and sewing were the means by which women and their families entered market activity.

The pre-industrial family was a production site, as well as, to a lesser degree, a consumption site, with women essential and central to early market production. Women were also the earliest tradespeople in providing essential utilities such as heat and light, by stoking hearths and keeping a constant supply of cut wood, and by making candles. And they worked on farms, caring for cows, carting water from streams, planting, picking, cutting, and harvesting. As the first medical and nursing practitioners, they delivered babies, helped care for the sick, and cared for the disabled or chronically ill. Industrialization had the consequence of *reducing* women's involvements in the market economy and transforming women into dependent housewives with their home-based work confined to the domestic realm.

Women's loss of access to market activity undermined the previous partnership between men and women in marriage. As the domestic division of labour sharpened and widened, husbands and wives were no longer economic partners and co-workers. One consequence is that women became more vulnerable to desertion by their husbands. There was less economic incentive to stick together and men often left to look for work in the new industrial economy. Women, left alone with children to care for, resorted to age-old reliance on small-scale agricultural production, something they knew and understood, and for many, their only economic option.

The trouble was that they did this in the rapidly growing cities of Montreal, Toronto, and Hamilton. Keeping pigs, cows, and chickens in city yards proved perplexing to authorities (Bradbury, 1984). **"Sanitary reformers,"** in the interest of health, began to work on bylaws prohibiting the keeping of farm animals in cities. Campaigns with such evocative names as "Death to the Pigs" (Bradbury, 1984:14) began. It was poor women's pigs (and cows and chickens) that were first outlawed. Bradbury reveals that one-quarter of the pigs kept in Montreal in 1861 were in one particularly poor ward, among cramped houses and factories where the pigs roamed alleyways and streets. No doubt the banning of farm animals from cities did improve hygiene, but it further limited the means by which women on their own could access market activity and have some degree of autonomy. Later the same restrictions to women's market activities occurred with zoning bylaws that prohibited non-family homes in some neighbourhoods, preventing separated, divorced, and widowed women from taking in boarders.

Labour-Saving Devices and Household Work

Legend has it that in the past, work in the home was tough and demanding. Now, with so-called labour-saving devices and "farming out" of tasks to the marketplace and to social institutions such as schools and hospitals, life on the home front is supposedly easier. However, this is not entirely the case.

It did, indeed, take more time and energy to survive in pre-industrial households. Many tasks such as candle making, bread making, and butter making that were previously done at home or on the farm have long since been taken over by the marketplace. However, in the past, this work was only partly domestic—that is, it was only partly for the family's consumption. It was also done as a market activity, as we have seen. What must be recognized when we talk about the market taking over domestic work is that there has also been a domestication or privatization of market work.

One example is food preparation in the home, which in pre-industrial times often involved a market component and now seldom does. The overall consequence is that domestic work may take less time, but the rewards and autonomy associated with it for women have lessened as well, and the standards have increased dramatically (see Schwartz Cowan, 1992).

Vacuum cleaners, for example, brought the possibility of cleaning a house more readily than by sweeping or taking heavy area rugs out to the yard to be beaten with brooms or paddles. Yet, expectations about cleanliness also increased with the capacities of a vacuum (or a Hoover, as the early vacuums were generically called) to suck up every bit of dust and dirt. Similarly, refrigerators replaced wells, cold storage areas, and iceboxes (which were kept cool by blocks of ice—brought by an iceman in towns and cities, or taken from lakes and creeks in the countryside). Fridges saved the worry and the trouble of food storage in homes but created the necessity to shop longer and with greater care because meals were expected to be more complex and elegant than they had been.

The availability of "labour-saving devices" increased time spent in shopping as the new devices had to be purchased, along with their accoutrements. Homes quickly shifted from small-scale production units into showplaces of consumer goods. Women's roles in the domestic division of labour were reshaped from producers of goods to sell on the market, to consumers of goods to make houses and living spaces "homey." This shift sharpened the domestic division of labour by gender. Cross and Szostak (1995:50) put it well:

> The unity of market work and domestic/family work was eventually sundered. With that separation came what we today call the 'traditional housewife' in her 'separate sphere' outside the workforce who was almost totally dependent on her husband's income.... The machine took a long time to empty the home of wealth-creating work and to make it a center of mass-produced consumer goods.

So-called labour saving machines in homes largely "saved" women from market labour and made their work fully domestic. This, no doubt, had time-saving effects, at the cost of women's connections to market work and its rewards. Women were expected to make their homes nice and attractive out of love rather than any interest in market rewards. The fusing of love with domestic consumerism and household duties for women changed forever the relations between the sexes on the domestic front.

Campaigns to promote the new household technologies recognized the love component of housework in working against the fear that women might abandon their domestic work with the **"mechanization" of housework** (Fox, 1993:151). Home economists worked to elevate the esteem of homemakers by promoting the idea that the new home technologies required skilled operators. Health came to be associated with extreme standards of cleanliness. Homemakers then were charged with technical work and health promotion, noble causes indeed but unpaid and immensely undervalued. The scientization of housework was complete, and women were cast into the role of maintaining the home as their central life work, with limited access through their homemaking skills to the markets they had enjoyed prior to industrialization.

The Worth of Housework

Housework and child care are too valuable to be paid for. This is one popularized view of the value of housework. Another is that housework and child care are drudgery, avoided by those in society who have the power to say they would prefer not to do drudgery, that is, mostly men (Wilson, 1996:68). Both approaches have been used by sociologists, but the latter is most frequent when housework is studied at all by sociology. Housework is almost as invisible in sociology as it is in life! When British sociologist Ann Oakley (1974) was launching her pioneering study of housework, she met with puzzlement from more established sociologists who could not understand why housework would be of interest to sociology. Some may still be puzzled today.

Shifting attitudes toward housework have resulted in serious attempts to measure the economic value of housework in market terms. In these efforts, Canada has been a world leader (see Statistics Canada, 1995). Some trace the work on measuring the worth of housework to a 1988 book by Marilyn Waring of New Zealand, *If Women Counted: A New Feminist Economics*, which argues that housework is real work and ought to be considered as part of a country's gross national product. Statistics Canada (1995:2) agrees that unpaid work at home matters and suggests that putting a value on it can "... foster a greater understanding of the economy and of the links between its market and non-market sectors." A Statistics Canada report (1995:3) credits Waring for the rekindled debate on including unpaid work, of which housework is a part, in estimates of economic productivity.

Attempting to assess the worth of housework is not a 1990s concept. It has a long history going back, surprisingly, to Adam Smith. By the middle of this century, it was generally agreed that it may be misleading or inappropriate to exclude domestic work from the economy, but it was thought impractical to try to measure its contribution (Statistics Canada, 1995:3). Some argued, in contrast, that housework could be measured but still should not be included as a market exchange since the work done by women at home ought to be freely provided. To make this point clearer, it was suggested that confusion could arise, since if a man married his housekeeper or his cook, the national dividend would be diminished!

When the calculations are done, housework in Canada is estimated to be valued at approximately $319 billion a year (Statistics Canada, 1995). This is about 30–46 percent of the gross domestic product (GDP) of Canada, an enormous portion of the economy. By contrast, Statistics Canada estimates that the so-called "informal economy," about which much is said but less is actually known, accounts for only 2.5 percent of the GDP.

What would happen if all housework became paid work? What would happen if all housework ceased tomorrow, and we all had to purchase housework services in the marketplace? The economic consequences of both scenarios are impressive, revealing that housework indeed counts, and counts a lot. Housework might someday be added to computations of gross national product. At present, however, too many challenges remain in estimating its economic worth and making official records historically compatible.

Paying Homemakers?

One way to show that housework is valued would be to pay homemakers a salary. The idea that domestic work deserves to be paid is not a 1970s notion, although it is sometimes portrayed that way. This idea has been around for over a century. Payment for housework would, it is argued, acknowledge that society values all the work done in families—overwhelmingly by women—in raising children, providing healthy home environments, and offering emotional support.

In a small way, **family allowances**, begun in Canada after World War II, were a way to give women compensation as well as recognition for child rearing. The monthly payments, based on the number of children at home, went to all women with children—but only to women, never to men. For many women who worked solely at home, this was their only independent income. Quebec alone now continues with some form of family allowances (LeBourdais & Marcil-Gratton, 1995). The federal program of family allowances was discontinued in 1992, replaced by the Child Tax Credit program, which targets low- and middle-income families. The Quebec program of baby bonuses is intended both to increase the numbers of births and to provide support for women raising children. The amounts paid in no way compensate for the costs involved in raising a child (discussed in Chapter 4).

Many have argued that paying for housework would not be in women's interests since it would do nothing to change the existing division of labour. Women would continue to do most of the housework, but it would be paid work instead of unpaid. Eichler (1988:250), however, suggests that if we could separate out the socially useful work from that which is privately useful, paying for the former might enhance women's status. She then argues that developing labour force re-entry programs for homemakers and displaced homemakers could aid in compensating women for the domestic work they do for the good of society. The debate is not yet over, although Eichler's recommendations as well as others (Armstrong & Armstrong, 1994) hint that it is taking new and different forms as the end of this century nears.

Unpaid Work Comes of Age

Unpaid work has been officially acknowledged recently in Canada in an important way—by being included for the first time in the Census of Canada.

The story of how this came to be is an important one that bears sharing here. On the 1991 Census of Canada (censuses in Canada are done every five years—in years ending with 1 and with 6), a Saskatchewan woman, Carol Lees, refused to answer the census question that asked how many hours she worked in the last week. That question specifically defined work as "not including volunteer work, housework, [home] maintenance or repairs." Yet, for 19 years, Carol Lees had been a person who did all the work excluded by the Census as work. She said at the time that she was "mighty annoyed."

Since refusal to answer a Census question in Canada is illegal, Lees found herself in the midst of a national firestorm over unpaid work. She formed a support group, the Canadian Alliance of Home Managers, which became a lobby group. Her push to have housework and unpaid work included on the Census was timely, since unpaid work was much discussed in the mid-1990s as paid work became more precarious and as voluntary work became more vital as governments cut back sharply on services. Lees' lobby was taken seriously, though it may not have gotten onto the Census but for the fortuitous intervention of timely sociological research.

One of your authors (McDaniel) serves on the highest level advisory board to Statistics Canada. Just before the 1996 Census questions were to be finalized, the questions on unpaid work came before this board. Evidence of their effectiveness from the Census pre-tests was inconclusive. Nonetheless, board members were thinking of scrapping the questions. McDaniel had been doing research on changing work and family over the period of the mid-1990s in Canada, including changes in both paid and unpaid work. Her presentation of those research findings about the growing importance of unpaid work among Canadians helped the advisory board decide to recommend that the questions be included on the 1996 Census. This advice was taken by both Statistics Canada and the federal Cabinet, which gives final approval to Census questions.

And so unpaid work was included in the 1996 Census, positioned *before* the questions on paid work. Canada is the first country in the world to include questions on unpaid work on its national census. Other countries will surely follow suit, giving housework and unpaid work a new legitimacy.

Double Days, Double Toil

A characterization of today's paid and unpaid work that has stuck is that we have a 1990s workplace with a 1950s division of labour at home. Arber and Ginn (1995:21) put it this way:

> In the late twentieth century there has been progress towards equality of occupational achievement between women who work full-time and men, but substantial gender inequalities in earnings remain

within occupational groups. However, in the private sphere of the household, gender inequalities of pay and occupational level between marital partners may be a more persistent source of inequality and be more influential in maintaining patriarchal power in society.

The portrayal of 1990s gender equality in work may still be a little optimistic. The 1996 Census of Canada (Statistics Canada, 1998a) reveals that although women have made gains in occupations, there remains a strong tendency for women to cluster in traditionally female occupations while men work in more traditionally male, and better paid, occupations. Data for 1998 (Statistics Canada, 1998e) show that among single people and young married people, the earnings of men and women are closer together than ever before (women earn $0.93 for every dollar men earn). The earnings gap among married women and men, however, remains high (married women earn $0.69 for every dollar married men earn). This gap lessens when education, years in the paid labour force, and age are the same for women and for men. This is fine for women who have education and experience comparable to men's, but many still do not.

Their wages, however, are often needed to keep the family from poverty.

> Dual-earning may help families stay above the low income cutoffs. Without the contribution of the spouse with lower earnings, the number of families with low income in 1994 would have more than doubled to 400,000 from 184,000 (Statistics Canada. 1996c:1).

On the home front, women continue to put in another day's work whether or not they also work outside the home. The consequence is that women are working harder and longer than previously since they are more often working outside the home, and still do the largest part of the work at home. And mothers of young children are entering the paid workforce at the highest rates. It's not surprising that people today so often use images of juggling or balancing to describe work and family.

The invisibility of women's unpaid work at home and their lower pay than men in the workforce underlines social attitudes toward women's roles. Women are seen as working at home out of love, due to the centrality of family to their lives, and as working for less pay in the workplace because of the priority they give to family. Armstrong and Armstrong (1994:225) argue compellingly that

> ... the nature of women's work in the home and in the labour force reinforces and perpetuates the division of labour by sex. Because women have the primary responsibility for domestic work, they are undertaking a double burden when they enter the labour force. Their job in the home means that some women are unable to work continuously or full-time in paid employment and all women face constraints on their work in both spheres.

Women are working longer and harder than previously, since more of them work outside the home while still doing the largest part of the work at home.

The conclusion is that women's unpaid work at home contributes in part to their lesser opportunities in the labour market and that society relies on women as a source of cheap, flexible labour, both at home and in the paid labour market. The implications for women, men, children, families, and societies are complex and important. The first step toward a solution seems to be to recognize that domestic work may be the key to enhanced gender equality.

Men contribute to domestic work too, most notably on household maintenance and repairs. Often, however, less time overall is spent on these kinds of tasks than women spend on day-to-day housework and child care. Two additional factors matter in how men's contributions to the home play out in society. First, these sorts of household tasks can often be postponed until time permits. Unless the leaking faucet threatens to flood the house (which can happen, but not often, thank goodness), it can wait until a Saturday to be fixed. Similarly, the lawn can be mowed on weekends, although snow may have to be shovelled more immediately. This means that men's work at home is a little less constraining than women's on a day-to-day basis.

Second, and importantly, men's work at home is not seen as defining them in the way that women's does. Men who fix up and maintain their homes are less often defined by that work, whereas some people still define women as wives and mothers first and workers second. So, while both men and women often contribute to domestic work, they contribute in different ways and their domestic work is seen differently by society at large.

How does this double day affect women? How does it affect couples? Women tend to experience stress. "The ensuing exhaustion of women encourages dissatisfaction, especially when their partners do not share the responsibility of work in the home" (Armstrong & Armstrong, 1994:227). Double days also are predictive of depression in both spouses (Windle & Dumenci, 1997). Studies, however, have shown that participation in the labour force can have benefits for some women, such as raised self-esteem, improved mental and physical health, and increased status and resources (Tingey, Kiger & Riley, 1996). How stressful the double day will be for a woman, and whether it will create stress within her family, depends partly on her sense of control as well as how the work at home is shared. Baker, Kiger and Riley (1996:173) find, significantly, that "husbands are more satisfied with household-task arrangements than are wives." They quickly add that "[T]he most obvious explanation for this finding is that wives continue to do the bulk of the household chores and husbands are satisfied with the arrangement" (Baker, Kiger & Riley, 1996:173). More on this in a moment.

Child Care: The Big Component of Domestic Labour

A study of the effects of parenthood on division of labour at home (Sanchez & Thomson, 1997:747) based on national U.S. data finds, not surprisingly, that "... there were no effects of parenthood ... on husbands' employment or housework hours." However, "[m]otherhood increases wives' housework hours and reduces employment hours." The conclusion is sharp: "Parenthood crystallizes a gendered division of labor, largely by reshaping wives', not husbands', routine." A Canadian study (Lupri & Mills, 1987) comes to similar conclusions, as does a 1991 Canadian survey. In Chapter 4 on entering parenthood, the possibility that children, under today's gender expectations, limit women's opportunities was considered.

As the work lives of women and men become more similar (although, as we have seen, not yet by any means identical), child care becomes the great divide on the domestic scene. As Baker & Lero (1996:103) argue

> ... the gender-structured nature of the labour market, differential use of parental and childrearing leave by men and women, and different gender expectations by families and communities preserve the unequal sharing of economic and social parenting.

It is not only that the presence of a child or children takes more time and adds to the domestic demands. It's also that parents tend to take on particular roles. Practical day-to-day parenting is seen as women's work, while men specialize in economic responsibilities for the children. This is partly a reflection of the gendered labour market, where women's paid work matters less to families because they are typically the lesser earners, while men's earnings matter more and they are paid more.

Child care is thus a central concern in the domestic division of labour. It is difficult indeed for women to work in the numbers they do in the paid labour force and to mind young children at the same time. Even if adequate child care arrangements are made, they tend to fall apart if the child falls ill, as most children do at some point. The best jugglers of work and family typically cannot continue juggling in a crisis. Such times reveal who is ultimately responsible for child care. "Care of a sick child is still considered women's work" (Wylie, 1997:41). Women are expected to take the time from work to do the caring, while men usually are not. The great fear of having a child fall ill or experience a crisis makes some employers reluctant to hire women with young children, particularly single mothers. The National Childcare Study in Canada (cited by Armstrong & Armstong, 1994:106) found that each additional child lowers the probability that a single parent will be employed.

Figure 6.1   **MOTHERS IN THE PAID WORKFORCE**

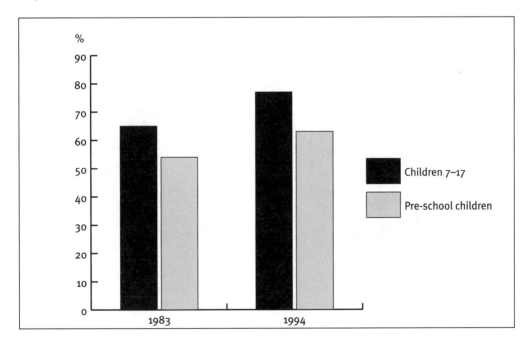

Source: Canadian Council on Social Development. 1996. *The Progress of Canada's Children*. Ottawa: 15.

Even without sick children or crises, child care is seldom equally shared by parents (Wilson, 1996:77). Child care is something women overwhelmingly undertake. Statistics Canada data (cited in Armstrong & Armstrong, 1994:110) reveal that women are almost three times as likely as men to provide physical care of children under the age of five, and 2.5 times as likely to provide care for children aged five to eighteen. A 1990 study by the Conference Board of Canada found that 76.5 percent of women reported that they had primary responsibility for child care, while only 4.1 percent of men reported this (Armstrong & Armstrong, 1994:110). Men in Quebec, interestingly, tend to do more housework and child care than men in other provinces, which some argue is related to the strong women's movement in that province.

With most mothers of young children in the paid labour force, as shown in Figures 6.1 and 6.2, care is needed for young children while parents work. The National Child Care Study (Baker & Lero, 1996:89) reports that care was needed for 64 percent of families with one child under age 13, 59.3 percent of families with two children under 13, and 48.3 percent of families with three or more children. The study also found that only 55 percent of parents of children under 13 work standard work weeks or standard hours. Most existing child care programs cannot accommodate irregular hours or different work schedules. The gap between demand (estimated to be 2.2

Figure 6.2 PROPORTION OF PARENTS WORKING

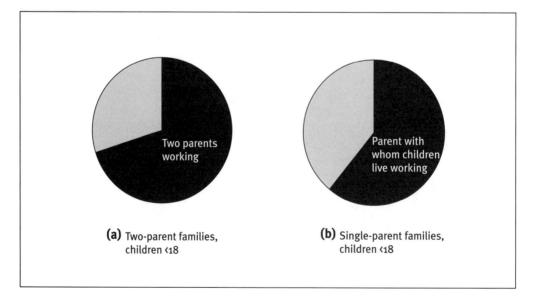

(a) Two-parent families, children ‹18

(b) Single-parent families, children ‹18

Source: Canadian Council on Social Development. 1996. *The Progress of Canada's Children*. Ottawa: 15.

million children age 12 and under) and supply of licensed child care spaces (333 000) means that only 15 percent of children who need care have access to it (Baker & Lero, 1996:91).

Pressure has been put on politicians for many years to address the child care issue. In 1987, the federal Conservative Government announced a strategy which essentially changed the ways child care is funded but did not address the child care shortage. The Liberal Government at the end of its first mandate in 1997 put forward a proposal for national child care to be cost-shared with the provinces. It did not fly and has yet to be reintroduced.

Child care, like other domestic work, has been defined largely as a private responsibility, leaving parents to scramble as best they can to find care for their children while they work. This creates enormous challenges for parents, as sociological research has shown—challenges relating not only to access but also to affordability and quality of care. Child care has been perceived mainly as babysitting, and not to be highly valued by society. In fact, many parents opt for babysitters, often because they have little other option. Babysitting may not address important issues of compatibility with the child's needs and skills, and with the family's culture, values, or language group.

A 1998 study by economists Gordon Cleveland and Michael Krashinsky (reported by Philp, 1998) looks at the issue of child care from the point of view of social problems and benefits. This is not entirely new thinking, but this study looks at the entire population benefits, and is receiving serious attention. In essence, the economists estimate that a public program of child care in Canada would be cost-effective if child care were seen as an investment. Their conclusion, as quoted by Philp (1998:A8):

> Basically, what we're saying, and this is why it's a radical finding, is not that child care is good for children who are disadvantaged or in some way neglected. The issue is that good educational care can have benefits spread across the entire population for children two to five years of age.

The rewards of good child care are estimated at $4.3 billion a year if lower school dropout rates, higher future incomes, and larger tax revenues are considered. If benefits to the economy are added in, such as more women joining the workforce, fewer career interruptions, and more women with higher incomes, the overall benefits total $6.4 billion.

The More Things Change ...

Women still do most of the housework. As can be seen in Table 6.1, wives, regardless of their employment status, consistently perform about twice as much housework as husbands do (Davies & Carrier, 1998; Marshall, 1990; 1993; Statistics Canada, 1998:16–18). This proportion has not changed much

TABLE 6.1   HOW MUCH TIME PARENTS SPEND WORKING

	WITH CHILDREN 5 YRS OLD		WITH CHILDREN 5+ YRS	
	WOMEN	MEN	WOMEN	MEN
Hours Spent per Day				
Paid Work	5.2	6.8	5.2	6.5
Domestic Work	2.4	1.4	2.6	1.5
Primary Child Care	2.2	1.2	0.7	0.3

Source: *1992 General Social Survey*. Abridged from Janet Che-Alfred, Catherine Allan, and George Butlin. 1996. *Families in Canada*. Ottawa and Toronto: Statistics Canada and Nelson Canada.

over time, despite the dramatic increase in women's paid labour force work. Nakhaie (1995) finds in an analysis of Canadian national data on the gender division of domestic labour that gender explains more of the variation in housework done than any other factor.

Yet, there are hints of change in the air. A study of 179 couples in the mid-1990s (Bernier, Laflamme & Zhou, 1996) finds that the amount of housework done by women has declined compared to earlier studies. Are men picking up the slack or is less attention being devoted to housework these days? The jury is still out. Hints of tendencies could be troubling, however. Nakhaie (1995) finds that when husbands' work hours increase beyond 30 hours a week, their contribution to housework decreases; when women's work hours increase beyond 30 hours a week, their contribution to housework *increases*.

Domestic work is a mirror of what society expects of men and of women (see Oakley, 1974). Couples may, in fact, not actually ever decide on who does what, but fall into expected gender patterns. Luxton, Rosenberg and Arat-Koc (1990:31) put it well:

> The most powerful myth surrounding housework is one which claims that a woman's place is in the home. This myth is based on the assumption that women's biological capacity to bear children means that they are the best caregivers for children and that they are "naturally" inclined to cook, clean, and manage the running of a household.

Getting beyond the power of this myth is not easy for couples, even for new age postmodern couples. Power relations in couples and in society are an important dimension of who does what on the home front. Davies and Carrier (1998), in a study of 2577 employed Canadians who have an employed spouse, find that gender inequalities in the paid work force matter to the domestic division of labour. They discover, for example, that the segregated nature of paid work into "male" and "female" jobs translates into doing male and female tasks at home. Interestingly, however, when the proportion of women in men's occupations increases, those men participate more in "female" housework such as grocery shopping, laundry, meal making, and house-cleaning.

In terms of decision-making about dividing household labour, gender inequities in the work world where men, on average, have higher earnings and more power, are found to translate into power differentials at home. In short, men's greater power at work can exempt them from the less desirable aspects of domestic work (Davies & Carrier, 1998). Since these tasks still need doing, women do them most often. It is an oversimplification to presume a simple and direct correspondence between power in the wider world and division of family work. Glenn (1987:373) describes family work as a "tangle of love and domination," an apt image for the complexity of close relations, even when the topic under dispute is who cleans the bathroom.

Mr. Mom, although a popular Hollywood image, is not that common in reality. In fact, research finds that men actively resist full participation in domestic work, let alone willingly taking charge. Luxton (1986) paints vivid pictures of how this works among couples she interviewed in Flin Flon, Manitoba. One man explains his approach to domestic division of labour:

> Look, I'm not interested in doing stuff around the house. I think that's her job, but since she's working she's been on my back to get me to help out so I say, 'sure I'll do it.' It shuts her up for a while and sometimes I do a few things just to keep her quiet. But really, I don't intend to do it, but it prevents a row if I don't say that (Luxton, 1986:50).

One woman describes how the kitchen sink is directly in the middle of the counter with the drain board usually on the left side and the dirty dishes on the right. She reports that her husband maintained that he was unable to do the dishes because he was left-handed and the sink was designed for right-handed people!

Because couples find it so difficult to negotiate openly who does what housework, they can get into situations where one manipulates the other into doing the work. Luxton (1986) cites an example of this. The woman began with reasoned discussion of how she was now working full-time and it seemed only right that he share the work at home. In principle, he agreed but resistance apparently got the better of him and he did little to help. So she began her campaign. She determined all the discrete steps involved in doing the laundry and set out to get him to do it one step at a time.

The first day she left the laundry basket of sorted clothes sitting at the top of the basement stairs. As he was going down to his workroom she asked him to take the laundry down and put it on top of the machine. She repeated this several times until he automatically took the basket down without being asked. She then asked him, as he went down with the basket, to put the laundry into the machine. Once that was learned, she asked him to put in the soap and turn the machine on. "Finally, it got so he would regularly carry the laundry down, put it in and turn it on. I never even had to ask him. So then I began getting him to pick up the dirty clothes." (Luxton, 1986:51)

Amusing as this story may be, there is a down side. The woman felt resentful and contemptuous of her husband for refusing to do part of the housework in the first place when she broached it with him. The husband refused to discuss it at all even after he had assumed complete responsibility for doing the laundry. Her efforts, although resourceful and successful, may not ultimately have positive consequences for the relationship.

What happens when roles are reversed, and women take on the role of workers outside the home and men take on the role of homemakers? Even if the parents work things out between them, the child's expectations may dictate that mother should do what Moms do in our society.

Many couples who reverse roles do not do so voluntarily. With huge changes in the work world through economic restructuring and downsizing in recent years, many men have been laid off and inadvertently cast into the role of stay-at-home husbands/fathers.

In research that one of the authors (McDaniel) is doing on work and

Mr. Moms and Ms. Dads

We've heard lots in recent years about stay-at-home dads, pioneers of role reversal who brave loss of income, jokes about their masculinity and the suspicion of mothers in tot lots to keep their kids out of day care.

Behind every Mr. Mom, it stands to reason, there must be a Ms. Dad. But we haven't heard much until recently from the breadwinner mothers. No wonder. It turns out that they've been busy.

According to a study presented last week at the American Psychological Association convention in Chicago, many of these breadwinner moms revert to traditional roles when they come home from work, making dinner, giving the baths and managing the

bedtime routine—even when their husbands stay home 45 hours a week or more. Unlike traditional fathers, the breadwinner moms tend to know their child's schedule, friends and classes even though they are at work all day.

Society still expects mothers to be primary caregivers, no matter how demanding their jobs are.

[Robert Frank (Loyola University), author of the study, suggests] "Our society says if the kids don't come out so good, there's a sense that the female didn't do a good job. And if the dad is not making big bucks and supporting his family, it's not being done right."

Lyn Smith. 1997. "Study Compares Home Roles of Mr. Moms and Ms. Dads," *The Edmonton Journal*, 30 August:G7.

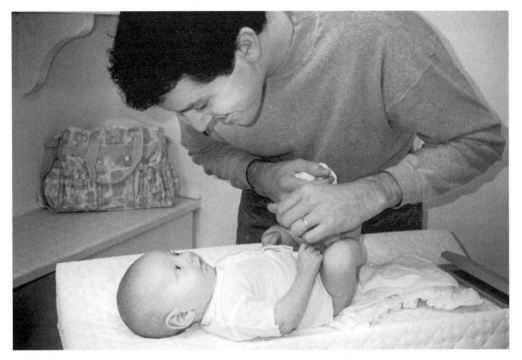

The popular Hollywood image of Mr. Mom is not very common in reality.

family in midlife, an unemployed man told about how he walked with his son in a stroller each day in his neighbourhood. He said he noticed several other fathers with babies in strollers or baby carriages walking too, but they never talked to each other. It is almost as if they were distancing themselves from acknowledging their roles as homeworkers and fathers, both to themselves and to other men. Or, as was pointed out by a male graduate student who spent a year as a full-time parent to his daughter, they may be assuming, as he often did, that these other men were working (paid work) and it was only he who was working at home with no paid work. He added that women, on average, tend to be more sociable both with other women and with men.

Conflicts over Housework

We have seen that conflicts over housework can be problematic for couples. A Canadian study of a nationally representative sample (Frederick & Hamel, 1998:8) finds that an unsatisfactory division of housework would be sufficient basis for seeking divorce among 17 percent of adults (for those over age 50, 21 percent; for those age 15–29, 12 percent). Who does what at home is not easily discussed either prior to marriage or afterwards. Factors such as differential power in the workplace and in society, beliefs about women's and men's natural roles, and the ways in which men and women are taught to see themselves and their families, all matter to how house and family work gets divided.

Division of domestic labour is not settled once and for all, however, as the examples above reveal. Once settled, things change—the woman may start a full-time job or return to school; the husband may be laid off or retire; the couple may have a baby or a child may grow up and leave home. These changes often call into question the existing agreement, even if it is unspoken.

Although a lot of sociological research has focused on the division of household labour, surprisingly little has looked at the process of dividing the labour, or specifically on conflicts created by that process. One Dutch study (Kluwer, Heesink & Van de Vliert, 1997) finds that discontent with who does what in the family can be destructive to a marriage. Usually, discontent leads to demand/withdrawal interactions between the couple: typically she makes demands and he withdraws. "The relationship between spouses' discontent with the division of labour and mutually integrative interactions [which strongly predict constructive outcomes] was either negative or nonexistent" (Kluwer, Heesink & Van de Vliert, 1997:648). This does not bode well for maintaining strong marriages in the face of unhappiness about the division of housework and unwillingness to discuss it. And that may be showing in the Canadian study cited above.

How, then, are such conflicts best resolved? Taking a problem-solving approach works best, and avoiding the "should" concept. Kluwer and his col-

Work–Family Conflict

A 1990s study of 27,000 Canadian employees reveals:

- 40% of working mothers & 25% of working fathers experience high levels of work/family conflict

- 50% of parents report high levels of difficulty managing family time

- 50% of working mothers & 36% of working fathers report high stress

- 40% of working mothers & 25% of working fathers report depression

- ‹ 50% of parents are highly satisfied with their lifestyles

Employers are feeling an impact on their "bottom line" from parents' difficulties in balancing work and family demands. A number of work-related problems have been found to be more common among employees with dependent or elder-care responsibilities, including increased lateness, more absenteeism, unscheduled days and emergency hours off, excessive use of the telephone, missed meetings, decreased productivity, lower quality of work, and lower morale and job satisfaction.

Source: Canadian Council on Social Development. 1996. *The Progress of Canada's Children*. Ottawa: 15.

leagues favour family education programs and/or therapy approaches that focus specifically on gender differences in conflict behaviours. Women's growing sense of entitlement to discuss reworking taken-for-granted divisions of labour may induce conflicts in couple relationships. This may be a fundamental part of social change, however. Kluwer and his colleagues express caution: women who press for changes in the domestic division of labour may open unresolvable issues. "Issues of housework that are not resolved constructively are bound to lead to aggravation and conflict time after time," note Kluwer, Heesink and Van de Vliert (1997:648).

The good news is that more egalitarian couples are more responsive to each other's statements about discontents. Although they experience more conflicts over housework, they are also more willing to negotiate making them more satisfied in their relationships. Traditional couples, by contrast, are more likely to maintain surface harmony, but let the discontent simmer into ultimate trouble in the relationship. Even interpersonal interactions in egalitarian relationships, however, tend toward reinforcement of traditional norms of who does what and to favour men, according to Zvonkovic and colleagues (1996). More research is needed on the long-term effects on relationships of conflicts over division of housework. Avoiding conflicts, however, is not the answer; nor is maintenance of the *status quo* which, with more and more women in the paid workforce, makes women's days even longer.

An interesting concluding note comes from a study by Karen Pyke and Scott Coltrane in California (reported in Furstenberg, 1996:38–39). Pyke and Coltrane interviewed 193 remarried men and women. More than half of them also had spouses who had been married previously. Even in remarriages, where one might expect a more equal division of labour, housework is optional for men. Remarried women, like their sisters who are married to their first husbands, do about twice as much of the housework as their husbands. Only one in ten husbands among this remarried sample contributes equally to the housework. Furstenberg (1996:38) notes, in discussing this study, that "Although many wives complain that their current husbands do not do enough of the housework, they often add that at least the men do more than previous husbands had done." First husbands who do little housework, beware!

Economic Independence and Domestic Work

Sociologists have found that women's increased labour market work alters authority patterns between husbands and wives. Decisions about major purchases, for example, are more often made jointly in two-earner families (Baker & Lero, 1996:97–98). Couples where both partners work for pay more often have separate bank accounts. Wives who work for pay see themselves as having more bargaining power in the relationship.

One theory of marital relationships holds that couples work out who has more power in any given situation through a complex set of equations. Known as personal resources theory, the idea is that if one knows that the other has greater knowledge of cars, for example, that person will defer to the more knowledgeable partner. However, if one partner is particularly attractive and the other is not, or sees him- or herself as less attractive, then the deferral pattern will tilt in the direction of the more attractive partner, possibly out of fear that he or she could leave otherwise. It has been argued, however, that resources such as knowledge, looks, education. or earning power are not randomly distributed. Couples tend to pair up based on their comparable or complementary resources. Differences between men and women are perpetuated and exaggerated by a marriage system in which women are typically younger, a little less well educated, and shorter than their husbands. Arber and Ginn (1995:40) spell out the connection:

> ... patriarchy has adapted to increased women's equality in the labour market, in terms of entry into higher status occupations, but without conceding equivalent economic changes. The persistence of male economic dominance in the public sphere is magnified in the family, reinforcing the ideology of women's subordination. There is a reciprocal relation between the labour market and the family, with women's economic disadvantages in the labour market influencing their domestic role in the family, which in turn reduces women's ability to participate to their full potential in the public sphere.

Despite gains toward equality in marital or cohabiting relationships, there are strong hints in the research literature that women's growing economic independence does not translate into independence from domestic work at all. In part this is because husbands typically remain the higher earners and can translate that into a sharp division of labour at home. " ... [P]atriarchal relations in the home are likely to be reinforced by the earnings dominance of the husband," argue Arber and Ginn. They continue,

> Women's lower earnings than their husbands mean that they have less power to influence the family decision-making, and their lower earnings are likely to hamper attempts to equalize the domestic division of labour (Arber & Ginn, 1995:39-40).

Recent evidence suggests that overall time spent on housework decreases with the wife's employment outside the home (Bernier, Laflamme & Zhou, 1996). This may be a compromise on standards that women or couples are willing to make. Or, it could be that the gap in getting housework done left by women working outside the home is not being filled by men. Or compromises are made with the help of technologies such as microwaves and dishwashers, or homes that require less maintenance such as no-wax flooring, condominium living, or smaller living spaces.

A particular concern and focus of research has been the consequences for children of mothers working outside the home. Significantly, people rarely question the effects on children of men's paid employment. The assumption is that men work and women look after children and family; and if women work as well, then their families are thought to suffer from neglect. A new, comprehensive study draws this conclusion, a conclusion based on research but not widely known:

> ... consistent with earlier research, for employed mothers, greater occupational complexity is predictive of diminished levels of child behavioral problems. The economic resources that accrue from employment, and opportunities for workplace autonomy that benefit parenting skills, appear to outweigh any disadvantages that stem from decreased time working mothers spend with their children (Cooksey, Menaghan & Jekielelek, 1997:658).

The Effects of Domestic Work on Paid Work

We have talked in this chapter about how paid work affects domestic work. But how does domestic work affect paid work? For women, large effects exist and are presumed. "A woman's work as wife and mother is frequently considered a sufficient explanation and justification for the segregated labour force and women's low wages" (Armstrong & Armstrong, 1994:182). Women are presumed to be primarily responsible for work at home—family work—and therefore are thought to have tentative connections with, and commitment to, the paid labour market. Whether this is true or not matters little to the prevalence of the perception and the realities it creates. For example, Canadian federal policies allow certain categories of skilled workers to enter the country under special permits, but prohibit their spouses from working. Only recently have governments begun to recognize that this prohibition makes the program unappealing to skilled workers (Church, 1998).

In no aspect of domestic work is the effect clearer than with reproduction and child care. The International Labor Organization has a stark description of the effects for women:

> In all parts of the world, working women who become pregnant are faced with the threat of job loss, suspended earnings and increased health risks due to inadequate safeguards for their employment (F.J. Dy-Hammar, Chief, ILO Conditions of Work Branch, International Labor Organization, 1998:1).

Women, not surprisingly, take greater advantage of parental and family leaves, flextime, and "family friendly" workplace policies than do men, largely to care for dependent children. Women also more often turn down work that requires travel, or decline transfers or promotions that mean a geographical relocation, because of their responsibilities for children and families.

For men, the effects of domestic responsibilities on paid work are clear and positive. Men are thought to be working to support their families, so the presence of family in men's lives is seen as a stabilizing force. That men's roles in family work remain largely economic is revealed in their increased employment work hours with the presence of more than one child (Sanchez & Thomson, 1997). Men contribute to family welfare by increasing their paid work rather than by increasing their contributions to domestic work. This has the effect of sharpening the gender division of domestic work: men become providers, and women caregivers.

Changes in Domestic Divisions over the Life Course

The life course perspective is a newcomer to sociology, but highly useful in following family and social dynamics through people's lives and changes. Power and dominance hierarchies do not remain static in families or anywhere else in society, but change with time. Couples who once had a sharp division of domestic responsibilities may find themselves questioning or changing those decisions as they age or as their life circumstances change. And with aging, hidden components of domestic work such as care giving and emotional work often become vivid and clear (McDaniel, 1996).

Retirement can precipitate such a reevaluation or a crisis. With hus-

Too Close for Comfort: Division of Labour in the RV

We both step into our rig after a nice morning golfing in the shirtsleeve spring weather of our chosen winter retreat.

"Oh migawd, what is that smell?" we gasp as one.

"Don't know," gasp, gasp, "maybe it's the garbage."

"Quick, get rid of it!" says Herself.

"Yeah, okay," I agree.

I don't even protest that in our division of chores, it's Herself who usually does the garbage detail as Minister of the Interior. That portfolio includes complete domination over a three-foot by four-foot section bordered by fridge, sink and stove.

I enter that domain at my peril. I get my own breakfast in the morning, while Herself feigns sleep. It is our way of avoiding conflict in our marriage.

Over 35 years of marriage, Herself was housewife and reigned supreme in the important areas of our home. My sphere of operations was confined to the Yard, the Garage and the Basement, and seeing that there was enough income to cover the outgo.

Source: Jack Wainwright. 1998. "Too Close for Comfort," in Let the Good Times Roll, RV gazette Winter: 45. Reprinted with permission of the RV gazette, Publisher, Wayfarer Explorer Company Limited, and Jack Wainwright.

bands more often entering retirement before their wives, given the average age differences between spouses, men often find themselves spending their days on what their wives consider their turf: the home. Mid-life men, too, may spend more time at home as "downsizing" leads to long-term unemployment. Conflicts can result.

"What am I going to do with him underfoot all day?" may be the question posed by women who work at home when their husbands leave their work world full-time. Resolutions can be amusing or poignant and can move toward or away from equality, but typically involve either renegotiation or acceptance of the *status quo*. Retirement may not be the event that causes this second look at domestic division of labour and the couple need not even be married or cohabiting.

An interesting example comes from an acquaintance. A well-to-do family composed of husband and wife and three children, one disabled, lived together with their long-time live-in housekeeper/nanny/governess, who had been with the husband's family since she was a young adult and he only a slightly younger child. Two of the kids grew up and left home; the disabled one went to live in semi-institutional care. The wife died after years of illness, during which the housekeeper nursed her. Left alone were the housekeeper and the widower. Soon after they were on their own, the man sat at the dining room table waiting for his breakfast, which never arrived. Instead, the housekeeper sat down to talk about renegotiating domestic arrangements. She wanted more freedom to do other things—by this time she was almost seventy, and he in his early sixties—and she thought that he might learn to cook. In fits and starts, he took up the challenge, eventually becoming a gourmet cook who often prepares meals for the two of them. She, meanwhile, took up art and gardening. They continue to share domestic responsibilities and are happy about the changes they made. It is never too late to renegotiate the domestic division of labour.

Other couples develop patterns of domestic relationships that are not so easily changed or adjusted with aging. These patterns may be mutually reinforcing and supportive of the earning power of one of them. Such is the case with the late W.O. Mitchell and his wife, Merna, as described by someone who knew them both well:

> He [W.O.] was, of course, only half a person. The other half was the redoubtable Merna Mitchell, known to most of us by the full appellation, 'Fercrissakesmerna.' As his loving, caring and remarkably tolerant wife of more than half a century, she deserves a book of her own. She was more than a glasses finder, a snuff box retriever, she was the Organizing Principle in his life, to the extent that any arrangement made with him was worthless unless entered into the agenda by Merna (Gibson, 1998).*

Reprinted with the permission of Douglas Gibson, Publisher, McClelland & Stewart.

Displaced Homemakers

The assumption that women are primarily responsible for domestic work means that women who spend their adult lives caring for families and homes do not have access to economic resources on the same basis as men. As Bergmann (1987) suggests, the problem for women and for society of "losing one's position" as homemaker through divorce or widowhood also affects married women who realize their precarious situation should something happen to the marriage.

That women's domestic work is tied together both with concepts of work and entitlement and with familial concepts of love and devotion makes the challenge of facing up to the realities of displaced homemakers perplexing. Some argue that they deserve "severance packages" and support from their ex-husbands in the case of divorce. Others see this as unrealistic and suggest that government ought to provide support, partly in recognition of the service homemakers provide to society and its future. Having no simple answer, many jurisdictions have done nothing. Women whose marriages end in divorce, after years of working as homemakers, all too often find themselves falling quickly into poverty. Widows who spent their adult lives in family work—including, increasingly, caring for a chronically ill or dying spouse—find themselves without any pension.

The landmark 1970 Royal Commission on the Status of Women (Wilson, 1996:72) recommended that changes be made to the Canada/Quebec Pension Plan to enable homemakers to contribute to it. This recommendation was never implemented, but has been periodically on the political table ever since. Some changes have been implemented enabling domestic work to be pensionable. For instance, in 1983 it became possible for women leaving the workforce in order to care for small children (under age 7) to receive continuous pension coverage. Since 1987 pension credits have had to be divided between married spouses on divorce and can be divided at the end of a common-law union, although it is rare for women in common-law relationships to ask for this.

The challenge is to find an equitable way to provide pensions to women who have spent their lives in unpaid work at home. Given that many women, but also some men, may spend portions of their working lives as homemakers or informal caregivers, the question is whether this work would also be credited. And there are the vast majority of women, and men too, who spend their entire adult lives combining paid work with family work. How do they contribute to pension plans for the unpaid work portion? These are thorny and thus far irresolvable questions.

Some analysts worry that providing pensions to full-time homemakers might increase rather than decrease inequalities among women. Equity questions aside, that a woman who spends her life caring for her family would have nothing on which to rely in her old age, is heartbreaking and unjust. Debates on the issue will continue, even as the issue itself becomes ever more complex as women's work and family lives become more complex.

Imported Homemakers

A new conceptualization of the division of domestic labour looks at housework, like paid work, as something that is increasingly internationalized. Bakan and Stasiulis (1995), for example, argue that housework in countries like Canada and the United States cannot be fully understood without addressing issues related to female migrant domestic labour—sometimes called **imported housewives**. These researchers conclude that Canada's crisis in the domestic sphere (where there is no one at home any more to do the housework and child care) is being resolved by importing the needed homemakers from developing regions of the world.

Arat-Koc (1992) sees the domestic crisis in Canada in terms of lack of government action on child care. Instead, she argues, government is willing to import domestic workers, a practice long ago used in Canada, to provide cheap domestic help to middle- and upper-class families. Although this is a solution to the domestic work problem for a limited number of women, the working conditions of those brought in and the denial of citizenship rights make it a poor solution. Bakan and Stasiulus (1995) agree and add that this system creates a racial aspect of domestic service that divides women against other women.

Domestic workers are admitted into Canada under special provisions. They work at the employers' behest and can be sent back at will or if they become ill. The homes in which they work often provide no time off, and they are expected to work long, long hours and be on constant call. Imported domestic workers are not permitted to bring their own families with them, so monies are often sent home to support their own children, who are left behind. They work in private and live in the homes in which they work, occasionally with the children they care for or in cramped quarters with limited privacy. They may be subjected to sexual harassment and assault; if they complain, they can be sent back home. The Philippines has had numerous domestics returned to their homeland from other countries in pine boxes after being killed by their employers.

Additionally, the domestic walks a fine line between being paid (very low wages), and doing the work that homemakers and mothers typically are expected to do for love. Sometimes they indeed grow attached to their young charges but have no defined relationship to them. Further, it is very difficult to enforce labour standards and codes of conduct between employers and employees when there are no job evaluations and the work takes place on demand in private homes.

The problem of lack of citizenship rights in the country of employment is most revealing of the contradictions of domestic work. Imported home-makers are thought to be good enough to care closely for children and households, but they are regarded with deep suspicion when they demand rights of access to labour laws, to human rights codes, to lives and families of their own, and—the big issue in Canada—to health care. Cases have come to light of nannies being sent home because they develop cancer and have no right to treatment in Canada. The plight of a secondary workforce reveals how society views housework and child care as ultimately secondary to "real" work. A captive labour force that is almost completely female and non-white is created, specifically to do housework.

Elder Care: An Emerging Challenge at Home

Several factors come together to make the care of aged and frail relatives a growing challenge in the domestic realm. Increased life expectancies, par-ticularly among the old-old (those over age 85) has meant that the demand for care has increased. Most people remain healthy into their old age. It is typ-ically very late in their lives that they need care and assistance. Dramatic cutbacks in both health and social services sectors have limited the options available for care (Fast *et al.*, 1997). People come home from hospital now "quicker and sicker" and often need help to manage. All this is compounded by the fact that many middle-aged women are now in the workforce, leav-ing few available for home-based care when needed. Other middle-aged daughters and daughters-in-law live far away, sometimes in other coun-tries, and are also unavailable for direct help to elders.

Additionally, family sizes have shrunk over recent generations, with the result that many of us have large numbers of older relatives while there are fewer of us to share the responsibilities of caring for them (Baker & Lero, 1996:102; McDaniel, 1996b).

Research with a representative sample of Canadians (McDaniel, 1994) has shown that women are called upon differentially to provide not only hands-on care but also emotional support to family members and friends of all ages, not only elders. Women themselves have little time for themselves, in light of all those who call on them for help. Men rely heavily on the women in their lives, particularly their wives, for emotional support. Sadly, many men report that if their wives were not an option, they would have no one to whom they could turn for emotional support.

The sharp gender division in emotional caring and the burden it places on women is a part of domestic work that is not often considered. The demands on women for emotional support increase in times of rapid eco-nomic change such as Canada in the 1990s, at the same time as there are many more older relatives in families who may need someone to depend on emotionally.

Women in Canada are called upon to provide care to family members of all ages, but elder care presents a special and growing challenge.

The consequences of all the demands for the well-being of middle-aged women and for their relationships and immediate families are not fully known. However, indications exist from sociological research. Lack of control is known to undermine well-being. A study by McDaniel (cited in 1996) found that when asked why they took on caregiving for elders, many women replied that there was no one else to do it. This is an admission to a loss of control over choice-making. Additionally, the overwhelming majority of middle-aged women said they had considered quitting their jobs or turning down a promotion or a transfer because of family responsibilities.

If even a portion of these women give up jobs to do informal caregiving, then the societal consequences down the road could be large, with fewer older women having pension entitlements, and possibly more poverty among older women. Since poverty, on average, is a greater risk for women than for men, and particularly for single mothers, then the potential problems over the life course for women who are asked to take on more caregiving for elders could be enormous.

Policy Debates and Challenges

Policy may not seem to come into the private division of unpaid work at home, but the domestic arena is central to many contemporary policy debates. Child care and, increasingly, elder care, are important points of policy discussion in the 1990s in Canada; so, too, is the expectation that a "third sector" (the volunteer sector) will pick up the bits and pieces of human needs left over from profit-making in the private sector and cost and program reductions in the public sector. Another area of policy challenge and debate is the "domestic crisis" in North America that brings together women of the first and third worlds in child care and domestic work (Bakan & Stasiulis, 1995). This makes domestic division of labour in North America (and, to some extent in Europe and in urban, highly developed parts of Asia) a global issue and challenge.

Can work–family conflicts—time crunches resulting from demands on women for family work at home—be resolved by advocating "family-friendly" workplaces with flextime, job sharing, and on-site daycare? This remains an open question (CBC, 1994). First, increasing numbers of Canadians work in smaller workplaces that, no matter what their predisposition, cannot afford to implement family-friendly policies. Such policies may be impractical in one- or two-person workplaces. Second, implementing policies that enable families to balance the double day tends to endorse—even if inadvertently—the existing division of labour at home. It is mainly women who take advantage of family-friendly policies, enabling them to better manage the double day, but without fundamentally changing the division of domestic labour.

Concluding Remarks

We end this discussion of domestic division of labour where we started. It may be the most important arena in which gains in equality have yet to be made. Couples forming relationships need to talk openly about their wishes and aspirations with respect to housework, child care, and elder care. Remote as it may seem to most young couples, this conversation could be fundamentally important to their future marital and life happiness. And they could vow to each other as part of the marriage ceremony, or an informal ceremony they have between them, that they will remain flexible on who does what as the demands on each of them change over time.

CHAPTER SUMMARY

In this chapter, we explored who does what on the home front. The domestic division of labour may be the issue over which most conflicts occur and the arena in which gender equality may ultimately rest.

Surprises were revealed about domestic divisions of labour in the past. Among the most notable are that men, not women, were largely responsible for child rearing in the past, and that men and women were partners in homes that were productive units. With industrialization, women lost autonomy and access to the market.

Unpaid work in the domestic realm has become of particular interest in the 1990s. The 1996 Census of Canada even includes a question about it. Attempts to measure the value of unpaid work have revealed that an enormous portion of the economy (30–46 percent) is devoted to unpaid work. Hours spent in unpaid work are equally impressive.

It is suggested that we have a 1990s division of paid work and a 1950s division of domestic work. Women still do the lion's share of the domestic work. Men are more likely to do the house maintenance tasks. Housework is largely invisible and taken for granted, requiring redoing over and over again.

Child care, the biggest component of domestic work, is also the most contentious both for couples and in the public sphere. There are many ways to see child care, including as a private responsibility of parents and as a public investment for society and its future.

Couples seldom discuss who will do what work on the home front, which often leads to conflicts and sometimes to separation and divorce.

Domestic work relates to policies such as the importing of domestic workers to fill in the gaps left at home, and the attraction of skilled labour along with working spouses. We also showed that division of domestic labour shifts over the life course.

KEY TERMS

Caring: Putting the needs of others, particularly of one's family, ahead of one's own. Or, the provision of support and assistance to others, often dependent family members.

Domesticity: The attribute of caring about home and family; considered to be characteristic of women.

Family allowances: A now-ended federal policy that provided some income to mothers of dependent children. The policy exists now only in Quebec.

Family work: All the various kinds of work needed to keep families going, including the menial chores of housework but also child care and child rearing.

Imported housewives: Nannies and domestics who are brought into North American and European homes to do the kind of family work that is not being done by the wives and mothers in those families. These people are not really housewives, but they do the work of housewives, often for little pay and under poor working conditions.

Mechanization of housework: Generally refers to the introduction of various technologies into households that make housework easier to do.

Sanitary reformers: Public health advocates who, in the late nineteenth and early twentieth centuries in Canada, urged bylaws preventing the keeping of farm animals in towns and cities.

SUGGESTED READINGS

Arat-Koc, Sedef. 1992. "In the Privacy of Our Own Home: Foreign Domestic Workers as a Solution to the Crisis of the Domestic Sphere in Canada," pp. 149-174 in M.P. Connelly and Pat Armstrong (Eds.), *Feminism in Action*. Toronto: Canadian Scholars Press. This article shows that the gap on the home front in housework and child care left when women work in the paid labour market is being filled by importing nannies and domestics from developing countries. The dilemmas this practice and policy poses for women and for society are discussed.

Armstrong, Pat and Hugh Armstrong. 1994. *The Double Ghetto: Canadian Women and Their Segregated Work* (3rd edition). Toronto: McClelland & Stewart. This book is the classic on paid and unpaid work by women in Canada. It shows, with data and theory, how paid and unpaid work are linked together for women, with unpaid work in families disadvantaging women's paid work, and women's paid work being seen as secondary to their more central roles at home, thereby disadvantaging women in the workplace.

Cross, Gary and Richard Szostak. 1995. "Women and Work Before the Factory," pp. 37-51 in Gary Cross & Richard Szostak, *Technology and American Society: A History*. Englewood Cliffs, New Jersey: Prentice Hall. This article looks at the historical changes brought to women's work in the home with the advent of industrialization. It reveals that what we think about labour market work freeing women from domestic drudgery may not have been so. Instead, industrialization may have deepened women's domestic roles by reducing women's opportunities to participate in market activities at home.

Luxton, Meg. 1986. "Two Hands for the Clock," pp. 14-36 in Meg Luxton & Harriet Rosenberg (Eds.), *Through the Kitchen Window: The Politics of Home and Family*. Toronto: Garamond. This now-classic study of families in Flin Flon, Manitoba follows the lives of several families over three decades. In this article, the second decade of the study reveals the ways in which couples work out, or don't, who will do what work at home. The study finds that most women, whether or not they work outside the home, do a much larger share of the housework than their spouses.

Nakhaie, M.R. 1995. "Housework in Canada: The National Picture," *Journal of Comparative Family Studies* 26(3):409-425. This article provides an analysis of national data in Canada on domestic division of labour. The findings are that relative income of the spouses, personal resources, time availability, and the presence of children affect who does what at home. Full-time paid working women are found to do most of the housework at the expense of their own leisure and personal care. The value of time seems to relate to one's power position in the household. For example, when men increase their paid work hours they do less housework, but when women increase their paid work hours they tend to do more housework.

Oakley, Ann. 1974. *The Sociology of Housework*. Bath: Martin Robinson. This book is the first sociological examination of housework ever done. It searches out the meanings of housework and provides explanations for why it is devalued and not paid.

REVIEW QUESTIONS

1. Over what issue does most marital and family conflict occur?

2. In the past, what was the concept of child rearing and who took the major responsibility?

3. How did industrialization alter women's roles and the significance of home-based work?

4. What is the most contentious component of domestic work, both in families and in the public arena?

5. What was the most notable effect of labour-saving devices on women's domestic work?

6. How did housework come to be seen as scientific?

7. Why does men's unpaid work at home affect paid work less than women's unpaid work at home?

8. What is the female/male ratio of hours spent on child care at home in Canada?

9. How much housework do women in Canada do in comparison to men?

10. What happens to authority patterns and division of domestic work in families where the women have paid employment?

DISCUSSION QUESTIONS

1. Why do you think that so much emotional energy is spent determining who does what at home to keep families going?

2. Discuss your images of how domestic discussion of labour worked among the early settlers in Canada and how these arrangements changed with contact with aboriginal peoples.

3. How did widowhood in the past offer women some opportunities for power and autonomy that they might otherwise not have had?

4. "Industrialization emptied the home of wealth-creating work." Explain this statement. Is this process still occurring? What do you think the future holds in this regard?

5. How does the gender division of labour in paid work matter to the gender division of labour at home?

6. How has child care come to be seen as a private responsibility? What would happen if it came to be seen as a public investment?

7. Why does myth and ideology play such a large role in the domestic division of labour?

8. What is the best means of resolving conflicts over housework and child care? How would you approach the challenge?

9. What are some policy implications of presumptions about the domestic division of labour?

10. How do you expect that the domestic division of labour might change for you and your spouse/partner over your life courses?

WEBLINKS

**http://www.jinjapan.org/stat/data/
19WME51.html**

An article discussing the sharing of housework (1986–1991).

**http://www.tcnj.edu/~unbound/news/old/
housewk.html**

An article discussing the issues related to
proposed compensation for housework.

CHAPTER SEVEN

Work and Family Life:

Balancing Conflicting Demands

In our society today, most adults work for pay. For a large portion of their lives, most people also live in families—either the one into which they were born, or one they formed as adults. Yet, often, these two major life activities—paid work and family life—fit together badly. The demands of work are often hard to reconcile with the demands of family life. In this chapter we look at problems that arise from the conflicting demands of work and family life. Then, we look at the strategies people use to balance these different demands—what shapes these strategies and what makes them effective. Finally, we consider some ways that work organizations and governments have tried to solve the problem.

For most of human history, people blurred the line between work and family life. In some families, this continues today. Consider, for example, families who run a small business: say, a corner variety store, laundry, or grocery. Such businesses, even today, are common in many ethnic urban communities, especially among immigrants. They rely on family labour, which is often unpaid and extremely reliable. This is what makes the business competitive. Think of the role children play as workers in small, labour-intensive businesses such as Chinese take-out restaurants (Song, 1995). How much and in what ways do children contribute their labour, and with what effects? How do children feel about helping out—sometimes willingly and sometimes not—as free labour and perhaps also as cultural and linguistic mediators for their parents? How does their work relationship affect their family relationships?

These are questions families still ask today. In the past, work was something most people did *only* within the context of family life. Husband, wife, children, kin, and other helpers worked together. Sometimes they did so willingly and sometimes not. Without this unpaid labour, the family business—typically, the family farm—could not have survived.

Before industrialization, the family unit was the primary unit of production. Most families were rural, and were either agricultural workers or connected directly to people who were. Work and family were found in the same place. A spouse primarily responsible for one activity could see and appreciate the work that the other spouse did. Since work and family occurred in the same place, the two were not separate. Even children helped to run the family business and keep the home running smoothly. Each person, old or young, had a role to play and society defined each person's role. The husband was usually responsible for representing the family to the rest of the world. However, people accorded the wife respect for the work that she did within the home.

Agricultural work also lent itself to the formation of extended families. In the first place, agricultural work—based on land and animals—was difficult to move, so people more often stayed put. Exceptions, of course, were non-inheriting children, who often migrated or emigrated in search of their own agricultural land. People who stayed formed strong bonds among neighbours and generations. This lent itself to the formation of a **gemeinschaft** type of community typical of pre-industrial rural life: that is, one in which everyone knows everyone else and people share common values. Since limited social safety nets existed, families largely had to take care of their own. Aging grandparents helped busy parents to provide care to the many children of the family and often provided housing and money when needed (McDaniel & Lewis, 1998).

Since work time and family time overlapped, people had no sense of "quality time," only of "quantity time." Meaningful discussions might have taken place as the family pitched hay or sowed the seeds for next year's harvest. Quality time, as we know it today in family life, was likely less important then. Shared tasks and hardships helped to cement the bonds within the family, but also dictated that these bonds are different from the ones we are used to today. Think about it. Every family member was around the others twenty-four hours a day, seven days a week. By today's standards, this arrangement might seem claustrophobic, with other family members always in your face. Nevertheless, members of pre-industrial societies accepted it as normal, perhaps even desirable, but certainly necessary for economic survival.

Not only did people have no sense of quality time, they had no sense whatever of time budgeting in the ways that we experience it today. Efficiency was not a major concern, nor was punctuality, conciseness, or brevity. The clock of the seasons and the weather determined agricultural, and sometimes human, timing. Predicting how much time people would give to any task was impossible. Too many factors were involved. People did what was necessary. People valued dedication, sociability, and the satisfaction of working together for the common good.

Industrialization changed all of this. First it drove many individuals and families out of the countryside and into the new towns and cities. Some families became migratory, following the work. As this was almost impossible to do with an extended family, the nuclear family became more common. This type of family was smaller and more compact, thus easier to move. It was also more specialized. Everyone had a role to fill, although the roles were different from those in an extended family.

Many nuclear families could not survive with only one or two members of the family working for pay. Typically, children worked in the factories or on the streets selling papers, shining shoes, or picking rags, or they took care of the younger children so that the mothers could work. In the early industrial period a significant portion of family income came from the work of children. However, factory work posed new problems for families. For example, children who were working in the factories with their parents often did not want to give their entire wages to their parents. They might even choose to move out. If they moved out, they would still be poor, but they would have control over their wages. Stay or leave, they had more independence from their parents' wishes than children had in an agricultural society. This meant a significant change in relations between older and younger generations, and a new image of childhood. Increasingly, children became a liability. Parents, behaving sensibly, started to have fewer children.

The Industrial Revolution, which began in Canada in the mid-1850s, moved the productive activity of men outside the household. Increasingly, people began to work *with* strangers and *for* strangers. Their family life became more of their private personal business, none of the boss's business. Their work life was, if they wished, not their family's business. There are those who argue that the private family is payment for selling one's labour in an alienating work environment. This relates to the concept of the home as a working man's castle, a concept with important negative consequences, as we shall see in Chapter 8. In any case, a clear line between work and family life, in the way that we perceive them today, appeared only with industrialization.

The Problem: Balancing Work and Family Life

The problem, in short, is this: both work and a family life make enormous demands on our time, energy, and emotions. Both form an important part of our identity, and both are the source of important rewards—financial, social, and psychological. But today, life often calls upon us to make choices between work and family, giving less time and energy to one so that we can give more to the other.

Two centuries have passed since this problem first arose. People in widely varying societies, doing different kinds of work, have tried to solve the problem in different ways. (We consider some of these solutions later.) Nevertheless the problem has worsened in the past decade, as many people have taken to working longer hours. People now routinely expect to work unpaid overtime. Many people with cell phones or e-mail are on call twenty-four hours a day, seven days a week. Throughout the industrial world, women's labour force participation and women's family lives have changed dramatically (Chafetz & Hagan, 1996).

Of course, by historical and comparative standards, most workers are not working more. The total number of hours a person works for pay in his or her lifetime has declined over the past century. Lengthier education has delayed entry into the workforce, and earlier retirement—both mandatory and voluntary—has hastened the exit. Work weeks have shrunk from 50 hours to 40 to close to 35 for many people who work for pay full-time. Finally, many workers work part-time—often not by choice. But many of the highly educated workers in full-time, **primary labour market jobs** (that is, well-paid, secure jobs with high qualifications) are returning to longer work weeks (Chafetz & Hagan, 1996). Though early retirement and a longer education shorten work over the lifespan, working hours during the prime working years have recently increased, especially for workers in high-paying occupations, such as law, medicine, and management.

Why do people work longer hours, if it means shortening the time they can spend with their families? The most obvious answer is the economic decline and growing job insecurity of the last two decades. After the recession of the late eighties and early nineties, incomes became less secure for many workers. To get and keep a job, people had to sell, or give up, an ever larger portion of their waking hours. To prove their worth and importance to an employer, more people began to work overtime, even if it meant stealing time from leisure and from their families. Employers, for their part, preferred to pay full-time workers overtime wages, or get more work from employees for the same or less pay, rather than hiring more workers. Doing so is cheaper, because employers have no need to spend on additional benefits or training.

As well, many women are working longer hours because, like men, they are now in jobs and careers where employers expect it of them. Many women value their careers and want to develop them, even if this means working longer hours. Finally, many women understand that earning an independent income increases the likelihood of equal treatment both within the household and in the larger society. It also provides security in case of problems with a spouse or partner.

Today, women make up about 44 percent of the paid labour force in Canada. As shown in Figure 7.1, by far the most common pattern is now for both spouses to work. Even women with preschool children generally work for pay. Yet, as we saw in the last chapter, women also continue to do most of the child care and housework. Sociologist Martin Meissner (1975: 237) has written: "Women carry more than 'half of the sky,' and half the work of Canadians is not in the market economy, but in the household" (see also Meissner, 1986).

Descriptions of the resulting problem fall into several categories: overload, culturally induced stress, and spillover. By **overload**, we mean the excessive amount of work many people—especially mothers—have to do. They are physically and emotionally unable to keep up with the burden of demands. Overloaded people simply have too much work and too little leisure. By **culturally induced stress** we mean that the workload, and the inability to get it all done, carry stress- and guilt-inducing meanings in our culture. The guilt quotient for failing to complete the workload is high. Finally, by **spillover**, we mean that workers bring home from the workplace strains and demands that the family struggles, often unsuccessfully, to meet.

Figure 7.1   THE CHANGING CANADIAN FAMILY

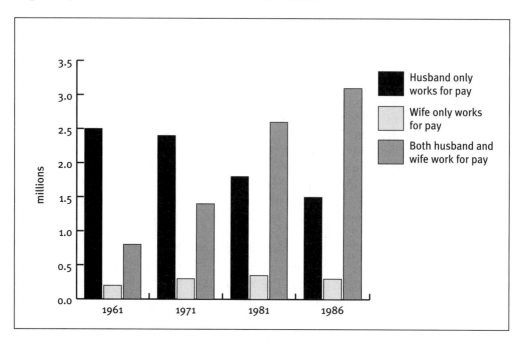

Source: *Transition*, a publication of the Vanier Institute of the Family, September 1993, based on data from the *Demographic Review*, Statistics Canada. Reprinted with permission.

Overload

As we saw in the last chapter, the unequal division of domestic labour dumps a large amount of work on the shoulders of women who also work for pay. Results include stress, resentment, and poor health. For example, many surveyed (female) nurses report heavy workloads at home. Nurses with the heaviest workloads and the least control over them suffer the worst health (Walters, Lenton *et al.*, 1996). The most vulnerable are nurses in their childbearing years who care for a dependent adult and children too. Social supports, such as close friendships, help these nurses shoulder the burden. Feeling satisfied with their professional work also helps the nurses cope with these stresses. Yet, supports and coping strategies do not eliminate the risk of health problems due to work overload. This example also highlights the wide gap between the domestic world and the work world: skills and talents that people routinely apply at work (as nurses, for example) do not necessarily find their way into the home.

The case of nurses puts this problem in its best light. After all, nurses are professionals who know how to care for people's health. They also enjoy a fair amount of social support at work, self-esteem due to their professional

A Model for Maintaining the Work–Life Balance

[Nora] Spinks doesn't like to be thought of as any kind of model for work–family balance, but there are plenty of people who would say she is. In her years of thinking about the juggling act so many of us play, she has developed some clever strategies to keep her own life sane.

Families are running on empty these days, she says over lunch with a reporter. One of the biggest challenges for work–life balance is the stress of never having time to sit back and figure out priorities. "I don't ever want to be in that fog," she adds, though admitting a moment later that she frequently does get dragged into it.

Her underlying philosophy: Control the things you can and you'll be better able to deal with surprises. "I can control the way I look at life," she says, "and nurture my body by getting enough sleep and eating sensibly. Then when things come at you that are out of your control, like the cancelled flight or a family member's illness, you can manage them better."

No one can go it alone, she adds. You need good workplace policies and community supports. Research also shows one of the keys to balance is a supportive spouse and a responsive family, "which I certainly have."

Source: Margot Gibb-Clark. 1999. Workplace Reporter, *The Globe and Mail*, Tuesday, January 5 (abridged).

status, and job satisfaction. Nonetheless, mothers who are nurses, like other mothers, suffer health problems because of a work overload.

Achieving balance takes close connections between men and women, and close connections between the workplace and home. Perhaps those connections are what the next generation—our students—can forge.

The findings on occupational stress are confusing. Statistics Canada reports no difference in occupational stress by sex. Yet other research shows that paid work stresses women more and causes women more absenteeism from work than it does men (Jacobson *et al.*, 1996). Women are more likely than men to hold paid jobs that are intrinsically stressful. Many of women's jobs combine heavy, continuing demands with a lack of decision-making authority. This combination causes higher than average risks of stress and cardiovascular disorders (Karasek and Theorell, 1990). Professional women, with more job autonomy, experience fewer harmful effects of work overload than female secretaries. However, compared with men, women are more likely to hold (high-stress) clerical and service jobs than (low-stress) professional jobs.

As well, most women have to work longer hours to earn the same amount as men, due to their lower overall earning power (called the **wage gap**). Finally, the demands of single-parenting stress many more women than men. What most women have in common is the challenge, discussed in the last chapter, of balancing a 1990s work pattern and a 1950s division of labour at home. Husbands and children—especially male children—still generally expect mothers to do most of the domestic work. So, women report heavy psychological demands in both their paid and family work, with time shortages being the most common problem they face.

Because women spend more combined time than men on paid work and domestic work, they experience more overload, especially during early parenthood. However, the extent of the problem varies over the family's life cycle. Particularly when their children are young, women in dual-earner families report more symptoms of distress than men. Women's jobs are still, on average, less satisfying and lower paid than men's. As we have discussed, in most households the domestic workload is both heavy and unequal. Mothers continue to do more of the work than fathers. Mothers' and fathers' situations do not become similar until the children approach adolescence (Higgins, Duxbury & Lee, 1994).

Sociologist Arlie Hochschild (1996) has suggested that the demands of family life are, for mothers, even less manageable and less egalitarian than the demands of paid work life. This, says Hochschild, accounts in large part for some women spending so much time at work. Many women fail to take advantage of corporate arrangements like part-time work and job-sharing that would allow them to spend more time with their families. They don't want to. Put simply, they like their jobs better than their families. More time off paid work would mean spending more time at home, doing more domestic work.

Cultural Sources of Distress

Even when men hold a paid job, do domestic work, and care for children, they suffer less stress than women with similar duties. Men do less, get some help and social support from others, and feel less guilty about their failure to achieve "supermom" status.

Women's aspirations and expectations vary from one culture to another, but they are generally different from men's. In Canadian society, parents increasingly encourage their daughters to set high goals for themselves. Yet, conflict, strain, and guilt—and also achievement—result when women try to combine traditionally feminine family ideals with traditionally masculine occupational goals. One researcher who studied schoolteachers shows this with cross-national data. Female Bulgarian and Israeli schoolteachers, who favour a traditional division of household labour, report higher levels of home–work conflict than American, Australian, and Dutch schoolteachers, who favour an egalitarian division of household labour (Moore, 1995). Both have similar amounts of actual work to do. The women who, for cultural reasons, continue to strive for high levels of homemaking experience the most conflict.

Housework, not paid work, may be the central problem facing women in more traditional marriages. This is still true throughout the Western world, where women have come to expect more equality between the sexes.

However, the problem is not only due to unmet (egalitarian) expectations. Even in a less-developed country like India, women spend more time than men on family work but just as much time as men on paid work. As a result, their work life interferes with family life, and vice versa. They suffer a work overload and a sense that neither the paid work nor the domestic work is done well—the same problem being reported by Bulgarian and Israeli school-teachers.

The problem women face is even worse in China, due to the centrality of work roles. In China, work stress has much more effect than family stress on people's psychological well-being. As well, the Chinese seem particularly vulnerable to stresses arising from interpersonal conflicts. Such stresses and conflicts, due to a combination of work overload and interpersonal conflict, can produce psychological distress.

Societies provide different roles for men and women. Our culture continues to hold women more responsible than men for the well-being of children and spouses, and for the avoidance or solution of marital problems. Ideologically, we portray family work as a shared responsibility in two-job families with children. In practice, most wives still do the domestic work with little help from their husbands and children. They typically report housework, not surprisingly, as unrewarding, monotonous, and boring. It is a major source of conflict and stress, and a limit on their leisure time (Gill & Hibbins, 1996). It is, finally, a source of guilt over roles—job-related, spousal, and parental—which they play imperfectly. Our culture teaches women to feel guiltier than men when work demands get in the way of marital relations or child care. If work for pay is socially defined more as what men do, then this can contribute to women's sense of guilt as well. This culturally induced guilt, not the workload or domestic inequality *per se*, causes women to feel more stress, and to experience more health consequences of stress, than men.

To repeat, in every culture for which we have evidence, women carry a heavier total burden of domestic and paid work than men. However, this burden has more harmful effects on women in some cultures than in others. This tells us that the effects of a work overload have cultural and psychological, not purely physiological, causes. It isn't the sheer amount of work that poses a problem so much as the meanings women attach to this burden, and the conflicts they produce. Again, what people perceive is what they respond to. Usually, effective family life depends on understanding, sharing, and changing our perceptions.

Many women, especially those who return to full-time professional jobs after the birth of a first child, express concern about their ability to manage multiple role demands. New parental responsibilities lead to psychological distress, particularly for new mothers who doubt their ability to manage the demands of their job and family roles. A woman's belief that her

Figure 7.2 CORRELATIONS BETWEEN REPORTED HEALTH AND JOB OR
MARITAL SATISFACTION FOR MEN AND WOMEN

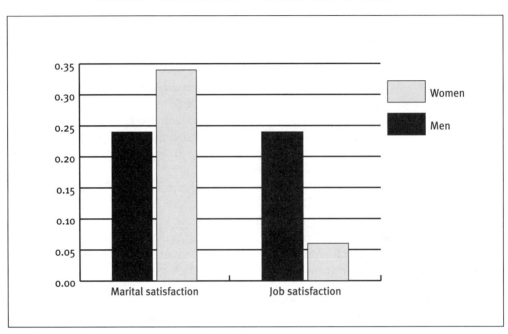

Source: Kas Wickrama, Rand Conger, Frederick Lorenz, and Lisa Mathers. "Role Identity, Role Satisfaction, and Perceived Physical Health." *Social Psychology Quarterly* 1995, 58 (4): p. 270.

spouse will help provide child care reduces much of this distress. Often, however, husbands don't provide the help we expect them to. As Figure 7.2 shows, marital satisfaction has much more effect on women's health than does job satisfaction.

Second, husbands' attitudes may also contribute to wives' health problems. Many studies find that paid employment improves women's mental health, and that multiple roles can have beneficial effects. However, that chiefly occurs when the husband is supportive. When husbands oppose their wives' paid employment marital conflict results, wiping out the potential health benefits of paid work. Other, related factors also cause stress among working mothers. For example, a husband's frustration with his own work, or a woman's dissatisfaction with child care arrangements, can produce stress.

The problem of overload may diminish in time, as more people become adept at juggling their duties (Tingey, Kiger & Riley, 1996). Already, people have become much better at this than we could have imagined. More than any generation before them, members of the baby boom generation have learned to work within conflicting cultural ideas, beliefs, and gender ideologies. Baby boom mothers have set high goals for themselves: to be a "perfect" wife, mother, boss, employee, daughter, friend, and lover, for example. Reaching perfection in any of these is, of course, impossible. Even with lower standards, it may take a generation for women to become great jugglers. Until then, our society's construction of feminine identities and conceptions of motherhood will pose a problem for women.

Workload problems also affect women differently, depending on their class or cultural group. Mothers in privileged social groups have a better chance to enter and stay in paid employment even if they have responsibility for children. Likewise, older and better educated mothers are more likely to be in high-status occupations. They are also more likely to earn enough to pay for child care, and to have their employer offer them on-site daycare, flextime, and other provisions for working mothers. In short, for a variety of reasons, high-income women are generally better able to deal with the dual burden of work and marriage. Conversely, the problem of a work–family overload is greatest for women who are already the most socially vulnerable.

Spillover

Researchers studying the connection between work and family often speak of "spillover." This term captures the notion that the products of one part of life intrude haphazardly on another part. As sociologists, we want to learn the reasons for this spillover, and its consequences (Skrypnek & Fast, 1996).

A study of female hospital workers and their families finds spillovers from paid work to the home, and to a lesser extent, from the home to work (Wharton & Erickson, 1995). A spillover in either direction least affects workers who possess the greatest sense of personal efficacy, or control, at work and at home. A sense that they can deal effectively with emotional exhaustion also helps them to avoid the harmful effects of a spillover. Simple exhaustion is one of the most important impacts of work on family life. Work-induced emotional exhaustion—along with work overload and mood shifts—profoundly affect people's state of mind. What is more, it persists unless people, groups, and organizations try to overcome it. Along with family conflict, emotional exhaustion increases the likelihood that work will interfere with family life by disrupting spousal and parenting relationships (Leiter & Durup, 1996).

Stress and tension vary across workplaces, with tension apparently being greater in small workplaces. Also, more demanding jobs spill over more into family life. On the other hand, workplaces vary in how much protection they offer against spillovers. Where support is more readily available, as for example where the organization provides benefits for working mothers, or employees feel close to their co-workers, women report less spillover from paid work to the family.

The spillover of stress from work to family occurs in different ways for men and women. Research finds that mothers whose work has stressed them are more likely to ignore their children. By contrast, fathers whose work has stressed them are more likely to generate conflict—to pick a fight—with their children. Both child neglect and conflict increase the likelihood of adolescent problem behaviour, as we saw in Chapter 5. Parent–adolescent conflict is highest when work stresses both parents.

Spillovers from family to work are also common and consequential. Women with children under age 12 most often report that their family responsibilities cause them to be absent, tardy, inattentive, inefficient, or unable to accept new work responsibilities (Crouter, 1984). Their most commonly cited reason for missing work, coming in late, or leaving early is caring for a sick child. Overall, women with children have higher work absenteeism rates than men with children do. Children are seen to be more women's responsibility than men's. As a result, fathers describe low levels of spillover from family to work, no matter what the age of their children (Burden & Googins, 1987).

Family responsibilities also shape parents' perspectives on work. In a study by Galinsky and Hughes (1986), 21 percent of the male respondents and 27 percent of the female report seeking less demanding jobs so they can have more time with their families. Thirty percent of the men and 26 percent of the women also say they have refused a transfer or turned down a promotion because it would have meant less time with their family. More recent research by McDaniel (1996b), cited in the last chapter, finds even higher proportions of midlife women potentially refusing transfers or pro-

Career Interruptions for Women

Women in the 1990s have been less likely than those of earlier decades to interrupt their careers for family or other reasons, according to data from the 1995 General Social Survey (GSS). In addition, those who did take a hiatus were more likely to return to paid work, and to return more quickly.

The GSS data showed that in 1995, almost two-thirds (62 percent) of all women who had ever had a paid job took at least six months off, compared with just over one-quarter of men (27 percent).

However, women's first completed work interruptions are now much shorter than they were in the past. Women aged 25 to 34 in 1995 reported an average hiatus from work of 1.4 years, compared with 8.1 years for those women aged 55 to 64.

Factors that may have influenced the trend to fewer and shorter paid work interruptions include lower fertility rates, delayed childbearing and changes in the workplace that have allowed women to resume work after childbirth.

The 1995 survey also found that university graduates were least likely to interrupt their careers. Those who did so returned to their jobs much more quickly than women without degrees.

Source: Statistics Canada. Adapted from *The Daily*, September 16, 1997. Catalogue No. 11-001. Reprinted with permission.

Men are becoming more willing to change their careers to increase family involvement.

motions because of family responsibilities.

Men are evidently more willing than they used to be to change their careers to increase family involvement. In 1985, just 18 percent of men interviewed said they would be interested in part-time work as a way of adapting to the needs of their children. Three years later in 1988, this percentage had almost doubled to 33 percent. In 1985, 27 percent of men said they would like sick leave policies to cover work missed to care for a sick child, and by 1988, this percentage had increased to 48 percent (Drago & Wooden, 1992; Roxburgh, 1998).

Work-Related Stress

As we have noted, paid work produces stress. Indeed, it is a key source of stress. Questionnaire data on nearly eighty thousand employees from 250 work sites in the U.S. reveals that the greatest sources of stress in people's lives are (1) job, (2) finances, and (3) family. Because of high stress levels, and the prevalent belief that women are responsible for the nurturance of children, spouse, and parents, women are absent from work more often than men (Jacobson, Aldana *et al.*, 1996).

However, what happens at work affects all workers who are family members and, particularly, affects how these workers relate to others in their families. As the workplace changes, so do the pressures on family life. In the past decade, three major changes in the workplace have put new pressures on family life. First, widespread downsizing in both the private and public sectors has produced high unemployment. Second, the spread of information technology throughout the work setting has increased the possibility of "teleworking" (or telecommuting). Finally, increased reliance on high-involvement team approaches has increased management control and worker accountability. All these changes affect work stress, social support on the job, and the extent to which workers experience job complexity and self-direction (Crouter & Manke, 1994).

Children are both sources of stress and contributors to well-being for women in the paid labour force. Once they become parents, men and women approach the workplace in different ways. Fathers are more likely to work extended hours, when possible. Mothers work shorter hours and require more flexibility in their working arrangements. Full-time working mothers are more likely to ask for and receive parental leave from their employers than fathers or part-time working mothers. As we have said repeatedly, the burden of organizing work and family life falls primarily on mothers. Research on professional women in Quebec working in traditionally male jobs illustrates this point. Whether they have a partner and children determines the number of hours they work each week and their sense of job involvement (Carrier, 1995). Partnered childless women work longer hours and feel more involved with their work than women with children.

Work-related stress is a major cause of marital problems in many families. When work increases the stress on a husband, it increases the likelihood of a hostile marital interaction. In that way, stress reduces the quality of both marital and family functioning (Larson, Wilson & Beley, 1994). Many people respond to a loss of job autonomy by becoming depressed and trying to control their spouses. Controlling your spouse may satisfy your desire to control your environment. However, it hurts your marital relations. As work increasingly interferes with family life, both emotional and practical support within the family deteriorate.

Yet, for all the problems associated with working, unemployment and job insecurity hurt families even more. Under conditions of unemployment and job insecurity, conflict intensifies and so does the risk of domestic violence. Unemployment harms the emotional health of the spouses, the quality of the marital relationship, the parent–child relationship, and family cohesion. We will have more to say about this in the next chapter on stress and violence.

Secure employment, on the other hand, generally benefits the family, even if it does increase people's overall workload. Some have claimed that maternal employment hinders a preschool child's development. However, current research does not support that view (Lamb, 1996). On the contrary, research shows that maternal employment has little impact on a child's development, or on the quality of interaction between a mother and her (preschool) child, and may be beneficial to the child's achievement and aspirations.

Of course, when maternal employment causes *too much* stress, it can hurt the child's development. Whatever its source, too much stress hinders children's well-being and parent–child interactions. However, many sources of stress are unrelated to the daily hassles of employment. For example, divorced and other single mothers report higher than average levels of stress, whatever their employment status. So do unemployed men. In both cases, the problem is likely a shortage of money. Simultaneously, divorced and hassled mothers report more instances of child behaviour problems. They also engage in more controlling, less supportive patterns of interaction with their preschoolers than their married and less hassled counterparts (Pett, Vaughan-Cole & Wampold, 1994). The problem to be solved in each case is not work or divorce, but stress. In other words, the sources of stress are many, and many kinds of stress are harmful. Work, like divorce, intensifies the problems associated with parenting, but it isn't alone in creating these problems.

Moreover, it is not *maternal* employment but *parental* employment that poses the problem in dual-earner families. We need to consider both parents' working conditions if we are to understand the effects of work on children's well-being. A mother's paid work does the family a great deal of good when it makes up for a father's difficulties with work such as an inadequate or insecure income (Grimm-Thomas & Perry-Jenkins, 1994). Parental paid work is more likely to harm the children when fathers are heavily involved in, and successful at, their own jobs, and mothers also work. Under those conditions, neither parent is paying the children much attention (Menaghan, 1993). Equally, the father's work does the family the most good when the mother's income is inadequate or insecure.

Strain and Preoccupation

Another way in which paid work affects family life is by preoccupying the thoughts and interactions of the spouses. Couples often discuss their work at home and, normally, both partners have an accurate view of their spouse's job. A survey of HIV/AIDS and cancer treatment staff in London, England found that one-third of the workers without long-term emotional relationships feel their work keeps them from becoming intimately involved with another person. Those in close relationships report spending much time discussing their work with partners. Work-related subjects lead to conflict for just under half. Indeed, four respondents in ten report their partners complain regularly about their commitment to their work. One-quarter report their relationship has suffered as a result (Miller & Gillies, 1996). Work-related strain creates anxiety, which leads to a withdrawal from marital interactions. It also leads to depression, which causes angry marital interactions (MacEwan & Barling, 1994).

Unlike many social conditions that transform people's lives slowly, work-related emotional exhaustion produces harm almost immediately (Leiter & Durup, 1996). Personal strain and exhaustion, due to job stress, make the parent more hostile and less responsive (Kinnunen, Gerris & Vermulst, 1996). Work-related stress strains parents' relations with their adolescents and, in this way, increases the likelihood of adolescent problem behaviour (Galambos, Sears *et al.*, 1995). (Recall the discussion in Chapter

---

Single Mother's Experiences Lead to Project to Identify Family-Friendly Work

Ah, the joys of September. Screaming kids being peeled off guilt-ridden parents as summer holidays give way to the demanding schedules of school and child care. You can tell the parents with jobs outside the home by their suits, uniforms and even cell phones—and by their furrowed brows as they weigh the psychological consequences of leaving little Johnny wailing at his first day of school against showing up late for work.

It's just this dilemma that led Barbara Cameron to set up a pilot project on family-friendly jobs. Its goal is to help parents who are trying to balance work and family responsibilities. The project has identified more than 40 family-friendly employers in the Lower Mainland and researched jobs and business opportunities that can be done from home.

In identifying family-friendly businesses, the most common denominator seems to be flexibility on the part of employers. Policies aren't entrenched, but usually more ad hoc arrangements suited to particular circumstances.

The options range from job sharing, flextime and telecommuting to on-site day care. They're not only geared to families with children at home, but to the changing demands individuals face in balancing home and work life.

Cameron says the advantages are not only to employees, but to employers as well. Citing absenteeism that costs companies $1.5 billion a year, Cameron says economic self-interest can be the catalyst behind family-friendly companies.

....

Source: Gillian Shaw, *In Business. The Vancouver Sun*, September 8, 1995 (abridged). Reprinted with permission.

---

5 of the link between parental involvement and juvenile delinquency.)

Of course, nothing about this process is mechanical or inevitable. That is, a stressful environment at home doesn't automatically cause adolescent misbehaviour. As with every social process, we must also take into account other factors, such as the parents' usual parenting style, the relationship that has developed over the years, the adolescent's personality, friends, and school environment, and the influence of social perception and labelling. We can only say that parental stress increases the risk of a stressful home environment and creates conditions that make misbehaviour more likely.

The major stressors that affect mothers of preschool children are lack of time, child-related anxieties (e.g., how is the child developing), and guilt (Rankin, 1993). Filling multiple roles does not necessarily cause stress. Whether a working mother feels she has control over her life is an important determinant of whether she feels stressed and whether the stress she feels has harmful effects for the family (Tingey, Kiger & Riley, 1996). Women who feel they have control over their home and work situations are less likely to suffer from stress. A strong sense of job control particularly benefits the mental health of women with children, since they are otherwise likely to feel stress about child care arrangements (Roxburgh, 1995). In this instance, then, *stress* is a medical word for **structural powerlessness**.

Many other aspects of paid work influence family life. Women who hold particularly demanding jobs report more spillovers from their paid work to their family life. Likewise, women who feel their workplace provides no support for working mothers or feel distant from their co-workers are more likely to report spillovers from work to family life (MacDermid, Williams & Marks, 1994).

Domestic inequality, work overload, and emotional stress all reduce the quality of people's marriages. As the conflict between work and family life increases, so does the psychological distress. In turn, psychological distress increases marital conflict and decreases the warmth and supportiveness of the marital relationship.

Given the risks to mental and physical health, is paid work a better choice than housework for women, if the choice is available? Put another way, are women who work for pay happier and better adjusted than those who do not? It's hard to say. The crucial variable is not so much paid employment (versus domestic employment), but whether the woman has a choice in working or not working. Equally, we could ask whether marriage is a good idea for working women—whether working women who marry are happier and better adjusted than those who do not marry. Again, the element of choice is likely to play a large part in people's satisfaction with their situation. So is their sense of control. People who feel they have more control over their lives, whether at work or at home, are happier than those who do not.

However, men married to homemakers have much higher marital satisfaction, family life happiness, and general happiness than the husbands of working wives (Chadwick & Chappell, 1980). Husbands in dual-earner marriages are generally less satisfied with their lives than other husbands. They experience relative deprivation when comparing themselves to men whose wives are homemakers (Stanley, Hunt & Hunt, 1986). They feel less successful as providers and also feel deprived of the services provided by wives who are homemakers. These male responses are **hegemonic**—the product of a patriarchal culture that raises men to expect domestic services from women.

The Reciprocal Relationship

Does maternal employment affect the emotional and psychological development of children, as some fear it does? The evidence on this question is mixed. Research finds that school-aged children and adolescents with working mothers hold fewer stereotyped ideas about male and female roles, and daughters of these mothers are more achievement-oriented. At the same time, some children whose mothers work for pay are more likely than other children to experience "insecure attachment" to their mothers. This implies that these children will grow up to be less secure in their social relations than the average person. Feelings of attachment are also linked to delinquent behaviour, as we saw in Chapter 5. Children's overall adjustment, however, seems to depend on their parent's attitudes toward the mother working, not on her employment alone. Enjoyable features of work—such as the complexity of work with people, the challenge, and the stimulation—all contribute to good parenting (e.g., less harsh discipline, more warmth and responsiveness). That is because anything that makes the parent happier and more secure is likely to improve the quality of parenting and thus the well-being of the child.

Not all the effects of paid work on family life are harmful. Full-time employed women are the most supportive of gender equality—a value most people today support. Paid work often liberates women's thinking. For mothers, paid work in a good job can increase self-esteem, even allowing for workload and caregiver strain. It works the other way round, too: mothers with a strong sense of mastery and self-esteem are the most able to deal with the demands of paid employment. Mothers whose qualifications are well suited to their current job have the most satisfaction with their work and maternal roles. Of all working mothers, they are the least anxious about being apart from their children.

Finding the proper balance between work and family remains a problem. For many North Americans, work devours not only their time but also their loyalties. Particularly among well-educated and successfully employed people, work identities supersede other identities. In part because of the new personal, portable technologies we discussed earlier, and in part because of our acquiescence to its claims on our loyalty, work has become an **imperial entity**. It affects family life, neighbourhood and community life, vacations, Sundays, marriage—even love and sex.

We see people using their cellular telephones while driving, in restaurants and concerts, in line-ups for movie tickets, in the park during a stroll with children—even in school classrooms. The omnipresence of the cellular telephone tells us that people are trying to be in two places at once. At least one of those two places is, usually, a workplace (or, at least, a **virtual workplace**, in the sense that it contains at least one work-related communicator).

Some research suggests that men and women who work for pay experience the imperialism of careers in similar ways. For example, a study of dual-earner couples in Hong Kong (Aryee & Luk, 1996) finds that husbands and wives are equally satisfied with their careers. Work-related variables have more impact than non-work variables on their career satisfaction. Moreover, perceptions of child-care quality, supervisor support, and skill use at work affect the career satisfaction of husbands and wives equally. Wives still experience more work–family conflict than their husbands. Nevertheless, work–family conflicts and multiple stresses do not affect career satisfaction, at least in this study.

Other research suggests that men and women experience careers, and the imperialism of careers, in different ways. For example, women in many traditionally male-dominated careers encounter what sociologists have called a **glass ceiling**—that is, a limit to their advancement up the career ladder. Where this **gender gap** remains, men and women use different strategies to maximize their career satisfaction. Even within a particular career—for example, as senior managers in the finance industry—men and women use different strategies to balance work and family. Workplace barriers ("glass ceilings") and legal pressures on these barriers also play a part.

Women who finished college in the late 1960s and early 1970s, for example, are less likely to have married, stayed married, and borne children than older and younger colleagues (Blair-Loy, 1996). Their careers conflicted with understandings of marriage and motherhood that were current when they graduated. In contrast, the women who finished college in the mid- to late 1970s show a resurgence of interest in marriage and childbearing. These younger women carry egalitarian cultural understandings, established in the workplace, into their expectations of family life.

Historically, women have had to put up with demands from others for flexibility and sacrifice. Consider, for example, research on clergy families who move. Wives of clergy who move report more stress, more negative views about their last move, fewer coping resources, and less well-being than their (clergy) husbands. Problems include a diminished opportunity to own and personalize a home, responsibility for reestablishing the family within the new community, a disruption of the wives' own employment patterns and informal social support networks and of children's social/friendship networks, an increased financial burden, and a lack of support from their husbands (Frame & Shehan, 1994). The spouses of other relocating workers, such as military personnel, commonly voice most of these same issues.

However many women cannot or will not move at a moment's notice. They have their own careers to run. Sometimes, fate turns the tables. Today, for example, many more Protestant clergy are women, and it will be at their request that families must consider moving.

Given changing levels of support to combine work and family, women use a variety of strategies which, in turn, influence their chances for success and upward mobility. Women vary in their labour force participation, quality of work, and adaptation to family demands, depending on when they entered the labour force and formed their families (Trappe, 1995). The considerable changes in women's employment patterns reflect changes in the social and organizational policies that shape women's opportunities.

Contemporary workplace demands require ever more ingenuity when, for example, they encroach on the choice of where to live. New personnel challenges are associated with dislocation, relocation, and adjustment to a new area. Families with not merely two jobs but two careers are not as transportable as they used to be. Concerns about children from past and present marriages, and about elderly parents, create enormous strains for today's workers. We can no longer assume that the primary mover is a male, that the trailing spouse is a female, or that the family of a moving worker will even move at all.

Efforts to Solve These Problems

How can people solve the problems of work overload, culturally induced stress, spillover, and concerns about child and elder care that we have been discussing? The strategies fall into at least two main categories: personal and familial (or **micro**) solutions, on the one hand, and corporate and state (or **macro**) solutions on the other hand. We will now consider each of these in turn.

Individual and Familial Efforts

People use a variety of strategies to deal with the conflicting demands of paid work and housework (Paden & Buehler, 1995; Wiersma, 1994).

One pattern, common for decades, has been for a parent, usually the mother, to stay at home to look after the young children. Thus, mothers are less likely than other women to work for pay.

However, for those parents who must balance both paid work and parenting, the question is how to do it, and here advice is in ample supply. Increasingly, the media offer practical advice as to ways that people can juggle their conflicting roles by more creative time management and prioritization. Time management is important for people who are coping with too many demands (Hessing, 1994). Yet, love relationships, particularly those involving children, cannot fit easily into the model of corporate careerism. Such relationships are, by their nature, too messy and inefficient. Children are more than objects that parents "manage." Caring for them is qualitatively different from meeting a business deadline. If love is to keep a secure place in our daily existence, people have to restore ways of thinking and acting that stem from sectors other than work (Pearcey, 1995).

The difficulty of conforming to workplace schedules and coordinating them with household needs is due, in large part, to the routinization of paid work hours, scarcity of discretionary time, and conflict in the time requirements of women's combined workload. Given these constraints, many women adopt timing strategies (McLaren, 1996). They prioritize paid work hours, manipulate time use, routinize daily tasks, synchronize household and workplace events, and prepare for contingency needs. The creative ways that women manage time help them to adapt to the demands of a combined workload.

Other strategies include having fewer children. For those who have gone ahead with childbearing, the most common methods are relying on extended family for support, doing less housework, or "outsourcing" the things that the family used to do by hiring extra help around the house. Some people redefine how much care their children really need. They rationalize that sending a three-month-old baby to daycare for a full working day is acceptable, since this teaches the child to be more independent, or provides the child with a "jumpstart on preschool"—which may be the case. Many families buy more services: for example, paying someone to clean the house, buying prepackaged dinners, hiring sitters to look after the children, or taking the children to daycare.

Another method of dealing with the problem is by restructuring the work arrangements of one or both parents. Part-time work and self-employment are increasingly attractive forms of contingent work that offer schedule flexibility, particularly important for women (Carr, 1996). Education, age, and past work experience all influence parents' willingness and ability to become self-employed. Obviously, a physician or lawyer can more readily exercise the option than a teacher or factory worker. It all depends on who controls the parents' **means of production**, the tools and conditions by which they make a living. Remember, however, that men and women both work and parent differently. Parenthood significantly reduces *women's* willingness to accept employment during nonstandard hours, though not *men's*—a signal that in our culture men can parent with less distraction to their work, in large part because women pick up the domestic responsibilities (Presser, 1995).

As we saw earlier, before the Industrial Revolution public and private spheres of activity were not always distinct. The home was a place of work too, not just a private retreat. With industrialization came the separation of the workplace from living space. It became more economically efficient to produce goods and services outside the realm of the family unit. Now the growth of home working makes it possible for women with few marketable skills, for example immigrant women with an inadequate knowledge of English, to work at home making clothes for big clothing manufacturers. Though paid low wages, these women can organize their paid labour around the needs of their families (Gringeri, 1995). Jobs like these with greater flexibility allow women more time for housework, for example. Part-week, part-year, and shift schedules increase the hours spent on domestic chores. Unlike employment outside the home, the number of hours spent on home-based work does not significantly reduce the number of hours spent on domestic chores (Silver & Goldscheider, 1994).The result, argue some analysts, is that this sort of home-based manufacturing works to reinforce women's lesser status both at work and at home.

Another adaptation is the home office. Now, in the so-called "post

Despite hopes to the contrary, home offices do not necessarily solve the problem of a work–family spillover.

industrial" era, new technologies have led to changes in thinking about work and home. Many tasks can be done just as efficiently in either a public workplace or a private one. As well, home work eliminates the need for an employer to pay overhead to supply its employees with a workplace. Consequently, workers can shift back to working out of the home through the aid of computers, fax machines, and e-mail.

With advances in communications technology over the past few years, many people in administrative positions can now work in the comfort of their own living rooms or **home offices**. They can keep in touch via telephone, e-mail, and fax, and only have to go into the office once a week or so, or even less.

Yet, despite hopes to the contrary, computer-supported **supplemental work at home (SWAH)** does not solve the problem of a work–family spillover. Employed parents who do computer-supported SWAH report more task variety and job involvement than other parents. However SWAH adopters also report higher levels of role overload, interference, and stress (Duxbury, Higgins & Thomas, 1996). Perhaps this shows that the new technology causes workers and employers to increase the expectations surrounding the job.

Consider the influence on family life of mobile **telework**—doing work away from the office via telecommunications equipment. Researchers compared teleworkers in a large national corporation with an equivalent group of office workers from the same corporation. Most mobile workers reported much more flexibility and some reported that their families thrived on this flexibility. However, other mobile teleworkers found that their families suffered because workplace and schedule flexibility blurred the boundaries between work and family life. This is especially problematic for teleworkers who have to care for elderly dependents in the home (Nazer & Salaff, 1996).

The reasons are easy to understand for anyone who has ever worked at home. The success people have in balancing work and family depends on drawing and maintaining a boundary between the two areas of life. As a result, "home" and "work" offer sociologists an opportunity to study **boundary work** across a range of relationships (Nippert-Eng, 1996). Boundary practices to distinguish between home and work often involve the use of different calendars and keys, clothing and appearances, eating and drinking, money, people and their representations (e.g., photographs and gifts), talk styles and conversations, reading materials and habits, and work breaks (e.g., lunches and vacations). In all these areas, people have to strive consciously, through their social practices, to give meaning to mental frameworks by placing, maintaining, and challenging cultural categories.

Apparently, teleworkers have a hard time enforcing the boundaries of their work area (and work-time) when they work at home. This is particularly challenging with the presence of young children, who often have difficulty respecting the boundaries of work and family spaces. Many people view work as something closer to leisure when it's done at home. Take a close-to-home example. Right now, one author is writing this chapter at

Home Office Politics

People who work at home trade office politics for the domestic variety, abandon regular pay cheques for cash-flow crises and set up shop in a vocational no man's land in which the boundaries between home and office, family and career are indistinguishable, a place that I call The Great DOZ—the domestic office zone.

What takes precedence, your son's homework assignment or the book review you promised to do overnight? Would you plead incompetence about the charts you can't print out, or confess that your grief-stricken daughter has used up all the toner reproducing funeral memorabilia for the family cat? And why is their need for the best computer invariably more pressing or deserving than yours? If you know the answers to these questions, then you are either immune to The DOZ or you are not working from home.

We slid into The DOZ big time about six years ago during a negotiated settlement over Nintendo and we've been trudging through moral relativity ever since. We bought a second computer—a 286—with a colour monitor, a video card and a slew of educational games, including a typing tutor (novice parents that we were), and set it up in our son's bedroom. It was his machine, but the rest of us could use it.

I know that the real solution to combining home and office will come soon enough. When my children grow up and move out, I'll have plenty of peace and quiet. But I will miss them terribly, along with their mess, their interruptions and their lively and spontaneous presence. Hey, maybe I can console myself with a Pentium processor.

Source: Sandra Martin, 1996. *The Globe and Mail*, November 30 (abridged). Reprinted with permission.

home. It's snowing and his spouse wants a ride to the subway. Can he refuse? His son comes in to ask what is for dinner, and to report on something momentous that happened at school. Being a good parent means listening politely, but if he listens too much, dinner may not materialize, or this chapter may not get finished until tomorrow. A charity telephones to ask for contributions. The dog starts barking crazily downstairs because of a furniture delivery next door (a dog bed for the neighbour's poodle). As the other author works on this chapter getting ready to send it off via e-mail to the publisher, she negotiates with her spouse, who is also on e-mail in the home office adjacent to hers. Children visiting a neighbour are yelping outside to be taken on the boat, which causes an enthusiastic response from the author's dog, who would rather go out on a boat with children than sit at a writer's feet while she types endlessly on the computer. Sometimes, the worker also violates work boundaries by trying to watch an infant, do a wash, or schedule a plumber's visit during work-time.

So, real family life ends up intruding on the supposed advantages of new working technologies. Worse, new expectations associated with this new technology may even intensify stress. The scope for overload is larger than ever before. Fax, voice-mail, and e-mail mean that colleagues expect a much faster response than they did in the days when people relied on telephones and "snail-mail" alone. And the volume of messages sent is greater, too, as more people expect instant communication. Since workers have access to these technologies at home, home workers are not spared these new stresses. And they may be expected to check for messages on their e-mails even while on holidays.

A home office may be either full-time or part-time. A part-time home office does not necessarily mean that the person is working part-time. It means that the individual goes out to work for a few hours each week, but completes the work at home. This form of work has become increasingly feasible as computers with modems provide an almost instantaneous link to the rest of the company.

Many organizations are moving to telework and see it as having few disadvantages. It is cheap, and because they have decentralized the work, workers don't know each other and the chances of unionization are reduced. Corporations do not pay the overhead and utilities but get the work done, sometimes in technically coordinated ways, by monitoring key strokes and so on. Think of this, however, from the worker's perspective; perhaps a worker who is at the same time sole caregiver for a toddler. As anyone knows who has minded a toddler, even temporarily, they can be very demanding and get into trouble or danger all too quickly. It is not so easy to be an efficient worker at the very same time as child-minding. This gives balancing work and family a new reality! The less-attractive features of home working strike us even more strongly if we consider low-level workers who do tedious work at home. It seems unlikely, therefore, that teleworking and home working are going to solve the home–family problem for all satisfactorily.

Some working parents try to reschedule their lives in a broader way, by putting things off "until the kids are older." The things put off may include a sex life, sleeping at night, hobbies, travel, and social and recreational activities. By doing this, many families miss potentially pleasurable experiences for the sake of time management and their kids. Other overloaded people split into two selves: the actual self, and the self they would be if they had more time. We've all done this, for example when we've bought tools for a project we never started, or planned for a trip that we've never taken. Prime-time TV enables, to some degree, this daydreaming and helps us create second selves. Daycare is a more practical solution to these problems.

The Daycare Debate

Ultimately, the kind of care working parents can provide to their children depends on their financial, cultural, and educational background. Parents with the resources—perhaps the wealthiest 5 percent—may hire nannies to provide at-home child care, and some of these nannies are very well-trained, skilled, and dedicated. There are reputable "nanny schools" in some parts of the world. Most nannies and au pairs (typically, young people from a foreign country), however, are paid little, have little or no training, and limited skills and commitment to the work.

Figure 7.3 shows the kinds of care that Canadian children receive. About one-quarter of parents leave their preschool children with a non-parental relative (for example, a grandmother). Some leave their preschooler in the home of the caregiver, who may or may not be tending her own infants and those of other parents as well. Corporate on-site daycare is typically of high quality, but is still rare and few children—especially, few children from poor families—have access to it. As well, with fewer and fewer Canadians working in large corporations, the opportunities for workplace daycare are fewer and fewer.

Private daycare centres provide a common form of child care. These centres vary widely in cost as well as quality. They vary enormously in the ages of children they accept, the staff-to-child ratio, the kinds of facilities that are available, and the quality of experience they provide for children. Some are more like preschools with many educational activities for the children. Others are more like large babysitting services where the children do little more than play and rest.

More highly educated and, typically, highly paid women are likely to place their children with non-kin caretakers. They are also more inclined to do so when the child is older. The availability of institutionalized, high quality child care and the parents' views on this type of care also affect their choice. Financial incentives (e.g., wages and the price of nonparental care)

Figure 7.3 PRIMARY CHILD CARE WHILE PARENTS WORK (CANADA 1988)

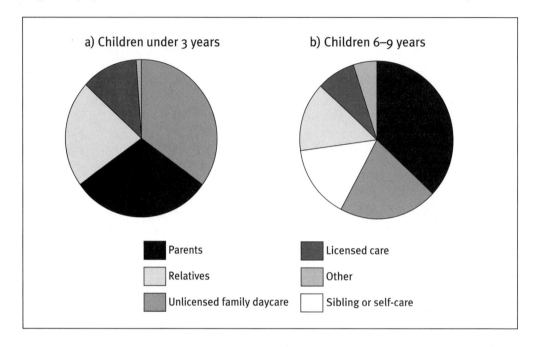

Note: Figures do not include school or kindergarten. *Licensed daycare* includes daycare centres, half-day preschool programs, before- and after-school programs, and licensed family daycare. *Unlicensed family daycare* refers to care by an unrelated unlicensed provider, either in the provider's home or the child's home.

Source: Donna S. Lero. 1993. "The Changing Patterns of Work, Family Life, and Child Care," *Transition*, a publication of the Vanier Institute of the Family, June, pp. 5, 7. Reprinted with permission.

affect the decisions of both "traditional" and "modern" parents.

As we've discussed in earlier chapters, most research supports the benefits for children of good quality nonparental daycare. Typically, children have no problems and no attachment anxiety. They usually develop better social skills and develop more rapidly than other children. Children of impoverished mothers benefit most from daycare in the area of cognitive performance. With smaller family sizes, children have fewer opportunities at home to socialize with other children, so daycare fulfils that need. Children in daycare exhibit better social skills than their home-raised peers due to a more varied social world (Broude, 1996).

German research finds that problems result from too early or extensive separation of children from parents, or exposure to illness in daycare situations. In sum, the quality of the mother-child relationship, influenced by the type of upbringing and personality of the mother, and by her and her husband's living circumstances, plays the most important role in the child's development (Laewen, 1989). Dutch research finds little evidence to support the hypothesis that children in group daycare are more aggressive or less socially competent than peers with other child care experiences (Goossens *et al*, 1991). Swedish research finds both girls and boys benefit from early daycare, especially boys who experience daycare at ages six to twelve months. Boys displaying learning or behaviour problems usually have been reared at home with no exposure to daycare or preschool (Anderson, 1996).

Some research on daycare shows positive but conditional results. Hennessy and Melhuish (1991) find four trends in a review of the literature. First, the age at which a child enters full-time daycare is frequently associated with later differences in cognitive and socioemotional functioning in the early school years. Typically, if daycare is of high quality, early entry improves later functioning. However, there is no consensus in these studies on "age of early entry." Second, children in centre-based daycare show small gains in intellectual abilities accompanied by increased aggressiveness, when compared with non-centre-based care. Third, better quality care is associated with better socioemotional outcomes. Finally, the effects of daycare are often gender-specific.

Perhaps the most decisive factor in the effectiveness of daycare is the degree of parents' and providers' satisfaction with the daycare situation (Van-Crombrugge & Vandemeulebroecke, 1991). Effective child care provides a seamless fit between home and daycare. Children's adjustment to daycare, and their ability to benefit from it, depends on a cooperative relationship between parents and centre staff. This affects both family life and the children's self-development (Sommer, 1992).

Clarke-Stewart (1991) notes significant differences between children in the various forms of daycare with respect to intellectual and cognitive abilities, social competence with strangers, independence from mother, and interaction with unfamiliar peers. However, the relationship between daycare and development depends on the particular measure used in each instance (King & MacKinnon, 1988). Some care providers establish meaningful relationships that have significant long-term effects on the children's personal and social development (Lamb, 1996). When the quality of care is poor or when there is no opportunity to establish meaningful relationships with stable care providers, nonparental care can lead to behaviour problems, including aggression and noncompliance.

In the first year or two of life, children are apparently most sensitive to nonparental care. Boys are more likely to be adversely affected than girls, as shown by behaviour problems in preschool, although as discussed above, boys are also more likely to benefit (i.e., boys respond more variably than girls). There is still debate about whether child-adult ratio and daycare settings are important factors. Research results provide little support for the contention that early nonparental care increases the risk of aggression in children (Belsky & Eggebeen, 1991). However, research does suggest that children's noncompliant behaviour is associated with early and extensive non-parental care. Maternal employment is not confirmed as a cause of child development problems, but it may be a risk factor for some children.

Considering the tender ages and vulnerability of preschool children, and the complexity of parenting situations, it is impressive that nonparental child care is so successful. It's easy to see why poor daycare can be bad for children. Leavitt (1991) completed an ethnographic study of infants and toddlers in six daycare centres and found "collective regimentation," with timetables in which flexibility and spontaneity are absent. Scheduled routines can take precedence over children's physical needs and inclinations. Such rigidity, while typical of technical rationalism, is new in its application to the very young. In the caregivers' repression of resistance, the development of autonomy is thwarted. Further, more rigid discipline only makes more discipline necessary as the children fight back against the discipline of the regime.

The important matter of achieving consensus between parents and caregivers is far from easy. Where consensus is lacking, conflicts and inconsistencies between the parent and caregiver can arise, with potentially harmful effects on the children. Kontos and Dunn (1989) report the results of a survey of one hundred three- to five-year-old children in ten different daycare centres. This study focused on the caregiver attitudes toward parental child-rearing abilities. The researchers found that children of parents perceived as doing a good job were more advanced (by the researchers' estimate) on three of six measures of cognitive, language, and social development skills. Mothers perceived as doing a poor job of parenting were likely to be single and less communicative with caregivers. They also had more traditional child-rearing and educational values, and more problems with daycare centre rules and regulations.

Possibly this study reveals that some mothers are less competent or attentive than others, and their children develop less rapidly as a result. An alternative interpretation is that caregivers have more and less favoured parenting styles, likely in part because of their own class and educational background, and tend to favour children raised in ways they approve of. The children of less favoured parents develop less rapidly, perhaps because they receive less nurturance from the caregivers but also because they come from less favourable family circumstances. (Note, however, that data obtained by interviewing the mothers supported the caretakers' assessment of the mothers.)

One study found that children who experience twenty or more hours a week of non-maternal care during their first year of life run a much higher risk of disciplinary problems later. Their parents are more likely to use controlling methods of discipline. They are least likely to mix control with guidance. Of all the parent groups studied, heavy daycare users report the most frequent defiance by their children. Resistance often explodes when they try to control the child (Belsky *et al*, 1996).

Maternal employment may produce acute problems when the mother experiences much stress at work and has little social support. Videotaped interactions show that when highly stressed mothers reunite with energetic preschoolers at the end of the workday, the mothers often withdraw emotionally and behaviourally. They speak less and offer the infant fewer signs of affection than less-stressed mothers. This withdrawal can be especially problematic, since children of stressed-out parents may also receive the most attention when they are misbehaving. This combination of too little positive attention and too much negative attention eventually leads to disciplinary problems and may encourage deviant attention-getting behaviour.

Largely, however, the research to date seems to say "No, children do not receive worse parenting when both parents are working for pay" (see, for example, Paulson, 1996; Beyer, 1995). True, parenting styles may change when women start to work for pay, so that children receive too little warmth, attention, or fostering of cognitive growth. Nonetheless, it is parenting style, not maternal employment, that causes the problem. Thus, research suggests that maternal employment is sometimes helpful to child development and sometimes harmful—depending on the quality of paid child care provided and on how well the parenting style adapts to new challenges and circumstances.

Often, problems in a dual-earner family are due to the parents themselves, especially if they feel insecure or guilty about leaving the child. Once again, people's perceptions of reality are what count most. If parents perceive that the use of outside child care is a problem, then it can become a problem. Research finds fathers and mothers reporting similar levels of separation anxiety. The spouses' concerns feed on each other. Thus, paternal separation anxiety is most strongly associated with fathers' perceptions of their wives' separation concerns. In short, people can worry themselves into unnecessary difficulty.

This peculiar behaviour—parents worrying themselves into trouble unnecessarily—is a result of guilt, which grows out of two conflicting cultural beliefs. On the one hand, people tend to believe that parents ought to be available and attentive to their children. On the other hand, people believe parents ought to develop themselves as individuals and provide a good standard of living for their children, even if it means working long hours away from home. In other cultures, people have other beliefs about parenting. Where children recognize that parental absences are normal, recurrent, involuntary, and interspersed with signs of genuine love for the children, absences are not as likely to produce guilt in the parent or a sense of rejection in the child.

Some parents use tactics aimed at eliminating the guilt they feel for not "being there" for their children. For example, some buy their kids extravagant numbers of toys. This may explain the curious fact that the toy industry is booming. In theory it shouldn't be, since fewer children are being born in our society, but of course, there are more relatives per child available now than ever before.

People try all sorts of tactics to reduce the pressure. They make plans, try to change the ways they think about work or family, find diversions, withdraw into a private reverie, develop social support networks, and so on. All these mechanisms work for some people, sometimes. Husbands are often psychically unavailable to their wives. Perhaps therefore, friends and family give working women the most important supports. They do this in practical ways, by cooperating and helping one another. Other forms of support are also important, contributing to both physical and emotional health.

Individual and familial coping responses are important and universal. No doubt, parents use as many different patterns of coping as there are families. However, individual and familial responses cannot solve all of the problems posed by the conflict between work and family life. The problems are societal and organizational, and social changes must address them. It is to these that we now turn.

Corporate Responses

Large corporations have, over the last twenty or so years, become more sensitive to the needs we are discussing here. As a result, many have changed their policies, provided new employee benefits and services, and even reformed their organizational culture—the way they think and talk about work issues. The changes have paid off. The more the organization supports employees with family responsibilities, the less strain employees experience between paid work and family roles. Supervisor flexibility and the provision of family-oriented benefits also reduce the level of work–family strain (Warren & Johnson, 1995; Thomas & Ganster, 1995). The provision of on-site child care and flextime helps workers, especially mothers, to deal better with the real demands of work and family life. It also increases work satisfaction; which, in turn, increases life satisfaction (Ezra & Deckman, 1996).

However, employers will not do this simply to increase employee satisfaction. They provide family benefits when they realize it is in their own best interest to do so (Seyler, Monroe & Garand, 1995). Employers become more likely to provide these benefits when they see they can reduce per-employee start-up costs such as training. They also provide them when work productivity is suffering because too many employees are stressed out by their family life. Generally, then, companies offer family-oriented benefits if they have a large number of employees, many of whom are women, and if keeping an existing employee is cheaper than training a new one (Seyler, Monroe & Garand, 1995). As Rosabeth Moss Kanter points out (1983), many innovative organizations adopt family-supportive policies because they profit by doing so.

Employers have good reasons to enact family-friendly policies that reduce the opportunity costs of having children. As we mentioned, the first incentive is the high cost of training. Providing paid **maternity leave** (which will typically last no more than six months) is less expensive than training a replacement for the mother.

Indeed, a survey of 4400 families with children under age 13 finds that the availability of employer policies affects how quickly working mothers re-enter the workforce after childbirth (Hofferth, 1996). A combination of parental leave laws, organizational policies, and the cost and quality of child care jointly determine how soon a mother will begin (or return to) working outside the home after childbirth. Mothers' family circumstances also matter, as do their own and their families' attitudes.

However, it takes political initiative to make organizations realize that it is in their own interest to embrace family-supportive policies. Such policies are most likely when human resource managers are enlightened, sympathetic, and capable of bringing in new policies (Kossek, Dass & DeMarr, 1994) and, more generally, when the corporate leadership is willing and able to see the big picture. Unions also play a large part in pressing for more workplace benefits and gender equality. In general, firm size and unionization are the most powerful determinants of family-responsive policies in North American, especially American, companies (Glass & Fujimoto, 1995). With large firms cutting back and union membership dropping in Canada, the prospects for family-friendly policies may be less bright.

Paternity leave may be an exception to this pattern. Paternity leave carries relatively little cost, since many men never request it. Most new fathers may take a few days of holidays after the birth of their child, but return to work within a short time. Paternity leave may have another, non-financial, purpose: it helps to recruit and keep employees. If the company cannot offer the same salary as a competitor, perks like the availability of paternity leaves can make a difference. Paternity leaves make a company seem progressive. Also, when employees feel that the company is taking an interest in their well-being, company morale and employee loyalty are enhanced. This, employers hope, increases productivity and dissuades employees from leaving to join the company's competitors.

Supportive family policies, especially flexible scheduling, and sympathetic supervisors increase employees' sense of control over their work and family matters. In turn, this sense of control produces lower levels of work–family conflict, job dissatisfaction, depression, somatic complaints, and blood cholesterol. By increasing employees' control, organizations help employees to be both healthier and more productive, committed employees (Thomas and Ganster, 1995).

However, organizational policies and practices often continue to be shaped by the views of typical male employees whose family commitments impinge marginally, if at all, on their work responsibilities. They continue to view women, as actual or potential mothers, as deviants from this male norm, whose family responsibilities are likely to hinder work performance and commitment. Assumptions like these condition the general treatment of women in careers and jobs. They also reinforce the prevailing domestic division of labour and maintain the belief that women's primary role is, or should be, familial and that their paid work is secondary (Jones & Causer, 1995).

Since most people do not want the problems associated with home offices or self-employment, they increasingly value **flextime** (see Figure 7.4). Flextime involves working the usual number of hours in the office, but having some freedom to decide when to work these hours. It doesn't involve a pay cut, or diminish chances for a promotion, so it is popular among parents, particularly women. Flextime can be formal or informal. Informal flextime, common among professionals, may mean as little as coming to work half an hour earlier to be able to take an hour and half lunch break to run errands.

Figure 7.4 PERCENT OF SURVEYED EMPLOYEES FINDING WORK ARRANGEMENTS APPEALING

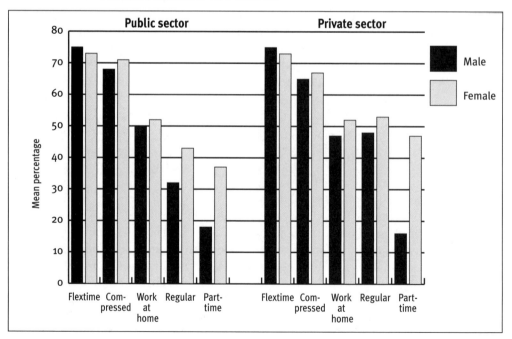

Source: Linda Duxbury, Christopher Higgins, and Catherine Lee, 1993. "Work–Family Conflict," *Transition*, a publication of the Vanier Institute of the Family, June: p. 14. Reprinted with permission.

Swapping shifts is another way of creating flextime, to allow the worker to be free for an appointment, for example. Yet shift work, despite its flexibility, carries costs. It disrupts circadian (bodily) rhythms, sometimes leading to physical and psychological ill health and domestic unrest. There is no such thing as an ideal shift system. But organizations can develop more effective ones if they take the time to find out their employees' needs and preferences, and adapt their systems to fit these needs (Snyder, 1995).

Formal flextime gives more flexibility, and a person can work extra hours one week and use them up the next by taking a day off. It seems likely, though unproven, that flexible work hours improve productivity and reduce conflicts between work and family life.

The use of flextime differs from one office to another. In some offices people frown on flextime, seeing it as evidence of lack of commitment on the part of the employee, and as causing problems. For example, if one employee leaves halfway through the day, co-workers have to cover if a client calls or a problem arises. Some researchers have speculated that primarily female offices adopt flextime more readily and use it more than offices that are male-dominated.

Where flextime is used, good communication is the key. Co-workers must know roughly when each worker is likely to come in, and that this scheduling is approved by the boss. Otherwise, the worker seems inconsistent or unreliable. If they know that the boss has approved the arrangement, the onus is on them to work around this schedule (e.g., to take messages or try to get in touch with the absent worker).

Part-time work is a policy even more widely used than flextime, for many reasons. Organizations like to put people on part-time work because then they don't have to pay full benefits and can fire the employee at will. For these and other reasons, employees generally don't like part-time work. Part-time status puts women who take advantage of it for domestic reasons on a "**mommy track**." Employers see the women on this track as less committed to their work and to their career and thus less promotable. As well, many families cannot afford the pay cut associated with going from full-time to part-time.

Other concerns include fears of being laid off. It may be cheaper for the employer to fire part-timers and distribute their work over many people, as overtime. This is especially true if the employer is paying full benefits to an employee who took advantage of an offer of part-time work. The same problem exists with **job sharing**, in which two people each work part-time to fill a job that used to be full-time. Though the two employees work the same number of hours and do the same amount of work as one full-time employee, the employer has to pay for benefits for both of them. This can become expensive, and so this form of part-time work, though increasing in prevalence, is still uncommon.

Some organizations have programs to support people with aging parents. The human relations departments of these organizations claim that the increase in efficiency in solving problems improves worker productivity more than the cost of the programs.

One of the most popular family-friendly workplace initiatives is onsite daycare for young children. This program does not change how parents have to work, but it relieves some of their anxieties. In dual-earner families, quality child care is critically important to the parents, who often feel guilty for not being with their children more. A quality child care program is particularly critical for lower-income families. However, usually only large organizations can afford to provide it. Therefore, not only must employers integrate such policies, but existing programs must be more accessible to all types of families of all socioeconomic backgrounds.

More workplaces are providing benefits packages for gay and lesbian families, including daycare for their children. Even the conservative Disney Corporation is doing so. However many lesbian and gay couples are unable to take advantage of these benefits because they do not reveal their sexual orientation to their employer, for fear of losing their jobs. The challenge is to get social attitudes updated to fit contemporary family realities.

For example, a gay or lesbian couple cannot benefit from a company-sponsored program that helps relocate spouses if the employer does not know about the relationship. Bias can also make it difficult for gay and lesbian couples to get parental leave. Therefore, gays and lesbians with children have a serious struggle to maintain a balance in their families and work lives.

Increasingly, men and women, whatever their sexual orientation, face many similar workplace challenges in caring for their families. Some employers provide little flexibility in work hours, arrangements, or responsibilities, forcing parents to use more sick leave than non-parents, for example. The increasing *casualization* of the workforce brings lower wages and fewer workplace benefits for both men and women. Deregulation of the labour market and pressures generated by global competitiveness are harming families and neighbourhoods and decreasing the options of balancing family and work lives.

Some researchers believe that, for their own good and the good of society, organizations need to allow for the wider responsibilities of employees beyond the workplace, such as caregiving to children and elders. For example, stronger legislation to limit overtime would send an important signal that priorities are changing in favour of families, thus boosting morale and reducing absenteeism.

Family Policies: A Cross-National Outlook

Family policies exist in many countries, in varying forms. Paid parental leave goes as far back as 1883 in Germany. From that time, industrialized countries have tried to incorporate policies because of their proven usefulness in helping correct the balance between family and work.

Maternity leave differs from one country to another. For example, Austria, Italy, and Sweden force employers to give all women employees maternity leave without precondition. In Canada, the United Kingdom, and Ireland maternity leave is limited to full-time employees.

Paternity leave is not available in all countries. However, the participation of men in child care and domestic work has grown with the struggle for equality of the sexes, and most industrialized countries have had to acknowledge the growing role that fathers play in the family. Among countries that have paternity leaves, Sweden, New Zealand, and Norway give fathers the longest leaves, while France, Spain, and Canada provide the shortest.

Sweden is an example of a country in which mothers are encouraged to participate in the workforce, through both widely available maternal leave and paternal leave. Sweden has a higher tax rate than Canada, so that more money can be spent on these policies. As well, Sweden has a century-long history of progressive policies on families and children. Sweden has also had a large proportion of lone-parent and divorced families for longer than Canada has. Perhaps Sweden's history points to the road ahead for Canada.

Many European countries have more liberal policies than Canada, but they achieve their family-supportive goals in a variety of ways. For example, Australia allows low-income support even when a family owns a home and car, which would disqualify a family in Germany.

In Japan, the law seems to support corporate interests against family and individual interests. For example, the law tends to side with the corporation when an employee resists a company's order to move. The husband must go, even if his family stays behind to sell the home, to maintain the

Bailing Out on Future Generations: Erosion of Social Programs Jeopardizes Prospects of Future Generations

It is revealing and, frankly, disappointing to hear those who have benefited most from public investment objecting, in their peak-earning years, to supporting public infrastructure and social investments through their tax dollars. It is that age group of people who have been remarkably privileged by all of that investment in education and health care. Members of this generation—my generation—have achieved their relative level of security and success on the basis of that investment. Now we are saying that we can't afford to pass on to our own children the gifts from which we so richly benefited ourselves. And, perversely, we say we can't afford to lay this burden of debt on our children.

If out of fear and anxiety we wind up dismantling what we as a society have built up through years of hard work and careful planning, we will be biting off our future to spite our past.

Source: Dr. Robert Glossop. 1996. Vanier Institute of the Family. *Transition*, March 1996. Reprinted with permission.

Paternity leave is not available in all countries. However, most industrial nations have acknowledged the role that fathers play in the family.

continuity of the children's education, or to care for elderly family members. Such transfers lead to loneliness for the transferee, a huge burden for the spouse left to care for household needs alone, and a heavy strain on the marriage itself. It also destabilizes the children, who grow up without the presence of the father figure.

What cross-national comparisons show us is that we can solve any problem in a variety of ways. The ways selected will reflect historical, cultural, and social differences between societies. It also tells us something about what the state can and cannot do to direct the interaction between families and work organizations. (For a useful comparison of organizational and institutional arrangements in six European countries, see Buchmann & Charles, 1995.)

State Responses

Because balancing work and family life is a huge burden for so many families and the source of both family and workplace problems, many governments have stepped in with policies designed either to give parents more time at home or to provide safe, affordable daycare.

A family issue of concern to every industrial state is population aging. As the Canadian population continues to be weighted toward the elderly (because of the decrease in birth rates), definitions of the family and of family policy are changing. Canadian companies and the Canadian government are witnessing an increase in pressure from various advocacy groups for better child care and fairer policies that will benefit all types of families. As the policies expand and improve, Canadians need to realize that it will benefit them and their families to take full advantage of them.

As women enter the labour force, whether by choice or necessity, the work traditionally allocated to women—providing care to children, the infirm, and the elderly—must be done in other ways. Societies like Sweden commodify caring and domestic work to some extent, paying for it and providing it to those who need it. In market-driven societies like the United States, caregiving has become more of a private service to be purchased by those who can afford it (Boje, 1995). However, it is still mainly women who provide the caring work. They do so either as paid female service industry workers, or as female family members who must work a second (or third) unpaid shift at home (where the **second shift** is traditional housework and child care and the third shift is elder care).

Many states are spending less money on public services such as health, education, and welfare that benefit families most directly. On the other hand, in many European countries the state has recognized the double burden women carry by giving them paid parental leave and state-run daycare centres, for example. Corporations have followed suit. France, Germany, Hungary, and Sweden have all been concerned with promoting childbearing and helping parents to balance work and family responsibilities. In addition, they have increased national responsibility for the provision of care and education of children aged between three and five years and employer responsibility for parental leave (Hofferth & Deich, 1994).

There are a variety of ways that the state can induce change in this area. Policy and law-making is one of these. However, policies are not effective unless they are enforced. Another effective way is to "lead by example" where policies are not legislated but are adopted by state-run agencies (in Canada, by Crown Corporations).

At both the governmental and corporate levels, the United States and Canada lag far behind in responding to the plight of working women, particularly single mothers. Unlike France, where child care is run by the state, the United States has a market-based system. Middle- and upper-income parents make choices and are repaid by the state for some of their expenses. Low-income parents receive targeted subsidies. Recent parental leave legislation brings the U.S. only marginally closer to Europe because leave in the U.S. remains unpaid.

As we have seen, for women—the traditional caregivers—managing the dual role of outside employment and caregiving is often highly stressful. In the U.S., women rely on institutional (i.e., corporate) and domestic support. In Japan, they rely on social traditions. Governments in both countries are attempting to ease the strains, particularly through enacting tax exemptions, workplace training and support, and community partnerships, though projects are more thoroughly integrated in Japan (Lechner & Sasaki, 1995).

Sweden and the United States demonstrate contrasting approaches to integrating family and work (Lundgren-Gaveras, 1996). In the United States, and to a lesser degree in Canada, most programs with this aim are privately run, while both the private and public sector are involved in Sweden. In both countries, programs are designed to serve the labour market. Thus, in the United States, where single mothers make up little of the labour market, they often cannot take advantage of these programs. For example, tax breaks don't benefit people who don't have employment income, and programs such as paternity leave that free up spouses for parenting don't help single mothers. The United States is unique among industrialized countries in its very limited state support for child-rearing mothers, its lack of state-guaranteed minimum payments, and its lack of programs (such as high-quality publicly funded daycare) that would help mothers increase earnings.

Currently being debated in the United States is a Help for Working Parents Proposal (HWPP). Its goal is to get all poor mothers out working for pay, though most will be working in low-skill, low-wage jobs. The policy does this in two ways. On the one hand, it reduces the attractiveness of not working (that is, of being on welfare). On the other hand, it provides child care, health insurance, and housing assistance for women who take these unattractive jobs. It guarantees health care and child care for working parents, thus supplying benefits not available in many low-wage jobs. It also increases benefits for at-home parents beyond the current system, through vouchers. HWPP does not make more low-wage jobs available. However, it does enable parents to survive with the available jobs (on this theme, see Hartmann & Spalter-Roth, 1996).

Historically, Canada has provided families and individuals with more and better social "safety nets" than the United States. However, many programs were cut severely or eliminated in the 1990s, in an effort to reduce public spending and public debt. Today, Canadian policies and programs are more similar to American ones than they were in the past.

The European, Canadian, and American approaches to thinking about work and family issues differ in many ways. However, they all point to the need for workplace culture to change in ways that incorporate the perspective of many interested parties (Lewis & Cooper, 1995). Clear thinking is needed on social policy. States must find some way to shape and predict the balance of housework (including child care) and outside work, to ease the recurrent conflicts felt by the general population. Doing so is in the national interest, and no one else is likely to do it. Private corporations have little interest in doing so, and overworked spouses are unable to do so.

Largely, how well we can solve the problem depends on how well we think about it. That is, it depends on the quality of our models of the family as an entity in the economic sector (and also the ritual, symbolic, and educational sectors). One reason existing policy does not meet the needs of Canadians is that it is based on outdated assumptions. In a recent book (1997), Canadian sociologist Margrit Eichler provides three models (patriarchal, individual responsibility, and social responsibility) and three conceptual models of the work–family relationship (separate sphere, spillover effects, and interactive). Thus, her starting point is to recognize the fact that

Women Find There's No Place Like ... Work

Working women have discovered what men have known for a long time—staying at work is a whole lot nicer than going home.

Home and work have changed places to the point where harried parents now feel more relaxed and appreciated at work, while their home life has become a constant hassle, sociologist Arlie Hochschild told a news conference yesterday.

Now, she said, the real competition isn't between North American companies and those in Germany or Japan, but "between North American companies and homes. Competition is in the currency of time and the company is winning."

Hochschild warns that children are becoming increasingly industrialized at home and the already fragile family is bound to suffer. "I fear we're adjusting to a lower level of emotional giving," she said, "and we may develop into less humane people. The question isn't can we adapt to the time famine at home, but do we want to?"

Governments should develop moral and financial incentives for companies who resist downsizing and replace it with work-sharing, and also develop a family protection agency, similar to the U.S. Environmental Protection Agency, because "families are an endangered species, too."

Source: Elaine Carey. Reprinted with the permission of The Toronto Star Syndicate. From an article originally appearing in *The Toronto Star*, August 12, 1997.

families and work–family relationships vary widely. So must models of the family and state responses to family life.

Pre-World War II legislation perpetuated female dependency on males, signifying the change from a family-based to a socially based patriarchy. After World War II, the state began to promote gender equity with policy and legislation designed to reduce inequality in the marketplace (Boyd and McDaniel, 1996). However, the "equal opportunity" package, focusing as it does on the rights of individual workers, is inadequate to deal with aging, changing family structure, economic restructuring, and immigration. We cannot hope to make satisfactory progress until we have adopted the right model for change, as has been done in other industrial societies (Burstein, Bricher & Einwohner, 1995).

Taking another approach, cross-national research on 15 industrial societies (Shaver and Bradshaw, 1995) finds that people commonly apply three models to the relation between family and work. In the *traditional* model, the wife is economically dependent on her husband. In the *modern* model, the wife remains outside the labour market while she has young children. In the *dual breadwinner* model the mother of young children is in full- or part-time employment. Welfare states typically embrace the dual breadwinner model. They provide support to women, whether or not they have young children and work for pay, though the levels of support vary greatly among welfare states.

Concluding Remarks

With North American workers putting in about 140 more hours on the job each year than they did twenty years ago, many find it difficult to relax and enjoy their family and friends regularly. Also, the increase in time spent at work has created a great deal of stress within the family. Household management is no longer simple, and even with outsourcing, someone has to co-ordinate the services. Financial insecurity also increases stress within the family, and the past twenty years have provided many opportunities for families to experience financial stress. We will discuss some results of this in the next chapter. We have already noted some consequences for mental and physical health.

For many individuals, the financial costs of family life are starting to outweigh the benefits. The consequences of family stress, bad parenting, and work disruption due to family concerns are significant public issues. Yet they are still, for the most part, problems to be remedied by individuals in the privacy of their homes.

To meet the demands that work is putting on parents, family time has become increasingly regimented, with "quality time" scheduled between the different family members. Increasingly, dual-career couples develop behavioural strategies to solve work–home conflicts. These coping behaviours are cooperative or social, in the sense that they transform the way the family system works to reduce pressures on one or more of the family's members. More individualistic coping strategies may also be tried, such as taking up yoga, getting time alone, developing friendships outside the family, which may or may not change the way the family operates. But neither type of strategy involves state expense; the state largely leaves to families the problem of adaptation.

In solving the problem of a balance between work and family, much depends on how effectively dual-earner spouses deal with the time shortage, work overload, and overall work–family conflict. Families that deal with their stresses well are typically satisfied with their family life, whether they have one breadwinner or two. Dealing with these stresses successfully usually means developing successful strategies for resolving conflicts. Here a problem arises, since attitudes about gender affect the ways that people think about work–family decisions and the interpersonal strategies they use to carry them out. Various socioeconomic factors also make it easier or harder for families to function. Because low-income or less educated parents have fewer opportunities, they experience greater difficulties and, eventually, more stress.

Each partner's ideology and interpersonal strategy affects the other partner's satisfaction with the relationship. Thus, a difference in gender ideologies—especially where one or both partners adopt confrontational problem-solving strategies—is likely to sharpen the conflict over work–family issues. Moreover, spouses affect each other's perceptions of "the job" and the fit between work and family, and this in turn affects the level of marital tension. Where one spouse thinks the fit is poor, the other is more likely to adopt this point of view too. This, in turn, increases marital tension (despite agreement about the nature of the problem).

The organizational and institutional standards in any society determine the context within which men and women make education, labour market, and reproductive choices. For example, irregular school schedules, limited shopping hours, and lack of child care services reflect a social and political belief—typically, a belief not shared by young working women—in the full-time homemaker. Therefore, women in such societies are forced to make a choice between family and work, a decision not forced on women in countries with more accommodating organizational structures.

For most of this chapter, we have concentrated on the negative aspect of work, especially that of work causing stress in the family. We should not leave the topic without acknowledging that work can also be a profoundly rewarding experience, with benefits for the entire family. For example, many studies of single mothers show that if the mother is in a job that she enjoys, the child often grows up unaffected by the absence of a father. Other studies show that professionals can sometimes apply to their family the problem-solving skills learned at work. This is an interesting aspect of the relationship between work and home that researchers should explore further.

Women and men also need to establish a new domestic economy. Too many men still believe they are entitled to full domestic service from their wives. Women should consider carefully whether to marry such men—or even to marry at all. Women who do marry ought to consider unfair treatment grounds for divorce. The whole question of what is fair in marriage—especially, though not exclusively, when both mates are working for pay and workers have children to care for—needs to be opened up for plenty of discussion. Men have had it their way for far too long. That's not only unfair, but it can ruin a relationship.

The "bargain" between the sexes needs to be renegotiated. In any society, the interests of men, women, and children, straight and gay, religious and secular, rich and poor need to be articulated and (metaphorically) brought to the bargaining table. In this respect, our book tries to document what the adult women's negotiating team would want to get accepted by society as a whole. We must be careful to ensure that we also hear the wishes of children. Men have already made their wishes known.

Thus, it is not work per se that is the problem, nor even work in the context of parenthood. The problem is gender inequality at home and at work. When we solve that problem, work and parenting will still require a lot of effort. However, they will not necessarily be incompatible, harmful to health, destructive of marriage, or an impediment to the growth of happy, productive children.

CHAPTER SUMMARY

In this chapter, we have stressed the problematic aspects of the connection between work and the family. We noted the family's evolution from the industrial revolution to the 1990s. The structure of the family has changed considerably with the change in work. Family size shrank, the roles of the individuals within the family changed, and the concept of quality time developed. We have seen a great change in the role that women play in the workforce, which has directly affected family structure. Families of the '90s face many obstacles. As people work longer hours, they find it difficult to balance work and family demands. Women carry a larger share of the burden than men because in many cases expectations of domestic roles have not changed to accommodate their greater participation in the paid workforce. When parents experience stress, children are also affected.

The balance that exists today between family and work is not an effective one. Work usually takes precedence over the family, and it has been work that has shaped the family since the Industrial Revolution. The powerful have not been interested in a work structure that effectively preserves the family, though the family is what makes work and workers possible. Family-friendly policies help to solve some problems. Some employers have realized that problems do exist and have introduced such things as maternity/paternity leave, flexible working hours, and part-time work to help families cope with everyday stressors associated with work. Home working and self-employment are also approaches to resolving work–family conflicts, but carry problems of their own. We looked at policies cross-nationally, and have seen that Canada has much catching up to do. We need more government intervention in building these policies and making sure that companies practise them.

KEY TERMS

Boundary work: The effort to draw and maintain lines between different spheres of life, such as family and work; often difficult for people who work at home.

Culturally induced stress: Stress from the guilt people feel when they cannot meet all the obligations of work and family they feel society expects from them.

Flextime: A variety of arrangements, formal or informal, that allow employees some freedom to decide when to work their allotted hours.

Gemeinschaft: The type of community typical of pre-industrial rural life, in

which everyone knows everyone else and people share common values.

Gender gap: Differences in men's and women's opportunities and treatment, for example in workplaces.

Glass ceiling: An unofficial but real barrier limiting women's advancement up a career ladder.

Hegemonic: Relating to a ruling or powerful group or class; men who have been raised in a patriarchal culture tend to expect the benefits of male dominance, including domestic services from women.

Home office: A workplace within a home, used by self-employed people or employed people who are able to work at home, usually on computer.

Imperial entity: An element that dominates all of a person's life and life decisions (used to describe work in modern life).

Job sharing: An arrangement in which two people work part-time to fill what would otherwise be a single full-time job.

Maternity leave: Time off work, especially paid or partly paid, to give birth or to care for a new child.

Means of production: The tools and conditions through which goods or services are produced and people earn a living.

Micro/macro: Referring to the different levels on which problems can be addressed: Micro refers to strategies carried out by individuals and families, and macro to strategies at the level of the organization or state.

Mommy track: A career path for women who work part-time or turn down additional responsibilities in order to care for children; can relegate them to lower status and reduce chances for promotion.

Overload: The excessive amount of work many people—especially mothers—have to do.

Paternity leave: Time off work, especially paid or partly paid, to allow a man to spend time with his new child.

Primary labour market: Jobs that are secure and well-paying and, typically, have entry requirements (e.g., educational credentials or specialized job experience) which relatively few people can satisfy.

Second shift: Housework and child care done by women who are also doing a full day of paid work.

Spillover: Strains and demands from the workplace brought into the family—or from the family into the workplace.

Structural powerlessness: Lack of control over their own home and work lives experienced by people because of social and economic factors related to the formal and informal structures of society.

SWAH: Supplemental work at home; work from home for people who also work out of an office.

Telework or telecommuting: Work done away from the office using telecommunications equipment.

Virtual workplace: The hypothetical place in which people work (especially by computer or telephone) without physically going to a workplace such as an office or factory.

Wage gap: The difference between men's and women's earning power.

SUGGESTED READINGS

Daly, Kerry J. 1996. *Families and Time: Keeping Pace in a Hurried Culture.* Thousand Oaks, CA: Sage. Offers a new paradigm of time control that shows that decisions about the control of time express value preferences. In the new "politics of time," families increasingly develop strategies to control time use. They must work out their mutual interests and make decisions about time so that they do not simply maintain the pace of the culture and come together in an exhausted, needy state.

Gerson, Kathleen. 1993. *No Man's Land: Men's Changing Commitments to Family and Work.* New York: Basic Books. Uses life-history interviews of men from varied social backgrounds to investigate how men are re-evaluating their commitment to work and family in today's society.

Shows that men are increasingly turning away from the "breadwinner" role toward either remaining single (or getting divorced) or getting actively involved in raising children.

Hanson, Susan and Geraldine Pratt. 1995. *Gender, Work and Space.* London: Routledge. A detailed picture of the history and relationships between family life and working life in Worcester, Massachusetts, using quantitative and qualitative analysis to link feminist geography and feminist theory. Themes include gendered social networks and cultures in relation to labour markets, and the ways household arrangements reflect patriarchy.

Hendershott, Anne B. 1995. *Moving for Work: The Sociology of Relocating in the 1990s.* Lanham, MD: University Press of America. Examines how relocations affect workers' careers and relationships. Of particular concern are the challenges associated with dislocation and adjustment to a new area, especially in the context of dual-career families, single-parent-

families, and worries about elderly parents.

Phizacklea, Annie and Carol Wolkowitz. 1995. *Homeworking Women: Gender, Racism and Class at Work.* London: Sage Publications, 1995. A critical overview of home-based work that challenges the view of home working as attractive. Original research in Great Britain shows that home working replicates existing racial, class, and gender divisions in the labour force. Differences experienced by clerical, manufacturing, and professional home workers are noted.

Sachs, Carolyn. 1996. *Gendered Fields: Rural Women, Agriculture and Environment.* Boulder, CO: Westview. Uses feminist theory to study rural women and their participation in work and family life, in the context of a changing global economy, shifting gender relations in both industrialized and developing countries, and changes in people's practices in the face of such problems as environmental degradation.

REVIEW QUESTIONS

1. In this chapter we have looked at three problems having to do with women taking on a double workload: "overload," "culturally induced stress," and "spillover." Discuss one of these in detail.

2. Briefly discuss what is meant by teleworking and how this affects the family.

3. What is flextime? How have corporations used it to their advantage?

4. What is meant by the term reciprocal relationship? Discuss some of the health/emotional problems that arise out of work-related stress.

5. Why has the recent trend of working longer hours developed? Why has work time become more concentrated into specific periods of the typical lifespan?

6. What is on average greater—home-to-work spillover or work-to-home spillover—and why?

7. Name some benefits that paid work has for women.

8. What do research findings show about the effects of daycare on child development?

9. Why is it often to the company's advantage to provide paid maternity leave? Paternity leave?

10. Why are gays and lesbians sometimes unable to take advantage of family programs offered in their workplaces?

DISCUSSION QUESTIONS

1. If you had to choose between a successful career or having many adorable children, toward which side would you lean?

2. The explosion of computers has made it easier to perform job-related duties at home, but has also changed job expectations and specific duties. Overall, is this a good thing?

3. If you were gay or lesbian and had a partner, would you reveal your sexual orientation to your employer? Is there any answer to the dilemma of gays and lesbians who want to benefit from family-oriented policies but are afraid of prejudice in the workplace?

4. "Top ranking officers in the Canadian forces are expected to have wives who are geographically mobile." Considering the importance of military men, is this expectation justified?

5. Do you feel parents are justified in placing their infants in daycare for a great proportion of the day in order to keep up with their careers?

6. Should paternity leave be given to all working fathers? Should they be entitled to leave even if their wives have taken maternity leave?

7. In Germany, a family eligible for low-income support must own very little. In Australia, low-income support is given even when a family owns a home and cars. Which country do you think has the fairer policy?

8. This chapter has outlined many courses of action that could help alleviate the problems of work–family conflicts. Can you think of any other solutions?

9. If you were the owner of a company, what arrangements would you make to ensure fairness to employees who were the mothers and fathers of young children?

10. At what age would you leave a child alone at home? For how long? How would you ensure the well-being of a child left at home, or what alternative arrangements would you consider?

WEBLINKS

**http://www.statcan.ca/english/Pgdb/
People/Labour/labor01a.htm**
Average incomes, by sex, for full-time workers.

**http://virtual.finland.fi/finfo/english/
work_family.html**
Combining work and family as a key issue for women. Policies on work and family, current trends in working life.

http://www.bpinews.com/hr/issues/rwf.htm
The national report on work and family, news on legislation, litigation, and employer policies.

**http://www.wa.gov.au/gov/doplar/
w percent26f/**
Western Australia Department of Productivity and Labour Relations
Work and family resources; back issues of work and family newsletters. Newsletter on balancing work and family.

http://www.mwfam.com/index2.html
This Web site on managing work and family has workshops, consulting services, links, and published works.

http://www.vikingsolutions.com/ misswork.htm

An article on more women taking more time off work than men, by Eric Beauchesne in *The Ottawa Citizen*.

http://ndsuext.nodak.edu/extpubs/yf/ famsci/fs514w.htm

Balancing work and family: working with your employer.

http://www.mot.com/Employment/motlife/ wrkfam.htm

A statement of an employer's "life vision" of balancing work and family, from Motorola.

http://www.ahri.com.au/hrinfo/hrmonthly/ abstracts/work.html

HRMonthly

Current abstracts on work and the family from a magazine aimed at human resources professionals.

CHAPTER EIGHT

Stress and Violence:

Unpleasant Realities of Family Life

Recently two boys in Arkansas filled a van with stolen guns and set a trap for their schoolmates. One pulled the school's fire alarm while the other lay in wait. As their mates poured into the schoolyard, the two boys began firing rifles. They killed one teacher and four girls. The hailstorm of bullets injured many others. Police quickly arrested the boys and, immediately, people began trying to make sense of this violence—not an isolated incident in the United States in recent years.

Their efforts to make sense are, as always, socially structured in predictable ways. As is typically the case, people who knew the accused expressed their shock and surprise: "They seemed like such nice, normal boys." As always, parents blamed the mass media for teaching children violent behaviour. Some, mainly non-owners of guns, called for the stiffer regulation of guns. The familiar analyses were partly right, but only partly so because each was incomplete. Each focused on the individual and his seemingly unique behaviour, or the seemingly unique incident. Each sought to blame someone or something else. Yet, in fact, the problem of violence is socially structured.

The urge to injure or kill is not as rare as we might like to think. Such urges are themselves socially structured. Frustration or despair motivates them, and these are also socially structured, as we have seen in several previous chapters. Some people's lives are more desperate and frustrating than others. This is, in large part, a result of the **class** and racial or ethnic **stratification** of societies. Beyond that, culture teaches us ways to deal with our frustration and despair. Many young people in our society take their own lives. Our culture also contains messages that condone violence against others—especially violence by men against women. It comes as no surprise that in the case described above the two killers were male, the five victims female. This is usually the pattern in mass murder.

Finally, society makes weapons of destruction differentially available. Guns are more readily available in some parts of the world, and in some parts of some countries. Legislation to ease or hinder the possession of guns is itself a "social fact" that needs explaining.

Society structures the motivation, the rationale, and the opportunity for public violence. It also structures the motivation, the rationale, and the opportunity for private or intimate violence. As we will see, stress is common in families but more common in some families than in others. Violence too is common in families, but more common in some families than in others. The translation of stress into violence cannot take place without the provision of a **cultural rationale**—typically, a **patriarchal value system**. It also requires plenty of opportunity, typically provided by people turning a blind eye to the escalating violence. Except in the mass media, families are danger zones.

In this chapter we examine various forms of family stress and violence. We consider what it is about family life that often leads to stress, and the ways that stresses affect family relationships. Finally, we examine the common forms of intimate or familial violence, especially child abuse and wife battering. Note that stress is not the only or even the main cause of domestic violence. Stress does not always lead to violence, nor does violence always result from stress. In fact, stress is more often an effect than a cause of family violence. The reason for including stress and violence in the same chapter is that both illustrate a gap between the idealized image of the family and the actual functioning of close relations in families.

Stress

Family stress is "a state that arises from an actual or perceived imbalance between a **stressor** (i.e., challenge, threat) and capability (i.e., resources, coping) in the family's functioning" (Huang, 1991:289). To explain the effect of stressor events on families, most current researchers employ a version of the **ABCX family crisis model** first elaborated by Hill (1949). In this model, A, which represents the stressor event, interacts with B, the family's crisis-meeting resources, and with C, the interpretation a family makes of the event, to produce X, the crisis.

This ABCX model focuses primarily on pre-crisis variables that make some families more or less able to cope with the impact of a stressor event. Researchers originally developed the model to study family adjustment to the crises of war-time separation and reunion (Hill, 1949). Sociologists have since used the model to examine differences in the ways families cope with a wide variety of difficult problems.

One factor that always influences stress is the nature of the stressor event itself, as measured by its severity, intensity, duration, and timing. We can evaluate stressor events as *objective* and *subjective* phenomena. An outsider, such as a researcher, using agreed-upon standards of measurement, provides an objective evaluation of the stressor, which corresponds to *A* in the model. Thus, an objective evaluation of *unemployment* for a given family, for example, might take into account the income-earning capacity of the other family members, the family's debt load, and the resources (e.g., property) the family has to fall back on. A researcher would measure the duration and timing of the stressor event: how long the unemployed period lasted, and the frequency with which it recurred. Typically, the longer a stressor event lasts, the more severe its effects. The more often it occurs, the more it strains a family's resources. Consequently, the harder it is for the family to cope successfully.

Family members themselves make a subjective evaluation, which corresponds to *C* in Hill's model. How family members view and define that event determines the way they react to it. Their subjective evaluation of an event may not correspond to the researcher's objective evaluation. In large

---

Farmers Today Face Urban-Type Stress

Since its founding more than a century ago, Brandon has been identified with agriculture.

Today, Brandon University has a psychologist who specializes in stress counseling for farmers.

"What we see in the farm environment is that financial pressures have exaggerated the stress level," said Dr. Lilly Walker during an interview in her university office. "That pressure makes all the other pressures that were there more intense."

In other words, after the drought and the rust and the smut and the grasshoppers and the flea-beetles and the sow thistles and the quackweed and the hail and the frost, there is still the interest to pay on the mortgage.

"There are some characteristics that define farmers," says Walker.

"One is independence and one is pride, and those two often have the effect of insulating them from admitting they have any problems at all.

"Now, because of the accumulation of crises, we see people who are forced to say: 'I need some help here.'"

At Brandon University, Walker will be watching the development of stress in farmers in terms of "negative coping"—drunkenness, overeating, wife-beating or other violent behavior.

"On stress scales, one of the things that is a major stressor is debt," she says.

Source: Patrick Nagle. 1985. Southam News, in the *Calgary Herald*, June 16, p. A12 (abridged). Reprinted with permission.

---

part, how they evaluate it is largely a product of their own sense of whether they can likely cope with the situation. Like any self-fulfilling prophecy, a belief in their ability to cope increases the family's actual ability to cope.

When sociologists study families living under conditions of stress, they do so in different ways than psychologists and psychiatrists. Since sociology is the study of social relationships and social institutions, sociologists are interested in learning how stress changes the system of roles and relationships that make up a family. For example, they study how stress changes the ways that spouses relate to each other, parents relate to children, children relate to parents, or siblings relate to one another. They investigate the ways stress affects patterns of communication and interaction, marital satisfaction, or parental competence within the family. How, they ask, does stress change the way that members of a family relate to extended kin, neighbours, community members, teachers, and employers? Finally, they investigate how stress changes a family's ability to socialize children, or provide a stable and healthy workforce.

Often, extreme stress reduces a family's ability to act well in these situations. For that reason, sociologists are interested in how family members cope and adjust to a long-term stressor. Some families and their members cope poorly by avoiding change as much as possible. Others cope better as individual members change their behaviours. Finally, others cope by changing their family relations. It is that change of family relations that interests sociologists most. How, sociologists ask, do families as a whole adjust their expectations and interactions to suit the new conditions of life and, in this way, reduce stress?

Consider, for example, how a family might adjust to the strains of civil war, as in Northern Ireland, Bosnia, or Rwanda. They cannot easily escape the dislocations caused by war—death, injury, unemployment, scarcity, fear, guilt, and so on. Nevertheless, some family members ignore them for as long as possible. Others cope by running away, drinking heavily, or hiding and sleeping. Some seek guidance and consolation from a friend, the local minister of religion, a teacher, or a medical doctor. Others, finally, discuss the problem with family members. Then, they may plan how, individually and collectively, they can maintain the supply of food, shelter, and other necessities of life, and how they will react to threats to the family as a group.

Ultimately, a family's success in coping with a stressor event will depend on the strength or quality of its crisis-meeting resources. As we will see, families that cope well with stresses are families that already had considerable resources—especially, cohesion and flexibility—before the stresses began. We will find systematic differences between the families that pull together and the families that fall apart under the strains of stressor events.

Causes of Stress

Common causes of family stress fall into at least four categories. They include **major upheavals** such as war and natural disasters (e.g., tornadoes, floods, and earthquakes) that affect many people simultaneously. Second, they include **major life transitions**—acute disruptions due to events that may affect some family members simultaneously, but not others—such as the birth of a child, the death of a parent, divorce, and retirement. Third, they include **chronic stressors** such as disability, chronic physical or mental illness, drug and alcohol abuse, occupational problems, unemployment, or imprisonment of a family member. Finally, they include **occasional stresses**, which may be temporarily severe but go away without permanent change. Examples of this would include a car accident, a burglary, a sudden illness or death of a family member, or even apparently pleasant but stressful stimuli like a holiday trip.

Major Upheavals

For North American families, the Great Depression of the 1930s was a near-universal stressor causing widespread unemployment and poverty. A classic study of family dynamics during the Depression (Cavan & Ranck, 1938) concluded that coping ability rests largely on a family's previous organization. Families reacted to the Depression in the same way as they had reacted to earlier problems. Thus, families who had been well-organized beforehand more readily recovered from the emotional strain caused early in the Depression. All families showed increasing strain as the Depression continued; however, the degree to which this strain was felt differed from one family to another.

World War II provided an example of a varied stressor. For many, the War reduced family stress by providing jobs for people who had been unable to find work during the Depression. It also allowed restless young men to leave home and join the military. Simultaneously, however, the dramatically increased wages that many teenagers brought home weakened parental control and increased delinquent behaviour. Also, the loss of a father to military service, or a mother's change of roles from homemaker to working woman, required all members of the family to adjust (Levy, 1945).

Recent studies of families in crisis conditions have highlighted other increasingly common sources of stress. Current research continues to examine the linkage between economic stress, poverty, and family dysfunction. Sociologists continue to find that economic pressure on a family increases parental unhappiness and marital conflict. It also increases parent–adolescent conflicts (Conger, Ge & Elder, 1994). High levels of irritability, combined with arguments about money, lead parents to show greater hostility toward their children. In turn, these hostile exchanges increase the risk of adolescent emotional and behavioural problems.

Economic stress resulting from unemployment poses additional problems. Job loss can cause psychological depression—especially in husbands who have been living under economic strain for a long time and have an erratic work history (Wright & Hoppe, 1994). Generally, mental health worsens as economic problems increase. Wives are even more likely than husbands to stay depressed under these conditions (Friedemann & Webb, 1995).

Research also continues to examine the effects of war on family functioning. Families living under long-term war conditions suffer considerable stress. Consider the families in West Beirut, Lebanon. After 12 years of war, they show a variety of stress-related problems: depression, interpersonal and marital conflict, and psychosomatic symptoms (Farhood et al., 1993). In Honduras, symptoms associated with **post-traumatic stress disorder (PTSD)** due to civil war and repression are particularly common among the families of "the disappeared" (those who were arrested, taken away, and never again seen). Symptoms characteristic of PTSD include psychological numbing, increased states of arousal and anxiety, and a tendency to re-experience the trauma mentally. PTSD can be more debilitating than grieving the death of a loved one. An atmosphere of fear and isolation prolongs these stress-related disorders long after the disappearance of the family members itself (Quirk & Casco, 1994).

War, like unemployment, brings family members closer together if they were already cohesive. However, it drives them apart if they were not.

During the 1991 Persian Gulf War, for example, residents of Haifa, Israel relied more on kin for immediate or direct aid than they did on their everyday networks of friends. Friends, by contrast, continued to provide comfort and advice. Thus, non-kin provide a specific form of social support, but people still turn to kin for survival (Shavit, Fischern & Koresh, 1994).

As we have said, crises can make or break a family. Thus, in the early 1990s, Israeli and Palestinian couples with a strong, shared ideological orientation agreed more often and reported an increase in cohesiveness. Other couples reported a deterioration of their relationship. They disagreed more about the meaning of the peace process and its effects on the family (Ben-David & Lavee, 1996). Crises test families, and many are found wanting.

Family Life Transitions

Like war and economic difficulty, migration has been a continuing source of family stress throughout this century. Immigrant families face **acculturative stress**, due to the strains of adapting to a new society. These include a lack of local language skills, low employment and economic status, and limited educational background (Thomas, 1995). Prolonged stress tends to harm a family. Therefore, time spent in a new homeland may increase the anxiety and depression of both parents and children, as young Indochinese refugees reported after settling in Finland (Liebkind, 1993). Reportedly, women are particularly stressed by immigration.

Typically, the children of immigrants assimilate more rapidly than their parents to local standards of behaviour. This often produces conflict between parents and their children. So, for example, Southeast Asian adolescents in the United States report experiencing a lot of parent-induced stress about academic performance (i.e., studying for a test, pressure to get good grades) and parental expectations (i.e., high expectations to do well). They fear failing to meet family expectations. Adolescent women are particularly susceptible to stress of this kind (Duong Tran, 1995).

Chronic Stressors

The three most common causes of chronic family stress are the demands of paid work, of parenting, and of caring for ill or infirm family members. We will briefly consider each of these sources of stress. As we have already discussed the stresses caused by parenting and by paid work, here we will focus on the stresses associated with caregiving.

As we have already seen, parenthood itself causes stress. The most important predictors of parental (especially maternal) stress are the age and sex of the infant. Under normal conditions, older infants and female infants are easier to handle (Sanik, 1993).

However, parental stress intensifies when children have special needs. Thus, one source of family stress that researchers have given much attention to is the need to care for a chronically sick child. This is a long-term stressor that cannot be fully eliminated by typically effective coping methods. Consider these examples:

- *Attention-deficit hyperactivity disorder (ADHD)*. A child with ADHD can challenge parenting resources and coping, thus risking the quality of family functioning. Parenting stress for mothers of children with ADHD is particularly intense when these children develop behaviour problems and "act out" (Baker & McCall, 1995).

- *Developmental disabilities*. Dealing with the disability itself and with behaviour problems stresses families of children with developmental disabilities. At highest risk of depression are fathers with male children and mothers with younger children. The quality of the marital relationship, and the level of parents' self-esteem, influence the development of depression in either parent (Trute, 1995). Among the continuing difficulties reported are a lack of time and limited professional assistance (Leyser, 1994). High levels of social support from spouses and friends, good health, and a sense of personal efficacy can reduce stresses (Snowdon, Cameron & Dunham, 1994). Over time, the adverse effects of a developmentally disabled child decreases. Family members (especially siblings) adjust.

- *Autism and other mental illness*. Autistic youngsters commonly have problems with communication, bonding, and sleeping, and exhibit unpredictable behaviour. Stress for parents and siblings is created by exhaustion, an increased financial burden, and changes in family routine (Norton & Drew, 1994). In these families, as in others with chronically ill children, parents may be distressed by what researchers have called "off-timedness," a feeling of intensified burden when their children fail to achieve the normal landmarks appropriate for their age, such as graduation or marriage (Pickett, Cook & Cohler, 1994).

- *Hospitalization*. Families find their own emotions and their problems in communicating, particularly with hospital professionals, to be the most stressful aspects of a child's long-term hospitalization. Parents employ a wide range of coping strategies to address these problems (Horn, Feldman & Ploof, 1995).

The effects of chronic illness vary from one family to another, partly due to variations in the illness itself. However, many similarities are also evident. Specifically, families with chronically ill children often suffer from a decline in the health of the parent who is most responsible for taking care of the sick child. Family members often experience a decline in the well-being of the family as a whole. This decline, caused by a chronic shortage of time and money, can show up in a variety of ways: physical exhaustion, irritability, depression, pessimism, seclusiveness, or a withdrawal of cooperation.

Two interacting causes of this decline are the *duration* of the illness and treatment, and the extent of *parental involvement* in caring for the ill child. The more severe the decline of the caretaker parent and the longer it goes on the more strain the entire family experiences, and the more difficult it is for the family to cope adequately.

Other family members suffer from emotional and psychic depletion too. Fully one-third of all children who become chronically ill by age 15 also suffer from serious psychological and behavioural problems as a result (Kashani *et al.*, 1981). Moreover, the tensions caused by long-term care can be permanently damaging. Dysfunctional coping responses such as depression, blame, denial, and guilt are common in all family members, including the sick child (Bruhn, 1977). In such families, the members often grow estranged from one another and the risk of divorce is high (Field, 1982).

Immediate shock, anger, and helplessness (Valman, 1981), as well as hopefulness (Mattson, 1972) disappear. They give way to a dazed state, a deep sense of apathy, and isolation from other family members and society. Researchers also know this state as "pseudo-narcotic" syndrome (Anthony, 1970). It has some features in common with post-traumatic stress syndrome, which we discussed earlier.

Families with chronically ill children often suffer from a decline in the health of the parent who is most responsible for taking care of the sick child.

The isolation family members feel from one another intensifies as each member goes through the grieving process, experiencing different emotions at different times. Often, family members fail to talk about the child's disease or his or her fears of death (Taylor, 1980). The ill child also becomes isolated from friends and society (Burnette, 1975). Often, silence reflects the family's inability to cope (Turk, 1964). The family as a whole refuses to adjust to an abnormal or difficult situation (Kaplan *et al.*, 1980). Many do not know where to begin.

When people take care of a chronically ill family member, the intensity of emotion is difficult to sort out or express in relationships with other family members. This produces some of the feelings of isolation. However, in some families, the illness also brings people closer. Thus, isolation and **enmeshment** can go hand in hand.

The presence of a chronically sick child also harms siblings in the home (Lademann, 1980). Just as fathers are often estranged from the mother-child relationship, siblings are left out of the intense relationship between the parents and their sick child (Larcombe, 1978). This provokes feelings of anger, resentment, and neglect (Valman, 1981). Children may try to compensate at school for lack of attention at home. However, lacking the communication skills of adults, they have a hard time giving voice to their feelings and desires; serious behavioural problems at school and at home may result. Adults and children in daily contact with these siblings often remain ignorant of the source of resulting behaviour problems.

Thus, many parents and siblings suffer uncommunicated fears, anxieties about the past and future, broken sleep, nightmares, bad eating habits, speech impediments, nail biting, accident-proneness, and more (Kanof *et al.*, 1972). Most of the literature reflects a high rate of dysfunctional response to child illness. However, as we mentioned earlier, chronic or fatal illness sometimes strengthens family ties (Motohashi, 1978). In some families, members talk meaningfully for the first time (Valens, 1975). People occasionally discover unknown and creative personal resources (Anthony, 1970). Though the obstacles posed by a child's illness are phenomenal, these family breakthroughs prove that successful coping is possible.

The problems that families encounter in trying to cope with a chronically ill child are often closely tied to problems that existed before the onset of illness (Kalnins, 1980). In short, a family's ability to cope is correlated with its previous level of functioning (Steinhauer *et al.*, 1984).

The Care of Ill Relatives

Problems posed by caring for a chronically ill child are similar to the problems posed by caring for a chronically ill spouse, parent, or other relative. Increasingly, as life spans lengthen, more adults devote more of their time to caring for ill adult relatives. As our society continues to age, care for adult relatives will become an ever larger portion of our caregiving activities.

Thus, it will become an ever larger source of family stress. This comes at a time when, because of declines in the fertility rate, most people have fewer siblings to help them care for their aged relatives, and fewer "social safety net" supports, or even medical resources, given the drastic cuts to the numbers of hospital beds and nurses.

Caring for frail, elderly parents puts an emotional strain on adult sons and daughters. Daughters experience more distress than sons, due to interference with work and a strained relationship with the parent (Mui, 1995a). So far, research provides little basis for estimating the extent of caregiving in the working population, or for accurately identifying types of work interference (Tennstedt & Gonyea, 1994; Carswick, 1997). Even so, it is clear that regular caregiving—for example, assisting in activities of daily living and elder care management, especially when crises arise—interferes significantly with the caregiver's work life. The common result is stress and costs to personal and job life (Gottlieb, Kelloway & Fraboni, 1994).

Caring for elderly family members often leads to burnout in women, for a variety of reasons. Unchanged gender-role expectations mean that many men do not accept responsibility for providing care. Formal caregiving services are limited and expensive. Caregiver burnout is a likely result. Note, however, that it is a societal problem: the result of a **culture lag**, a lack of fit between changes in our material conditions of life and our cultural values and norms (Alford-Cooper, 1993). Since it is a societal problem, it won't improve significantly without significant improvements in social policy.

Additionally, caregiver burnout and other psychosomatic symptoms may occur because people charged with caring for an ill or aged parent have never resolved conflicts or ambivalent feelings toward their parents. As we saw in Chapter 5, poor parenting can produce a variety of problems in children; yet these are the same children who may be called upon to care for their parents a few decades later. Showing attentive affection to parents who elicit feelings of anger or resentment will, in the long run, take a toll on the caretaker's mental health. Such problems are bound to become more common with the continuing increased longevity of parents and the diminished number of children.

Consider these stress-producing situations that arise out of providing care to adult relatives:

> • *Dementia (e.g., Alzheimer's disease)*. Caring for a parent or spouse with dementia usually affects the caregiver's mental and physical health, and often also the health and well-being of other family members: spouses, children, and in-laws. As the illness progresses, its effects cascade through the family network. However, using many caregiving or social services can mitigate the effects (Lieberman & Fisher, 1995).

> Caregivers report that in the first two years of caring for parents with

dementia, friends are the most important source of emotional support. Siblings are the greatest source of both practical help and interpersonal stress. Friends or relatives who have cared for elderly family members themselves are more likely than anyone else to provide continuing practical help. In time, however, they become less important as sources of emotional support (Suitor & Pillemer, 1995).

Family caregivers who put their relatives in nursing homes experience immediate relief from feelings of overload and tension. However, a continuing concern and sense of guilt leads to long-term stress (Zarit & Whitlatch, 1993).

• *Cancer.* A diagnosis of cancer in a parent is particularly distressing when the child is still young, and especially for females. So, for example, adolescent girls whose mothers develop cancer report more symptoms of anxiety and depression than girls whose fathers have cancer, or boys whose mothers or fathers have cancer. Largely, this is because of identification with the stricken parent, and the need to take on tasks which have fallen on their shoulders (Grant & Compas, 1995).

• *Heart surgery.* For spouses of patients undergoing open-heart surgery, the worst stressors are chronic illness, sleep disturbance, and fear of death. Caregivers report that, after surgery is complete, they urgently need support groups and referrals to community services. Largely, this is due to considerable alterations in work schedules after surgery, as well as diminished satisfaction with sex and spousal communication (Monahan, Kohman & Coleman, 1996).

• *HIV/AIDS.* Added to the factors already discussed, the stigma associated with HIV/AIDS leads to depression and a sense of burden among family members (Demi, Bakeman, & Moneyham, 1997). Family and friends of an HIV-infected patient often react emotionally to the disease. Stigmatization and isolation are major stressors. Fear, shame, dependency, and hopelessness complicate bereavement (Lippman, James & Frierson, 1993). In heterosexual couples with an HIV-positive partner, two-thirds report that at least one family member is aware of the HIV-positive condition. Of the family members who are aware, only half are supportive.

Gender is the only predictor of psychological distress where this condition is concerned. After controlling for race, age, and education, women experience far more psychological distress than men, on a variety of dimensions. Women have particular emotional difficulties in dealing with this illness (Kennedy *et al.*, 1995).

Overall, unpaid caregivers to the disabled—whatever the relationship or cause of disability—have a distinctive profile. Most are women, aged 30

Deadly Stress

There has been a stark increase in suicide rates and depression in North America over the past 60 years, perhaps by as much as 3,000 per cent. Indeed, there have been increases—although less dramatic ones—in the rates of all stress-related illness.... The epidemic far outweighs the challenge posed by any virus.

The increasing rates of stress-related illnesses have led many to conclude that life these days is more harsh and demanding than it was in the days of our parents. However, this is not an idea that is readily embraced by an older generation that survived economic depression, world wars and, in many cases, emigration....

Let me offer you another possibility. Life is no more stressful than in previous eras, but there has been a decline in the resources the individual has available to meet the emotional slings and arrows that life hurls in our direction. I refer to one resource in particular: what behavioral scientists call our social support systems.

So how does the presence of friendly co-workers, supportive siblings, cheery neighbors, forever loving (and forgiving) parents and spouses enhance health, and lessen the likelihood of chronic disease? By buffering us against the effects of stress. The scientific data are surprisingly clear on this point.

Stress produces any number of unwanted changes in physiology, and in almost all instances these effects are more dramatic in people who are lonely and without social support.... Researchers found that the incidence of heart disease and adult-onset diabetes were three to five times greater in individuals who were low on measures of social interactions.... The social environment was as good a predictor of heart disease as was smoking, and substantially better than even obesity, physical exercise and cholesterol in predicting the incidence of heart disease. Think for a moment on the emphasis we place today on fat and nutrition. Not for a moment would I question such convictions. But it does beg the question of why we ignore the social aspects of our lives.

Source: Michael Meaney. 1995. Special to *The Gazette*, Dossiers, Montreal, September 23 (abridged).

to 59, and married, and most are the child, parent, or partner of the care recipient. Of care recipients, the vast majority have multiple problems, frequently age-related. Except for caregivers whose relatives are in residential care, few receive any formal assistance, although many receive informal support from family and friends. Nearly half the caregivers report they have experienced major health problems of their own in the past year. Indeed, two-thirds say they feel exhausted at the end of each day. Half feel they have more to do than they can handle (Schofield & Herman, 1993).

Coping with Stress

As we have seen, family life is full of stresses. However, many families deal with them successfully: family functioning returns to normal, though the stressor may still be present. Families learn to cope by taking advantage of the resources they have available and by organizing their lives around handling their problems. Support from family, friends, and community agencies buffers the impact of caregiving, work, and family role strain. A supportive work environment also reduces physical and emotional strains (Lechner, 1993).

Two types of resources ease the burden for caregivers: assistance from other caregivers and support from people outside the caregiving situation. Overall, caregivers with larger support networks—especially of women and kin—report lower levels of stress. Close relationships with people who are both personal supporters and caregivers lighten the load of caregiving (Wright, 1994).

Two broad categories of resources—material and emotional/psychological—are key in deciding which families can withstand crises successfully. **Material resources** are easiest to define. They include money, time, and energy. Stressor events always use up large amounts of all these resources. When a family member develops a chronic illness, families have to pay for costly medication (even in Canada if the person is not in hospital, which happens more and more with health care cutbacks) and family members have to take time off from work to look after the ill person. Time and money alleviate the strain. **Psychological and emotional resources** are more difficult to define. They include the ability to accept that the stressor event has taken place, talk honestly about one's reactions, begin the process of adjustment soon afterward, and acknowledge the need for help from others.

Family members commonly bring both resources to the family unit. Individuals bring their money and cooperation to the common pool of resources. Family members contribute to material resources, for example, by aiding in household chores or earning an additional income. However, they may drain them by wasting time and money. Family members may build up the emotional resources of others by listening well and offering encouragement. This role is especially important in the spousal relationship. The strongest influence on mothers of disabled children is the degree of marital satisfaction. It successfully predicts maternal coping 70 percent of the time (Freidrich, 1979).

Certain kinds of families are better than others at providing support. Other things being equal, flexible and cohesive families have the highest level of well-being. In **cohesive** families, members feel attached to the family, and to one another. In **flexible** families, members can change their ideas, roles, and relationships as the situation demands. Even families with adolescents (typically a predictor of diminished well-being) show high levels of well-being if they are cohesive and flexible.

Families in which cohesion and flexibility are weak have the least ability to cope with stress, because they can give their members the least support. Even with the support and assistance of others, many still have trouble handling the stresses life throws their way. Often, attempts at coping are unsuccessful. In these cases, the family situation deteriorates, communication worsens, and unhappiness increases. When the family's ability to cope breaks down, individuals in that family each try to handle the stress on their own. Their individual efforts often end up increasing the stress and discomfort of the family as a whole. Intense and prolonged stress of this kind can lead to the breakup of the family.

We can even see the decision to break up the family as a form of coping. However, this is personal coping. The family is unable to cope as a social unit of interacting individuals. That is why one or more members of the family decide they must separate from the unit to help them cope better. Precisely what we mean by a **dysfunctional family** is a social unit that works so badly that its members are better off on their own.

Social and psychological disturbances characterize dysfunctional families with chronically ill children. Poor family communication and lack of support within the family by one or both parents are indicators of the problem (Jurk et al., 1980). Dysfunctional families are notable for chronic conflict, child abuse or medical neglect, psychiatric pathology, or alcoholism (White et al., 1984).

Families under the strain of chronic illness and treatment often reproduce and magnify their most troublesome characteristics. Families that were happy and healthy continue to be happy and healthy. However, in families with histories of drinking, marital strife, sibling rivalry, or financial instability, problems that begin as minor ones may explode into major ones.

Violence

Violence among family members is probably as old as the institution of the family itself. However, the systematic study of family violence is a new branch of academic research. It only emerged in the 1960s, launched by the publication of the first detailed case studies of seemingly inexplicable physical injuries that young children had suffered.

How big a problem is family violence in our society? No one knows for sure. A large part of the difficulty in determining the extent or prevalence of family violence is methodological. To begin with, we have the problem of defining violence. Students of family violence come at the issue from a host of disciplines that include anthropology, sociology, psychology, social work, medicine, and criminology. Within each discipline, there are competing definitions of what counts as family violence, and a variety of ways of measuring its extent. Thus, the studies that they conduct are often hard to compare.

The term "family violence" did not even exist before 1930 (Busby, 1991: 336). People may have been aware that violence did occur within families. Almost certainly police, doctors, novelists, and nosy neighbours knew. However, an overwhelming social consensus sanctified family privacy, thus keeping researchers from asking, and victims from talking about, family violence. For a variety of reasons, that consensus broke down in the 1960s.

Table 8.1 **MILESTONES ON THE ROAD TO STOPPING FAMILY VIOLENCE**

1965	Ontario became the first province to require reporting of child abuse
1970	First Royal Commission report on the Status of Women (no mention of violence)
1970	First women's studies course offered (University of Toronto)
1972	Canada's first shelter for abused women opened in Vancouver
1973	Canadian Advisory Council on Status of Women (CACSW) established
1973	Newfoundland's Neglected Adults Welfare Act became the first North American adult protective legislation
1976	House Standing Committee held hearings and issued a report on child abuse and neglect
1980	National Advisory Council on Aging established
1981	Media reports of laughter in House of Commons over report on prevalence of wife abuse prompted public outcry
1982	National Clearinghouse on Family Violence established
1982	Canada's Solicitor General urged police to lay charges in cases of wife battering when they had reasonable grounds to believe that an assault had taken place
1983	Broad amendments made to Canadian sexual assault legislation including an amendment making sexual assault in marriage a crime
1984	Speech from the Throne included wife battering as a priority concern
1984	The Committee on Sexual Offences Against Children and Youth (Badgley Committee) released report
1986	Health and Welfare Canada created Family Violence Division
1987	CACSW released report, *Battered But Not Beaten: Preventing Wife Battering in Canada*
1989	Eight women killed in Montreal in what became known as the "Montreal Massacre"
1989	First major Canadian survey on the extent and nature of elder abuse
1990	Special Advisor on Child Sexual Abuse to the Minister of National Health and Welfare released report, *Reaching for Solutions*
1993	Canadian Panel on Violence Against Women released report, *Changing the Landscape: Ending Violence, Achieving Equality*
1993	Statistics Canada conducts Violence Against Women Survey

Source: "Stopping Family Violence: Steps Along the Road." 1995. *Transition*, a publication of the Vanier Institute of the Family, September: p. 6. Reprinted with permission.

As shown in Table 8.1, public concern about family violence has grown, along with initiatives to put a stop to it.

Family violence is an umbrella term covering a range of different kinds

Figure 8.1 PHYSICAL ASSAULT, BY RELATIONSHIP OF ASSAILANT

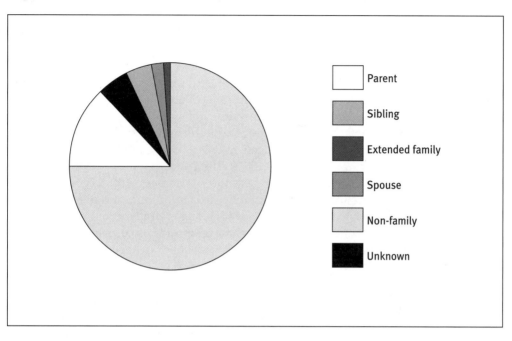

Note: Extended family includes others related by blood or marriage (e.g., grandparents, aunts, uncles, cousins, in-laws).

Source: Statistics Canada. 1998. *The Daily*, May 28.

of violence, among different sets of family members. The oldest recognized form of violence is physical violence: the intentional use of physical force that one family member aims at hurting or injuring another family member (Busby, 1991:335). It ranges from such acts as slapping, shaking, pushing, punching, and kicking to using (or threatening to use) a weapon, such as a knife or a gun or even a baseball bat, with the intention of scaring, hurting, maiming, or killing. It is estimated, as shown in Figure 8.1, that at least 20 percent of all physical assaults are carried out by family members, most commonly by parents.

In addition, we need to include sexual violence, such as child sexual abuse, incest, and marital rape, which is likely to have a component of physical violence as well. Due to its qualitatively different nature, researchers categorize sexual violence separately from non-sexual physical violence and study it in its own right.

Researchers also study nonviolent forms of emotional and psychological abuse. These include anything from emotional neglect to psychological torture. The reasons for including nonphysical forms of abuse in studies of family violence are twofold. First, emotional abuse often accompanies violent acts. Second, emotional abuse is often as painful or destructive of the self-esteem and healthy emotional development of its victims as physical violence.

As to neglect, it may seem that no attention at all is better than the excessive negative attention involved in abuse. However, neglect can be just as damaging to a family member, especially to a dependent child or elderly parent. Sexual abuse, neglect, and physical violence are different forms of violence and often stem from different causes. In the discussion that follows, we will focus on physical violence.

Sociologists see two additional problems in determining the prevalence of family violence. We generally lack access to hospital records and to cases gathered by social workers. These records and cases are confidential, and so they are off-limits even to researchers with the most benign motives. Moreover, adequate sampling and measurement is difficult. Family violence has, to a considerable degree, been dragged out of the closet. However, it remains a source of shame for most of its perpetrators as well as for its victims. Therefore, family violence continues to be hidden, to a large degree, from public view.

Even if people were completely forthright about what goes on behind closed doors in their families, measurement would still be complicated by the variation in what counts as violence, from one culture to another and often from one family to another. For example, in the early part of our century, many parents disciplined misbehaving children by beating them with a belt or ruler. For their part, the Sioux peoples considered the white settlers' slapping and beating of their own children as childish and reprehensible (Erikson, 1950). Some Muslim cultures still practise female circumcision. Most North Americans would consider this practice a severe form of cruelty.

Is female circumcision family violence? If it is, what about infant male circumcision? This procedure, originally a Jewish religious practice, was at one time virtually universally adopted by North Americans, for supposed hygienic reasons, and is still routinely performed. However, many experts find no medical justification for this surgical procedure. When done without anaesthesia it is undoubtedly painful and traumatic, but until recent research proved this people doubted the infant's pain.

In spite of the difficulties in identifying family violence, sociologists have developed better techniques for estimating its prevalence. According to one such estimate, "(a)t least one form of physical violence (slaps and pushes) occurs in more than half the homes in the United States" (Busby, 1991:374). Consider these facts about the extent of **domestic violence** in our society:

> • Domestic violence remains the leading cause of injuries to women aged 15 to 44: more common than muggings, auto accidents, and cancer deaths combined (Dwyer, Smokowski & Bricout, 1995).

- Many male abusers, including incest offenders, use physical, non-sexual violence directed toward both partners and children living within their homes (Stermac, Davidson & Sheridan, 1995).

- The lifetime danger of physical and sexual assault in the histories of episodically homeless, seriously mentally ill women is so high that rape and physical battery are normal experiences for this population (Goodman, Dutton & Harris, 1995).

- Among runaway and homeless adolescents, reports of parental neglect, rejection, violence, and sexual abuse are commonplace. Admissions by the parents or caregivers themselves support the credibility of these reports (Whitbeck, Hoyt & Ackley, 1997).

- When sexually abused girls under age 18 complain to their parents, in over half the cases the incest continues for more than a year following disclosure. Parents typically meet the disclosure with disbelief or blame of the girl (Roesler & Wind, 1994).

- Hispanic women report more serious childhood sexual abuse than non-Hispanic white women. The perpetrator is, more often than for non-Hispanic women, a member of their extended family rather than a nuclear family member or outsider (Arroyo, Simpson & Aragon, 1997).

- Though they are similar in many ways to younger abused women, women over 50 who are abused by partners or adult children are inaccurately perceived. As a result, current intervention systems often fail to help them (Seaver, 1996).

- Lesbian violence is common, though abuse in lesbian relationships is more frequently nonphysical than physical (Lockhart, White & Causby, 1994).

Most commonly used today in measuring the extent of domestic violence—especially, for purposes of criminal justice intervention—is Straus's **Conflict Tactics Scales**, developed in 1979. The first reliable and valid scale for measuring family violence, the Conflict Tactics Scales measure verbal aggression and physical violence on a continuum. This, in conjunction with a checklist to identify high-risk cases, focuses on two specific criteria. One is whether there have been three or more instances of violence in the previous year. The other is the violence of the act or acts. Factors used to rate violence include the use of a weapon; injuries requiring medical treatment; the involvement of a child, an animal, or a nonfamily member; drug or alcohol involvement; extreme dominance, violence, or surveillance; forced sex; extensive or repeated property damage; and police involvement (Straus, 1996).

How common is family violence? As we have said, this question is hard to answer. However, violence is sufficiently common to pose a problem for family researchers who need a nonviolent control group. Holtzworth-Munroe and colleagues (1992) report having collected questionnaire and scale data on over 550 respondents recruited through newspaper advertisements and from among couples seeking marital therapy, for example. Findings from five such studies suggest that husband violence has occurred in up to one-third of couples who do not report distress with their marriage and one-half of maritally distressed couples.

As we have mentioned, sociologists are limited in the study of intimate violence and abuse. Violence typically takes place in private, as part of an ongoing intimate relationship. We lack widely accepted and widely applied definitions of the key terms involved. Also lacking is a widely accepted definition of what is a family (Gelles, 1994).

Finally, recognize that much of what occurs between intimates within marriage also occurs between intimates outside marriage. Consider date rape: a survey was conducted on 44 college and university campuses across Canada by sociologists Walter DeKeseredy and Katherine Kelly (1993; 1995; Kelly & DeKeseredy, 1994). It found that four women in five claimed they had been subjected to abuse by a dating partner. Overall, nearly as many men admitted having acted abusively toward their dates.

The validity of the findings was attacked because the study listed a very wide range of behaviours under the heading of "abuse" (Gartner & Fox, 1993). These behaviours included insults, swearing, accusations of flirting with others or acting spitefully, as well as violent and grotesque acts such as using or threatening to use a gun or knife, beating, kicking or biting the dating partner. So it is best to separate out the violent from the less violent abuses before we attempt to analyze the results.

When we do this, certain patterns fall into place. Where *violent* abuses are concerned, women are more than twice as likely as men to acknowledge their occurrence. Where less violent abuses are concerned, men and women acknowledge them equally often. For example, 65 percent of women report being insulted or sworn at by a date, and 63.6 percent of men report having insulted or sworn at a date. On the other hand, 11.1 percent of women report being slapped by a date, yet only 4.5 percent of men report slapping a date. Likewise, 8.1 percent of women report being kicked, bitten, or hit with a fist, yet only 2.4 percent of men report having done any of those things. This consistent discrepancy leads to one of three possible conclusions. Either (1) violent and abusive men date a lot more women than gentle, non-abusive men, (2) women tell a lot of lies about their dates, or (3) many men are ashamed to admit the things they have done to their dates.

The data also show that violent abuses on dates are not only physical, they are also sexual. As with physical violence, male respondents are only about one-half or one-third as likely to report doing these things as women are to report having them done.

Bear in mind that most instances of forced sexual activity occur between people who know each other. The result is, too often, that women blame themselves for the experience. Because they know the assailant, they react passively to the sexual assault. Because they react passively, they blame themselves for not reacting more forcefully. A few even continue the dating relationship.

Sexual harassment is another form of sexual assault, and is especially prevalent in schools and workplaces. In the halls of their schools, female high school students regularly experience harassment, which ranges from unwanted staring and rude or embarrassing remarks, to unwanted touching. The result is a frequent, if not constant, sense of discomfort, even dread, about being at school.

Part of the problem is that perceptions of sexual harassment vary by gender. High school boys may have little idea just how much they are upsetting the girls. College-aged men are much less likely to label behaviour "harassment" than their female peers. But after exposure to the workforce, men's awareness grows and they, too, come to see certain behaviour as harassment. Overall, women label more behaviours as harassing than men do, but this discrepancy decreases with experience in the workforce, as women become accustomed to "the norm."

Causes of Violence

Violence between spouses may be the most perplexing form of violence, as it raises so many questions. The most obvious is, Why do spouses abuse their partners? Of equal theoretical interest is the question, Why does an abused spouse stay with her or his abuser?

We use the term **spousal violence** in this chapter, but unmarried couples also inflict violence on each other. In fact, one study found severe violence to be five times more likely among cohabiting than married couples (Yllo & Straus, 1981). Other, more recent research confirms that cohabitors are still more likely than spouses to engage in violent relationships (Jackson, 1996).

Researchers debate the causes of family violence (for a text that reviews many controversies in the literature, see Gelles & Loseke, 1993). Possible contributors range from personal factors, such as stress level or a history of abuse, to cultural ideologies of families and "discipline." We are still unable to detect the relative contribution of any single factor. We can identify correlates of violent behaviour, but a correlate is not necessarily a cause.

Some argue that the same social conditions produce both domestic violence and violent crime outside the household: poverty, inadequate housing, unemployment, and the social acceptance, even glorification, of violence. Others argue that a high crime rate fosters an acceptance of aggression and hastens the deterioration of the family unit, both of which increase domestic violence. The variables most strongly associated with domestic violence are age, income, work status, religion, urban versus rural residence, and ethnic group (Straus, Gelles & Steinmetz, 1980). According to this research, the safest homes are those with fewer than two children, little stress, and a democratic system of decision making.

Other variables likely to distinguish husbands who batter their wives are presence of alcohol abuse, low education, frequent arguments with spouse, and frequent drug use. Abusing husbands typically also have a (childhood) background of family violence and marital arguments (Coleman, Weinman & Bartholomew, 1980).

Status inconsistency (inconsistency between one's education and occupation) is another risk factor associated with increased psychological and physical abuse, and an even greater risk of life-threatening violence. Perceived under-achievement by the husband and over-achievement by the wife are also factors. In contrast, over-achievement by the husband decreases abuse risks (Hornung, McCullough & Sugimoto, 1981). Violent men typically have lower levels of self-esteem than nonviolent men from either stressed or happy marriages (Goldstein & Rosenbaum, 1985). Violent men also consider their wives' behaviour toward them to be more damaging to their self-esteem.

The single best predictor of violent behaviour toward a partner is the experience of violence at the hands of a partner. If your partner hits you, you will likely hit him or her back. After that, having been the tar-

Why do spouses abuse their partners? Why does an abused spouse stay with her or his abuser?

Domestic Violence Has Soared Since Ice Storm, Police Say

One of the darkest aspects of the week-long black-out around Montreal has been a marked increase in cases of domestic violence. To make matters worse, shelters have been closed for lack of power and hot-lines for victims have been disrupted.

Montreal Urban Community Police Chief Jacques Duchesneau said cases of domestic violence have "soared" since the ice storm began on Jan. 4. Though he could not provide precise figures, the chief said one in four calls in the past week has been from battered women.

Gabriel Larivière, a counselor at the Centre for the Prevention of Sex Crimes in Longueuil, Que., on the hard-hit South Shore, said his greatest concern is the inability of women to get help.

He stressed that the difficult conditions do not make men more violent, but rather that "conditions are such that abusers might be more abusive." Mr. Larivière said the "violence is already there. But when you lock people up in cold, stressful conditions for long periods of time, it can trigger some very bad situations."

Source: André Picard, Quebec Bureau, *The Globe and Mail*, 1998 (abridged). Reprinted with permission from *The Globe and Mail*.

get of parental violence during childhood most increases the risk of child abuse in adulthood. Excessive use of alcohol is a significant, though modest, predictor of both intimate-partner violence and child abuse (Merrill, Hervig & Milner, 1996).

Marital violence is a major predictor of physical child abuse. Men who abuse their wives often abuse their children as well; and the more often a spouse uses violence against a spouse, the more likely that spouse is to also use violence against a child. This relationship is particularly strong for men. The probability of child abuse by a violent husband increases from 5 percent with one act of marital violence to near certainty with fifty or more such acts (Ross, 1996). Thus, children in abusive households are likely to both witness and experience domestic violence firsthand. Witnessing violence between parents increases the likelihood that children will use violence against their own spouses when they grow up.

Children learn, by observation, to use violence to resolve disputes and vent frustration. We must stress the importance of early childhood experience in forming people's attitudes toward violence. Childhood experience doesn't explain all incidents of abusive behaviour, but it does account for many. According to Murray Straus (1992:685), the more physical punishment a man experiences as a child, the higher is his probability of hitting a spouse. For it is in the family that children learn the normative legitimacy of family violence.

Some of the effect of childhood exposure is a reaction to the shock of witnessing violence. In this sense, it is due to the creation of mental health problems in the child—problems of shame, guilt, low self-worth, and depression. However, many children who suffer or witness abuse never become abusive adults. Despite their violent histories, men who perceive threats from significant others (e.g., threats of rejection by their beloved) tend to be nonviolent if they are strongly attached to their spouse (Lackey & Williams, 1995). Thus, a strong adult attachment can often undo, or partly undo, the damage done by a violent childhood.

A second factor that affects whether a person will use violence against intimates is sex. The childhood experience of violence affects girls differently from boys. Girls typically internalize their problems, as depression and anxiety. Boys typically externalize their problems, as aggression and rule-breaking. Girls who suffer abuse as children are more likely to become victims of abuse in adulthood, whereas boys who suffer abuse as children are more likely to become abusers.

Women's shelter records show five main types of battered women, determined by types of violence used and experienced: (1) women in stable low-violence relationships, who are likely to be violence instigators; (2) women in unstable relationships who suffer severe and often sexual violence; (3) severe and chronically abused women who have also seen their children abused; (4) women who were not abused but whose children were; and (5) chronically abused women who have grown to accept it. This last type is the most likely to return to the assailant after a period in the shelter (Snyder & Fruchtman, 1981).

Some view domestic violence as a defence of patriarchy by men who fear that women's increasing economic and social independence is eroding their dominance. So, for example, an income disparity between husband and wife predicts the occurrence of wife abuse (McCloskey, 1996). An income bias that favours women predicts more frequent and severe violence by men toward their wives. Since employment is a symbolic resource in relationships—a source of status, power, and economic resources—spousal violence against women is most common when the wife has a job and the husband does not. Risks are low when neither partner is employed or only the husband has a job (Macmillan & Gartner, 1996).

Men are more likely to batter—or kill—to protect what they think of as their sexual property, whereas women are only likely to batter or kill to protect themselves. (For a contrary view, see Straus (1992), who argues that women too may be violent to men when they are not acting out of self-defence; however this is mainly characteristic of the less-serious "common couple violence.") Men are likely to kill themselves after killing their "property." Women are not. They only kill a partner who has battered them systematically and who they fear will batter them even more. Compared with non-battered women, battered women in spousal conflict use more violence, receive lower levels of social support, and experience higher levels of self-blame. Battered women, therefore, are more likely to use violence on their spouse when they feel they are receiving little social support, and even if they feel they are to blame for the conflict (Barnett, Martinez & Keyson, 1996).

The vast majority of battered women in jail for killing their partner share a few distinctive characteristics. Typically, they were sexually assaulted during childhood, dropped out of high school, have an erratic work history of unskilled jobs, cohabited with their partner, experienced a drug problem, attempted suicide by drug overdosing, and/or had access to the batterer's guns. These findings, based on in-depth interviews, help to explain why battered women kill their mates. After brutal, repeated assaults and death threats, and after failing in their attempts to escape through alcohol or drug abuse—even through attempted suicide—they see killing their abuser as the only way out (Roberts, 1996).

Women jailed for killing or assaulting their abusers are usually older, in the relationship longer, and have experienced a longer duration of violence in the relationship. They have also experienced more frequent and severe battering (including sex assaults) and sustained more injuries than a comparison group of battered women incarcerated for other offences. Furthermore, battered women who killed or seriously assaulted their partners were more likely to believe that their lives were in danger. They were less likely to use violence against their partners and less likely to have a prior criminal record or to have served time previously than battered women jailed for other offences (O'Keefe, 1997). In many venues, these cases are being reconsidered as self-defence.

Some researchers note that, on occasion, both husbands and wives are violent. They argue, in effect, that violence is an *interactional problem*—a result of marital dysfunctioning. For example, Brinkerhoff and Lupri (1988) state, on the basis of a survey conducted in Calgary, that husband-to-wife, wife-to-husband, and mutual violence occur in families at every socioeconomic, educational, and income level (see Figure 8.2). The strongest predictors of violence are interactional—meaning that they arise from relationship processes such as marital conflict, customary modes of expressing aggression, and stresses induced by work. Accordingly, Lupri (1993) uses data from a representative national sample of Canadians to argue that male violence in the home is a widespread and, in that sense, "normal" element of marital interaction. Over the life course, partners negotiate and renegotiate their ways of interacting and dealing with conflicts, with the result that patterns of violence change with age. (On the importance of age and marital conflict, see also Lupri, Grandin & Brinkerhoff, 1994.)

Indeed, Grandin and Lupri (1997) state that common-couple violence— the "normal" product of many U.S. and Canadian households—is characterized by gender symmetry. According to this research, and contrary to common belief, wife-to-husband violence is frequent, and Canadian couples are more likely to engage in domestic violence, both severe and minor,

Figure 8.2 SPECIFIC VIOLENT ACTS BY SEX AMONG 562 CALGARY COUPLES

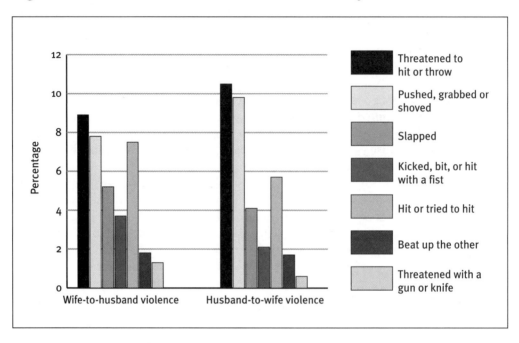

Source: Merlin B. Brinkerhoff & Eugen Lupri. 1992. "Interspousal Violence," in *Debates in Canadian Society*, ed. Ronald Hinch.
Scarborough: Nelson Canada.

than are American couples.

Psychologically abusive women show the same personality profiles as abusive men, characterized by jealousy, suspicion, immaturity, and insecurity. As to physical abuse, researchers reported that more than 70 percent of these women have been physical to the point of shoving their husband or boyfriend or destroying their partner's possessions in anger (Stacey, Hazlewood & Shupe, 1994:124). Their spouses' superior strength kept them from more direct forms of assault, but many women nonetheless punched, slapped, kicked, or used a weapon against their partner. In such relationships violence is two-sided. As Macmillan and Gartner (1996) have noted, "**interpersonal conflict violence**" is extremely common and symmetrical, with equal numbers of male and female perpetrators.

A woman may instigate the violence, for example, by hitting the man during an argument, to which he responds by hitting back. Though the man does more damage (up to five times more physical injuries) to his partner, both partners may be guilty of uncontrolled tempers. As we have said, some women also lash out in self-defence. Often, this occurs in the anticipation of violence from the man after long experience with his violence. Occasionally,

Family Violence in Canada: A Statistical Profile

The 1993 Violence Against Women Survey lends itself to analysis of a number of factors that affect the risk of being the female victim of spousal assault. The strongest risk factor is the presence of emotional abuse by male spouses, particularly degrading name-calling. Other factors increasing the risk of victimization are the age of the couple (18–24 years of age), living in a common-law relationship, long-term unemployment on the part of the male partner, and witnessing violence as a child (by either the man or the woman).

In 1996, children under 18 years of age were victims in 22% of the violent crimes reported to police.

Family members were responsible for one-fifth of physical assaults and one-third (32%) of sexual assaults on children.

Parents were the most likely perpetrators in cases of family-related physical (64%) and sexual (43%) assaults against children. Fathers were responsible for 73% of physical assaults and 98% of sexual assaults committed by parents.

The likelihood of being physically assaulted by a family member increases with age for girls, reaching a peak at age 17. For boys, the peak age for physical assault is 13, and then it declines.

Source: Statistics Canada. 1998. *The Daily*, May 28.

it comes as retaliation after the fact, as with Lorena Bobbitt, who cut off her husband's penis, or Francine Hughes, who set her abusive husband's bedroom on fire while he slept, or the long-abused woman in Nova Scotia who shot her husband in his truck. (A National Film Board film was made about this very sad case.)

In a continuously and symmetrically abusive relationship, the line between instigation and self-defence blurs. Sometimes, the perception of women as victims and men as perpetrators is a false analysis of the situation. A better view might be the **circular causal model**, in which both partners contribute to the escalation of the abuse. But it still may be that the partners do not have equal power in the relationship or in society, generally making women more vulnerable. In these cases, therapy should focus on the treatment of both partners or on the peaceful end of the relationship.

Alcoholism and drug abuse are also important factors in explaining spousal violence. Many drugs (including alcohol) are disinhibitors, causing people to relax their inhibitions, including those against violent behaviour. Other drugs increase adrenaline levels and, in this way, may cause anger or frustration levels to get out of control. Thus, some people who wouldn't otherwise resort to violence when they are sober may engage in it when they are under the influence of drugs. Macmillan and Gartner (1996: Table 5) show that drinking, for example, is a significant predictor of **systematic abuse** and of attempts at coercive control.

A lack of sufficient *coping resources* also increases the likelihood of violence in a family relationship. In one study, 90 percent of the violent families examined had serious problems such as financial difficulties and poor family cohesion. These families were also poorly integrated into society, showing a lack of social support (Bryant *et al.*, 1963). **Social isolation**, or lack of social support, is a common predictor of physical child abuse. Mothers at the greatest risk of physically abusing their children are, typically, more socially isolated than others. Practical support from work or school associates, and emotional support from supportive, nurturing people both help to decrease the potential for physical child abuse (Moncher, 1995).

Cultural attitudes that support violence as a whole, or violence directed against women and children in particular, also contribute to domestic violence. A society that condones violent behaviours may end up encouraging them.

It is unclear whether societies that condone family violence have higher rates of violence than those that do not. However, these societies offer fewer options to abuse victims. In the past, cultural myths prevented Canadian society from accepting domestic violence as a serious problem, and therefore recognizing the need for laws and institutions to protect women. These myths included the belief that women typically provoke violence, and that family violence is a "private affair" and therefore police should stay out of it. The recognition of a "battered-wife syndrome" was a big step toward condemning wife abuse (Fineman & Mykitiuk, 1994).

Thus, to understand the prevalence of domestic violence in our society, we must understand ordinary people's attitudes toward intimacy, gender, and violence. Even those who are innocent of violent behaviour may unwittingly support violence by their ways of thinking.

In short, we note a variety of "causes of violence" in the literature. The reason for so many causal candidates is, mainly, that we are confusing three different types of spousal violence. Macmillan and Gartner (1996:25) identify them as

> (1) *interpersonal conflict* violence, that almost exclusively involves pushing, shoving, grabbing and slapping; (2) *non-systematic abuse*, which involves a greater variety of violent acts, including threats, the throwing of objects, kicking and hitting; and (3) *systematic abuse*, which involves a relatively high risk of all types of violent acts, including life-threatening violence such as beating, choking, and attacks with knives or guns.

In their analysis of data from the Canadian Violence Against Women Survey (Statistics Canada, 1993), Macmillan and Gartner (1996) examine the effects of such proprietary or "coercively controlling" attitudes on domestic violence. The jealous husband doesn't want his wife to talk to other men. He tries to limit her contact with family or friends, insists on knowing who she is with and where she is at all times, and prevents her from knowing about or having access to the family income, even if she asks. We can say that a woman whose partner possesses all these traits has a coercively controlling husband.

Often, psychologically and physically abusive men fear the loss of their partner, whom they consider sexual and emotional property. These abusive men show a high degree of jealousy and always try to monitor their spouse or girlfriend. They insult and belittle her yet display an extreme fear of being left by her. Although they rationalize their behaviour by blaming their partner, alcohol, or various other sources for their rages, "[m]any men, particularly those at their meetings for counseling, were self-conscious, embarrassed, and ashamed" (Stacey, Hazlewood & Shupe, 1994:60). They recognize their behaviour as aberrant.

High levels of reported coercive control predict all three types of domestic violence and predict the most serious, systematic abuse most strongly (Macmillan & Gartner, 1996: Table 5). The more jealous and possessive a partner, the more dangerously and consistently abusive he is likely to be. In our culture, men can find justification for such pathological behaviour in the belief that it is appropriate for a man to protect his woman's purity and innocence (sometimes interpreted as ignorance). Today, the remnants of antiquated notions of chivalry do not protect women (if, indeed, they ever did); rather, they are used to justify gender inequality and hence domestic violence against women.

Also, because of cultural conceptions of masculinity, men are more tolerant of domestic violence than women. This too squares perfectly with the patriarchal model, which says that men are in charge and they use violence to stay that way. **Traditional family values** of male dominance, gender-based division of labour, and parental discipline of children are associated with high levels of family violence, including child sexual abuse (Higgins & McCabe, 1994). A review of previous studies finds that assaultive husbands are likely to support a patriarchal ideology, including positive attitudes toward marital violence and negative attitudes toward gender equality. For their part, assaulted wives usually hold more liberal gender attitudes than non-assaulted wives (Sugarman & Frankel, 1996). Usually, people in our society who hold egalitarian sex-role beliefs are more sympathetic to battered women than are traditionalists (Coleman & Stith, 1997).

Here's another window into our culture: researchers asked college students to assign verdicts to fictional court cases based on vignettes describing battered women who killed their husbands. They found some kinds of women guilty more often than others. Specifically, verbal aggression by the woman, and her characterization as a bad or dysfunctional wife or mother, increased the likelihood that the students would support a guilty verdict. The husband's use of a weapon against the woman did not significantly decrease the number of guilty verdicts (Follingstad, Brondino & Kleinfelter, 1996).

The effects of traditionalism on beliefs about domestic violence are even more evident in recently industrializing countries. For example, residents of Singapore disapprove of wife beatings, even when extramarital affairs or child abuses by women are involved. However, beatings are more acceptable if people see the wife as violating her prescribed sex role, particularly in failing to be the "good mother" and the "loyal wife" (Choi & Edleson, 1996).

Women themselves have a hard time escaping from these traditional notions. For example, many Indian immigrant women in North America show the effects of patriarchal training in their acceptance of domestic violence. Indoctrinated from childhood to believe that a good wife and mother sacrifices personal freedom and autonomy, they gain little sense of empowerment even from a professional job and economic independence. Further, they feel responsible for the reputation of their families in India and are eager to avoid compromising their families' honour by divorcing. As well, they operate under the added pressures of preserving traditions and presenting an unblemished image of their ethnic community to the North American mainstream (Dasgupta & Warrier, 1996).

Finally, as we mentioned before, *stress* also contributes to violence. Perceived stress, verbal aggression, and marital conflict—all stressful—are all factors present in abusive relationships, according to an analysis of data from the 1985 U.S. National Family Violence Survey (Harris, 1996). High levels of marital conflict along with low socioeconomic status and a history of witnessed violence in the family of origin also increase the likelihood of long-term abusive behaviour (Aldarondo & Sugarman, 1996). High levels of depression and reported life stressors are among the significant predictors of male violence toward female intimates (Julian & McKenry, 1993).

Stress also increases the risk of child abuse by mothers. For example, child disabilities, such as we discussed earlier in this chapter, increase the risk of abuse (Ammerman & Patz, 1996). Mothers with disabled children and low levels of social support and coping skills score higher on child abuse potential than do other mothers. Likewise, in Hong Kong, abusive mothers demonstrate significantly more stress on a Parenting Stress Index. They also have much lower levels of neighbourhood support, spousal support, community involvement, and emergency help (Chan, 1994). However, as we noted earlier, stress is also an effect of domestic violence, and it is only one of many causes.

Types of Abusive Relationships

In 1946, the case study of a child with a mysterious head injury led researchers to examine the external cause of the injury. Out of their investigation came the phrase **battered-child syndrome**. Before that, people often merely labelled beating a child "strict discipline." In 1962, Kempe and colleagues watched hospitals and found 302 (known) cases of child abuse in one year. Of these children, 33 died and 85 suffered permanent brain injury. The syndrome could affect children at any age but mainly affected children under the age of three. This study led to the first legislation that required professionals working with children to report suspected cases of abuse.

As we mentioned earlier, abused children often grow up to be abusive adults. Also, child abuse contributes to the risk of delinquent behaviour. As shown in Figure 8.3, the majority of young offenders had suffered childhood abuse of some kind, and among those young offenders classified as psychopathic (meaning that they are incapable of internalizing moral standards or forming deep attachments) the level of childhood abuse was even higher.

Even if the abused child grows up to be nonviolent, he or she is unlikely to be well-adjusted. Elmer and Gregg's (1967) study found that, out of twenty abused children, only two measured normally in all five areas of interest: physical, emotional, and intellectual, development speech capability, and physical defects. Few of these children went on to become capable adults.

Unfortunately, it may not be possible to provide a valid estimate of the population affected by parent–child violence. Thus, saying whether this is a major determinant of the adult criminal or mentally ill population may not be possible. However, for speculation on this topic, see Lykken (1996).

Figure 8.3 YOUNG OFFENDER ABUSE HISTORY

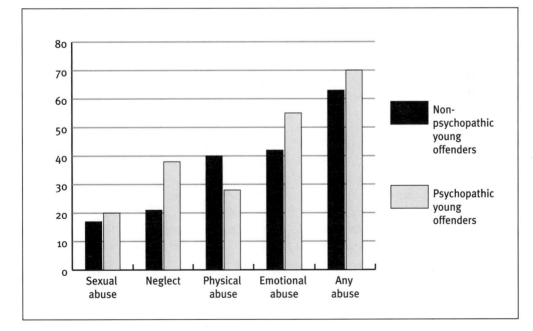

Source: Adelle Forth & Fred Tobin. 1995. "Psychopathy and Young Offenders: Rates of Childhood Maltreatment," *Forum*, 7 (1). From *Online*: http://198.103.98.138/crd/forum/e07/e071f.hi. Reprinted with permission.

Spare the Rod, Spoil the Child?

"While most physical discipline does not result in abuse, most abuse begins with physical discipline." So says Joan E. Durrant, a psychologist and assistant professor of family studies at the University of Manitoba in the Winter of 1993 edition of the newsletter of the York University Institute for Social Research.

Studies have shown that there is strong support for physical discipline in the U.S., but little research has been done on this subject in Canada. Professor Durrant reports on a recent effort in Toronto to survey the attitudes there. Of 298 adult respondents, a majority (59%) believed that physical discipline is ineffective in improving children's behaviour. Yet 75% also said that physical discipline is appropriate, at least under some conditions.

"Self-endangerment, commission of physical harm to others and violation of property rights were seen as behaviours most deserving of physical punishment," she writes. "Interestingly, two of the misbehaviours for which corporal punishment was most frequently viewed as appropriate involved hitting others." She notes the apparent "contradiction inherent in hitting a child in an attempt to teach that hitting is wrong."

Parents felt that the most frequent outcome of physical punishment is guilt in the parents. "Further, almost one-half of the sample stated that physical discipline rarely increases children's respect for their parents and almost one-third believed that it frequently leads to long-term emotional upset in the child."

Source: "Family Matters." 1993. *Transition*, a publication of the Vanier Institute of the Family, June.

Child homicide by parents offers an extreme but well-documented version of child abuse. In the first few weeks of a child's life, the risk of being killed by a parent is about equal for males and females. In the first few weeks or months, mothers are usually the perpetrators. The main causes of death are asphyxiation or drowning. It is only as the child's age increases that guns and knives become predominant. Then, too, fathers become ever more likely to commit the murder, committing 63 percent of all homicides among the 13- to 15-year age group and 80 percent for the 16- to 18-year age group. From one week to 15 years, males are the victims in about 55 percent of all parent–child homicides. In the 16- to 18-year age groups, this proportion increases to 77 percent (Kunz & Bahr, 1996).

Both child abuse and elder abuse arise from attempts by the caregiver to control behaviour they find problematic. Male abusers typically use physical violence, whereas female abusers tend toward neglect (Penhale, 1993). Finally, both these kinds of abuse often pass from one generation to another (Biggs, Phillipson & Kingston, 1995). In some cases of elder abuse, adult children are now abusing the parents who abused them in childhood.

Though common in North America, this has often also been the case in rural China, where very young women traditionally move in with their husband's family after marriage (Gallin, 1994). Young women are treated poorly by their husband's mother, only to become abusive when they must look after these women in their old age (Kwan, 1995).

Research shows that **elder abuse** cases fall into three categories, determined by the type of mistreatment (physical, psychological, financial, or neglect), the relationship between victim and perpetrator, and the sex and race of the victims and abusers. Profiles include (1) physical and psychological abuse perpetrators, who are likely to be financially dependent on the victim; (2) neglect victims, who are likely to be dependent on the perpetrator; and (3) financial abuse victims, who are often lonely, with few social contacts (Wolf, 1996).

Unlike child abuse, elder abuse receives little attention in our society, partly because it is less common, and perhaps also because we have less interest in elders than in children. Most would acknowledge that children are our future, however, many see elders as burdens we must put up with until they pass on (Biggs, Phillipson & Kingston, 1995). Another reason may be the economic prosperity of the past few decades, which allowed many seniors to provide for their own needs, instead of being dependent on their children. However, with the aging of the baby boom population and the decrease of available pension funds, we may see an increased interest in the well-being of elders.

The most common form of domestic violence is one that is considered natural, and therefore most acceptable in our society: namely, between-sibling violence (Steinmetz, 1977). We often excuse violence committed between children by saying they "don't know better." Or, we may see the injuries they do one another as less serious than those inflicted by adults. For whatever reason, little research is done on **sibling abuse**. Future studies may discover it is a more serious difficulty that we have previously thought.

Effects of Violence

Both perpetrators and victims of violence are less likely to verbalize their feelings than are nonviolent people. Thus, for example, female victims are much less aware of their emotional states, and possess and express significantly fewer positive feelings than the average adult woman. Though some researchers may view this condition as a cause of domestic violence, we view it as an effect we spoke of earlier, called post-traumatic stress disorder (PTSD).

More than four in five battered women meet the criteria for a diagnosis of PTSD, as do two in three verbally abused women (Kemp, Green & Hovanitz, 1995). Compared to other battered women, those with PTSD have been the victims of more physical abuse, more verbal abuse, more injuries, a greater sense of threat, and more forced sex. Besides the battery itself, other factors contributing to PTSD are the experience of other distressing life events and a lack of perceived social support.

Battered women are three times as likely to suffer from PTSD as are women who are maritally distressed but have not suffered battering. Both groups have similar rates of previous traumatic experiences. However, women showing PTSD—whether battered or not—are more likely to report having experienced childhood sexual abuse. They also report more previous traumas than women without PTSD.

Though little research has been done on the linkage between spousal abuse and PTSD, a great deal of research has documented other symptoms of domestic violence that are similar to symptoms of PTSD. For example, women whose partners initiate violence or force them to have sex have more fear of future assaults than other women (DeMaris & Swinford, 1996).

Abused women typically have less faith in their own efficacy, are more depressed, and have less self-esteem than non-abused women. Further, as physical abuse increases in severity, so does the woman's level of depression (Orava, McLeod & Sharpe, 1996). At a domestic violence shelter, more than four women in five are at least mildly depressed, and over half are still depressed six months later. Feelings of powerlessness, experiences of abuse, and insufficient social support all contribute to the persistence of this depression (Campbell, Sullivan & Davidson, 1995).

Psychological factors aside, social and economic factors also conspire to make women fear their vulnerable and dependent condition. Typically, battered women live in an oppressive ("coercively controlling") environment. Powerlessness, social isolation, and economic dependency characterize their lives (Forte, Franks & Forte, 1996). As we saw earlier, abusive husbands try to isolate their spouses and hide domestic conflict (Lempert, 1996a).

Jacobson, Guttman and colleagues (1996) find that only 38 percent of couples separate or divorce in the two years following an initial assessment of severe husband-to-wife violence. What about the other 62 percent? In some cases, the abuse continues—particularly where the husband has been domineering, negative, and emotionally abusive toward the wife at intake.

Women remain in abusive relationships for a variety of reasons. For example, women are taught that they should forgive and forget, that they ought to help their spouses be better people and support them through stresses. Also, abuse that is coercively controlling creates feelings of powerlessness and hopelessness (Aguilar & Nightingale, 1994). Most women who continue to feel closely attached to their partners, even after leaving them, have a negative self-image and tend to feel fearful or preoccupied about the relationship. In turn, preoccupation with the relationship is associated with more frequent previous separations from the relationship, continuing emotional involvement with the partner after separation, and more frequent sexual contact with the partner (Henderson, Bartholomew & Dutton, 1997).

Battered women have, typically, lost the ability to make decisions about their relationship in their own best interest. However, some research (e.g., Campbell, Miller & Cardwell, 1994) rejects a "learned helplessness" model for most women experiencing abuse. In their view, most abused women just need practical help and advice to be able to break with their past. They argue in favour of supporting battered women seen in the health care and social services systems, so that they can more easily decide the status of their relationship.

Feelings of commitment to an abusive partner are strongest among women who have limited economic alternatives and are more heavily invested in their relationships. Thus, women with little education—and therefore little chance of achieving economic independence—are more "committed" to their abusive relationship. Likewise, women with preschool children are more "committed" since they have more invested in the relationship than women without young children. Level of commitment predicts which women will return to their partners immediately after leaving a shelter, although most do so many times before finally deciding to leave.

Children also suffer from spousal violence, possibly even more than adults (Engle, Castle & Menon, 1996). Witnessing violence between one's parents harms the emotional and behavioural development of children (Kolbo, Blakely & Engleman, 1996). For example, exposure to family violence produces behavioural problems in girls and reduces self-worth in boys (Kolbo, 1996).

As we noted earlier, parent–child violence is common in families where parent–parent violence occurs. Both parent–child violence and exposure to interparental violence are significant predictors of adolescent behaviour problems (O'Keefe, 1996). Exposure to physical abuse produces open hostility in children and a tendency to flare up in anger without a specific provocation. (Exposure to *emotional* abuse is more likely to produce shame, hostility, and anger, both expressed and unexpressed.) Often, the outcomes of domestic violence are gender-specific. Females tend to internalize their emotions, reporting higher levels of shame and guilt. Males usually externalize their emotions, expressing higher levels of hostility and anger (Hoglund & Nicholas, 1995).

Like battered women, battered children show signs of post-traumatic stress disorder (Wind & Silvern, 1994). Motta (1994) suggests that a rise in family violence, violence within schools, and a variety of other stressors are leading to the characteristic PTSD symptoms increasingly observed among children.

A reported one-quarter to one-third of all female children suffer sexual abuse before their eighteenth birthday, and at least one-half of all the women with severe mental illness acknowledge such events. An even higher percentage of mentally ill homeless women have a history of childhood victimization (Rosenberg, Drake & Mueser, 1996). Among adolescent psychiatric patients, family dysfunction and trauma are more marked in those who have been sexually abused (Wherry *et al.*, 1994). Sexual abuse, parental assault, and kidnapping experiences are particularly strong predictors of depression and PTSD-related symptoms in 10- to 16-year-olds studied over

Domestic Violence Often Tolerated in Pakistan

Wrapped in a blood-caked shawl, her nose covered by a dirty gauze bandage, Nusrat Parveen trembled as she recalled the horrific morning when her husband cut off her nose.

Enraged because she had complained about his bad temper to his mother, he slammed her against their bed. He threw her on her back, tied her legs to the bed and her hands behind her back. For a brief moment he disappeared, but when he returned he was carrying scissors, a knife and a sharpening tool.

Ancient tradition in Pakistan says that to cut off a woman's nose is the greatest humiliation, a sign she is scorned by her husband, an outcast.

Nothing happened to her husband. She went to the police, but her husband said she was an evil woman and police refused to file charges. In Pakistan's male-dominated society, often ruled by conservative traditions, domestic violence is tolerated.

In the hospital bed next to Parveen lay Tasneen Bibi, 25. The left side of her face was bright red and contorted, her eye was partially closed and below it a wound festered. She said her in-laws threw acid on her face while she slept. "I just screamed and screamed. It hurt and hurt. I couldn't do anything," she said. She has had several operations, one to pry her head from her shoulders where it had joined.

Source: Kathy Gannon. 1997. Associated Press, *The Toronto Star*, November 3, D3 (abridged). Reprinted with permission.

a long period (Boney-McCoy & Finkelhor, 1996).

Parental substance abuse, family conflict, and exposure to both child and adult abuse set in motion a vicious circle that predicts substance abuse in later life. It also continues abusive family patterns into successive generations (Sheridan, 1995). In short, a **cycle of abuse** exists—a tendency for abused girls and daughters of abused mothers to become abused women, and for male children of abusive fathers to become abusive fathers themselves. The connection between childhood abuse and adult abuse may lie in interpersonal functioning. Children who grow up in abusive families don't learn how to conduct their lives, or their marriages, in non-abusive ways, or how to prevent the escalation of violence or abuse (Weaver & Clum, 1996). They may also have a history of depression and low self-esteem, both predisposing them to violence and victimization (Cascardi, O'Leary & Lawrence, 1995).

Concluding Remarks

What do we learn from research about the best ways to intervene to solve problems of family stress and violence? For reasons of brevity we will consider only a few conclusions.

First, we learn that violence is a major factor causing women to leave marriages. It often continues throughout the separation and divorce process, affecting negotiations for assets and custody (Kurz, 1996). Protective measures need to be put in place by government during divorce or other proceedings. Some even argue that we must exclude abusive relationships from mediation procedures (Raitt, 1996).

Second, programs that attempt to address abuse directly—such as civil restraining orders, treatment programs for batterers, and policies requiring mandatory arrest and no dropped charges—are generally not effective in solving the problem of domestic violence (Davis & Smith, 1995). By contrast, treatments aimed at reducing alcohol and drug abuse may make a long-term difference to the likelihood of future violence (O'Farrell & Murphy, 1995; Brannen & Rubin, 1996).

Third, we must actively address problems like stress and violence. If we want to reduce family stresses, we must create a society that is family-friendly, with increased social support and practical assistance to working parents with small children. The same is true for violence. A culture like ours, which enshrines a predatory notion of masculinity, will regularly produce men who batter their wives and children. It is not clear how we might change this cultural pattern, except through gradual education.

Fourth, research shows us that the health and social service professions are, sadly, far behind the times. To deserve the respect and rewards that they avidly seek, these professionals are going to have to move more decisively into understanding and intervening in modern relationships. Specifically, this means educators must change the programs that train and certify people for work in which they are likely to contact people who are stressed, violent, or the victims of stress and violence.

Fifth, research shows us that personal lives, and families, are increasingly diverse. That means that they have varied problems. Recently arrived immigrant and refugee women, for example, have needs that differ markedly from most battered women in the general population, involving language, cultural, and immigration issues (Huisman, 1996). Along similar lines, lesbians are less likely than heterosexual women to use traditional battered women services that were designed for male–female relationships. Workers in the health and social service professions have done little to make lesbians feel welcome and respected (Renzetti, 1996; Istar, 1996). Gay men face similar problems.

Problems like these call for more institutional flexibility and resourcefulness. As far as we can tell, there never has been a society whose families were completely free from stress and violence, and there never will be. We can, however, work to reduce and prevent such problems. As family members, we need to understand and deal with such problems more openly and carefully than in the past. For their part, service providers need to know more about the variety and complexity of family life and create more effective treatment methods.

The recognition of domestic violence as an important social issue, and mobilization against it (e.g., the Zero Tolerance campaign, cf. Mackay, 1996), owes much to grassroots coalitions of feminist and other movements. Women established in relevant local institutions (e.g., the press, government) make a big difference, especially when support from local politicians is available (Davis, Hagen, & Early, 1994; Abrar, 1996). We must all be alert to new problems, and to new solutions.

In the end, however, we must recognize that there will be no major decline in the violence against family members until societies reduce the stresses on family members. Yet governments and corporations have been *adding* to the stress by downsizing (recall that a risk factor is men being unemployed while their wives are employed). Societies must also dismantle the cultural justifications for domestic violence, and deprive the violent of opportunities to hide or repeat their behaviour. Ending domestic violence must be a societal project, no less complex than dealing with unemployment, illiteracy, AIDS, or any of a dozen other recognized social problems.

CHAPTER SUMMARY

We have examined the various forms of family stress and violence in this chapter. In the ABCX model, A, which represents a stressor event, interacts with B, the family's crisis-meeting resources, and with C, the interpretation a family makes of the event, to produce X, the crisis. Common causes of stress include major upheavals such as wars and natural disasters, life transitions, such as immigration, poverty and unemployment, and dealing with a disabled or chronically ill child or caring for an ill relative. We focused on chronic illness, which can lead to stress through a shortage of time or money, disappointment, and a feeling of stigma. Family well-being declines with duration and parental involvement in the stressor event. Families cope best when they have time, money, social support, and emotional resources, and are both cohesive and flexible.

We then focused on violence and the family. The level of family violence is difficult to determine both because it is often hidden and because researchers use varying definitions. During the twentieth century, family violence has emerged from the private sphere to the public sphere. The Straus Conflict Scale is often used to categorize degrees of violence.

Family violence is an umbrella term that covers many specific types of interpersonal violence. We discussed child, spousal, elder, and (briefly) sibling abuse. Three types of spousal abuse were identified: interpersonal, non-systematic, and systematic. Predictors of violence within a family include childhood experience or witnessing of family violence, low self-esteem, alcohol and drug abuse, a lack of coping resources and social support, stress, and cultural attitudes that justify inequality and violence. Too often family violence can lead to a "cycle of abuse" that continues from generation to generation. Our attention shifted away from seeing the violent interactions between family members as strictly between a victim and an abuser, as we explored the idea behind violent interactions between both family members.

We closed with a look at the effects of violence, including a discussion of post-traumatic stress disorder, as well as exploring the commitment of victims to their abusive relationships.

KEY TERMS

ABCX family crisis model: A model that explains family crisis in terms of a stressor event A, the family's crisis-meeting resources B, the family's interpretation of the event C, and the resulting crisis X.

Acculturative stress: Stress caused by the difficulties of adapting to a new society, such as the need to learn a new language and a new set of social behaviours and problems in obtaining employment.

Battered-child syndrome: The condition of children traumatized, physically and mentally, by severe abuse.

Chronic stressors: Ongoing factors that increase stress, such as poverty, disability, and chronic physical or mental illness.

Circular causal model: A model of family violence that views both partners in an abusive spousal relationship as contributing to the escalation of the abuse.

Class stratification: A social system in which some groups have significantly more material goods, opportunities, and social status than others.

Cohesion: Attachment of family members to each other and to the family itself.

Conflict Tactics Scales: An instrument developed by Murray Straus to measure the extent of domestic violence based on frequency and severity of incidents.

Cultural rationale: Justification for a behaviour based on beliefs commonly held within a culture.

Culture lag: A lack of fit that results when our material conditions in life change faster than our cultural values and norms.

Cycle of abuse: A tendency for family violence to replicate itself from one generation to the next, as abused girls and daughters of abused mothers grow up to become abused women, and abused boys or sons of abusive fathers grow up to become abusive husbands or fathers.

Domestic violence: Family violence; violence against any member of the household, including a child, spouse, parent, or sibling.

Dysfunctional family: A family that works so badly that its members would be better off on their own.

Elder abuse: Physical violence, psychological cruelty, or neglect directed at an older person, usually by a caregiving family member.

Enmeshment: Very close relationships that blur appropriate boundaries between family members.

Flexibility: Ability within a family structure to allow members to change their ideas, roles, and relationships as the situation demands.

Interpersonal conflict: Violence that almost exclusively involves pushing, shoving, grabbing, and slapping.

Major life transitions: Disruptions to family life caused by changes such as the birth of a child, the death of a parent, divorce, and retirement.

Major upheavals: Disruptions that affect many people simultaneously, such as war and natural disasters.

Material resources: The tangible things people need to deal with whatever life brings, such as money, time, and energy.

Non-systematic abuse: Abuse that involves relatively serious violent acts, such as threats, throwing objects, kicking, and hitting.

Patriarchal value system: A set of standards for behaviour within a culture that takes for granted the natural rightness of male dominance.

Post-traumatic stress disorder (PTSD): An anxiety disorder experienced by people who have survived or witnessed some very disturbing event, such as war, natural disaster, accident, or abuse, characterized by psychological numbing, increased arousal, and a tendency to relive the trauma repeatedly.

Psychological and emotional resources: The internal strengths people need to be able to deal with whatever life brings, including adaptability, the ability to understand what is happening and to talk about it, and willingness to accept help.

Sibling abuse: Violence by one sibling against another.

Social isolation: A lack of social support from kin, friends, co-workers, etc.

Spousal violence: Physical abuse between spouses. It may be reciprocal ("common couple violence") or directed by one partner against the other, and may occur between cohabitors as well as legally married couples.

Status inconsistency: Lack of congruence between the various indicators of social class, such as education and occupation, or wealth and prestige.

Stressor: A challenge or threat to a person or group that can cause stress.

Systematic abuse: Abuse that involves a high risk of life-threatening violence such as beating, choking, and attacks with knives and guns.

Traditional family values: A term commonly used by those who hold such views to describe support for male dominance, the gender-based division of labour, and strong parental discipline of children.

Suggested Readings

Baumrind, Diana. 1995. *Child Maltreatment and Optimal Caregiving in Social Contexts* New York, NY: Garland Publishing. This book reviews the literature on child abuse and normal family functioning to argue that maltreatment of children is directly linked to sociostructural rather than psychological factors. Family contexts that potentially contribute to child abuse include maternal youth and inexperience, marital discord and divorce, single parent status, and how demanding or responsive the mother is.

Buzzawa, Eve S. and Buzzawa, Carl G. (Eds.) 1996. *Do Arrests and Restraining Orders Work?* Thousand Oaks, CA: Sage. A collection of essays by researchers and practitioners that discuss issues related to domestic abuse, including the proper role of the police, prosecutors, and other officers of the court. Also included are recent findings on differential arrest practices for victims of domestic and stranger assaults.

Cheal, David. 1996. *New Poverty: Families in Postmodern Society*. Westport, CT: Greenwood Press. Despite the myth that the modern welfare state is benevolent, state income supports in Canada and the United States do little to protect families with children. The least secure families are those with low, unstable incomes. Female-headed families are in a particularly precarious financial situation, with few savings and low rates of home ownership.

Ellis, Carolyn. 1995. *Final Negotiations: A Story of Love, Loss, and Chronic Illness*. Philadelphia, PA: Temple U Press. This personal account of the author's nine-year love relationship with a man dying of emphysema includes the intricate details and difficulties of caregiving. Examines the emotional roller-coaster accompanying physical decline, negotiations with medical professionals, embarrassment, fear, and grief, and highlights the social processes of chronic illness and dying.

Fleisher, Mark S. and Robin F. Meier. 1995. *Beggars and Thieves: Lives of Urban Street Criminals*. Madison, WI: U of Wisconsin Press. Drawing on life histories and field observation of nearly 200 informants in jail, prison, and on the streets, this book shows how street criminals are enmeshed in a life cycle that comprises running away from home, membership in a gang, serving time in jail, residence in a shelter or prison, and homelessness. This experience provides a "sociocultural grammar" that makes normal life almost impossible.

Gordon, Linda. 1988. *Heroes of their Own Lives: The Politics and History of Family Violence, Boston, 1880–1960*. New York, NY: Viking. This book shows that family violence has been well known to social workers and reformers for a century but the realities of family violence have been concealed behind images that alternately pathologize or normalize it, making it seem the inevitable by-product of predispositions and stresses. Gordon reminds us that institutional records and institutional responses to violence are both cultural and political.

REVIEW QUESTIONS

1. Describe and give an example for each component of the ABCX model of stress.

2. What are the three main types of stressor? List at least two examples for each major type.

3. Name the two characteristics that are common to families that cope with stress well.

4. Name and elaborate on two kinds of resources that might help a family cope with a stressor.

5. What difficulties does a sociologist attempting to do a comprehensive study of family violence face?

6. Explain when and why family violence began to be publicly acknowledged as a social issue.

7. List some ways in which a child's development can be affected by experiencing family violence, whether as a victim or a witness. How do the effects on boys and girls differ?

8. The term "family violence" covers many different types of intimate relation violence. List the various types covered in this chapter and explain one thoroughly.

9. List three types of spousal violence and briefly explain the differences between them.

10. What social and cultural factors contribute to family violence, and how?

DISCUSSION QUESTIONS

1. Recall that the availability of certain resources significantly improves a family's ability to cope with a crisis; one of these resources is family structure. Why would certain family structures (i.e., those with the most flexibility and cohesiveness) allow for increased coping by the family unit? What sort of inhibitions to coping might an opposite structure impose?

2. Other than the direct physical effects of the illness itself, what sort of obstacles—inside and outside the family — stand in the way of a chronically ill child leading a "normal" life?

3. What particular stressors might accompany a family's emigration to a country very different from the one in which it originated? What stressors would be added with the coming of the first generation born in the new country?

4. As a researcher studying stress, you must weigh both objective and subjective stresses; your measure must reflect their significance in the situation being studied. In studying, for example, unemployment's effects on family, what sorts of measures might be appropriate? How might objective and subjective perspectives differ?

5. All abuse is, by nature, damaging to the victim. "Non-violent" forms of child abuse—psychological abuse and neglect—are usually considered less serious than physical violence and sexual assault. However, one might argue that they are equally damaging to a child's sense of self-worth and ability to cope in the world. Do you think the law should be paying equal attention to these two types of violence?

6. We are already changing the once commonplace opinion that grade school bullying is a far cry from criminal assault. Should we also be considering the impacts of sibling abuse more seriously? Should the legal system involve itself, or should sibling abuse remain an issue for parents to deal with?

7. Why might certain relationship conditions (such as cohabitation versus marriage) affect the rate of family violence?

8. We mentioned earlier that much intimate partner violence is more or less reciprocal. With this in mind, should we alter the way we approach domestic violence cases? Should men who have beaten their wives receive lighter (or no) sentences if the women were also physically aggressive? Should an abused wife who kills her husband in his sleep be able to claim "self-defence"?

9. Some people feel the traditional structure of some societies facilitates the abuse of women, children, or the elderly in that society. Others feel it is the breaking down of traditional structures, leaving a society trapped between ancient norms and modern realities, that causes family conflicts and violence. What arguments could you make for either side? (Give examples if you can!)

10. In what respects is violence between family members similar to violence between warring countries? In what respects is it different, and why?

WEBLINKS

http://home.whitleynet.org/somebodycares/family.htm

This site contains a family stress test. It is interesting to find out if you fall into the category of high stress.

http://hammock.ifas.ufl.edu/txt/fairs/30920

A very general site on stress and family development.

http://housecall.orbisnews.com/sponsors/aafp/topics/mental_health/stress/pageo.html

Published by the American Association of Physicians, this site provides some general answers to questions such as, What causes stress? What changes may be stressful?

http://www.uia.org/uiademo/pro/d8130.htm

A very informative site that gives some statistics, and also provides information on such things as children and stress, and family violence.

http://www.mes.umn.edu/Documents/D/E/Other/familystress.html

A very good site with publications available on things such as how to deal with stress, and communication during stressful times.

http://www.famvi.com/

Information on family violence, including statistics, information on what can be done, and links to other family violence sites.

http://hwcweb.hwc.ca/main/hc/web/datahpsb/ncfv/pubs/factfam.htm

The Family Violence Facts Sheet

A good site published by Health Canada.

http://www.ama-assn.org/public/releases/assault/fv-guide.htm

Published by the American Medical Association, this site contains very good information on the clinical and medical aspects of family violence.

http://www.icfs.org/bluebook/sio00052.htm

A wide range of links to information on family violence.

http://www.acjnet.org/docs/famvidoj.html

A wide range of information on family violence, especially in rural and remote Canada.

CHAPTER NINE

Divorce:

A Legal End to a Marriage

Researchers using 1996 statistics estimate that 37 percent of all first marriages in Canada will eventually end in divorce (Statistics Canada, 1998f). The divorce rate is higher in some provinces (e.g., Quebec) than others. The rate is also higher for second marriages, and higher still for third marriages. On the other hand, the overall divorce rate is falling, compared with 1995 statistics. Indeed, divorce rates and numbers of divorces have been declining in Canada since 1987, and in the United States since 1980.

Divorce Rates

What do we mean by the "divorce rate"? There are several ways to compute divorce rates, and the interpretations depend very much on the method of calculation. The *crude divorce rate*, for example, is calculated as the number of divorces in a given year (say, 1998) divided by the midyear population in 1998, with the result multiplied by 100 000. This procedure yields relatively low rates—indeed, underestimates divorce—because the denominator includes everyone in the population, many of whom are not at all at risk of divorce, since they are children, single, or already divorced.

By contrast, another measure of divorce tends to err on the high side. It divides the number of *divorces* in 1998 by the number of *marriages* in 1998. This procedure overestimates divorce and lends itself to attention-catching statements (e.g., "Two-thirds of all current marriages will end in divorce") which titillate but do not really inform us since those being married in 1998 are *not* usually those at risk of divorce in 1998!

Better measures of a divorce rate, though too rarely provided for public discussion, consider the entire population at risk of a divorce, and only that population. Thus, the population at risk of a divorce in 1998 are those (and only those) who are married at the beginning of 1998 and earlier. This estimate can be improved by standardizing for age and other social characteristics that are known to influence people's propensity to divorce. Since older people tend to divorce less than younger people, for example, we would do well to compute divorce rates on a "standard population" with the same hypothetical age structure at two points in time. Only in this way would we know whether divorce-proneness was increasing, or changes in population make-up were causing the appearance of more divorce-proneness.

Another approach is to calculate a rolling divorce rate which measures the number of people in the population ever divorced as a fraction of the population ever married. This method of measurement carries its own advantages and disadvantages compared to other methods; for example, large cohorts of people (like the baby boom generation) have a disproportionately large effect on this estimate.

One final measurement, to our knowledge never tried, would calculate the number of adult years lived outside marriage. If our purpose in computing divorce statistics were to gauge people's desire to be married and stay married, nothing would demonstrate the societal rejection of marriage more clearly than a continuous decline in the amount of time people actually spend being married. However, the goal of computing divorce rates is not only to measure societal rejection of marriage. These rates also help sociologists make and test theories about the factors that contribute to the survival and breakdown of actual marriages. In turn, this helps us understand something about the conditions that make for better and worse family functioning.

A lot more could be said about the calculation of divorce rates. Demographers spend a great deal of time perfecting these measures, and the consumers of rates, like the readers of this book as well as policy makers, should be careful to know what is being measured and how. As a general rule, the best measured rate is one that correctly measures the risks of experiencing something such as divorce. It is wise never to devise a rate without knowing what question you are trying to answer; equally, never accept a rate as valid unless you know how it was created and what it really indicates.

Divorce and Society

Why do people divorce and what are the effects? Why do the rates vary over time and from one region to another and from one social group to another? But first, why should you care about the answers to these questions? Well, for one thing, the chances are high that your own parents are divorced or that your friends' parents are divorced. You may have already spent time thinking about the reasons why. Many children think, deep down, that they are somehow to blame, for example. Or, they blame one parent and not the other. This has important consequences for their self-esteem and life chances as well as their relations with one or both parents.

Maybe your parents didn't divorce, but you suspect they might have been happier if they had. The information in this chapter may help you make sense of the reasons people *don't* divorce as well as some of the reasons they do.

Finally, you should care because the chances are not negligible that, despite your best hopes and efforts, *you* will experience divorce. Or if not you, then your brother or sister or best friend may divorce at some time. Divorce usually solves some problems and creates other problems, problems between people and their children, their parents, siblings, or friends. You may have already witnessed some of these problems up close and want to understand them better and prevent similar problems from occurring in your life.

Sociologists are interested in divorce for similar (though usually less personal) reasons. They hope to learn important things from research on divorce about the nature of social bonding, the effects of economy and culture on personal relations, and the causes and consequences of divorce. At the micro-level, sociologists try to understand why individual couples get divorced. To do this, they examine family dynamics and interaction patterns, the expectations people have about married life, who they choose to marry and why, and people's subjective assessments of available alternative mates. They also examine the effects on divorcing spouses, their children, and other family members. Then, they consider how people may individually work to reduce the harmful effects of divorce.

At the macro-level, sociologists debate how to measure divorce, how to measure "a marriage or relationship breakdown," and how to find out the relationship between breakdown and divorce. Typically relationships break down long before divorce occurs, so separation may be a better indicator than divorce of marital problems. With dramatic increases in cohabitation, divorce rates are no longer the reliable indicators of relationship breakdown they once were (although, even in the past, they may not have been good indicators). With higher rates of cohabitation, we have fewer official records of marriage and divorce, and thus fewer records of "breakdown."

Macrosociologists have examined the social, cultural, economic, and political forces that shape the institution of marriage. Their goal has been to find out what accounts for the long-term increase in divorce rates (until recently, as we noted) in all industrialized countries over this century. To find out, they examine such large-scale processes as industrialization and urbanization, the increasing participation of women in the labour force, and changes in the societal norms regulating marriage and family life. They also study the macro-level effects of high divorce rates on family and social life, on parenting, and on the distribution of income.

Despite high divorce rates, the family is still the most important and most fundamental institution in society. So it is understandable that some may interpret high divorce rates as a sign of societal breakdown. This interpretation, favoured by political conservatives today, began with the work of the nineteenth-century sociologist Émile Durkheim in works like *Suicide* and *The Division of Labour in Society*.

Conservative sociologists note that, even today, high divorce rates are associated with high suicide rates, suggesting that the divorce rate measures distress or disorganization in the general population. Positive correlations between divorce rates, suicide rates, and alcohol consumption per capita suggest a broad-based social characteristic: a **social pathology**, as early sociologists would have called it. This produces a variety of stress-related behaviours, of which divorce is (supposedly) one.

However, liberal sociologists deny that divorce rates necessarily show **social disorganization**. High divorce rates can coexist with a healthy family and social life if clear norms specify what is to happen to the husband, wife, and children after a divorce. In societies that handle divorce well, such as Sweden, children continue to live with their kin: often, with their mother and her relatives. They do not suffer unduly from the separation of their parents. In this instance, divorce produces few stress-related behaviours. There are examples of relatively smooth divorce arrangements in our own society.

All too often in our own society, however, the macro- and micro-level problems supposedly caused by divorce—problems we associate with what thirty or forty years ago were called "broken homes"—are due to an inadequate institutionalization of divorce or a lack of societal support for those experiencing divorce. Modern North Americans don't handle divorce well as individuals, nor does our society. While that remains largely the case, high divorce rates will likely continue to result in social and personal problems. Conceivably, the problems will diminish when people receive more support—both material and normative—in the event of a divorce.

It must be added here that it is not only divorce that causes problems for individuals and society. Unhappy, abusive, unequal marriages can also cause great pain for individuals, for society, and for children. Sorting out the causes of social and individual problems in relation to divorce is not an easy task. Often many problems go together, making it unwise to attribute any or all subsequent problems to the divorce in particular.

People in our society have trouble thinking about divorce in a calm, dispassionate way. Why do they sometimes view it in dramatic terms, as a "pathology" or "societal breakdown"? Perhaps it is because no one really prepares for divorce as they do for other major adult life experiences, like education, employment, and marriage. Most couples still marry with the expectation that their marriage will last forever. Although the odds still favour marriages lasting, many do not. People wrongly organize their lives and societal roles/policies around the belief that long-term marriage is the only reasonable expectation. Beliefs about marriage and divorce have not changed, though historical and cross-national data show us that divorce practices surely have!

A Historical, Cross-National Overview of Divorce

In industrial societies, divorce rates hit a peak in the second half of the twentieth century. This peak occurred because of changes in the structure of social, economic, and legal institutions that shape family life and individual expectations of marriage. Divorce is nothing new, however, nor is it limited to Western industrial societies (see Phillips, 1988). What follows is a thumbnail sketch of the relevant sociohistorical processes.

Social Changes

To understand the reasons for these changes, we have to step back from our present lives. We must try to imagine life as people lived it for most of human history. In pre-industrial times, most families were rural, land-based, self-sufficient units. They produced most of what they needed to feed, clothe, and house their own members. The division of labour was simple. Tasks and responsibilities were allocated according to age and gender. *Social differentiation* beyond that was slight.

As we noted in Chapter 5, with the onset of the Industrial Revolution about two hundred years ago (mid-nineteenth century in Canada), the modern Western family lost its function as a productive unit. Many people were forced off the land. They moved to towns and cities, where they took wage-paying jobs. Most economic production thus moved out of the household and into factories and (later) offices. Individual family members still worked to sustain themselves and their families. However, the family lost its function as the basic social unit of production. Work and family were no longer the same thing.

These changes affected the strength of family ties, and the family's ability to control its members. When people earn their living from wages paid for work done outside the family, they may (though they do not always) effectively escape control by the family head. They no longer depend completely for their futures on getting a share of land or any other asset that is typically under the control of family elders. Jobs in the market economy allow people to earn a living as individuals, not family members. Workers receive their own wages. They may be able to spend them independently of their elders, and of their spouses. People's lives become more individuated and governed by market forces. People can lead highly individualistic, independent lives if they want to.

In the last hundred years, other functions of the family, such as the education and training of the young, increasingly have become the responsibility of the state. In Canada, compulsory education was the state response to unruly youth of the early industrial period. The interest was less in educating children than in controlling them. The state grew larger, taking responsibility for more of our lives—health, education, and welfare. This meant that the family was no longer a locus of production or a major source of personal economic security. Of course, that period of state expansion is now largely at an end. With increasing job and material insecurity (in pensions, social assistance, etc.), families may once again be becoming a crucial source of security for individuals.

To be sure, the family was always, and is still, important. In fact, throughout the industrial era the family continued to be a crucial economic unit. Even today, perhaps especially today, it is only by pooling their members' incomes that many families keep themselves out of poverty and off social assistance. Immigrant family members, in particular, tend to pool their resources to achieve collective upward mobility. Nonetheless, in the second half of the twentieth century, the family is much less necessary for edu-

When Love Dies, the Legal Battle Begins

Experts say that while society has formal routines and rituals for mourning death, there is no such structure for the grief that accompanies divorce. George Awad, a Toronto psychiatrist who works in family counseling and custody assessments, says one of the hardest tasks for divorcing couples is to separate emotionally and psychologically. If they do not, and they stay "enmeshed," bitter divorce cases result, he says.

"Though society has accepted divorce, it has not accepted responsibility for providing the support divorced families and single parents need," Jannie Mills, executive director of New Directions says.

By far one of the biggest problems for divorcing couples is our legal system, experts say. Lawyer Al Weisbrot has given up family law litigation and now works as a mediator in such cases. "The system is no good," he says. "At the end of one court case where we were very successful, I looked at the father. He said, 'We won. We won!' I thought 'What did we achieve? I took every effort to destroy that poor woman.'"

Source: Robin Harvey. Reprinted with permission of The Toronto Star Syndicate. From an article originally appearing in *The Toronto Star*, December 6, 1997, L1, L2.

cational and some other purposes than it was a century ago. As a result, people may invest less in the family. And, the looser their ties become, the easier it is to sever them when problems arise or attractive alternatives beckon. So, divorce rates tend to be high.

By this historical reckoning, higher divorce rates are the result of a change in the ties that bind family members to one another. Where family ties once rested on life-and-death economic dependence and co-dependence, today they rest more often on emotions of love and liking. Since emotional ties are by their nature more fragile than ties of economic dependence, we more easily sever them. However, not every couple that falls out of love gets a divorce, since divorce is a legal process and not simply a social or emotional one. Some couples, as we shall see, may not wish to enter the social and legal realm in ending their marriages.

Legal Changes

To understand divorce as a legal process, we must understand the laws governing divorce and how they have changed. Divorce laws in Canada and other Western countries have gradually liberalized over the past two centuries. For example, during the colonial period in North America divorce was completely illegal in the southern United States and Quebec. It was only granted elsewhere under narrowly defined circumstances such as adultery or after seven years of desertion. Even then, it was nearly impossible to get a divorce granted. Canadian law up until fairly recently required an Act of Parliament for each divorce to be granted. Not surprisingly, divorces were granted most often to the well-to-do and the influential.

Increasingly over the twentieth century, North American governments have granted divorces upon ever-widening grounds. A turning point occurred in the late 1960s and early 1970s with the introduction of **no-fault divorce** laws in Canada and some jurisdictions in the United States. In Canada, the 1968 Divorce Act enlarged the "fault grounds" under which a divorce could be granted, but also allowed divorce without accusations of wrongdoing in the case of "marital breakdown," which required three years of living apart, or five if both spouses did not agree to divorce. The 1985 Divorce Act, which is still in effect, considers marriage breakdown to be the only ground for divorce, though the older grounds such as adultery or cruelty are considered evidence of breakdown. It is no longer necessary for one spouse or the other to accept moral blame for the breakdown of the marriage. As a result of this change in approach, society has gradually redefined divorce. No longer does divorce have to be a rare or stigmatizing process where one party is held responsible under the law. On the contrary, we now may be more likely to look critically at marriages that survive even though they are emotionally dead. These are marriages that we now think could end, freeing their participants to try again to find emotional fulfilment.

Both these laws were reflected in immediate changes to Canadian divorce rates (see Figure 9.1). The greater access to divorce rates made possible in 1968 led to a fivefold increase in divorce between the late 1960s and the mid-1980s. Immediately following the 1985 Act, divorces again rose sharply, but much of this increase appears to have been accounted for by people who put off divorcing in 1984 and 1985, in anticipation of the revised legislation, and then initiated proceedings once the new law was enacted. By the late 1980s the rate was declining.

No-fault divorce laws implicitly define as unacceptable marriages in which couples are "incompatible" or have "irreconcilable differences." Divorce, according to no-fault laws then, could end marriages that are "irretrievably broken." The grounds for no-fault divorce are based almost entirely on the loss of emotional essentials. In earlier times, many marriages may have broken down emotionally or may never have been emotionally based in the first instance. It is only recently that the legal system has come to view this as sufficient reason to end a marriage.

These changes did not come to all parts of the English-speaking world at the same time. For example, divorce remained illegal in Ireland until 1995. A referendum on the topic in that year defeated existing laws by a narrow margin. The pressure to liberalize Irish divorce laws contributed to a wide-ranging discussion of **secularization** (a move away from religion as an organizing principle of society) and the nature of social and familial change. People have also been forced to reconsider the relationship between moral and constitutional matters, or church and state. Ireland is not yet a sec-

Figure 9.1 DIVORCES PER 100 000 POPULATION, 1968–1990

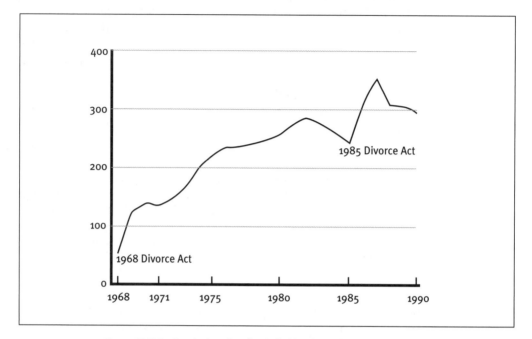

Source: Statistics Canada, from *Canadian Sotical Trends*, Catalogue No. 11-008, Summer 1993, No. 29, p. 14.
Reprinted with permission.

ular society. However, Ireland is more pluralistic and tolerant than it was a decade ago. Individual Catholics, in Ireland as elsewhere, no longer embrace completely all the doctrines of the Church (though it may well be that, in practice, they never did so entirely).

Cultural Changes

The liberalization of divorce laws has contributed to a steady increase in divorce rates over the past two centuries—until recently. Where divorce is still illegal, or merely hard to get, couples who would otherwise do so cannot end their union. The divorce rate is correspondingly low or nil. However, where divorce is easier, more couples divorce. Rising divorce rates are correlated with easier divorce laws. Couples long separated will seek a divorce when the laws allow. Yet, in and of themselves, easier divorce laws do not cause the increase in divorce any more than the building of a McDonald's causes hamburger-eating, although consumption of both hamburgers and divorce may increase with the widening of opportunities.

The increase in divorce is largely attributable to economic development (industrialization or modernization), which stimulates individualism in every area of life. Culture, including religion, also affects divorce. Some parts of the culture come to accept divorce more easily than other parts. In this respect, the legal system changes faster than the religious system. In any event, culture does not seem to override the general increase in divorce brought by development. That is why we see a liberalization of divorce laws—and rising divorce rates—wherever societies industrialize, whether they started life as Protestant, Catholic, Jewish, Muslim, Buddhist, or Confucian.

Today, *family* includes a vast array of increasingly diverse and complicated relationships and values. Both men and women enter marriage expecting less from it in terms of financial security but more in terms of interpersonal communication, intimacy, and sexual gratification. More people today think of marriage as a place for self-actualization and empathetic companionship. However, such aspirations have a downside. People who think that close relations are about intense emotions are more likely to cohabit—and if they do marry, more likely to divorce—than people who think that close relations are about practical living arrangements. Wherever people put a strong emphasis on intimate partnership as the ideal behind marriage, they are slower to marry and quicker to divorce if necessary.

As well, women's economic independence, the growth of civil rights, and the development of modern contraception have all led North Americans to assess marriage in non-traditional ways. Each cultural change affects marriage in a different way. Taken together they have all made marriage more discretionary. Both men and women feel less compelled by parents and friends, social norms, or cultural ideals, to marry. If married, they feel less compelled to stay married. And certainly, women now have other avenues of activity open to them if they choose not to make a career of marriage and parenthood.

Therefore, more liberal divorce laws and higher divorce rates both stem from the same sources. Changing values and norms in the larger society, alterations in economic opportunities, political ideologies, and even the models presented by the mass media all play a part. Liberal divorce laws are merely tools for the ready user. As Goode (1993:322) explains:

> Under any legal system, some people try to leave their marriages under the existing laws, but many will also press toward new laws with fewer restrictions. If we remove some barriers, some people get divorced who would not have done so before. But, if the deeper social forces that drive both actions become stronger, then still other people will try to dissolve their unions under restrictions they now consider hard and some will work toward even fewer barriers.

What, then, has propelled so many people toward demanding and using liberal divorce laws?

Causes of Divorce

To describe the social changes associated with changes in divorce rates may be taken to imply an explanation of those changes. However, a description should not be mistaken for an explanation. Let us consider the supposed causes of divorce, and changes in divorce practice, more systematically. (For a detailed discussion of the causes of divorce, see Guttman, 1993.)

In the discussion that follows, we speak of "causes" but, often as not, we might as well be using the words **determinants** or **predictors**. That is because many supposed causes of divorce intertwine with other causes. Their distinct, separate influence is hard to discover. The most we can say with certainty is that these are predictors—correlates that typically precede divorce and influence the likelihood of divorce. In that limited sense, they are causes of divorce.

We also distinguish among three levels of causal explanation: the micro-, meso-, and macro-levels. By **micro-level** causes, we mean something close to the lived experience of people who divorce: attitudes, perceptions, sentiments, beliefs, and the like. We include the experiences of rejection, infidelity, and marital dissatisfaction in this category. By **macro-level** causes, we mean societal changes like social integration, women's involvement in the workforce, and changes in divorce laws. These are the kinds of variables that Durkheim and his fellow classical macrosociologists studied and first called to people's attention.

Finally, "middle-range" or **meso-level** causes of divorce are, typically, demographic predictors—that is, characteristics of people who are at a high risk of divorce. It is unclear in many cases whether these characteristics are causes, determinants, or merely predictors. For example, people who marry at an early age, or after only a short relationship, run a particularly high risk of divorce. The cause? Probably not youth or unfamiliarity *per se*. Perhaps it is the stress, conflict, and dissatisfaction that arise when two immature strangers try to work out a life together.

Precisely what we call the "cause" in any situation will vary from one analyst to another. Let us begin with the microsociological causes of divorce. We have already discussed some of these at length in Chapter 3. They are the easiest causes to understand intuitively.

Microsociological Causes

We commonly cite two kinds of microsociological "reasons." The first are grounds that people use when they file for divorce (see Figure 9.2). Depending on the jurisdiction, the most common are alcoholism or drug abuse, infidelity, incompatibility, and physical and emotional abuse. These "grounds" may have value in a court of law (though no longer in Canada, where living apart for a year is considered sufficient proof of marriage break-

Figure 9.2   MARITAL BREAKDOWN IN CANADA 1991: GROUNDS FOR
DIVORCE UNDER THE 1985 DIVORCE ACT

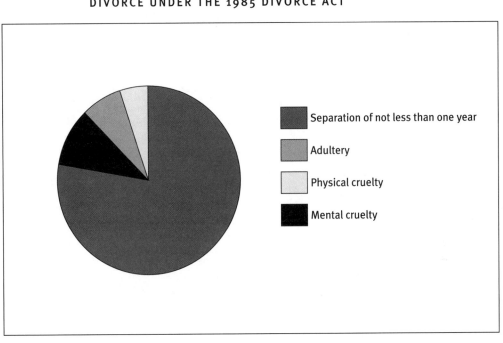

- Separation of not less than one year
- Adultery
- Physical cruelty
- Mental cruelty

Source: Statistics Canada, Cat. 84-213.

down), but sociologists find them largely unrevealing.

We learn more from the personal "accounts" of individuals who have undergone divorce. "Respondents' accounts of their own divorces illuminate several factors that receive little attention in the empirical literature ..." (White, 1990:908). They tell us a lot about the state of mind of the divorcing people, and the ways they make sense to themselves of what has happened. However, people often do not really understand the reasons for their own behaviour. As well, "(b)ecause these studies only include divorced respondents, they can tell us little about the extent to which these factors predict divorce" (ibid.). Table 9.1 shows some of the issues that Canadians say would lead them to consider divorce. It is interesting that older people consider such issues as disagreement over finances more important than do younger people, probably because they have a more realistic, practical view of marriage.

The second kind of microsociological reasons people cite to explain divorce typically describe the dynamics of the marriage relationship. As we said in Chapter 3, the quality of a relationship largely determines the stability of a marriage. Marriages likely to end in divorce have a typical profile. Usually, they are characterized by poor communication and poor conflict-

Table 9.1 ATTITUDES TOWARD DIVORCE BY REASONS (CANADA 1995)

	15–29	30–49	50+
Fundamental Issues			
Abusive behaviour	95	95	94
Unfaithful behaviour	89	85	89
Lack of love/respect	86	87	87
Partner drinks too much	68	73	80
Experiential Issues			
Constant disagreement over finances	28	40	49
Unsatisfactory sexual relationship	21	37	45
Unsatisfactory division of household tasks	12	16	21
Conflict about how children are raised	14	17	21
Would stay for the children	44	39	52

Respondents were asked whether they would consider the above issues valid reasons for divorce.

Source: Statistics Canada. 1995 General Social Survey. Abridged from Judith Frederick & Jason Hamel. 1998. "Canadian Attitudes to Divorce," *Canadian Social Trends* Spring: 8.

resolution skills as well as a lack of commitment to the spouse and/or to the institution of marriage. In these marriages the spouses have few shared values and interests, and there is often a perceived inequity between spouses and less than average respect, love, and affection on the part of one or both spouses. These are overall average traits and of course will not characterize each situation. However, these dynamics help us explain why particular couples end their marriages. We can imagine people in such relationships wanting and getting a divorce. Yet, because they are such common problems of married life, they rarely help us predict *which* couples are going to celebrate a fiftieth anniversary together and which ones are going to break up next week. Even those on the inside of the relationship often cannot make that prediction.

Consider, instead, some life-course (demographic) variables that make certain people more divorce-prone than others. They are better than microsociological variables at identifying conditions that produce tension and unhappiness—which, in turn, increase the likelihood of divorce. That is, even if they do not seem to explain divorce as well, they are better at predicting it.

Mesosociological Causes

Not everyone who marries, divorces. Moreover, the probability of divorce is spread unevenly throughout the population. Thus, to understand the causes of divorce we must look at who gets divorced and why. As Lynn White explains:

> A shift in the lifetime divorce probability from 10 percent to well over 50 percent cannot be explained at the micro level. In addition to asking why some marriages are more likely to fail than others, we also need to examine changes in the social institutions that structure individual experience (White, 1990:904).

Major life course and demographic variables correlated with a high divorce risk include young age at marriage, cohabitation before marriage, second or subsequent marriage, parental divorce, premarital pregnancy and/or childbearing, childlessness or, conversely, having a large number of children, early stage of marriage, urban residence, residence in western North America (or in Quebec), absence of religious belief or affiliation, and low socioeconomic status.

Age at Marriage

Age at marriage is probably the strongest predictor of divorce in the first five years of marriage. People who enter marriage at the youngest ages do so with the greatest risk of leaving marriage by divorce. Risks are particularly high for people who marry in their teens. Various explanations of this have been ventured: for example, young people lack the emotional maturity needed for marriage, and they have ill-founded expectations of what married life holds in store. They are also more likely to become disappointed and disillusioned with marriage, especially when they come upon plentiful alternatives to their current spouse. As well, some of the effects of youthful marriage on marital dissolution are the result of the harmful effects of early marriage on educational achievement. Young marriers divorce more often because they have less education, therefore a lower income, and perhaps fewer communications skills—which, in turn, can result in more marital conflict.

Ironically, though young marriers in our own society have high rates of divorce, young-marrying societies, in which the average age at marriage is low, have low rates of divorce. Typically, countries with low average ages of marriage have other features—for example, high rates of childbearing, strongly institutionalized religion, extended families, and restrictive divorce laws—that keep the divorce rates low for people of all ages. The Latin American and Islamic societies share these features.

Cohabitation

Cohabitation before marriage has, as we've said in earlier chapters, also been strongly correlated with a higher risk of divorce. This finding runs counter to common sense, which would suggest that people who marry after they live together should have a lower divorce rate. After all, they are basing their decision to marry on more knowledge about each other than most people who marry. Couples who marry without first living together lack important information about the compatibility of their spouse. Therefore, they should have higher divorce rates—but they don't!

The best current explanation for this finding is **adverse selectivity**. Historically, "the kinds of people who flout[ed] convention by cohabiting [were] the same kinds of people who flout[ed] normative marital behaviour, [had] lower commitment to marriage as an institution, and disregard[ed] the stigma of divorce" (White, 1990:906). Cohabitation does not affect marital stability when the effects of selectivity are removed (Lillard, Brien & Waite, 1995). Other things being equal, cohabitation neither increases nor decreases the likelihood that a couple will stay together. What this means is that, as more people—and more varied people—cohabit, cohabitation no longer predicts a high risk of divorce. So, cohabitation is a predictor variable that is probably on the way out of sociological theories about marriage, although of course not all sociologists are of one mind in seeing it this way.

Second Marriages

Other things being equal, second marriages are more likely than first marriages to end in divorce. The probability that third marriages will end in divorce is higher still. (As well, remarriages that end in divorce end more quickly than first marriages.) When remarriages show a lower divorce rate, it is typically because the remarried people are older than average. Older people are less likely to divorce. Young people who remarry are more likely to divorce than older people who remarry. Holding age constant, remarriers are more likely to divorce than people in a first marriage (Clarke & Wilson, 1994).

Again, this violates our common sense. One would expect remarriages—like cohabiting relationships—to have a lower divorce rate. People who had already gone through one divorce would, we imagine, be more careful choosing their next mate. They would try harder to make their marriage work, to avoid the problems and costs associated with divorce. However, this is not so. Adverse selectivity may again be the explanation. The kinds of people who get a first divorce may be more willing to get a second, then a third. People who divorce and remarry are more likely to divorce a second time because they are the kinds of people who are prone to divorce. That is, "people in remarriages carry with them the characteristics (early age at first marriage, lower education, and so on) that raised the probability of their first marriage dissolving" (White, 1990:906). Or, they are the kinds of people for whom divorce is an option, as shown by the fact that they got a divorce the first time around. Of course, given the frequency of divorce, the "kinds of people" argument includes more and more kinds of *us*.

A competing theory argues that the stresses and strains of a remarriage—which often involve the (difficult) integration of stepchildren into reconstituted families, and forced interactions with ex-spouses—are greater than those of first marriages. This makes the former more prone to divorce. Both theories are compelling. We need more research to decide which of these two explanations is better, or whether both factors come into play.

Parental Divorce

People whose parents divorced are also more likely to divorce. However, the mechanism that transmits this inheritance is unclear. Perhaps, people whose parents divorced are less likely to believe that marriages can last. That makes them more likely to opt for divorce when things get tough. They may have married before they were ready, out of fear that they would end up alone (like their parents). They may have feared that they would have to take care of someone else's kids if perhaps their parents did this. They may have married before they really understood what marriage was all about, because their parents' marriage didn't last long enough for them to find out. Or they may simply have been the victims of over-optimism.

People whose parents are divorced are more likely to divorce themselves—possibly because they are less likely to believe that marriages can last, or because they may marry before they are ready (like their parents).

Or, again, the correlation may be due to adverse selectivity. People whose parents divorced were once a small minority. Today, they are not. Their parents' divorce stigmatizes them less and leaves them less ignorant about the variety of possible adaptations to marital conflict. They know that just about anyone can survive divorce, and many people are better for doing so. If this explanation is correct, we can expect the divorce rates to continue to remain high. More and more people will have "learned how to divorce" from their parents. However, demographically speaking, as the average age of the population increases, and as older people remarry less often and cohabit more often, we may see a decline in second and third divorces.

Childbearing, Before and After Marriage

For people who marry after producing a child, the risk of divorce is high. However premarital pregnancy does not, by itself, predict a later divorce. Presumably, the reason premarital childbearing increases the likelihood of divorce is that the parents marry for the wrong reasons. Couples who marry after discovering that they are expecting a child are more likely to marry to legitimate the birth of their child than because they are committed to one another. The good news is that "shotgun" weddings are less common than they used to be.

The relationship between the birth of children within marriage and the likelihood of divorce is strong, but hardly straightforward. Women with small or medium-sized families have the lowest rates of divorce. Women with no children or large families have the highest divorce rates (Thornton, 1977, 1996). On the one hand, people who have no children are freer to divorce than couples with children. Both childlessness and divorce are most common early in marriage. Thus, the relationship between them may be only apparent, not real—a result of both variables being attached to a third (common) variable.

On the other hand, people with many children undergo a higher degree of stress (whether emotional, or financial, or both) than do people with fewer children. Both the number of children affected by divorce and the proportion of divorces involving children have been increasing. Thus, children are clearly no longer—if indeed they ever were—an effective deterrent to divorce.

One of the most interesting findings in the literature on the demographic correlates of divorce is that the sex of the child or children influences divorce-proneness. Data from the Current Population Survey in the U.S. show that sons reduce the risk of marital disruption by 9 percent more than daughters. Fathers apparently get more involved in raising sons than daughters, which creates more attachment and a stronger sense of obligation. Having at least one son also lowers the mother's perception of the likelihood of separation or divorce, as paternal involvement is higher with boys than girls. This increased paternal involvement fosters the idea that the fathers have more invested, and therefore more to lose as a result of divorce (Katzev et al., 1994).

However, some findings suggest that child-related variables, such as the presence of a male child in the family, play no role whatever in predicting or causing divorce (Devine & Forehand, 1996). Like other variables we discuss, this apparent discrepancy may reflect a change over time, as divorce becomes more common. When divorce was an unusual behaviour, it was relatively easy to pinpoint predictor variables. As divorce became culturally "normal," the characteristics of divorcing couples became more varied, and the predictive value of any particular characteristic diminished.

Stage of Marriage

The longer a marriage has lasted, the less likely people are to divorce. The explanation for this finding is that the more time and energy people invest in their marriage, the higher the costs of abandoning it and starting a new life. Conversely, divorce risks are highest early in a marriage. Divorce rates peak around the third year of marriage, since the factors responsible for divorce (e.g., emotional dissatisfaction) carry more weight in the early years. For example, couples are more aware of being badly matched early in the marriage. After about three years, relationships stabilize and many partners adjust to their situation. Investments in marriage accumulate with time and make divorce less attractive after a certain point.

On the other hand, the longer a marriage goes on, the older the spouses are likely to be, and the more likely they are to have grown up with cultural values in which marriage had much greater normative pull than it does today. We must wait another few decades before we find out the strength of this **cohort effect**. (A cohort effect is something that influences everyone of roughly the same age. World War II or the Depression might be such influences.)

Place of Residence

People living in urban centres are much more likely to divorce than people in rural settings. On the one hand, these findings reflect a higher probability of divorce under conditions of urban living. However, in part these statistics also reflect adverse selectivity—specifically, the tendency for rural people to migrate to urban areas before, during, or after a divorce. A family farm can be a difficult place for divorced people, particularly divorced women. They may be attracted to the more diverse neighbourhoods of cities, where married and unmarried people live nearer to one another.

The effect of urban living is sometimes confounded by the divorce-increasing role of migration. Thus, for example, Puerto Rican women who have lived on the U.S. mainland have markedly higher rates of divorce and separation than those with no U.S. life experience (Landale & Ogena, 1995). When we control for many possible explanatory factors, rates of marital instability are strongly related to recent and lifetime migration experience. The weak social ties of migrants appear to provide less social support for their unions and fewer barriers to union disruption. An alternative explanation is that when immigrants from countries in which marriage is seen primarily as a practical arrangement come to North America and encounter the expectation that marriage should be based on passion and companionship, they look at their own marriage from a different point of view, and become dissatisfied. A third possibility is that selectivity explains the finding. People who take the initiative of moving to a new country are risk takers, willing to confront challenges and make changes in their lives; it seems reasonable that they would be more willing to consider divorce than the more cautious people who stay behind.

Divorce rates vary across regions in any given country, too. In both Canada and the United States, divorce rates increase as one moves from east to west. An exception is posed by Quebec, which is in the centre of Canada, yet has relatively high rates of divorce (and also of cohabitation, as we noted in Chapter 2). One factor explaining this east-west pattern is a difference in attitudes and values. Something of a frontier tradition that includes rootlessness seems to characterize the West in both Canada and the United States. The age distribution of the population also differs, with younger (and thus more divorce-prone) people being found in the West. People in the West have also tended to move away from the stabilizing influences of extended families and family traditions in search of jobs.

Religion

The ethnic and religious composition of the population has something to do with the east-west pattern of divorce. The more religious people are, the less likely they will be to opt for divorce, even if they are unhappy in their marriages. Sharing the same religious affiliation also plays a part. Couples in which the spouses belong to different religions are more likely to divorce than couples who belong to the same religion. Couples in which neither spouse has a religious affiliation tend to have even higher rates of divorce (Goode, 1993:320).

The percentages of regular churchgoers and fundamentalists in a state or region also correlate negatively with the divorce rate (Sweezy & Tiefenthaler, 1996). As Durkheim would have predicted, the percentage of Catholic residents in any American state or region correlates negatively with the divorce and suicide rates (Joubert, 1995). Catholic belief does not sanction either divorce or suicide. We know from Durkheim's research, discussed in earlier chapters, that low divorce rates cause low suicide rates (due to an inverse correlation between social integration and suicide).

Socioeconomic Status

The divorce rate increases as one moves down the socioeconomic ladder. Study after study confirms that, whatever the index of socioeconomic status used—income, occupation, or education—we observe an inverse correlation between **socioeconomic status** (SES) and divorce rates.

The relationship between social class (or SES) and divorce rates may be explained, on the one hand, by the higher level of financial insecurity that lower-income people face. Economic stresses produce marital stresses. Simultaneously, the poor have less to lose from divorce and less to gain from staying married. In other words, compared to more prosperous people, their material investment in marriage may be lower, so divorce "costs" them less. However, differences in divorce rates by socioeconomic status generally tend to be decreasing. This is in part a function of an increase in the

Are the Seeds of Divorce Lying in Our Genes?

Over the past 20 years a group of psychologists at the University of Minnesota has been looking at the lives of identical and non-identical twins with an eye to separating mother nature from mother nurture. The researchers' most famous work involves parsing the lives of identical twins from around the world who were adopted at birth by different families.

Among divorced identical twins, in 45 per cent of the cases both twins in the family were divorced. Among divorced fraternal twins, in 30 percent of the cases both twins in the family were divorced. "Our data implicate the importance of genetic fac-

tors in the prediction of divorce risk," says the paper. The psychologists also make the case that divorce is a genetic predisposition that parents pass on to children.

My belief is that the Minnesota professors don't appreciate how human history humbles genetic theorists—particularly when, as in the present case, there are no actual genes being studied. "There is no question that [someone] couldn't come up with societal sanctions that reduce [our] divorce rate down to nil," Prof. McGue admits, but doesn't see how this stands all his genetics-underlies-divorce thesis on its head.

Source: Stephen Strauss. n.d. *The Globe and Mail* (abridged) . Reprinted with permission from *The Globe and Mail*.

divorce rate among middle- and upper-class people.

Sociologist William Goode has an interesting explanation for both the finding that divorce rates diminish as one moves up the socioeconomic ladder, and that the divorce rate for middle- and upper-middle class couples is on the rise. He notes that in the 1950s,

> lower-class women had relatively less to lose economically from divorce because they were more likely to be close to the wages of their husbands. Middle- and upper-class women, in contrast had a much greater economic stake in the stability of their marriages and much more to lose from a divorce. There was likely to be a much greater discrepancy between their own income (which was often nonexistent since few middle-class women with children were employed in those days) and the income of their husbands.

> If the relationship between class position and proneness to divorce has been changing, the change is likely to be the result of a shift in the strongest variable in this pattern: the discrepancy between the husband's and the wife's incomes. Now that more married women from the middle and upper classes are likely to be employed, and more likely to be employed in occupations and professions similar to their husbands, there is less discrepancy between their incomes. With less discrepancy (and with independent incomes), those women now look — sociologically — more like the lower-class women of the past in that they will not experience as great a loss of income if they divorce. The same variable may also account for part of the higher divorce rate among Afro-Americans, since it determines how great a loss the wife would experience if a divorce occurred (Goode, 1993:331)

By suggesting that the divorce rate is higher because more women can afford to get divorced than once could, Goode assumes that women are more likely to want out of marriage than men. The more economically independent women become, the more likely they will be to leave their marriages when they want. We would have to look further at who initiates separation or files for divorce, to confirm this hypothesis. The implication is that marriage, though seemingly about love or emotional union, is a way for women to gain economically, or at least to survive.

Some research finds that increases in wives' socioeconomic status and labour force participation do indeed increase the probability of marriage disruption. When the wife's work status is higher than her husband's, instability is more likely (Tzeng & Mare, 1995). We may know of situations where this occurs. However, other research finds no support for this hypothesis. Improvements in the wife's status usually increase marital stability, perhaps by reducing economic stresses in the family, or by increasing the wife's **autonomy** and fulfilment.

Most couples with more education and a stronger attachment to the workforce have more stable marriages. It is also these couples who are most likely to be egalitarian. Given the importance of work in stabilizing marriage, it is no surprise that unemployed people have higher divorce risks than employed people. The receipt of family-support income also (slightly) increases the likelihood that a married woman will become divorced (Hoffman & Duncan, 1995). This does not mean that social transfers cause marital instability, but only that economic and other instabilities may be correlated.

Macrosociological Causes

It should be clear by now that, although the decision to divorce is one made by an individual couple, that decision is influenced strongly by large processes in the structure of society over which people have little, if any, control.

The institution of the family has changed a great deal over the past two centuries. The ties of authority and economic dependence that bind family members together have weakened considerably. In addition, the legal structure forcing people to remain together has loosened, making divorce an attainable option for many people. Other important macro-level determinants of divorce include wars and migrations, economic cycles, sex ratios, gender roles, social integration, and cultural values. We will look at each of these factors in turn.

Wars

Sharp increases in divorce rates usually follow wars. Divorce rates usually then return to the prewar levels. This is likely because war separates many couples for long periods. Sometimes, couples who were formerly close grow apart—or are torn apart. Some migrate to other regions or countries, never to return to their home countries or their spouses. In other cases, wartime separation merely establishes separate lives for couples whose marriages had been held together only by inertia. In addition, war throws together many lonely people under conditions that encourage involvement. Few people institute divorce actions while a war is in progress. Many do so when wars end and people readjust. Finally, the strains of postwar reunion themselves are often great. Some formerly stable marriages break under this additional strain.

Economic Cycles

People are less likely to divorce during recessionary periods than during periods of economic prosperity. People feel freer to strike out on their own when economic opportunities exist. They are more wary of leaving a familiar home or relationship, even if it is unpleasant, in times of economic uncertainty. This may help to explain why divorce rates declined slightly in the difficult late 1980s and 1990s.

Moreover, divorce is costly. It requires establishing separate households, dividing the property, and establishing specific terms for the support of children. These requirements tax most people's financial resources even during prosperity and often become prohibitive in bad times. Great financial hardship may draw together some couples who might otherwise become isolated from each other. If this happens, apparently the effect is short-lived. Although divorce rates drop during depressions, they rise rapidly when the depression ends.

On the other hand, according to White's review of the sociological literature on divorce published in the 1980s, "(t)he most sophisticated analysis of American time series data ... finds that the effect of prosperity is to slightly reduce divorce" (White, 1990:905). Although prosperity may make divorce more feasible, the benefits of prosperity outweigh this effect on personal relationships (South, 1985). Indeed, as we noted in the last chapter, financial insecurity places a great deal of stress on any marriage. It can add enough strain to break marriages that would otherwise survive under conditions of prosperity. Thus, divorce rates may fall because financial security adds stability to personal relationships.

Sex Ratios

One of the more provocative and controversial findings in the literature on macro-level determinants of divorce is that the ratio of women to men in a given society affects the divorce rate. Among non-Hispanic whites, the risk of divorce is highest where either wives or husbands have the option of many potential mates. Despite strong cultural norms against extramarital relations, many people remain open to alternative relationships while married. The supply of spousal alternatives in the local marriage market seems to increase the risk of divorce. The jury is still out on how much of a factor this is, however.

Gender Expectations

When social structures allow women more economic independence from men and families, women have more freedom to divorce. A growing similarity of women's and men's lives and roles may produce less marital cohesion than complementary, reinforcing roles do. Both of these processes imply that the more women become financially independent, the higher the divorce rate will be.

Evidence, both from time series studies in the United States and from cross-cultural studies, overwhelmingly finds that as women's participation in the labour force increases, so does the divorce rate. This may be more correlation, however, than causation. It is unclear whether the critical factor is extra-familial opportunities, economic independence, growing similarity of gender roles, the worldwide trend toward more modern marital relationships based on higher expectations, or some other factors. However, the rise in divorce rates is not likely due to a blurring of gender roles, or more gender equality.

Evidence suggests that the most satisfying and stable marriages are those in which gender roles are egalitarian, men are sensitive and nurturing, and husbands and wives share equally in making the decisions that affect their lives. Antill & Cotton (1987) studied 108 couples and found that when both spouses are high on "feminine" characteristics such as nurturance, sensitivity, and gentleness, couples are happier than when one or both spouses are low on this cluster of characteristics. "**Femininity**" of both wives and husbands is positively associated with a smooth marital adjustment (Kalin & Lloyd, 1985). The explanation is that many qualities and characteristics that make up femininity are conducive to positive interpersonal relationships. Relationships that both spouses view as equitable have the best marital adjustment. The greater the perceived inequity, the poorer the marital adjustment, and thus the higher the risks of divorce.

The nature of the relationship between gender expectations and divorce proneness remains unclear. Are divorce rates and rates of female participation in paid work intrinsically related? Is the divorce rate as high in countries that have had a longer history of female participation in the labour force? Historical and cross-cultural research is addressing these questions. (See, for example, Popenoe's research on Sweden and other advanced industrial countries.)

Social Integration

Another macro-level determinant of divorce is a society's degree of **social integration**. The higher the social integration, the lower the divorce rate.

Aggregate-level studies in the United States and Canada uniformly find that community instability, whether measured by migration or by **social mobility**, is the best predictor of aggregate divorce rates. In a stable, highly integrated community, consensus on social rules is strong and rule-breakers are punished. This happens especially when the rules broken bear on social institutions as central to the community life as "the family." The highly integrated community typically supports a variety of "pro-family" ideals bearing on marriage, premarital or extramarital sexuality, or child obedience. Social integration decreases the likelihood that people will divorce by increasing the costs of divorcing and divorce. By getting a divorce, people risk incurring a social stigma for flouting social norms. In highly integrated communities, this is scary stuff and a definite deterrent to any kind of "deviance," including divorce.

Cultural Values

Researchers have given a lot of attention to the postwar shift in cultural values from an emphasis on community to the primacy of the individual. Today, it is argued, we invest less in familial commitments, whether to parents, spouses, or children, than was once the norm.

Since the 1960s, the cultural value placed on marriage has been declining. Many scholars argue that formal marriage has lost its normative support. This means it is no longer something that one *ought* to do, but is simply a matter of personal choice or preference. Distinctions between marital and nonmarital childbearing, marriage, and cohabitation have lost their normative force. We have reduced marriage and divorce to mere formalities, or sets of lifestyle choices.

Effects of Divorce

Divorce, like the breakup of any important relationship, is usually messy and painful. Most couples decide to divorce only reluctantly over a long period. For most of them, considerable trauma is involved. A minority experience some discrimination and may be, for a time, almost without friends. Some, notably women, suffer economic deprivation.

Effects on Both Spouses

One of the major effects of divorce is economic: for men and women, but especially women, incomes fall. For both men and women, patterns of credit use change and debt problems increase after divorce. The material effects of divorce should not be underrated: economic distress is a large contributor to generalized psychological distress. Controlling for financially caused stress reduces the estimated effect of divorce or separation. However, economic distress is only one aspect of divorce and its aftermath. The other side is the emotional stress of interpersonal conflict. This begins well before the divorce, and may reach its peak then. In the years immediately preceding divorce, people experience higher-than-usual levels of distress. But conflict does not always end with divorce. The effects of divorce, both material and emotional, are surprisingly long-lasting, often as strong after four to eight years as they are within the first four years (Mastekaasa, 1995).

Some people take longer than others to recover from the effects of divorce. For example, people who experience high levels of guilt have more trouble adjusting to their new situation following divorce, as measured by depression, role strain, and continuing attachment to the ex-spouse. A majority report some level of contact with their former spouse. This is particularly likely if they have children, of course. Also, a majority hold similar views about the desirable level of contact, and behave in conformity with these views.

By contrast, some former spouses disagree on the involvement of non-custodial parents in co-parenting. An overwhelming majority of residential parents feel they have problems with the issue of visitation rights. A smaller but still substantial percentage of non-residential parents do too. Moreover, these problems don't go away quickly. For residential parents, usually the mother, visitation problems are connected to feelings of hurt and anger about the divorce. They are also connected with concerns about the ex-spouse's parenting abilities, child support, and sometimes about abuse of the child.

The process of changing role-identities during divorce and post-divorce interactions is different for initiators than for non-initiators, or what Hopper (1993) calls "dumpers" and "dumpees," although both pass through a series of predictable stages on the way to recovery (Duran-Aydintug, 1995). Each person's network of social relationships helps to shape the effects of divorce and adjustments to it.

After divorce, the satisfaction people feel with their current family situation or (subsequent) marriage is influenced by a variety of things, including the contact they have had with relatives since the divorce. Participation in organizations and clubs also helps people feel that life is better afterwards than during the divorce. It may be simply that people feel that they have seen the worst and survived it.

Having acknowledged that men and women have some similar experiences during divorce, we will now focus on the different effects for each after divorce. Particularly, we will consider the difficulties women face with divorce, which tend to be greater than those for men.

Effects on Women

This section emphasizes the adverse effects of divorce. However, let's begin by acknowledging that divorce may also have benefits. For example, divorced mothers whose marriages were difficult, and sometimes abusive, are typically relieved that their marriages are over. However, even among those who are happy to be out of a bad or intolerable relationship, a majority express concern about the conditions they face after divorce. They tend to be angry about diminished opportunities and their perceived second-class treatment as divorced women (Kurz, 1995).

Though the end of a marital relationship, whether by death or divorce, is almost always traumatic, the way the relationship ends also makes a difference, particularly for women. German research suggests that, for women, the actual loss of the marital partner is not as important as the circumstances under which the partner was lost (Maas, 1995). Divorced women are financially worse off than recently widowed women, for example. They also report more health problems.

Because women and men have different experiences after a divorce, they behave differently. After divorce, both male and female suicide rates rise. However, the effect is far stronger for men than for women. Separated men are six times more likely than married men to commit suicide (especially in the younger age groups), while separated women do not have much higher suicide rates. Thus, as Durkheim said, marriage protects both sexes, but it does so differently. Women with more children have lower suicide rates than women with fewer children, for example. It is possible that their child-rearing responsibilities protect women against suicide. This protection erodes as their children become independent.

Divorce depresses both women and men. However, women undergoing divorce show greater increases in rates of depression. Men whose marriages are breaking up typically show higher rates of alcohol problems but not of distress. Women report more distress but not more alcohol problems. These findings support the idea that men externalize their problems in response to circumstances that lead women to internalize. Women also show more symptoms of distress before the separation, whereas men display more symptoms afterwards. In short, men and women respond to the stresses of divorce differently. Therefore, researchers must measure men's and women's well-being differently and therapists must help them in ways appropriate to the problems they face.

After divorce, women usually suffer a decline in their standard of living. A classic American study by Lenore Weitzman (1985) estimated a decline of 73 percent in women's standard of living, compared to a 42 percent decline for men in the first year after divorce. (For comparable Canadian data, see Finnie, 1993, which will be discussed in a moment. For more recent American data, see Arditti, 1997. For a re-analysis of Weitzman's data and less dramatic findings, see Peterson, 1996.) This drop in living standard occurs even among less-advantaged subgroups, such as African-American and Hispanic low-income adults. Most young minority men fare poorly after divorce in

Both men and women experience a decline in their standard of living after a divorce, but that of women drops twice as much, on average.

absolute economic terms. However, young minority women fare even worse, a disparity that stems, either directly or indirectly, from women's roles as primary child caretakers (Smock, 1994).

Finnie's (1993) Canadian research also demonstrates that both men's and women's standard of living drops as a result of divorce, but women's drops twice as much, on average. Men tend to recover economically more quickly than women in the aftermath of divorce. Thus, divorce is much more likely to plunge divorced women into poverty, and keep them there for longer. This is particularly true if they have children for whom they are solely or largely responsible.

After a couple separates, the husband's per capita income goes up, since there are fewer people sharing his income. However, his expenses also go up, as do his wife's, for there are now two households to run. After spending on necessities (rent, home furnishings, utilities) less money remains for both the man and the woman. (That is one good reason why people move in together in the first place, and why they stay together.)

Yet, of the two, husbands typically have a better standard of living than wives after separating, since they typically have a higher income to start with. And, after allowing for monthly child support payments (which many of them fail to make) separated husbands have less to spend their money on than their wives.

Women usually experience a greater decline in their standard of living both because they typically earn less than men in the paid labour force and because they usually get custody of the children. And women may have taken time out of paid employment to bear children or stay with them while they are young, thus reducing their years of income and work experience. Low income is the cause of higher levels of life strains reported by separated women, according to a six-year longitudinal study (Nelson, 1994).

Women's economic disadvantage after divorce is largely due to the traditional practice of investing male human capital in the wage labour market and female human capital in the family and home. The latter greatly disadvantages women after divorce, when women are likely to receive inadequate compensation for time spent out of the wage labour market. Even women with almost the same educational background as men are at a disadvantage, leaving women, who had invested heavily in their families, vulnerable because of divorce (James, 1996).

This effect is even more dramatic as single women grow older. Elderly women who divorced twenty years ago or more are worse off than long-term widows, despite their (typically) higher education. This is in part because they have not had the benefit of much shared income. In the past—even the recent past—widows were treated with more respect by policy and by law than divorced women, having greater access to their deceased husband's pensions, for example, and greater rights to own property on their own and to get mortgages. Divorced women are also more likely to lack informal support systems and to rely on paid helpers (Choi, 1995).

The gender-related problems we are discussing are nearly universal. For example, divorced women in India and the United States experience similar problems with economic adequacy, social support, and psychological well-being. Furthermore, the predictors of divorce adjustment are similar in both societies. However, for a combination of cultural and economic reasons, Indian women suffer more hardship than American women. Three factors are responsible for this pattern: Indian women's extreme economic dependence on men, traditional Indian cultural beliefs about women and marriage, and the patriarchal organization of the Indian family.

The impact of divorce is often lifelong. The healing process takes time. For divorced mothers, for example, stressful events and depressive symptoms heighten dramatically soon after the divorce. They then decline over the next three years. Healing is influenced by such variables as age of mother and child, potential for remarriage, coping skills, social networks, and income changes. Having a steady, satisfying job is associated with higher self-esteem and lower distress among divorced women. A good job provides meaning, social interaction and support, positive distraction, and, of course, income. Spirituality helps some women. Others change their behaviour to reduce stress. They may take up exercise or otherwise focus on nurturing a healthy body; they may take classes or take up hobbies to improve their mental well-being; they may revamp their personal appearance to give themselves a boost. (For more on this theme, see Wallerstein & Blakelee, 1990.) We will discuss more about life after divorce in Chapter 10 when we consider fresh family starts.

Effects on Children

Traditionally, many couples avoided divorce and stayed together "for the sake of the children." Their concern was, in some respects, justifiable. Divorce may have harmful effects for the children involved. However, as we will see, recent research suggests that many couples might think in terms of breaking up "for the sake of the children." The research shows repeatedly that the effects of divorce, for children as well as for parents, depend very much on what is happening in the family before divorce. If the family is violent, for example, then divorce might provide needed relief.

Since the early 1970s, more than a million North American children have experienced parental divorce each year (Ducibella, 1995). Divorce is associated with a variety of adverse psychological and health effects in these children. For example, children of divorced parents can display poorer social and psychological adjustment than children from non-divorced homes (Kunz, 1992:352). When they grow up, they are much more likely than those from intact families to think their own marriage is in trouble.

Parental divorce increases the risk of adolescent depression in two ways. First, it is a source of many secondary problems and stresses that cause depression. Second, it alters youths' reactivity to these stresses, sometimes increasing the depressive effects. Economic hardships, a common outcome of divorce for children, also increase the risk of depression, thus accounting for the greater vulnerability of youths in single-parent families to depression (Aseltine, 1996).

Children of divorced parents show higher levels of depression and lower levels of self-esteem than children from intact families. In particular, children with irrational beliefs and feelings about divorce are most likely to develop behavioural and psychological problems (Skitka & Frazier, 1995). This shows the need for counselling that puts the divorce in perspective. As well, children who blame themselves for their parents' problems seem to have particular difficulty adjusting to the separation. The more recent the separation, the less likely children are to accept it and the worse they feel about it. As they settle into their new living arrangement, distress diminishes (Bussell, 1995).

Adolescents from lone-parent and step-parent families generally suffer from lower self-esteem, more symptoms of anxiety and loneliness, more depressed moods, more suicidal thoughts, and more suicide attempts than children from intact families. Among adolescent children with divorced parents, boys appear to have more emotional problems in step-parent families while girls have more problems in lone-parent families (Garnefski & Okma, 1996).

To the extent that children do suffer from divorce, much of the ill effect stems from one of two sources. One is a diminished sense of personal security; the other is worse parenting. After divorce, some children living in relatively happy homes report no change in security and happiness, while others feel less security and less happiness. Much of the decreased sense of security may reflect a temporary decline in the parenting provided. This can be due to parental unhappiness or depression, or due to a reduction in the number of parents present.

Divorced parents may experience problems in raising their children. Research shows that children in homes where one parent is missing through divorce are more likely to display problems than children in two-parent families. Sometimes, the reason is that separation and divorce fail to end the conflict between parents.

Separated and divorced parents often have difficult problems to solve. They may become frustrated when they choose, or are forced, to make decisions that conflict with their own desires and beliefs. For example, the court may grant a father the right to visit his children periodically, though the mother deems the father incompetent or even dangerous. Because the mother opposes the visits, she may be extremely frustrated, especially if the children exploit parental differences. For example, children may tell their mother, "Well, Daddy lets us." This causes the mother to feel insecure about her parental practices as she struggles to both fulfill the child's needs and be the "favourite" parent, or at least a liked parent. Given her often reduced financial circumstances, she may not be able to buy the food or clothes or entertainment that the child's father can afford. This adds to the frustrations.

Because of these conflicts and frustrations, parents are often too preoccupied to meet their children's needs completely. Failure to agree on custody is a common source of problems after divorce or separation. The child or children can become a pawn in a never-ending war between the parents, sometimes making repeated court appearances. Some parents see the child as a prize rather than a person with needs of his or her own. Visitation or access and child support are often the touchstone issues. Moreover, these problems fail to improve much over time. We consider custody issues a bit more in Chapter 10 when we discuss new family starts.

On the other hand, separation and divorce can improve family functioning, especially if custody rules are clear and agreed-upon, and civility is attained. Peaceful order benefits both parents. Compared with sole custody mothers, mothers with joint custody report lower levels of parenting stress and better co-parental relations. This produces a happier set of parents, which will no doubt lead to better parenting.

The effects of divorce vary by sex. For women, marriage and parenthood are distinct institutions, and women tend to provide for children's needs whether or not they are married to their children's father. For men, marriage tends to define their responsibilities to children. When men divorce, they often disengage from their biological children. Also, men are more likely than women to remarry quickly and have new children, whom they help to support. Thus, their first family children are liable to feel rejected and to be neglected. (However, for a contrary view on this topic, see David Popenoe's (1996) *Life Without Father*.)

Teens from divorced families tend to be less well-adjusted than teens from intact families (Muransky & DeMarie-Dreblow, 1995). Due to loss of access or reduced access to a biological parent, they may feel less intimately connected with their fathers. They may feel they have less social support (Clifford & Clark, 1995). Also, they may have assumed more family responsibilities which cut into time they might spend with friends, on sports, or with school work (Gonzalez, Field & Lasko, 1995).

However, it is not the process of divorce *per se* that shapes the children's adjustment but the family environment—the degree of parental conflict, paternal indifference, or lack of involvement (Weiner, Harlow & Adams, 1995). Children in divorced families are children from families that have experienced spousal conflict and dissatisfaction. So we should not focus too much attention on divorce as a cause of children's problems. Instead, we should emphasize what went on and what goes on between family members. As we have said repeatedly within this book, the processes within a family matter more than what the family looks like.

The previously mentioned problems suffered by children of divorced parents persist in adulthood. Rodgers (1994) notes that in childhood, few behavioural differences exist between girls from divorced and intact families. Later, large differences emerge in premarital pregnancy, job-changing during early careers, and marital breakdowns. A higher-than-expected incidence of "problems" is found among the adult children-of-divorce who are never-married, divorced, or remarried.

To the extent that divorce is associated with health problems in children, it is the conflict between parents that is most harmful to the emotional and psychological development of children. Indeed, "parental conflict has a greater impact on the social and psychological adjustment of children than divorce" (Kunz, 1992:353). The negative effect of parental divorce is eliminated once parents' past marital quality is considered (Cooney & Kurz, 1996). This suggests that living in conflict-free homes with one divorced parent is better for children than living in conflict-ridden intact homes.

Thus, the effects of parental divorce depend greatly on parental marital conflict before divorce. In high-conflict families, children have higher levels of well-being as young adults if their parents divorced than if they stayed together. However, in low-conflict families, children have higher levels of well-being if their parents stayed together than if they divorced (Amato, Loomis & Booth, 1995).

Other things being equal, marriage is better than divorce. Children living in single-mother families with no parental conflict, and with much contact with the non-residential father, still have lower levels of well-being than children who live in two-parent families without parental conflict. However, the well-being of children living in peaceful single-mother families is higher than that of children living in two-parent families with much parental conflict. The degree of parental conflict after divorce is more important for the well-being of children than contact with the departed father. That is to say, it is better for the children of divorce if Father doesn't come around if parental arguments break out when he does come around (Dronkers, 1996).

Parental divorce, as we have seen, is correlated with a variety of mental health stresses in children, due mainly to the conflict that precedes divorce. The conflict-and-divorce process influences how children view the world and view their place in it. However, we must be careful not to exaggerate the size of that influence.

Beyond the effects on thinking and feeling, divorce is correlated with variations in children's behaviour. So, for example, in a family that is not abusive, divorce leads to deterioration in children's school performance; increased proneness to crime, suicide, and out of-wedlock births; worsened

Pilot Project Puts the Needs of Children First

In Alberta, attendance at a six-hour workshop is now mandatory for parents before they can proceed with an application for divorce. The workshops were the brainchild of Madame Justice Marguerite Trussler, Court of Queen's Bench, and Kent Taylor, co-ordinator of the Edmonton and Northern Alberta custody mediation program. The sessions, free to those who attend, have been offered since February of 1996.

The number of contested custody trials heard by Edmonton courts dropped the following year from 1,200 to 800, according to Trussler. "What the lawyers tell me ... is that their clients are more reasonable when they come back from the course and it makes it easier to settle."

"We wanted to get to them as soon as we possibly could to tell them what damage they could do to their children if they got into this sort of a hassle." It's a sobering lesson for parents, says Fred Sudfeld, a therapist with The Family Centre in Edmonton, who along with a lawyer conducts the workshops, attended by anywhere from 35 to 50 adults.

With videos and talk, he shows how younger kids internalize parents' tensions and blame themselves, how older children may try to become "pleasers" so they won't be rejected like mommy or daddy, or how some become demoralized hearing arguments about money and think parents care more about that than them.

Source: Tonda MacCharles. 1998. *The Toronto Star*, Ottawa Bureau, December 11. Reprinted with the permission of The Toronto Star Syndicate. From an article originally appearing in *The Toronto Star* (December 11, 1998).

adult work performance; and likelihood of the children themselves becoming divorced later in life (Galston, 1996). The experience of divorce may weaken trust in people and institutions, and impede the capacity to form stable, enduring relationships.

Parental divorce and remarriage have strong effects on children's attitudes toward premarital sex, cohabitation, marriage, and divorce. These effects persist even after controlling for parental attitudes (Axinn & Thornton, 1993). Thus, children do not merely replicate their parents' values and attitudes toward non-marital sex, marriage, and divorce but develop an approach that incorporates their lived experience.

Children of divorce typically marry earlier, cohabit, achieve less economically, and hold more pro-divorce attitudes. All these factors account for some intergenerational transmission of divorce. However, holding these constant, interpersonal behaviour problems account for the biggest share of the transmission. It seems likely that children of couples who end up divorcing learn to behave in ways that hinder or destabilize intimate relationships: that is, they learn to behave like their parents (Amato, 1996). They don't learn how to contain or reduce conflict, solve interpersonal problems, or share their feelings.

Increased interparental conflict and parental divorce predict decreased self-esteem among children of divorce. This, in turn, predicts poorer peer-adolescent relationships, which predict poorer adult interpersonal competence (Armistead *et al.*, 1995). Likewise, family disruption, marital conflict, and disengaged parent-child relations all increase antisocial behaviour in childhood, though few of these effects generally continue into adulthood (Sim and Vuchinich, 1996).

Despite all the information on how divorce negatively affects children, recent research on this topic provides little basis for concern that divorce will inevitably produce problem behaviour. Neither exposure to parental divorce nor exposure to parental conflict affects the quality of attachment to adult intimates, nor the quality of parenting (Taylor, Parker & Roy, 1995). Adolescence and early adulthood may present many challenges—more to women than to men. Coming from a divorced family may contribute to those pressures. However, coming from a divorced family does not, in the end, diminish an individual's ability to cope with new challenges.

Relations with Parents

Since divorce often results in the departure of the biological father from the family, it affects father–child relationships most. Increasingly, children maintain an ongoing relationship with their fathers after the divorce. However, on average, adolescents in divorced families get less advice from their fathers and feel less satisfied with paternal support. Adolescents from intact families say they have more positive emotional relationships with their fathers than do adolescents from divorced or remarried families. It is true that adolescents who live with both parents fight their fathers to achieve independence. Ironically, this can be a good thing, related to the development of more self-esteem and a stronger ego-identity (McCurdy & Scherman, 1996).

Amato and Booth (1996) used data from a 12-year longitudinal study of marital instability to examine the effects of divorce on parent–child relationships. They found that problems in the parent–child relationship before divorce, and low quality in the parents' marriage when children were (on average) 10 years old, led to low parental affection for the children when they were (on average) 18 years old. Divorce continued to undermine affection between fathers and children, although not between mothers and children. Thus, the break in a father–child relationship may predate divorce by many years of turbulence and indifference.

The father's departure in a divorce greatly reduces the likelihood his child will name him as someone to whom the child would go for help with a stressful event. Departure may reduce the child's access to his or her father. However, those fathers who maintain contact remain important functional people in their children's lives and an important source of support in times of stress (Munsch, Woodward & Darling, 1995).

High marital quality predicts a similar relationship with both parents. However, when marital quality is low, children usually "choose a parent" to be close to. For example, the father–daughter tie is particularly vulnerable after divorce. By contrast, the mother–daughter tie is especially resilient (Booth & Amato, 1994). This suggests that the way in which poor marital quality and divorce affect adult child–parent relations is by polarizing children, forcing them to take sides when they are young.

Compared with those who grew up in two-parent families, the adult children of divorced parents perceive their relationships with both mothers and fathers to be of lower quality. The quality is generally two or three times lower for fathers than for mothers. Usually, memories of parental conflict or other family problems can explain the effect of parental divorce on relationship quality. Children of divorce also have much less current contact with their parents than adults from two-parent families (Webster & Herzog, 1995). Children generally evaluate their relationships with mothers more positively than those with fathers. They generally evaluate pre-separation relationships more positively than post-separation relationships, with some recovery after the passage of time. As already noted, a positive relationship with one parent contributes negatively to the evaluation of the other parent after separation, suggesting that separation typically polarizes loyalties (Hoffman & Ledford, 1995).

Effects on Parents

After divorce, most fathers and mothers are unprepared for the unique problems they will face, and the inadequacy of counselling and support services that are available. Separated parents often choose or are forced to make decisions that conflict with each other's desires and beliefs. Further, children can exploit parental differences and parents' desire to be the favourite parent. Custodial parents often fail to realize the impact of a move on the other parent, and remarriage or new partnerships complicate interactions between biological parents (Weiss, 1996).

Remarriage, discussed in the next chapter, complicates the situation. It is associated with less frequent co-parental interaction, less reported parenting support from the former spouse, and more negative attitudes about the other parent. For men, remarriage predicts lower levels of parenting satisfaction and less involvement in children's activities (Christensen & Retting, 1995).

Non-custodial fatherhood has increased due to trends in divorce and out-of-wedlock births. The standard divorce—i.e., the mother with custody, father with child support responsibilities and visitation rights—is most common in cases of longer marriage, higher male income, and younger children. In other circumstances, relationships may be less predictable and less stable. Visitations are essential to non-custodial parents and, as we have seen, the nature of visitation rights is crucial to the quality of the subsequent father–child relationship. Visitation and child support are complementary—fathers who visit regularly also tend to keep up with support—and joint custody improves support compliance. Non-custodial fathers benefit from successful resolution of issues of autonomy, connectedness, and power that can confront men after divorce, and from social supports that encourage moving beyond gender and **role polarization** (Fox & Blanton, 1995).

Divorce has a variety of effects on fathers, and on their children. For example, it affects non-custodial fathers' views of their parental role. Common themes among non-custodial fathers include divorce-related emotional distress; dissatisfaction with custody, visitation, and child support arrangements; perception of divorce proceedings as unfair; and ongoing conflicts with former spouses (Dudley, 1996). The father often views himself as a victim of his spouse. Moreover, his disempowerment, loss of legal custody, and relegation to the role of an economic provider have a profound impact on his masculine identity (Mandell, 1995). This may be another way of saying that "real men" in our culture are not supposed to let themselves get pushed around by their wives or ex-wives. It has recently taken a decidedly political turn with father's rights groups pushing the government to revise legislation on custody and post-divorce settlements.

Fathers typically have limited contact with their children after divorce, and this contact decreases over time. As fathers develop new relationships, they reduce the involvement with their children from their previous marriage. Not so for mothers. Their remarriage affects only the probability of fathers having weekly contact with their children. For the most part, characteristics of the mother and of the children do not affect post-divorce visitations except that fathers are more likely to see preschool-age children every week than school-age children (Stephens, 1996).

Why the reduced contact and visitation by so many fathers? Researchers have offered many reasons. One is that non-residential fathers feel less competent and less satisfied in the role of father. Typically, fathers who identify strongly with the role of father are more frequently involved with their children. Non-residential fathers identify less strongly with the role (Minton & Pasley, 1996). Overall, fathers who do not want contact with their children are more apt to have been less involved with child rearing, to feel indifferent about their children, or to have been in a violent relationship (Greif, 1995).

In contrast to the majority, nine non-custodial fathers studied by Arendell (1995) have developed strategies more congruent with their aim to parent their children actively. Child-centredness prevails in their accounts and actions. Each of these men has established, with their former wives, some type of parenting partnership. They actively seek to create "best case scenarios" in divorce and are absorbed with family relationships, their main-

Modernization and Divorce: Contrasting Trends in Islamic Southeast Asia and the West

During the 1960s and 1970s, when Western divorce rates were rising sharply, divorce rates in Islamic Southeast Asia declined dramatically, despite rapid urbanization and industrialization. According to demographer Gavin Jones, several factors associated with industrialization increased the potential to break away from unsatisfactory marriages in the West, while in Islamic Southeast Asia these same factors allowed people to avoid unsatisfactory marriages in the first place, thereby lowering the divorce rate.

"Any argument ... that development of an urban-industrial economy and improved educational and employment opportunities for women correlates with rising levels of divorce is stood on its head by the experience of the Malay-Muslim world" notes Jones.

Rising women's labor force participation in the West appears to have encouraged divorce by making women financially independent, by raising spousal stress levels over household management arrangements, and by exposing them to potential partners in the workplace. Rising women's labor force participation in Islamic Southeast Asia had those potential effects too, but they appear to have been overwhelmed by other divorce-reducing effects.

The ideational change that accompanied rapid urbanization and industrialization increased the social acceptability of divorce in the West, where declining religious belief led to individual self-fulfillment and permissiveness in the legal framework. By contrast, in Islamic Southeast Asia, ideational change stressed the autonomy of young people and their right to choose their own life partner, but in a context of increasing religious orthodoxy. Thus the avenues for improvement of women's well-being stressed in the two regions differed: in the West, increased potential to break away from unsatisfactory marriages; in Islamic Southeast Asia, avoidance of unsatisfactory marriages in the first place.

Source: Gavin Jones. 1997. *Population and Development Review*, March. (Population Council News Release; abridged). Reprinted with permission.

tenance, repair, and nurture. Unlike most respondents, these men are satisfied, even pleased with their parenting. Simultaneously, they see themselves as defying the norms of masculinity, which has led them on occasion to question their identity as men. Thus, self-confidence and uncertainty coexist for these innovative fathers.

In sum, for children, parents, and other relatives, divorce, like other major life events, can be stressful. With divorce, the stresses include economic hardship, parental adjustment, interpersonal conflict, or parental loss. However, we must be careful not to exaggerate the extent or permanence of harm done. Developing resources and protections can reduce the negative effect of these stressors. Higher levels of coping resources support a greater optimism about the future, fewer financial problems, more confidence in parenting ability, and a more satisfactory relationship with the former spouse (O'Leary, Franzoni & Brack, 1996).

The impact of divorce on children varies enormously depending on many factors, including the responsiveness of parents, schools, and community adults. Overall, young adults are optimistic about marriage, and their parents' divorce has not had a large impact on their attitudes toward marriage and divorce (Landis *et al.*, 1995).

Factors that reduce the adverse effect of divorce on children include a strong and clear sense that both parents still love them, an understanding that they are not to blame for the divorce, and regular visits with the non-custodial parent. Children of divorce may need some help coming to terms with irrational beliefs about divorce and feelings of sadness, guilt, and anxiety (Skitka & Frazier, 1995). Involved and caring parents can produce a good child adjustment to divorce. Parental distance, on the other hand, is likely to produce maladjustment. Parental conflict, as we have said so often, has a bad effect in both intact and divorced families (Weiner, Harlow, Adams & Grebstein, 1995).

Though divorce may sometimes cause problems, it sometimes also solves problems. It may even bring benefits. People whose parents divorced during their adolescent years display a much higher level of moral development than those whose parents did not divorce (Kogos & Snarey, 1995). Underlying the development of moral judgement is an increased perspective-taking, necessary for children of divorce who witness differences in opinions between their parents.

Concluding Remarks

As we have seen, divorce is both a micro- and a macro-level phenomenon, with both micro- and macro-level effects. Little synthesis between macro- and micro-level analyses has been achieved. We are still far from having a comprehensive theory that predicts who will get divorced and why.

The past 25 years have not fulfilled legislators' objectives in adopting no-fault divorce. There is no improved family life, and no expanded choice and happiness, at least in the eyes of critics (see, for example, Stanton, 1996). Some have remarked on how the combined effect of increased divorce rates and escalating levels of unwed childbearing have ensured that over half the children born in the 1980s will be raised in single-parent homes for all or part of their lives. The decline of marriage has also led to paternal disinvestment in children. Allegedly, unmarried men are less likely to support children financially. Increased maternal earning capacity or improved public investment has not compensated for the decline in paternal support (Whitehead, 1996).

The conservative approach to these problems of increased divorce rates, teen pregnancies, suicides, violence, and substance abuse is to blame the emerging culture of tolerance and the expanded welfare state, contending that they undermine the benefits of self-reliance and community standards. The conservative definition of family values is, in our view, too narrow. However, the perspective rightly emphasizes the role of the family in child-rearing education. Liberals, for their part, do recognize that increased unemployment, rising competition, and the need for dual-earner households have threatened the family.

However, they overemphasize the extent to which government services can replace effective family bonds (Giele, 1996). According to conservatives, strategies to encourage the re-institutionalization of the family would include restricting the legal benefits of family life to legally married couples and their children, exerting tighter controls on entry into marriage, making divorce more difficult, protecting children from divorce, and changing the nature of family law so that we define marriage as a moral obligation between partners rather than a personal contractual decision (Schneider, 1996).

Though it is not the job of sociologists to favour one side or the other, it is part of our responsibility to collect and examine data that would help evaluate these views. Here, sociology has an important role to play in the process by which a democratic society makes the policies and laws that govern family life.

The evidence shows us that divorce is correlated with unhappiness and trouble. The question is, does divorce cause the unhappiness and trouble, or does unhappiness and trouble cause the divorce? Further, does divorce prolong unhappiness and trouble or cut it mercifully short? While it is foolhardy to generalize about all divorces, certainly there is no evidence to show that, generally, divorce is the cause of most family-related unhappiness, nor that divorce tends to prolong unhappiness that might be otherwise cut short. Though it is true that people benefit from stable family lives when those families are functioning well, it is also true that people suffer from family lives when those families are functioning badly.

For better or worse, it is up to the participants to determine whether their family life is functioning well or badly. Outsiders' impressions count for little. Remember, as we have pointed out so often throughout this book, what counts is a person's perception. If the people involved think the family is working well, then to all intents and purposes, it really is. If not, and efforts to remedy the situation don't work, then divorce makes good sense—for the sake of the children as well as the spouses themselves. After all, a child can get good parenting without father and mother living together. On the other hand, conditions of stress, violence, unhappiness, and depression make good parenting almost impossible. We must assume, and probably can assume, that the vast majority of parents take these factors into account when they decide to stay together or divorce. This being so, the conservative viewpoint on divorce has little to offer us.

CHAPTER SUMMARY

In this chapter we looked at the rise in divorce experienced in the second half of the twentieth century in most industrial societies. As social scientists, we look at the nature of social bonding, and our discussions on divorce cover not only some of the reasons behind increased divorce rates, but the effects this increase has had on individuals and society as a whole. Although these trends indicate a dramatic change in family structure and the functions the family plays in our lives, research has shown that our beliefs and attitudes regarding the role of the family have not kept pace. This makes the task of assessing the real impacts of divorce a bit more difficult, yet all the more needed.

Historically, divorce has worried social scientists and policy-makers alike. This concern has become heightened with the recent explosion of divorce rates worldwide. Social, legal, and cultural changes have all played a part in the development of these trends.

Generally, causes of divorce should more accurately be called predictors, since it is easier to note relationships between variables than to pin down a cause-and-effect relationship. Factors influencing the likelihood of divorce are found at the micro-, meso-, and macro- levels. Micro-level factors include poor communication, poor conflict-resolution skills, lack of commitment, lack of shared interests, and perceived inequity. Meso-level factors include age, marital duration, location, religiosity, class, and race. Macro-level factors include war, economic cycles, and cultural values.

The effects of divorce were then considered. Divorce is a time of distress for spouses and children. Both men and women suffer a decline in standard of living, but men's incomes drop less and rebound faster. This effect is particularly important for women, since they are most commonly the prime caregivers of the children after a divorce. Typically, fathers gradually disengage from children, though some do remain closely involved in parenting. Children are distressed immediately after a divorce, but gradually adjust.

The harmful effects of divorce are often talked about. Yet it is important to recognize that many of the harmful effects observed stem not from divorce *per se* but from poor family interactions prior to, during, and after the divorce.

We concluded with a look at some popular political viewpoints on divorce. There is a movement urging legal and policy changes to discourage divorce, in an attempt to alleviate some of the social burdens that divorce produces. We find many of the proposed solutions incomplete and ineffective, because of the narrow interpretation of the problem, which labels divorce as the culprit rather than dysfunctional family interactions.

KEY TERMS

Adverse selectivity: A tendency for people who choose to engage in a given behaviour to be, by nature of the kind of people they are, also at risk for a given outcome; selectivity may create the appearance of cause-and-effect relationships where they do not exist.

Autonomy: Independence; ability to make choices and direct one's own life.

Cohort effect: An effect that influences everyone of roughly the same age, such as a war, depression, or industrial change.

Determinant: A factor that contributes to an outcome (such as divorce) without necessarily being the direct or principal cause.

Femininity: A cluster of characteristics, such as nurturance, sensitivity, and gentleness, traditionally considered natural to women, but which can be found in men or women; couples where both spouses have these characteristics tend to be well adjusted.

Macro-level: The broad level of examining a social phenomenon, focusing on changes that affect society as a whole.

Meso-level: A middle range at which a social phenomenon may be examined, focusing on demographics: the characteristics of the people affected.

Micro-level: The smallest level at which a social phenomenon may be examined, the level of interactions between individuals and effects on individuals.

No-fault divorce: Divorce granted on the basis of marital breakdown rather than of specific wrong-doing (e.g., adultery) on the part of one spouse or the other.

Predictor: A characteristic that is correlated with and precedes an outcome but may or may not be a cause.

Role polarization: A tendency to view male and female roles as fixed and separate.

Secularization: A move away from religion as an organizing principle of society

Social disorganization: A breakdown of societal functioning.

Social integration: The state of societies that are closely knit and stable, in which people hold similar world views and there is a strong consensus on social rules.

Social mobility: The potential for an individual or family to experience significant change in their social status.

Social pathology: A broad-based distress or disorganization within society.

Socioeconomic status: Class; standing in society in terms of income, education, and prestige.

Suggested Readings

Friedman, Debra. 1995. *Towards a Structure of Indifference: The Social Origins of Maternal Custody*. Hawthorne, NY: Aldine De Gruyter, Between 1880 and 1920, in all Western countries that permitted divorce, there was a legal shift of huge importance: fathers ceded custodial rights to mothers. Responsibilities for children were split between mother (nurture), father (financial support), and state (schooling), indicating a growth of indifference towards children.

Kurz, Demie, 1995. *For Richer For Poorer: Mothers Confront Divorce*. New York: Routledge. 1995. This book explores the impact of divorce on U.S. women, detailing the reasons women are leaving their marriages and the hardships they face afterward. It also discusses benefits, such as freedom from domination, violence, and destructive emotions. Thus, divorce is an experience with both good and bad aspects. Domestic violence and hardships due to poverty remain problems to solve.

Maccoby, Eleanor E. and Robert H. Mnookin. 1992. *Dividing the Child: Social and Legal Dilemmas of Custody*. Cambridge, MA: Harvard University Press. Combines data obtained via quantitative surveys and qualitative research to show the links between class and gender in divorce actions.

Vaughan, Diane. 1986. *Uncoupling: Turning Points in Intimate Relations*. New York: Oxford University Press. A description of the series of transitions people go through in ending a relationship, and the similar pattern displayed in all breakups. Based on the author's personal experience of a divorce and on interviews with married and unmarried, straight and gay people who had separated or were separating from their partner. "Uncoupling" is viewed as a process of individual and joint resocialization.

Weitzman, Lenore J. 1985. *The Divorce Revolution: The Unexpected Social and Economic Consequences for Women and Children in America*. New York: Free Press. The now-classic study of the economic and familial consequences of no-fault divorce laws, based on an analysis of divorce records and interviews with family lawyers, among others. Demonstrates that the post-divorce standard of living rises for men and falls for women and children.

Review Questions

1. Define no-fault divorce. How does it differ from what preceded it?

2. Outline the difference between macro- and micro- reasons for divorce.

3. Describe the changes in families (family structure, division of labour, functions of the family, etc.) that occurred as a result of industrialization and urbanization.

4. Define adverse selectivity.

5. What is the relationship between divorce rates and socioeconomic class, race, age, and religious affiliation?

6. Discuss the role that female participation in the work force played in the changing of the divorce rates. Was there an increase or decrease as more women participated?

7. What happens to the divorce rate after a large-scale war? Why?

8. What are some of the consequences of divorce for children?

9. Describe the lifelong effects of divorce on women.

10. Give some reasons why many couples ought to break up "for the sake of the children."

Discussion Questions

1. Why does society have an interest in whether people get divorced or stay married? Isn't this a personal, private matter?

2. Can you imagine any way in which Western societies could have industrialized and urbanized—in short, modernized—without having eventually caused an increase in the divorce rates? Did this actually happen anywhere?

3. How can a predictor of divorce not be a cause of divorce? Is any cause of divorce not also a predictor of divorce? Give some specific examples in answering.

4. Discuss how adverse selectivity affects other areas of life besides the family—for example, the correlation between cigarette smoking (or drug use) and school performance, or between social protest and church attendance.

5. Why does the presence of children sometimes increase and sometimes decrease the risk of divorce? On balance, is childbearing a good strategy for keeping a shaky marriage together?

6. Would a 10 percent decrease in the gap between men's and women's average incomes be likely to lead to a 10 percent increase in the divorce rate? Why or why not?

7. Movies about wartime often depict emotional intensity and romance between men and women. Would you expect wartime marriages to be long-lived or short-lived? Why? Do you think movies depict this reality? Why or why not?

8. Why are the effects of divorce different for men and women? Is there any evidence that this disparity is changing? Why might we expect such a change?

9. Under what circumstances does divorce improve the relations between parents and their children? Under what circumstances is it likely to worsen them?

10. How can our society make divorce less damaging and painful for divorcing spouses and their children? What is the evidence that this might work?

Weblinks

http://www.divorceinfo.com/

An excellent source of information on a variety of topics related to divorce. The site has advice on helping children cope, coping with the pain of divorce, life after divorce, and the costs involved.

http://www.divorce-online.com/

Articles, general information, and psychological and professional help with regards to divorce. This site is also quite helpful as a search engine.

http://www.divorcemag.com/

Divorce Magazine

Up-to-date statistics and data on divorce as well as the latest topics and issues surrounding divorce. One can also find the latest issue of the magazine at this site.

http://www.hec.ohio-state.edu/famlife/ divorce/demo.htm

Demographics of divorce, with graphs depicting some of the concepts we have discussed in this chapter.

http://www.hughson.com/

General information on divorce, including information on law (American) and divorce, and children and divorce, as well as a good reading list.

CHAPTER TEN

Fresh Starts:

One-Parent Families, Remarriage, Step-Families and Empty Nests

Chapter Outline

Transitions into parenthood are momentous and perplexing moments in one's life and the life cycle of families. Transitions to different family situations can be just as challenging and momentous. The phrase "fresh start" implies happy transitions to a new life and a wiping of the family-experience slate clean. Yet some new starts are stale starts, or redoing the old start without much that is new. Some fresh starts prove impossible. Others are indeed fresh and new, reflective of learning from mistakes and regrets of the past. Fresh starts can involve reinventing close relations, customizing social ideals to best fit one's particular needs and situation.

We explored in the previous chapter the many challenges posed by family dissolution. In this chapter, we focus on life *after* separation or divorce, or widowhood. We also consider some of the ways people rediscover or reinvent families. We look at the multiple ways in which people and families make fresh starts, examining what is possible and what we can learn from the heroic efforts of many to make fresh starts.

Fresh Starts in the Past

When we think of fresh starts for families, we often see this phenomenon as something recent that rarely or never happened in the past. In reality, making fresh starts is nothing new. With massive flows of immigrants out of strife-torn, and in some cases poverty-stricken Europe throughout the first half of this century, many people started families afresh in North America. Immigrants and refugees from Europe are still coming, as strife recurs, and have now been joined by people from Africa, Asia, and Latin America fleeing an old life or seeking new opportunities in Canada, Australia, and the United States.

Immigrants built new families in various ways in their new situations. They may have brought families with them as well as maintaining family ties with those left behind. But life in the new country does not allow all the ways in which families live, or the ways their children form their own families, to remain totally unchanged. Fresh family starts are necessitated by the process of immigration and the contact with new ways to live in close relations.

In a historical study of Methodist missionaries in northern Manitoba in 1869–1876, Brown (1992) recounts the central and formative role played by a Cree nurse known as Little Mary, who cared for the boy, Eddie. As the first white child born into the region, Eddie was largely raised by the indulgent Little Mary, who modified strict Victorian practices of child rearing to raise Eddie more as a Cree boy than as the son of a missionary. Eddie's life was given a fresh start by his introduction to her world view and culture. It led to hilarity and conflict when Eddie performed for his parents as a young Cree boy. When he was revealed by a stocking that would not stay up, revealing a white leg (his description in later life), his parents became dismayed. Eddie, in later life, attributed much that he valued in his character to the socializing influence of Little Mary which softened his parents' strictness. His upbringing is an example of a new form of child rearing combining two cultural approaches.

Another example of a fresh family start also comes from early Canada, where the voyageurs and fur traders lived with native wives according to the customs of the aboriginal people with whom they associated. This was called **"à la façon de la pays"** or **"the custom of the country"** (Van Kirk, 1992). Some of the men were already married and had left their first wives in France, Scotland, or eastern Canada. Once the native woman became a country wife, she was treated with respect by other fur traders who then referred to her as "Madame." What emerged was not only a fresh start in family for individuals, but also a new family form (Van Kirk, 1992:72).

Both the fur trader men and the native women made fresh starts, sometimes spectacularly so, as in the case of Robert Pilgrim's native wife, Thu a Higon, who accompanied him when he returned to England, along with their infant son (Van Kirk, 1992:72). One can imagine the adjustment challenges she must have faced in Victorian England, and wonder what fresh starts their family made. Other fur traders were denied the possibility of taking their native wives and families back to the old country by company policies. Many were left behind in Canada, sometimes with pensions provided by the "husband" or the company (Hudson's Bay Company or The Northwest Company). This may be the first known example of pensions for homemakers, discussed in Chapter 6.

Still others among the voyageurs/fur traders decided to solemnize their marriages on the retirement of the "husband" from active service. One couple, William Hemmings Cook and his wife Agatha, made a fresh start by marrying, after living together according to the "custom of the country" for a long time. Van Kirk (1992:79) cites one of the guests at the wedding as observing, "old Cook had stood manfully forth ... bringing his 35 years courtship to an early close." Living together is not so new as a family form, and marrying as a fresh start after a long cohabitation is not so modern either.

Another more recent historical example of a fresh family start related to immigration is evident in the story of Maria, who came to Toronto in 1956 from a peasant farm in southern Italy to join her husband, Eneo, who had come a year earlier (Iacovetta, 1992). Within two days, she had a job as a steam press operator, for which she was paid $37 a week. She worked for the rest of her life at various low-skill, low-pay jobs to help support her family in their adopted country. The fresh start for Maria and Eneo is the new kind of marriage she, and others like her, made with their husbands in the new country where men and women both contributed economically to their families, and yet women had no prescribed public role. The almost constant supervision of women, prevalent in southern Italy in the 1950s and earlier, had to be abandoned in part in the new situation, according to Iacovetta (1992:286). Fresh starts were made by couples in their new country, with varying degrees of success and difficulty.

The higher mortality rates of the past often meant that families experienced the death of one or both spouses/parents while the children were still young, creating the possibility or the need for fresh family starts. Remarriage after the death of one's first spouse was frequent, as were step-parents, adoption, and fostering of children. Fresh family starts were more characteristic of families in the past than we sometimes acknowledge today. In some ways, widows in the past were similar to single mothers today in the economic vulnerability they and their children faced, and in the social challenges they posed (Gordon & McLanahan, 1991).

Nor did marriage failure and divorce begin recently, as some might think. Men deserted their families; some women deserted too; and couples agreed mutually to separate (Gordon & McLanahan, 1991). Some Canadians went to the U.S. to seek divorces when divorce was not as attainable in Canada (Bradbury, 1996:72–73). In some provinces, such as Quebec where divorce was almost impossible to obtain until well into the mid-twentieth century, and was frowned upon strongly, some women slipped into Ontario and declared themselves widows.

Sometimes the women had been victims of spousal abuse or found themselves in intolerable marriages from which there was little escape. Because family was seen as largely women's responsibility in the past, women were more often trapped in difficult marriages, for if they left they would be stigmatized, socially and legally, as the deserters of families. Escapes for women included close friendships with other women, charity and community work, sometimes illnesses or frailties that were seen as romantic, and often drugs and alcohol. It is not well known that in nineteenth- and early twentieth-century Canada, as well as in the United States, middle-class women were the most common drug addicts. Failed marriages and attempts to make new starts are not only a modern-day phenomenon.

What Is a Fresh Start in Family?

The beginning of a new family can be a step filled with hope and dreams for a wonderful shared future. The strength of this hope is evidenced in social research, which shows that most young people expect never to be divorced. This may be indicative of their sense of commitment to a life-long relationship, but their hopeful expectations may blind them to the known risks of divorce. A fresh start at family can be any happy young couple on the brink of establishing themselves as a couple, whether married or not, gay/lesbian or heterosexual. That first kind of fresh start we discussed earlier on in

Chapter 2, so will not focus on it here.

Fresh family starts of interest in this chapter are second or subsequent starts at families or familial relationships. The processes through which this start comes about are various. It can be a flight from violence in a family of origin or a conjugal family/relationship, an escape from an abusive practice sanctioned by the prevailing culture, a mutually agreed upon separation or divorce, a death, or a myriad of other family changes over the life course. It can be a rediscovery of one's roots and a new basis on which to found and maintain a family, or even a discovery of cultural roots in a new setting or country. It can involve a personal reinvention of family to meet one's particular needs.

Fresh starts are possible because things did not work out as planned, expected, or hoped for the first time around. Fresh family starts can be begun reluctantly as one's idealism about family is tarnished by family dissolution. In this way, fresh starts reflect change, both individual and social, as well as personal learning and adaptation. It is an adventure to explore the complex ways in which people make families afresh, and the new ways for people to have close relations.

One of the themes in this book is that families are immensely varied. Perhaps at no point is this clearer than when families make fresh starts. The multiple pathways of fresh starts include shrinking of family to its smallest unit, a single-person household with non-household-based families, or to a parent with a child. It can also involve non-residential parenting, and the development of intricate and large extended kin or non-kin networks. Another theme highlighted in this book is that family processes rather than forms provide the rewarding focus of family studies. In considering fresh family starts, we observe families and individuals actively engaging in family as process, in designing families anew, in negotiating family and in striking bargains with former family members on how to endure as family. It is family dynamics in process, active development of new solutions to family challenges.

Multiple Fresh Starts

In today's world of long life expectancies and rapidly changing families, people may expect to make not one but multiple fresh starts in family over the course of their lives. Think of those who marry or live together after having lived alone or as an adult in the parental home. They have already experienced two kinds of fresh family starts: first the transition to new ways of being family when they became adults and continue to live with their parents, and then marriage. And the fresh starts are likely to continue throughout their lives, with possible separation, divorce, remarriage, perhaps following a period of cohabitation, then possibly widowhood and maybe another later life relationship or marriage.

Within each of these states of family life, there can be phases that mark other kinds of fresh family starts: into parenthood, into or out of working parenthood, from being in a two-earner to a one-earner (or no-earner) family, to grandparenthood, step-parenthood, and so on. In families today, diversity is now the norm, with almost endless possibilities. The **SNAF** (standard North American Family) no longer exists.

Singlehood as a Fresh Start

Most, or at least many, people who experience the end of a marriage or a committed relationship become single before becoming any other kind of family. Some may move directly from one relationship to another. Is singlehood a fresh start in family life? Some might respond that a single person is not a family. True enough. But, is a single person without family? A few rare people may be, but most of us have families even if we live alone or are living separately from our spouses or partners. This raises an important dimension of fresh family starts, one to which we will return as a theme in this chapter: that family is not equivalent to household. Families and close relations can and do exist, and even thrive, across households.

Living solo is an option growing in popularity. The 1996 Census of Canada reveals a 14.9 percent growth in one-person households since 1981 (Statistics Canada, 1998:2). The largest proportion living alone occurred among those aged 65 and over; 35.5 percent lived alone in 1996 compared with 33.7 percent in 1981. Significant proportions of those 30-49 (32.8 percent) also lived alone, a substantial increase from 22.5 percent in 1981. Among younger Canadians (under age 30), preference for living solo dropped like a stone; only 12.1 percent lived alone in 1996 compared to 23.9 percent in 1981.

Living by oneself does not mean that one is isolated from family. Findings from a national survey in Canada (McDaniel, 1994) reveal that 35 percent of adult children live within walking distance of their mothers, while another 19 percent live within 50 kilometres. Visiting between parents, particularly mothers, and adult children is frequent, as is contact by phone or letter. Even among adult children who live more than 1000 kilometres from their parents, one out of five is in weekly contact, and fewer than 10 percent have limited or no contact with parents. Among siblings, there is even more regular contact. These findings reveal the extent of family ties and connections across households and generations, regardless of the living arrangements of those involved. However, a clear pattern emerges: mothers have more contact than fathers and are more often sought out by adult children.

For some, singlehood is a transitional stage to a new committed relationship. We will discuss that in a moment. For increasing numbers of North Americans, however, living alone is a life choice, a preference, or better than other alternatives. The diversity of solo living, however, prevents us from making many solidly based generalizations about it. People living alone include older people who are widowed, middle-aged professionals, and poor people who may have little prospect for marriage. This group also still includes young people, although, as we have seen, the numbers of young people able to live alone has declined recently.

The growth in living alone may reflect, more than anything else, the capacity to do so. In the past, living on one's own was often not an option, particularly for women. Recent analyses find that even in a place as reputedly family-centred as pre-Confederation Newfoundland, there was a strong preference for living alone when old, if possible, but it was often not feasible (McDaniel & Lewis, 1997). One should *not* conclude, however, as some have, that the growth in living alone is indicative of disinterest in family or growing individualism. Research evidence does not support such a claim.

A U.S. study (Marks, 1996) of the Wisconsin Longitudinal Study (sample size of 6876) finds that unmarried men who live alone are more disadvantaged than unmarried women. Although the picture of living singly is complex, with advantages and disadvantages for both men and women, single women are found to score higher on personality characteristics associated with better psychological well-being than married women. Single men, however, do not compare so favourably with married men.

One-Parent Families

In the past, as we have seen, one-parent families were most frequently just that, one living parent with dependent children (Morton, 1992b). There was no other parent living. Tough as it no doubt was (and still would be) to be a widow or widower with young children, these families really were one-parent families. Today's one-parent families, created as they are most often by separation, divorce, or relationship dissolution, are often families where one parent lives with the children and one parent does not. In that sense, they are really two-parent families where the parents do not share a household.

We have seen in Chapter 9 that some fathers do not maintain family ties with their children once they are divorced or remarried after divorce. The reality that children have two parents who remain as parents but no longer live together raises a number of complex challenges in determining who takes what responsibility for the children.

It also raises a crucial clarifying point about families, discussed in detail by Eichler (1997): *family* and *household* are not congruent. "One household," argues Eichler (1997:96), "may encompass people who belong to two (or maybe more) family units that are not shared by other household members." An example would be a boy who lives with his biological mother and her husband and his two children from a previous marriage. The boy's biological father may continue to parent him, but does not live in the same household. A portrait of the boy's family, seen from his viewpoint, would involve at least two households. If he has a sister away at university who comes "home" to both his own principal residence and his father's, he might see himself as having a family that crosses three (or even more) residences. The assumption that a family is bound by the walls of a household may no longer be valid or appropriate.

Marital or relationship dissolution can be the start of single parenthood, but it is not the only pathway. There has been growth in the numbers of people having children without being in a committed couple relationship. This, as we have seen in Chapter 4, can occur in a variety of ways. One of those, the deliberate seeking of parenthood on one's own, will be considered in the next section as a kind of fresh family start. Here, we will focus on the more common pathway to lone parenthood, as a result of marriage or relationship breakdown.

Before discussing single parenthood as a fresh start, it is important to shed some light on the perplexing problem of defining single parents. Typically, estimates of the numbers of single parents are based on a one-time sample, such as a census or a survey, and are looked at from the view-

Figures 10.1 & 10.2 **FAMILIES BY FAMILY STRUCTURE (CANADA, 1996)**

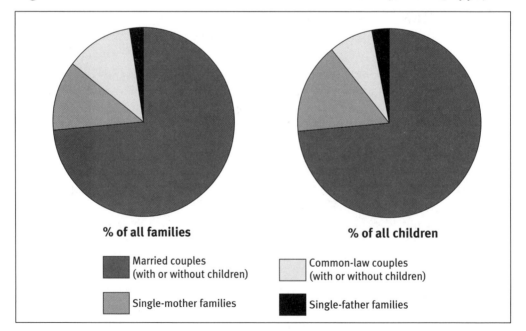

% of all families   **% of all children**

- Married couples (with or without children)
- Common-law couples (with or without children)
- Single-mother families
- Single-father families

Note: Rounding may mean that percentages do not add up to 100.

Source: Statistics Canada. "1996 Census: Marital Status, Common-Law Unions and Families," *The Daily* 14 October 1997: 4.

point of adults. The research question asked is: What proportion of adults at this moment are living in single-parent families? Three problems, at least, are apparent in this approach. The first is that it often remains unknown whether single parents of children are indeed living on their own and how many are cohabiting.

Figure 10.1 shows the proportions of Canadian families that involve marriage, common-law relationships, or lone parenting. Figure 10.2 shows the proportion of children living in various family structures; approximately one child out of five lives in a single-parent family. A U.S. study based on a sample from the 1990 U.S. Census finds that 2.2 million children (3.5 percent of all children) live in cohabiting couple families, and generally are less well off than children in married families (Manning & Lichter, 1996). This is a "chicken and egg" issue: do less well-off people prefer cohabitation, or does cohabitation lead to being less well off? Research evidence favours the former explanation. Second, without considering single parenthood from a life course perspective, it is not possible to see it as a process rather than a state, to see how the experience affects adults and children, and to distinguish between transitional and permanent arrangements. Third, and importantly, examining single parenthood in terms of adult relationships tends to divert attention away from single parenthood as it affects children.

One innovative Canadian study (Marcil-Gratton, 1993) turns data, collected from the Census and a social survey at single points in time, into studies of children's family experiences by generations (or cohorts). This allows an important look at single parenthood over time from the child's standpoint. Although the children followed are not the same children, it is possible to observe changes in patterns of children's exposure to single-parenting. The findings are striking and worth summarizing:

> • In 1975, the proportion of "out-of-wedlock" births in Quebec was lower than elsewhere in Canada, but the proportion boomed to 19 percent in 1980, climbed to 33 percent in 1988, and reached an astounding 38 percent of all births in 1990.

> • More children than ever experience life in a single-parent family in Canada. By age 20, one out of four children from the 1961–63 cohort had experienced single parenthood; the same proportion was reached at age fifteen for the 1971–73 cohort. By age fifteen, 18 percent of the 1961–63 cohort had experienced single parenthood; the same proportion was reached at age six for the 1981–83 cohort.

Single parenthood has increased dramatically in recent decades. In Canada, the number of single-parent families tripled between 1961 and 1991, to 14 percent of all families (Lero & Brockman, 1993:92). The number has continued to increase more, to 19 percent in 1996 (Statistics Canada, 1998b:4). In the United States in 1990, nearly 25 percent of all families were single-mother families (17 percent of white families, and 53 percent of African-American families) (McLanahan & Garfinkel, 1993:16). The overwhelming majority of lone parents in both Canada and the U.S. are mothers.

The incidence of poverty is high among single parents, particularly single mothers. In Canada in 1993, 59.6 percent of lone-mother families were below the low income cutoffs, making these families the group with the highest incidence of family poverty in Canada (Eichler, 1997:37), poverty that is most resistant to remedy (Dooley, 1993:117). This compares with a poverty rate of 12.5 percent among husband–wife families with children under age 18 living at home. "Among the surging number of single mothers who have taken refuge in temporary shelters [recently] are an entirely new class of homeless—formerly secure career women," notes a recent report (Gadd, 1997:D1). Among the new homeless are single mothers who have lost their jobs and are not able to find new ones.

Many women with dependent children tumble into poverty when their marriage ends. This occurs for a number of interconnected reasons. Marriage, in our society, is a presumed economic alliance between a man who can earn more and a woman who is to be economically subordinate or dependent while devoting herself to childbearing and child rearing. When the marriage ends, women find (as noted in Chapter 9) that the initial disparity in income and potential income has widened. As well, a woman with young dependent children and perhaps fewer work skills, less training or education, and sole responsibility for children, may not seem like a good prospect to an employer. And on separation, the considerable benefits of having the combined incomes of two earners no longer exists.

Housing is a further challenge for many single mothers, who may be unable to find reasonably priced housing. The upshot is that they quickly become poor, and tend to remain so, with disadvantages both for themselves and for their children (McDaniel, 1993). Not surprisingly, the consequences to men of divorce are seldom as financially bleak.

Children in single-parent families are known to suffer both directly from the disadvantage of their family situations—particularly poverty—and from society, which stigmatizes them and expects less from them. The two forces work together to create lower achievement prospects that tend to become self-fulfilling. These factors, though powerful, are not deterministic. Many children from single-parent families achieve at high levels indeed, among them Eartha Kitt and Charles Chaplin, to cite but two world-famous examples. Nonetheless, making opportunities for children from single-parent families is often not easy for the mothers, the children themselves, or society.

The positive experiences of living in a single-parent family, for both mothers and their children, are not to be discounted. Among other things, they may learn the value of interdependence, of invention and innovation, of self-reliance, of mutual interdependency, and how to value women in a world that too often fails to do so (Colllins, 1991; Ferri, 1993). Children from deprived situations where love persists can learn to persevere, to aim high in their expectations, and to deny themselves for future gain.

These lessons can be beneficial in a world where many have so much that they do not see a need to struggle to succeed. A longitudinal study in Britain (Ferri, 1993:289) finds that "[m]any of those who had grown up in lone parent families had done as well, if not better, than their peers who had enjoyed more stable family lives." This is a hopeful and not often heard message that bears noting. Knowledge of this sociological finding by family research can go a long, long way toward encouraging children in single-parent families to strive for success in life.

Latchkey children, children who are regularly left for some part of the day without adult supervision, epitomize both the best and the worst of resilience. Not all latchkey children are from single-parent families. Many are from two-income families where no one is home when they return from school each day. Both good and bad consequences are found for latchkey children in one study (Leung *et al.*, 1996). The positive outcomes include learning to be independent and responsible, as well as learning useful skills such as how to start dinner for the family, how to grocery shop, etc. Among the negatives are loneliness, fear, boredom, underachievement in school, and perhaps drug or alcohol abuse.

Single parenthood after divorce or separation is a fresh start plagued with perils, as we saw in the previous chapter. Not the least of the challenges is the stigma, both social and economic. It does not help that poverty and economic insecurity are generally associated with single motherhood, but there is more to the stigma than economic deprivation and its labels. The negative attribution may start with the social sense of women's inadequacies as women and as mothers, and then move to the threat, both social and economic, that women having children without men pose to the society.

> [T]here is a tendency for minority arrangements like lone-parent families to be seen as something of an affront to established beliefs about the nuclear family. If they can be seen to 'work,' they undermine the credibility of the nuclear family, and this has subversive implications for the dominant economic and moral order which to a great extent depends on the nuclear family and in its turn endorses it (Collins 1991:159).

The transition into single parenthood can cause a woman in particular to question her identity as a woman, and her understandings and assumptions about family and the society in which she lives. This can also occur with men, but men less often have as much invested in their identity as spouse and parent as women do.

One transition to single motherhood not as often considered is when the marriage or relationship ends because the husband "comes out" as gay.

This is a more frequent occurrence than might be imagined, particularly with the societal encouragement of the recent past to deny same-sex attractions and marry anyway. Few marriage partners expect a change in sexual identity in their partners when they marry.

In one study of this experience, French (1991) finds that some couples agree to stay together after the "coming out" while others separate but maintain active parental involvement with the children. French points out how becoming a lone parent can be a means of problem-solving for women in this situation. She further reveals that sexuality, like family, is not static and given, but a process sometimes worked through in family as the means to new identities and lifestyles. Interestingly, French's study shows that as the men came to grips more and more with their gay identities, their interest in maintaining their father role continues, sometimes even intensifying.

Increasingly in Canada, single mothers have become the targets for cutbacks to social assistance.

Self-help groups for women married to gay men have formed and can prove helpful to women, if primarily to provide support and to indicate that they are not alone in their experiences. The study reveals that family is indeed a process and that husbandhood and fatherhood need not be synonymous, and need not be only heterosexual roles.

Single mothers in the United States, and increasingly in Canada, have become the targets for cutbacks to social assistance (welfare in the U.S.) and vicious public labels. They are variously termed slothful, manipulative, inadequate mothers, irresponsible women, and selfish takers of public monies. Some are even labelled as women who use their sexuality and reproduction to get public subsidies. That little of this has any basis in fact does not seem to matter. It has a reality of its own in belief systems that favour more and deeper cuts to social assistance and so-called incentives to single mothers to work outside the home, even though there are no jobs and few child-care options for them. The campaigns against single mothers also have a clear basis in efforts to preserve the nuclear family against other family forms, as we have seen earlier in this chapter.

Single-parent families have posed perplexing problems for policy makers because of their persistent and deepening poverty. Many countries, including Canada and the United States, have had policies that have been explicitly or implicitly built in the belief that women and children are the responsibilities of husbands and fathers (Baker, 1995:13). Only when this fails do states believe they must act, reluctantly and under pressure. State family policies have ranged from providing incentives to single mothers to parent full-time (in the Netherlands, for example) to offering incentives for them to work in the paid labour force (Sweden and Australia) (Baker, 1995). Europe, on average, does far more for single-parent families than does North America (Kamerman & Kahn, 1988), enabling them to balance work and family responsibilities by a variety of supports.

Behind social policies oriented to single-parent families are three models. The first is the private family approach, characterized by the United Kingdom and the United States, where family is believed to be a private institution that ought to look after itself, with the state stepping in only on a casualty basis (Lesemann & Nicol, 1994:117). This contrasts with the family-oriented model (France and Quebec) which sees the state as having a public interest in families. The third is the state-based model (Sweden) which sees state intervention as important not to help families but to promote socio-economic participation as fully as possible. Canada is caught between these models, using a little of each in its approach to policies for single parents.

Much attention has been devoted recently to how to provide the means to move lone mothers away from social assistance. An interesting and innovative Canadian study of 150 single mothers on social assistance offers some important insights (Gorlick & Pomfret, 1993). Focussing on women's exit strategies from social assistance, Gorlick and Pomfret find that the main predictors of successful exits are social supports, including information, and the women's aspirations. The research finds that single mothers on social assistance in Canada are actively involved in an extensive range of social and economic strategies to exit social assistance. They are realistic and hopeful about the possibilities, but feel that they could benefit from useful supports and information to assist them.

Deliberately Seeking Parenthood on One's Own

The largest growth in childbearing outside of marriage or cohabiting relationships is occurring among women in their late twenties and early thirties (Ram, 1990:33), although the rates of non-marital childbearing have increased for most age groups. The exception, surprisingly, has been births to teens, which in Canada fell throughout the first half of the 1990s (though it did rise slightly in 1997). If mature women are having births without being married, several factors could be at work. There could be accidental pregnancies, as there always are. More women who accidentally become pregnant now choose to keep and raise their babies instead of giving them up for adoption. This is a deliberate choice in favour of motherhood, even if the conception itself may not have been planned. There is also evidence that some women are seeking motherhood on their own without the traditional step of marriage or being in a committed relationship.

Few studies have looked at unmarried single mothers, women who *begin* single parenthood without being married. One study (Clark, 1993) finds that the social and economic costs of unmarried single motherhood are evident ten years after the first child is born. Although there are no effects on likelihood of marrying, the risks of poverty are greater than for married mothers. As well, there is lessened opportunity to pursue education, thus further disadvantaging the unmarried mothers. As the children grow, however, the initial discrepancies between unmarried and married mothers decrease. Age at first unmarried motherhood matters greatly: the younger one is, the greater the disadvantage and the less likely one is to catch up later on. Children born to younger unmarried mothers do less well in school and in IQ tests than other children.

In deliberately seeking motherhood on one's own as a fresh family start, options exist today that did not exist previously. We introduced some of these options in the scenarios in Chapter 4. With the stigma lessened of having a child outside marriage, it may not be surprising that some women are going for it. This may be a generation of women who have been taught to go after what they aim for in life, rather than waiting for all their dreams to fall into place by luck or chance. Some are successful, educated, thoughtful career women who know their own minds. Others may have become infertile earlier in their lives, but not given up their dreams of motherhood. Options now include new reproductive technologies, including **artificial insemination** and *in vitro* **fertilization**, informal means to access sperm for conception, private adoptions, and foreign adoptions.

Let's look first at adoption, although in reality, women often look at adoption only after considering the option of giving birth to a baby. Adoption not long ago was carefully controlled by churches and the state. For good or for bad, it was thought that adoptive parents should be married and matched in religion, region, and ethnicity/race as much as possible to the adopted child. This left out single women, single men, cohabiting couples, lesbians and gays. It also often left out the non-religious. Adoption has opened up considerably in recent years, most notably in private adoptions whereby the birth mother (or parents) can know and sometimes select the adoptive family for the baby/child. More single people have been able to adopt children too, although the waiting lists are lengthy and the screening tight and sometimes unnecessarily judgmental about lifestyle.

A new option that has opened things up for couples and single women wishing to adopt—and some single men, too—has been foreign adoptions. These occur for numerous reasons. One is that strife and disruption in various world regions have created unwanted babies and children, either as war orphans or as a result of policies such as the forbidding of birth control and abortion in Romania a few years ago (see Chapter 1). The one-child policy in China has led to numbers of babies, primarily girls, being adopted by Canadians and others, as many Chinese choose, for cultural reasons, to have a boy if they can have only one child. There is the concern that some babies or children may be taken from their parents for the lucrative foreign adoption market, or brought into the world for the purposes of the adoption market. It is not fully known whether this occurs and, if so, to what extent.

The opening up of foreign adoption has meant that more Canadians can adopt who may not meet, or not wish to meet, the requirements of domestic adoption agencies. International adoption is costly and time-consuming, with lengthy screening and often frustrating international negotiations, but it is possible for a small minority of people to make a fresh start by becoming the adoptive parent of a child born elsewhere.

The not-so-new reproductive technologies have also opened possibilities for fresh starts for single people, and to some extent, gays and lesbians. For example, artificial insemination has been used for a long time by women and by doctors to inseminate their patients. It has not been so routinely discussed until recently, however. Surrogate motherhood can be found in the Old Testament, but has lately become more popular in North America, although regulation has lagged behind practice. *In vitro* fertilization, or test-tube conception, has a low success rate, but has been used to help women and couples conceive if one or both have fertility problems. These technologies have created new families and challenged the bases on which nuclear families have traditionally been built.

As a result of changing families, with multiple family fresh starts as well as the new reproductive technologies, new types of fatherhood have been created. Eichler (1997:72) notes that there are now nine kinds of fathers:

- biological, social, exclusive, full fathers

- non-biological but social, exclusive full fathers

- biological but not social fathers

- biological, social, exclusive, partial fathers (where the father is non-custodial)

- biological, social, non-exclusive, partial fathers (a non-exclusive father is one where the mother has a new partner)

- non-biological but social, exclusive, partial fathers

- non-biological but social, non-exclusive, partial fathers

- gay co-fathers, non-biological, social, non-exclusive fathers

- post-mortem biological fathers (where the man's sperm is taken for impregnation after his death)

Not much is known about men seeking fatherhood outside marriage or committed relationships. Some gay men who are single, as well as some in committed relationships, have been pushing for the option of adoption in several provinces in Canada. It is not known how many men on their own are seeking fatherhood. It might be anticipated, however, that as men's self-images with respect to families and fatherhood change, more men might seek to have children outside of marriage or a committed relationship. It also might be predicted that, even with contemporary social changes, fewer men than women would deliberately seek single parenthood. Existing practices, such as surrogate motherhood (whereby a woman agrees to conceive and gestate a baby for a fee), are more readily available to men, given their greater average purchasing powers.

Custody and Non-Custodial Parenting

When spouses separate, divorce, or part ways, an important question arises: Who will have what responsibilities for the children in the new families that emerge? Custody decisions are often amicable and made by the couple without resort to the courts, but also can be the basis for immensely heated emotions, nasty court battles, and highly charged policy forums. The latter have been seen in Canada with the 1998 Senate committee hearings on divorce and custody. Successes of fresh starts in families following divorce or separation can depend on custody arrangements being satisfactory for all family members involved. Custody involves the children's entire well-being, including day-to-day care, control and protection, instilling of values, and future opportunities. Custody issues can relate to, and overlap with, issues of access to children by the non-custodial parent as well as issues of child support.

Short of King Solomon's solution—dividing the child in half—there is no simple solution to child custody disagreements. Debates about the rights of mothers relative to the rights of fathers and the rights of grandparents often overlook what is in the best interests of the child(ren), and how those interests can best be achieved. Even the concept of "custody" itself might bet-

Tears, Sneers, and Accusations

There were tears, sneers and accusations in Toronto last week as advocacy groups for battered women, non-custodial fathers. and grandparents unleashed pent-up resentments and complaints before the Special Joint Committee of the Senate and the House of Commons on Child Custody and Access. The hearings are part of a compromise reached last year when the Senate held up approval of a tough new bill to force delinquent parents — mostly fathers—to make good on their child support commitments....

Stories abound of lonely and distraught grandparents, of mothers leaving town with the kids to elude brutal former partners, and of fathers who have been denied visitation rights by mothers who wield access like a weapon to extort money.

... Some practical suggestions, such as requiring parents to take pre-divorce education courses, to draw up parenting plans as part of legal separation agreements, and giving all parents access to mediation, will work only if fairness to both parents is guaranteed. The way to do that is to ensure that children have open and ample access to both parents and to other family members.

Source: "Where Kids Sit When Families Split," Editorial, *The Globe and Mail*, 6 April 1998:A20. Reprinted with permission, *The Globe and Mail.*

ter suit families if it were abandoned in favour of something that indicates a child-centred focus. "Parenting responsibilities" is one alternative. "Primary caregiver" has been another helpful suggestion (Richardson, 1996:232). Others might be devised.

Joint custody is rapidly increasing in both Canada and the United States. Many think (Drakich, 1993; Eichler, 1997, for example), however, that it is unlikely to work successfully except in those cases where the marriage breakdown was amicable. Joint custody requires negotiations in good faith by both partners, and the capacity of each to have the best interests of the children at heart. It has clear benefits in good situations, but can create problems, too. For instance, the child(ren) can continue to be socially parented by both parents, which can help their development and their adjustment to the disruption of the separation and divorce. However, if the mother and father have different standards of living, the kids may blame one or the other for the relative deprivation the child endures in that household. If Mom and Dad live in different regions, there can be a lot of travel and shuffling back and forth, creating a sense of rootlessness for the child. And if the child has regular contact with both parents but the parents don't coordinate their parental roles well, the child can play one parent off against the other.

Some parents, as we noted in Chapter 9, effectively stop parenting once they live in a household separate from the child. Others continue to act as parents. A major challenge for divorced families is that there is no clear model for non-residential parenting. The relation of parenting with custody issues is, in part, what makes custody such a political hot button, particularly for men's rights groups.

Divorced Dads as "Non-Parents"

Separated and divorced families are a growing reality in today's society, [Ron] Kuban [past President of Children and Parents Equality Society] told a small audience. So, divorced families, including fathers, require more attention and support. If they don't receive it, the consequences will be costly to all levels of society....

Right now, fathers don't get much support, he said ... "The courts are now saying to the one parent, who has traditionally been the mom, for whatever reason or for whatever bias, you continue to be the parent. The non-custodial parent suddenly ceases to be the parent in the traditional sense. He or she now becomes the access parent. But the access parent is a misnomer for a large babysitter."

Source: Tom Arnold. 1997. "Divorced Dads Treated as Non-Parents," *The Edmonton Journal*, June 11:B4. Reprinted with the permission of *The Edmonton Journal*.

Remarriage

Most divorced people remarry (Baker, 1996:30). In fact, the proportions of marriages in which one or both of the partners has been previously married is increasing. In Canada in 1967, for example, only 12.3 percent of marriages involved a previously married partner; by 1991, the proportion was 32.3 percent (Baker, 1996:30). Remarriage of divorced people is so common now that some see it as normative. Called "conjugal succession" or "recycling the family" (Richardson, 1996:243), it seems here to stay. More than anything else, the extent of remarriage after divorce underlines people's desire to have committed, emotionally involving relationships. Divorce rates would only mark a decline in family if few divorced people remarried, or subsequently became involved in long-term unions. A trend is discernible toward a lesser rate of remarriage now in Canada than in the 1980s, as shown in Table 10.1, but it should be remembered that marriage rates overall have declined.

Table 10.1 PROBABILITIES OF REMARRIAGE FOR DIVORCED PERSONS BY AGE AND SEX (CANADA)

	1981	1986	1991
Males			
25–35	.885	802	.647
35–50	.780	718	.614
Females			
25–35	.791	.737	.657
35–50	.578	.536	.483

Source: Statistics Canada. 1996. *The Decline in Marriage in Canada, 1981–1991*. Ottawa: Statistics Canada. Catalogue no. 84-536-XPB, p. 10.

Figure 10.3 FORMING A NEW UNION AFTER SEPARATION (CANADA 1987–1993)

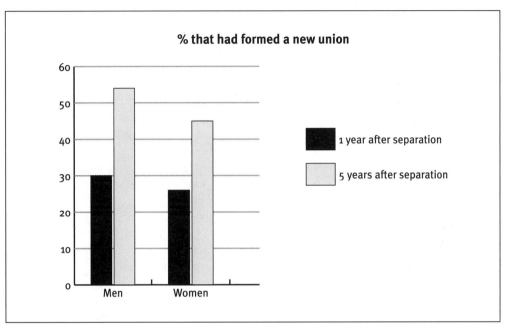

% that had formed a new union

Source: Statistics Canada. 1997. *Family Income After Separation*. Ottawa: Statistics Canada. Catalogue no. 13-588-MPB, no. 5, p. 7.

More divorced men than women remarry (Baker, 1996:30), as shown in Figure 10.3 and Table 10.1, and the likelihood of remarrying following divorce is reduced if one has children, particularly for women. In the United States, more people marry, more divorce, and more remarry than in Canada (Adams & Nagnur, 1990:144). Although still popular, the overall rate of remarriage has declined a little in Canada recently, corresponding with the lower marriage rate.

Second marriages, as we noted in Chapter 9, have a higher risk of divorce than do first marriages. The reasons for this could be many. One is that those who are divorced may have fewer of the social supports and the values that keep couples together. For example, they may be less willing to tolerate unhappiness or violence to preserve the marriage. Another reason is more psychological; people entering a second marriage may not have resolved the personal problems that led to problems in the first marriage. They may thus bring "baggage" into the second relationship, or choose the wrong kind of partner again the second time. A third reason is that in some situations, conflicts between first and second families are too difficult to work out. We will talk more about the particular challenges of blended families in a moment.

Most explanations for the higher risk of divorce in remarriages are sociological. When couples marry or form a committed relationship, they begin a process of "social construction of marriage," by which they create together their own shared traditions and memories. Over time, they create together a shared new definition of themselves in relation to the world around them. When a marriage ends, this social construction of self-identity in relation to marriage becomes shaky but it does not get forgotten.

In remarrying, different and new social constructions must be developed through negotiation, agreeing to new social roles and divisions of labour. The imprints of the past relationship are shadowed by the new relationship, but always provide implicit comparisons. Since the former relationship is in the past, memories of it can be either overly rosy or overly bleak, with no reality checks. Both types of memories can have implications for the present relationship and make it more challenging to maintain. When children are involved, the increased number of relationships and the need to maintain an ongoing relationship with the ex-spouse can make remarriage even more challenging.

A study based on a national survey in Canada (Wu, 1994) finds that adaptation to a second marriage is related to the particular type of marital dissolution, age at marital dissolution, religion, and gender.

Less is known about remarriage after widowhood. One Canadian study (Wu, 1995), using event history analysis, has found huge differences between men's and women's probabilities of remarriage after widowhood. Remarriage is significantly higher for men (almost twice as high), and in particular, for men who are better off financially. Prospects for remarriage of widows and widowers has dropped recently, particularly for young widowers (Nault & Belanger, 1996:11). The drop was less for young widows. Nault and Belanger (1996:13) conclude, "The chances of widowed persons remarrying are consequently much lower, in particular for women who at older ages find themselves facing a marriage market strongly slanted against them."

Little is known about the extent to which obligations to members of the ex-spouse's extended family remain after divorce and remarriage. One of the few studies which has looked at this question finds that among 190 women and 93 men who divorced and remarried, most feel that they are obligated to help family members in need, if possible (Coleman, Ganong & Cable, 1997). They perceive their obligations to the younger generation as stronger than those to elders.

The majority of couples succeed in meeting the challenges of a second marriage. What works is, not surprisingly, similar to what works in a successful first marriage: good communication, realistic expectations, honesty, a shared sense of humour. Meyerstein (1997) suggests that advance preparation is highly useful in a good second marriage. It helps to recognize that a second marriage is not the same as a first, and that the first marriage cannot be repressed and forgotten but should be mined for lessons learned. Beyond these sensible approaches, the couple needs to work to develop the marital relationship and to establish and maintain the new loyalties to each other (Kheshgi-Genovese & Genovese, 1997).

Cohabitation as a Fresh Start

Assessing the degree to which cohabitation is a fresh start after dissolution of a first relationship is not easy. Cohabitation, unlike marriage, does not have a clear date of beginning and ending, thus errors in estimates of cohabitation are probable. Language is also elusive in satisfactorily capturing cohabitation arrangements, making accurate estimation even more challenging. Terms used include common-law unions, cohabitation, living together, persons of the opposite sex sharing living quarters (known as **POSSLQ**—or **PSSSLQ** for same-sex partners), and in French, "**union libre,**" as well as street-language terms such as "shacking up," "living in sin," and "trial marriage." Whether these terms connote similar kinds of living arrangements is far from clear. No matter how definitions are spelled out on surveys and census forms, people's own self- and social definitions of what is and is not cohabitation come into play in their responses.

Despite these measurement challenges, data on divorce and remarriage suggest that there is a reduced tendency for men and women to enter a second marriage after the failure of a first relationship (Marcil-Gratton, 1993:88). This is not surprising. There is the sense that marriage may not be for them after all, or alternatively, there are the attractions of singlehood or lone parenthood, both of which offer some autonomy and independence—although a parent can never be fully independent. Nonetheless, "[c]ohabitation is replacing marriage as the framework to begin life as a couple, to give birth to children and start a family, and to reconstitute another unit when the first one has failed" (Marcil-Gratton, 1993:89).

Growing proportions of Canadian children experience a fresh family start when one or both of their parents start a new family by cohabitation. "Three-quarters of the children from broken unions whose parents have ever engaged in cohabitation have at age sixteen experienced at least one new two-parent family and the integration of the new partner" (Marcil-Gratton, 1993:87–88). The proportion of children born to at least one parent who has ever lived in cohabitation has risen dramatically in the last thirty years. The phenomenon barely existed in the early 1960s (2.5 percent of 1961–63 birth cohorts), increased to 9 percent for children born in 1971–73, climbed to 32 percent for those born in 1981–83, and reached 43 percent for those born in 1987–89 (Marcil-Gratton, 1993:76).

Fresh starts at family based on cohabitation seem to be more fragile than those based on marriage (Desrosiers, LeBourdais & Laplante, 1995). A cohabiting family in which one or both partners is divorced is less likely to break up if there is a pre-school child or children at the time of the formation of the new union, if a child is born to the newly formed couple, or if only the man brings children into the new relationship (Desrosiers, LeBourdais & Laplante, 1995).

Fleeing into Fresh Starts

Some people, with immense courage and fortitude, create entirely fresh family starts for themselves after suffering not only marital disruption, but family at its worst. Two of these kinds of fresh family starts are discussed here: fleeing from family abuse, and fleeing from an abusive cultural practice. Both involve journeys of self- and family discovery. Other examples could easily have been included.

Fleeing into fresh starts at family and at life itself is not limited to the kind of pain Florence experienced.

Growth and Triumph

I am from the Peigan Nation. I was adopted out when I was an infant so I have never had the opportunity to live on my reservation. Eleven years ago I was reunited with my birth parents, and that is where my healing began....

I grew up in ... an average, middle-class white family ... In school, "squaw" was a label that was always applied to me. Sexual abuse, disruption in our home and my own longing to know who I was welled up inside me and I began to run away from home ... I grew to be ashamed of who I was and remained so until I understood Canadian history, until I understood the circumstances of my birth, until I understood that I was loved and until I understood that racism was a reflection of ignorance....

I was suicidal and I either ran away at every opportunity or slashed my wrists in hope that someone would care. I spent the rest of my teens ... in a haze of drugs, alcohol and all the evils that street life can offer to a teenager....

In Vancouver, I met the man I would stay with for twelve years; he was twenty-two and I was seventeen. We were both on the streets and we learned to exist together, but neither of us really knew how to love or respect each other because we were both searching for some part of ourselves. We had a daughter and eventually a son but our relationship deteriorated—fighting, alcohol and drugs were always present and we patterned our lives this way for many years until we separated for the last time.

If I were to sum up my lifetime, I would have to say that the first half has been about pain and the rest about healing ... I am now in university and working on a degree in native studies. It has been a struggle with myself ... I have had to give up drinking and drugs, kicking and screaming and it is hard to keep that commitment ... It has taken a long time for the street to leave me but those survival skills have carried me through a lot of years.

Source: Florence Shone, 1998. "It Became Important..." *Our Voice*, April:8. Reprinted with permission, *Our Voice*.

Do They Hear You When You Cry?

... [A] happy, spoiled little girl in the tiny West African country of Togo, Fauziya ... is the favourite youngest daughter of a well-to-do businessman who is traditional enough to have stature in his community but progressive enough not to let his four girls be "circumcised" according to tribal tradition.

Then he dies ... Within a year, the ambitious 17-year-old's education has been scrapped and she's been gift-wrapped as a fourth wife for an old man who won't take delivery of his new bride until her "woman's parts" have been removed to ensure her "cleanliness" and fidelity.

... Fauziya flees the night before the butchers are to come for her ... is delivered from her room by her eldest sister, who smuggles her out of the house and to the airport, where she boards a flight to Germany using papers provided by a shabby "fixer."

Source: Jane Gadd. 1998. "A Harrowing Escape from Genital Mutilation," *The Globe and Mail*, 4 April 1998: D13. Reprinted with permission, *The Globe and Mail*.

What comes through in both of these examples is the strength of survival, the skills and confidence that enabled both women to become stronger and to create new selves along with new families. These are truly inspiring fresh family starts.

Not the Brady Bunch: The Challenges of Blended/Step-Families

The number of blended families is not fully known. **Blended families** are remarried families in which one or both partners brings children into the new relationship. In 1990, there were thought to be 343 000 blended families in Canada, or 7 percent of all families (Eichler, 1997:32). Eichler compellingly argues that this number should be doubled, since there is another person often (but not always) involved too, a non-custodial parent who may still parent the children in another blended family. From the perspective of numbers of children in different kinds of families, it is estimated that in 1994 in Canada about 5 percent of children lived in some sort of blended family (Peters, 1997). In the United States, it has been estimated that 20 percent of children will have lived in some kind of step-family by the age of 18 (Church, 1996:82).

The terminology of blended families is as challenging as that for cohabiting couples. The terms "blended" or "reconstituted" make new families sound almost strange, in contrast to "regular" families. One suggestion is the term "**binuclear family**" (Church, 1996:83), which also has drawbacks. Using the descriptor "blended," "reconstituted," or "binuclear" highlights differences rather than similarities with other families that have not experienced divorce and remarriage.

Similarities are likely large, and when differences are found, the question must be asked whether they are due to the blended family experience,

Good-bye 'Daddy' and 'Mommy'

The terms "mommy" and "daddy" are to be banned from schools in Ireland as part of a drive by the Roman Catholic Church to ... recognize the growing number of one-parent families.

A new church program aimed at four- and five-year olds in Catholic schools throughout Northern Ireland and the Irish Republic asks teachers to use phrases such as "the adults who live in your house" and "the people who look after you" instead of referring to mothers and fathers.

Source: "Good-bye 'Daddy' and 'Mommy.'" 1997. *The Edmonton Journal*, 17 October :A6.

to the divorce experience, or to family problems that might have occurred anyway. These are not easy questions to sort out in research. However, the emphasis we tend to give to "blended" families as different may cause us to search there for the source of family or child problems, appropriately or not.

Making fresh families is not easy or straightforward. What to call non-biological parents is one challenge, for example, along with what to call the children of the step-parent. The terms can be perplexing for both children and parents.

Additionally, there are the mythologized images of the immensely happy Brady Bunch of TV fame and the opposite, but strongly compelling images of the wicked stepmother of folklore and fairy tales. Cinderella's stepmother (and stepsisters) are vivid images for children of what step-families can be and what they would not want (Valpy, 1998). Stepfathers do not fare too well either in some children's literature, with images of stern taskmasters, of negligent men, or of propensities toward abuse, particularly sexual abuse.

There is also the contemporary reality of biological fathers and mothers who are not only alive, but often a continuing part of the child's life. The child may make comparisons between the two "mothers" or "fathers,"

Don't Expect the Brady Bunch

When Marianne Libertella married Ray Massi, a divorced father of three, she thought she was prepared for her new life and her new step family.

But after two years' experience ... "I was really going into it naive. I was 40. I had never had children. I thought this was going to be the family I had never had."

Reality hit at a family gathering that included both mother and stepmother. The child favoured her mother, ignoring her stepmother.... Since then, Marianne Massi has become a close friend to her stepchildren, a role better suited to stepparents ... say experts.

Source: Lini S. Kadaba. 1998. "Don't Expect the Brady Bunch," *The Edmonton Journal*, 5 April:G3.

or play one against the other, or deny that the step-parent is really a parent after all. Step-parents, too, may make comparisons, experience self-doubts about their parenting, or find that the necessary ongoing relationship with the absent parent is challenging.

A particular challenge of life in blended families is the sharing of children at special family events, such as Christmas or Chanukah or Ramadan. Children we may think of as ours are away at the other parent's place for some holidays, which creates the need for regular negotiations and close collaboration among the various parents and their other family members. Some parents, too, may deeply feel the absence of their children at important family times. Mother's Day and Father's Day can also highlight differentness and create longings among children and parents.

At the same time, living in a blended family is not all bad by any means. One little boy who lived with his mother, stepfather, and younger brother thought his situation much better than that of his younger brother since he had two Dads while his brother had only one!

Family research is helpful in identifying what works successfully in blended families. A popular research strategy is to compare reconstituted families with so-called "intact" families. This research design has its problems, in that the two kinds of families may not be comparable. Members of blended families may have been through family disruption and, for good or bad, have learned strategies for dealing with problems, while "intact" families may not have had such lessons. It may also be that in comparing "intact" and blended families, the implicit standard is set by the "intact" families, leading to inappropriate and prejudicial comparisons.

Nonetheless, the findings of what works well in blended families from such studies bears sharing. A significant predictor of success is the degree of consensus on parenting between the new spouse and the child's parent

Without Our Most Precious at the Holidays

This Christmas we'll be without our two of our most precious gifts. A daughter and a son.

The sting of separation is familiar to those in "non-traditional" families. There are more than one million children in this country living with one parent, or a parent and a step-parent, or dual-custody parents. Step siblings abound.

What it all adds up to for many families is a certain amount of confusion. A certain amount of anxiety. And a lot of pain.

At no time is this more evident than at Christmas. In this season of joy and sharing and coming together the pain of being apart is keenly felt ... Since moving to this city eight years ago, our family has faced this painful reality every other Christmas. One year, the kids are with us. The next, they're gone. It never gets easier. Our three children are my wife's from her first marriage. Their father lives in Saskatchewan.

Source: Rick McConnell. 1996. "It's a Lot to Ask ..." *The Edmonton Journal*, 15 December: G1. Reprinted with permission, *The Edmonton Journal.*

(Saintjacques, 1995). Preparation for the step-parent role is also important, including accepting the reality that both the new spouse and stepchildren had a previous family life which did not, and never can, include the step-parent (Richardson, 1996:244). Step-parents also need to recognize that they ultimately have limited control over whether the child(ren) accept them.

Trying too hard can be a mistake. Since women face more obstacles and challenges in becoming stepmothers than men do in becoming stepfathers (Valpy, 1998), it is important that women prepare more and understand some of the particular challenges they face in advance (Morrison & Thompson-Guppy, 1986). For instance, Valpy (1998), in citing research done by David Cheal in Canada, notes step-parenting can be stressful, especially with the vivid wicked stepmother imagery that we all seem to have. Added to this is the fact that women have traditionally borne the major responsibilities for child care and child rearing, meaning more contact with stepchildren and more points at which to encounter tender feelings on both sides. This makes stepmothering more challenging than stepfathering.

In research that focuses on couples in mutual support groups as they make the transition from being lone parents to becoming blended families, Collins (1991) finds that there are both private, personal issues and social challenges. Unlike most researchers, Collins does not compare blended families with intact families but looks at fresh starts as process. He particularly examines the interplay between individual lives and dominant ideologies about marriage and families.

Two forces draw lone parents to remarry, according to Collins: first, there is the desire to escape from the "cheerless life" of the lone parent; and second, "the widespread view in Western societies that the nuclear family is the proper setting in which to bring up children" (Collins, 1991:159), or what Church (1996:87) refers to as filling the "kin vacuum." Recognition in the light of day that lone parenthood has distinct advantages, and that the nuclear family is not all that it is deemed to be for children or for anyone else, gets crowded out by the power of ideological beliefs that restoring "order" to what is seen as a deviant family form is to be desired. In deciding whether to make the transition to step-parenthood or blended family, single mothers must balance the roles of mother versus woman, and are influenced by the "herd" notion that marriage must be good because most people do it.

Negotiating the dilemmas of parenthood responsibilities, personal preferences, and ideological pushes is the basis on which families begin life as a blended family. Their success in working out these dilemmas will relate to the success of their new family (Church, 1996).

Research with 105 stepmothers in Canada (Church, 1996) finds that stepmothers define family in more fluid terms than members of other kinds of family. They do not see household and family as directly equivalent. And roles, including gender roles in family, are seen as more flexible. Church concludes that step-parents may not want to try to be parents to their stepchildren immediately but rather wait and see what new family relationships emerge.

From the child's viewpoint, there may be a need to establish new relationships with the step-parent, and perhaps with step-siblings, but also with both the custodial and non-custodial parent, as all the relationships adjust to the new family arrangement. Conceptions of who is family and who is not matters to how these relationships develop and to their ultimate success. Shared parenting can produce a broader and sometimes more accepting view of what family is, and can be. In situations where there is a distinct difference in level of socioeconomic status between the homes of the two parents, there can be ambivalence and even guilt, which can cause the child to wonder about families and gender, but can also expand the child's horizons.

A crucial, but under-researched, aspect of the success or failure of blended families is the degree to which they are socially institutionalized, or provided with everyday supports, guidelines, and societal acceptance. If, in fact, blended families are viewed, or see themselves, as less able to draw on society's resources and rewards, they may be disadvantaged. The judgment is self-fulfilling: if we expect less of blended families, we give less and get less in return. There is some evidence emerging that this may be the case (Richardson, 1996:245). However, as marital disruption becomes more normative, or widely accepted as happening to many of us, it may be that the institutional supports for remarried and blended families will strengthen.

Discontinuity of relationships between children in blended families and their grandparents (the parents, usually, of the non-custodial parent) has not been the subject of much research. It is, however, of growing policy and legal importance as grandparents increasingly express their rights to have access to their grandchildren after divorce and after remarriages. One study (Kruk, 1995) discovers that grandparents whose adult children are non-custodial (mostly paternal grandparents) are at high risk for contact loss. The primary mediators in ongoing grandparent/grandchild relationships are the daughters-in-law. Disrupted contact between grandparents and grandchildren is found to have adverse consequences for the grandparents. It is not fully known whether the consequences are as adverse for the grandchildren.

Widowhood as a Fresh Start

Widowhood is now seen as an expectable life event. Given the difference between men's and women's life expectancies, a woman who marries or establishes a lasting relationship can realistically anticipate that she will be left a widow. The good news, however, is that widowhood is occurring later than it used to (Moore & Rosenberg, 1997:31). In Canada, almost 80 percent of women aged 85 or over are widowed, while even at age 70 to 74, 40 percent are widowed. Since most men at advanced ages are still married (55.7 percent of men aged 85+), while most women are widowed at these ages, the implications for fresh starts are clear.

Older women, mainly widows, are much more likely than men to make a change in their living arrangements late in life. Usually, these changes are related to health status, but they also relate to family. A man with health problems more often has a built-in caregiver at home, while a woman with health problems, even at the same age, is less likely to have that benefit. Hence, she is more likely to move in with relatives or into an institution. Widowed women, as mentioned earlier, are less likely to remarry than widowed men (Gee & Kimball, 1987:89).

Myths abound about widows. Mainly they are seen as sad and depressed. Depression does strike some, and at times it is debilitating. But it is not the only reality for widows. Eighteen months or so after the spouse's death, most widows are ready to start life over for themselves (Gee & Kimball, 1987:90). Most often this means reaching out to friends, siblings, adult children, and others such as clergy or even lawyers. Some develop active new hobbies or interests. Contact with their peers seems to provide the most satisfaction for widows. Some even note that this is the first time they have felt independent and that they enjoy it.

Fresh Family Starts in Later Life

Most research on fresh family starts has focused on people under the age of 50. But with increasing life expectancy and divorce likelihood, the proportions of those over age 65 who are divorced has risen. Moore and Rosenberg (1997:31) note that 5 percent of men and 6.1 percent of women aged 65 to 74 in 1991 in Canada were divorced, compared with 0.3 percent of men and 0.1 percent of women in 1951. People older than 50 remarry with increasing frequency, and establish new non-married families as well. In France, for example, in 1992, 1.8 percent of all marriages involved a man over the age of 60 (Caradec, 1997:47).

Some older couples who are alone after widowhood or divorce may choose to cohabit but keep separate households in order to maintain continuity in their living arrangements and to avoid fuss by their offspring about loyalties and inheritance. An unusual study in France (Caradec, 1997:65) of conjugal arrangements among those 60 years and older finds "a great diversity of conjugal lifestyles: some couples live together in marriage, some outside marriage (showing that cohabitation is not reserved for the young in age), and others have adopted more novel forms of union, intermittent or alternating cohabitation."

This may suggest two things: first, as Caradec (1997:65) argues, an **intergenerational contagion** whereby non-marital unions have become diffused from young to old; and second, the need for different people—in this case people at different stages in the life course—to customize relationships to fit their particular needs. It is notable, however, that available statistical data routinely collected by censuses, vital statistics, or most social surveys in North America may not truly capture the immense diversity possible in fresh starts.

Gay/Lesbian Fresh Starts

We talked earlier about gay men who stay married, and about women who become lone mothers after a marriage to a gay man ends. Here, we look at the fresh start of coming out as a gay or lesbian family. There have always been gay fathers and lesbian mothers, usually those who have become parents in a heterosexual marriage or relationship or, in the case of lesbians, in some instances through sexual assault or coercion. What is newer is gay and lesbian couples having children together and raising them as a family unit. What is also relatively new is for the gay and lesbian couples that form after the end of a heterosexual relationship or marriage, along with the children of one or both partners, to live together as a *family*. Here, we will discuss gay and lesbian parents raising children in families, however they formed, as well as gay and lesbian couples in committed relationships, as fresh family starts.

Diversity exists among gay and lesbian families, as among all families. With respect to gay and lesbian families, there is an added dimension of diversity: whether or not they are "out" as a family, or in other words open about their relationship with all they know and meet. Miller (1996:132), in describing his own gay family, has this to say:

> The family I live in as a father is also the family I live **out** in as a gay man. I call it an 'out family' for three reasons: its openness to homosexual membership; its opposition to hetero sexist conformity (the prejudicial assumption of heterosexuality as normal and proper); and its overtness within the contemporary lesbian and gay movement.... Mine is a family that opens out, steps out, and stands out. It opens out to people traditionally excluded from the charmed circle of Home; it steps out beyond the police and policed borders of the Normal; and it stands out as a clear new possibility on the horizon of what used to be called ... the Just Society (Miller, 1996:132).

Not all gay and lesbian families are "out" in this or any other sense. Some remain cloaked in secrecy out of fear for the children or themselves.

Lesbian families with children have been seen as a contradiction: women having children without heterosexual relations. Or they are seen as threats,

Lesbian couples deciding to give birth to a child must negotiate which one will become pregnant, and then agree on the process.

women without the need for men. Lesbian mothers became more visible in the 1970s and 1980s, according to Epstein (1996:109), because they chose to claim their identities as both mothers and lesbians. She notes, with sadness, that the claiming often occurred in courtrooms in custody hearings, where lesbians were typically defined as unfit mothers. The risk of losing custody of their children still gives lesbian mothers a strong motivation to conceal their orientation. A recent example occurred in Alberta where a long-time, highly successful foster mother, referred to in media reports as Ms. T, was denied foster children when it was discovered that she was lesbian (Abu-Laban & McDaniel, 1998:82).

Gay and lesbian families challenge the family status quo in several fundamental ways, according to recent family research. First, both gay and lesbian families may provide important developmental learning for children in the possibilities of resisting confining gender role expectations (Epstein, 1996:111). Second, lesbians can teach daughters, in particular, how not to compete with other women but to bond with them to work together. Third, both gays and lesbians force a questioning of the assumptions and values of heterosexist nuclear families. Fourth, gay families raise vital questions about the presumptions we make about masculinity in families and in society. And fifth, gay and lesbian families are an effective force of change in family policies.

Challenging family policies by gays and lesbians goes beyond gaining access to the same benefits that heterosexual couples have, although this is important. Epstein (1996:108) asks readers to imagine what it is like to face the following situations:

> • Your child is in a medical emergency and you are not allowed to make any decisions about the care the child is to receive.

The Zoo

I can remember a time long ago when my father took me and my sisters to the zoo with "Joe" and his small children. Entering the gates my Dad could not help but see an ad stating that families could buy a pass that would reduce costs for he and "Joe" significantly. Delighted by this, he nicely asked the cashier for one family pass. She reacted by saying, "I'm sorry, sir but we only sell passes to families." Well, this infuriated my Dad and he demanded that he should be able to buy the pass. He and the cashier continued to argue over whether or not he could buy a pass. Then finally Dad stopped and yelled, "Listen, 'Joe' and I are gay lovers and these are our children." The cashier's face went bright red and she immediately handed my Dad the family pass while apologizing.

Source: Personal communication to one author from the child, now a teenager.

- Your child's teacher will not speak to you about your child's progress at school.

- You are assumed to be a single parent even though you live and parent with your partner.

- The courts grant custody of your child to your mother because your sexual relationship with your partner is deemed immoral.

The challenges involve rethinking what families are, what spouses are and do, and what parenting is. These are profoundly important sociological endeavours at reconceptualizing families. It was, in large part, this sort of rethinking that has led, in recent years, away from defining family by form and instead defining families broadly on the basis of processes: what families *do* rather than what they *are*.

Gay and lesbian families, in not reproducing the heterosexual model of family, tend not to be structured hierarchically by gender. They therefore do not have the same divisions of labour by gender that many heterosexual families have. They are chosen families, characterized by fluid boundaries, new roles, little institutionalized symbolism. They can be creative in making families and in devising new ways to be familial.

Lesbian couples deciding to give birth to a child must negotiate which one will become pregnant, and then agree on the process. This necessitates closeness in talking openly about their feelings and innermost desires and longings. Nelson (1996) reveals in her study of lesbian mothers, to which we referred in an earlier chapter, the intricacy and beauty of reproductive decision-making. Epstein (1996) refers to parenting roles in lesbian couples being based on personality attributes rather than gender, so one parent is the funny one, or the hard-liner, or the one pushing academics. One of Epstein's (1996:119) respondents puts it well, "We're not modelling male–female power dynamics, we're modelling women doing everything that needs to be done in order to maintain life." Miller (1996:155) talks about shared and solidifying humour when one of his daughters, Alice "tactfully informed Jennifer (who was babysitting) that if she was looking for a husband at our house, she was 'barking up the wrong tree.'"

Yet, there are tensions in the fresh starts of lesbian and gay families. These occur at several levels, emanating in part from the lack of acceptance of gays and lesbians in some of society and the reality of having no blue-prints on how to be. One respondent in a study of lesbian mothers puts it this way:

> We don't presume that we are a family. And I think that has created
> a closer, ah, an opportunity for closeness that would not have been
> there if I had just assumed that we were a family and dammit behave
> like one! Because it gives you no choice (Nelson, 1996:105).

Epstein (1996:122) cites homophobic behaviours of family members such as disowning family membership, or a lesbian partner showing pref-erence for biological links, by taking her own child somewhere for a spe-cial occasion but not her partner's children. And Miller (1996:150) notes that his children endure taunts such as, "'We don't want you on the team because you're a **fag** like your dad'" [bold in original]. On the home front, Dad sug-gests the following comeback, "Come on, just because my dad's gay does-n't mean I am, and even if I turn out to be gay, what difference would that make to my pitching arm?" (1996:151).

Post-gender families is a description of relationships in which gender forms no part of the household or the domestic division of labour. This kind of relationship raises important questions about the social concept of "cou-pledom" as well as about the ways in which gender determines much of what we are and do in families, and how a commitment to non-sexist prin-ciples as the basis on which to build families can create new sorts of family fresh starts. Oerton (1997) explores these issues among lesbian couples in an article she evocatively entitles, "Queer Housewives?" Her conclusion is that gendering processes may so intertwine with all domestic labour, and all that we are in family, that inventing family without it is challenging but not impossible. She argues that creative new solutions to family processes, par-ticularly divisions of labour, might be found in closer study of lesbian and gay couples. Risman (1998) argues that some of these new solutions can be found among heterosexual couples as well.

Risman and Johnson-Sumerford (1998) examine heterosexual "post-gender" marriages in which the partners share equally in paid and unpaid family work without regard for gender. They find that there are four path-ways to such relationships: a dual-career household, a dual-nurturer rela-tionship, a post-traditional relationship, and external forces that open relationships to egalitarianism. Egalitarianism is likely to affect both the power balance and the emotional quality of the relationship, Risman and Johnson-Sumerford suggest, for the good.

Transitions out of Parenting: Empty Nests

Even without marital dissolution, fresh starts in family occur. A fresh start that many families experience (and increasing numbers of others may wish to) is the empty nest. An empty nest, ideally, occurs when all the children grow up and move away. Children are still growing up, but they are moving away with less and less frequency. Findings from the 1996 Census of Canada show that an amazing 55 percent of those aged 15 to 29 lived in their parental homes (Statistics Canada, 1998). This is up from 47 percent in 1981. This, suggests Statistics Canada, is one reason for the overall decline in the proportion of households headed by people under age 30 in Canada.

Census data in Canada reveal that most people over age 65 either live alone or with a spouse only (Desjardins & Dumas, 1993:67). So, empty nests are a reality for most Canadians. Among some elderly, there are a minority who feel that there is no one, or only one person, on whom they could rely for help (Moore & Rosenberg, 1997:47). Among most, however, there are numbers of friends and family, both close and far, on whom they rely. Family networks are more geographically dispersed than are friends, so in essence family and friends may be reversed as older people build family-like relationships with networks of friends.

Finally, an Empty Nest ... Maybe

When our older son was little he used to say, "Mommy, when I grow up, I'm going to live with you forever."

He kept his word! Like so many in these times, he left home for a while, then came back and scotch-taped himself to the basement suite for 20 more years—and bought a dog!

But, truly, hope springs eternal ... I looked forward to getting rid of Kid and Dog. I could foresee many joys in my life with him outta there ... finally, Kid bought a house. He's gone! In case he ever thinks of moving back, his old bedroom has been turned into my sewing room....

But he drops off Dog each day so she—and we!—won't be lonely ... Now there is doggie doo in two backyards ... On his way home from work, he picks up Dog. It smells good in here, he says—every day! He goes to the stove and lifts the lids of all the pots. He hangs around. He watches us eat....

But (other hand again!), he still mows the "old folks'" lawn. He still shovels our walk.

Source: Edith Kirby. 1998. "Finally—An Empty Nest," *The Edmonton Journal*, 3 April:15. Reprinted with permission, Edith Kirby.

People in mid-life who have responsibility for both the young and the old are sometimes called the "sandwich generation."

Sandwiched Families and Cluttered Nests

Recently, there has been a shift in living arrangements and family lives that in some ways constitutes a fresh family start. It takes two forms. One is the return to the family home of adult children, as well as the presence of adult children who never left in the first instance. This has become a common living arrangement, as indicated above by the 1996 Census data. In fact, some researchers argue that "[i]t is now commonly understood that midlife parenthood often comprises prolonged periods of coresidence with grown adults" (Mitchell, 1998:2). The other is elders living with middle-aged children (Rosenthal, Martin-Matthews & Matthews, 1996). People in midlife who live with or have responsibilities for both the young and the old are sometimes called the "sandwich generation." It is rare for three or more generations of adults to share living quarters, but it is far from rare for them to be dependent on each other in a variety of ways, even when they maintain separate households.

Concerns have been raised that refilled nests are a crisis for those whose homes are being refilled, struggling as they are with work, caring for elders, looking after themselves, their homes, and their communities. The common perception seems to be that young people are sponging off parents and are lay-abouts. Recent research by Mitchell (1998) shows that this is an incorrect presumption. Generations living together in families provide mutual support and generally get along well. Middle generations receive valued companionship and the satisfaction of facilitating their child's transition into adulthood.

On the other side, adult children receive a number of valuable services, such as free or low-cost housing, food, and access to a car perhaps. In other research (Mitchell & Gee, 1996a), even marital satisfaction is unaffected by the presence at home of adult children, provided the kids do not leave and return home multiple times.

Young adults are more likely to leave the parental home when they live in step-families than when they live in either single-parent or two-parent biological families (Mitchell, 1994). This raises the important question of long-term implications for social inequalities. If some young adults increase their disadvantage by leaving the family home earlier than others, then the ultimate outcome could be widening social inequalities. If combined with early pregnancies, early family starts, or leaving school to support oneself, the long-term consequences are magnified.

In terms of social policy, it seems that the family home is becoming a kind of safety net for youth who cannot establish themselves in independent residences (Mitchell & Gee, 1996b). Families that cannot afford, in economic or social terms, to take adult children into their homes may be forced to cut the net for their children. In times of sharp reductions in social transfers, this may force the young people to seek low-wage employment rather than education or training in order to support themselves. "Not being able to return to the security and comforts of home could have a devastating effect on the lives of young adults who are not psychologically prepared to be launched as adults" (Gee & Mitchell, 1996:68).

With respect to older relatives living with those in midlife, the issues are remarkably similar. In Canada, with reductions in health care dollars, those who are hospitalized return home "quicker and sicker." This often means, for elders, temporary or permanent reliance on their adult children for assistance.

Created Families

A crisis, such as a life-threatening illness, can challenge one's idea of family and precipitate the interesting positive outcome of a fresh family start in creative new directions. One study of the perceived families of persons living with HIV/AIDS reveals exciting new family options (Wong-Wylie & Doherty-Poirier, 1997). When a number of people with HIV/AIDS were asked who or what they considered to be family, the results were surprising.

For this group of respondents, family as process was paramount. To be considered family, an individual must have *a reciprocal relationship* with the defining person (the HIV/AIDS person), and must be *accepting, supportive*, a source of *health and wellness resources*, and an *inspirational influence*. What kinds of people met these criteria for the respondents? They listed seven categories of people altogether as comprising their created families (not every respondent had family from each category): families of origin, health care professionals, friends, other people with HIV/AIDS, deceased friends, family caregivers, and valued material objects.

Some specific examples fill in the human faces and the diversity of created family. One male respondent with HIV/AIDS saw his family as large and diverse. His closest family consisted of his partner (male), his daughter and his partner's daughter, and his ten good friends, both male and female (two of whom were deceased). Beyond that, family to him was members of the HIV/AIDS Society, his parents and their siblings and friends, numbering 13 in all, and then his grandparents on both sides, three of whom were also deceased. Another respondent (female) saw her in-laws as being as important to her as family as her husband and father. Her many friends, both gay and straight (four of whom also had HIV/AIDS) were also part of her created family.

Another included his physician in his self-defined family in an equal place with his wife and son. In his case, all but one of the friends included in his family definition also had HIV/AIDS. Significantly, he specifically excluded some members of his blood family, such as his mother, from his family definition. Yet another person with HIV/AIDS defined his family as consisting of computers, bridge, his ex-partner, and the "gay world" writ large, only incidentally noting his mother, brother, and sister.

These findings emphasize the limitations of assuming we know what family is, or examining families by structure alone. Family processes matter, and we all possess the power to define family for ourselves. Most importantly, this study shows that family, however we define it, is becoming more rather than less important as this century and millennium draws to a close. This is a point we have made throughout this book in a variety of ways, and with numerous examples.

It need not take the crisis of HIV/AIDS for us to create new families. Many of us create families for ourselves—in a new land, in situations where we have lost our families through war or time, when we have irresolvable disputes with families, or when our memories of our families of origin are too horrid to forgive. In these cases, and endless others, we make families of our friends, our neighbours, our communities, those with whom we share something important, or even our pets, plants, work, computers, and sporting equipment.

Concluding Remarks

We have explored multiple and varied fresh starts to family in this chapter. With family being placed increasingly in the realm of ideology and politics, it sometimes seems as if different approaches to family are in competition for our hearts. The fresh starts to family discussed here are not arranged in sequence for the most part, nor are they arranged like a smorgasbord for us to choose what we like best. For most of us, the kinds of families we live in choose us. This is true for families arranged along the life course. It is also true for gay and lesbian families. And it is true in many single-parent families, because sometimes, as the old phrase has it, life happens. We do not necessarily make informed and deliberate choices about the ends of marriages or relationships. Sometimes the choice is not ours, but our partner's or spouse's. Sometimes, we flee from violence or an intolerable situation to something unknown but safer.

In our various kinds of families, however, we do make choices. We engage in and develop processes that define us as families. We do our best within the opportunities and constraints society offers. It is these choices that matter most to our outcomes and the outcomes of our children, and to our happiness. It is not the shape our families take.

In the contest over which kind of family is preferable or most sanctioned by society or religions, we can lose track of the reality that all of us in families are sharing and caring for each other. Single- and two-parent families, for example, are not the great divide. Nor are heterosexual and gay/lesbian families. The similarities in daily family living far outweigh the differences.

CHAPTER SUMMARY

This chapter discusses transitions to different family situations of many sorts: singlehood, one-parent families, remarriage, step-families, empty nests, flights from family situations into new ones, and fresh starts that are inventive and creative of new kinds of families. We learn that some fresh starts can bring new ways to behave and to live in close relations. Others could better be called stale starts, since they merely lead to a repetition of old patterns and of old relational problems.

Starting new families is not a new phenomenon in human society. With large-scale immigration and high death rates in the past in North America, many single-parent families and orphans existed.

The perils of fresh starts in family include high risks of poverty for single mothers and their children after separation and divorce. Similar risks exist for women who choose to have children on their own without partners, a phenomenon growing in popularity. At the same time, teens who become pregnant are much more likely to keep their babies rather than give them up for adoption, as in the past, which creates risks of poverty and lifetime or long-term underachievement among young mothers. Adoption of children from other countries can have perils as well; the children face the cultural challenges of adapting to the new family's customs and the lingering effects of trauma experienced in early childhood.

Becoming a parent without a partner as a deliberate choice is a fresh family start, one which makes for multiple kinds of parenthood and families. Custody arrangements also create new kinds of parents, most notably in shared or joint custody situations in which a non-residential parent is involved in active parenting. The news here is that families can extend beyond the walls of a household.

Remarriage is more common for men than for women; for both, the risks of divorce are higher with a second marriage. Social pressures toward remarriage are more ideological than material; people want to be like other couples in society and to avoid stigma. Cohabitation after divorce is growing as the fresh family start of choice in Canada.

Blended families pose challenges to the ways we think of families, for numerous reasons. New vocabularies to describe relationships must be invented. And the numbers of familial relationships both inside and outside the household multiply.

We learn that not all fresh family starts are choices. Some people flee from abuse, or from culturally sanctioned violence against them into new lives, in the process creating new families.

Living solo is a growing option for many people who maintain close family ties but not in their own households. Counter to this is the sandwich family, which involves both youth and elders living together with the middle generation, or cluttered nests, a variant on this theme where youth either never leave the family home or return home to live.

With aging, families change and fresh family starts are made. Changing times have enabled post-gender families to develop and some same-sex families to live more openly.

KEY TERMS

Artificial insemination: A process of introducing semen into a woman's body without sexual intercourse; can be a medical process but may not be.

Binuclear family: A term used to describe a blended family, or a family where the spouses each bring children and non-residential parents into a new family. This term enables the capturing of the concept of family as extending beyond household.

Blended family: Typically describing a family comprising two previously married spouses with children who marry each other and bring their children together in a new family.

Custom of the country/ à la façon de la pays: The long-standing practice among early fur traders in Canada to take aboriginal "wives," who were known as "country wives."

In vitro **fertilization**: Generally known as test-tube fertilization; conception that occurs by bringing together ova and sperm in medical procedures.

Intergenerational contagion: A process by which trends that begin in one generation may be adopted by other generations. An example is cohabitation, which was mostly a youthful phenomenon, but has now been adopted by people of all generations.

POSSLQ: Person of the opposite sex sharing living quarters.

Post-gender families: Families in which the division of labour is not based on gender.

PSSSLQ: Person of the same sex sharing living quarters.

SNAF: An acronym meaning Standard North American Family, or mother, father, two kids, and usually a dog or a cat.

Union libre: Widely used term for common-law union in Quebec.

SUGGESTED READINGS

Collins, Stephen. 1991. "The Transition from Lone-Parent Family to Step-Family," pp. 156–175 in Michael Hardy & Graham Crow (Eds.), *Lone Parenthood: Coping with Constraints and Making Opportunities in Single-Parent Families*. Toronto: University of Toronto Press. This article explores in detail the important transition out of lone parenthood and into becoming a step-family. It shows that both material issues (poverty) and ideological issues (the desire to avoid the stigma of single motherhood for both mother and children) play a role, but that the ideological pull of remarriage is stronger. Collins also shows how much women's status in life is determined both by labour market activity and by their family status.

Eichler, Margrit. 1997. *Family Shifts: Families, Policies and Gender Equality*. Toronto: Oxford University Press. This book introduces and explores the various models of family. It reveals how complex families have become in their everyday lives and how many family relationships now exist. A key point, emphasized and demonstrated throughout the book, is that family and household are not synonymous.

Ferri, Elsa. 1993. "Socialization Experiences of Children in Lone Parent Families: Evidence from the British National Child Development Study," pp. 281–290 in Joe Hudson & Burt Galaway (Eds.), *Single Parent Families: Perspectives on Research and Policy*. Toronto: Thompson. An original study based on a long-term follow-up of children in lone-parent and two-parent families in Britain. The findings show only minimal differences between the two groups of children. Much of this difference can be attributed to differences in income, housing, and labour market experiences of lone parents rather than family structure or parenting styles.

Risman, Barbara J. & Danette Johnson-Sumerford. 1998. "Doing It Fairly: Study of Postgender Marriages," *Journal of Marriage and the Family* 60:23–40. This article is an original study of what the authors see as a new kind of family in which gender roles are not the primary basis for deciding who does what. The concept of post-gender marriages enables analysts to see the institutional and structural gender contexts in which families exist but defines them as not determining of all our behaviours. Risman explores this in greater depth in her 1998 book, *Gender Vertigo: American Families in Transition*. New Haven, Connecticut: Yale University Press.

REVIEW QUESTIONS

1. Give two examples of how immigration can produce family fresh starts.

2. Is it true that fresh starts in families began largely in the 1970s?

3. What was a "Quebec widow" in Ontario earlier in this century?

4. Why is it expectable now that people will make multiple fresh family starts over their lives?

5. Which family members tend to maintain communications and ties among family members across households most?

6. Do men or women do better living alone?

7. What are some of the problems with the way we measure single parenthood?

8. What are the reasons single mothers often experience poverty?

9. In what age group is childbearing outside marriage growing fastest?

10. What are some problems in comparing blended families with other nuclear families?

DISCUSSION QUESTIONS

1. In what ways were widows in the past similar to and different from single mothers today?

2. Are there other ways than those discussed here by which fresh starts in families can occur?

3. What are some of the challenges faced by families in which parents live separately but continue to be active in parenting?

4. What can all of us do to try to ensure that children from single-parent families are encouraged and not stigmatized?

5. What would happen if single mothers one day were no longer stigmatized? Would poverty among this group lessen?

6. Why are more women deliberate seeking to bear a child outside of marriage or a committed relationship?

7. Discuss some of the pressures to remarry after divorce. What implications might they have for second marriages?

8. What are the future implications of an increasing number of divorced older people?

9. Are fresh starts in family part of family living or are they something new and different?

10. What are some insights gained into families and close relations by understanding more about gay and lesbian families? About post-gender families?

WEBLINKS

http://www.parentswithoutpartners.org/sup1.html

Facts about single-parent families.

http://nces.ed.gov/pubs97/97981.html

An article that shows that children in single-parent families are more likely to experience early school problems and are less likely to participate in early literacy activities than children in two-parent families

http://www.ed.gov/PressReleases/10-1997/father.html

An article showing that children do better in school when their fathers are involved.

http://www.nig.nl/congres/3rdeuropeancongress1995/abstract/063-1114.html

Information on the effects of family changes (including step-families) on the elderly.

http://www.childtrends.org/dadvar2.htm

A summary of key research findings on how social, economic, and cultural factors influence fathers' involvement with their children.

http://www.relationships.com.au/living.htm#link1

A discussion of myths about step-families and how they differ from other families.

http://www.weber.edu/chfam/topics/NINE.STEPS.HTML

Nine steps toward healthy step-families.

http://www.stayhealthy.com/hrdfiles/hrd00081.html

Problems, including health problems, faced by members of step-families.

A Glimpse into the Future:

Trends and Challenges

"Of all things, the future is the hardest to predict," Nobel Laureate John Polanyi has said. Indeed, humans do not have a good record in predicting the future, despite the growth in future studies and futurologists. The latter seem generally to take up their trade late in life, perhaps to avoid being around when their predictions are not realized. This failure to predict accurately is not surprising, since all of our knowledge is about the past, and our decisions are about the future. There is—to say the least—a problematic relationship between past and future in an era of rapid change such as our own.

The record of social scientists is not much better. Demographers, for example, sometimes looked to as modern-day gurus, failed to predict both the baby boom and the subsequent baby bust. The Chief Statistician of Canada, Ivan Fellegi (1997:28) notes that, "High profile examples of misdiagnoses [of the future] abound." He then cites his personal favourite: "... the statement made by Lincoln Steffens, the American journalist, when he returned from a visit to the Soviet Union in 1919, 'I have seen the future; it works...' " Clearly, seeing the future, or at least seeing it with any precision, is a major challenge.

What should a "glimpse into the future" of families look like? What are some appropriate goals for this chapter? Noted sociologist and student of the future Wendell Bell tells us in his classic work *Foundations of Futures Studies: Human Sciences for a New Era* that this "glimpse" could take many forms. Adapting what Bell (1997:111) says about future studies in general to the study of families in particular, we could pursue any of the following topics:

> 1. *The study of possible futures.* What could a family possibly look like in the future? How widely could it vary and still be considered a family—whether in our own current thinking, or in the thinking of people who live in such families one hundred, five hundred, or a thousand years from today? For example, will a person who lives with a dozen clones of himself or herself be living in a family?

> 2. *The study of probable futures.* A family made up solely of John Smith and his clones is, at least to our current thinking, possible but quite improbable. So we might prefer to focus on more probable futures. To do this, we would identify current trends and imagine them continuing, largely unchanged, into the distant future. What would this thought experiment predict for families?

> 3. *The study of images of future families.* People are the actors whose actions create societies—past, present, and future—and people often imagine what they are doing before they do it. Thus, we may most effectively glimpse the future by looking at the ways people imagine future families: for example, how they imagine their adult families will differ from the families they grew up in, or their grandchildren's or great-grandchildren's families will differ from their own.

4. *The study of the knowledge foundations of future families.* Some who consider the future of families are concerned with the methodological or epistemological issues involved: that is, with questions about how it is possible to know what we think we know. A difficult undertaking in any area of research, this question is particularly difficult when it relates to the future. Where families are concerned, it gets into questions about what aspects of family are not merely unknown but unknowable. For example, can we ever really know how two spouses feel about each other?

5. *The study of the ethical foundations of family life.* Discussing the future of family life provides a golden opportunity to consider some questions about what we would hope people are trying to accomplish in their roles as spouse, parent, or sibling. Are we humans living at the start of the twenty-first century making a good job of families, ethically speaking? And if we are doing a bad job, how can we imagine improving our family lives and then go about actually improving them? Typically, sociologists shy away from such questions, but these questions remain intensely interesting to many others.

6. *Interpreting the past and orienting the present.* Usually, our predictions and imaginings of the future are based on our understanding of the past and present. But sometimes we use our thinking about the future—about what is possible and what is probable, what is knowable and what is desirable—as a basis for rethinking families of the past and present. How would today's or yesterday's families look to someone three hundred years in the future?

7. *Integrating knowledge and values for designing social action.* Thinking about the future gives us a good opportunity to bring together scientific hunches and ethical concerns, theories about the past, and images of preferred futures. Ideally, once we have carefully thought through and debated the kinds of families we want, we will design social policies that make it more likely these families will come into being.

8. *Increasing democratic participation in imagining and designing the future.* Our ability to design social policies that produce the kinds of families we want in the future will depend, in large part, on our ability as members of society to hear each other's views and implement plans that are democratically based. Doing this requires that we empower the powerless, pay equal attention to all family members, and allow for diversity.

9. *Communicating and advocating a particular image of the future.* Imagine that we have succeeded in glimpsing the future of families, and have devised procedures for supporting new kinds of family life. Our job

as futurists, then, is to communicate and advocate our thinking—in effect, to bring the fruits of our science and scholarship to the people whose lives will be affected and who must, therefore, decide what kinds of families they want to support.

As you can see, these varied approaches to glimpsing the future of families all have merit. In some respects they are also interlinked, although most family researchers who think about the future emphasize only one or two of these approaches. This chapter will touch on various approaches. Let us start with possible and probable scenarios for change in family life within the foreseeable future.

The future is what the present used to be. In thinking about the future, it is often useful to think along historical lines (after all, we have no other source of empirical data). What would the present be if written by future family sociologists or family historians? What is the future if seen from the past? Possibilities open up for different vantage points on the future, not as something that unfolds without our creative input but as something that is created socially.

Take a look at Figure 11.1 and think about what future it predicts for families. Over the course of the twentieth century, families have left farming communities for cities, households have shrunken in size (with the reduction

Figure 11.1 **THE CHANGING FAMILY, THE CHANGING SOCIETY**

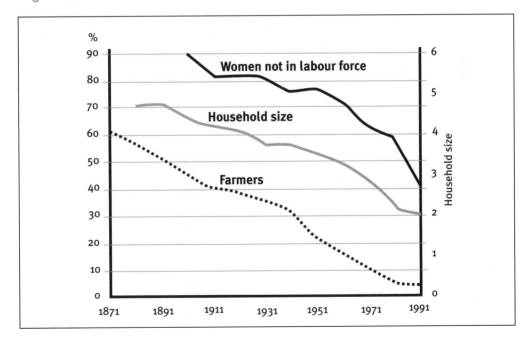

Source: Health and Welfare Canada, 1989. *Charting Canada's Future: A Report of the Demographic Review.* Catalogue No. H21-105/1-1989, p. 16.

in childbearing), and women have entered the paid workforce. We have purposely left out any data after 1991; see if you can find the most up-to-date statistics needed to complete this chart up to the present.

Now, what of the future? If we extrapolate the future from the past more or less mechanically, we have to conclude that at some time in the future, no one in Canada will be farming, no women will still be outside the paid workforce, and the average household size will be 1 (it can't be less than 1 and still be considered a household).

What problems do you have with this picture of the future? Do you have difficulty imagining a Canada in which we have to import all our food since we don't produce any of it ourselves; in which the concept of house-wife or stay-at-home mother has completely died out, and in which even 90-year-old women have paid jobs; in which people don't live with other people as spouses, parents, siblings, or even friends? Such a country is hard to imagine, but it is a country implied by these data.

Now, conversely, let us suppose that the trends represented in Figure 11.1 will level off or will even reverse (i.e., farming will become a growth occupation, women will start bearing large families again, and paid work will become a mainly male activity). What theories that we have discussed in this book—or indeed, that you can find in any sociology book—support such a prediction? The answer is, none. In fact, all of sociology is predicated on the notion that economic development—whether we call it industrial-ization, modernization, or globalization—tends in one direction: that is, toward urbanization, gender blurring, and decreasing fertility (plus, more choice in the entry into and exit from social relationships). What this exercise illustrates is that, both as participants in our own lives and as sociologists, we are hard-pressed to imagine any family life very different from the one we are living right now. We have a hard time imagining the future, or even accepting the implications of our own best theories.

So, you can see that much of what we are going to put forward in this chapter's "glimpse into the future" will be tentative, cautious, and even somewhat unimaginative. After all, just think of what people would have said in the year 1900 (or even in 1950) if we had correctly predicted for them family life as we experience it in the year 2000. Two views of history (both of which include the present and the future, as well as the past) are directly relevant to our glimpse into the future of families. First, there is the image of the present as the peak of human progress to date. We see ourselves emerg-ing from a grim, dreary past into a bright present where we are smarter, wiser, and happier than our ancestors. The future holds more of the same improvements and advances over the present. A contrasting view, equally prevalent, is that we used to have, or be, something wonderful, but with time, what was good slipped away, replaced by a society with less-clear values, more social problems, less stability, and less certainty. The list is expanded or contracted to fit occasions and needs.

Although contradictory, both of these views are so prevalent that they can be stated, within moments, by the same person. You may have heard examples on the street, in your family, or from politicians. In this chapter we look at competing visions of present-day families and project them into the future, looking at how social scientists are changing their studies of families, at challenges to family security, at new ways to be family, at contemporary trends developed into futuristic scenarios, at select policy challenges, and at a few "what ifs."

Family Futures: Competing Visions

Family has gone public in recent decades. It is at the heart of politics, of religion, of our hopes for the future. This is particularly so in the United States, but increasingly true in Canada as well (see, for example, Richards (1998) and Marks (1998)). In a late 1990s reflection on future challenges by top-level public servants in Canada (Fellegi, 1997), family issues such as the continued evolution of family as a basic social unit and the human development role of family, both for children and adults, were highlighted as central future challenges of society and policy.

Several debates and visions connect and collide on the issue of families, what they are, what they could be, and what they should be. The key debates, in our view, centre on gender and on technological change. We will look at these issues, as well as the effects of increased mobility.

Feminism and Gender

At the heart of the wars over family and what family is to be in the future are feminism and gender arrangements. Stacey (1990), for example, argues that feminism and gender are at the core of today's deeply polarized debate about North American life. Popenoe (1996) also suggests that gender is central to the future of family, but he comes at it from a different place than does Stacey. Berger and Berger (1983), whose book is entitled *The War Over the Family*, have this to say:

> Among those who came to see the family as a problem, there developed a relatively negative faction and a more positive one, as it were. Some took a mainly negative view of the family, as an obstacle to realization of human liberty, full individuality, and the like. Others took a more positive view, in which the family itself, albeit with some tinkering here and there, was evolving in such a way as to realize these ideals ... when one hears the proposition that 'the family (or this or that type of family) has become a problem,' one ought immediately to ask, '*Says who?*' Likely, one will find that those who say so come from a specific class location in society (Berger & Berger, 1983:8–9).

Eichler (1997:1) notes that "[t]he ground on which families are built has shifted." She suggests that one such shift has been "the introduction of gender equality as a legal and moral principle" on which families should be structured. In the past, she argues, families were based on gender differentiation. It is the incorporation of gender into the study of family that led to British social theorist Anthony Giddens' comment (Cheal, 1991:1) that the study of family has moved from what he calls the most boring of endeavours to the most exciting.

Contrast the gender equality view of family with that of those who espouse "family values," popular in the United States. There are large differences among family values advocates, just as there are among those who support gender equality. One "family values" view was expressed strongly by 1988 presidential contender Pat Robertson in his comments on the Equal Rights Amendment:

> It is about a socialist, anti-family, political movement that encourages women to leave their husbands, kill their children, practice witchcraft, destroy capitalism and become lesbians. ("The Year We Said No," *The Globe and Mail*, 2 January 1993:D1).

Other takes on family values are apparent in public debates in the United States over recent sociological studies, such as Hochschild's *The Time Bind* ... (1997). The thesis of Hochschild's study, based on interviews in an actual company that she calls Amerco, is simple but perplexing: that the positions of the home and workplace in people's lives have been reversed. Hochschild's conclusion, as described in Chapter 7, is that family is no longer a haven from work, but that people are seeking solace from family in work.

Hochschild's conclusion began a headline-grabbing public discussion in the United States with cover stories in both *Newsweek* and *U.S. News and World Report*. The hotly contested vision of families and gender was made vivid in the subsequent debate about values, women's roles, and effects on children and families of working mothers. Hochschild was the target of critics for implying that women who work for pay have no choice, or that women who work at home are making the wrong choice. Little of the debate centred on what Hochschild actually said in her book, but rather on the interpretations and implications of her findings and their meanings for gender and family values issues.

Another perspective on families and gender comes from a social movement of Christian men called the Promise Keepers. Characterized as "the largest and most controversial men's movement in the United States" (Phillips, 1997:52), the Promise Keepers argue that "many social ills—fatherless families, drugs, infidelity, even putting work ahead of family and God—stem from the failures of men" (Phillips, 1997:53). The Promise Keepers draw huge numbers of men together in sports stadiums to take themselves back to family and to God. According to Promise Keepers founder Bill

McCartney (known as "Coach" in Promise Keepers' circles), using stadiums is no coincidence. He is known to favour a blend of sport and military metaphors to reach his audience of largely white men. In a statement entitled *Man of His Word: The New Testament, New International Version: 3*, the Promise Keepers declare:

> Men tend to be 'fix it myself' people. We can admit we're weak in establishing relationships. We admit we are far from perfect ... The problem is that our theme song is 'I did it my way.' When we do it our way, we remain isolated by our own sins. We separate ourselves not only from God, but also from right relationships with our families and others. In our relationship with God, we can't be do-it-yourselfers. We can't fix what's wrong by our own efforts.

Whether the group's vision of families and gender arrangements is favourable to women is the source of debate and controversy. Promise Keepers argue that the movement is a yearning for spiritual values by men, and that their wish to take their family and social responsibilities seriously poses no threat to women. In that, they have supporters, one of which is Canada's self-proclaimed national newspaper:

> Saturday's huge Washington, D.C. rally of the Christian men's group Promise Keepers revealed the surprising rise of a new mass movement in America ... Whether the need is for spiritual guidance, or perhaps for a renewal of a sense of personal responsibility, it's a pervasive middle-class craving that the fiercely secular, me-generation mavens of popular opinion have yet to understand (*The Globe and Mail*, 1997).

On the other hand, the U.S. National Organization of Women says that Promise Keepers' real agenda is for women to return to their secondary roles in families and in society. One Promise Keeper is quoted as saying that "men should sit down with their wives and say something like this: 'Honey, I've made a terrible mistake. I've given you my role. I gave up leading this family. Now I must reclaim that role'" (Phillips, 1997:53).

Distant Relationships

Separation and distance from our parents (and other close kin) will affect most of us in our lifetime. Whether due to career changes, leaving home for college, getting married, or retirement, long-distance relationships have become increasingly common for families. In his book *Distant Parents*, Jacob Climo (1992) explores the effects of distant living and separation on parent–child relationships in America. Climo aims to show that the distant child–elderly parent relationship is unique and must be treated as such.

Let's explore the reasons for the establishment of distant child–elderly parent relationship. They can be broken down into two categories: external and internal forces. External forces are generally economic pulls, social mobility, and education. Children leave home for college, get married, or move in search of better jobs. Climo attributes the desire for upward mobility to the American culture, which puts great emphasis on improving one's status.

Children from rural areas are particularly likely to migrate because of a lack of economic opportunity in their home town. Distant relationships are also more common among middle-class than among lower-class families, because the former can afford to send their children away to school or to move to retirement regions.

Many reasons for leaving home are *not* due to external forces, but to what Climo calls internal forces. These differ from one person to the next, but include a desire for growth and for emotional, behavioural, and value autonomy. Climo asserts that the isolated nuclear family represents the clearest expression of our cultural norm which encourages generation differences and independence. Yet, if mobility is encouraged to improve status, why are people displeased and ambivalent about their relationship with distant parents?

In interviews with distant children, some express a sense of void, loneliness, and stress. There are usually unresolved conflicts with parents, both from the past and arising from the distant relationship. Yet oddly, Climo states, we have not yet recognized distant living as a social problem that can tear the generations apart. Only when we abandon inappropriate assumptions and recognize these difficulties can we alleviate people's isolation and stress. Climo sees the solution in technological advances, such as the video phone, that could allow face-to-face interactions, and in improved social services.

People have accepted several assumptions about long-distance (or "distant") relationships without thoroughly investigating their validity. The first is that geographic distance reflects emotional distance. In fact, research suggests that distant children feel no less emotional attachment than nearby children. The second is that near and distant emotional attachments are similar: that the quality and feelings of parents and children remain the same and do not vary with distance. This can also be the case for spouses in commuter marriages, as discussed in an earlier chapter. However, distance diminishes contact frequency, a fact that we will discuss later.

A third assumption is that children living nearby provide more assistance to their parents than children living more at a distance. This presumption is only valid in the sense that there is a decrease in communication between distant parents and their children. However, distant children often help their parents in various ways.

If these assumptions are not necessarily true, in what ways *does* distance affect child–elderly parent relationship? In answering this question, Climo focuses on three ideas embedded in Western culture: the development of the interpersonal self, independence and separation, and ambivalence toward love and distance.

The "interpersonal self" establishes a sense of emotional attachment to our social world. This attachment, in turn, is important for the integration of individuals into society. The parent–child relationship is the primary means by which individuals develop the interpersonal self. Climo argues that physical distance between parents and their children produces a lack of interpersonal self-development, thus producing an individualized self which is isolated and incomplete. The incomplete development of an interpersonal self because of distance hurts our social relationships and the growth of the individuals involved.

Alongside the development of the interpersonal self is the development of the "independent self." Post-industrial societies encourage emotional and economic independence from the nuclear family. Philosophers believe individual freedom is necessary if people are to achieve success in such a society. This freedom allows parents and children to be as close or distant as they want to be. People can also find and form significant bonds outside the family. However, these bonds, as Climo explains, are often difficult to build and sustain. The human need for an intimate relationship with parents is often stressful and requires that children and parents go to great lengths to make the relationship work. Prolonged separation at a distance makes maintaining this bond even more difficult. For this reason, most children and parents experience great stress in trying to keep the bond strong whatever the distance that separates them. This stress has a significant impact on distant relationships.

The desire to maintain a close and intimate bond with parents is further complicated by what Climo calls ambivalent feelings between the two generations. In distant relationships, children experience mixed feelings of both love and hate. One reason is that geographic distance allows for more conflict, misunderstanding, and highly emotional relationships which may feel both good and bad at various times. In his interviews, Climo found distant children expressing strongly opposed emotions toward their parents in the same interview.

These influences of the need for an interpersonal self, independence, and ambivalence all adversely affect distant relationships. However, distant relationships between parent and children also differ between individuals. Some are satisfied with their relationships, while others are unhappy and say they have a hard time maintaining a close bond. In his study, Climo identified three distinct groups with varying degrees of emotional attachment to their parents, based on the degree of emotional bonding with their parents.

Climo calls the most emotional group "displaced children." These "displaced" children are generally dissatisfied with distant living and want to reunite with their parents. They dislike distant living and complain about the harm that separation has done to their relationship with their parents. The "displaced" children attribute most of their conflicts to distance and believe that living closer would benefit both parties.

The second group, "well-adapted" children, are similar to displaced children in the sense that they too have a positive relationship with their parents. Although they feel that distance has complicated communication, they are generally happy with their relationship and do not want to change it. This group feels secure in their relationship with their parents.

The third group, "alienated" children, are different from the first two. Because of negative emotions toward their parents, they choose to live as far away as possible. The "alienated" children express both open hostility and anger, which can usually be attributed to past conflict. The relationship with their parents is both unsatisfactory and strained, yet they have no desire to change their circumstances. As we will see later, these three groups deal with the problems arising from distant living in different ways, and each group has a different relation with their elderly parents.

All three kinds of relationship are common in North American society. They are delicate and people must expend great effort to keep alive the bond between a parent and a child when hundreds of miles separate them. Unsatisfactory distant relationships are harmful to both parents and children and can lead to depression and alienation. So, distant communication has gained importance in the lives of distant parents and children. The various forms of communication include routine telephone calls, visits, and letters. Increasingly, one supposes, e-mail will offer greater numbers of parents and children a fast, cheap mode of communication. People consider letter-writing as the least satisfactory form of communication since the writer must wait for a reply. Far more immediate, and therefore more satisfying, is the telephone call, to which we now turn our attention.

The telephone has developed into the preferred form of interactive communication. Parents and children living far apart speak on the telephone once a week on average. These conversations are important to both parties and allow for regular contact. Although the telephone represents the most satisfying form of distant communication, it is limited by a lack of visual stimulation. In face-to-face conversations, people pick up on non-verbal cues. Lacking visual contact, telephone conversations leave room for misinterpretation and ambiguity. A simple sentence may turn into a heated conversation if the meaning does not come across as intended.

Another limit to telephone conversation is the time element; many people cannot afford to speak for a long time. They may feel obliged to limit themselves to conveying information about finances, health, or business affairs, rather than freely exchanging information about everyday life events and expressing emotions and sentiment.

Cost also limits the frequency of telephone calls. We generally assume that the more frequent the telephone calls, the greater the importance of that relationship. However, Climo states that the frequency of calls is not indicative of the significance of the relationship or the satisfaction people take in it. Far more important is the emotional content of the conversation.

E-mail offers the quickness of telephone communication minus the cost. Those who are connected can feel free to communicate as often as they want, and at any time. However, e-mail lacks not only visual cues but the information conveyed by tone of voice and rhythm of speech, and messages are not as carefully composed as in postal letters. For these reasons, e-mail is particularly subject to misinterpretation, especially about emotional matters. The full effects of this new medium on distant parent–child relations are not yet clear, since many older people have been slower to adopt computer technology.

Factors affecting how often children call home are the distance, parent's age, health status, and cost. The farther away the parent from the child, the less frequent are the calls, presumably because of cost. Yet, despite the cost, children call more often when parents are ill, usually to check on their health. Parents' age also affects the frequency of calling. However, the older the parents, the less children want to call home, perhaps because the conversations are less satisfying or more stressful.

Despite all its limitations, the telephone is still the most important tool for communication between children and their distant parents. Despite their importance, the telephone and e-mail do not replace the desire to visit. The average child visits his or her parents twice a year. Distant children and parents put much emphasis on their time spent together during visits. Visits are important to both parents and children. Distance, cost, and time constraints do limit the length and frequency of visits. However, for the most part they are satisfactory for both parties in the displaced and well-adapted group. For the alienated group, visits are stressful and the children are usually glad to leave.

As parents age and experience life-cycle transitions, most distant children respond by helping their parents. Retirement is an important shift in the lives of their parents and, most of the time, the children want to help their parents as much as possible. So far, there has been no tradition established which explains how to deal with life-cycle transitions from a distance. During these transitions, the distant child feels a sense of helplessness resulting from the long distance. Factors that affect the distant child's capacity to help the parents include the stage in the life cycle of the child. An adult child with a family of his or her own experiences divided responsibilities and often feels torn between conflicting duties. Some children try to help elderly parents by communication with social workers, doctors, and priests in their parents' town.

In the end, several things become clear from Climo's survey of distant parents. One is that we do not yet know enough about the strengths and weaknesses of distant-family relationships—whether between parents and children, between spouses, or between siblings—to know how geographic mobility will continue to affect the meaning and conduct of family life in the twenty-first century. More research needs to be done on the varieties of adaptation to this problem of distance.

Second, it seems clear from Climo's work that, at least when he did his research in the early 1990s, the existing means of distance communication were no substitute for face-to-face contact. Ultimately, close relationships had to be secured and revived by periodic visits, thus putting an emphasis on high-speed travel technology, not high-speed communication technology. It remains to be seen whether, in the twenty-first century, electronic media will conquer the distance between intimates or whether, for example, the solution to the distance problem will prove to be an instantaneous people-transporter.

Finally, to the extent that distant family relationships are maintained or activated to deal with crises of aging, poor health, and infirmity, improvements in health technology and social services may transform family life in the twenty-first century. There is no denying that both health and social services have changed dramatically in the twentieth century, so they are likely to continue changing dramatically. On the other hand, it is also clear as we end the twentieth century that most Western governments have lost a taste for large-scale spending on health and social services. So, in the end, public care may not be a future substitute for family care after all. Families may still prove indispensable for the old and infirm.

Technology on Fast Forward

Now consider the role of technological innovation: what it has done and can do to our concepts of family. The major challenge to family life as we know it comes from changes in reproductive possibility through the application of reproductive technologies. But that is not the entire story. Other technological innovations are affecting ways in which we form families, communicate in families, provide for our basic needs, and entertain ourselves.

The pace of technological change in the late 1990s has been daunting to even the most technologically aware people. This fact is captured well in "The Hitchhikers Guide to Cybernomics" (1996:8):

> If cars had developed at the same pace as microprocessors over the
> past two decades, a typical car would now cost less than $5 and do
> 250,000 miles to the gallon.

Computers and the Internet are changing the ways in which families structure their time. On the one hand, e-mail may allow some distant family members more-frequent contact than expensive long-distance calls. On the other hand, the solitary nature of much computer work and play may separate family members into their own individual spaces. Recent evidence on this little-studied development suggests that this might put families at risk (Brehl, 1998). With technological developments, it may be that television will be unified with Internet technologies to make Internet exploration somewhat more sociable.

Microwave ovens and pre-prepared, fast-frozen foods have meant that family dinners are less common. Each individual may eat alone, standing in the kitchen, before racing off to the next activity. This is another step in the march of technological change that has moved families away from the central hearth in homes, once the only source for heat and cooking.

Reproductive technologies have also developed quickly, as seen in Chapter 4. It is now possible for some who are clinically infertile to give birth. We are almost at the point of being able to clone ourselves. This gives new meaning to producing "an heir and a spare." And the role of family and of gender and sexual relations are changed too. These technologies raise fundamental questions and challenges for families in the future, questions for us all, not only those who make use of reproductive technologies. It is not simply a question of who is related to whom and in what ways. Questions extend to whether technology is changing the essential nature and meaning of family.

Technology is changing meeting and mating too, as was seen in Chapter 2. There are computer dating services, ways to contact potential mates across the world on Internet chatlines. The realm of cybersex even makes it possible for people to be "intimately involved" without ever having met. This opens immense possibilities, both good and bad, and will no doubt be the subject of debate in the future. There have already been examples of people falling in love as a result of Internet exchanges and starting happy non-virtual relationships. There are also examples of people being unhappily surprised to meet their virtual loves in the non-virtual world.

There is even an example reported in the media in which the woman with whom a man had been communicating turned out to be a man. In the absence of physical bodies, all things are possible via cybersex. Important questions arise about the bases of love and attraction.

Computer technology has been blamed for creating family problems. There have been cases in the news of women and men neglecting their families because of their "addictions" to surfing the Net. A new problem related to technology has appeared with the introduction of video lottery terminals (VLTs) in bars and pubs in several provinces in Canada. Quick and easy access to a gambling computer that accepts cash, together with the inhibition-breaking effects of liquor, has resulted in huge profits for governments. Concerns are now being raised about problem gamblers who gamble away their wages, leaving families to suffer deprivation. A generational problem is raised when adolescent children learn video gambling from their parents. Recent evidence in Alberta suggests that teens make up a disproportionate number of problem gamblers, relying particularly on VLTs. Public concern runs so high in Alberta that petitions forced the Alberta government to add a question on the October 1998 municipal election ballot on the banning of VLTs.

Technologies of various sorts are offering families new possibilities at the same time as they pose new challenges. Likely, families will survive, as they have throughout the ages. Just as likely, however, they are being transformed in fundamental ways.

The Future of Family Studies

The future holds more for the study of families than did the past. Cheal (1991) suggests that there has been a "big bang" in our theories and approaches to the study of families. This virtual explosion is based on two changes: the diversification of family types and experiences, and a broadening of the perspectives used to analyze families in their diverse social contexts.

Formidable tasks face family researchers who must see and try to understand aspects of family lives that are often hidden or invisible. This task is made even more difficult when contemporary family sociology is still haunted by traditional images of family life, and is undertaken on a stage of strong political and public interests. Family sociology in the 1990s and beyond is searching for ways to be inclusive of the various different experiences people have in families, including the different experiences of individuals within the same family. The search for new ways to study families is also challenged to move beyond the assumptions, spoken and unspoken, that traditional family sociology made about the nature of family.

For example, family research from the 1950s to the 1970s often took one member's view of family as real for all other members. Typically, it was the woman who was interviewed, on the presumption that she was the family specialist, while men specialized in work roles. Standard sociological approaches took the view that the nuclear family was normal and expected, and that within that family structure, members did different but complementary things. The goal of this approach was to assess the fit between family and society. Questions were seldom asked about whether a fit existed, whether conflicts in family occurred, or whether different members of the same family might see and experience their families differently.

Further, family was conceptualized as private, separate from the world of work, a place of retreat from the stresses of the work world. This may have been true for men in families, but was less so for women, for whom home was the workplace. What occurred in the private place of home was considered incidental to society's *real* activities, which took place in board rooms and political offices, typically involving important decisions made by men. This kind of thinking is revealed in the popular 1950s concept of

Family research in the past often involved interviewing only the mother, since it was assumed she was the family specialist.

"bedroom communities," suburbs where people were "stored" and restored before returning to the more important parts of cities where work took place.

Seeing families as a chorus of voices singing different parts of the same song, but always in harmony, misrepresented the realities of many families. Defining the vital societal work that families do as incidental to the real work of society also prevented us from seeing families as important. And defining as secondary and unimportant the places where women worked, often as skilled managers, trivialized their work and contributions.

From the 1960s, women began challenging some of the approaches and assumptions made in family sociology. Change did not occur overnight. Gradually, the concept of family itself came to be critically examined. The assumption that all family members thought as one was critiqued and reconsidered. New research methodologies developed that involved open-ended interviews with several members of the same family. Men's perceptions of family were essentially heard for the first time. Even relationships between the subject of the research and the interviewer/researcher were questioned, examined, and transformed.

Family research in the 1990s is actively building on this critical base. A **postmodern** perspective (one that involves a general distrust of grand theories and ideologies) on families (always plural) starts with the view that there is no consensus about what families are and do. There is no longer one dominant family form from which all other forms are thought to deviate. The concept of the logical progression of family, based on grand theory, breaks down. What families *are* becomes what they *say* they are. Exploratory analysis of what families and individuals in families do and are becomes the central goal. Diversity is to be expected. Family experiences differ by gender, age, class, race, and ethnicity, as well as by numerous other social factors yet to be explored. Voice and identity are crucial components of the postmodern analysis of families. *Voice* is essentially one's capacity for being heard, and *identity* is how we define ourselves in society and in relation to others.

What does a postmodern family look like? There are many visions; here is one: a Christmas 1997 photo of ten adults sent to one of the authors (McDaniel) by a close friend. "Alice" (a woman in her late forties) is next to her daughter, age 23, from Alice's now-ended marriage. Also in the photo are Alice's current male partner (to whom she is not married and with whom she does not live), his two adult children from a now-ended marriage, one of them with a boyfriend, Alice's good friend (another woman about 45 or so), that woman's ex-husband, his adult child from his first marriage (to a woman other than Alice's friend), along with the girlfriend of that child. To round out the photo is the mother of Alice's friend, a lively-looking woman in her sixties. All are happy and smiling broadly. Postmodern Christmas holidays do not match the images of families we held in the 1950s. But they are happy holidays nonetheless, particularly if the participants do not pine away for some image of an ideal family that they may never have experienced.

The Challenges of Security for Families

> Security, the chief pretense of civilization, cannot exist where the worst of dangers, the danger of poverty, hangs over everyone's head.
> (George Bernard Shaw, *Major Barbara*).

Families are being pinched in many ways in North America today, ways that shape what they will become in the future. Families are expected to play more central roles in caring for the young, the old, the infirm, the unemployed, the disabled, and the criminal. Yet the resources society provides, both through government programs and through labour markets, are diminishing. Canada and the United States do not have a good record on family poverty compared to most other industrialized countries, with the U.S. at the bottom and Canada near the bottom (Baker, 1996). And the gap is widening. Figure 11.2 shows that between 1993 and 1996, net income, after tax and transfer payments, rose for the higher-income Canadian families but fell

Figure 11.2 CHANGES IN NET FAMILY INCOME, 1993–1996

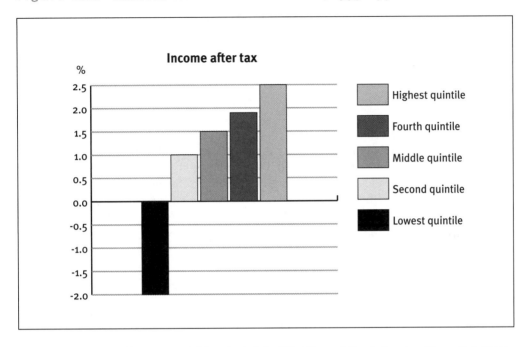

Note: Incomes are calculated in constant 1996 dollars. A quintile is a fifth of the population; the lowest quintile constitutes the 20 percent of the population with the lowest incomes and the highest quintile is the 20 percent with the highest incomes.

Abridged from: Statistics Canada, Income after tax, distributions by size in Canada, 1996, Catalogue no. 13-210-XPB, p. 21.

for lower-income families.

Zill and Nord (1994) conclude that making ends meet is one of the central challenges to families now and in the future. Families with limited incomes and resources risk long-term health and social problems. Eradication or reduction of long-term poverty ought to be a societal goal. Zill and Nord argue that for "the forgotten half" of the population (the poor, the less educated, and more isolated), the risks to life chances are large and serious, especially for children. Similar concerns are expressed by the National Forum on Family Security in Canada (McDaniel, 1993c:1) which argues in its keynote paper that:

> The central issue of our times is the feeling of insecurity felt deeply by many Canadian families.... If Canadians do worry about the deficit, family breakdown, or global competition, or retraining, it is not because they have an overriding interest in any one of them, but rather because of what these might mean for the security of their families and for their children's futures.

Judith Maxwell (1996) extends this point with her theory that social capital is as central to society as economic growth. She sees social cohesion and justice as resting on enabling families, particularly children, to develop themselves as societal resources. O'Neill (1994) makes the essential point that the foundations of society cannot be market contracts but must be shared interdependent relationships, such as those we find in families. McDaniel (1997) takes this idea further, suggesting that family interdependencies extend beyond the household and nuclear family and into intergenerational commitments, some of which are global.

That gains have been made in reducing poverty among seniors is often touted as an achievement by government. As shown in Table 11.1, since 1980 there has been a reduction in low income among seniors in Canada, by about one-half for men who are unattached, and by about one-third for women who are unattached. However, for both, the proportions of those with low income remains high (33.3 percent for men, and 53.4 percent for women). Whether this is completely a good news story depends on whether one sees the glass half empty or half full. Whatever one's perspective, more than half of unattached women over age 65 lived below the low-income

Table 11.1 **INCIDENCE OF LOW INCOME* BY SELECTED FAMILY TYPES (CANADA)**

	1980	1985	1990	1996
Family type %				
Married couple only				
1 earner	11.9	13.8	11.6	12.8
2 earners	1.6	3.2	3.4	4.0
2 parents with children				
1 earner	16.6	21.1	23.2	25.0
2 earners	5.8	7.8	6.5	6.6
3+ earners	3.6	5.0	2.6	3.4
Lone parent				
Male	25.4	26.9	25.5	31.3
Female	57.3	61.1	59.5	60.8
Elderly unattached				
Male	60.7	50.2	41.0	33.3
Female	71.6	64.1	53.8	53.4

*Low income cut-offs used here are based on an analysis of 1992 Family Expenditure data collected by Statistics Canada. Families who usually spend 54.7% or more of their income on food, shelter and clothing are considered below the low income cut-off, which is differentiated by region and family size.

Source: Statistics Canada. 1997. *Income Distributions by Size in Canada, 1996*. Ottawa: Statistics Canada. Catalogue No. 13-207-XPB, Text Table IV:34-35.

cutoff in 1996.

Gender is, in fact, crucial to income in Canada and in the United States. Women, whether in families or unattached, have a higher likelihood than men of living in poverty. The highest risk of poverty is among female-headed lone-parent families: in 1996 in Canada, more than 60 percent of such families lived below the low-income cutoff. This proportion has actually risen a little over the past 15 years. The economic prospects for single fathers are better but are not entirely rosy either—almost one in three live below the low-income cutoff.

The next highest risk for poverty occurs for married couples with children and one earner, one-quarter of whom were in poverty in 1996 in Canada, compared to 16.6 percent in 1980. Families facing insecurity of income may respond by sending out more members into paid employment. This has the effect of spreading risks and pooling resources, and may be a major trend in families in the 1990s and into the future. This is what families were known to have done at the time of industrialization as well as during other economic crises such as the Depression.

Without the security and stability of a solid base of resources, families struggle to survive day to day and to build lasting relationships. Without safe

Figure 11.3 CHILDREN IN LOWER-INCOME FAMILIES MOST LIKELY TO HAVE BEHAVIOURAL PROBLEMS OR REPEAT A GRADE

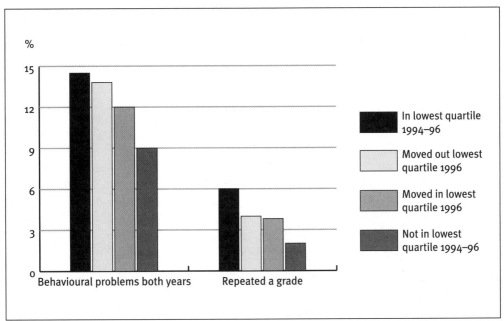

Source: Adapted from Statistics Canada. 1998. *The Daily*, Catalogue #11-001,October 28.

and healthful housing, nutritious food at regular intervals, and warm, dry clothes, the well-being of both children and adults is compromised. One measure of the effect of poverty on children is school performance. As Figure 11.3 shows, children whose families had incomes in the lowest quartile (i.e., the bottom 25 percent of the population by income) are more likely to have behaviour problems at school and more likely to repeat a grade. The experience and the stigma of poverty can test and tatter a family's shared pride in sticking together in hope and love. Stress takes its toll on insecure families. Their chances of surviving intact are reduced. And yet, as we have seen, families develop new ways to cope with the insecurity they face, one of which is to send out more workers to earn income. This is an example of families determining their own destinies rather than being corks on a river of change; but, like any adaptation, it has costs. Families whose members all need to work to survive may have little time together. Adolescents and children who are working part- or full-time may be shortchanging their education or sleep time. They may chafe under the burden of having to provide for their families, and resent their parents for not providing them with the more carefree life enjoyed by better-off peers.

Not Only New Family Forms

When people today discuss family, they talk about two things. They emphasize that families, and what happens with families, matter to them. They also talk of the diversity of families today in comparison to the past. The

Formation of First Common-Law Unions

The majority of Canadians now live common-law in their first conjugal relationship. Between 1990 and 1995, 57% of people who entered their first union chose to live together rather than marry. The probability of living common-law was significantly higher for women born between 1971 and 1980, and for women employed in a paid job. The probability of entering a first common-law union was also higher for women living in Quebec whose mother tongue was French, and for women who had already had a child.

The marital history of their parents also exerted a major influence on the type of first union that daughters chose. The probability for women entering a first common-law union was 75% higher if their parents had separated or divorced (before they were 15 years old) than if their parents had remained married.

Women who had a child before their first conjugal union had a 50% greater chance of entering a common-law relationship than women without children. This result is consistent with recent research in the United States, which found that the birth of a child decreases the likelihood of entering a first marriage, but increases the likelihood of entering a first common-law union.

Source: Statistics Canada. 1997. Adapted from *The Daily*. December 9. Catalogue No. 11-001. Reprinted with permission.

Figure 11.4 CANADIANS LIVING IN COMMON-LAW UNIONS

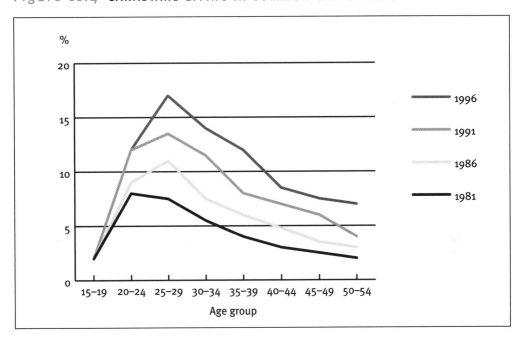

Source: Statistics Canada. Adapted from *The Daily*, December 9, 1997. Catalogue No. 11-001. Reprinted with permission.

diversity to which most people refer is a range of family forms, defined by legal and living arrangements of spouses, whether or not children are present, and even by the definition of who is a spouse. (As Figure 11.4 shows, the incidence of common-law couples is increasing, especially among young people.) So, we hear about married couples with or without children, common-law or cohabiting couples with or without children, female- or male-headed single-parent families, adoptive families, foster families, empty nesters, gay or lesbian families, and the list goes on. At times the impression seems to be that a smorgasbord of choices about how to live in families exists. All you need do is pick the one that suits you.

Yet this apparent diversity may be deceiving. People do not typically make informed choices about which family form they would prefer, matching their preferences with their personal characteristics and needs. Most people in families other than two-spouse families are there as a result of family life-cycle change, such as kids growing up and leaving home, or marriage/relationship breakdown. Heterosexual people do not say "let's form a gay or lesbian family." The only family forms that involve true choice may be common-law couples or adoptive or foster families.

Looking at family diversity only in terms of structures may have another, more fundamentally deceptive aspect. Diversity *within* various family forms may be overlooked or underestimated, suggesting that families are more uniform than they actually are. This view diminishes the potential lessons that might be learned from looking at real families, regardless of the form they take, and observing how the successful ones remain so. Form is not in itself the key to living well in families, nor is it the key to maintaining close relations over the long term.

Family and Circles: Innovation in Caring

The term *family* itself may be too restrictive, eliminating everyone to whom we are not related by blood or marriage. A student once told one of the authors (McDaniel) on his return from a weekend family reunion, "If I weren't related to these people, I would likely have nothing to do with them!" It may be that our restrictive idea of family takes away from us other ways to care for those we like. For example, we may parcel out our love and caring cautiously, thinking that family has a monopoly on caring. Yet, research by family sociologists on who people turn to in crisis or need (McDaniel, 1994, for one example) shows that people see many non-family individuals as family. Such individuals have been referred to as **fictive kin**, the idea being that they act like relatives even though they are not. The curiosity in this term is the suggestion that relatives act as relatives should (whatever that means!), or that the social distinction between family and friends is a clear one.

African-American, single, female-headed families are inventing a new way to be familial. Stacey (1990) argues, on the basis of a study of working-class families in California, that it is *not* middle-class families with their well-aired problems of balancing work and family, deciding whether or not to have children, and struggling to raise quality children who are the innovators in family, but working-class families. Indeed, white, middle-class families are more the beneficiaries than the creators of family change. It is, argues Stacey (1990) African-American and Chicano working-class women who are the postmodern family pioneers, who draw on traditional family networks at the same time as they create new ones to meet new needs.

Other-mothering is one such family innovation, which permits extended relations or friends to mother children and moves beyond the nuclear, biological family. Other-mothering is

> ... revolutionary in American society because it takes place in opposition to the ideas that parents, especially mothers, should be the only child rearers.... This kind of shared responsibility for child care can only happen in small community settings where people know and trust one another. It cannot happen in those settings if parents regard their children as their 'property,' their possession (hooks, 1984:144).

Beyond Families "At Risk"

A popular way to see families that face challenges and to help them move toward a better future is to define these families as being "at risk." The **"at risk"** label has been applied to couples who have divorced parents who themselves might be seen to be "at risk" for divorce. It has been applied to children in families where the parents are survivors of childhood abuse. And it has been applied frequently to families in poverty and to single-parent families.

Helpful critiques have been put forward of "at risk" thinking about families by African-American and other minority sociologists in the United States. Swadener and Lubeck (1995:ix) argue that "... oppressed groups have reframed home and community as sources of strength and the dominant society as a source of barriers to advancement." They suggest instead that family, or **homeplace**, is a site of resistance to the power of the dominant society. This change in labelling can be empowering for families and for children, who then can draw from their communities the strength they need to move into the future.

Trends into Scenarios

Thinking about the future as an extension of the present, for better or worse, takes us back to the beginning of this chapter and the concept that the future evolves from the present and the past. Several current trends are considered here as they move into the future. Of the many that could be selected, we will attempt to shed light on three: dual- or multiple-income families, refilled nests, and family diversity across the life course.

Dual-Income Families

Dual-income families are seen as an important pattern of family change. It is not that women in the past did not work—they did, many of them for pay in the workforce, as well as at home. What is new in the late twentieth century in North America is the proportion of women with families who work outside the home. The fastest-growing labour-force participation rate between 1981 and 1991 in Canada occurred among mothers of preschool children. Maternal employment is no passing fad that will cease because some politicians or conservative forces try to push the clock back to the 1950s. The economy needs the wages and skills of women too much. And governments need the taxes women contribute.

That most couples will be working when they get together is a given these days. Career and job commitments may lead to postponed weddings and to more commuting relationships in the future. More husbands may follow their spouses' career or job opportunities in the future. Childbearing may be more delayed in the future but the emotional value placed on children will mean that most couples will indeed have children at some point.

With children and dual incomes will come the challenge to both work and family for both men and women. It could be that with changes in the global marketplace, men's work may not be as privileged as it was in the past, when men were seen as primary family providers. Women increasingly are taking on the role of provider in the 1990s in families where a man is present, as men's work becomes more precarious and insecure. This means changes in the roles and expectations of spouses and in the ways children come to see what mothers and fathers are and do.

Refilled Nests

What are refilled nests and what is the present and future trend for such nests? For a time it was the common pattern that children grew up and left the family home as soon as they reasonably could make their own way in the world. It may be that children still do this, but the age at which they are able to make their own way in the world has advanced considerably. Boyd and Pryor (1989) suggest that couples who thought that their children had grown up and "flown away" soon discover that the family home (nest) has been refilled with adult children who are: returning to school (or have never left school); having trouble finding or keeping jobs; getting separated or divorced; or even having children of their own. Family nests can refill readily when adult children bring their own children and possibly spouses back to the family home.

What does this trend mean when developed into a future scenario? In some ways, it could be a harkening back to the past, when extended families were presumed to share one home. In fact, this seldom occurred in reality since life expectancy was lower and there were not many three-generation families around, or around for long. It is also the case that many people did not prefer to live in multiple-generation families anyway and did so only when they had little choice (McDaniel & Lewis, 1997). The future may be, then, like the past: some families live in refilled nests only out of necessity and do not see themselves as creating anything new, merely pooling housing and resources to survive. Others, however, may see huge creative possibilities in refilled nests—for child care, for example, by grandparents while parents work; for sharing housework among more family members; for reducing environmental problems by having fewer accommodations; for developing new ways of intergenerational caring for elders. The probability is high that the range of options presented by and created in refilled nests will widen into the future, and that the phenomenon will not go away anytime soon.

Diversity across the Life Cycle

A different take on family diversity than discussed thus far is to consider diversity across the life cycle. One useful way to examine this diversity is to look at families in midlife, the period in which family diversity is widest. It could be, for example, that in midlife men are retiring early and women are beginning careers or education, some couples are having grandchildren, and others are having children for the first time. Some may be focusing on family as a priority for the first time in their lives, while others are focusing on work after a long time of attention to family. Some marriages may be breaking up, others just beginning.

The trend toward diversity in close relations across the life cycle reveals a clear pattern of individualization of family life. People live longer now than ever before. In the lifetime allotted to each of us, we can—and likely will—live in many kinds of family situations. This is true even if our family lives are stable and secure. Children have a tendency to grow up and leave home eventually—even if it takes them a longer time to do so! Couples find themselves in different family situations simply by living year after year. The longer we live, the more diversity of family we will face. Mix in other changes, such as divorce, remarriage, possibly living common-law at some point, and we quickly realize that the various kinds of family forms that

The trend toward diversity in close relations reveals a pattern of individualization of family life.

have been discussed in this book may actually take place for one person in his/her lifetime. The life-cycle perspective offers a different view of diversity and one well worth considering, if for no other reason than to promote tolerance of other ways of being close in families.

The Growth of Individualization

Let us focus on one particular aspect of this change—what we call the *individualization* of people's lives (Jones *et al.*, 1990; also Beck-Gernsheim, 1983; Schultz, 1983; and Herlyn & Vogel, 1989). With individualization, there is more variety, fluidity, and idiosyncrasy in all of the major demographic processes: in migration, marriage, divorce, childbearing, family decision-making, and the relation of work life and family life. This is because, with individualization, we expect people to be self-sufficient actors in their economic, household, leisure, and intimate relationships.

Individualization of social roles means the empowerment of women, through higher levels of formal education and more participation in the paid labour force. The rise of a service economy creates more employment opportunities for women and, in this way, speeds up the process. Ultimately, the growth in jobs that free people from family dependency and control is what increases the variety, fluidity, and idiosyncrasy of people's private lives. But they still need and want the support, the emotional attachments of family lives. What is it that families still offer people in this age of individualization? Why, given the choice, do most North Americans still value and desire marriage and children?

Intellectuals have always been quick to predict an end to "traditional," non-rational concerns like religion, ethnicity, and nationalism, among others; and they have usually been wrong. None of these has disappeared and some have increased in strength and importance around the world, with both good and bad consequences. Repeatedly, they have changed form and resurfaced. Today, the forces of religion, ethnicity, and nationalism remain among the most potent factors in people's lives. Rational economic or political concerns do not diminish them, nor are they mere justifications for imperialism or responses to discrimination. Anyone who is religious, feels nationalistic, or has an ethnic identity knows better than that. These things have a reality and a meaning of their own to both individuals and to society.

Family life is similar in that it is, to some degree, more emotional than rational. It, too, gives an important sense of belonging and identity. There is no sign that the human need for belonging is going to disappear. Yet there are also strong signs of *rationality*. People show signs of wanting to maximize their happiness by choosing their own destinies. When people have an opportunity to choose their own lives—for example, their mate, their living arrangement, or the number of children they will bear—they exercise this choice. In doing so they may ignore customary norms and expectations, or bend them to fit their own needs. This produces enhanced personal satisfaction but also social changes.

However, more personal choice also produces uncertainty and ambivalence about how, and when, to limit personal choice. Do we tolerate or celebrate the marriages of same-sex couples; support or oppose birth control awareness among teenagers; allow abortion in the situation of sexual abuse or violent sexual assault but not in other situations when it is sought? These lines are indeed difficult to draw and it is not clear in societies that are increasingly diverse and individualized who is drawing them, or whether lines should be drawn at all.

Not surprisingly, there is a strong conservative reaction to this uncertainty. Emotion-laden images are evoked of current family arrangements—for example, the growing participation of men in family life—or of the pleasures of family life in the "old days." Whether or not these are solidly based arguments does not affect their power to sway public opinion. Supporting this conservative reaction is a part of the population that has been spared much of the recent changes. For example, rural people are more likely to support resistance to contemporary family change.

The outcome of these struggles for and against change in family life is hard to predict. Generally, the ratio of facilitating to resistant responses will be determined by the rate at which opportunities for independence are increasing (for example, through a growth of jobs for women). Anything that (1) slows down the growth of opportunities after an initial growth, or (2) increases the individualization of lives faster than the creation of new cultural meanings and norms, or (3) otherwise produces uncertainty (for example, a war or environmental disaster) will increase support for a backward-looking mythology of the family.

How do people cope with the ambivalence and uncertainty of intimacy and close relations these days? Typically, they develop new social forms and invent new lifestyles to deal with the uncertainties they face. The struggle to create new rules is especially important for women, who have been kept from a wide range of choices in the past. Solutions to the problem of uncertainty include both formal and informal changes. *Formal* changes include laws and policies, such as new legislation to define marriage and its rights and obligations, to support gender equity and affirmative action for women, to improve daycare, and encourage fertility control. *Informal* changes include efforts people make in their own lives to negotiate new social roles and norms. For example, people work out new ways of disciplining the children of their spouse's first marriage, interacting with their mother's new boyfriend, or getting to know a co-worker's same-sex spouse.

A New Culture of Intimate Life

Out of all these efforts a new culture of intimate life emerges. Social and cultural changes, in turn, bring pressure for further structural changes by government and business. For example, the growth in part-time work, work sharing, and workplace child care all reflect, in part, new ideas about the relationship between work and family life. So do pressures on employers to pay health, retirement, or death benefits to non-traditional "spouses." In turn these changes further increase choice, uncertainty, and cultural change, so the cycle of family change continues.

With few exceptions, this cycle works similarly in all societies. However there are suppressers and enhancers at work. Bearing that in mind, what kinds of families are likely to result from this ongoing process of individualization? At least four main kinds of nuclear family are likely to appear; they differ along two main dimensions: (1) role separability and (2) personal interchangeability.

Role separability in families refers to the separation of being a spouse from being a parent. Many North American households are made up of cohabiting couples with children, or reconstituted or blended families, where spouses may or may not parent one another's children.

A second dimension, **personal interchangeability**, refers to the choosing of a spouse on the basis of ability to perform certain roles rather than for the individual's unique characteristics. People who marry for love choose a mate for his or her unique characteristics. People who marry for instrumental reasons are more interested in a mate who is a good provider, or who can produce healthy offspring. Personal interchangeability is well-suited to societies with high rates of mortality. By contrast, purely romantic marriages are unpredictable and unstable. They are a luxury best enjoyed in prosperous times.

Now we can cross-classify nuclear families along these two dimensions. Doing so yields four possibilities: we call them the (1) corporate, (2) collected, (3) concatenated, and (4) cyclical family, respectively (see Figure 11.5).

The **corporate family** is characterized by inseparable family roles and personal interchangeability. In this kind of family people can come and go without changing the essential structure of the family. The husband serves as father to the younger generation in the household—children, apprentices, and household servants—and the wife serves as mother, whoever the natural parents of these children may be.

This type includes what Zimmerman called the Trustee Family and what Ogburn called the Multifunctional Autonomous Family (see Goldenberg, 1987:131). It is only in a society dominated by this kind of family that people can reasonably think and speak of "the family" as a well-defined social institution. The institution of "the family" is protected in

Figure 11.5 FOUR TYPES OF FAMILY

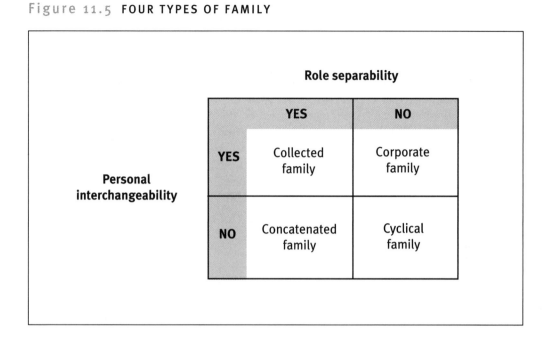

religion as well as by the state. In culture and by law, "the family" has social importance, enjoys its own resources, and commands its members' loyalties.

This kind of family emphasizes its members' duty to the group. As Sacks says, such families only exist because of choices people do *not* make:

> To be a child is to accept the authority of parents one did not choose. To be a husband or wife is to accept the exclusion of other sexual relationships. To be a parent is to accept responsibility for a future that I may not live to see (Sacks, 1991: 56–7).

In fact this kind of family is best suited to a theocratic, undifferentiated social structure. There, the state, the law, and religion are closely tied together and lean the same way on family matters. In societies where the corporate family dominates, competing models of life—for example, notions that individuals have rights and liberties—and competing institutions (like the secular school) hold little sway.

This "corporate family" existed among the nineteenth- and early twentieth-century European and North American middle classes. As we now know, its survival was aided by hypocrisy about the keeping of mistresses, involvements with prostitutes, visits to brothels, and carefully hidden homosexuality. It is a patriarchal family in which a double standard prevails and in which men are dominant. Today, the corporate family is still the dominant model in Western societies. However it is gradually losing support in law and public opinion.

By contrast, the **collected family** is characterized by separable roles and interchangeable performers. It is similar to Duberman's (1975) "reconstituted" family, which follows the remarriage of partners who have children from previous unions. Like the corporate family, the collected family requires family members to conform to traditional notions of husband, wife, father, mother, and child. However, given the complexities of remarriage, family members concede the impossibility of compelling mates to be both good spouses *and* good parents to the resident children.

In these families, it is not the family as a whole but the component roles that are the locus of loyalty, meaning, and resources. Children are permitted to feel close to their mother, for example, without feeling obliged to love her spouse or call him "Daddy." Mothers can feel they are doing their duty as a "good mother" even if they select a partner who, they have reason to believe, will not excel as a parent; and so on.

Societies like our own, with growing numbers of reconstituted families, are beginning to recognize the peculiar character and special needs of collected families. For example, the state increasingly delivers benefits to spouses or parents or children, not to the "family head" of earlier days. In this system, one cannot assume that the family has a "head." Nor is it thought proper to invent one for the purposes of dispensing state funds. The Census of Canada long ago changed from referring to "head of household" to simply calling one person in the household—whoever the person filling in the Census chooses—"Person 1." In 1988, the Canadian government began to send out family allowance cheques made payable to the custodial parent of a child, typically the mother. This change recognized the crucial difference between a corporate family and a collected family.

Such legal rethinking has commanded a great deal of attention over the 1980s and it is still going on in many jurisdictions. However this change is opposed by people who live in, or idealize, corporate families. After all, it concedes that corporate families are becoming less common; opponents argue that accepting this change makes families normatively less important to people's lives than they once were.

A third kind of family, the **concatenated family**, is exactly opposite to the corporate family, since it is characterized by separable roles and unique performers. From the outside, the concatenated family looks like a chance event, a slow collision of individuals in time and space. Indeed, the concatenated family is nothing more than a household at a particular moment in time. Here, meanings, loyalties, and resources are vested in individuals, not roles. Families exist only through the sharing of these meanings and resources. As a result, family members must constantly affirm and renegotiate the bases for this sharing.

Here, the meaning of *spouse* or *parent* is no longer certain. It is highly idiosyncratic from one person to another, hence from one household to another. Occasionally definitions will mesh for long periods of time. Sometimes, a shortage of alternatives will keep the household from dissolving despite a failure of definitions to mesh. In any event we cannot assume, in these families, that members will have a permanent commitment to "the family" or even to their current spouse and children.

The concatenated family is an extreme version of radical individualism. It assumes that people ought to have unlimited free choice in their living arrangements. This freedom is subject only to the legal protection of minors from the consequences of family breakdown and the protection of all family members from household violence. Family life is perceived as a lifestyle or individual choice—so far as the adults are concerned, a kind of supermarket for intimate relations.

In this system, mating is motivated mainly by considerations of the spouse's unique characteristics, which may not continue to allure. Childbearing is motivated by a biological drive to reproduce or by personal self-expression—a form of psychic consumption of children for personal pleasure. Under these conditions, marital dissolution will likely be frequent, because of the high premium on varied experience. Childbearing continues, but at lower levels, because it is expensive, reduces marital satisfaction, and makes household dissolution more difficult.

Not surprisingly, this family system creates an enormous number of potential kinship connections (Gross, 1987). Along with this goes a lot of confusion about parenting responsibilities and property rights. However, more mothers than fathers will remain with their children in the event of a divorce. So in practice, concatenated families (with children) tend to be more matrifocal. Women and children remain, men come and go.

In North America and Europe, concatenated families are still far from the average. Yet they are common in certain sub-groups (for example, the poorest and wealthiest classes, and among migrant or artistic communities). They may become an increasingly common though transient experience in many people's lives. That is, many people will spend a part of their lives in concatenated families (just as they spend a part of their lives in collected or corporate families).

Like the corporate family, the **cyclical (or recycled) family** features traditional (inseparable) roles. But unlike the corporate family, there is no interchangeability in the cyclical family. Instead, the performances of its members are unique. Indeed, each is a "return engagement" occurring *because of* the unique relationship of the members. This return engagement may be a second marriage of the same people, which is rare but occurs. More often, it is a second parenthood, during which people are called upon to parent their now-adult children (occasionally called "boomerang children") a second time.

For example, in Canada since 1981 the percentages of men and women between ages 20 and 34 years living with parents has risen significantly. The result is a complex household that *looks* like a corporate family but has none of the predictability or normative power of that older arrangement. Many reasons account for the return of adult children. They include unemployment, insufficient income for accommodation, or the need for additional education or babysitting help.

Unique family situations result from an interaction between the reasons for return and expectations of the children and parents. For example, the parents may expect their grown children to be tidy, follow curfews, and be independent. The children may expect to be looked after, even to receive an allowance. Yet they violate household rules regarding the use of cars, stereo systems, home space, and so on. Naturally, conflicts can arise from these differences. There can also be mutual support and benefit for both generations.

Alongside these differences in expectations, problems also arise out of feelings of guilt or a desire to maintain good relations with one another (usually, parents trying to maintain good relations with their children). Norms to guide behaviour in these circumstances are not yet established, so we witness what amounts to a series of unique performances.

What If ...?

Sorting out what is likely to happen with families in the future from hype and hope is not an easy task, even for those most familiar with current research and trends. Nonetheless, it is part of the human process to speculate. One way to think about the future is to imagine what would happen if the things some people hope for actually came to pass. Based on existing knowledge, what would the consequences be? The editors of *American Demographics* (1997) have done just this, but unfortunately not for families specifically.

Let's take one example. Some wishful thinkers want (and some policy-makers seem to be encouraging) mothers of preschool children to leave the workforce and devote their adult lives to family. What would happen if they did? All answers are based on the best available data in the United States and Canada. Family incomes would drop 32 percent in the United States (*American Demographics*, 1997:39), and 27 percent in Canada (Statistics Canada, 1997b:3). Even after taking into consideration costs that would not be incurred, such as for daycare and other work-related expenses, families would still suffer a net loss of income.

The loss would be greatest for those dual-income families in which the wife earns more than the husband (22 percent of dual-earner families in the U.S., 15 percent in Canada). There would be reduced overall spending too (except on food at home), which would slow down the economy. Employers would lose valuable employees and suitable substitutes among men would be hard to find. And lastly, the editors of *American Demographics* mention what might happen to the women themselves who leave paid employment for family:

> We're talking about a generation of women for whom a job is much more than a paycheck ... 63 percent of married women with children under age 6 work because it pays, one way or another. There's nothing to suggest they won't keep doing so (*American Demographics*, 1997:40).

Policy Challenges

Societies are not particularly wise in anticipating the challenges that will face them in a few years time. Nor are they fully able to figure out what steps to take in policy to meet these challenges, or even if policy is the best method. Nonetheless, even in these times of government lessening in North America, policy, both public and private, matters to our plans. Business plans involve anticipating changes and, hopefully, developing in the directions of those trends, however approximately. It is now recognized that society's ultimate objectives—good quality of life and long life for as many of its citizens as possible, together with a productive and growing economy—do not lend themselves readily to direct intervention. Nevertheless, some issues and challenges are emerging out of the mists of the future, which we ignore at our peril. We will focus on a few of these as distinct family policy challenges.

Growing family inequalities pose one such challenge. If all families in Canada are divided into five equal groups by income level, some interesting current trends emerge in the 1995–96 period. The top group with the highest incomes actually increased their family incomes most (Statistics Canada, 1997b:20), while the lowest group with the lowest family incomes lost most. The result is increasing family income inequality in Canada, a trend apparent since 1980. Since many more families in the lowest income groups depend on government sources for at least part of their income (about 59 percent in 1996 according to Statistics Canada (1997c:18)), it is decreasing government contributions that account most for the growth in inequality. At the same time, government support and tax policies continue to have the effect of reducing family income inequalities (Statistics Canada, 1997c:21). The concern for the future is whether continuing declines in government support for low-income families will further increase family inequality in Canada. The unfortunate conclusion is that this is likely.

Some might wonder whether family inequality is a problem at all. Research evidence suggests that it is, and a significant problem, too—not only for those families with low income, but for all of society. In groundbreaking research, Wilkinson (1994) has shown that mortality rates and life expectancies in the industrialized world are more related to the degree of income inequality than to *per capita* income or *per capita* economic growth. What factors are involved here and how are they related to family?

> The importance of relative income to health suggests that psychological factors related to deprivation and disadvantage are involved. That is to say, it is less a matter of the immediate physical effects of inferior material conditions than of the social meanings attached to those conditions and how people feel about their circumstances and about themselves (Wilkinson, 1994:70).

McDaniel (1998a) shows how meanings given to relative deprivation filter through families. Poor children in affluent societies feel negatively about themselves and often blame their families for the relative deprivation. This has severe implications for their life chances and potential to contribute to society. Cheal (1996:xv) adds that the higher risk of being poor while a child and the fact that government programs seem to do so little for low-income families with children is a huge cause for concern about families and society in the future. Poor children often grow up to be poor adults or adults whose early deprivation prevents them from catching up on growth, education, skills acquisition, or lost hope.

If mothers of young children continue to work for pay in the numbers they currently do, society will have to find a way to care for those children.

A second major emerging policy challenge is child care. If mothers of young children continue to work for pay in the numbers they currently do, and if "motherwork" remains a woman's domain primarily, some solution to caring for children while mothers work must be found. In the lengthy public deliberation on the pros and cons of daycare, children who need care while mothers work are not getting the kind of care they need. The capacity of all care facilities and options combined in both the U.S. and Canada represents only a fraction of the demand. The large baby boom generation does not make this mismatch any easier. Pressures are likely to increase on businesses as well as on governments to provide child care at the worksite or in the home neighbourhood, as well as to continue to develop means to meet working people's family needs such as parental leaves, flexible work hours, recreational facilities for children, and after-school programs.

This issue is central to the future of families, since without some solution, couples may have little choice but to restrict their childbearing even further or forgo parenthood altogether. As with growing family inequality, all of society would suffer as a result. Child care is also crucial to gender equality, since without access to affordable child care, women who become mothers may be forced to restrict themselves to lower-paying or part-time work rather than contribute to society in ways commensurate with their talents and education. This flies in the face of deeply held values of equality of opportunity for all, and the idea that education should pay off for individuals, who take advantage of its opportunities and for society, which reaps the rewards of a creative, contributing, and educated workforce.

Family policy challenges are complex and diverse but may be central to the future of families and of us all. We openly acknowledge the centrality of families to our individual lives and happiness as well as to our collective futures, and yet we seem reluctant to meet the needs of families in developing creative solutions. Lesemann and Nicol (1995:124) argue that "It is paradoxical that the family seems simultaneously to be recognized and supported by the government ... and abandoned by it...."

Concluding Remarks

We conclude this examination of the future of close relations in families with two seemingly contradictory ideas. The first is that the ways in which we form and maintain close relations with others are a product of the times in which we live and the larger contexts in which families exist. The second is that we ourselves make our own families and in doing so, contribute to the strength of the society in which we live. The contradiction is that we are both created by and create society in families. Let us look at the second idea first.

We make our future; it is not made for us. This is nowhere more true than with close relations, where our choices and the means by which we relate to those closest to us determine so much of what we are, our life chances, and our happiness and well-being. Close ties among people are not going to go out of style anytime soon, despite the deeply felt concerns some might have about the demise of family as they might know it, or wish it to be. People need the security, the "warm fuzzy" feeling that close relations with others bring; they will not quickly abandon committed and permanent bonds. The forms that those bonds might take, however, will likely not be what they were in the past.

Family sociology has come to see people and people's important actions as central to their futures as well as our collective future. Nowhere is this more the case than in close relations. One way to see choices in a framework is to imagine individuals and societies with sociocultural "toolkits" with which they work as carpenters, constructing their family worlds with care and expertise. They occasionally hit their thumbs with a tool or make mistakes but they learn from those mistakes. Practice, communication, new habits, beliefs, and symbols all constitute the tools by which we build strong, healthy, enabling families.

At the same time, close relations and the possibilities they entail for us are shaped by the times and circumstances in which we live. Challenges to families are large, and sometimes global—in terms of security, balancing work with family, balancing the needs of individual family members with the needs of the family overall, changing technologies, and keeping families going and together in the face of forces that tear them apart, such as immigration, war, poverty, violence, and drugs. The meaning of family is changing in a rapidly changing world.

In the intersection of large-scale social changes and the individual choices we make about close relations exists the opportunity for connection with others, for creating a new and better world, for realizing our deepest dreams. Choices are always made within social contexts and constraints. The more we know and understand those contexts and constraints, the better our choices can be. Our hope is that this book will at least make each of you think more deeply about close relations and what they can be.

CHAPTER SUMMARY

We contemplate, in this chapter, the future of close relations, beginning with a clear understanding that social prediction is far from a perfect science or art. Contesting visions of families in the future are considered. We look at the effects of gender, distant relationships caused by greater mobility, and technological change. Shedding light on the centrality of gender to families has opened new possibilities for studying, understanding, and explaining how and why families change. Relationships between adult children and their parents are challenging when they live far apart. Technologies can be complex and contradictory in their effects.

The future of family studies involves huge, but exciting, challenges to those seeking to explain and understand family change. The study of families remains haunted by vested interests in particular ways to be familial. Family research into the future is being built on a critical perspective on families and close relations, which means not a critique of family, but of the ways in which we studied families in the past. There may be no grand theory that can encompass all the ways of being a family.

Challenges for families in the future include providing themselves with material security, a challenge increasing of late as more and more families are pinched by economic change. Another challenge is to see clearly the diversity of ways to be family, not only the different forms but different ways to relate and give meaning to close relations within the same family forms. A third challenge is to move beyond what is widely called the "families at risk" way of thinking.

Lastly, several current trends are developed into future scenarios and we ask what would happen if mothers actually did stay home with their small children.

The chapter ends with some consideration of policy challenges into the future.

KEY TERMS

Collected family: One characterized by separable roles and interchangeable performers.

Concatenated family: One characterized by separable roles and unique performers.

Corporate family: One characterized by inseparable family roles and personal interchangeability.

Cyclical family: One characterized by traditional (inseparable) roles and unique performers.

Families at risk: Usually a concept applied to families where the spouses are separated, divorced, never married, and living in poverty; and/or to abusive, deprived situations.

Fictive kin: People who are not relatives but who act like family.

Homeplace: A term used first by African-Americans and sociologists in the United States to describe the home/family/close relations as a place of resistance to the power of dominant society.

Other-mothering: Taking on mothering roles and responsibilities for someone other than one's own child.

Personal interchangeability: The degree to which a person, such as a spouse, is chosen for the ability to fill a certain role (e.g., being a good provider) rather than for unique personal characteristics.

Postmodern: A general distrust of grand theories, ideologies, and explanations that purport to explain all social behaviours.

Role separability: In families, the separation of being a spouse from being a parent.

SUGGESTED READINGS

Cheal, David. 1996. *New Poverty: Families in Postmodern Society*. Westport, Connecticut: Greenwood Press. This book explores in detail the relationships between current family challenges and the risks of poverty today. In particular, the focus is on poverty that is related to modernization or globalization.

Hochschild, Arlie Russell. 1997. *The Time Bind: When Work Becomes Home and Home Becomes Work*. New York: Metropolitan Books. This book reports on an original study of people employed in one corporation in the United States. It explores through qualitative interviews the ways in which people see families and work. The big finding is that people in this workplace tend to see work as a refuge from family and its pressures.

Mann, Susan A., Michael D. Grimes, Alice Abel Kemp, & Pamela J. Jenkins. 1997. "Paradigm Shifts in Family Sociology? Evidence from Three Decades of Family Textbooks," *Journal of Family Issues* 18(3):315–349. This article examines family sociology texts over thirty years and dis-

covers some changes in the ways family is approached and studied. However, the study also finds that traditional images of families and old theories still colour how family sociology is taught.

McDaniel, Susan A. 1997. "Intergenerational Transfers, Social Solidarity, and Social Policy: Unanswered Questions and Policy Challenges," *Canadian Public Policy/Canadian Journal on Aging* (Joint issue):1–21. This article looks with a broad lens at intergenerational transfers and develops a conceptual framework for filling in what we do not as yet know about these transfers. Intergenerational transfers are argued to be at the heart of social continuity and cohesion, as well as the core of social policy challenges. It points toward policy questions that need addressing, such as inequalities in society that are perpetuated over generations, the relation of private and public transfers of wealth and resources, and the degree to which the experiences of today's generations approximates those of tomorrow's.

REVIEW QUESTIONS

1. What are two views of historical change, either or both of which can influence how the future of close relations is seen?

2. What are two major issues for the future of close relations and families?

3. In the family / work realms of our lives, which is generally solace from which, according to new research?

4. What is the main premise of the social movement, The Promise Keepers?

5. What are some of the effects on close relations of computers and the Internet?

6. Why is it that the future of family studies may depend on a postmodern approach?

7. List two central challenges that families in the future will face.

8. Which families are at greatest risk for low income? Which families are at the lowest risk?

9. Why is it said in this chapter that the term "family" may be too restrictive?

10. What is the main thesis of those who oppose the "families at risk" concept?

DISCUSSION QUESTIONS

1. What would you write about families and close relations today, if you were a social historian looking back on the 1990s in 2020?

2. Why has family become such a public issue recently? Do you anticipate that such public debate will continue into the foreseeable future?

3. What do you suppose are the next political dimensions families will face / experience?

4. How could a study be designed to measure the effects (both good and bad) of one new technology on close relations? Be creative in your approach.

5. If "families at risk" approaches are discarded, what could usefully replace them?

6. If you were in charge, how would you begin to improve financial security for all families?

7. Looking at families across the life course opens new possibilities for seeing our own family futures. Outline what you would like your family future to be as you age. Then outline what you think it will be.

8. How can we in society make the kinds of futures we wish families to have?

9. What steps can be taken to ensure that people forming families begin with the skills and resources they need for this challenging undertaking?

10. If you were writing this last chapter on the future of families and close relations, what would you add to the future challenges families face?

WEBLINKS

http://www.sc.edu/ifis/

The Institute for Families in Society seeks to enhance family well-being through interdisciplinary research, education, and consultation at community, state, national, and international levels. For the Institute's *Family Futures Magazine*, see

http://www.sc.edu/ifis/web6.html

http://www.ag.ohio-state.edu/~ohioline/ lifetime

Life Time

A quarterly newsletter to help employed people balance work and family, published by Ohio State University Extension.

GLOSSARY

ABCX family crisis model: A model that explains family crisis in terms of a stressor event A, the family's crisis-meeting resources B, the family's interpretation of the event C, and the resulting crisis X.

Acculturative stress: Stress caused by the difficulties of adapting to a new society, such as the need to learn a new language and a new set of social behaviours and problems in obtaining employment.

Adverse selectivity: A tendency for people who choose to engage in a given behaviour to be, by nature of the kind of people they are, also at risk for a given outcome; selectivity may create the appearance of cause-and-effect relationships where they do not exist.

Affective nurturance: Caring for another with emotional attachment.

Amae: In Japanese culture, a desire for bodily closeness with family and friends developed by frequent and intense bodily contact between parents and infants.

Anomie: A state of normative confusion; a lack of rules and regulations.

Arranged marriage: A marriage in which the bride and groom are chosen for each other by their relatives.

Artificial insemination: A process of introducing semen into a woman's body without sexual intercourse; can be a medical process but may not be.

Attachment: A state of intense emotional dependence on someone (especially a parent); a social bond involving affection and a feeling of belonging.

Authoritarian parenting: A style of parenting characterized by low acceptance (i.e., little liking and respect is shown for children) and high control.

Authoritative parenting: A style of parenting characterized by high acceptance (i.e., liking and respect for children) and high control.

Autonomy: Independence; ability to make choices and direct one's own life.

Battered-child syndrome: The condition of children traumatized, physically and mentally, by severe abuse.

Bilateral: Referring to a kinship system in which descent or lineage is traced through the families of both the mother and the father.

Binuclear family: A term used to describe a blended family, or a family where the spouses each bring children and non-residential parents into a new family. This term enables the capturing of the concept of family as extending beyond household.

Blended family: Typically describing a family comprising two previously married spouses with children who marry each other and bring their children together in a new family.

Boundary work: The effort to draw and maintain lines between different spheres of life, such as family and work; often difficult for people who work at home.

Caring: Putting the needs of others, particularly of one's family, ahead of one's own. Or, the provision of support and assistance to others, often dependent family members.

Chronic stressors: Ongoing factors that increase stress, such as poverty, disability, and chronic physical or mental illness.

Circular causal model: A model of family violence that views both partners in an abusive spousal relationship as contributing to the escalation of the abuse.

Class stratification: A social system in which some groups have significantly more material goods, opportunities, and social status than others.

Cohesion: Attachment of family members to each other and to the family itself.

Cohort effect: An effect that influences everyone of roughly the same age, such as a war, depression, or industrial change.

Coitus interruptus: A natural contraceptive method whereby the man withdraws from sexual intercourse prior to ejaculation.

Collected family: One characterized by separable roles and interchangeable performers.

Companionate marriage: Marriage in which the partners are in love and find pleasure in each other's company.

Concatenated family: One characterized by separable roles and unique performers.

Conflict Tactics Scales: An instrument developed by Murray Straus to measure the extent of domestic violence based on frequency and severity of incidents.

Control and supervision: The extent to which parents monitor and influence their children's behaviour.

Convergence theory: A sociological theory that holds that social forces such as urbanization, industrialization, and education lead inevitably to changes in social and family structure, so that ultimately family structures will be much the same the world over; and that these changes are beneficial.

Corporate family: One characterized by inseparable family roles and personal interchangeability.

Crude birth rate: Number of live births per 100 000 population.

Cultural gap: Conflict between parents and children based on differing expectations that occur either in a rapidly changing culture or among immigrants.

Cultural rationale: Justification for a behaviour based on beliefs commonly held within a culture.

Culturally induced stress: Stress from the guilt people feel when they cannot meet all the obligations of work and family they feel society expects from them.

Culture: The language, perspective, and skills, the likes and dislikes, and the cluster of norms, values, and beliefs that characterize a group of people.

Culture lag: A lack of fit that results when our material conditions in life change faster than our cultural values and norms.

Custom adoption: Adoption of a child, especially among First Nations peoples, which does not proceed through legal processes but instead is based on traditional understandings and customs.

Custom of the country/ à la façon de la pays: The long-standing practice among early fur traders in Canada to take aboriginal "wives," who were known as "country wives."

Cycle of abuse: A tendency for family violence to replicate itself from one generation to the next, as abused girls and daughters of abused mothers grow up to become abused women, and abused boys or sons of abusive fathers grow up to become abusive husbands or fathers.

Cyclical family: One characterized by traditional (inseparable) roles and unique performers.

Debriefing: Conversation between spouses about what happened during the day, which may serve both to convey information and to share support.

Demographers: Researchers who study the processes of population, most notably fertility, mortality, and migration.

Determinant: A factor that contributes to an outcome (such as divorce) without necessarily being the direct or principal cause.

Discipline: The enforcement of rules to control children's behaviour (not necessarily through punishment).

Domestic violence: Family violence; violence against any member of the household, including a child, spouse, parent, or sibling.

Domesticity: The attribute of caring about home and family; considered to be characteristic of women.

Dysfunctional family: A family that works so badly that its members would be better off on their own.

Elder abuse: Physical violence, psychological cruelty, or neglect directed at an older person, usually by a caregiving family member.

Endogamy: Marriage to a partner from the same social group or geographical locale (village, area, etc.).

Enmeshment: Very close relationships that blur appropriate boundaries between family members.

Exogamy: Marriage to a partner from outside one's social group or geographical locale.

Extended family: A multigenerational family in which grandparents, parents, children, and perhaps other relatives (aunts, uncles, cousins, etc.) share a household; or a description of such relatives even if they do not live together.

Families at risk: Usually a concept applied to families where the spouses are separated, divorced, never married, and living in poverty; and/or to abusive, deprived situations.

Family allowances: A now-ended federal policy that provided some income to mothers of dependent children. The policy exists now only in Quebec.

Family cohesion: Sticking together as a family, with its own group identity, social life, and activities that involve the members.

Family household: A household whose members are related to each other by blood, marriage, or adoption.

Family work: All the various kinds of work needed to keep families going, including the menial chores of housework but also child care and child rearing.

Femininity: A cluster of characteristics, such as nurturance, sensitivity, and gentleness, traditionally considered natural to women, but which can be found in men or women; couples where both spouses have these characteristics tend to be well adjusted.

Fictive kin: People who are not relatives but who act like family.

Flexibility: Ability within a family structure to allow members to change their ideas, roles, and relationships as the situation demands.

Flextime: A variety of arrangements, formal or informal, that allow employees some freedom to decide when to work their allotted hours.

Gemeinschaft: The type of community typical of pre-industrial rural life, in which everyone knows everyone else and people share common values.

Gender gap: Differences in men's and women's opportunities and treatment, for example in workplaces.

Gender socialization: The part of the socialization process through which people learn gender-based habits of behaviour, as they learn to associate gender with their personal identity and with distinctive activities.

Glass ceiling: An unofficial but real barrier limiting women's advancement up a career ladder.

Hegemonic: Relating to a ruling or powerful group or class; men who have been raised in a patriarchal culture tend to expect the benefits of male dominance, including domestic services from women.

Heterogamy: Marriage between people who are significantly different in race, religion, or sociocultural background.

Home office: A workplace within a home, used by self-employed people or employed people who are able to work at home, usually on computer.

Homeplace: A term used first by African-Americans and sociologists in the United States to describe the home/family/close relations as a place of resistance to the power of dominant society.

Homogamy: A tendency for people to marry people from similar socioeconomic and cultural backgrounds, partly because they have more opportunities to meet such people.

Identity support: Parents' respect, acceptance, and emotional support for a child.

Idioms: Expressions that form a private language for a couple, including pet names, inside jokes, and special words or phrases for intimate or special activities.

Imperial entity: An element that dominates all of a person's life and life decisions (used to describe work in modern life).

Imported housewives: Nannies and domestics who are brought into North American and European homes to do the kind of family work that is not being done by the wives and mothers in those families. These people are not really housewives, but they do the work of housewives, often for little pay and under poor working conditions.

In vitro fertilization: Generally known as test-tube fertilization; conception that occurs by bringing together ova and sperm in medical procedures.

In loco parentis: Literally, "in the place of parents"; refers to the assumption of parent-like responsibility by public institutions, such as schools, or by individuals such as step-parents, grandparents, or other caregivers.

Induction: A type of discipline based on teaching good behaviour by example and rewarding imitation.

Instrumental communication: The frequency with which an adolescent talks to his/her parents about problems, plans, etc.

Intergenerational contagion: A process by which trends that begin in one generation may be adopted by other generations. An example is cohabitation, which was mostly a youthful phenomenon, but has now been adopted by people of all generations.

Internal moral control: Control of one's own behaviour because of a feeling of right and wrong, rather than to avoid punishment.

Interpersonal conflict: Violence that almost exclusively involves pushing, shoving, grabbing, and slapping.

IUD (Intrauterine Device): A contraceptive device medically inserted into a woman's uterus that prevents conception.

Job sharing: An arrangement in which two people work part-time to fill what would otherwise be a single full-time job.

Kibbutz: A quasi-communal, usually agricultural community in Israel; in early kibbutzim children were largely raised communally in a vast social experiment at replacing the family with the community as the chief socializing influence.

Kin-keeper: The family member who keeps the family in contact through holidays, special occasions, letter-writing or phone calls, arranging family reunions, or by other means.

Kinship group: A group of people who recognize a blood relationship and have positions in a hierarchy of rights over the property.

Latchkey youth: Children who are home alone two or more days per week.

Looking-glass self: A self-concept constructed from the way we appear to others, which is then reflected back to us.

Love withdrawal: A type of discipline based on threatened emotional punishment (withholding parental affection) for a child who does not comply with rules.

Macro-level: The broad level of examining a social phenomenon, focusing on changes that affect society as a whole.

Major life transitions: Disruptions to family life caused by changes such as the birth of a child, the death of a parent, divorce, and retirement.

Major upheavals: Disruptions that affect many people simultaneously, such as war and natural disasters.

Marriage gradient: The tendency of men, on average, to marry someone who is a little younger, a little less well educated, a little lower in socioeconomic status and slightly shorter than they are; or conversely, of women to marry men who are a little older, a little more educated, a little higher in socioeconomic status, and slightly taller than they are. This results in a gradient of marriage partners that leaves out tall women and short men differentially, as well as very well-educated, well-off women and poor men with little education.

Material resources: The tangible things people need to deal with whatever life brings, such as money, time, and energy.

Maternity leave: Time off work, especially paid or partly paid, to give birth or to care for a new child.

Matriarchy: A society of family type/system in which women have more power or authority than men.

Matrilineal: Referring to a kinship system in which descent or lineage is traced through the family of the mother.

Means of production: The tools and conditions through which goods or services are produced and people earn a living.

Mechanization of housework: Generally refers to the introduction of various technologies into households that make housework easier to do.

Meso-level: A middle range at which a social phenomenon may be examined, focusing on demographics: the characteristics of the people affected.

Micro-level: The smallest level at which a social phenomenon may be examined, the level of interactions between individuals and effects on individuals.

Micro/macro: Referring to the different levels on which problems can be addressed: Micro refers to strategies carried out by individuals and families, and macro to strategies at the level of the organization or state.

Mommy track: A career path for women who work part-time or turn down additional responsibilities in order to care for children; can relegate them to lower status and reduce chances for promotion.

Monogamy: The system of marriage in which one is married to one person to whom one is expected to be loyal and faithful.

Neolocal residence: Wife and husband (bride and groom) live in a residence separate from their parents.

Neonaticide: The murder of a newborn.

No-fault divorce: Divorce granted on the basis of marital breakdown rather than of specific wrong-doing (e.g., adultery) on the part of one spouse or the other.

Nonfamily household: A household containing unrelated individuals or people who live alone.

Non-systematic abuse: Abuse that involves relatively serious violent acts, such as threats, throwing objects, kicking, and hitting.

Other-mothering: Taking on mothering roles and responsibilities for someone other than one's own child.

Overload: The excessive amount of work many people—especially mothers—have to do.

Parental involvement: Emotional and practical commitment of parents to children, shown by spending time with them, talking with them, and thinking and talking about them.

Paternity leave: Time off work, especially paid or partly paid, to allow a man to spend time with his new child.

Patriarchal value system: A set of standards for behaviour within a culture that takes for granted the natural rightness of male dominance.

Patriarchy: A society or family type / system in which men have more power and authority than women.

Patrilineal: Referring to a kinship system in which descent or lineage is traced through the family of the father.

Permissive parenting: A style of parenting characterized by high acceptance (i.e., liking and respect for children) and low control.

Personal interchangeability: The degree to which a person, such as a spouse, is chosen for the ability to fill a certain role (e.g., being a good provider) rather than for unique personal characteristics.

Polygamy: A system of marriage in which adults are allowed to marry more than one person at time, even if they do not actually do so.

POSSLQ: Person of the opposite sex sharing living quarters.

Post-gender families: Families in which the division of labour is not based on gender.

Postmodern: A general distrust of grand theories, ideologies, and explanations that purport to explain all social behaviours.

Post-traumatic stress disorder (PTSD): An anxiety disorder experienced by people who have survived or witnessed some very disturbing event, such as war, natural disaster, accident, or abuse, characterized by psychological numbing, increased arousal, and a tendency to relive the trauma repeatedly.

Power assertion: A type of discipline based on threatening to punish a child for noncompliance with rules.

Predictor: A characteristic that is correlated with and precedes an outcome but may or may not be a cause.

Primary labour market: Jobs that are secure and well-paying and, typically, have entry requirements (e.g., educational credentials or specialized job experience) which relatively few people can satisfy.

Primary socialization: Learning that takes place in the early years of a person's life.

Propinquity theory: The theory that people tend to associate with and eventually marry those who live near them or work or go to school or university with them.

PSSSLQ: Person of the same sex sharing living quarters.

Psychological and emotional resources: The internal strengths people need to be able to deal with whatever life brings, including adaptability, the ability to understand what is happening and to talk about it, and willingness to accept help.

Relationship dynamics: The patterns of interaction, communication styles, expressions of emotion, and intimate practices between spouses.

Role polarization: A tendency to view male and female roles as fixed and separate.

Role separability: In families, the separation of being a spouse from being a parent.

Romantic love: Idealized or sentimental love.

Sanitary reformers: Public health advocates who, in the late nineteenth and early twentieth centuries in Canada, urged bylaws preventing the keeping of farm animals in towns and cities.

Second shift: Housework and child care done by women who are also doing a full day of paid work.

Secularization: A move away from religion as an organizing principle of society

Sexual double standard: Social rules governing appropriate sexual conduct that differ markedly for men and women, and typically also by class, race, and ethnicity.

Sexual script: The social rules of sexual behaviours for men and for women.

Sibling abuse: Violence by one sibling against another.

SNAF: An acronym meaning Standard North American Family, or mother, father, two kids, and usually a dog or a cat.

Social disorganization: A breakdown of societal functioning.

Social integration: The state of societies that are closely knit and stable, in which people hold similar world views and there is a strong consensus on social rules.

Social isolation: A lack of social support from kin, friends, co-workers, etc.

Social mobility: The potential for an individual or family to experience significant change in their social status.

Social pathology: A broad-based distress or disorganization within society.

Socialization: The social learning process a person goes through to become a capable, functioning member of society.

Socioeconomic status: Class; standing in society in terms of income, education, and prestige.

Spillover: Strains and demands from the workplace brought into the family—or from the family into the workplace.

Spousal violence: Physical abuse between spouses. It may be reciprocal ("common couple violence") or directed by one partner against the other, and may occur between cohabitors as well as legally married couples.

Status inconsistency: Lack of congruence between the various indicators of social class, such as education and occupation, or wealth and prestige.

Stressor: A challenge or threat to a person or group that can cause stress.

Structural powerlessness: Lack of control over their own home and work lives experienced by people because of social and economic factors related to the formal and informal structures of society.

SWAH: Supplemental work at home; work from home for people who also work out of an office.

Systematic abuse: Abuse that involves a high risk of life-threatening violence such as beating, choking, and attacks with knives and guns.

Telework or telecommuting: Work done away from the office using telecommunications equipment.

The revenge of the cradle: A historical term used to describe Quebec's long-standing high birth rates as "revenge" against perceived social injustices felt by the Quebec people surrounded as they were (and are) by an anglophone country and continent.

Thomas Dictum: The observation that a situation that is believed to be real is real in its consequences.

Traditional family values: A term commonly used by those who hold such views to describe support for male dominance, the gender-based division of labour, and strong parental discipline of children.

Unengaged parenting: A style of parenting characterized by low acceptance (i.e., little liking and respect is shown for children) and little control.

Union libre: Widely used term for common-law union in Quebec.

Virtual workplace: The hypothetical place in which people work (especially by computer or telephone) without physically going to a workplace such as an office or factory.

Wage gap: The difference between men's and women's earning power.

References

Abrar, Stefania. 1996. "Feminist intervention and local domestic violence policy," *Parliamentary Affairs* 49 (1):191–205.

Abu-Laban, Sharon McIrvin & Susan A. McDaniel. 1998. "Beauty, status and aging," pp. 78–102 in Nancy Mandell (Ed.), *Feminist Issues: Race, Class and Sexuality* (2nd edition). Scarborough: Prentice Hall Allyn and Bacon.

Adams, Gerald R., Thomas Gullotta & Mary Anne Clancy. 1985. "Homeless adolescents: A descriptive study of similarities and differences between runaways and throwaways," *Adolescence* 20: 715–724.

Adams, Jeffrey M. & Warren H. Jones. 1997. "The conceptualization of marital commitment: an integrative analysis," *Journal of Personality and Social Psychology* 72(5):1177–1196.

Adams, Owen B. & Dhruva Nagnur. 1990. "Marrying and divorcing: A status report for Canada," in Craig McKie & K. Thompson (Eds.), *Canadian Social Trends*. Toronto: Thompson Educational Press.

Adelmann, Pamela K., Kirsten Chadwick & Dana Royce Baerger. 1996. "Marital Quality of Black and White Adults Over the Life Course," *Journal of Social and Personal Relationships* 13(3):361–384.

Adlaf, Edward M., Yola M. Zdanowicz & Reginald G. Smart. "Alcohol and other drug use among street-involved youth in Toronto," *Addiction Research* 4(1)11–24.

Aguilar, Rudy J. & Narina Nunez Nightingale. 1994. "The impact of specific battering experiences on the self-esteem of abused women," *Journal of Family Violence* 9 (March): 35–45.

Alberta Advisory Council on Women's Issues. 1996. *Breadmakers and Breadwinners ... The Voices of Alberta Women*. Edmonton: Alberta Advisory Council on Women's Issues.

Aldarondo, Etiony & David B. Sugarman. 1996. "Risk marker analysis of the cessation and sersistence of wife assault," *Journal of Consulting and Clinical Psychology*. 64 (Oct.)1010–1019.

Alford-Cooper, Finnegan. 1993. "Women as family caregivers: An American social problem," *Journal of Women and Aging* 5(1):43–57.

Allen, Mike & Nancy Burrell. 1996. "Comparing the impact of homosexual and heterosexual parents on children: Meta-analysis of existing research," *Journal of Homosexuality* 32(2):19–35.

Allison, David B., Michael C. Neale, Melissa I. Kezis & Vincent Alfonso, "Assortative mating for relative weight: Genetic implications," *Behavior Genetics* 26(2):103–111.

Amato, Paul R. 1994. "The impact of divorce on men and women in India and the United States," *Journal of Comparative Family Studies* 25 (summer).

Amato, Paul R. 1996. "Explaining the intergenerational transmission of divorce," *Journal of Marriage and the Family* 58 (Aug.).

Amato, Paul R & Alan Booth. 1995. "Changes in gender role attitudes and perceived marital quality," *American Sociological Review* 60 (Feb.).

Amato, Paul R. & Alan Booth. 1996. "A prospective study of divorce and parent-child relationships," *Journal of Marriage and the Family* 58 (May).

Amato, Paul R., Laura Spencer Loomis & Alan Booth. 1995. "Parental divorce, marital conflict and offspring well-being during early adulthood," *Social Forces* 73(3).

Amato, Paul R. & Sandra J. Rezac. 1994. "Contact with nonresident parents, interparental conflict and children's behavior," *Journal of Family Issues* 15 (June).

American Demographics Editors. 1997. "What If...?" *American Demographics* (Dec.):38–45.

Ammerman, Robert T & Richard J. Patz. 1996.

"Determinants of child abuse potential: Contribution of parent and child factors," *Journal of Clinical Child Psychology* 25 (Sep.): 300–307.

Anderson, B.E. 1995. "Children's development related to day-care, type of family and other home factors," *European Child and Adolescent Psychiatry* 5,(suppl. 1):73-75.

Angenent, Huub L., Balthasar M. Beke & Paul G. Shane. 1991. "Structural problems in institutional care for youth," *Journal of Health and Social Policy* 2(4):83–98.

Angus Reid Group. 1994. *The State of the Family in Canada*. Angus Reid Group: Toronto.

Anthony, E.J. 1970. "The impact of mental and physical illness on family life," *American Journal of Psychiatry* 127:138–145.

Antill, John K. & Sandra Cotton 1987. "Self disclosure between husbands and wives: Its relation to sex roles and marital happiness," *Australian Journal of Psychology* 39(1):11–24.

Arat-Koc, Sedef. 1990. "Importing housewives: Non-citizen domestic workers and the crisis of the domestic sphere in Canada," pp. 81–104 in Meg Luxton, Harriet Rosenberg & Sedef Arat-Koc (Eds.), *Through the Kitchen Window: The Politics of Home and Family (2nd enlarged edition)*. Toronto: Garamond.

Arat-Koc, Sedef. 1992. "In the privacy of our own home: Foreign domestic workers as a solution to the crisis of the domestic sphere in Canada," pp. 149–174 in M.P. Connelly & Pat Armstrong (Eds.), *Feminism in Action*. Toronto: Canadian Scholars Press.

Arber, Sara & Jay Ginn. 1995. "The mirage of gender equality: occupational success in the labour market and within marriage," *British Journal of Sociology* 46(1):21–43.

Arendell, Terry J. 1995. "Fathers in divorce: 'Best case scenarios'," *American Sociological Association*.

Arditti, Joyce A. 1997. "Women, divorce, and economic risk," *Family and Conciliation Courts Review* 35(1).

Armistead, Lisa, Rex Forehand, Steven R.H. Beach & Gene H. Brody. 1995. "Predicting interpersonal competence in young adulthood: The role of family, self and peer systems during adolescence," *Journal of Child and Family Studies* 4(4).

Armstrong, Pat & Hugh Armstrong. 1994. *The Double Ghetto: Canadian Women and Their Segregated Work (3rd edition)*. Toronto: McClelland & Stewart.

Aronson, Jane. 1994. "Women's sense of responsibility for the care of older people: 'But who else is going to do it?' pp. 175–194 in Victor Marshall & Barry McPherson (Eds.), *Aging: Canadian Perspectives*. Peterborough, Ontario: Broadview Press.

Arroyo, Judith A., Tracy L. Simpson, & Alfredo S. Aragon. 1997. "Childhood sexual abuse among Hispanic and non-Hispanic white college women," *Hispanic Journal of Behavioral Sciences* 19 (Feb):57–68.

Aryee, Samuel & Vivienne Luk. 1996. "Balancing two major parts of adult life experience: Work and family identity among dual-earner couples," *Human Relations* 49 (4): 465–487.

Aseltine, Robert H. Jr. 1996. "Pathways linking parental divorce with adolescent depression," *Journal of Health and Social Behavior* 37 (June).

Atwood, Joan D. & Madeline Seifer. 1997. "Extramarital affairs and constructed meaning: A social constructionist therapeutic approach," *The American Journal of Family Therapy* 25 (spring).

Aube, Jennifer & Richard Koestner. 1995. "Gender characteristics and relationship adjustment: Another look at similarity complementarity hypotheses," *Journal of Personality* 63(4).

Averill, Patricia & Thomas G. Power. 1995. "Parental attitudes and children's experiences in soccer: Correlates of effort and enjoyment," *International Journal of Behavioral Development* 18(2):263-276.

Axinn, William G. & Arland Thornton. 1993. "Mothers, children, and cohabitation: The intergenerational effects of attitudes and behavior," *American Sociological Review* 58(2):233–246.

Bahr, Howard M. & Bruce A. Chadwick. 1980. "Sex and social change in Middletown," in Stephen J. Bahr (Ed.), *Economics and The Family*. Lexington, Mass: Lexington Books.

Bakan, Abigail & Daiva K. Stasiulis. 1995. "Making the match: Domestic placement agencies and the racialization of women's household work," *Signs* 20(2):303–335.

Baker, David B & Kevin McCall. 1995. "Parenting stress in parents of children with attention deficit hyperactivity disorder and parents of children with learning disabilities," *Journal of Child and Family Studies* 4(Mar.):57–68.

Baker, Maureen. 1994. *Canada's Changing Families: Challenges to Public Policy*. Ottawa: Vanier Institute of the Family.

Baker, Maureen. 1995. *Canadian Family Policies: Cross-National Comparisons*. Toronto: University of Toronto Press.

Baker, Maureen. 1996a. "Introduction to family studies: Cultural variations and family trends," pp. 3–34 in Maureen Baker (Ed.), *Families: Changing Trends in Canada (3rd Edition)*. Toronto: McGraw Hill Ryerson.

Baker, Maureen. 1996b. "The future of family life," pp. 299–317 in Maureen Baker, *Families: Changing Trends in Canada (3rd edition)*. Toronto: McGraw Hill Ryerson.

Baker, Maureen & Donna Lero. 1996. "Division of labour: Paid work and family structure," pp. 78–103 in Maureen Baker (Ed.), *Families: Changing Trends in Canada*. Toronto: McGraw-Hill Ryerson.

Baker, Robin, Gary Kiger & Pamela J. Riley. 1996. "Time, dirt and money: The effects of gender, gender ideology and type of earner marriage on time, household-task and economic satisfaction among couples with children," *Journal of Behavior and Personality* 11(5):161–177.

Balakrishnan, T.R., Evelyne Lapierre-Adamcyk & Karol J. Krotki. 1993. *Family and Childbearing in Canada: A Demographic Analysis*. Toronto: University of Toronto Press.

Barnett, Mark A., Steven W. Quackenbush & Christina S. Sinisi. 1996. "Factors affecting children's, adolescents', and young adults' perceptions of parental discipline," *Journal of Genetic Psychology* 157(4):411–424.

Barnett, Ola W., Tomas E. Martinez, & Mae Keyson. 1996. "The relationship between violence, social support, and self-blame in battered women," *Journal of Interpersonal Violence* 11 (June):221–233.

Belsky, J. 1990. "Parental and nonparental child care and children's socioemotional development: A decade in review," *Journal of Marriage and the Family* 52:885–903.

Belsky, Jay & David Eggebeen. 1991. "Early and extensive maternal employment and young children's socio emotional development: Children of the National Longitudinal Survey of Youth," *Journal of Marriage and the Family* 53(4):1083–1098.

Belsky, Jay & Michael Rovine. 1990. "Patterns of marital change across the transition to parenthood: Pregnancy to three years postpartum," *Journal of Marriage and the Family* 52(1):5–19.

Belsky, Jay, Sharon Woodworth and Keith Crnic. 1996. "Trouble in the second year: Three questions about family interaction," *Child Development* 67(2):556–78.

Belt, William & Richard Abidin. 1996. "The relation of childhood abuse and early parenting experiences to current marital quality in a nonclinical sample," *Child Abuse and Neglect* 20 (Nov.):1019–1030.

Ben-David, Amith & Yoav Lavee. 1996. "Between war and peace: Interactional patterns of couples under prolonged uncertainty," *The American Journal of Family Therapy* 24 (winter):343–357.

Bennun, Ian. 1997. "Systemic marital therapy with one partner: A reconsideration of theory, research and practice," *Sexual and Marital Therapy* 12(1).

Berger, Brigitte & Peter L. Berger. 1983. *The War*

Over the Family: Capturing the Middle Ground. London: Hutchinson.

Bergmann, Barbara. 1987. *The Economic Emergence of Women.* New York: Basic Books.

Bernard, Jessie. 1973. *The Future of Marriage.* New York: Bantam.

Bernardes, Jon. 1993. "Responsibilities in studying postmodern families," *Journal of Family Issues* 14(1): 35–49.

Bernier, C., S. Laflamme & R.M. Zhou. 1996. "Housework: Reductions in gender division and development of a complicated problem," *Canadian Review of Sociology and Anthropology* 33(1):1–21.

Bernier, Leon, Anne Morisette & Gilles Roy. 1992. "A need for love, or feelings gone awry," *Revue internationale d'action communautaire* 27(67): 101–115.

Berry, Mary Frances. 1993. *The Politics of Parenthood: Child Care, Women's Rights and the Myth of the Good Mother.* New York: Viking.

Beyer, Sylvia. 1995. "Maternal employment and children's academic achievement: parenting styles as mediating variable," *Developmental Review* 15(2):212–253.

Biggs, Simon, Chris Phillipson & Paul Kingston. 1995. *Elder Abuse in Perspective.*

Bischoff, Richard J; McBride, Andrea. 1996. "Client perceptions of couples and family therapy," *American Journal of Family Therapy* 24(2).

Blair-Loy, Mary F. 1996. "Career and family patterns of executive women in finance: Evidence of structural and cultural change," American Sociological Association, Association paper.

Boje, Thomas P. 1995. "Introduction to Part III," *International Journal of Sociology* 25(2):1–8.

Boney-McCoy, Sue & David Finkelhor. 1996. "Is youth victimization related to trauma symptoms and depression after controlling for prior symptoms and family relationships? A longitudinal, prospective study," *Journal of Consulting and Clinical Psychology.* 64 (Dec.):1406–1416.

Booth, Alan & Paul R. Amato. 1994. "Parental marital quality, parental divorce and relations with parents," *Journal of Marriage and the Family* 56 (Feb).

Bosman, Rie. 1994. "Educational attainment of children in mother-headed families: The impact of socialization," *Netherlands Journal of Social Sciences* 30(2):148–169.

Boyd, Monica & Susan McDaniel. 1996. "Gender inequality in the Canadian policy context: A mosaic," *Revista Mundial de Sociologia* 2:25–50.

Boyd, Monica & Edward T. Pryor. 1989. "The cluttered nest: The living arrangements of young adult Canadians," *Canadian Journal of Sociology* 14(4): 461–477.

Bradbury, Bettina. 1984. "Pigs, cows and boarders: Non-wage forms of survival among Montreal families, 1861–91," *Labour/Le Travail* 14:9–46.

Bradbury, Bettina. 1996. "The social and economic origins of contemporary families," pp. 55–77 in Maureen Baker (Ed.), *Families: Changing Trends in Canada (3rd Edition).* Toronto: McGraw Hill Ryerson.

Brannen, Stephen J. & Allen Rubin. 1996. "Comparing the effectiveness of gender-specific and couples groups in a court-mandated spouse abuse treatment program," *Research on Social Work Practice* 6(4): 405–424.

Bray, James H. & Ernest N. Jouriles 1995. "Treatment of marital conflict and preventions of divorce," *Journal of Marital and family Therapy* 21(4).

Brehl, Robert. 1998. "Internet can be a home wrecker," *The Globe and Mail,* 23 February: A1,A5.

Brinkerhoff, Merlin B. & Eugen Lupri. 1988. "Interspousal violence," *Canadian Journal of Sociology* 13 (4):407–434.

Bronstein, Phyllis, Paula Duncan & Adele D'Ari. 1996. "Family and parenting behaviors predicting middle school adjustment: A longitudinal study," *Family Relations* 45 (Oct.):415–426.

Broude, Gwen J. 1996. "The realities of daycare," *Public Interest* 125(fall):95–105.

Brown, Jennifer S.H. 1992. "A Cree nurse in the cradle of Methodism: Little Mary and the Egerton R. Young family at Norway House and Berens River," pp.93–110 in Bettina Bradbury (Ed.), *Canadian Family History: Selected Readings.* Toronto: Copp Clark Pitman.

Bruce, N. 1970. "Delinquent and non-delinquent reactions to parental deprivation," *British Journal of Criminology* 10:270–276.

Bruhn, J.G. 1977. "Effects of chronic illness on the family," *Journal of Family Practice* 4:1057–1067.

Brumberg, Joan Jacobs. 1998. *The Body Project.* New York: Random House.

Brunstein, Joachim C., Gabriele Dangelmayer & Oliver C. Schultheiss. 1996. "Personal goals and social support in close relationships: Effects on relationship mood and marital satisfaction," *Journal of Personality and Social Psychology* 71(5).

Bryant, H.D. *et al.* 1963. "Physical abuse of children: An agency study," *Child Welfare* 42:125–130.

Burton, Roberta & Michael McGee. 1996. "The relational systems model: An analysis of Gottman's findings on marital success," *Journal of Family Social Work* 1(4):3–17.

Burden, D. & B. Googins. 1987. "Vulnerability of working parents: Balancing work and home roles." *Social Work* 32 (4): 295–299.

Buss, David M. & Todd K.Shackelford. 1997. "From vigilance to violence: Mate retention tactics in married couples," *Journal of Personality and Social Psychology* 72(2).

Buchmann, Marlis & Maria Charles. 1995. "Organizational and institutional factors in the process of gender stratification: Comparing social arrangements in six European countries," *International Journal of Sociology* 25(2):66–95.

Buntain-Ricklefs, Joanne J., Kathi J. Kemper, Michelle Bell & Thomas Babonis. 1994. "Punishments: What predicts adult approval?" *Child Abuse and Neglect* 18(11):945–955.

Burden, D. & B. Googins.1986 Boston University *Balancing Job and Homelife Study: Managing Work and Family Stress in Corporations.* Boston: Boston University School of Social Work.

Burnette, B.A. 1975. "Family adjustments to cystic fibrosis," *American Journal of Nursing* 75 1986–1999.

Burstein, Paul, R. Marie Bricher & Rachel L. Einwohner. 1995. "Policy alternatives and political change: Work, family, and gender on the congressional agenda, 1945–1990," *American Sociological Review* 60(Feb.): 67–83.

Busby, Dean M. 1991. "Violence in the family," pp. 335–385 in Stephen J. Bahr (Ed.), *Family Research: A Sixty-Year Review, 1930–1990, Volume 1.* New York: Lexington Books, Maxwell Macmillan International.

Buss, David M. 1985. "Human mate selection," *American Scientist* 73(1): 47–51.

Bussell, Danielle A. 1995. "A pilot study of African American children's cognitive and emotional reactions to parental separation," *Journal of Divorce and Remarriage* 24(3–4).

Butler, Ruth and Nurit Ruzany. 1993. "Age and socialization effects on the development of social comparison motives and normative ability assessment in kibbutz and urban children," *Child Development* 64(2):532–543.

Call, Vaughn R A, Susan Sprecher & Pepper Schwartz. 1995. "The incidence and frequency of marital sex in a national sample," *Journal of Marriage and the Family* 57 (Aug.).

Campbell, A. 1980. "The sense of well-being in America: Recent patterns and trends." New York: McGraw-Hill.

Campbell, Jacquelyn C, Paul Miller & Mary M. Cardwell. 1994. "Relationship status of battered women over time," *Journal of Family Violence* 9 (June):99–111.

Campbell, Rebecca, Cris Sullivan & William S. Davidson. 1995. "Women who use domestic violence shelters: Changes in depression over time," *Psychology of Women Quarterly* 19 (June):237–55.

Canadian Council on Social Development. 1997.

The Progress of Canada's Children. Ottawa: Canadian Council on Social Development.

Cancian, Francesca. 1987. *Love in America.* New York: Cambridge University Press.

Caradec, Vincent. 1997. "Forms of conjugal life among the 'young elderly,'" *Population: An English Selection* 9:47–74.

Carr, Deborah. 1996. "Two paths to self-employment? Women's and men's self-employment in the United States, 1980," *Work and Occupations* 23(1):26–53.

Carrier, Sylvie 1995. "Family status and career situation for professional women," *Work, Employment, and Society* 9(2):343–358.

Carstensen, Laura L., John M. Gottman & Robert W. Levenson. 1995. "Emotional behavior in long-term marriage," *Psychology and Aging* 10 (Mar).

Carswick, Kelly. 1997. "Canadian caregivers," *Canadian Social Trends*, 2 (winter).

Cascardi, Michele, K. Daniel O'Leary, Erika E. Lawrence. 1995. "Characteristics of women physically abused by their spouses and who seek treatment regarding marital conflict," *Journal of Consulting and Clinical Psychology* 63:616–623.

Cashdan, Elizabeth. 1994. "A sensitive period for learning about food," *Human Nature* 5(3):279–291.

Cavan, R. & K.R. Ranck. 1938, *The Family and the Depression*, Chicago: University of Chicago Press.

CBC News, "The Family-Friendly Workplace: A Look at Two Companies," 23 March 1994.

Cernkovich, S.A. & Peggy C. Giordano. 1987. "Family relationships and delinquency," *Criminology* 25:295–321.

Chadwick, B.A. & C.B. Chappell, 1980. "The two-income family in Middletown, 1924–1978," in *Economics and The Family.* Stephen J. Bahr (Ed.) Lexington, Mass: Lexington Books.

Chafetz, Janet Saltzman & Jaqueline Hagan. 1996.

"The gender division of labor and family change in industrial societies: A theoretical accounting," *Journal of Comparative Family Studies*, 27 (summer):187–219.

Chan, Anna Y & Ken. R. Smith. 1996. "A comparison of the marital quality and stability of interracial and same-race marriages," American Sociological Association.

Chan, Yuk-Chung. 1994. "Parenting stress and social support of mothers who physically abuse their children in Hong Kong," *Child Abuse and Neglect* 18 (Mar.):261–269.

Chao, Ruth K. 1994."Beyond parental control and authoritarian parenting style: Understanding Chinese parenting through the cultural notion of training," *Child Development* 65(4):1111–1119.

Chao, Ruth K. 1996. "Chinese and European American mothers' beliefs about the role of parenting in children's school success," *Journal of Cross Cultural Psychology* 27(4): 403–423.

Cheal, David. 1991. *Family and the State of Theory.* Toronto: University of Toronto Press.

Cheal, David. 1993. "Unity and difference in postmodern families," *Journal of Social Issues* 14(1):3–19.

Cheal, David. 1996. *New Poverty: Families in Postmodern Society.* Westport, Connecticut: Greenwood Press.

Cheal, David. 1997. "Hidden in the household: Poverty and dependence at different ages," Paper presented at the Conference, Intergenerational Equity in Canada, 20–21 February. Statistics Canada, Ottawa.

Cherry, Andrew. 1993. "Combining cluster and discriminant analysis to develop a social bond typology of runaway youth," *Research on Social Work Practice* 3(2):175–190.

Chilton, R.J. & G.E. Markle. 1972. "Family disruption, delinquent conduct and the effect of subclassification," *American Sociological Review*, 37:93–99.

Choi, Alfred & Jeffrey L. Edleson. 1996. "Social Disapproval of Wife Assaults: A National

Survey of Singapore," *Journal of Comparative Family Studies* 27(1):73–88.

Choi, Namkee G. 1995. "Long-term elderly widows and divorcees: Similarities and differences," *Journal of Women and Aging* 7(3).

Christensen, Donna-Hendrickson & Kathryn D. Rettig. 1995. "The relationship of remarriage to post-divorce co-parenting," *Journal of Divorce and Remarriage* 24(1–2).

Church, Elizabeth. 1996. "Kinship and stepfamilies," pp. 81–106 in Marion Lynn (Ed.), *Voices: Essays on Canadian Families*. Scarborough, Ontario: Nelson.

Church, Elizabeth. 1998. "Ottawa relaxes work rules on foreign spouses," *The Globe and Mail* 2 October 1998:B23.

Clark, Roger & Terry Clifford. 1996. "Towards a resources and stressors model: The psychological adjustment of adult children of divorce," *Journal of Divorce and Remarriage* 25(3–4).

Clark, Susan M. 1993. "Support needs of the Canadian single parent family," pp. 223–238 in Joe Hudson & Burt Galaway (Eds.), *Single Parent Families: Perspectives on Research and Policy*. Toronto: Thompson.

Clarke, Sally & Barbara Wilson. 1994. "The relative stability of remarriage; a cohort approach using vital statistics," *Family Relations* 43(July).

Clarke-Stewart, K. Allison. 1991. "Does day care affect development?" *Journal of Reproductive and Infant Psychology* 9(2-3):67–78.

Clifford, Terry & Roger Clark. 1995. "Family climate, family structure and self-esteem in college females: The physical vs. psychological-wholeness divorce debate revisited, *Journal of Divorce and Remarriage* 23(3–4).

Climo, Jacob. 1992. *Distant Parents*. New Brunswick, NJ: Rutgers University Press.

Coleman, H.H., M.L. Weinman, & P.H. Bartholomew. 1980. "Factors affecting conjugal violence," *Journal of Psychology* 105:197–202.

Coleman, Marilyn, Lawrence Ganong & Susan M.

Cable. 1997. "Beliefs about women's intergenerational family obligations to provide support before and after divorce and remarriage," *Journal of Marriage and the Family* 59 (February):165–176.

Coleman, Jean U. & Sandra M. Stith. 1997. "Nursing students' attitudes toward victims of domestic violence as predicted by selected individual and relationship variables," *Journal of Family Violence*. 12 (June):113–138.

Collier, Linda M., Juliet Dee, Douglas Fraleigh & Joseph J. Hemmer. 1995. "Interact: A symposium of responses to the Hate Speech Forum," *Howard Journal of Communications* 5(4):317–330.

Collins, Patricia Hill. 1990. "Mammies, matriarchs and other controlling images," pp. 67–90 in *Black Feminist Thought: Knowledge, Consciousness and the Politics of Empowerment*. Boston: Union Hyman.

Collins, Randall. 1975. *Conflict Sociology: Toward an Explanatory Science*. New York: Academic Press.

Collins, Stephen. 1991. "The transition from lone-parent family to step-family," pp. 156–175 in Michael Hardy & Graham Crow (Eds.), *Lone Parenthood: Coping with Constraints and Making Opportunities in Single-Parent Families*. Toronto: University of Toronto Press.

Coltrane, Scott. 1998. *Gender and Families*. Thousand Oaks, California: Pine Forge Press.

Conger, Rand D., Xiaojia Ge & Glen H. Elder, Jr. 1994. "Economic stress, coercive family process, and developmental problems of adolescents," *Child Development*. 65(Apr.): 541–61.

Conte, Anthony E. 1994. "The discipline dilemma: Problems and promises," *Education* 115 (2):308–331.

Contreras, Raquel, Susan S. Hendrick & Clyde Hendrick. 1996. "Perspectives on marital love and satisfaction in Mexican American and Anglo-American couples," *Journal of Counseling and Development* 74(4).

Cook, Donelda A. & Michelle Fine. 1995. "Motherwit: Childrearing Lessons from African-

American Mothers of Low Income," pp. 118–142 in Beth Blue Swadener & Sally Lubeck (Eds.), *Children and Families "At Promise": Deconstructing the Discourse of Risk.* Albany: State University of New York Press.

Cooksey, Elizabeth C., Elizabeth G. Menaghan & Susan M. Jekielek. 1997. "Life course effects of work and family circumstances on children," *Social Forces* 76(2):637–667.

Cooney, Teresa M. & Jane Kurz. 1996. "Mental health outcomes following recent parental divorce: The case of young adult offspring," *Journal of family issues* 17(4).

Coontz, Stephanie. 1992. *The Way We Never Were: American Families and the Nostalgia Trap.* New York: Basic Books.

Corak, Miles. 1998. "Death and Divorce: The Long-Term Consequences of Parental Loss," Paper presented at the 2nd CILN Conference, Burlington, Ontario, 27–28 September 1998.

Correa, Sonia. 1994. *Population and Reproductive Rights: Feminist Perspectives from the South.* London: Zed Books.

Cortex, J.B. & F.M. Gatti. 1972. *Delinquency and Crime: A Biopsychosocial Approach*, New York: Seminar Press.

Cote, Marguerite Michelle. 1992, "A painful situation still crying out for a solution: Montreal's street youth," *Revue internationale d'action communautaire* 27(67):145–152.

Cowan, Carolyn Pape & Philip A. Cowen. 1995. "Interventions to ease the transition to parenthood: Why they are needed and what they can do," *Family Relations* 44(Oct.).

Cox, Chante L., Michael O. Wexler, Caryl E. Rusbult & Stanley O. Gaines, Jr. 1997. "Prescriptive support and commitment processes in close relationships," *Social Psychology Quarterly* 60(1):79–90.

Creamer, Mark & Ian M. Campbell. 1988. "The role of interpersonal perception in dyadic adjustment," *Journal of Clinical Psychology* 44 (3):424–430.

Crohan, Susan E. 1996. "Marital quality and conflict across the transition to parenthood in African American and white couples," *Journal of Marriage and the Family* 58 (Nov.).

Cross, Gary & Richard Szostak. 1995. "Women and work before the factory," pp. 37–51 in Gary Cross & Richard Szostak, *Technology and American Society: A History.* Englewood Cliffs, New Jersey: Prentice Hall.

Crouter, Ann C. & Beth Manke. 1994, "The changing American workplace: Implications for individuals and families," *Family Relations* 43(Apr.):117–124.

Crouter, Ann C. 1984. "Spillover from family to work: The neglected side of the work-family interface," *Human Relations* 37(6):425–441.

Currie, Dawn. 1988. "Rethinking what we do and how we do it: A study of reproductive decisions," *Canadian Review of Sociology and Anthropology* 25(2):231–253.

D'Emilio, John & Estelle B. Freedman. 1988. *Intimate Matters: A History of Sexuality.* New York: Harper Row.

Daly, Martin & Margo Wilson. 1985. "Child abuse and other risks of not living with both parents," *Ethology and Sociobiology* 6(4):197–210.

Dasgupta, Shamita Das & Sujata Warrier. 1996. "In the footsteps of 'Arundhati': Asian Indian women's experience of domestic violence in the United States," *Violence Against Women* 2(3): 238–259.

Davies, Lorraine & Patricia Jane Carrier. 1998. "The importance of power relations for the division of household labour," *Canadian Journal of Sociology* 23(4).

Davis, Liane V., Jan L. Hagen & Theresa J. Early. 1994. "Social services for battered women: Are they adequate, accessible, and appropriate?" *Social Work* 39:695–704.

Davis, Phillip W. 1996. "Threats of corporal punishment as verbal aggression: A naturalistic study," *Child Abuse and Neglect* 20(4):289–304.

Davis, Robert C. & Barbara Smith. 1995. "Domestic

violence reforms: Empty promises or fulfilled expectations?" *Crime and Delinquency* 41 (Oct.) 541–552.

Degliantoni, Lisa. 1997. "I love you just the way you are," *Psychology Today* 30 (Mar./April).

DeKeseredy, Walter S. & Katharine D. Kelly. 1995. "Sexual abuse in Canadian university and college dating relationships: The contribution of male peer support." *Journal of Family Violence* 10 (1): 41–53.

DeKeseredy, Walter S. & Katharine D. Kelly. 1993. "The incidence and prevalence of woman abuse in Canadian university and college dating relationships." *Canadian Journal of Sociology* 18 (2): 137–159.

DeKeseredy, Walter S. & Martin D. Schwartz. 1994. "Locating a history of some Canadian woman abuse in elementary and high school dating relationships," *Humanity and Society* 18(3):49–63.

DeMaris, Alfred & Steven Swinford. 1996. "Female victims of spousal violence: Factors influencing their level of fearfulness," *Family Relations* 45 (Jan.):98–106.

Demi, Alice, Roger Bakeman & Linda Moneyham. 1997. "Effects of resources and stressors on burden and depression of family members who provide care to an HIV-infected woman," *Journal of Family Psychology* 11 (Mar.):35–48.

Demo, David H & Alan C. Acock. 1996. "Single-hood, marriage and remarriage: The effects of family structure and family relationships on mothers' well-being," *Journal of Family Issues* 17(3).

Desjardins, Bernard & Jean Dumas. 1993. *Population Aging and the Elderly, Current Demographic Analysis*. Ottawa: Statistics Canada. Catalogue no.91-533E.

Desrosiers, Hélène, Celine LeBourdais & Benoit Laplante. 1995. "The Breakup of Reconstituted Families: The Experience of Canadian Women," *Recherches Sociographiques* 36(1):47–64.

Devine, Danielle & Rex Forehand. 1996. "Cascading toward divorce: The roles of marital and child

factors," *Journal of Consulting and Clinical Psychology* 64 (April).

Devine, John. 1995. "Can metal detectors replace the panopticon?" *Cultural Anthropology* 10(2):171–195.

Dixon-Mueller, Ruth. 1993. *Population Policy and Women's Rights*. Westport, Connecticut: Praeger.

Doherty, William J.& Deborah S. Simmons. 1996. "Clinical practice patterns of marriage and family therapists: A national survey of therapists and their clients," *Journal of Marital and Family Therapy* 22(1).

Dooley, Martin. 1993. "Recent changes in the economic welfare of lone mother families in Canada: The roles of market work, earnings and transfers," pp. 115–132 in Joe Hudson & Burt Galaway (Eds.), *Single Parent Families: Perspectives on Research and Policy*. Toronto: Thompson.

Douglass, Frazier M.& Robin Douglass. 1995. "The marital problems questionnaire (MPQ): A short screening instrument for marital therapy," *Family Relations* 44 (July).

Duong Tran, Quang, Serge Lee & Sokley Khoi. 1996. "Ethnic and gender differences in parental expectations and life stress," *Child and Adolescent Social Work Journal* 13 (Dec.) 515–526.

Drakich, Janice. 1993. "In whose best interest? The politics of joint custody," pp. 331–341 in Bonnie Fox (Ed.), *Family Patterns, Gender Relations*. Toronto: Oxford.

Dronkers, Jaap 1996. "The effects of parental conflicts and divorce on the average well-being of pupils in secondary education," American Sociological Association,.

Ducibella, John, S. 1995. "Consideration of the impact of how children are informed of their parents' divorce decisions: A review of the literature," *Journal of Divorce and Remarriage* 24 (3–4).

Dudley, James R 1996. "Noncustodial fathers speak about their parental role," *Family and Conciliation Courts Review* 34(3).

Dunne, G. 1997. *Lesbian Lifestyles: Women, Work and the Politics of Sexuality.* Toronto: University of Toronto.

Duran-Aydintug, Candan. "Former spouses exiting role identities," *Journal of Divorce and Remarriage* 24(3–4):195.

Duran-Aydintug & Marilyn Ihinger-Tallman. 1995. "Law and stepfamilies," *Marriage and Family Review* 21(3–4):169–192.

Durkheim, Émile. 1915/1957. *The Elementary Forms of the Religious Life.* New York: Free Press.

Durodoye, Beth A. 1997. "Factors of marital satisfaction among African American couples and Nigerian male/African American female couples," *Journal of Cross-Cultural Psychology* 28(1).

Duxbury, Linda Elizabeth, Christopher Alan Higgins & D. Roland Thomas. 1996. "Work and Family Environments and the Adoption of Computer-Supported Supplemental Work-at-Home," *Journal of Vocational Behavior* 49 (1):1–23.

Dwyer, Diane C; Paul R. Smokowski, John C. Bricout. "Domestic violence research: theoretical and practice implications for social work," *Clinical Social Work Journal* 23 (summer):185–198.

Easterlin, Richard & Eileen Crimmins. 1991. "Private materialism, personal self-fulfillment, family life and public interest: the nature, effects and causes of recent changes in the values of American youth," *Public Opinion Quarterly* 55:499–533.

Eells, Laura Workman & Kathleen O'Flaherty. 1996. "Gender perceptual differences in relation to marital problems," *Journal of Divorce and Remarriage* 25(2).

Ehrensaft, Mirian K. & Dina Vivian. 1996. "Spouses' reasons for not reporting existing marital aggression as a marital problem," *Journal of Family Psychology* 10(4).

Eichler, Margrit. 1988. *Families in Canada Today: Recent Changes and Their Policy Consequences (2nd Edition).* Toronto: Gage.

Eichler, Margrit. 1997. *Family Shifts: Families, Policies and Gender Equality.* Toronto: Oxford University Press.

Eichstedt, Jennifer L. 1996. "Heterosexism and gay/lesbian/bisexual experiences: Teaching strategies and exercises," *Teaching Sociology* 24:384–388.

Ek, Carl A. & Lala Carr Steelman. 1988. "Becoming a runaway: From the accounts of youthful runners," *Youth and Society* 19(3):334–358.

Elder, Glen H. Jr. 1992. "Models of the Life Course," *Contemporary Sociology* 21:632–635.

Ellison, Christopher G. 1996. "Conservative Protestantism and the corporal punishment of children: Clarifying the issues," *Journal for the Scientific Study of Religion* 35(1):1–16.

Ellison, Christopher G. , John P. Bartkowski & Michelle L. Segal. 1996. "Conservative Protestantism and the parental use of corporal punishment," *Social Forces* 74(3):1003–1028.

Elmer, E. & G. Gregg. 1967. "Developmental aspects of abused children, *Pediatrics* 50: 596–602.

Emanuels-Zuurveen, Lineke & Paul M.G Emmelkamp. 1996. "Individual behavioral-cognitive therapy v. marital therapy for depression in maritally distressed couples," *British Journal of Psychiatry* 169(2).

Emanuels-Zuurveen, Lineke & Paul M. G. Emmelkamp. 1997. "Spouse aided therapy with depressed patients," *Behavior Modification* 21(1).

Engle, Patrice L. Sarah Castle & Purnima Menon. 1996. "Child Development: Vulnerability and Resilience," *Social Science and Medicine* 43(5): 621–635.

Epstein, Rachel. 1996. "Lesbian Families," pp. 107–130 in Lynn, Marion (Ed.), *Voices: Essays on Canadian Families.* Toronto: Nelson Canada.

Erel, Osnat & Bonnie Burman. 1995, "Interrelatedness of marital relations and parent-child relations: A meta-analytic review," *Psychological Bulletin* 118 (July).

Erel, Osnat, Gayla Margolin & Richard S. John.

1998. "Observed sibling interaction: Links with the marital and the mother-child relationship," *Developmental Psychology* 34(2):288–298.

Erikson, Erik H. 1950. *Childhood and Society*. New York: Norton.

Ezra, Marni & Melissa Deckman. 1996. "Balancing work and family responsibilities: Flextime and child care in the federal government," *Public Administration Review* 56 (Mar/Apr.): 174–179.

Family Matters: Papers in Post-Confederation Canadian Family History. Toronto: Canadian Scholars Press.

Farhood, Laila, Huda Zurayk, Monique Chaya, Fadia Saadeh, Garbis Meshefedjian, & Thuraya Sidani. 1993. "The impact of war on the physical and mental health of the family: The Lebanese experience," *Social Science and Medicine* 36(12):1555–1567.

Fast, Janet E., Norah C. Keating, Leslie Oakes, & Deanna L. Williamson. 1997. *Conceptualizing and Operationalizing the Costs of Informal Elder Care*. NHRDP Project No. 6609–1963-55. Ottawa: National Health Research and Development Program, Health Canada.

Fellegi, Ivan. 1997. "Statistical services: Preparing for the future," Chief Statistician of Canada's presentation to the United Kingdom Statistics Users Conference, 11 November 1997, London.

Ferri, Elsa. 1993. "Socialization Experiences of Children in Lone Parent Families: Evidence from the British National Child Development Study," pp. 281–290 in Joe Hudson & Burt Galaway (Eds.), *Single Parent Families: Perspectives on Research and Policy*. Toronto: Thompson.

Field, B. 1972. "The child with spina bifida: Medical and social aspects of the problems of a child with multiple handicaps and his family," *Medical Journal of Australia* 2:1294–1287.

Fineman, Martha Albertson & Roxanne Mykitiuk (Eds.) 1994. *The Public Nature of Private Violence: The Discovery of Domestic Abuse*. New York, NY: Routledge.

Finklehor, David, Nancy Asdigian & Gerald Hotaling. 1996. "New categories of missing children: Injured, lost, delinquent, and victims of caregiver mix-ups," *Child Welfare* 75(4): 291–310.

Finnie, Ross. 1993. "Women, men, and the economic consequences of divorce: Evidence from Canadian longitudinal data," *Canadian Review of Sociology and Anthropology* 30(2):205–241.

Fisher, H. 1992. *Anatomy of Love: A Natural History of Mating, Marriage and Why We Stray*. New York:Fawcett.

Fiske, Jo-Anne & Rose Johnny. 1996. "The Nedut'en Family: Yesterday and Today," pp. 225–241 in Marion Lynn (Ed.), *Voices: Essays on Canadian Families*. Toronto: Nelson.

Follingstad, Diane R, Michael J. Brondino & Kathryn J. Kleinfelter. 1996. "Reputation and behavior of battered women who kill their partners: Do these variables negate self-defense?" *Journal of Family Violence* 11(Sept.):251–267.

Forte, James A., David D. Franks & Janett A. Forte. 1996. "Asymmetrical role-taking: Comparing battered women," *Social Work* 41(Jan.):59–73.

Forthofer, Melinda S., Howard J. Markman & Martha Cox. 1996. "Associations between marital distress and work loss in a national sample," *Journal of Marriage and the Family* 58 (Aug.).

Fowers, Blaine J., Eileen M. Lyons & Kelly H. Montel. 1996. "Positive marital illusions: Self-enhancement or relationship enhancement?," *Journal of Family Psychology* 10(2).

Fowers, Blaine J., Kelly H. Montel & David H. Olson. 1996. "Predicting marital success for premarital couple types based on PREPARE," *Journal of Marriage and Family Therapy* 22(1).

Fowers, B.J. & D.H. Olson. 1986. "Predicting marital success with PREPARE: A predictive validity study," *Journal of Marital and Family Therapy* 12:403–413.

Fox, Bonnie. 1993. "The Rise and Fall of the Breadwinner-Homemaker Family," pp.147–157 in Bonnie Fox (Ed.), *Family Patterns/Gender Relations*. Toronto: Oxford.

Fox, Greer-Litton & Priscilla White Blanton. 1995. "Noncustodial fathers following divorce," *Marriage and Family Review* 20(1–2).

Frame, Marsha Wiggins & Constance L. Shehan. 1994. "Work and well-being in the two-person career: Relocation stress and coping among clergy husbands and wives," *Family Relations* 43(Apr.):196–205.

Franks, Melissa M. & Mary Anne Paris Stephens. 1996. "Social support in the context of caregiving: Husbands' provision of support to wives involved in parent care," *Journals of Gerontology Series B: Psychological Sciences and Social Sciences* (Jan.).

Frederick, Judith & Jason Hamel. 1998. "Canadian Attitudes to Divorce," *Canadian Social Trends* Spring:6–11.

Freidrich, W.N. 1979. "Predictors of the coping behavior of mothers of handicapped children," *Journal of Consulting and Clinical Psychology*, 47:1140–1141.

French, Maggie. 1991. "Becoming a Lone Parent," pp. 126–142 in Michael Hardy & Graham Crow (Eds.), *Lone Parenthood: Coping with Constraints and Making Opportunities in Single-Parent Families*. Toronto: University of Toronto Press.

Friedemann, Marie Louise & Adele A. Webb. 1995. "Family health and mental health six years after economic stress and unemployment," *Issues in Mental Health Nursing*, 16(1):51–66.

Furstenberg, Frank F. Jr. 1996. "The Future of Housework the Second," *American Demographics* June:34–40.

Furstenberg, Frank F., Jr., J. Brooks-Gunn & P. Morgan. 1987. *Adolescent Mothers in Later Life*. New York: Cambridge.

Gadd, Jane. 1997. "The Drift to the Bottom," *The Globe and Mail* 21 June: D1,D2.

Gaines, Stanley O. Jr. 1996. "Impact of interpersonal traits and gender-role compliance on interpersonal resource exchange among dating and engaged/married couples," *Journal of Social and Personal Relationships* 13(2).

Galambos, Nancy L., Heather A. Sears *et al.* 1995. "Parents' work overload and problem behaviour in young adolescents," *Journal of Research on Adolescents*, 5(2): 201–223.

Galinsky, E. & D. Hughes. 1986. *The Fortune Magazine Child Care Study*. New York: Bank Street College.

Galinsky,Ellen, Diane Hughes & Judy David. 1990. "Trends in Corporate Family-Supportive Policies," *Marriage and Family Review* 15 (3–4):75–94.

Galin, Rita S. 1994. "The intersection of class and age: Mother-in-law/daughter-in-law relations in rural Taiwan," *Journal of Cross Cultural Gerontology* 9 (2):127–140.

Galston, William A 1996. "Braking divorce for the sake of children," *The American Enterprise* 7 (May/June).

Garnefski, Nadia & Sjoukje Okma 1996. "Addiction risk and aggressive/criminal behaviour in adolescence: Influence of family, school and peers," *Journal of Adolescence* 19(6):503–512.

Garnett, Gale. 1997. "Joni Mitchell: Our sad-eyed lyricist of love," *The Globe and Mail*, 6 December:D19.

Gartner, Rosemary & Bonnie J. Fox. 1993. "Commentary and debate," *Canadian Journal of Sociology* 18 (3): 313–324.

Gee, Ellen M. 1986. "The life course of Canadian women: An historical and demographic analysis," *Social Indicators Research* 18:263–283.

Gee, Ellen M. 1990. "Preferred timing of women's life events: A Canadian study," *International Journal of Aging and Human Development* 31(4):279–294.

Gee, Ellen M. 1993. "Adult outcomes associated with childhood family structure: An appraisal of research and an examination of Canadian data," pp. 291–310 in Joe Hudson & Burt Galaway (Eds.), *Single Parent Families: Perspectives on Research and Policy*. Toronto: Thompson.

Gee, Ellen M. 1995. "Contemporary Diversities, " pp. 79–110 in Nancy Mandell & Ann Duffy

(Eds.), *Canadian Families: Diversity, Conflict and Change*. Toronto: Harcourt Brace.

Gee, Ellen M. & Meredith M. Kimball. 1987. *Women and Aging*. Toronto: Butterworths.

Gelles, Richard J. 1996. "Constraints against family violence: How well do they work?" pp. 30–42 in Eve S. Buzzawa & Carl G. Buzzawa (Eds.), *Do Arrests and Restraining Orders Work?* Thousand Oaks, CA: Sage Publications.

Gelles, Richard J. 1994. "Introduction: Part of a special issue on family violence," *Journal of Comparative Family Studies*. 25 (spring):1–6.

Gelles R. & D. Loseke (Eds.). 1993. *Current Controversies on Family Violence*. Newbury Park, CA: Sage.

Giele, Janet Zollinger. 1996. "Decline of family: Conservative, liberal and feminist views," in David Popenoe, Jean Bethke Elshtain & David Blankenhorn (Eds.), *Promises to Keep: Decline and Renewal of Marriage in America*, Lanham, MD: Rowman and Littlefield Publishers, Inc.

Gibson, Douglas M. 1998. "Requiem for a Master Storyteller," *The Globe and Mail* 28 February:C3.

Giles-Sims, Jean. 1994. "Family structure and corporal punishment," *International Sociological Association*, Association paper.

Gill, Gurjeet & Ray Hibbins. 1996. "Wives' encounters: Family work stress and leisure in two-job families," *International Journal of Sociology of the Family* 26(2):43–54.

Gillmore, Mary Rogers, Steven M. Lewis, Mary Jane Lohr, Michael S. Spencer & Rachelle D. White. 1997. "Repeat Pregnancies Among Adolescent Mothers," *Journal of Marriage and the Family* 59(Aug.):536–550.

Glass, Jennifer & Tetsushi Fujimoto. 1995. "Employer characteristics and the provision of family responsive policies," *Work and Occupations* 22(4):380–411.

Glenn, Evelyn Nagano. 1987. "Gender and the Family," in Beth B. Hess & Myra Marx Ferree (Eds.), *Analyzing Gender: A Handbook of Social Science Research*, Newbury Park: Sage.

Glenn, E. N. 1994. "Social Constructions of Mothering," pp. 1–29 in E.N. Glenn, G. Chang & L.R. Forcey (Eds.), *Mothering, Ideology, Experience and Agency*. New York: Routledge.

Glenn, Norval D. 1975. "The contribution of marriage to the psychological well-being of males and females," *Journal of Marriage and the Family* 37(3): 594–601.

Glenn, Norval D. 1990. "Qualitative research on marital quality in the 1980s: A critical review," *Journal of Marriage and the Family* 52:818–831.

Glenn, Norval D. 1998. "Closed hearts, closed minds: The textbook story of marriage," *Society* 35(3):69–79.

The Globe and Mail, 1993 "Should governments try to make marriage more robust?" 22 March:A17.

The Globe and Mail,. 1997. "Is it Wrong to Keep a Promise?" Editorial, 7 October:A20.

Goldberg, Margaret E., Barbara W. Lex & Nancy K. Mello. 1996. "Impact of maternal alcoholism on separation of children from their mothers: Findings from a sample of incarcerated women," *American Journal of Orthopsychiatry* 66(Apr.):228–238.

Goldenberg, Sheldon. 1987. *Thinking Sociologically*. Belmont, CA: Wadsworth.

Goldstein, D. & A. Rosenbaum. 1985. "An evaluation of the self-esteem of maritally violent men," *Family Relations* 34: 425–428.

Golombok, Susan & Fiona Tasker. 1994. "Children in lesbian and gay families: Theories and evidence." *Annual Review of Sex Research* 5:73–100.

Gonzalez, Ketty P., Tiffany M. Field & David Lasko. 1995. "Adolescents from divorced and intact families," *Journal of Divorce and Remarriage* 23(3–4,).

Goode, William. 1993. *World Changes in Divorce Patterns*. New Haven: Yale University Press.

Goodman, Lisa A., Mary Ann Dutton & Maxine Harris. 1995. "Episodically homeless women with serious mental illness: Prevalence of physical and sexual assault," *American Journal of Orthopsychiatry* 65(Oct.):468–478.

Goossens, Frits A., Geertruud Ottenhoff &Willem Koops. 1991. "Day care and social outcomes in middle childhood: A retrospective study," *Journal of Reproductive and Infant Psychology* 9(2-3):137–150.

Gordon, Linda & Sara McLanahan. 1991. "Single Parenthood in 1900," *Journal of Family History* 16(2):97–116.

Gordon, Robert A. 1996. "Parental licensure and its sanction," *Society* 34(1):65–69.

Gordon, Sean & Tony Sesku.1997. "Mom's Side of Family Known for Large Numbers," *Edmonton Journal*, 21 November:A12.

Gorlick, Carolyne A. & D. Alan Pomfret. 1993. "Hope and circumstance: Single mothers exiting social assistance," pp. 253–270 in Joe Hudson & Burt Galaway (Eds.), *Single Parent Families: Perspectives on Research and Policy*. Toronto: Thompson.

Gottlieb, Benjamin H., E. Kevin Kelloway & Anne Martin-Matthews. 1996. "Predictors of work–family conflict, stress, and job satisfaction among nurses," *Canadian Journal of Nursing Research* 28(2):99–117.

Gottlieb, Benjamin H., E. Kevin Kelloway & Maryann Fraboni. 1994. "Aspects of eldercare that place employees at risk," *The Gerontologist*. 34 (Dec.):815–821.

Gottlieb, Laurie N., Ariella Lang & Rhonda Amsel. 1996. "The long-term effects of grief on marital intimacy following an infant's death," *Omega* 33(1).

Gottman, J.M. 1979. *Marital Interaction: Experimental Investigations*. New York: Academic Press.

Gottman, John M. 1982. "Emotional responsiveness in marital conversations," *Journal of Communication* 3(summer):108–120.

Gottman, J.M. 1994. *What Predicts Divorce? The Relationship between Marital Processes and Marital Outcomes*, Hillsdale, NJ: Lawrence Erlbaum Associates.

Gottman, John M, Howard Markman & Clifford Notarius. 1977. "The topography of marital conflict: A sequential analysis of verbal and nonverbal behavior," *Journal of Marriage and the Family* 39(3):461–477.

Gottman, John M. & Albert L. Porterfield. 1981. "Communicative competence in the nonverbal behavior of married couples," *Journal of Marriage and the Family* 43(4): 817–824.

Gove, W.R. & R.D. Crutchfield. 1982. "The family and juvenile delinquency," *Sociological Quarterly* 23:301–319.

Grandin, Elaine & Eugen Lupri. 1997. "Intimate violence in Canada and the United States: A cross-national comparison." *Journal of Family Violence* 12 (4):417–443.

Grant, Kathryn E. & Bruce E. Compas. 1995. "Stress and anxious–depressed symptoms among adolescents: Searching for mechanisms of risk," *Journal of Consulting and Clinical Psychology*. 63(Dec.):1015–1021.

Gray, John. 1996. "Domesticity, Diapers and Dad," *Globe and Mail* 15 June:D1.

Gray-Little, Bernadette; Donald H. Baucom & Sherry L. Hamby. 1996. "Marital power, marital adjustment and therapy outcomes," *Journal of Family Psychology* 10(3).

Greif, Geoffrey L. 1995. "When divorced fathers want no contact with their children: A preliminary analysis," *Journal of Divorce and Remarriage* 23(1–2).

Greenstein, Theodore N. 1995. "Gender ideology and perceptions of the fairness of the division of household labor: Effects on marital quality," American Sociological Association paper.

Grimm-Thomas, Karen & Maureen Perry-Jenkins. 1994. "All in a day's work: Job experiences, self esteem, and fathering in working class families," *Family Relations*, 43(Apr.):174–181.

Grindstaff, Carl F. 1990. "Long-term Consequences of Adolescent Marriage and Fertility," in *Report on the Demographic Situation in Canada 1988*. Ottawa: Statistics Canada, Catalogue no. 91–209.

Gringeri, Christina. 1995. "Flexibility, the family

ethic, and rural home-based work," *Affilia* 10(1):70–86.

Grissett, Barbara & Allen L. Furr. 1994. "Effects of parental divorce on children's financial support for college," *Journal of Divorce and Remarriage* 22(1–2).

Groat, H. Theodore, Peggy C. Giordano, Stephen A. Cernkovich, M.D. Pugh, & Steven P. Swinford. 1997. "Attitudes toward childbearing among young parents," *Journal of Marriage and the Family* 59:568–581.

Gross, Penny. 1987. "Defining post-divorce remarriage families: A typology based on the subjective perceptions of children." *Journal of Divorce* 10 (1,2): 205–217.

Guttman, Joseph. 1993. *Divorce in Psychosocial Perspective: Theory and Research.* Hillsdale, NJ: Lawrence Erlbaum Associates.

Halli, Shiva & Zachery Zimmer. 1991. "Common-law unions as a differentiating factor in the failure of marriage in Canada," *Social Indicators Research* 24:329–345.

Hannah, Mo Teresa, Wade Luquet & Joan McCormick. 1997. "COMPASS as a measure of the efficacy of couples therapy," *The American Journal of Family Therapy* 25 (spring).

Harrell, W.A. 1995. "Husbands' involvement in housework: Effects of relative earning power and masculine orientation," *Psychological Reports* 77(3):1331–1337.

Harris, Kathleen Mullan. 1997. *Teen Mothers and the Revolving Welfare Door.* Philadelphia: Temple University Press.

Harris, Maxine. 1996. "Treating sexual abuse trauma with dually diagnosed women," *Community Mental Health Journal* 32: 371–385.

Harris, Sarah B. 1996. "For better or for worse," *Journal of Elder Abuse and Neglect* 8(1):1–33.

Hartmann, Heidi & Roberta Spalter-Roth. 1996. "A feminist approach to public policy making for women and families," *Current Perspectives in Social Theory* 16:33–51.

Hayes, Donald P. & Margaret G. Ahrens. 1988. "Vocabulary simplification for children: A special case of 'motherese'?" *Journal of Child Language* 15(2): 395–410.

Hays, Sharon. 1997. *The Cultural Contradictions of Motherhood.* New Haven: Yale University Press.

Hays, Sharon. 1998. "Reconsidering the 'choice': Do Americans really prefer workplace over home?" *Contemporary Sociology* 27(1):28–32.

Heinicke, Christopher M. & Donald Guthrie. 1996. "Prebirth marital interactions and postbirth marital development," *Infant Mental Health Journal* 17(2).

Heitlinger, Alena. 1993. *Women's Equality, Demography and Public Policies.* New York: St. Martin's.

Henderson, A. J. Z., K. Bartholomew & D.G. Dutton. "He loves me; he loves me not: Attachment and separation resolution of abused women," *Journal of Family Violence* 12 (June):169–191.

Hendrick, C & S. Hendrick. 1996. "Gender and the experience of heterosexual love," pp. 131–148 in J.T. Wood (Ed.), *Gendered Relationships.* Mountain View, Colorado: Mayfield.

Hennessy, Ellis & Edward C. Melhuish. 1991. "Early day care and the development of school-age children: A review," *Journal of Reproductive and Infant Psychology* 9 (2–3):117-136.

Henripin, Jacques & Yves Peron. 1971. "Demographic transitions in the province of Quebec," in David Glass & Roger Revelle (Eds), *Population and Social Change.* London: Edward Arnold.

Hensley, Robert 1996. "Relationship termination and the Fisher divorce adjustment scale: A comparative study," *Journal of Divorce and Remarriage* 25(1–2).

Heriot, Jessica. 1996. "Maternal protectiveness following the disclosure of intrafamilial child sexual abuse," *Journal of Interpersonal Violence* 11(2):181–194.

Hessing, Melody. 1994. "More than clockwork: Women's time management in their combined workloads," *Sociological Perspectives* 37(winter):611–633.

Hier, Sally J., Paula J. Korboot & Robert D. Schweitzer. 1990. "Social adjustment and symptomatology in two types of homeless adolescents: Runaways and throwaways," *Adolescence* 25(100): 761–771.

Higgins, Christopher, Linda Duxbury & Catherine Lee. 1994. "Impact of life-cycle stage and gender on the ability to balance work and family responsibilities," *Family Relations* 43 (Apr.): 144–50.

Higgins, Daryl J. & Marita P. McCabe. 1994, "The relationship of child sexual abuse and family violence to adult adjustment: Toward an integrated risk-sequelae model," *The Journal of Sex Research* 31(4): 255–266.

Hill, R. 1949. *Families Under Stress: Adjustment to the Crises of War Separation and Reunion*, New York: Harper and Bros.

Hobart, Charles. 1996. "Intimacy and Family Life: Sexuality, Cohabitation, and Marriage," pp. 143–173 in Maureen Baker (Ed.), *Families: Changing Trends in Canada (3rd edition)*. Toronto:McGraw-Hill Ryerson.

Hochschild, A. 1983. *The Managed Heart*. Berkeley: University of California Press.

Hochschild, Arlie Russell. 1997. *The Time Bind: When Work Becomes Home and Home Becomes Work*. New York: Metropolitan Books.

Hock, Ellen, Mary-Beth Schirtzinger & Wilma J. Lutz. 1995. "Maternal depressive symptomatology over the transition to parenthood: Assessing the influence of marital satisfaction and marital sex role traditionalism," *Journal of Family Psychology* 9 (March).

Hofferth, Sandra L. & S.G. Deich. 1994. "Recent U.S. child care and family legislation in comparative perspective," *Journal of Family Issues* 15 (Sept.):424–448.

Hoffman, Charles D. & Debra K. Ledford. 1995.

"Adult children of divorce: Relationships with their mothers and fathers prior to, following parental separation, and currently," *Journal of Divorce and Remarriage* 24(3–4).

Hoffman, Martin L. 1979. "Development of moral thought, feeling, and behavior," *American Psychologist* 34(10):958–966.

Hoffman, Saul & Greg Duncan. 1995. "The effect of incomes, wages and AFDC benefits in marital disruption," *The Journal of Human Resources* 30 (winter).

Hoglund, Collete L. & Karen B. Nicholas. 1995. "Shame, guilt, and anger in college students exposed to abusive family environments," *Journal of Family Violence* 10 (June): 141–157.

Holdaway, Doris M. & JoAnn Ray. 1992. "Attitudes of street kids toward foster care," *Child and Adolescent Social Work Journal* 9(4):307–317.

Holman, Thomas B. & Bing Dao Li. 1997. "Premarital factors influencing perceived readiness for marriage," *Journal of Family Issues* 18(2):124–144.

Holtzworth-Munroe, Amy, Jennifer Waltz, Neil S. Jacobson, Valerie Monaco, Peter A. Fehrenbach & John M. Gottman. 1992. "Recruiting nonviolent men as control subjects for research on marital violence: How easily can it be done?" *Violence and Victims* 7(1):79–88.

Hooks, Gwen. 1997. *The Keystone Legacy: Recollections of a Black Settler*. Edmonton, Alberta: Brightest Pebble.

Hooks, Bell. 1984. *Feminist Theory: From Margin to Centre*. Boston: South End Press.

Hopper, Joseph. 1993. "The rhetoric of motives in divorce," *Journal of Marriage and the Family* 55(Nov.):801–813.

Horn, Janice D., Heidi M. Feldman & Dianna L. Ploof. 1995. "Parent and Professional Perceptions about Stress and Coping Strategies during a Child's Lengthy Hospitalization," *Social Work in Health Care* 21(1) 107–127.

Hornung, C.A., B.C. McCullough & T. Sugimoto. 1982. "Status relationships in marriage: Risk factors in spouse abuse." *Journal of Marriage and the Family* 42:675–692.

Huang, I-Chiao. 1991. "Family stress and coping," pp. 289–334 in Stephen J. Bahr (Ed.), *Family Research: A Sixty-Year Review, 1930–1990, Volume 1*. New York: Lexington Books, Maxwell Macmillan International.

Hudson Joe & Burt Galaway (Eds.), *Single Parent Families: Perspectives on Research and Policy*. Toronto: Thompson.

Huisman, Kimberly A. 1996. "Wife battering in Asian American communities: Identifying the service needs of an overlooked segment of the U. S. population," *Violence Against Women* 2(3):260–283.

Iacovetta, Franca. 1992. "From contadina to worker: Southern Italian immigrant working women in Toronto, 1947–62," pp. 281–303 in Bettina Bradbury (Ed.), *Canadian Family History: Selected Readings*. Toronto: Copp Clark Pitman.

International Labor Organization. 1998. "Gap in employment treatment for men and women still exists," *ILO News*, 15 February.

Isralowitz, Richard E. "The kibbutz in transition: The influence of child sleeping arrangements on work and leisure attitudes and behavior," *Israel Social Science Research*,1993, 8, 1, 91-107.

Isralowitz, Richard E. & Michal Palgi. 1992. "Work attitudes and behaviors of kibbutz parents with familial and communal child sleeping arrangements," *Journal of Social Psychology* 132(1):121–123.

Istar, Arlene. 1996. "Couple assessment: Identifying and intervening in domestic violence in lesbian relationships," *Journal of Gay and Lesbian Social Services* 4(1):93–106.

Jackson, Nicky Ali. 1996. "Observational experiences of intrapersonal conflict and teenage victimization: A comparative study among spouses and cohabitors," *Journal of Family Violence* 11(3):191–203.

Jacobson, Bert H. & Steven G. Aldana *et al*. "The relationship between perceived stress and self-reported illness-related absenteeism," *American Journal of Health Promotion*, v. 11, no. 1, Sept–Oct 1996:54–61.

Jacobson, Neil S. 1989. "The politics of intimacy," *The Behavior Therapist* 12(2):29–32.

Jacobson, Neil S., John M. Guttman, Eric Gortner, Sara Berns & JoAnn Wu Shortt. 1996. "Psychological factors in the longitudinal course of battering: When do the couples split up? When does the abuse decrease?" *Violence and Victims* 11(4): 371–392.

James, Adrian L. 1995. "Social work in divorce: Welfare, mediation and justice," International *Journal of Law and the Family* 9(3).

James, Simon. 1996. "Female household investment strategy in human and non-human capital with the risk of divorce," *Journal of Divorce and Remarriage* 25(1–2).

Janus, Mark David, Anne W. Burgess & Arlene McCormack. 1987. "Histories of sexual abuse in adolescent male runaways," *Adolescence* 22,(86):405–417.

Janus, Mark David, Francis X. Archambault, Scott W. Brown & Lesley A. Welsh. 1995. "Physical abuse in Canadian runaway adolescents," *Child Abuse and Neglect* 19(4):433–447.

Jekielek, Susan M. 1996. "The relative and interactive effects of parental conflict and parental marital disruption on child well-being," American Sociological Association.

Johnson, Sheri L & Theodore Jacob. 1997. "Marital interactions of depressed men and women," *Journal of Consulting and Clinical Psychology* 65(1).

Johnson, Sue. 1997. "A critical review of marital therapy outcome," *Canadian Journal of Psychiatry* 42(3).

Johnson, Susan M. & E. Talitman. 1997. "Predictors of success in emotionally focused marital therapy," *Journal of Marital and Family Therapy* 23(2).

Jones, Carol & Gordon Causer. 1995. "'Men don't have families': Equality and motherhood in technical employment," *Gender, Work and Organization* 2(2): 51–62.

Jones, Fiona & Ben Fletcher. 1993. "An Empirical study of occupational stress transmission in working couples," *Human Relations* 46 (7):881–903.

Joubert, Charles. 1995. "Catholicism and indices of social pathology in the states," *Psychological Reports* 76(April).

Julian, Teresa W. & Patrick C. McKenry. 1993. "Mediators of male violence toward female intimates," *Journal of Family Violence* 8(1):39–56.

Jurk, Imas *et al.* 1980. "Family responses to mechanisms of adjustment following death of children with cancer," *Australian Pediatric Journal:* 85–88.

Kalin, Rudolf & Carol A. Lloyd. 1985. "Sex role identity, sex-role ideology and marital adjustment," *International Journal of Women's Studies* 8(1):32–39.

Kalnins, Ilze *et al.* 1980. "Concurrent stresses in families with a leukemic child," *Journal of Pediatric Psychology* 5 (1):81–92.

Kamerman, Sheila B. & Alfred J. Kahn. 1988. "What Europe does for single-parent families," *The Public Interest* 93(Fall):70–86.

Kanof, A., B. Kutner & N.B. Georeon. 1972. "The impact of infantile amaurotic familial idiocy (Tay-Sachs disease) on the family," *Pediatrics* 49:37–45.

Kanter, Rosabeth Moss. 1983. *The Change Masters: Innovations for Productivity in the American Corporation.* New York: Simon and Schuster.

Kaplan, D.M., A. Smith, R. Grobstein & S. Fischman. 1980. "Family mediation of stress," pp. 475–488 in P.W. Power & A.E. Dello-Orto (Eds.), *Role of the Family in the Rehabilitation of the Physically Disabled,.* University Park Press, Baltimore, MD.

Kaplan, Elaine Bell. 1997. *Not Our Kind of Girl: Unravelling the Myth of Black Teenage Motherhood.* Berkeley, CA: University of California Press.

Karasek, Robert & Tores Theorell. 1990. *Healthy Work: Stress, Productivity, and the Reconstruction of Working Life.* New York: Basic Books.

Karney, Benjamin R. & Thomas N. Bradbury. 1995. "Assessing longitudinal change in marriage: An introduction to the analysis of growth curves," *Journal of Marriage and the Family* 57(4):1091–1108.

Kashani, J.H., R. Venzke & E.A. Millar. 1981. "Depression in children admitted to hospital for orthopedic procedures," *British Journal of Psychiatry* 138:21–35.

Kashubeck, Susan, Sheila M. Pottebaum & Nancy O. Read. 1994. "Predicting elopement from residential treatment," *American Journal of Orthopsychiatry* 64, 1, Jan, 126-135.

Katz, Jennifer, Ileana Arias, Steven R.H. Beach, Gene Brody & Paul Roman. 1995. "Excuses, excuses: Accounting for the effects of partner violence on marital satisfaction and stability," *Violence and Victims* 10(4).

Katzev, Aphra R., Rebecca L. Warner & Alan C. Acock. 1994. "Girls or boys? Relationship of gender to marital instability," *Journal of Marriage and the Family* 56(Feb):89–100.

Kelly, Katharine D. & Walter S. DeKeseredy. 1994. "Women's fear of crime and abuse in college and university dating relations," *Violence and Victims* 9 (1):17–30.

Kemp, Anita, Bonnie L. Green & Christine Hovanitz. 1995. "Incidence and correlates of posttraumatic stress disorder in battered women: Shelter and community samples," *Journal of Interpersonal Violence* 10 (Mar.):43–55.

Kempe, C.H., F.N. Silverman, B.F. Steele, W. Droegmueller & H.K. Silver. 1962. "The battered-child syndrome," *Journal of the American Medical Association* 181:17–24.

Kennedy, Cheryl-Ann, J.H. Skurnick, M. Foley & D.B. Louria. 1995. "Gender differences in HIV-related psychological distress in heterosexual couples," *AIDS Care* 7(suppl. 1):S33–S38.

Keyfitz, Nathan. 1986. "The Family That Does Not Reproduce Itself," *Population and Development Review* (suppl. 12):139–154.

Keyfitz, Nathan. 1988. "On the wholesomeness of marriage," in L. Tepperman & J. Curtis (Eds.),

Readings in sociology: An introduction. Toronto: McGraw-Hill Ryerson.

Kermeen, Patricia. 1995. "Improving postpartum marital relationships," *Psychological Reports* 76 (June).

Kheshgi-Genovese, Zareena & Thomas A. Genovese. 1997. "Developing the spousal relationship within stepfamilies," *Families in Society: The Journal of Contemporary Human Services* 78(3):255–271.

King, Donna & Carol E. Mackinnon. 1988. "Making difficult choices easier: A review of research on day care and children's development," *Family Relations* 37(4):392–398.

Kinnunen, Ulla, Jan Gerris & Ad Vermulst. 1996. "Work experiences and family functioning among employed fathers with children of school age," *Family Relations* 45(Oct.):449–55.

Kirk, H. David. 1984. *Shared Fate: A Theory and Method of Adoptive Relationships.* New York: Free Press.

Kirk, H. David. 1988. *Exploring Adoptive Family Life.* Port Angeles, Washington & Brentwood Bay, British Columbia: Ben-Simon Press.

Kirk, H. David & Susan A. McDaniel. 1984. "Adoption policy in Great Britain and North America," *Journal of Social Policy* 13(1):75–84.

Kluwer, Esther S., Jose Heesink & Evert Van de Vliert. 1996. "Marital conflict about the division of household labor and paid work," *Journal of Marriage and the Family* 58(Nov.).

Kluwer, Esther S., Jose A.M. Heesink & Evert Van De Vliert. 1997. "The marital dynamics of conflict over the division of labor," *Journal of Marriage and the Family* 59(August):635–653.

Knudson, Martin Carmen & Anne R. Mahoney. 1996. "Gender dilemmas and myth in the construction of marital bargains: Issues for marital therapy," *Family Processes* 35 (2).

Kochanska, Grazyna. 1991. "Socialization and temperament in the development of guilt and conscience," *Child Development* 62(6):1379–1392.

Kochanska, Grazyna, Darcie L. Padavich & Amy L. Koenig. 1996. "Children's narratives about hypothetical moral dilemmas and objective measures of their conscience: Mutual relations and socialization antecedents," *Child Development* 67(4):1420–1436.

Kogos, Jennifer L. & John Snarey. 1995. "Parental divorce and the moral development of adolescents," *Journal of Divorce and Remarriage* 23(3–4).

Kohli, Martin. 1986. "Social organization and subjective construction of life course," pp. 271–292 in A.B. Sorenson, F.E. Weinhert & L.R. Sharrod (Eds.), *Human Development and the Life Course.* Hillsdale, California: Erlbaum.

Kolata, Gina. 1997. "March of progress: Yesterday's never is today's why not," *Edmonton Journal*, 7 December :B4.

Kolbo, Jerome R. 1996. "Risk and resilience among children exposed to family violence," *Violence and Victims* 11(2): 113–128.

Kolbo, Jerome R., Eleanor H. Blakely & David Engleman. 1996. "Children who witness domestic violence: A review of empirical literature," *Journal of Interpersonal Violence* 11 (June):281–293.

Kontos, Susan & Loraine Dunn, 1989. "Attitudes of care givers, maternal experiences with day care, and children's development," *Journal of Applied Developmental Psychology* 10(1):37–51.

Kossek, Ellen Ernst, Parshotam Dass & Beverly DeMarr. 1994. "The dominant logic of employer-sponsored work and family initiatives: Human resource managers' institutional role," *Human Relations* 47(Sept.):1121–1149.

Kozuch, Patricia & Teresa M. Cooney. "Young adults' marital and family attitudes: The role of recent parental divorce, and family and parental conflict," *Journal of Divorce and Remarriage* 23(3–4):1995.

Kposowa, Augustine. 1995. "Risk factors for divorce in the United States," *American Sociological Association.*

Kruk, E. 1995. "Grandparent grandchild contact loss: Findings from a study of grandparent rights members," *Canadian Journal on Aging* 14(4):737–754.

Kufeldt, Kathleen & Margaret Nimmo. 1987. "Youth on the street: Abuse and neglect in the eighties," *Child Abuse and Neglect* 11(4): 531–543.

Kufeldt, Kathleen & Philip E. Perry. 1989. "Running around with runaways," *Community Alternatives* 1(1):85–97.

Kumar, Pramod & Jayshree Dhyani. 1996. "Marital adjustment: A study of some related factors," *Indian Journal of Clinical Psychology* 23(2).

Kunz, Jennifer & Stephen J. Bahr. 1996. "A Profile of Parental Homicide against Children," *Journal of Family Violence* 11(4): 347–362.

Kunz, Jenifer & Phillip R. Kunz. 1995. "Social support during the process of divorce: It does make a difference," *Journal of Divorce and Remarriage* 24(3–4).

Kurtz, Linda. 1995. "The relationship between parental coping strategies and children's adaptive processes in divorced and intact families," *Journal of Divorce and Remarriage* 24(3–4).

Kurz, Demie. 1995. *For richer or for poorer: Mothers confront divorce.* New York: Routledge.

Kurz, Demie. 1996."Separation, divorce, and woman abuse," *Violence against Women* 2(1).

Kwan, Alex Yui-huen. 1995. "Elder abuse in Hong Kong: A new family problem for the Old East?" *Journal of Elder Abuse and Neglect* 6 (3–4):565–580.

Lackey, Chad & Kirk R. Williams. 1995. "Social bonding and the cessation of partner violence across generations," *Journal of Marriage and the Family* 57:295–305.

Lademann, A. 1980. "The neurologically handicapped child," *Scandinavian Journal of Audiology* 10 (suppl.): 23–26.

Laewen, Hans Joachim. 1989. "A discussion of day care for children up to age three," *Zeitschrift fur Padagogik* 35(6):869–888.

Lamb, Michael E. 1996. "Effects of nonparental child care on child development: An update, " *Canadian Journal of Psychiatry* 41(6):330–342.

Landale, Nancy S. & Nimfa B. Ogena. 1995. "Migration and union dissolution among Puerto Rican women." *International Migration Review* 29 (3): 671–692.

Landis, Kleine, Linda Foley & Loretta Nall. 1995. "Attitudes toward marriage and divorce held by young adults," *Journal of Divorce and Remarriage* 24(3–4).

Landolt, Monica A., Martin L. Lalumiere & Vernon L. Quinsey. 1995. "Sex differences in intra-sex variations in human mating tactics: An evolutionary approach," *Ethology and Sociobiology* 16(1):3–23.

Landry, Yves. 1992. *Les filles du roi au xviie siècle: Orphelines en France, pionières au Canada,* Montreal: Lemeac.

Lapierre-Adamcyk, Evelyne. 1987. "Mariage et politique de la famille," paper presented at the Association des Demographiques du Québec, Ottawa, May.

Larcombe, E.S. 1978. "A handicapped child means a handicapped family," *Journal of the Royal College of General Practice* 28, 46–52.

Larson, Jeffrey H., Stephan M. Wilson & Rochelle Beley. 1994. "The impact of job insecurity on marital and family relations," *Family Relations,* 43(Apr.):138–43.

Laub, J.H. & R.J. Sampson. 1988. "Unraveling families and delinquency: A reanalysis of the Glueck's data," *Criminology* 26: 355-380.

Lauer, Robert H., Jeanette C. Lauer & Sarah T. Kerr. 1990. "The long-term marriage: Perceptions of stability and satisfaction," *International Journal of Aging and Human Development* 31(3):189–195.

Laumann, E.O, J.H.Gagnon, R.T. Michael & S. Michaels. 1994. *The Social Organization of Sexuality: Sexual Practices in the United States.* Chicago: University of Chicago Press.

Lavee, Yoav, Shlomo Sharlin & Ruth Katz. 1996. "The effect of parenting stress on marital quality: An integrated mother-father model," *Journal of Family Issues* 17.

Laws, Judith Long & Pepper Schwartz. 1977. *Sexual*

Scripts: The Social Construction of Female Sexuality. Hindsdale, Illinois: Dryden.

Leavitt, Robin Lynn. 1991. "Power and resistance in infant-toddler day care centers," *Sociological Studies of Child Development* 4:91-112.

LeBourdais, Celine & Nicole Marcil-Gratton. 1994. "Quebec's pro-active approach to family policy," pp. 103–116 in Maureen Baker (Ed.), *Canada's Changing Families: Challenges to Public Policy.* Ottawa: Vanier Institute of the Family.

Lechner, Viola M. 1993. "Support systems and stress reduction among workers caring for dependent parents," *Social Work* 38(4,):461–469.

Lechner, Viola M. & Masahito Sasaki. 1995. "Japan and the United States struggle with who will care for our aging parents when caregivers are employed," *Journal of Gerontological Social Work* 24(1–2):97–114.

Leiter, Michael P. & Marie-Josette Durup. 1996. "Work, home, and in-between: A longitudinal study of spillover," *Journal of Applied and Behavioural Science* 32(1):29–47.

Lempert, Lora Bex. 1996a. "Language obstacles in the narratives of abused women," *Mid-American Review of Sociology* 19(1–2):15–32.

Lempert, Lora Bex. 1996b."Women's strategies of survival: Developing agency in abusive relationships," *Journal of Family Violence* 11(3):269–289.

Leonard, Suzanne. 1995. "Love stories," *Psychology Today* 28(Nov./Dec.).

Lero, Donna S. & Lois M. Brockman. 1993. "Single parent families in Canada: A closer look," pp. 91–114 in Joe Hudson & Burt Galaway (Eds.), *Single Parent Families: Perspectives on Research and Policy.* Toronto: Thompson.

Lesemann, Frederic & Roger Nicol. 1994. "Family policy: International comparisons," pp. 117–125 in Maureen Baker (Ed.), *Canada's Changing Families: Challenges to Public Policy.* Ottawa: The Vanier Institute of the Family.

Leung, A.K.C., W.L.M. Robson, H. Cho & S.H.N. Lim. 1996. "Latchkey children," *Journal of the Royal Society of Health* 116(6):356–359.

Levan, Chris. 1998. "Learning the rules on how to fight fairly," *Edmonton Journal* 31 January:F4.

Levine, Robert, Suguro Sato, Tsukasa Hashimoti & Jyoti Verma. 1995. "Love and marriage in eleven cultures," *Journal of Cross-Cultural Psychology* 26(5 (Sept).

Levy, D.M. 1945. "The War and Family Life: Report for the War Emergency Committee, 1944." Reprinted in *American Journal of Orthopsychiatry,* 15:140–152.

Lewin, Alisa & Yeheskel Hasenfeld. 1995. "Divorce: Does warfare policy reduce the gains from marriage?," American Sociological Association.

Lewis, Jane. 1997. "Gender and welfare regimes: Further thoughts," *Social Politics* (summer).

Lewis, Suzan & Cary L. Cooper. 1995. "Balancing the work/home interface: A European perspective," *Human Resource Management Review* 5(4):289–305.

Leyser, Yona. 1964. "Stress and adaptation in Orthodox Jewish families with a disabled child," *American Journal of Orthopsychiatry.* 64(July):376–85.

Lieberman, Morton A. & Lawrence Fisher. 1995. "The impact of chronic illness on the health and well-being of family members," *The Gerontologist* 35(Feb.):94–102.

Liebkind, Karmela. 1993. "Self-Reported Ethnic Identity, Depression and Anxiety among Young Vietnamese Refugees and Their Parents," *Journal of Refugee Studies* 6(1):25–39.

Lillard, Lee, Michael Brien & Linda Waite. 1995. "Premarital cohabitation and subsequent divorce: A matter of self-selection?," *Demography* 32(Aug.).

Linden, E. & J.C. Hackler. 1973. "Affective ties and delinquency," *Pacific Sociological Review* 16: 27-46.

Lippman, S. B., W. A. James, R.L. Frierson. 1993. "AIDS and the family: Implications for counseling," *AIDS Care* 5(1):71–78.

Livingston, Mary J., Kim Burley & Thomas P. Springer. 1996. "The importance of being feminine: Gender, sex role, occupational and marital role commitment, and their relationship to anticipated work-family conflict," *Journal of Social Behavior and Personality* 11(5): 179–192.

Lobo, Francis & Glen Watkins. 1995. "Late career unemployment in the 1990s: Its impact on the family," *Journal of Family Studies* 1(2):103–113.

Lockhart, Lettie L., Barbara W. White & Vicki Causby. 1994. "Letting out the secret: Violence in lesbian relationships," *Journal of Interpersonal Violence* 9 (Dec.):469–492.

Luker, Kristin. 1996. *Dubious Conceptions: The Politics of Teenage Pregnancy*. Cambridge, MA: Harvard University Press.

Lundgren-Gaveras, Lena. 1996. "The work-family needs of single parents: A comparison of American and Swedish policy trends," *Journal of Sociology and Social Welfare*, 23(1):131–147.

Lupri, Eugen. 1993. "Spousal violence: Wife abuse across the life course." *Zeitschrift für Sozialisationforschung und Erziehungssoziologie* 13 (3): 232–257.

Lupri, Eugen & James Frideres. 1981. "The quality of marriage and the passage of time: Marital satisfaction over the family life cycle," *Canadian Journal of Sociology* 6:283–305.

Lupri, Eugen, Elaine Grandin & Merlin B. Brinkerhoff. 1994. "Socioeconomic status and male violence in the Canadian home: A reexamination." *Canadian Journal of Sociology* 19 (1):47–73.

Lupri, Eugen & Don Mills. 1987. "The household division of labour in young dual-earner couples," *International Review of Sociology* 2:33-54.

Luster, Tom, Harry Perlstadt & Marvin McKinney. 1996. "The effects of a family support program and other factors on the home environments provided by adolescent mothers," *Family Relations* 45(July): 255–264.

Luxton, Meg. 1986. "Two hands for the clock," pp. 39–55 in Meg Luxton & Harriet Rosenberg (Eds.), *Through the Kitchen Window: The Politics of Home and Family*. Toronto: Garamond.

Luxton, Meg & Ester Reiter. 1997. "Double, dou-ble, toil and trouble. Women's experience of work and family in Canada, 1980–1995," pp. 197–221 in Patricia M. Evans & Gerda R. Wekerle (Eds.), *Women and the Canadian Welfare State: Challenges and Change*. Toronto: University of Toronto Press.

Luxton, Meg, Harriet Rosenberg & Sedef Arat-Koc (Eds.). 1990. *Through the Kitchen Window: The Politics of Home and Family*. Toronto: Garamond.

Lye, Diane N. & Ingrid Waldron. 1997. "Attitudes toward cohabitation, family and gender roles: Relationships to values and political ideology," *Sociological Perspectives* 40(2):199–225.

Lykken, David. 1996. "Psychopathy, sociopathy, and crime," *Society* 34(1):29-38.

Maas, Ineke. 1995. "Demography and aging: Long-term effects of divorce, early widowhood, and migration on resources and integration in old age." *Korea Journal of Population and Development* 24(2):275–299.

MacDermid, Shelley M., Margaret Williams & Stephen Marks. 1994. "Is small beautiful? Work family tension, work conditions, and organisational size," *Family Relations*, 43(Apr.):159–67.

MacDonald, Andrea. 1998. "Course looks at kids' lit from gay angle," *The Edmonton Journal*, 9 January 1998:H6.

MacEwen, Karyl E. & Julian Barling. 1994. "Daily Consequences of Work Interference with Family and Family Interference with Work," *Work and Stress* 8(3): 244–254.

Mackay, Fiona. 1996. "The zero tolerance campaign: Setting the agenda," *Parliamentary Affairs* 49(1):206–220.

Mackey, Wade C. 1995. "U.S. fathering behaviors within a cross-cultural context: An evaluation by an alternate benchmark," *Journal of Comparative Family Studies* 26(3):445-458.

Macmillan, Ross & Rosemary Gartner. 1996. "When she brings home the bacon: Labour force participation and the risk of spousal violence against women," unpublished mss., Toronto: Department of Sociology, University of Toronto.

Mak, Anita S. 1996. "Adolescent delinquency and perceptions of parental care and protection: A case control study," *Journal of Family Studies* 2(1):29–39.

Mandell, Deena. 1995a. "Fathers who don't pay child support: Hearing their voices," *Journal of Divorce and Remarriage* 23(1–2).

Mandell, Deena. 1995b. "Non supporting divorced fathers: The problem in context," *Canadian Social Work Review* 12(2).

Mann, Susan A., Michael D. Grimes, Alice Abel Kemp & Pamela J. Jenkins. 1997. "Paradigm shifts in family sociology? Evidence from three decades of family textbooks," *Journal of Family Issues* 18(3):315–349.

Manning, W. & D.T. Lichter. 1996. "Parental cohabitation and children's economic well being," *Journal of Marriage and the Family* 58(4):998–1010.

Marano, Hara-Estroff. 1997. "Love lesson: 6 new moves to improve your relationship," *Psychology Today* 30(Mar./Apr.).

Marcenes, Wagner & Aubrey Sheilham. 1996. "The relationship between marital quality and oral health status," *Psychology and Health* 11(3).

Marcil-Gratton, Nicole. 1993. "Growing up with a single parent: A transitional experience? Some demographic measurements," pp. 73–90 in Joe Hudson & Burt Galaway (Eds.), *Single Parent Families: Perspectives on Research and Policy*. Toronto: Thompson Educational Publishing.

Margolin, Gayla & Richard S. John. 1997. "Children's exposure to marital aggression: Direct and mediated effects," pp. 90–104 in Glenda Kaufman Kantor and Jana L. Jasinski (Eds.), *Out of Darkness: Contemporary Perspectives on Family Violence*, Thousand Oaks, CA: Sage Publications.

Marks, Lynne. 1998. "When in doubt, it seems, blame the mothers," *The Globe and Mail,* 26 January:A21.

Marks, N.F. 1996. "Flying solo at mid-life: Gender, marital status and psychological well-being," *Journal of Marriage and the Family* 58(4):917–932.

Marshall, Katherine. 1990. "Household chores," *Canadian Social Trends* (spring):18–19.

Marshall, Katherine. 1993. "Employed Parents and the Division of Housework," *Perspectives on Labour and Income* (autumn):23–30.

Mastekaasa, Arne. 1995. "Divorce and subjective distress: Panel evidence," *European Sociological Review* 11(2).

Matthews, Lisa S., Rand D. Conger & K.A.S. Wickrama. 1996. "Work-family conflict and marital quality: Mediating processes," *Social Psychology Quarterly* 59(1):62–79.

Mattox, William R. Jr. 1996. "Marital bliss," *The American Enterprise* 7(May-June).

Mattson, A. 1972. "Long-term physical illness in childhood: A challenge to psychosocial adaptation," *Pediatrics* 5:801–811.

Maxwell, Judith. 1996. "The Social Dimensions of Economic Growth," Eric J. Hanson Memorial Lecture. Edmonton: University of Alberta, Department of Economics.

McCloskey, Laura A. 1996. "Socioeconomic and coercive power within the family," *Gender and Society* 10(Aug.): 449–463.

McCloskey, Laura A., Aurelio Jose Figueredo & Mary P. Koss. 1995. "The effects of systemic family violence on children's mental health," *Child Development* 66(Oct.):1239–1261.

McCormack, Arlene, Ann Wolbert Burgess & Peter Gaccione. 1986. "Influence of family structure and financial stability on physical and sexual abuse among a runaway population," *International Journal of Sociology of the Family* 16(2): 251- 262.

McCormack, Arlene, Mark David Janus & Ann Wolbert Burgess. 1986. "Runaway youths and sexual victimization: Gender differences in an adolescent runaway population," *Child Abuse and Neglect* 10(3):387-395.

McCurdy, Susan J & Avraham Scherman. 1996. "Effects of family structure on the adolescent separation-individuation process," *Adolescence* 31(122).

McDaniel, Susan A. 1988. "Women's roles, reproduction and the new reproductive technologies: A new stork rising,"in Ann Duffy & Nancy Mandell (Eds.), *Reconstructing Canadian Families: Feminist Perspectives*, Toronto: Butterworths.

McDaniel, Susan A. 1989. "Reconceptualizing the nuptiality/ fertility relationship in Canada in a new age," *Canadian Studies in Population* 16(2):163–186.

McDaniel, Susan A. 1993a. "Single parenthood: policy apartheid in Canada," pp. 203–211 in Burt Galloway & Joe Hudson (Eds.), *Single Parent Families: Canadian Perspectives on Research and Policy*, Toronto: Thompson Educational Publishing.

McDaniel, Susan A. 1993b. "The changing Canadian family: Women's roles and the impact of feminism," pp. 422–451 in Sandra Burt & Lorraine Code (Eds.), *Changing Patterns: Women in Canada (2nd edition)*. Toronto: McClelland & Stewart.

McDaniel, Susan A. 1993c. "Where the contradictions meet: Women and family security in Canada in the 1990s," pp. 163–180 in *Family Security in Insecure Times*. Ottawa: National Forum on Family Security.

McDaniel, Susan A. 1994. *Family and Friends* 1990: General Social Survey Analysis Series. Ottawa: Statistics Canada, Minister of Supply and Services. Catalogue No. 11–612E, No. 9, ISBN 0-660-15354-8.

McDaniel, Susan A. 1995. *Families Function: Family Bridges from Past to Future*. Occasional Paper Series, No. 19/1995. Vienna: United Nations Secretariat for the International Year of the Family.

McDaniel, Susan A. 1996a. "Family/work challenges among older working Canadians," pp. 195–214 in Marion Lynn (Ed.), *Voices: Essays on Canadian Families*. Toronto: Nelson.

McDaniel, Susan A. 1996b. "The family lives of the middle-aged and elderly in Canada," pp. 195–211 in Maureen Baker (Ed.), *Families: Changing Trends in Canada (3rd edition)*. Toronto: McGraw-Hill Ryerson.

McDaniel, Susan A. 1996c. "Toward a synthesis of feminist and demographic perspectives on fertility," *The Sociological Quarterly* 37(1):83–104.

McDaniel, Susan A. 1997. "Intergenerational transfers, social solidarity, and social policy: Unanswered questions and policy challenges," *Canadian Public Policy/Canadian Journal on Aging* (Joint issue):1–21.

McDaniel, Susan A. 1998a. "Towards Healthy Families," pp. 3–42 in National Forum on Health, Determinants of Health: Settings and Issues. Volume 3. Ste.-Foy, Québec: Editions Multimodes.

McDaniel, Susan A. 1998b. "Families, feminism and the state," in Wayne Anthony & Les Samuelson (Eds.), *Power and Resistance: Critical Thinking About Canadian Social Issues (2nd edition)*. Toronto: Fernwood.

McDaniel, Susan A. & Lewis, Robert. 1998c."Did they or didn't they? Intergenerational supports in families past: A case study of Brigus, Newfoundland, 1920–1945," pp. 475–497 in Chambers, Lori & Edgar-Andre Montigny (Eds.), *Family Matters: Papers in Post-Confederation Canadian Family History*. Toronto: Canadian Scholars Press.

McIlroy, Anne. 1998. "One way to build better families," *The Globe and Mail*, 29 September: A1, A6.

McKenna, James J. 1996. "Sudden infant death syndrome in cross-cultural perspective: Is infant-parent cosleeping protective?" *Annual Review of Anthropology* 25:201-216.

McKie, Craig. 1993. "An overview of lone parenthood in Canada," pp. 53–72 in Joe Hudson & Burt Galaway (Eds.), *Single Parent Families: Perspectives on Research and Policy*. Toronto: Thompson.

McLanahan, Sara & Irwin Garfinkel. 1993. "Single motherhood in the United States: Growth, problems, and policies," pp. 15–30 in Joe Hudson & Burt Galaway (Eds.), *Single Parent Families: Perspectives on Research and Policy*. Toronto: Thompson.

McLaren, Angus & Arlene McLaren. 1986. *The Bedroom and the State: The Changing Practices and Politics of Contraception and Abortion in Canada, 1880–1980*. Toronto: McClelland & Stewart.

McLaren, Arlene Tigar. 1996. "Coercive invitations: How young women in school make sense of mothering and waged labour," *British Journal of Sociology of Education* 17(3):279–298.

McLeod, Jane D., Candace Kruttschnitt & Maude Dornfeld. 1994. "Does parenting explain the effects of structural conditions on children's antisocial behavior? A comparison of blacks and whites," *Social Forces* 73(2): 575-604.

McMahon, Martha. 1995. *Engendering Motherhood: Identity and Self-Transformation in Women's Lives*. New York: Guilford.

McMahon, Martha & Ellen Pence. 1996. "Replying to Dan O'Leary," *Journal of Interpersonal Violence* 11 (Sept.).

McManus, Michael J. 1996. "The marriage-saving movement," *The American Enterprise* 7 (May/June).

Meeks, Suzanne, Diane B. Arnkoff, Carol R. Glass & Clifford J. Notarius. 1986. "Wives' employment status, hassles, communication and relational efficacy: Intra- versus extra-relationship factors and marital adjustment," *Family Relations* 35(2): 249–255.

Meissner, Martin. 1986. "Estrangement from Sociability and the Work of Women in Canada." International Sociological Association.

Meissner, Martin. 1975. "On the division of labour and sexual inequality." *Sociologie du Travail* 17 (4): 329–50.

Menaghan, Elizabeth G. 1993. "The Long Reach of the Job: Effects of Parents' Occupational Conditions on Family Patterns and Children's Well-Being," American Sociological Association, Association paper.

Merrill, Lex L., Linda K. Hervig, & Joel S. Milner. 1996. "Childhood parenting experiences, intimate partner conflict resolution, and adult risk for child physical abuse," *Child Abuse and Neglect* 20(11):1049–1065.

Merskin, D.L. & M. Huberlie. 1996. "Companionship in the Classifieds: The adoption of personal advertisements by daily newspapers," *Journalism and Mass Communication Quarterly* 73(1):219–229.

Meyerstein, Israela. 1997. "The problem box ritual: Helping families prepare for remarriage," *Journal of Family Psychotherapy* 8(1):61–65.

Millar, Wayne & Surinder Wadhera. 1997. "A perspective on Canadian teenage births, 1992–94: Older men and younger women?" *Canadian Journal of Public Health* 88:333–336.

Miller, A. Therese, Colleen Eggertson-Tacon & Brian Quigg. 1990. "Patterns of runaway behavior within a larger systems context: The road to empowerment," *Adolescence* 25(98): 271–289.

Miller, David & P. Gillies. 1996. "Is there life after work? Experiences of HIV and oncology health staff," *AIDS Care* 8(2):167–82.

Minkler, Meredith & Relda Robinson-Beckley, Jr. 1994. "Raising grandchildren from crack-cocaine households: Effects on family and friendship ties of African-American women," *American Journal of Orthopsychiatry* 64(1):20–29.

Minkler, Meredith & Kathleen M. Roe. 1996. "Grandparents as surrogate parents," *Generations*, 20 (spring):34–38.

Minton, Carmelle & Kay Pasley. 1996. "Fathers' parenting role identity and father involvement: A comparison of non-divorced and divorced, nonresident fathers," *Journal of Family Issues* 17(1).

Mitchell, Barbara. 1994. "Family structure and leaving the nest: A social resource perspective," *Sociological Perspectives* 37(4):651–671.

Mitchell, Barbara. 1998. "The Refilled Nest: Debunking the Myth of Family-in-Crisis," Paper presented at the 9th Annual John K. Friesen Conference, The Overselling of Population Aging, Simon Fraser University, 14–15 May 1998.

Mitchell, Barbara A. & Ellen M. Gee. 1996a. "'Boomerang kids' and midlife parental marital satisfaction," *Family Relations* 45:442–448.

Mitchell, Barbara A. & Ellen M. Gee. 1996b. "Young adults returning home: Implications for social policy," pp.61–71 in Burt Galaway & Joe Hudson (Eds.), *Youth in Transition: Perspectives on Research and Policy*. Toronto: Thompson Educational Publishing.

Molseed, Mari J. 1995. "In loco parentis: An elaboration of the parental relationship form," *Symbolic Interaction*, 1995 18(3):341-354.

Monahan, D. J, L. Kohman, & M. Coleman. 1996. "Open-heart surgery: consequences for caregivers," *Journal of Gerontological Social Work* 25(3–4):53–70.

Moncher, Frank J. 1995. "Social isolation and child-abuse risk," *Families in Society* 76(Sept.):421–433.

Mongeau, P.A. & C.M. Carey. 1996. "Who's wooing whom: An experimental investigation of date initiation and expectancy violation," *Western Journal of Communication* 60(3):195–213.

Monk, Timothy H., Marilyn J. Essex, Nancy A. Snider, Marjorie H. Klein, et al. 1996. "The impact of the birth of a baby on the time structure and social mixture of a couple's daily life and its consequences for well-being," *Journal of Applied Social Psychology*.

Moogk, Peter. 1982. "Les Petits Sauvages: The Children of Eighteenth Century New France," In Joy Parr (Ed.), *Childhood and Family in Canadian History*. Toronto: McClelland and Stewart.

Mookherjee, H.N. 1997. "Marital Status, Gender and Perception of Well-Being," *Journal of Social Psychology* 137(1):95–105.

Moore Lappé, Frances. 1985. *What To Do After You Turn Off the TV? Fresh Ideas for Enjoying Family Time*. New York: Ballantine Books.

Moore, Dahlia. 1995. "Role conflict: Not only for women? A comparative analysis of 5 nations," *International Journal of Comparative Sociology* 36(1–2):17–35.

Moore, Eric G. & Mark W. Rosenberg, with Donald McGuiness. 1997. *Growing Old in Canada: Demographic and Geographic Perspectives*. Toronto & Ottawa: Nelson & Statistics Canada. Catalogue no. 96–321-MPE, no. 1.

Morrison, Kati & Airdrie Thompson-Guppy, with Patricia Bell. 1986. *Stepmothers: Exploring the Myth*. Ottawa: Canadian Council on Social Development.

Morton, Suzanne. 1992a. "The June bride as the working class bride: Getting married in a Halifax working class neighbourhood in the 1920s," pp. 360–379 in Bettina Bradbury (Ed.), *Canadian Family History: Selected Readings*. Toronto: Copp Clark Pitman.

Morton, Suzanne. 1992b. "Women on their own: Single mothers in working-class Halifax in the 1920s," *Acadiensis* XXI(2):90–107.

Motohashi, S. 1978. "A record of a mother of a handicapped child," *Japanese Journal of Nursing* 42:968–970.

Motta, Robert W. 1994. "Identification of characteristics and causes of childhood posttraumatic stress disorder," *Psychology in the Schools* 31(1):49–56.

Mui, Ada C. 1995a."Caring for frail elderly parents: A comparison of adult sons and daughters," *The Gerontologist* 35(Feb.): 86–93.

Mui, Ada C. 1995b. "Multidimensional predictors of caregiver strain among older persons caring for frail spouses," *Journal of Marriage and the Family* 57(Aug.):733–740.

Mulhall, Peter F., Donald Stone & Brian Stone. 1996. "Home alone: Is it a risk factor for middle-school students?" *Journal of Drug Education* 26(1):39-48.

Munsch, Joyce, John Woodward & Nancy Darling. 1995. "Children's perceptions of their relationship with coresiding and non-coresiding fathers," *Journal of Divorce and Remarriage* 23(1–2).

Muransky, Jean M., Darlene DeMarie-Deblow. 1995. "Differences between high school students from intact and divorced families," *Journal of Divorce and Remarriage* 23(3–4).

Murray, Sandra L, John G. Holmes & W. Dale. 1996. "The benefits of positive illusions: Idealization and the construction of satisfaction in close relationships," *Journal of Personality and Social Psychology* 70(1).

Myers, Scott M. & Alan Booth. 1996. "Men's retirement and marital quality," *Journal of Family Issues* 17(3).

Nakhaie, M.R. 1995. "Housework in Canada: The national picture," *Journal of Comparative Family Studies* 26(3):409–425.

Nathan, Michael, Aliza Schnabel-Brandes & Harvey Peskin. 1981. "Together and apart: Kibbutz children, twelfth grade graduates in 1969, after ten years: A follow-up study," *Kibbutz* 8:105-115.

Nault, Francois & Alain Belanger. 1996. *The Decline in Marriage in Canada, 1981–1991.* Ottawa: Statistics Canada. Catalogue no. 84-536-XPB.

Nazer, Nancy & Janet Salaff. 1996. "Telework and taking care: The elderly," Society for the Study of Social Problems.

Nelson, Fiona. 1996. *Lesbian Motherhood: An Exploration of Canadian Lesbian Families.* Toronto: University of Toronto Press.

Nelson, Geoffrey. 1994. "Emotional well-being of separated and married women: Long-term follow-up study," *American Journal of Orthopsychiatry* 64 (Jan.).

Nippert-Eng, Christena. 1996. "Calendars and keys: The classification of 'home' and 'work'," *Sociological Forum* 11(3):563–582.

Nock, Steven L. 1995. "Commitment and dependency in marriage," *Journal of Marriage and the Family* 57(May).

Noller, Patricia. 1996. "What is this thing called love? Defining the love that supports marriage and family," *Personal Relationships* 3 (1):97–115.

Norton, Pamela & Clifford Drew. 1994. "Autism and potential family stressors," *The American Journal of Family Therapy* 22(spring): 67–76.

Notarius, Clifford I. & Jennifer S. Johnson. 1982. "Emotional expression in husbands as wives," *Journal of Marriage and the Family* 44(2):483–489.

O'Connor, Pat. 1995. "Understanding/variations

marital sexual pleasure: An impossible task?," *Sociological Review* 43(2).

O'Donohue, William & Julie L. Crouch. 1996. "Marital therapy and gender-linked factors in communication," *Journal of Marital and Family Therapy* 22(Jan.).

O'Farrell, Timothy J. & Christopher M. Murphy. 1995. "Marital violence before and after alcoholism treatment," *Journal of Consulting and Clinical Psychology* 63(Apr.):256–262.

O'Keefe, Maura. 1996. "The differential effects of family violence on adolescent adjustment," *Child and Adolescent Social Work Journal* 13(1): 51–68.

O'Leary, Micky, Janet Franzoni & Gregory Brack. 1996. "Divorcing parents: Factors related to coping and adjustment," *Journal of Divorce and Remarriage* 25 (3-4):85-103.

O'Neill, John. 1994. *The Missing Child in Liberal Theory: Towards a Covenant Theory of Family, Community, Welfare and the Civic State.* Toronto: University of Toronto Press.

Oakley, Ann. 1974. *The Sociology of Housework.* Bath: Martin Robinson.

Odegaard, Paul 1996. "Empathy induction in the couple treatment of depression: Shifting the focus from self to other," *Families, Systems and Health* 14(2).

Oerton, Sarah. 1997. "'Queer Housewives?': Some Problems in Theorising the Division of Domestic Labour in Lesbian and Gay Households," *Women's Studies International Forum* 20 (3):421–430.

Oppenheim, David, Frederick S. Wamboldt, Leslie A. Gavin, Andrew G. Renouf *et al.* 1996. "Couples' co-construction of the story of their child's birth; Associations with marital adaptation," *Journal of Narrative and Life History* 6(1).

Oppenheimer, Valerie Kincade. 1997. "Women's employment and the gain to marriage: The specialization and trading model," *Annual Review of Sociology* 23:431–453.

Orava, Tammy A., Peter J. McLeod & Donald Sharpe. 1996. "Perceptions of control, depressive symptomatology, and self-esteem of women in transition from abusive relationships," *Journal of Family Violence* 11 (June):167–186.

Orbuch, Terri L., James S. House & Pamela S. Mero. 1996. "Marital quality over the life course," *Social Psychology Quarterly* 59(June).

Orloff, Ann Shola. 1993. "Gender and the social rights of citizenship: The comparative analysis of gender relations and welfare states," *American Sociological Review* 58(3):303–328.

Osterman, Paul. 1995. "Work/family programs and the employment relationship," *Administrative Science Quarterly* 40:681–700.

Paden, Shelley & Cheryl Buehler. 1995. "Coping with the dual-income lifestyle," *Journal of Marriage and the Family* 57:101–110.

Palgi, Michal. 1993. "Kibbutz woman: Gender roles and status," *Israel Social Science Research* 8(1):108-121.

Papps, Fiona, Michael Walker, Antonietta Trimboli & Carmelina Trimboli. 1995. "Parental discipline in Anglo, Greek Lebanese, and Vietnamese cultures," *Journal of Cross-cultural Psychology* 26(1):49–64.

Parcel, Toby L. & Elizabeth G. Menaghan. 1993. "Family social capital and children's behavior problems," *Social Psychology Quarterly* 56 (2):120–135.

Paredes, Maceda Catherine. 1995. "Filipino women and intermarriages," *Asian Migrant* 8(4) (Oct.-Dec.).

Parker, Seymour & Hilda Parker. 1992. "Male gender identity in the Israeli kibbutz: Reflections on 'protest masculinity'," *Ethos* 20(3):340-357

Pasch, Lauri A. & Thomas N. Bradbury. 1998. "Social support, conflict, and the development of marital dysfunction," *Journal of Consulting and Clinical Psychology* 66(2):219–230.

Paulson, Sharon E. 1996. "Maternal employment and adolescent achievement revisited: An ecological perspective," *Family Relations* 45 (Apr.):201-208.

Payne, Malcolm. 1995. "Understanding 'going missing': Issues for social work and social services," *British Journal of Social Work* 25(3):333-348.

Pearcey, Nancy R. 1995. "Laboring at love," *The American Enterprise* 6(Sept.): 40–42.

Peiser, Nadine C. & Patrick C.L. Heaven. 1996. "Family influences on self-reported delinquency among high school students," *Journal of Adolescence* (Dec.):557–568.

Penhale, Bridget. 1993,. "The abuse of elderly people: Considerations for practice." *British Journal of Social Work* 23(2):95–112.

Perez, J.F. 1978. *The Family Roots of Adolescent Delinquency*, New York: Van Nostrand.

Peters, Alice. 1997. "Canadian Children in the 1990s: Selected Findings of the National Longitudinal Survey of Children and Youth," Paper presented at the Canadian Population Society meetings, St. John's, Newfoundland.

Peters, John F. 1995. "Canadian families into the year 2000," *International Journal of Sociology of the Family* 25(1):63–79.

Peterson, Richard, R. 1996a. "A re-evaluation of the economic consequences of divorce," *American Sociological Review* 61(3).

Peterson, Richard, R. 1996b. "Statistical errors, faulty conclusions, misguided policy: Reply to Weitzman," *American Sociological Review* 61(3).

Pett, Marjorie A., Beth Vaughan-Cole & Bruce E. Wampold. 1994, "Maternal employment and perceived stress: Their impact on children's adjustment and mother–child interaction in young divorced and married families," *Family Relations*, 43(Apr.):151–158.

Phillips, Andrew. 1997. "Christian men on the march," *Maclean's* 6 October :52–53.

Phillips, Lisa. 1995. "'The family' in income tax policy," *Policy Options/Options Politiques* 16(10):30–32.

Philp, Margaret. 1998. "Public day care pays off for whole society," *The Globe and Mail* 5 March:A8.

Phillips, Roderick. 1988. *Putting Asunder: The History of Divorce in Western Society*, New York: Cambridge University Press.

Pickett, Susan A., Judith A. Cook, & Bertram J. Cohler. 1994. "Caregiving burden experienced by parents of offspring with severe mental illness: The impact of off-timedness," *Journal of Applied Social Sciences* 18(2):199– 207.

Pina, Darlene L. & Vern L. Bengston. 1995. "Division of household labor and the well-being of retirement-aged wives," *The Gerontologist* 35,(June).

Plass, Peggy S. & Gerald T. Hotaling. 1995. "The intergenerational transmission of running away: Childhood experiences of the parents of runaways," *Journal of Youth and Adolescence* 24(3):335–348.

Pogrebin, Letty C. 1983. *Family Politics*. New York: McGraw Hill.

Pomerleau, Andree, Gerard Malcuit & Colette Sabatier. 1991. "Child-rearing practices and parental beliefs in three cultural groups of Montreal: Québécois, Vietnamese, Haitian," pp. 45-68 in Marc H. Bornstein (Ed.), *Cultural Approaches to Parenting: Crosscurrents in Contemporary Psychology*.

Popenoe, David. 1988. *Disturbing the Nest: Family Change and Decline in Modern Societies*. New York: A. de Gruyter.

Popenoe, David. 1996a. "Modern marriage: Revising the cultural script," pp. 247–270 in David Popenoe, Jean Bethke Elshtain & David Blankenhorn (Eds.), *Promises to Keep: Decline and Renewal of Marriage in America,*. Lanham, MD: Rowman and Littlefield Publishers, Inc.

Popenoe, David. 1996b. *Life Without Father*. New York: Free Press.

Powers, Jane Levine, John Eckenrode & Barbara Jaklitsch. 1990. "Maltreatment among runaway and homeless youth," *Child Abuse and Neglect* 14(1):87-98.

Presser, Harriet B. 1995. "Job, family, and gender: Determinants of nonstandard work schedules among employed Americans in 1991," 32, Nov.:577–598.

Price, Virginia Ann. 1989. "Characteristics and needs of Boston street youth: One agency's response," *Children and Youth Services Review* 11(1):75-90.

Promise Keepers. 1996. *Man of His Word: New Testament*. Colorado Springs, Colorado: International Bible Society.

Quirk, Gregory J. & Leonel Casco. 1994. "Stress disorders of families of the disappeared: A controlled study in Honduras," *Social Science and Medicine* 39(12):1675–1679.

Rabin, Claire & Giora Rahav. 1995. "Differences and similarities between younger and older marriages across cultures: A comparison of American and Israeli retired nondistressed marriages," *American Journal of Family Therapy* 23(3).

Radziszewska, Barbara, Jean L. Richardson, Clyde W. Dent & Brian R. Flay. 1996. "Parenting style and adolescent depressive symptoms, smoking and academic achievement: Ethnic, gender, and SES differences, " *Journal of Behavioral Medicine* 19(3):289-305.

Raitt, Fiona. 1996. "Domestic violence and divorce mediation," *Journal of Social Welfare and Family Law* 18(1):11–20.

Ram, Bali. 1990. *New Trends in the Family: Demographic Facts and Features*. Ottawa: Statistics Canada. Catalogue no.91-535E.

Rank, Mark & Larry Davis. 1996. "Perceived happiness outside of marriage among black and white spouses," *Family Relations* 45(Oct.)

Rankin, Elizabeth Anne DeSalvo. 1993. "Stresses and rewards experienced by employed mothers," *Health Care for Women International* 14(6): 527–537.

Reitsma-Street, Marge. 1991. "Girls Learn to Care: Girls Policed to Care," in Carol Baines, Patricia Evans & Sheila Neysmith (Eds.), *Women's Caring: Feminist Perspectives on Social Welfare*. Toronto: McClelland & Stewart.

Renaud, Marc. 1997. "Statement to the Standing Committee on Industry, House of Commons, on behalf of the Social Sciences and Humanities Research Council of Canada," 11 December.

Renzetti, Claire M. 1996. "The poverty of services for battered lesbians," *Journal of Gay and Lesbian Social Services* 4(1):61–68.

Richards, John. 1998. "The case for subsidizing the 'Traditional Family'," *Globe and Mail*, 26 January:A21.

Richardson, C. James. 1996. "Divorce and remarriage," pp.215–248 in Maureen Baker (Ed.), *Families: Changing Trends in Canada (3rd Edition)*. Toronto: McGraw-Hill Ryerson.

Riches, Gordon & Pamela Dawson. 1996. "An intimate loneliness: Evaluating the impact of a child's death on parental self-identity and marital relationships," *Journal of Family Therapy* 18(1).

Richmond, Virginia P. 1995. "Amount of communication in marital dyads as a function of dyad and individual marital satisfaction," *Communication Research Reports* 12(2):152–159.

Riege, M.Gray. 1972. "Parental affection and juvenile delinquency in girls," *"British Journal of Criminology* 12:55-73.

Risman, Barbara. 1998. *Gender Vertigo: American Families in Transition*. New Haven:Yale University Press.

Risman, Barbara J. & Danette Johnson-Sumerford. 1998. "Doing it fairly: Study of postgender marriages," *Journal of Marriage and the Family* 60:23–40.

Roberts, Albert R. 1996. "Battered women who kill: a comparative study of incarcerated participants with a community sample of battered women," *Journal of Family Violence* 11 (Sept.): 291–304.

Rodgers, Bryan. 1994. "Pathways between parental divorce and adult depression," *The Journal of Child Psychology and Psychiatry and Allied Discipline* 35(Oct.).

Rodrigues, James R. & Tricia L. Park. 1996. "General and illness-specific adjustment to cancer: Relationship to marital status and marital quality," *Journal of Psychosomatic Research* 40(1).

Roesler, Thomasa A. & Tiffany Weissmann Wind. 1994. "Telling the secret; Adult women describe their disclosures of incest," *Journal of Interpersonal Violence* 9:327–338.

Rorty, Marcia, Joel Yager & Elizabeth Rossotto. 1995. "Aspects of childhood physical punishment and family environment correlates in bulimia nervosa," *Child Abuse and Neglect* 19(6):659-667.

Rosenberg, Stanley D., Robert E. Drake & Kim Mueser. 1996. "New directions for treatment research on sequelae of sexual abuse in persons with severe mental illness," *Community Mental Health Journal* 32:387–400.

Rosenthal, Carolyn. 1999. "Changing families, life-course and aging," in Ellen M. Gee & Gloria Gutman (Eds.), *The Overselling of Population Aging: Apocalytic Demography and Intergenerational Challenges*. Toronto: Oxford University Press.

Rosenthal, Carolyn J., Anne Martin Matthews & Sarah H. Matthews. 1996. "Caught in the middle? Occupancy in multiple roles and help to parents in a national probability sample of Canadian adults," *Journal of Gerontology* 51B(6):S274-S283.

Ross, Susan M. 1996. "Risk of physical abuse to children of spouse-abusing parents," *Child Abuse and Neglect* 20(7):589–598.

Rotherham-Borus, Mary J. 1993. "Suicidal behavior and risk factors among runaway youths," *American Journal of Psychiatry*, 150(1): 103-107.

Rotherham-Borus, Mary Jane, Karen A. Mahler, Cheryl Koopman& Kris Langabeer. 1996. "Sexual abuse history and associated multiple risk behavior in adolescent runaways," *American Journal of Orthopsychiatry* 3(July): 390-400.

Roxburgh, Susan J. 1995a. "Job Stress and the Well-Being of Women in the Paid Labor Force: An Integration of the Job Stress Models of Kohn and Schooler and Robert Karasek," American Sociological Association (ASA), Association paper.

Roxburgh, Susan J. 1995b. "The Effect of the Quality of Home and Work Roles on the Mental Health of Women in the Paid Labor Force," American Sociological Association (ASA), Association paper.

Ryan, Kristapher. 1990. *From We to Just Me, A Birth Mother's Journey: Decision-Making, Letting Go, Grieving, Healing*. Winnipeg, Manitoba: Freedom To Be Me Seminars.

Ryder, Norman B. 1992. "Reproductive retrenchment in Canada and in the United States," *Proceedings, The Peopling of the Americas. International Union for the Scientific Study of Population.* 3:155–170.

Sabourin, Teresa Chandler. 1995. "The role of negative reciprocity in spouse abuse: A relational control analysis," *Journal of Applied Communication Research* 23(4).

Sabourin, Teresa Chandler & Glen H. Stamp. 1995. "Communication and the experience of dialectical tensions in family life: An examination of abusive and nonabusive families" *Communication Monograph*s 62(3).

Sacks, Jonathan, 1991. *The Persistence of Faith: Religion, Morality and Society in a Secular Age. The 1990 Reith Lectures.* London: Weidenfeld and Nicolson.

Sagi, Abraham; Marinus H. Van-Ijzendoorn, Ora Aviezer, Frank Donnell & Ofra Mayseless,. 1994. "Sleeping out of home in a kibbutz communal arrangement: It makes a difference for infant-mother attachment," *Child Development* 65 (4):992-1004.

Saintjacques, M.C. 1995. "Role strain prediction in stepfamilies," *Journal of Divorce and Remarriage* 24(1–2):51–72.

Sanchez, Laura & Elizabeth Thomson. 1997. "Becoming mothers and fathers: Parenthood, gender and the division of labour," *Gender and Society* 11(6):747–772.

Sanik, Margaret Mietus. 1993. "The effects of time allocation on parental stress," *Social Indicators Research* 30(2–3):175–184.

Schlesinger, Benjamin 1998. "Strong families: A portrait," *Transition*. Ottawa: The Vanier Institute of the Family, June:4–7.

Schneider, Carl E. 1996. "The law and the stability of marriage: The family as a social institution," pp. 187–213 in David Popenoe, Jean Bethke Elshtain & David Blankenhorn, (Eds.) *Promises to Keep: Decline and Renewal of Marriage in America*, Lanham, MD: Rowman and Littlefield Publishers, Inc.

Schofield, Hilary & Helen Herrman. 1993. "Characteristics of carers in Victoria," *Family Matters* 34(May): 21–26.

Schumm, Walter R., Anthony P. Jurich, Stephan R. Bollman & Margaret A. Bugaighis. 1985. "His and her marriage revisited," *Journal of Family Issues* 6(2):221–227.

Schwartz Cowan, Ruth. 1992. "Twentieth century changes in household technology," pp. 82–92 in Arlene Skolnick & Jerome Skolnick (Eds.), *Family in Transition* (7th edition). New York: Harper Collins.

Schwartz, Pepper & Virginia Rutter. 1998. *The Gender of Sexuality*. Thousand Oaks, California: Pine Forge Press.

Scott, Katherine. 1996. *The Progress of Canada's Children*. Ottawa: Canadian Council on Social Development.

Scott-Little, M. Catherine & Susan D. Holloway. 1994. "Caregivers' attributions about children's misbehavior in child-care centers," *Journal of Applied Developmental Psychology* 15(2):241–253.

Seaver, Carol. 1996. "Muted lives: Older battered women," *Journal of Elder Abuse and Neglect* 8(2):3–21.

Seltzer, Judith A. 1994, "Consequences of marital dissolution for children," *Annual Review of Sociology* 20:235–266.

Sev'er, Aysan. 1990. "Mate selection patterns of men and women in personal advertisements," *Atlantis: A Women's Studies Journal* 15(2):70–76.

Seyler, Dian L., Pamela A. Monroe & James C. Garand. 1995. "Balancing work and family: The role of employer-supported child care benefits," *Journal of Social Issues* 16(Mar):170–193.

Shadish, William R; Kevin Ragsdale & Renata R. Glaser, Renata R 1995. "The efficacy and effectiveness of marital and family therapy: A perspective from meta-analysis," *Journal of Marital and Family Therapy* 21(4).

Shane, Paul G. 1989. "Changing patterns among homeless and runaway youth," *American Journal of Orthopsychiatry* 59(2):208-214.

Shane, Paul G. 1991. "A sample of homeless and runaway youth in New Jersey and their health status," *Journal of Health and Social Policy* 2(4):73-82.

Shaver, Sheila & Jonathan Bradshaw. 1995. "The recognition of wifely labour by welfare states," *Social Policy and Administration* 29(1):10–25.

Shavit, Yossi; Claude S. Fischer & Yael Koresh. 1994. "Kin and nonkin under collective threat: Israeli networks during the Gulf War, *Social Forces* 72(4):1197–1215.

Shek, Daniel T.L. 1995a. "Gender differences in marital quality and well-being in Chinese married adults," *Sex Roles* 32(June).

Shek, Daniel T.L. 1995b "Marital quality and psychological well-being of married adults in a Chinese context," *Journal of Genetic Psychology* 156(1).

Sheridan, Michael J. "A proposed intergenerational model of substance abuse, family functioning, and abuse/neglect," *Child Abuse and Neglect* 19(May):519–530.

Shucksmith, J., L.B. Hendry & A. Glendinning. 1995. "Models of parenting: Implications for adolescent well-being within different types of family contexts," *Journal of Adolescence* 18(3):253-270.

Shupe, Anson D., William A. Stacey & Lonnie R. Hazlewood. 1987. *Violent Men, Violent Couples: The Dynamics of Domestic Violence.* Lexington: Lexington Books.

Silver, Hilary & Frances Goldscheider. 1994. "Flexible work and housework: Work and family constraints on women's domestic labor," *Social Forces* 72(June):1103–1119.

Silverman, Eliane Leslau. 1984. *The Last Best West: Women on the Alberta Frontier 1880–1930.* Montreal: Eden Press.

Sim, Hee-Ong & Samuel Vuchinich. 1996. "The declining effects of family stressors on antisocial behavior from childhood to adolescence and early adulthood," *Journal of Family Issues* 17(May).

Simmons, Deborah S. & William J. Doherty. 1995. "Defining who we are and what we do: Clinical practice patterns of marriage and family therapists in Minnesota," *Journal of Marital and Family Therapy* 21(1).

Simons, Ronald & Les Whitbeck. 1991. "Running away during adolescence as a precursor to adult homelessness," *Social Science Review* 65(2):224-247.

Skitka, Linda & Michele Frazier. 1995. "Ameliorating the effects of parental divorce: Do small group interventions work?" *Journal of Divorce and Remarriage* 24 (3–4).

Skolnick, Arlene. 1991. *Embattled Paradise: The American Family in an Age of Uncertainty.* New York: Basic Books.

Skrypnek, Berna J. & Janet E. Fast. 1996. "Work and family policy in Canada: Family needs, collective solutions," *Journal of Family Issues* 17(6): 793–812.

Smith, Dorothy. 1993. "The Standard North American Family: SNAF as an ideological code," *Journal of Family Issues* 14(1):50–65.

Smith, Jane E., V. Waldorf & D. Trembath. 1990. "Single white male looking for thin, very attractive...," *Sex Roles* 23(11&12):675–683.

Smock, Pamela J. 1994. "Gender and the short-run economic consequences of marital disruption," *Social Forces* 73(Sept.).

Snarey, John & Linda Son. 1986. "Sex-identity development among kibbutz-born males: A test of the Whiting hypothesis," *Ethos* 14(2):99-119.

Snell, James G. 1983. "'The White life for two': The defence of marriage and sexual morality in Canada, 1890–1914," *Histoire sociale/Social History* 16(31):111–128.

Snow, Catherine E. 1991. "The language of the mother-child relationship," pp. 195–210, in Martin Woodhead, Ronnie Carr & Paul Light

(Eds), *Becoming a Person: Child Development in Social Context*, Vol. 1.

Snowdon, Anne W. Sheila Cameron & Katherine Dunham. 1994. "Relationships between stress, coping resources and satisfaction with family functioning in families of children with disabilities," *Canadian Journal of Nursing Research* 26(3):63–76.

Snyder, D.K. & L.A. Fruchtman. 1981. "Differential patterns of wife abuse: A data-based typology," *Journal of Consulting and Clinical Psychology* 49: 878–885.

Snyder, Robert A. 1995. "One man's time warp is another (wo)man's treasure: The importance of individual and situational differences in shift work tolerance and satisfaction," *Human Resource Development Quarterly* 6(4):397–407.

Sogner, Solvi. 1993. "Historical features of women's position in society," pp. 145–184 in Nora Federici, K.O. Mason & Solvi Sogner (Eds.), *Women's Position and Demographic Change*. Oxford: Clarendon.

Sommer, Dion. 1992. "A child's place in society: New challenges for the family and day care," *Children and Society* 6(4):317-335.

Song, Jung Ah, Betsy M. Bergen & Walter Schumm. 1995 "Sexual satisfaction among Korean-American couples in the Midwestern United States," *Journal of Sex and Marital Therapy* 21(3).

Song, Miri. 1995. "Children's labor participation in Chinese take-away businesses in Britain," American Sociological Association, Association paper.

South, Scott 1985. "Economic conditions and the divorce rate: A time-series analysis of the children," *Journal of Marriage and the Family* 47(1): 31–42.

South, Scott 1995. "Do you need to shop around? Age at marriage, spousal alternatives and divorce," *Journal of Family Issues* 16(July).

South, Scott & Kim Lloyd. 1995. "Spousal alternatives and marital dissolution," *American Sociological Review* 60(Feb.).

Spanier, Graham B. 1979. "The measurement of marital quality," *Journal of Sex and Marital Therapy* 5(3): 288–300.

Spillane-Grieco, Eileen. 1984. "Characteristics of a helpful relationship: A study of empathic understanding and positive regard between runaways and their parents," *Adolescence* 19(73): 63–75.

Sprott, Julie E. 1994. "One person's 'spoiling' is another's freedom to become: Overcoming ethnocentric views about parental control," *Social Science and Medicine* 38(8):1111-1124.

Stacey, Judith. 1990. *Brave New Families*. New York: Basic Books.

Stacey, William A., Lonnie R. Hazlewood & Anson D. Shupe. 1994. *The Violent Couple*. Westport, Conn: Praeger.

Stanley, Sandra C. Janet G. Hunt & Larry L. Hunt. 1986. " The relative deprivation of husbands in dual-earner households," *Journal of Family Issues* 7(1): 3–20.

Stanton, Glenn T. 1996. "The counter-revolution against easy divorce: New rumbling in the states," *The American Enterprise* 7(May/June).

Statistical Record of Women Worldwide. 1991. Detroit: Gale Research.

Statistics Canada. 1992. *Families, Number, Type and Structure*. Ottawa: Statistics Canada, Catalogue no. 93–312.

Statistics Canada. 1993. "The Violence Against Women Survey," *The Daily*, 18 November.

Statistics Canada. 1995. *Households' Unpaid Work: Measuring and Valuation*. Ottawa: Statistics Canada. Catalogue no. 13-603E, no. 3.

Statistics Canada. 1996a. "Life Events: How Families Change," *Labour and Income Dynamics* 5(1). Ottawa: Statistics Canada.

Statistics Canada. 1996b. "Canadian Families: Diversity and Change," *The Daily*, 19 June.

Statistics Canada. 1996c. "Dual-Earner Families," *The Daily*, 6 June.

Statistics Canada. 1997a. "Formation of First Common Law Unions," *The Daily*, 9 December.

Statistics Canada. 1997b. "Earnings Characteristics of Two-Partner Families," *The Daily*, 26 August:2–3.

Statistics Canada. 1997c. *Income Distributions by Size in Canada, 1996*. Ottawa: Statistics Canada. Catalogue no. 13-207-XPB.

Statistics Canada. 1998a. "1996 Census: Labour Force Activity, Occupation and Industry, Place of Work, Mode of Transportation to Work, Unpaid Work," *The Daily* 17 March.

Statistics Canada. 1998b. "1996 Census: Marital Status, Common-Law Unions and Families," *The Daily* 14 October.

Statistics Canada. 1998c. "1996 Census: Aboriginal Data," *The Daily*, 13 January.

Statistics Canada. 1998d. "1996 Census: Private Households, Housing Costs and Social and Economic Characteristics of Families," *The Daily*, 9 June.

Statistics Canada. 1998e. "Earnings of Men and Women, 1996," *The Daily* 23 March.

Statistics Canada. 1998f. "Marriages and Divorces, 1996," *The Daily*, 29 January.

Statistics Canada. 1998g. "Sterility,"*The Daily*, 24 January.

Statistics Canada. 1998h. "1996 Census: Ethnic Origin, Visible Minorities," *The Daily*, 17 February.

Steinberg, Laurence, Susie D. Lamborn, Nancy Darling, Nina S. Mounts & Sanford M. Dornbusch. 1994. "Over-time changes in adjustment and competence among adolescents from authoritative, authoritarian, indulgent, and neglectful families," *Child Development* 65(3):754–770.

Steinhauer, *et. al.* 1984. "The process model of family functioning," *Canadian Journal of Psychiatry* 29(March):77–88.

Steinmetz, S.K. 1977. *The Cycle of Violence: Assertive, Aggressive, and Abusive Family Interaction*, New York: Praeger.

Stephens, Linda S. 1996. "Will Johnny see Daddy this week? An empirical test of three theoretical perspectives of post-divorce contact," *Journal of Family Issues*12(4).

Stermac, Lana, Alison Davidson & Peter M. Sheridan. 1995. "Incidence of nonsexual violence in incest offenders," *International Journal of Offender Therapy and Comparative Criminology* 39(summer):167–178.

Stern, Susan B. & Carolyn A. Smith. 1995. "Family processes and delinquency in an ecological context," *Social Service Review* 69(4):703-731.

Stiffman, Arlene Rubin. 1989a. "Physical and sexual abuse in runaway youths," *Child Abuse and Neglect* 13(3):417-426.

Stiffman, Arlene Rubin 1989b. "Suicide attempts in runaway youths," *Suicide and Life Threatening Behavior* 19(2):147-159.

Stohs, Joanne Hovan. 1995. "Predictors of conflict over the household division of labor among women employed full-time," *Sex Roles* 33(3-4).

Straus, M., "Family Violence," in Edgar F. Borgatta & Marie L. Borgatta (Eds.), *Encyclopedia of Sociology,*. New York: Macmillan Publishing Co, 1992, vol. 2.

Straus, Murray A. 1996. *Identifying Offenders in Criminal Justice Research on Domestic Assault*. Beverley Hills: Sage Publications.

Straus, M.A., R.J. Gelles & S.K. Steinmetz. 1980. *Behind Closed Doors: Violence in the American Family*, Garden City, NY: Doubleday.

Sugarman, David B. & Susan L. Frankel. 1996. "Patriarchal ideology and wife-assault: A meta-analytic review," *Journal of Family Violence* 11(1):13–40.

Suitor, J. Jill & Karl Pillemer. 1995. "Changes in Support and Interpersonal Stress in the Networks of Married Caregiving Daughters: Findings from a 2–Year Panel Study," ASP, Association paper.

Sullivan, Kieran T & Thomas N. Bradbury. 1997. "Are premarital prevention programs reaching couples at risk for marital dysfunctions?" *Journal of Consulting and Clinical Psychology* 65(1).

Susser, Ezra S., Shang P. Lin, Sarah A. Conover & Elmer L. Struening. 1991. "Childhood antecedents of homelessness in psychiatric patients," *American Journal of Psychiatry* 148(8):1026-1030.

Swadener, Beth Blue & Sally Lubeck. (Eds.). 1995. *Children and Families "At Promise": Deconstructing the Discourse of Risk.* Albany, New York: State University of New York Press.

Sweeny, Megan 1996. "The decision to divorce and subsequent remarriage: does it matter which spouse chose to leave?" American Sociological Association.

Sweezy, Kate & Jill Tiefenthaler. 1996. "Do state-level variables affect divorce rates?," *Review of Social Economy* 54(1).

Sydie, Rosalind A. 1986. *Natural Women, Cultured Men: A Feminist Perspective on Sociological Theory.* Toronto: Methuen.

Szinovacz, Maximilian. 1996. "Couples' employment/retirement patterns and perceptions of marital quality," *Research on Aging* 18(2).

Tannen, Deborah. 1993. *Gender and Conversational Interaction.* New York: Oxford University Press.

Tasker, Fiona & Susan Golombok. 1995. "Adults raised as children in lesbian families." *American Journal of Orthopsychiatry* 65 (2): 203–215.

Tayler, Lyn, Gordon Parker & Kay Roy. "Parental divorce and its effects on the quality of intimate relationships in adulthood," *Journal of Divorce and Remarriage* 24(3–4).

Taylor, Lorraine C., Ivora D. Hinton & Melvin N. Wilson. 1995. "Parental influences of academic performance in African-American students," *Journal of Child and Family Studies* 4(3):293-302.

Taylor, S.C. 1980. "Siblings need a plan of care too," *Pediatric Nursing* (Nov.-Dec.): 9–13.

Teare, John F., Karen Authier & Roger Peterson. 1994. "Differential patterns of post-shelter placement as a function of problem type and severity," *Journal of Child and Family Studies* 3(1):7–22.

Tennstedt, Sharon L. & Judith G. Gonyea. 1994. "An agenda for work and eldercare research:

methodological challenges and future directions," *Research on Aging* 16(1):85–108.

Tepperman, Lorne. 1994. *Choices and Chances: Sociology for Everyday Life (second edition).* Toronto: Holt - HBJ.

Theriault, C. & M. Cyr. 1996. "Relation between satisfaction linked to three social roles and satisfaction with life among housewives," *Canadian Journal of Behavioural Sciences* 28(2):79–85.

Thomas, Geoff, Garth J.O. Fletcher & Craig Lange. 1997. "On-line empathetic accuracy in marital interaction," *Journal of Personality and Social Psychology* 72(4).

Thomas, Linda Thiede & Daniel C. Ganster. 1995. "Impact of family-supportive work variables on work–family conflict and strain: A control perspective," *Journal of Applied Psychology* 80(Feb.):6–15.

Thomas, Nancy L. 1991. "The new in loco parentis," 23(5):33–39.

Thomas, Tania N. 1995. "Acculturative Stress in the Adjustment of Immigrant Families," *Journal of Social Distress and the Homeless* 4(2):131–142.

Thompson, Suzanne C., Louis J. Medvene & Debra Freedman. "Caregiving in the close relationship of cardiac patients: exchange, power and attribution perspectives on caregiver resentment," *Personal Relationships* 2(2):1995.

Thornberry, Terence P., Carolyn A. Smith & Gregory Howard. 1997. "Risk Factors for Teenage Fatherhood," *Journal of Marriage and the Family* 59(August):505–522.

Thornton, Arland. 1977. "Children and marital stability." *Journal of Marriage and the Family* 39 (3) Aug.: 531–540.

Thornton, Arland. 1996."Comparative and historical perspectives on marriage, divorce and family life," pp. 69–87 in Popenoe, David, Jean Bethke Elshtain & David Blankenhorn (Eds.), *Promises to Keep: Decline and Renewal of Marriage in America*, Lanham, MD: Rowman and Littlefield Publishers, Inc.

Tingey, Holly, Gary Kiger & Pamela J. Riley. 1996.

"Juggling multiple roles: Perceptions of working mothers," *Social Science Journal* 33(2):183–191.

Tocqueville-Review / Revue-Tocqueville; 1980–81, 3, 1, fall–winter, 5–41.

Tower, Roni-Beth & Stanislav V. Kasl. 1996. "Gender, marital closeness and depressive symptoms in elderly couples," *Journals of Gerontology, Series B, Psychological Sciences and Social Sciences* 51B(3).

Trappe, Heike. 1995. "Women's changing life courses in the German Democratic Republic (GDR)," American Sociological Association, Association paper.

Trost, Jan. 1988. "Conceptualising the family," *International Sociology* 3(3):301–308.

Trudel, Gilles, Lyne Landry & Yvette Larose. 1997. "Low sexual desire: The role of anxiety, depression and marital adjustment," *Sexual and Marital Therapy* 12(1).

Trute, Barry. 1995. "Gender differences in the psychological adjustment of parents of young, developmentally disabled children," *The Journal of Child Psychology and Psychiatry and Allied Disciplines*. 36(Oct.):1225–1242.

Turcotte, Pierre & Alain Belanger. 1997. "Moving in together: The formation of first common-law unions," *Canadian Social Trends* 47(Winter):7–10.

Turk, J. 1964. "Impact of cystic fibrosis on family functioning," *Pediatrics* 34:67–71.

Tzeng, Jessie & Robert Mare. 1995. "Labor market and socioeconomic effects on marital stability," *Social Science Research* 24(Dec.).

United Nations. 1991. *Building the Smallest Democracy at the Heart of Society*. Vienna: United Nations International Year of the Family Secretariat.

United States Bureau of the Census.1995. *Statistical Abstract of the United States*. Washington, D.C.: U.S. Department of Commerce.

Jane Urquhart. 1997. *The Underpainter*. Toronto: McClelland and Stewart: 300.

Valens, E.G. *The Other Side of the Mountain*, New York, Warner Books, 1975.

Valman, H.B. 1981. "The handicapped child," *British Medical Journal* 283:1166–1169.

Valpy, Michael. 1998. "Out of the darkness of Cinderella," *Globe and Mail* 9 January:A21.

Van Crombrugge, Hans & Lieve Vandemeule-broecke. 1991. "Family and center day care under three: The child's experience," *Community Alternatives* 3(2):35–58.

Vanier Institute of the Family. 1994. *Profiling Canada's Families*. Ottawa: Vanier Institute of the Family.

Van Kirk, Sylvia. 1992. "'The Custom of the Country': An examination of fur trade marriage practices," pp. 67–92 in Bettina Bradbury (Ed.), *Canadian Family History: Selected Readings*. Toronto: Copp Clark Pitman.

Van Roosmalen, Erica & Susan A. McDaniel. 1989. "Peer group influence as a factor in smoking behavior of adolescents," *Adolescence* XXIV (96):801–816.

Van Roosmalen, Erica & Susan A. McDaniel. 1992. "Adolescent smoking intentions: Gender differences in peer context," *Adolescence* 27 (105):87–105.

Van Voorhis, P., F.T. Cullen, R.A. Mathers & C. Chenoweth Garner. 1988. "The impact of family structure and quality on delinquency: A comparative assessment of structural and functional factors," *Criminology* 26: 235-261.

Vangelisti, Anita & Mary A. Banski. 1993. "Couples' debriefing conversations: The impact of gender, occupation and demographic characteristics," *Family Relations* 42(Apr.).

Vanier Institute of the Family. 1994. *Profiling Canada's Families*. Ottawa: Vanier Institute of the Family.

Vansteenwegen, Alfons. 1996a "Individual and relational changes seven years after couples therapy," *Journal of Couples Therapy* 6(1–2).

Vansteenwegen, Alfons. 1996b. "Who benefits from couple therapy? A comparison of successful and unsuccessful couples," *Journal of Sex and Marital Therapy* 22(1).

Vansteenwegen, Alfons. 1997. "Do marital therapists do what they say they do? A comparison between experiential and communication couples therapy," *Sexual and Marital Therapy* 12(1).

Veenhoven, Ruut. 1983. "The growing impact of marriage," *Social Indicators Research* 12(1):49–63.

Veevers. Jean E. 1980. *Childless by Choice*, Toronto: Butterworths.

Veevers, Jean E. 1975. "The moral careers of voluntarily childless wives: Notes on the defense of a variant world view," *Family Coordinator* 24(4): 473–487.

Vergun, Pamela Bea, Sanford M. Dornbusch & Laurence Steinberg. 1996. "'Come all of you turn to and help one another': Authoritative parenting, community orientation, and deviance among high school students," American Sociological Association paper.

Vinokur, Amiran D., Richard H. Price & Robert D. Caplan. 1996. "Hard times and hurtful partners: How financial strain affects depression and relationship satisfaction of unemployed persons and their spouses," *Journal of Personality and Social Psychology* 71.

Volling, Brenda L. & Jay Belsky. 1991. "Multiple determinants of father involvement during infancy in dual-earner and single-earner families," *Journal of Marriage and the Family* 53(2):461–474.

Waite, Linda. 1995. "Does marriage matter?" *Demography* 32(4):483–507.

Waldron-Hennessey, Rebecca & Ronald M. Sabatelli. 1997. "The parental comparison level index: A measure for assessing parental rewards and costs relative to expectations," *Journal of Marriage and the Family* 59(4):824–847.

Walker, Karen E. & Frank F. Furstenburg. 1994. "Neighborhood Settings and Parenting Strategies," American Sociological Association, Association paper.

Wallerstein, Judith S. 1996. "The psychological tasks of marriage: part 2," *American Journal of Orthopsychiatry* 66(Apr.).

Wallerstein, J. & S. Blakelee. 1990. *Second Chances: Men, Women, and Children A Decade After Divorce*. New York: Ticknor and Fields.

Walters, Vivienne, Rhonda Lenton, *et al.* 1996. "Paid work, unpaid work and social support: A study of the health of male and female nurses," *Social Science and Medicine* 43(11):1627–1636.

Ward, Peter. 1990. *Courtship, Love and Marriage in Nineteenth Century English Canada*. Montreal & Kingston: McGill-Queen's University Press.

Waring, Edward M., Charles H. Chamberlaine & Claudia Carver. 1995. "A pilot study of marital therapy as a treatment for depression," *The American Journal of Family Therapy* 23(spring):3–10.

Waring, Marilyn. 1988. *If Women Counted: A New Feminist Economics*. San Francisco: Harper & Row.

Warren, Jennifer A. & Phyllis J. Johnson. 1995. "The impact of workplace support on work-family role strain," *Family Relations* 44(Apr.):163–169.

Watkins, Susan C. 1993. "If all we knew about women was what we read in *Demography*, what would we know?" *Demography* 30(4): 551–577.

Weaver, Terri L. & George A. Clum. 1996. "Interpersonal violence: Expanding the search for long-term sequelae within a sample of battered women," *Journal of Traumatic Stress* 9(4):783–803.

Webster, Pamela S. & Regula A. Herzog. 1995. "Effects of parental divorce and memories of family problems on relationships between adult children and their parents," *Journal of Gerontology, Series B: Psychological Sciences and Social Sciences* 50B(Jan.).

Webster, Pamela S., Terri L. Orbuch, James S. House. 1995. "Effects of childhood family background on adult marital quality and perceived stability," *American Sociological Association* 101(Sept.).

Weiner, Jennifer, Lisa Harlow & Jerome Adams. 1995. "Psychological adjustment of college students from families of divorce," *Journal of Divorce and Remarriage* 23(3–4).

Weisfeld, G.E., R.J.H. Russell, C.C. Weisfeld & P.A. Wells. 1992. "Correlates of satisfaction in British marriages," *Ethology and Sociobiology* 13 (2):125–145.

Weiss, Robert S. "Parenting from separate households," pp. 215–230 in *Promises to Keep: Decline and Renewal of Marriage in America*, David Popenoe, Jean Bethke Elshtain & David Blankenhorn, (Eds.) Lanham, MD: Rowman and Littlefield Publishers, Inc., 1996.

Weitzman, Lenore. 1985. *The Divorce Revolution: The Unexpected Social and Economic Effects for Women and Children in America*, New York: Free Press.

Weitzman, Lenore J. 1996."The economic consequences of divorce are still unequal: Comment on Peterson," *American Sociological Review* 61(3).

Wells, L.E. & J.H. Rankin. 1988. "Direct parental controls and delinquency," *Criminology* 26: 263-285.

Wells, Mona & Harjit S. Sandhu, 1986. "The juvenile runaway: A historical perspective," *Free Inquiry in Creative Sociology*14(2):143–147.

Weston, K. 1991. *Families We Choose: Lesbians, Gays, Kinship*. New York: Columbia University Press.

Wharton, Amy S. & Rebecca J. Erickson. 1995. "The consequences of caring: Exploring the links between women's job and family emotion work," *Sociological Quarterly* 36(2):273–296.

Wherry, Jeffrey N., John B. Jolly, John F. Aruffo, Greg Gillette, Lela Vaught & Rebecca Methony. 1994. "Family trauma and dysfunction in sexually abused female adolescent psychiatric and control groups," *Journal of Child Sexual Abuse* 3(1):53–65.

Whitbeck, Les B., Danny R. Hoyt & Kevin A. Ackley. 1997. "Families of homeless and runaway adolescents: A comparison of parent/caretaker and adolescent perspectives on parenting, family violence, and adolescent conduct," *Child Abuse and Neglect* 21(6):517-528.

Whitbeck, Les B. & Ronald L. Simons. 1990. "Life on the streets: The victimization of runaway and homeless adolescents," *Youth and Society* 22(1):108-125.

White, Lynn. 1990. "Determinants of divorce: A review of research in the eighties," *Journal of Marriage and the Family* 52(4):904–912.

White, James M. 1992. "Marital status and well-being in Canada: An analysis of age group variations," *Journal of Family Issues* 13(3):390–409.

White, Kimberly *et al.* 1984. "Unstable diabetes and unstable families: A psychosocial evaluation of diabetic children with recurrent ketoacidosis," *Pediatrics*, 73(6):749–755.

Whitehead, Barbara Dafoe. 1990. "The family in an unfriendly culture," *Family Affairs* 3:1–2.

Whitehead, Barbara Dafoe. 1996. "The decline of marriage as the social basis of childbearing," pp. 3–14 in David Popenoe, Jean Bethke Elshtain & David Blankenhorn (Eds.), *Promises to Keep: Decline and Renewal of Marriage in America*, Lanham, MD: Rowman and Littlefield Publishers, Inc.

Wiersma, Uco J. 1994. "A taxonomy of behavioral strategies for coping with work–home conflict," *Human Relations* 47(Feb.):211–221.

Wilkinson, Richard G. 1994. "From material scarcity to social disadvantage," *Daedalus: Journal of the American Academy of Arts and Sciences* 123(4): 61–77.

Wilkinson, Ross B. 1995. "Changes in psychological health and the marital relationship through childbearing: Transition or process as stress?" *Australian Journal of Psychology* 47(2).

Willen, Helena & Henry Montgomery. 1996. "The impact of wishing for children and having children on attainment and importance of life values," *Journal of Comparative Family Studies* 27(3): 499–518.

Williams, Lee & Joan Jurich,. 1995. "Predicting marital success after five years: Assessing the predictive validity of FOCCUS," *Journal of Marital and Family Therapy* 21(Apr.).

Willoughby, Jennifer C. & Laraine Masters Glidden. 1995. "Fathers helping out: Shared child care and marital satisfaction of parents of children with disabilities," *American Journal on Mental Retardation* 99(4).

Wilson, S.J. 1996. *Women, Families and Work (4th edition)*. Toronto: McGraw-Hill Ryerson.

Winch, Robert F. *The Modern Family*. New York: Holt, 1962.

Wind, Tiffany-Weissmann & Louise Silvern. 1994. "Parenting and family stress as mediators of the long-term effects of child abuse," *Child Abuse and Neglect* 18 (May):439–453.

Windle, Michael & Levent Dumenci. 1997. "Parental and occupational distress as predictors of depressive symptoms among dual-income couples: A multilevel modeling approach," *Journal of Marriage and the Family* 59(Aug.): 625–634.

Wissenstein. Michael. 1997. "Is number of newborn killings rising?" *The Gazette* (Montreal) 19 November :B1.

Wolf, Rosalie S. 1996. "Elder abuse and family violence: Testimony presented before the U. S. Senate Special Committee on Aging," *Journal of Elder Abuse and Neglect* 8(1): 81–96.

Wong-Wylie, Gina & Marianne Doherty-Poirier. 1997. "Created Families: Perspectives From Persons Living with HIV/AIDS," paper presented at the Canadian Home Economics Association, Victoria, B.C.

Worthington, Everett L, Michael E. McCullough & Joanne L. Shortz. 1995. "Can couples assessment and feedback improve relationships? Assessment as a brief relationship enrichment procedure," *Journal of Counseling Psychology* 42(Oct.).

Wright, Mareena McKinley & Sue Keir Hoppe. 1994. "Integrating Stress and Life Course Perspectives in the Study of Psychological Response to Job Loss," an association paper for the Society for the Study of Social Problems.

Wu, Zheng. 1994. "Remarriage in Canada: A social exchange perspective," *Journal of Divorce and Remarriage* 21(3–4):191–224.

Wu, Zheng. 1995. "Remarriage after widowhood: A marital history study of older Canadians," *Canadian Journal on Aging* 14(4):719–736.

Wylie, Betty Jane. 1997. *Family: An Exploration. Canada* (no place of publication listed): Northstone.

Xiaohe, Xu & Martin King Whyte. 1990. "Love matches and arranged marriages," *Journal of Marriage and the Family*, 52(3):709–722.

Yelsma, Paul. 1996. "Affective orientations of perpetrators, victims, and functional spouses," *Journal of Interpersonal Violence* 11(June):141–161.

Yllo, K. & M.A. Straus. 1981. "Interpersonal violence among married and cohabiting couples," *Family Relations* 30: 339–347.

Zachariah, Rachel. 1996. "Predictors of psychological well-being of women during pregnancy; replication and extension," *Journal of Social Behavior and Personality* 11(1).

Zarit, Steven H. & Carol J. Whitlatch. 1993. "The effects of placement in nursing homes on family caregivers: Short and long term consequences," *Irish Journal of Psychology* 14(1):25–37.

Zhang, Sheldon X. 1995. "Measuring shaming in an ethnic context," *British Journal of Criminology* 35(2):248-262.

Zill, Nicholas & Christine Winquist Nord. 1994. *Running in Place: How American Families are Faring in a Changing Economy and an Individualistic Society*. Washington, D.C.: Child Trends.

Zimmerman, Shirley. 1988. *Understanding Family Policy: Theoretical Approaches*. Beverly Hills, California: Sage.

Zinsmeister, Karl. 1996. "Family meltdown in the classroom," *The American Enterprise* 7(Sept./Oct.): 42 45.

Zvonkovic, A.M., K.M. Greaves, C.J. Schmiege & L.D. Hall. 1996. "The marital construction of gender through work and family decisions: A qualitative analysis," *Journal of Marriage and the Family* 58:91–100.

INDEX

PHOTO CREDITS

W.P. Wittman Ltd., p. 1; Fred Cattroll, p. 15; W.P. Wittman Ltd., p. 23; W.P. Wittman Ltd., p. 27; W.P. Wittman Ltd., p. 43; W.P. Wittman Ltd., p. 53; W.P. Wittman Ltd., p. 64; W.P. Wittman Ltd., p. 72; W.P. Wittman Ltd., p. 81; W.P. Wittman Ltd., p. 93; The Slide Farm/Al Harvey, p. 106; W.P. Wittman Ltd., p. 117; W.P. Wittman Ltd., p. 124; The Slide Farm/Al Harvey, p. 135; W.P. Wittman Ltd., p. 141; W.P. Wittman Ltd., p. 154; W.P. Wittman Ltd., p. 160; W.P. Wittman Ltd., p. 174; W.P. Wittman Ltd., p. 188; W.P. Wittman Ltd., p. 200; W.P. Wittman Ltd., p. 208; The Slide Farm/Al Harvey, p. 219; W.P. Wittman Ltd., p. 227; W.P. Wittman Ltd., p. 237; Tony Stone Images/ Steven Peters, p. 243; The Slide Farm/Al Harvey, p. 255; Tony Stone Images/Vincent Oliver, p. 264; Dick Hemingway, p. 278; Dick Hemingway, p. 289; Tony Stone Images/Bruce Ayres, p. 297; CP Picture Archive (CBC), p. 310; Tony Stone Images/ Bruce Ayres, p. 332; W.P. Wittman Ltd., p. 347; The Slide Farm/Al Harvey, p. 358; First Light, p. 375; Dick Hemingway, p. 386; Dick Hemingway, p. 404; Dick Hemingway, p. 408; W.P. Wittman Ltd., p. 416; W.P. Wittman Ltd., p. 431; Dick Hemingway, p. 441; The Slide Farm/Al Harvey, p. 450.